The Regulation of Psychotherapists
Volume I

Series on The Regulation of Psychotherapists

Daniel B. Hogan
with a Series Foreword by Ralph Slovenko

- **Volume I. A Study in the Philosophy and Practice of Professional Regulation.**

  A concise history of psychotherapy, including an analysis of its effectiveness, dangers, and the skills needed for therapeutic competence. Using the findings of social science research, the author argues that traditional forms of regulation, such as licensure, have not protected the public and may have had significant negative impact. He proposes a comprehensive, alternative framework for professional regulation.

- **Volume II. A Handbook of State Licensure Laws.**

  A comprehensive analysis of all laws potentially regulating psychotherapists, including physicians, psychologists, social workers, and marriage and family counselors.

- **Volume III. A Review of Malpractice Suits in the United States.**

  A description of malpractice law, followed by an examination of the impact of malpractice suits on professional practice generally and psychotherapy in particular. 300 decisions involving psychotherapeutic diagnosis, treatment, and care are analysed.

- **Volume IV. A Resource Bibliography.**

  More than 3,000 references on professional regulation, the development of the professions in society, and the nature of the psychotherapeutic process. Each area is divided into detailed subcategories preceded by an introductory discussion. The author provides a list of journals and other sources of information useful to those conducting research.

The Regulation of Psychotherapists
Volume I

A Study in the Philosophy and Practice of Professional Regulation

Daniel B. Hogan
Harvard University

Ballinger Publishing Company ● Cambridge, Massachusetts
A Subsidiary of Harper & Row, Publishers, Inc.

 This book is printed on recycled paper.

Publication of this book was made possible by a grant from the Maurice Falk Medical Fund, Pittsburgh, Pennsylvania.

International Standard Book Number: 0-88410-501-6

Library of Congress Catalog Card Number: 78-11291

Printed in the United States of America

Library of Congress Cataloging in Publication Data

Hogan, Daniel B
  A study in the philosophy and practice of professional regulation.

  (His The regulation of psychoterhapists ; v. 1)
  Includes indexes.
    1. Psychotherapists—Legal status, laws, etc.—United States. 2. Psychotherapists—Licenses—United States. 3. Psychotherapists—Malpractice—United States. I. Title. [DNLM: 1. Psychotherapy—Stands. 2. Licensure, Medical—United States. WM420.3 H714r
KF2910.P75H63 vol. 1   344'.73'017618914s   78-11291
ISBN 0-88410-501-6   344'.73'017618914

To Jean

Contents in Brief

Table of Contents

Series Foreword

The most critical issue facing the professions today is how they should be regulated. Various alternatives have been proposed. Professional associations have argued that self-regulation is the only appropriate method, reasoning that the public does not have the ability to judge professional competence. The result has been a regulatory framework dominated by the professions, with little public input or control. In the licensing field administrative boards are composed almost solely of members of the profession regulated. In the judicial sphere, malpractice law is based on a standard of care very much determined by what professionals consider acceptable practice. More important, professional associations wield tremendous power through their direct and indirect influence on nearly all aspects of regulation.

A regulated trade is a guarantee against unwanted competition, a closed shop sanctioned by the state. The pursuit of monopoly is an old one. As far back as medieval times, barbers and butchers, the only professions with ready access to sharp instruments, clashed for the exclusive right to perform surgery. (The barbers triumphed, and the blood-stained sheets they hung outside after their ministrations evolved into the barber pole.) In the mental health field a number of professional associations are attempting to achieve the type of control that the American Medical Association and American Bar Association possess in their respective fields. Thus, the American Psychological Association and the National Association of Social Workers have urged the enactment of licensing laws granting them the nearly exclusive right to practice psychotherapy. At the same time, the American Psychiatric Association argues that even these groups, should only be allowed to practice psychotherapy under appropriate medical supervision. Other professions, such as marriage and family counseling, worried about their own right to practice, have begun to lobby for additional licensing laws of their own.

According to theory, in return for a monopolistic right of practice, there is a reciprocal commitment to admit only individuals of proven competence, to insist on the observance of an ethical code of conduct, and to protect the public against bungling and extortion. In virtually every profession, however, disciplinary enforcement is virtually nonexistent. The little enforcement that there is does not act as a deterrent and is often done to protect the reputation or the economic interest of the group rather than to protect the public from harm.

The public is growing increasingly dissatisfied with the quality and cost of professional services. Malpractice suits against physicians, psychiatrists, psychologists, lawyers, and other professionals have multiplied in the last decade. Jury verdicts have escalated in size. In addition, the public has begun to demand a role on licensing boards and in the formulation and implementation of regulations involving the professions.

The question, of course, is whether any of these proposed methods of regulation are likely to prove effective. In the mental health field the problems are especially complex. The process of psychotherapy is notoriously difficult to define, the standard of competent practice is open to serious dispute, and methods of training and selection are only in their infant stages of development. It is problematic whether traditional legislative methods such as licensing or judicial methods such as the malpractice suit will prove fruitful.

What is most needed at this juncture, especially in the field of psychotherapy, is a thoughtful analysis of the impact of current efforts to regulate professional practice, along with constructive recommendations. As a first step in this process, data are necessary on the extent and impact of current regulatory efforts, including the degree to which state licensing or certification laws cover therapeutic practice and the extent to which malpractice suits have been used against psychotherapists. Such data have been almost impossible to obtain until the publication of this series, which provides the first comprehensive review of psychotherapeutic regulation.

In Volume I Daniel Hogan has constructed his recommendations for the regulation of psychotherapists. He has provided a compelling analysis of the psychotherapeutic process, documenting the extreme difficulties involved in defining and measuring therapeutic competence. He has demonstrated that academic credentials bear little if any relationship to that competence. His arguments are provocative and persuasive. The evidence marshalled by Hogan strongly suggests that licensing laws, malpractice suits, and the activities of the major professional associations have not done much to protect the public. Indeed, he suggests that the quality of services provided by licensed practitioners is no better than would be provided if there were no licensing laws.

Volumes II–IV constitute invaluable reference tools for those interested in licensing, malpractice, or regulation in general. These volumes serve as the informational base on which Hogan has constructed his recommendations for the regulation of psychotherapists.

While many have criticized current regulatory efforts, Hogan is one of the first to propose a well-thought-out and systematic alternative. I especially appreciate his emphasis on education of the public, his recommendation to require therapists to fully disclose all relevant information to clients, his view of the regulatory process as one of facilitating interaction rather than controlling behavior, and his insistence on the inclusion of the public in the formulation and implementation of any set of regulations. His analysis of how professionals develop and the evidence that psychotherapy is still a very young field of organized practice provides strong support for his ideas.

For those who are in fundamental agreement with Hogan's views, these four volumes provide excellent evidence and argument in support of their position. For those who do not, Hogan's work should encourage a sharper understanding of the issues and an examination of previously unquestioned assumptions. This latter point needs emphasis. One cannot help but be deeply impressed with the tone in which this book was written. Instead of a polemic, Hogan has chosen to present his views as one way of looking at the problem—he recognizes its limitations, and his writing reflects a respect for those with opposing points of view. Since the problem of professional regulation requires a great deal of thought and is likely to be with us for some time, it is essential that all those concerned continue to engage in constructive, dialectical discussion.

Dan Hogan has contributed an impressive study on the regulation of professions. He is to be congratulated.

Ralph Slovenko
Professor of Law & Psychiatry
Wayne State University
Detroit, Michigan
October, 1978

Foreword

I first met Dan Hogan in a seminar on human relations training I was conducting at Boston University in 1971. During the next year I worked closely with him on his law school essay, "The Regulation of Human Relations Training," written at the Harvard Law School.

I was particularly impressed with several qualities in his work, all of which are still apparent in this current volume. First, Mr. Hogan has done an excellent job of integrating his legal background with his experience in the field of psychology and human relations. This is not an easy task, and too often lawyers have approached the field of therapy without an adequate understanding of its relationship to law. Second, he has not been satisfied to write of processes about which he lacked direct experience. Instead, Hogan has enriched his book-knowledge through participation as a member and leader of T-groups and through clinical experience as a counselor. Third, Hogan has insisted on examining both the intended and unintended consequences of actual and proposed regulatory practices. Because of the dramatic impact that public policies are likely to have on the structure and development of psychotherapy, this insistence is especially critical.

Over the past seven years Mr. Hogan's work has expanded significantly. He has widened the scope of his research to include the full range of traditional therapies, as well as encounter groups and the newer humanistic therapies. In addition to statutorily prescribed licensure, Hogan has broadened his view of the regulatory process to include judicial regulation through professional liability suits, various programs of self-regulation by professional organizations, and regulation through education of the public.

This considerable expansion in subject matter has not resulted in any loss of quality or comprehensiveness. Hogan has continued to explore both the positive and negative effects of regulation. He has a clear commitment to the development of a regulatory framework that will protect clients from the risks involved in psychotherapy, particularly at its lunatic fringe. But he is equally committed to protecting the public from regulatory measures that only benefit the vested interests of the established professions.

Mr. Hogan has not been content to summarize and synthesize critiques of various regulatory practices in the complex and variegated field of psychotherapy, although his summaries and syntheses are painstaking and exhaustive. He has gone further to offer his own recommendations. These recommendations encompass preventive as well as curative practices in mental health. Moreover, they involve the education of the public and clients with respect to the risks and benefits of various forms of psychotherapy. In fact, they suggest ways of empowering the public to offset the potential ill effects of vested interests masquerading as the public interest in health affairs. This may well represent one of his most enduring contributions.

It is my hope that all those concerned with mental health, and with the broader field of public regulation of professionals generally, will not only study Dan Hogan's outstanding work, but will also implement his recommendations in social and public policies.

Kenneth D. Benne
Professor of Philosophy and Human
  Relations, Emeritus
Boston University
Boston, Massachusetts
October, 1978

Acknowledgments

This study of professional regulation contains the final fruits of a long-term research project on psychotherapeutic regulation. It would not have been possible without the support of a variety of individuals and institutions. My greatest debt is to the Maurice Falk Medical Fund and its President, Philip Hallen. The Fund originally provided a grant for nine months to conduct research on the regulation of encounter group leaders, a project that had grown out of my third-year legal thesis at Harvard Law School. The scope of work expanded rapidly, however, and soon encompassed psychotherapy as well.

Perhaps more important, my interest began to focus on the generic issue of professional regulation. Research on a project of this scope required considerably more time and effort, and the Falk Fund continued to provide the financial support to enable successful and timely completion. In addition to the Falk Fund's willingness to expand grant support, Philip Hallen's constant belief in the project's importance has been of significant moral support. The Fund, of course, should not be understood as endorsing any statement made or expressed herein.

Equally deserving of thanks are Geoffrey Gunn and Karl Oehlgeschlager of Ballinger Publishing Company, who at long last have a manuscript for publication. The original contract with Ballinger called for a six-month reworking of my legal thesis to be published as a one-volume work. That has since stretched into five years and the publication of a four-volume series. The staff at Ballinger has provided tremendous moral support, in addition to its skilled editorial assistance. Carol Franco and Sid Seamans, in particular, have given me patient guidance in the fine art of writing.

A third institution that has provided invaluable help is Harvard University, where I have been a Research Fellow in the Department of Psychology and Social Relations for the past three years. Among the faculty, David McClelland, Freed Bales, Herbert Kelman, Brendan Maher, and Pat Patullo have given support that has been greatly appreciated. Among the student body, many undergraduates and graduates did painstaking and often tedious research, proofing, and editing. David Barnard deserves special mention for his insightful criticisms of various portions of this manuscript, as does Hal Chapel, who did an outstanding job in developing and administering the computer program for analyzing the malpractice suits contained in Volume III. Other students who contributed significantly in a variety of ways were Richard Bashner, Grady Bolding, Juanita Carroll, Chris Cornog,

Lou Cozolino, Dorothy Figueira, David Heller, Richard Ismach, Eric Larson, Chris Moylan, Chris Rutkowski, Dorit Schutzengel, Tom Tweed, and Randy Wilkinson.

My particular gratitude goes to Jennifer Lyons for her outstanding administrative and typing assistance. Her willingness to spend long hours preparing tables and lists, and her ability to decipher my sometimes unintelligible scribbles, have significantly eased the task of completing this manuscript. Also assisting in the preparation of this manuscript, Ann Seamans did a magnificent job of indexing, especially given the severe time constraints imposed by publishing deadlines.

Unfortunately, a complete list of those who deserve recognition is impossible in the space provided. Others who must be mentioned, however, include Dick Hopkins, for his recommendation of Ballinger as a publisher; Alan Stone, for his advice and guidance on my initial research on encounter group regulation and his continued support since then; the Foundation for Applied Social Science, which has administered the grants from the Maurice Falk Medical Fund; and Ken Benne and Malcolm Knowles, both formerly of Boston University, whose wisdom has helped me understand the therapeutic process. Paul Pottinger, the Executive Director of the National Center for the Study of Professions in Washington, D.C., has been particularly helpful with his careful reading of and comments upon portions of the manuscript. The work he himself is undertaking represents an important step in implementing many of the recommendations suggested in this volume. David Matts, George Kohlreiser, Rolf Lynton, Ken Benne, and Jean Haley all read initial drafts of this book and I am thankful for their suggestions, which have improved the final product substantially.

The encouragement and faith of family and friends, especially Ann Coles, Robert Fischelis, Kent Nelson, Horace Seldon, and Barbara Westman, have been especially important. Finally, the love and faith of Jean Haley has made this long enterprise tremendously rewarding and fulfilling.

Chapter 1

Prologue

The regulation of practitioners in the mental health field is a controversial and significant issue. The most convincing argument for immediate regulatory action of some kind has been the pervasive allegation that psychotherapy entails significant risks. At the encounter group end of the spectrum, stories of nude marathons, suicides, and psychotic episodes, as well as evidence of economic fraud, have frequently created a furor. Even in more traditional individual psychotherapy, reports of sexual abuses have been rife.

These dangers have been the cause of serious concern, even alarm. Major newspapers and magazines,[1] including the *New York Times*[2] and *Wall Street Journal*,[3] have devoted substantial space to warn the public about the potential dangers involved in participating in encounter groups. The American Medical Association (1971), American Psychological Association (1973), and various other professional organizations[4] have issued position statements and guidelines on such groups. New York City (1971) has held extensive hearings on the alleged dangers of group leaders, while New York State (1972) has done the same for unregulated therapists in general. The call for regulation of some of the newer psychotherapies has even been raised at the federal level, where a member of Congress

(Rarick, 1969) has had fourteen pages of testimony written into the *Congressional Record* to demonstrate that encounter groups are a Communist conspiracy to brainwash U.S. citizens.

The concern about dangers, nonetheless, represents only one of the reasons why an investigation of regulatory proposals is critical. The mental health profession is playing an increasingly prominent role in U.S. society. The implementation of any set of regulations, therefore, is liable to have a significant economic and social impact. Some statistics will illustrate the potential degree of this influence.

Mental illness has long been acknowledged as the nation's number one health problem.[5] For years, more than half of all occupied hospital beds in this country have been filled by the mentally ill (Fein, 1958: 3). In addition, the number of people suffering from mental illness exceeds all other forms of illness (Fein, 1958: 4). Sophisticated epidemiological studies estimate that the percentage of the population suffering from psychiatric disorders ranges from 11 to 64 percent, with a median of 18 percent (Dohrenwend, 1975; see also Srole et al., 1962, and the President's Commission on Mental Health, 1978).

The cost of mental illness to society is staggering. In 1956 it was estimated to be

1

in excess of $3 billion, including both direct and indirect costs (Fein, 1958: xii). By 1971 the figure had risen to more than $25 billion (Levine and Levine, 1975), much of which represents payment for psychotherapeutic services, which is the predominant method of treating mental illness in the United States (Cowen and Zax, 1967: 12).

The increase in expenditures for mental health care parallels the considerable expansion of the entire health field in general. According to the Department of Health, Education and Welfare, the proportion of the gross national product related to health care spending grew from 5.9 percent in fiscal year 1966 to 8.3 percent in 1975; the total national health care expenditure was $118.5 billion in that year (U.S., HEW, 1976: 1). The portion of the GNP devoted to health could well reach 10 percent by 1980 (U.S., HEW, 1976: 30).

This increasing investment in health care has been accomplished by a redefinition of what health care is, its transformation from a privilege to a right, and a reevaluation of the services that ought to be incorporated into primary health care. Mental health is rapidly gaining a legitimate place in this overall picture. Many private insurance carriers and federal health insurance programs currently provide coverage for the treatment of mental health problems, including psychotherapeutic services designed to alleviate those problems (Reed, 1975).

Because psychotherapy now offers substantial monetary rewards, professional groups other than physicians are attempting to establish their right to deliver such services, and to do so without medical supervision. Psychologists, social workers, and marriage counselors have been the most forceful groups in this regard. Their main vehicle for legitimation has been licensing laws, the impact of which is having profound effects on the ability of the mental health profession to provide the

public with an adequate supply of practitioners, among other things.

In addition to the need for psychotherapeutic services in the treatment of mental illness, a burgeoning interest among U.S. citizens in self-actualization and emotional fulfillment has created a powerful demand for diverse forms of psychotherapy. As affluence and leisure time expand, this demand will almost certainly grow. The human potential movement, represented in its most concrete form by the encounter group and a variety of new psychotherapies, has become the primary vehicle through which to participate in this development. Psychologist Carl Rogers (1970: 1) has stated that the encounter group is "the most rapidly spreading *social* invention of the century, and probably the most potent. . . ." It has been estimated that a million individuals participate in some type of intensive group experience each year, and perhaps as many as 10 million people have experienced one or another form of human-relations training in the last twenty-five years (Benne et al., 1975: 11).

While there are people who contend that interest in mental health—and especially in encounter groups—is a passing fad, a persuasive argument can be made that this trend will continue. Philosophical theories and psychological studies of human nature support the contention that people become increasingly concerned with feelings, self-awareness, and self-actualization as a society develops (see, e.g., Maslow, 1971, 1968). The structure of U.S. society may well be undergoing such a transformation at this time (see, e.g., Leonard, 1972). Martin Krieger (1971) at the Center for Advanced Study in the Behavioral Sciences in Stanford, California, suggests that the United States may soon enter a "beyond post-industrial society," in which the critical resource is not land, as it was in agrarian times, or capital, as it was during the Industrial Revolution, or knowledge, as in today's post-industrial society. Instead the possession of "affect" may become the critical resource, which Krieger (1971: 10, 18) defines in part as the ability to be self-aware, understanding, and sensitive to others. In such a society personal services would be highly valued, and a dramatic increase in the number of psychotherapists, counselors, and others in the helping professions would doubtless result. Personal-growth groups, T-groups, and other groups designed to help expand sensory awareness would proliferate since, as Krieger (1971: 55-67) has demonstrated, they offer an economical means of producing this resource.

Beyond these readily apparent developments lie two other less discernible but perhaps more significant trends, each of which makes an examination of regulation in the mental health field especially timely. First, professional and occupational regulation has undergone disturbing developments in the past century. State licensing has become the major means of regulating a multitude of occupations and professions, from plumbing to medicine. Licensing laws have proliferated at an astronomical rate. By mid-century seventy-five occupations were licensed in one or more states, with fourteen licensed in all states (Council of State Governments, 1952). By 1970 the health field alone licensed thirty professional groups, with twelve of these regulated in every state (U.S., HEW, 1971).

In the mental health field all states presently license psychologists, while social workers are licensed in twenty-one states, marriage and family counselors in six, and various other states license social psychotherapists, pastoral counselors, and psychiatric aides. The medical profession argues that the practice of psychotherapy is already controlled by the state medical practice acts; indeed, virtually all of these laws expressly or by interpretation contain psychotherapy in all its forms within their definition of professional practice.

The economic impact of licensing and its effect on the quality of professional services are two of the most significant issues that must be examined in a study of professional regulation. Licensing laws are now estimated to have a direct effect on one-third to one-fifth of the work force (*Behavior Today*, 1976). Increasingly they require rigid academic credentials and frequently they rely on successful completion of difficult written examinations. Alternative modes of determining competence are generally ignored. The negative impact such laws may be having on the supply of professional personnel, the cost and organization of professional services, and the utilization of paraprofessionals—as well as their discriminatory effect—has caused considerable concern on the part of political scientists and other students of government. They argue that the requisite conditions have been created for a guild-type society reminiscent of the Middle Ages (*see, e.g.*, Gellhorn, 1976, 1956; Gilb, 1966; and Lieberman, 1970). The situation in the health field has become so severe that HEW (U.S., HEW, 1971), the American Medical Association (1970), the American Hospital Association (1971), and a number of other major professional associations have recommended a moratorium on licensing any new categories of health personnel.

The proliferation of licensing laws is largely the result of a second and more significant development—the rise in power of the professional class, of which psychotherapists are a part. The professions are increasingly assuming a central and critical role in society, a role far more important than hitherto imagined. In large part this is due to technological innovations, which are making the possession and communication of knowledge a more valuable asset than control of capital (Krieger, 1971). Since the professions have historically been the repositories of knowledge vital to the well-being of society, the control of access to that knowledge provides the professions with considerable power (Reiff, 1974). In fact, sociologist Talcott Parsons (1968: 545) has concluded:

The professional complex . . . has already become the most important single component in the structure of modern societies. It has displaced first the "state" in the relatively early modern sense of that term, and, more recently, the "capitalistic" organization of the economy. The massive emergence of the professional complex, not the special status of capitalistic or socialistic modes of organization, is the crucial structural development in twentieth-century society.

Each of the factors identified above—the alleged dangers involved, the importance of the mental health profession to society, the proliferation of licensing laws, and the increasingly central role of the professions in society—makes it crucial to develop a sound regulatory policy for psychotherapists and the professions generally. This study uses the findings of social science research and other empirical data to evaluate the effectiveness of traditional modes of regulation, such as licensing, malpractice suits, and professional self-regulation.

A close analysis of licensing laws reveals that they have significant problems in performing their intended purpose of public protection. It is questionable whether the current credentials required in most such laws have much relationship with competent practice. It is indisputable that licensing boards have done a poor job of disciplining incompetent or unethical practitioners. At the same time, evidence exists that licensing may decrease the supply of practitioners available, increase the cost of professional services, restrict innovations in professional practice, education, and the ways in which professional services are organized, and discriminate against minorities, women, and the aged. In addition, a consensus is growing that judicial regulation of the professions through malpractice suits has proved ineffective, as have the attempts by professional associations to regulate themselves.

If traditional methods of regulation have been deficient, improvements and alternatives must be suggested. This book presents a regulatory framework designed to obviate the problems of traditional regulation, while at the same time providing the public with adequate protection. It also proposes recommendations to improve existing licensing laws and other regulatory mechanisms.

A basic premise of this book is that restrictive licensing laws are only advisable when a professional field is clearly defined and a consensus has been reached based on sound scientific evidence as to the standards and criteria appropriate for determining who is qualified to practice. In other words, the profession must be fully mature before restrictive licensing is advisable. Psychotherapy has not yet achieved this status. Hence it becomes critical to develop regulations that protect responsible experimentation with diverse standards of practice and methods of organizing services. What is needed, then, is a system of regulation that will allow a careful determination of professional training and other qualifications that are necessary to protect the public from harm.

For these reasons the most desirable regulatory model is a system of registration in which all practitioners are required to register with the state, but are not required to possess any particular credential to practice. Protection against harm would be accomplished through a disciplinary board overseen by representatives of the profession, the public, consumers, and other relevant constituencies. Harmful conduct, either unethical or incompetent, would subject practitioners to penalties, including the loss of the right to practice.

In such a system professional associations would have a significant role to play, but one substantially different from traditional conceptions of that role. Since so little consensus exists as to appropriate standards and criteria for measuring the competence of therapists and group leaders, government policy should encourage research and controlled experimentation. Support should be provided for the development of a variety of professional associations and accrediting agencies, each with its own standards and criteria for measuring competence. At the same time domination by one professional association should be discouraged. Careful research should document which set of standards and criteria are most effective and in what circumstances.[6] In all cases the goal should be to establish standards and criteria clearly related to competent practice.

Augmenting this system would be laws requiring therapists to disclose all relevant information to potential clients and laws requiring truth in advertising. A comprehensive campaign to educate the public about the effective selection and utilization of mental health professionals would be essential. Professional liability suits would be used to prevent gross abuses and to encourage full and truthful disclosure of information. Perhaps as important, efforts to reorganize the delivery of mental health services and to improve professional training programs should be initiated, since these indirect methods of regulation are likely to have a more positive impact on the quality of professional services than direct methods, such as restrictive licensing laws.

Finally, careful and comprehensive research needs to be conducted to determine what makes a therapist effective and what methods of regulation are most likely to provide positive public protection. In order to do this, an adequate system for collecting and disseminating knowledge must be instituted.

The proposals contained in this book emphasize the regulation of output (what the practitioner does), rather than input (what standards the practitioner must meet before being allowed to practice). They focus on the value of educating the public, as opposed to making decisions for that public. They are based on a view of regulation that defines it as an interactive process, whose purpose is to order and facilitate the interactions of people with one another, not simply to achieve social control.[7] As such, regulatory methods, including licensing laws, must not only be designed to protect the public from harm, but should also help ensure that the needs of the public are met. Implicit in these proposals is an effort to demystify and demythologize the mental health profession. Also implicit is a commitment to the value of paraprofessionals in the delivery of professional services and the importance of a regulatory system developed and controlled by all relevant constituencies, not professionals alone.

NOTES

1. For a sample of the popular-media articles on the dangers of encounter groups, see Beldoch's (1971) "The False Psychology of Encounter Groups" in *Intellectual Digest;* Chesler's (1969) "Playing Instant Joy in the Lonely Crowd" in *The Village Voice;* Gorner's (1973) "Encounter Groupies, Beware!" in the *Chicago Tribune;* Maliver's (1971) "Encounter Groupers Up Against the Wall" in the *New York Times Magazine;* and Wysor's (1971) "Encounter Games: A Dangerous New Trend" in *Harper's Bazaar.* For psychotherapy, see *Time Magazine*'s (1975) article entitled "Love Thy Analyst." A number of best-selling books have been devoted to warning the public of the dangers involved in both psychotherapy and encounter groups. See Church and Carnes's (1972) *The Pit: A Group Encounter Defiled;* Maliver's (1973) *The Encounter Game;* and Tennov's (1976) *Psychotherapy: The Hazardous Cure.*

2. *See, e.g.,* Maliver (1971) and Peterson (1972).

3. *See, e.g.,* Calame (1969).

4. *See, e.g.,* the statements by the following groups: American Group Psychotherapy

Association (1971); British Columbia Medical Association (1970); California State Psychological Association (1969); Colorado Psychological Association (undated); Long Island Psychoanalytic Society (1970); Maine Psychological Association (1973); and New York County District Branch of the American Psychiatric Association (1973).

5. As far back as 1953 mental illness was considered the most important health problem that this country faced (U.S., Congress, House Committee on Interstate and Foreign Commerce, 1953).

6. It might eventually be concluded that no single set of standards is capable of defining the competent practitioner. Instead, evidence may document that a variety of people with varying skills may be effective in particular situations, although perhaps ineffective in others.

7. This is in line with Lon Fuller's (1969) philosophical theories as to the nature of the legal process.

REFERENCES

American Group Psychotherapy Association. *Position Statement on "Non-Therapy and Therapy Groups."* New York: American Group Psychotherapy Association, 1971.

American Hospital Association, Special Committee on Licensure of Health Personnel. *Statement on Licensure of Health Care Personnel.* (Approved by AHA, November 18, 1970.) Chicago: American Hospital Association, 1971.

American Medical Association, Council on Health Manpower. *Licensure of Health Occupations.* (Adopted by AMA House of Delegates.) Chicago: American Medical Association, 1970.

American Medical Association, Council on Mental Health. "Sensitivity Training." *Journal of the American Medical Association.* 1971, n. 217, pp. 1853-54.

American Psychological Association. "Guidelines for Psychologists Conducting Growth Groups." *American Psychologist.* 1973, v. 28, p. 933.

Behavior Today. "The Complexities of Licensure and Certification." *Behavior Today*, October 25, 1976, pp. 6-7.

Beldoch, M. "The False Psychology of Encounter Groups." *Intellectual Digest*, 1971, v. 2, pp. 85-88.

Benne, K.D.; Bradford, L.P.; Gibb, J.R.; and Lippitt, R.O. (Eds.) *The Laboratory Method of Changing and Learning: Theory and Application.* Palo Alto, Calif.: Science and Behavior Books, 1975.

British Columbia Medical Association, Section of Psychiatry. "Some Guidelines on Non-Medical Groups." *British Columbia Medical Journal.* 1970, v. 12, p. 187.

Calame, B.E. "The Truth Hurts: Some Companies See More Harm Than Good in Sensitivity Training." *Wall Street Journal*, July 14, 1969, pp. 1 and 15.

California State Psychological Association. "A Statement about Sensitivity Training from CSPA." Mimeographed. Los Angeles, Calif., 1969.

Chesler, P. "Playing Instant Joy in the Lonely Crowd." *The Village Voice*, December 25, 1969, pp. 9 and 41.

Church, G., and Carnes, C.D. *The Pit: A Group Encounter Defiled.* New York: Outerbridge and Lazard, E.P. Dutton and Co., 1972.

Colorado Psychological Association. "Psychology and Sensitivity Training Activities: A Position Statement of the Colorado Psychological Association." Mimeographed. Denver, Col., undated.

Council of State Governments. *Occupational Licensing Legislation in the States: A Study of State Legislation Licensing the Practice of Professions and Other Occupations.* Chicago: Council of State Governments, 1952.

Cowen, E.L., and Zax, M. "The Mental Health Fields Today: Issues and Problems." In

E.L. Cowen, E.A. Gardner, and M. Zax, *Emergent Approaches to Mental Health Problems.* New York: Appleton-Century-Crofts, 1967, pp. 3-29.

Dohrenwend, B.P. "Sociocultural and Social-Psychological Factors in the Genesis of Mental Disorders." *Journal of Health and Social Behavior.* 1975, v. 16, pp. 365-92.

Fein, R. *Economics of Mental Illness.* New York: Basic Books, 1958.

Fuller, L.L. *The Morality of Law.* (2nd ed., rev.) New Haven, Conn.: Yale University Press, 1969.

Gellhorn, W. "The Abuse of Occupational Licensing." *University of Chicago Law Review.* 1976, v. 44, pp. 6-27.

Gellhorn, W. *Individual Freedom and Governmental Restraints.* Baton Rouge, La.: Louisiana State University Press, 1956.

Gilb, C.L. *Hidden Hierarchies: The Professions and Government.* New York: Harper and Row, 1966.

Gorner, P. "Encounter Groupies, Beware!" *Chicago Tribune,* April 28, 1973.

Krieger, M.H. "Planning for an Affect Based Society: Prediction, Indicators and Structure." Working Paper 144B. Mimeographed. Institute of Urban and Regional Development, University of California, Berkeley, 1971.

Leonard, G.B. *The Transformation: A Guide to the Inevitable Changes in Humankind.* New York: Delacorte Press, 1972.

Levine, D.S., and Levine, D.R. *The Cost of Mental Illness—1971.* Washington, D.C.: U.S. Government Printing Office, 1975.

Lieberman, J.K. *The Tyranny of the Experts: How Professionals Are Closing the Open Society.* New York: Walker and Co., 1970.

Long Island Psychoanalytic Society. "Position Paper on T-Groups and Related Groups." Mimeographed. Great Neck, N.Y., 1970.

Maine Psychological Association. "Guidelines for Psychologists Engaged in Personal Growth Group Practice." (For membership approval, November 3, 1973.) Mimeographed. Portland, Me., 1973.

Maliver, B.L. *The Encounter Game.* New York: Stein and Day, 1973.

Maliver, B.L. "Encounter Groupers Up Against the Wall." *New York Times Magazine,* January 3, 1971, pp. 4-5, 37-41, 43.

Maslow, A.H. *The Farther Reaches of Human Nature.* New York: Viking Press, 1971.

Maslow, A.H. *Toward a Psychology of Being.* (2nd ed.) New York: Van Nostrand Reinhold Co., 1968.

New York City. *Hearings on Encounter Groups.* (Before the Council of the City of New York.) May 20-22, 1971.

New York County District Branch of the American Psychiatric Association. "Psychotherapy, Encounter, and Sensitivity-Training Groups: Present Status of Group Practice." *New York State Journal of Medicine.* 1973, v. 73, pp. 2369-71.

New York State. *Hearing on Abuses by Unregulated Therapists in the Mental Health Field.* (Before Louis J. Lefkowitz, Attorney General of the State of New York.) December 15, 1972.

Parsons, T. "Professions." In D.L. Sills (Ed.) *International Encyclopedia of the Social Sciences. Vol. 12. New York: Macmillan* 1968, pp. 536-47.

Peterson, I. "State Finds Quacks in Mental Therapy." *New York Times,* December 7, 1972.

President's Commission on Mental Health. *Report to the President.* Washington, D.C.: U.S. Government Printing Office, 1978. (4 vols.)

Rarick, J.R. "Sensitivity Training." *Congressional Record,* June 10, 1969 (H4667), pp. 15322-35.

Reed, L.S. *Coverage and Utilization of Care for Mental Conditions under Health Insurance—Various Studies, 1973-74.* Washington, D.C.: American Psychiatric Association, 1975.

Reiff, R. "The Control of Knowledge: The Power of the Helping Professions." *Journal of Applied Behavioral Science.* 1974, v. 10, pp. 451-61.

Rogers, C.R. *Carl Rogers on Encounter Groups.* New York: Harper and Row, 1970.

Srole, L.; Langner, T.S.; Michael, S.T.; Olper, M.K.; and Rennie, T.A.C. *Mental Health in the Metropolis: The Midtown Manhattan Study.* New York: McGraw-Hill, 1962.

Tennov, D. *Psychotherapy: The Hazardous Cure.* Garden City, N.Y.: Anchor Press, Doubleday, 1976.

Time Magazine. "Love Thy Analyst." *Time Magazine,* March 24, 1975, p. 76.

U.S. Congress. House Committee on Interstate and Foreign Commerce. *Health Inquiry.* Washington, D.C.: U.S. Government Printing Office, 1953. Cited by R. Fein, *Economics of Mental Illness* (New York: Basic Books, 1958), p. 4.

U.S. Department of Health, Education, and Welfare (DHEW). *Forward Plan for Health: FY 1978-82.* Washington, D.C.: U.S. Government Printing Office, 1976.

———. *Report on Licensure and Related Health Personnel Credentialing, June, 1971.* (Report to the Congress of the United States.) Washington, D.C.: U.S. Government Printing Office, 1971.

Wysor, B. "Encounter Games: A Dangerous New Trend." *Harper's Bazaar,* June 1971, pp. 60-61.

✷ *Part I*

The Psychotherapist in Perspective

Chapter 2

An Overview of Psychotherapy, I: Traditional Schools

The discussion of the increasing concern with mental health given in Chapter 1 indicated the growing importance of psychotherapy in the United States. The amount spent on professional psychotherapeutic services is rapidly escalating. Today three major groups provide therapy explicitly and directly: psychiatrists, clinical psychologists, and psychiatric social workers. Each of these groups has its own professional training program, standards, and accrediting bodies. A number of related professions provide therapeutic services as part of their regular practice, including psychiatric nurses, occupational therapists, rehabilitation counselors, and drug abuse workers. Significant therapeutic services are performed by such diverse professionals as the clergy and lawyers (Gurin et al., 1960). Even nonprofessionals and minimally trained paraprofessionals have been active in delivering therapeutic services.

Psychotherapy is conducted in a wide variety of settings, including Veterans Administration hospitals, school systems, private offices of psychiatrists, and drop-in centers. It has become increasingly accepted as a form of medical treatment. Many health insurance companies now offer some form of insurance for psychotherapy, and serious consideration is being given to its inclusion as a form of medical treatment under proposed systems of national health insurance. Most psychotherapy has been conducted on a one-to-one basis, but the recent burgeoning of group therapy, influenced by the growth of encounter groups, has changed this picture. The result has been to make the therapeutic process available to many who before could not afford it and to provide such service to a far greater number than previously could be treated by the individual practitioner.

Nonetheless, psychotherapy remains an amorphous and vaguely defined process with wide variations in theory and technique. Its history is enmeshed in the histories of religion, science, and magic. Currently there are those who view psychotherapy as a distinctly medical process and as a profession on a par with surgery or obstetrics. Others argue that it is but one form of education. Its rapid growth attests to the value that troubled individuals have found in it, but whether psychotherapy is effective is subject to debate, for the question of its effectiveness has not been definitively answered. Its potential for abuse and the possibility of negative effects from incompetent practice have only recently been scientifically examined.

An exploration of each of these aspects

of psychotherapy—defining its nature, examining its history, analyzing its theory and practice, establishing its value and effectiveness, and determining its risks and dangers—is essential in any effort to regulate those who practice as therapists. Without such exploration, seemingly appropriate regulatory policies may be totally misguided. For instance, if research indicates that therapy is not particularly helpful, but also not especially dangerous, the best regulation may be no regulation at all.

The ensuing analysis is meant to provide a basis for a sound regulatory program. Through a discussion of the history and value of psychotherapy, along with its special dangers, it should become clear that traditional methods of regulation are not likely to protect the public. In part, this lack of protection stems from the fact that psychotherapy cannot be adequately defined for legal purposes and because the dangers of therapy are only vaguely understood. Because traditional individual psychotherapy has generally been distinguished from the more recent encounter groups and humanistic therapies, these two schools of therapy will be dealt with separately.

DEFINITIONS AND DESCRIPTIONS

The earliest use of the term psychotherapy was by J.C. Reil in 1803 in an article entitled "Rhapsodies in the Application of Psychic Methods in the Treatment of Mental Disturbances" (Veith, 1958: 2). Since then the term psychotherapy has become a lexicographer's nightmare. Definitions abound, though few have much in common with each other and many are antithetical.[1]

Two major problems exist in defining psychotherapy. First, no consensus exists as to what processes should properly be labelled psychotherapeutic. Many practitioners argue that only verbal therapies

ought to be included, eliminating such methods as dance or art therapy. Others argue that therapies focusing on self-actualization, as opposed to those designed to ameliorate suffering, are not rightly regarded as psychotherapy. Second, phrases generally used in these definitions—such as "the modification of feelings, attitudes, and behavior" or "the use of psychological techniques"—cannot be precisely defined in themselves. The result is a large gray area in which one cannot be sure whether a given practice falls within a particular definition.

Yet narrow attempts at definition arbitrarily exclude many practices that are rightfully considered therapeutic.[2] One professional has wittily stated that psychotherapy is "an unidentified technique applied to unspecified problems with unpredictable outcomes. For this technique we recommend rigorous training" (Raimy, 1950: 93).

No attempt will be made here to formulate a precise definition of psychotherapy. Apart from the impossibility of such a task, constructing a narrow definition is unnecessary, since the findings and recommendations about regulation apply regardless of the particular definition adopted. Rather, certain broad and reasonably generic features will be identified. As an initial definition, Jerome Frank (1973: 2-3) provides a solid starting point, since his conception of the psychotherapeutic process has been widely recognized and accepted. He considers as psychotherapy only those types of influence exerted by a trained, socially sanctioned healer on a person who is suffering and seeking relief. The influence must be exerted through a circumscribed series of contacts in which the healer, often with the aid of a group, attempts to induce changes in the patient's emotional state, attitude, or behavior. Physical and chemical methods may be employed, but the healing influence is mainly achieved through verbal communication, acts and rituals.

The term psychotherapy as used here is somewhat broader than Frank's definition. He believes that a trained, socially sanctioned healer must be involved before something is properly termed psychotherapy. Since many nonsanctioned practitioners exist, and since they are perhaps the ones most in need of regulation, they will be included as well. Even though many of those involved in the self-actualization therapies do not perceive themselves as suffering, they too are included, since they do feel they need outside assistance. In this sense they "suffer" from self-perceived inadequacies that they wish to have "healed."

HISTORICAL AND THEORETICAL PERSPECTIVES

History

Even a brief look at the history of psychotherapy provides insights that have significant implications for its regulation.[3] Most historians agree that its roots lie in a number of intertwined and centuries-old traditions. In particular, the magical tradition, stemming from the human quest for omnipotence; the religious tradition, arising from humanity's quest for salvation; and the scientific tradition, deriving from the quest for knowledge and mastery of the universe, have strongly influenced the therapeutic process and have incorporated aspects of that process into their traditions (Ehrenwald, 1976: 20).

The writings contained in the Assyrian and Babylonian tablets, as well as the Papyrus Ebers, indicate that magic has played a strong role in psychotherapy for at least 4,500 years (Bromberg, 1975: 4). The earliest psychotherapists were the shamans and witch doctors of ancient and primitive societies who invoked supernatural forces to cure those seized by what they considered to be devils and other evil beings. The healing powers of St. Francis of Assisi, the curative effects of the "royal touch," and the cures achieved by the "laying on of hands" have been attributed to magical powers and illustrate how the therapeutic process continues to contain magical elements even in more modern times.

The religious tradition has contributed much to psychotherapy, and in turn has aspects and performs functions that bear remarkable resemblances to the therapeutic function. Since the inception of ancient Hindu, Taoist, and Buddhist doctrines in the Far East and early Greco-Roman and Judeo-Christian civilization in the West, religious healers have attempted to relieve the mental suffering of individuals and groups through essentially psychological means. By sustaining or inducing hope and faith, and using ritual and magic, the religious practitioner has employed techniques remarkably similar to modern-day psychotherapy.

Unfortunately, the religious tradition has also been responsible for some of the more bizarre methods of treating the mentally ill. The most horrifying example occurred at the end of the Middle Ages and the beginning of the Renaissance, when the persecution of witches reached its apex. The infamous *Malleus Maleficarum*, better known as the *Witches' Hammer* and authored in 1484 by two Dominican monks named Heinrich Kramer and James Sprenger, served as the moral justification for the ruthless killing of hundreds of thousands of women accused of practicing witchcraft.

This use of torture and killing in dealing with the problem of witchcraft illustrates the wide range of approaches possible in handling the problem of mental illness, and demonstrates the lengths to which society may go in explaining it. Throughout history society has tended to exclude and condemn the mentally ill. There has also been a recurrent tendency to view the mad as possessed by the devil.

Only in the last 200 years has a distinct effort been made to explain insanity on the basis of physical or psychological factors and to treat systematically the mentally ill through psychological means. Scientific efforts to explain and treat mental illness date back to the time of Hippocrates,[4] who viewed epilepsy as arising from natural causes and who castigated those who ascribed its symptoms to the works of the devil (Grimm, 1838: 211). Such attempts were not widespread, however, and for the most part the scientific world and the medical profession developed neither elaborate explanations of mental illness nor rational methods of treating it until the recent scientific age.

The writings of Johan Weyer may be viewed as the precursor to this new age. In 1550 he published a small book refuting the concept of demonism advocated and promulgated in the *Malleus Maleficarum.* Weyer forcefully argued that deviant behavior was caused by physical illness. Some 200 years later William Cullen enlarged on this theory when he coined the term "neurosis" to describe illnesses of a mental nature. Along with Hughlings Jackson, the eminent British neurologist, Cullen developed an explanation of behavioral disorders, theorizing that they were caused by defects in the central nervous system (Sarason and Ganzer, 1968: 507).

At the turn of the nineteenth century Benjamin Rush, considered the father of American psychiatry, was also conducting his landmark studies on the diseases of the mind. Over time physicians began developing classification schemes for psychiatric disorders. These culminated in the monumental work of Emil Kraepelin in the late nineteenth and early twentieth century, who developed a system containing more than 100 diagnostic categories for explaining mental illness on the basis of hereditary and organic factors.

Attempts to explain mental illness on a scientific basis were proceeding at roughly the same time that a new trend in treating the mentally ill was gaining momentum. After witchhunting had run its course, the mentally ill were relegated to madhouses, one of the earliest of which was Bedlam, built in 1377. There they received virtually no treatment and were generally locked in chains. Pinel (1745-1826) in France, Tuke (1732-1822) in England, and Dorothea Dix (1802-1877) in the United States, however, began what came to be known as the "moral treatment" of the insane. They recommended freeing mental patients from their chains and the other inhumanities of the early mental hospitals, and they advocated kindness, concern, and caring as effective treatment procedures.

By the late eighteenth century this development, in conjunction with the rudimentary scientific explanations of mental disease that were being explored, saw Mesmer's use of hypnosis to cure patients of specific emotional symptoms. He was one of the first to use a psychological technique to cure an emotional problem, where the use of the technique was based on scientific theory, not the use of magical forces, and where the purpose was to cure the patient of an illness, not to provide religious salvation. The use of these techniques by Mesmer represented the first true appearance of psychotherapy as a distinct form of healing (Frank, 1973: 4).

In the modern era Sigmund Freud stands as the grandparent of the current profession of psychotherapy. He was the first person to develop a widely accepted, viable, and comprehensive theory of mental illness. In addition he developed the technique of psychoanalysis as a treatment for emotional disorders. Freudian psychoanalysis has probably been the most important force in the history of modern psychotherapy. From its Viennese roots, Freud brought psychoanalysis to the United States in the early part of this century, where it became subsumed within the medical profession. This allowed it to obtain an eminence and prestige that would not otherwise have been possible, but resulted in its firm entrenchment as a medical process.

Freud's contribution to legitimating medical control of psychotherapy was two-edged. "It is generally agreed that the introduction and entrenchment of the concept of mental health as part of a general health-disease model is due to Freud" (Macklin, 1973: 53). In support of this view are the following facts. Freud's background was in medicine. He conducted his psychoanalytic practice in his doctor's office, making it appear that psychoanalysis must be a medical practice. Freud was thoroughly imbued in the medical tradition, and was strongly attracted to medical science because of its objectiveness. Despite his explanations of neurotic and psychotic disorders as being precipitated by early childhood conflicts and traumas, Freud believed that organic causes would ultimately be found for most major behavioral disorders (Sarason, 1968: 508). Freud also believed that psychoanalytic theory was appropriately a part of medicine.

At the same time Freud vehemently maintained that psychoanalysis as a method constituted an educational process, not treatment:

The internal development of psychoanalysis is everywhere proceeding contrary to my intentions away from lay analysis and becoming a pure medical specialty, and I regard this as fateful for the future of analysis. [Jones, 1957: III, 297.]

Freud apparently distinguished psychoanalysis as an explanatory theory of human behavior from psychoanalysis as a technique. His attempts to keep the technique of psychoanalysis separate from the medical profession were, however, defeated. In large measure the defeat stemmed from the efforts of the American branch of the International Psychoanalytic Association. In 1926 the New York legislature passed a bill making the practice of lay analysis illegal, and in 1927 the New York Society of Psychoanalysis issued a resolution condemning all forms of lay analysis (Siegler and Osmond, 1974: 49). With the rise in power of the American branch during and after World War II (because of the large number of psychoanalysts who left Europe for America), psychoanalysis and most of psychotherapy has become firmly entrenched as a medical specialty.

This development has been most unfortunate. A study of history clearly indicates that psychotherapy has roots in several traditions. Those who have been responsible for treating the mentally ill have come from a variety of professions. The religious healer, the shaman, and the witch doctor are prime examples of nonmedical people performing the tasks of psychotherapy. Over the course of time they have played a more significant part in creating and performing the therapeutic role than the medical doctor. While scientific explanations of mental illness may properly be the province of the medical profession, history argues that the treatment of mental illness does not lie exclusively within its domain.

Theory and Practice

Psychotherapeutic theory has been the driving force in the creation of new therapeutic techniques.[6] Prior to the twentieth century, however, attempts to formulate such theories and to develop such techniques were sporadic, incomplete, and rested on extremely shaky foundations. Mesmer's theory of animal magnetism, known as Mesmerism, is typical.[7] In the 1770s Mesmer began to achieve highly successful therapeutic results using his method, which he explained on the theory that the universe was filled with a magnetic fluid that must be distributed in the right amount in human beings. Mesmer achieved his cure by the "laying on of hands" and through physical contact with specific objects, thereby redistributing the universal magnetic fluid.

While Mesmer achieved considerable popular success, his work was the focus of much professional criticism and accusations of charlatanism. Nonetheless it represented one of the first attempts to develop a comprehensive explanatory theory of mental illness with an attendant therapeutic technique.

During the nineteenth century, as the physical sciences rose in importance, medical theory stressed the somatic bases of mental illness. This perspective was reinforced by the enormous advances in neuro-anatomy and neuro-physiology made by scientists such as Remak, Hall, and Dubois-Reymond, as well as the translation of this perspective into clinical practice by physicians such as Oppenheim and John Hughlings Jackson (Ackerknecht, 1959: 72). The result was a deemphasis of any form of verbal therapy, and moral treatment rapidly fell into disfavor. A very few nevertheless continued to experiment with hypnosis. These included Charcot, who used hypnotic techniques on a number of severely hysterical patients at the Salpetrière in France.

The experiments with hypnotism, begun a century earlier with the work of Mesmer and continued by Charcot, finally came to fruition in the research of Sigmund Freud. After his early work with Breuer on hysterics, Freud formulated the fundamental tenets of psychoanalytic theory.[8] Basic to Freud's theory was the belief that neurotic behavior was the result of sexual experiences in early childhood. Freud developed his now well-known concepts of the id, ego, and the superego to describe the psychic processes in human beings. Neurotic and psychotic behavior was the result of repressed memories and feelings related to the events of early childhood. As a result of this repression, these feelings became unconscious, although they still influenced behavior in the form of neurotic or psychotic symptoms, which Freud viewed as evidence of the underlying conflict. He developed the technique of psychoanalysis as the vehicle for assisting a patient in uncovering past conflicts and for successfully working them through. Critical to the process was the process of free association, the interpretation of these associations, and an analysis of the transference relationship. Psychoanalysis became a very lengthy process, lasting two to three years and involving four or more sessions per week.

Psychoanalytic theory and technique came to dominate modern psychotherapy until the 1950s, both in the United States and Europe. From its original Freudian roots, many different branches grew, including the individual psychology of Adler (1932), the analytic psychology of Jung (1966, 1933), and the analytic theory of Horney (1950). The large number of schools deriving from Freudian theory was chiefly the result of Freud's lack of toleration for disagreement. His anger and hostility toward those who dissented from his views made it virtually impossible for those with opposing ideas to remain within Freud's camp. Thus Jung's belief that dream life should be interpreted in relation to primitive archetypes held in common by various cultural groups, as opposed to the erotic symbolism prevalent in Freudian theory, along with the Jungian assumption of the primary place of the mother in the psychic development of the child, helped precipitate the eventual split between these two men. Similarly, Horney's emphasis on existential anxiety as the basis of neurosis was difficult to tolerate within the rigid tenets of the Freudian framework, and forced her to leave the fold. Adler, Stekel, Rank, Ferenczi, and Reich also parted ways with Freud quite quickly, and were soon followed by Sullivan, Fromm, and a host of others.

Generally, disagreement with Freudian theory centered on the importance of sexual conflicts as a determinant of mental illness, the importance of childhood in the development of the mature person, and the role of the therapist in the psychoanalytic process. On the latter issue, critics dispute the requirement of therapist aloofness and detachment, maintaining that a close rapport is desirable to encourage the client's (or patient's) self-exploration. There is also dispute over the role of catharsis in the curative process, and the value of focusing on strengthening the ego.

The fact that so many varieties of psychoanalytic theory have existed over time without any one proving itself superior, either in explanatory or curative power, is indicative of significant problems in the formulation of the theories themselves. Apart from evidentiary problems, much analytic theory lacks the prerequisites for either proof or disproof, since it is impossible to deduce determinate consequences from the assumptions of the theory, or to disprove the theory on the basis of experimental evidence.[9]

Until the 1950s Freudian analysis was mainly attacked from within—that is, from competing schools of analytic thought. In the past quarter-century the attacks have increasingly come from without. Today psychoanalysis, both as technique and theory, is increasingly viewed as anachronistic. Perhaps the biggest threats to the analysts have come from the behaviorists, who theorize that emotional disturbances can be alleviated without resort to lengthy analytic treatment.[10] They argue that many of the symptoms of mental illness do not imply a deeper underlying conflict, but are simply the result of improper learning or incorrect habits. They have gathered together an impressive array of research to demonstrate the efficacy of their treatment processes with a number of symptomatic problems, especially phobias.[11] Their theories and methods have challenged many of the cornerstones of psychoanalytic theory and have provided significant treatment alternatives.[12]

As client-centered therapy, Gestalt therapy, and the many other contemporary therapies continue to proliferate,[13] the mental health field is rapidly entering what Thomas Kuhn (1962) has termed a "scientific revolution." So many problems and unexplained phenomena exist with psychoanalytic and other theoretical formulations of the human condition, the effectiveness of any given treatment procedure is so open to question, and the claims to both explanation and cure of each school are so divergent, that "chaotic" becomes the most appropriate word to describe the state of the art.[14] The recent rise of community psychiatry and social psychiatry, with their emphasis and claim that social conditions are the primary cause of emotional illness and hence should be the primary focus of prevention and treatment, has only furthered the divisions within the already fractionalized psychotherapeutic community. Thus, despite the significant advances in research over the past thirty years, in many respects psychotherapy is more questioned today than ever before.

EVIDENCE OF VALUE AND EFFECTIVENESS

At the turn of this century psychotherapy was barely recognized and even less respected as a method of treatment among physicians and by the public. This was due to its relative infancy and the stigma attached to mental illness. Today psychotherapy is reasonably well established and well recognized. It is used to treat the chronically and severely mentally ill, the criminal offender, the relatively normal neurotic, and even extremely healthy individuals who see it as a vehicle for achieving further personal growth. The fact that many health insurance companies now reimburse policy holders for psychotherapeutic treatment is perhaps the most emphatic statement about its acceptance.

Whether psychotherapy is of value, however, and the extent to which it is effective, are empirical questions that have yet to be definitively determined.

Considerable research has been conducted bearing on these matters,[15] and this research has been thoroughly reviewed and analyzed by social scientists. Perhaps the best method of evaluating the effectiveness of psychotherapy is to review these reviews. Since 1950 more than twenty have appeared. By examining and comparing the best of these, a reasonably accurate picture emerges of the potential value of psychotherapy.

Hans J. Eysenck (1965, 1952), The Effects of Psychotherapy

In October 1952 Hans Eysenck published one of the first reviews of the literature on the effectiveness of psychotherapy, and thereby started one of the most acerbic, long-lasting, and emotionally charged debates in the history of research on psychotherapy.[16] The cause of the furor lay in his conclusions: while two-thirds of all neurotics who entered therapy improved considerably within two years, a similar proportion who received no treatment improved to the same extent (Eysenck, 1966). In other words, a neurotic was just as likely to improve without therapy as with it. Thirteen years after his original article,[17] Eysenck (1966: 40) updated his data and came to virtually the same conclusions: "Current psychotherapeutic procedures have not lived up to the hopes which greeted their emergence fifty years ago."

Eysenck's initial conclusions have been scrutinized intensely (see, e.g., Bergin, 1971, 1963; Luborsky, 1954; Rosenzweig, 1954). The most even-handed and thorough criticism is by Bergin (1971), who went to the trouble of reanalyzing all of Eysenck's data. After pointing out the methodological problems and flaws in the original data, Bergin's reanalysis led him to somewhat different conclusions. Whereas Eysenck concluded that 39 percent of those in psychoanalysis improved, Bergin's figure was 91 percent, although for eclectic psychotherapies his results hardly differed from Eysenck's

64 percent. Noting that Eysenck applied very stringent criteria for improvement, Bergin concludes that both his figures and Eysenck's are valid and justifiable. The differences stem from subjective interpretation of data that lend themselves to multiple interpretations.

As for Eysenck's 1965 conclusions, seventeen of the leading researchers in the field were invited to respond to them in the same issue of the journal in which Eysenck's article appeared. Their reactions ranged from outrage to hearty support. One of the most freqent criticisms concerned Eysenck's assertion that further research would not prove the efficacy of therapy. According to most researchers, his review was too limited to justify such a sweeping statement. Perhaps the most stinging and substantial criticism came from Kellner (in Eysenck, 1966: 86–91), who elaborately and effectively argued that: (1) Eysenck's reading of the literature was biased (in some instances Eysenck cited data from a particular study that supported his position, while ignoring data from other research of precisely comparable quality); and (2) Eysenck ignored a number of well-controlled studies that tended to demonstrate the effectiveness of psychotherapy.

Allen E. Bergin (1966), "Some Implications of Psychotherapy Research for Therapeutic Practice"

In the same year that Eysenck's pessimistic conclusions were reprinted in book form, Allen Bergin (1966) published a brief paper that has been widely hailed as one of the most important in the psychotherapeutic literature in the last twenty years. Much of the research in the 1950s had been characterized as a "flight from outcome into process," in which the effects of psychotherapy were ignored in favor of studying what went on in therapy. In the early 1960s this trend changed, and Bergin had been able to track down a number of studies that explained Eysenck's negative findings and provided further support for Kellner's assertion that psychotherapy could be effective. Bergin's (1966) specific conclusions can be summarized as follows:

1. Most forms of psychotherapy make some patients worse and some patients better. This accounts for the fact that many studies find no average difference between treated patients and controls.
2. Patients who do not receive formal psychotherapy improve, at least symptomatically, with the passage of time.
3. Client-centered therapy is the only school of interview-oriented therapy that has consistently demonstrated positive research results.
4. The most important therapist characteristics are warmth, empathy, adequate adjustment, and experience. Documentation of this stems primarily from the research of the client-centered therapists.
5. Certain kinds of patients are not amenable to interview-oriented psychotherapy.
6. Behavior therapy has been shown to be effective with certain types of symptoms.

Bergin based his conclusions on a comparative handful of studies, but these were carefully culled from all the existing research, and their quality was uniformly excellent. Each of his conclusions was supported by several studies, most of which had been adequately replicated.

Donald J. Kiesler (1966), "Some Myths of Psychotherapy Research and the Search for a Paradigm."

In this lengthy review of the literature, which appeared in the same year as Bergin's, Kiesler concluded that psychotherapy research was prolific but disorganized. In addition, methodological problems had severely weakened the impact of many studies. The inability of research to demonstrate the effectiveness of therapy was more related to these problems than to any inherent weakness in the therapeutic process itself. In particular, Kiesler attempted to show how three myths had been especially harmful. The first he labeled the "uniformity assumption." Because of this myth researchers had ignored the heterogeneity of patients and therapists. Schizophrenia research, for instance, had failed to take into account findings that patients diagnosed as schizophrenic were more different than alike. Similarly, differences in therapists' personalities were generally ignored in most research designs, despite the voluminous literature demonstrating the importance of specific therapist characteristics such as empathy. Failure to recognize these differences means that research results may prove negative because important variables have been incorrectly grouped together.

The second myth concerned "spontaneous remission," a term that arose to explain instances in which mentally ill people became healthy without formal psychotherapeutic help. The fact that some research evidence indicated that nearly the same percentage of sick people would improve whether they received therapy or not had been a mainstay of Eysenck's argument that psychotherapy was ineffective. Kiesler demonstrated how little sound evidence existed on which to base this assertion. The final myth revolved around the notion that present theoretical formulations were adequate for the conduct of research. None of the then-current theories explaining the psychotherapeutic process, such as Freudian, Rogerian, or learning theory, included all the known factors that influenced the course of therapy. Additionally, they were not sufficiently specific about independent variables and their relationship to outcome criteria, they frequently did not make a distinction between process and outcome, and they were based on classification schemes for mental illness that were neither valid nor reliable. Kiesler concluded that research based on the question, "Is psychotherapy effective?" would probably continue to yield poor results. He recommended that research be based on the more exact question, "What kind of psychotherapy under what conditions with what sorts of clients using which specific techniques yields what outcomes?"

Charles B. Truax and Robert R. Carkhuff (1967), Toward Effective Counseling and Psychotherapy

For years Carkhuff, Truax, and their associates have been concerned with measuring the effectiveness of psychotherapy. Working with Carl Rogers, they have developed operational measures for the curative factors in psychotherapy, as well as methods of measuring therapeutic results. As part of their work Truax and Carkhuff have synthesized the results of a large number of the better-conducted research projects, including thirty-seven studies utilizing control groups. They emphatically agree with Eysenck in their belief that the average counselor or psychotherapist does not help clients any more than they would be helped without therapy.[18] They hasten to add, however, that several relatively well-controlled studies demonstrate that certain types of counselors do produce beneficial effects beyond those observable in control groups. In their opinion many of the equivocal findings have arisen because good and bad therapists have not been properly controlled for.

Julian Meltzoff and Melvin Kornreich (1970), Research in Psychotherapy

Malan (1973: 723) has called Meltzoff and Kornreich's book-length study "the review to end all reviews." They have carefully analyzed virtually every single piece of important research prior to 1968.

They divided the research literature into "adequate studies" and "question-

able studies." Adequate studies met the following criteria: (1) there were no major design flaws that might make conclusions invalid; (2) the sample size had to be adequate and the control group appropriate; (3) the study had to be relatively unbiased; (4) measures had to be reasonably objective, reliable, and valid; and (5) the data had to be suitably analyzed and interpreted (Meltzoff and Kornreich 1970: 76). "Questionable studies" were of similar high quality, but failed to meet the above criteria in one or two respects. Thus, Meltzoff and Kornreich included analogue studies that might not be widely generalizable, or studies that had data relevant to psychotherapy research, but which were not conducted as evaluation research.

Meltzoff and Kornreich also divided each study according to results. *Positive* results were those that distinctly favored the treatment group; *null* results favored neither the treatment nor the control group; and *negative* results distinctly favored the control group. Since this latter category involved so few studies, they were lumped together. Finally, Meltzoff and Kornreich divided the studies according to whether the results were "major-primary-central-multiple" or "minor-secondary-peripheral-limited." This polarity classified results according to whether the treatment group showed major changes along dimensions that were central to improvement, or whether the changes were merely peripheral and perhaps other than what was originally desired.

After an exhaustive evaluation of 101 studies meeting their criteria, Meltzoff and Kornreich (1970: 174–77) summarized their findings. They pointed out that the total number of outcome studies had increased in every five-year period since 1950. The quality of the research conducted had improved in almost every respect. According to their breakdown, 80 percent of their studies yielded positive results, with the remaining 20 percent showing null or negative results. Of the adequate studies that failed to produce results, about 50 percent involved the failure of verbal therapies to help schizophrenic patients; another 33 percent were failures with regard to delinquency prevention, drug addiction, and enuresis. Of those studies not yielding positive results, patients in comparison groups receiving other than verbal forms of therapy improved more than untreated controls. The better the quality of research, the more positive were the outcomes.

Meltzoff and Kornreich concluded that far more often than not psychotherapy of a wide variety of types and applied to a broad range of disorders had been demonstrated to produce significant positive changes under controlled conditions. According to them, these changes could not be explained by the passage of time alone, and the therapist was a crucial factor in determining results. As a group the therapists upon whom research had been conducted were not chosen because of their excellence. In fact, many were inexperienced, and they worked in a wide variety of settings. Yet these therapists achieved distinctly positive results. On the other hand, Meltzoff and Kornreich recognized that the accumulated evidence still did not allow any statement about the degree of effectiveness of psychotherapy, or whether therapy was a worthwhile process. Since their main conclusions were so at variance with other reviews, Meltzoff and Kornreich attempted to account for this difference. In essence, they argued that their evidence was far more complete. Where the same research was involved they acknowledged that they had simply interpreted and evaluated the data differently.[19]

Allen E. Bergin (1971), "The Evaluation of Therapeutic Outcomes"

Allen Bergin has consistently offered more conservative and circumscribed conclusions on the efficacy of psychotherapy than reviewers such as Meltzoff

and Kornreich. This is clearly evident in his updated and considerably expanded 1971 review, which appeared in Bergin and Garfield's (1971) *Handbook of Psychotherapy and Behavior Change.* Strupp and Bergin (1969) had been commissioned by the National Institute of Mental Health to develop an exhaustive bibliography of the research on psychotherapy. Using this as a base, Bergin chose fifty-two studies as being of adequate design. Twenty-two of these emerged as positive,[20] fifteen in doubt, and fifteen negative concerning the effectiveness of psychotherapy. These results were comparable to the findings of Kellner (1967, 1965) and Jonckheere (1965), according to Bergin, and were in substantial agreement with his figures for research conducted prior to 1952. He concluded: "While the methodological sophistication and precision of studies have improved markedly, the evidence continues to yield the general conclusion that psychotherapy, on the average, has modestly positive effects" (Bergin, 1971: 228). In agreement with Truax and Carkhuff, Bergin attributes the modesty of these results to the failure of most research to take into account that some therapists do a significantly better job than others. In comparison with Eysenck's pessimistic conclusions, Bergin's more positive views on psychotherapy are attributable to his different analysis of the research on spontaneous remission. Instead of the two-thirds figure used by Eysenck, Bergin (1971: 241) concluded that "the median rate appears to be in the vicinity of 30 percent" (emphasis omitted).

David H. Malan (1973), "The Outcome Problem in Psychotherapy Research"

Malan's article, which appeared in the *Archives of General Psychiatry*, was not simply a review of the empiric literature, but a review of reviews. His basic position was close to Bergin's—more positive than Eysenck, and less optimistic than Meltzoff and Kornreich. The grounds for his qualified optimism rested largely on the research indicating a greater variability in outcome for those in therapy than for those who receive no treatment. This finding indicated that psychotherapy must be a powerful phenomenon, even though its effects were not always positive.

Yet Malan was not optimistic about the effects of the typical psychotherapy as performed by the ordinary practitioner, and here he took strong issue with the conclusions of Meltzoff and Kornreich. Of the one hundred one studies used by the latter, Malan argued that less than forty were adequately designed. In their criteria for adequacy Meltzoff and Kornreich omitted the requirement of long-term follow-up, which meant that many of the positive results they found may have been ephemeral or due to the placebo effect.[21]

If the requirement of follow-up is added to the other criteria of Meltzoff and Kornreich for determining adequacy, the number of studies with a major positive result is reduced to eleven. If a further limitation is established of requiring the treatment group to be both patients and non-psychotic adults, the number of studies is further reduced to four. These four studies were all of patients with psychosomatic illnesses such as ulcerative colitis. When Malan examined Meltzoff and Kornreich's adequately designed studies with positive but minor results, he found only one adult nonpsychotic outpatient with long-term follow-up, but even there the control group was questionable. In the category of adequate studies yielding null or negative results, only one met Malan's additional criteria. In other words, "as the reader will see, studies of dynamic psychotherapy on adult *psychoneurotic* outpatients are entirely absent" (Malan, 1973: 724).

After reorganizing Meltzoff and Kornreich's data, Malan came to some interesting conclusions. Five controlled studies of psychotherapy for psychosomatic conditions all gave positive results. The methods of therapy were all different. Malan stated that these studies demonstrate that psychotherapy can be effective with psychosomatic conditions, although they do not prove that psychotherapy is necessary or that a specific treatment process is recommended. He went on to comment, "Thus, we reach the almost bizarre conclusion that dynamic therapies seem to have been more or less validated for psychosomatic conditions, and for no other conditions whatsoever" (Malan, 1973: 725).

Edward S. Bordin (1974), Research Strategies in Psychotherapy.

In contrast to Meltzoff and Kornreich, Bordin was not so much interested in the general effectiveness of psychotherapy (which he bypassed completely), as in "what we know about different processes and parts of processes in the hands of different kinds of therapists with different persons" (Bordin, 1974: vii). In his analysis of research strategies Bordin examined the ways in which various factors influence the therapeutic process, such as the personality of the therapist and the patient. He concluded that "there is respectable evidence of short- or long-term effects of various aspects of the psychotherapeutic situation and of the functional relations among various components of it" (Bordin, 1974: 219). He admitted that the precisional level of most studies was not very advanced, but believed that the future was bright for innovation and progress. His review revealed that few studies had examined the effectiveness of competing theories and practices, and little research had been conducted on such critical variables as the transference and countertransference relationship. Also, a number of psychotherapies had been virtually ignored, including neopsychoanalytic, Gestalt, and the existential therapies.

Lester Luborsky, Barton Singer, and Lise Luborsky (1975), "Comparative Studies of Psychotherapies: Is It True that 'Everyone Has Won and All Must Have Prizes'?"

Luborsky, Singer, and Luborsky continued the tradition of Bordin in avoiding the broad question, "Is psychotherapy effective?" Their basic approach was to compare various therapeutic modalities: psychotherapy versus group psychotherapy, time-limited versus time-unlimited therapy, client-centered versus traditional therapies, and so on. Only studies of reasonable quality were chosen, and these were graded on the basis of twelve criteria. More than a hundred studies were included. Their basic conclusions were that different forms of psychotherapy do not make significant differences in the proportion of patients who improve by the end of psychotherapy, and most patients who go through any form of psychotherapy gain from it. Of thirty-three studies comparing psychotherapy with no therapy at all, twenty favored therapy, thirteen indicated no difference, and none concluded that no therapy was better than some form of therapy. Luborsky, Singer, and Luborsky explained the lack of difference in effectiveness among the major therapies as a result of the major common elements operative in each (especially the personality of the therapist) and the difficulty of a particular therapy appearing more effective when all appear to have significant effectiveness.

Gene V. Glass (1976), "Primary, Secondary, and Meta-Analysis of Research"

Perhaps the most brilliant review of the research on psychotherapy has been conducted by Gene Glass. He describes his review as meta-analysis, which he defines as "the statistical analysis of a large collection of analysis results from individual studies for the purpose of integrating the findings" (Glass, 1976: 2). Such an analysis is in contradistinction to casual, narrative discussions of research studies, which generally suffer from significant methodological difficulties.[22]

Glass's review is exceedingly comprehensive. He and his associates inspected more than a thousand studies, retained five hundred as appropriate, and fully analyzed the results of three hundred seventy-five controlled investigations.[23] No effort was made to screen out poorly designed studies, since Glass found that such studies were as valid as well-designed ones. Unlike most reviewers, Glass thoroughly investigated dissertations.

Psychotherapy was broadly defined, although drug therapy, hyponotherapy, bibliotherapy, occupational therapy, milieu therapy, and encounter groups were eliminated. Each of the 375 studies was quantified according to more than two dozen features, and sophisticated statistical techniques were then applied to analyze the aggregated data.

Glass's findings are persuasive. On average the typical study showed a two-thirds standard deviation superiority of the treated group over the control group. This means that the average client in therapy was significantly better off than three-fourths of those who did not receive treatment. Changes were most marked in the area of fear and anxiety, in which the results of therapy left patients better off than 83 percent of the people who received no treatment. Therapy was also more beneficial than no therapy in the area of self-esteem (nine-tenths of a standard deviation), adjustment (roughly six-tenths of a standard deviation), and school or work achievement (approximately three-tenths of a standard deviation). Concluded Glass: "If therapy is completely ineffective, the extant outcome evaluation literature represents either an epidemic of methodological naiveté or else self-delusion of gargantuan proportions" (Glass, 1976: 18).

The Annual Review of Psychology (1955-1975).

The *Annual Review of Psychology* has devoted considerable space to evaluating the effectiveness of psychotherapy and its various aspects. The change in the nature of the conclusions from early to later years is instructive about the progress of psychotherapy research, and parallels the changes in the conclusions of literature reviews in general. In 1955—three years after Eysenck's initial article—Paul Meehl reviewed the psychotherapy literature for the *Annual Review*. His basic conclusion was that no one had properly answered Eysenck by providing adequate studies of the effectiveness of therapy: "The lesson would seem to be that we know so little about the process of helping that the only proper attitude is one of maximum experimentalism. The state of theory and its relation to technique is obviously chaotic whatever our pretensions" (Meehl, 1955: 375). More than ten years later Dittman's (1966: 74) review indicated that some, but not much, progress had been made: "My impression is that studies of the outcome of psychotherapy have finally allowed us to draw conclusions on other bases than intuition, but that the conclusions, themselves, are modest, and are, moreover, diluted by confusion." The research was beginning to indicate that general research on effectiveness was not the answer: "The variability in results, even of the good studies, is so great that no one could possibly believe that psychotherapy is a unitary phenomenon" (Dittman, 1966: 74). Rosalind Cartwright's review in 1968 took this into account; the focus of her review was on discovering the ingredients of good psychotherapy, and she virtually assumed that psychotherapy was effective, at least in some instances.[24]

The trend toward research that attempts to identify the responsible factors for effectiveness, rather than questioning whether therapy is effective at all, has continued to the present. Bergin and Suinn's (1975) recent review is illustrative, as they conclude that "the weight of evidence and the views of reviewers support the notion of significant improvement . . . in psychotherapy, with improvement rates averaging about 67% . . ." (p. 518, references omitted).

Cost/Benefit Analysis of Psychotherapy

Those who have reviewed the research on psychotherapy have concentrated on the changes that it brings about and whether those changes are greater than for similar people who do not receive therapy. Perhaps even more important is the issue of whether the benefits of therapy are greater than its costs, and by how much (Conley et al., 1967). Ideally such a cost-benefit analysis would be expressed in dollars and cents figures, allowing a comparison of the effectiveness and efficiency of various modes of therapy. This type of quantification is exceedingly difficult (Panzetta, 1973), and has rarely been done. Where it has been, the indications are that psychotherapy is a financially sound proposition.[25] A frequent finding appears to be that medical utilization decreases significantly where increased psychiatric services are provided.[26] The reason appears to be that many visits to physicians for physical complaints and symptoms are a consequence of emotional distress for which psychotherapy is a more effective remedy (Cummings and Follette, 1976).

Conclusion

Over the past thirty years psychotherapy research has progressed considerably. In the 1950s the lack of outcome studies prevented definitive conclusions from being drawn either for or against the effectiveness of psychotherapy. By the mid-sixties this situation was changing, although reviewers such as Eysenck despaired of ever proving its value.

In the last ten years research has become increasingly sophisticated. In particular the recent reviews by Glass (1976),

Luborsky, Singer, and Luborsky (1975), and Bergin and Suinn (1975) indicate that psychotherapy is an effective process and does bring about an improvement in the mental health of many of those who participate in it. This means that the therapeutic process has potential value to society and that regulatory proposals must be framed in such a way as to protect that value. Arbitrary and unvalidated standards for determining psychotherapeutic competence may weaken or destroy these positive benefits.

RISKS AND DANGERS

Central to the problem of regulating psychotherapists is the degree of risk and danger involved in the psychotherapeutic process. The demand for regulation rests largely on this alleged danger, and the constitutionality of many licensing laws hinges on an adequate demonstration of significant risk.

Determining the degree of danger is more complex than first appears. The seemingly simple task of defining what constitutes an adverse result is in fact very difficult.[27] Determining whether psychotherapy is responsible for precipitating suicide or severe emotional distress is not an easy matter. Subtler still is the question of the duration of emotional injury, since negative effects may only be transitory. Often ignored is the necessity of comparing the level of danger in psychotherapy with that in other activities for which no demand for regulation exists. This section explores the types of dangers involved in traditional psychotherapy and attempts realistically to assess their likelihood.[28]

General Risks and Dangers

The formal practice of psychotherapy has been in existence for nearly a century. As a result, it is more generally accepted than encounter groups, and less outcry exists about its potential dangers.[29] While traditional psychotherapy was earlier attacked as radical, today it is more often accused of fostering establishment values and maintaining the status quo.[30] Nevertheless, as with encounter groups, many aspects of the psychotherapeutic process lend themselves to irresponsible use, with the possible consequence of harm to the client. For instance, since most therapies promote anxiety, at least to a certain degree, some clients may become too anxious and undergo destructive psychological decompensation. In the more active and directive therapies a tendency for intemperate verbal and physical assaults on clients may result in serious emotional disturbance (Lambert et al., 1977; Strupp et al., 1976: 56–57). Psychoanalytic writers have noted that the handling of the transference relationship is a delicate matter, whose inadequate resolution can lead to harmful and lasting dependency on the analyst (Chapman, 1964). Even successful resolution of a particular problem may be harmful, if the result is the reappearance of symptoms in a different area. Finally, the nature of the therapeutic process places great power in the hands of the therapist, and offers ample opportunity for unethical activities and other abuses.

Anecdotal Reports

Anecdotal reports provide evidence that these dangers are at least occasionally realized. Perhaps the most dramatic evidence is provided by the more highly publicized malpractice cases. In *Hammer v. Rosen* (1960), for instance, evidence was offered that the defendant psychiatrist had, as part of the treatment process, beaten the patient on a number of occasions. One of the nurses stated, in fact, that after one session the patient's body was covered with bruises and her clothes were torn and disheveled. In *Zipkin v. Freeman* (1968), a psychiatrist advised the plaintiff that she needed further treatment in the form of personal and social contacts with him. These contacts consisted in part of convincing the patient to steal her husband's property, participating with her in nude swimming parties, and carrying on illicit sexual intercourse with the patient over an extended period of time. Other reports of iatrogenic harm have appeared in a number of professional journals, and offer further evidence of the dangers that psychotherapy can pose (*see*, *e.g.*, Bergin, 1971: 250-52; Chapman, 1964; Schmideberg, 1963).

Survey Studies and Informed Estimates

Recently a questionnaire survey was undertaken to determine the prevailing views of expert clinicians, theoreticians, and researchers on negative effects in psychotherapy (Hadley and Strupp, 1976; Strupp et al., 1976). Virtual unanimity existed that the problem of harm was very real. Judgments as to its frequency ranged from moderate to extremely common (a few dissenters believed that no persuasive evidence of harm existed).

Two related categories of negative effects were frequently mentioned. The first consisted of the exacerbation of presenting symptoms such as a depressive breakdown, destructive acting out, or increased guilt. The second was the appearance of new symptoms that were more dysfunctional than the old ones (such as a shift from somatic complaints to paranoia). The most extreme instance of harmful results was the precipitation of suicide or a psychotic break.

Several professional organizations have also attempted to determine the degree of danger connected with psychotherapy. In investigating the feasibility of a model statute licensing the practice of psychotherapy, a task force of the American Orthopsychiatric Association (Harrison et al., 1970: 558) concluded that "the extent to which the public is hurt by quackery under the rubric of psychotherapy appeared to be minimal." On the other hand, the New York State Psychological Association (Schillinger, 1974) has conducted a long and sustained campaign to demon-

strate that unlicensed practitioners or practitioners with bogus degrees are causing significant and extensive harm. An investigation by the New York Attorney General's Office (New York State, 1972) into the unregulated practices of people in the mental health field demonstrated the existence of widespread abuses.

Surveys have documented the existence of specific problems in psychotherapy, especially sexual abuses. Taylor and Wagner (1976), for instance, examined every instance in the empirical literature on the effects of sexual relationships between therapist and client. Of the thirty-four cases found, 47 percent resulted in a negative outcome to either the client, the therapist, or both.[31] In another survey 1,000 randomly chosen California physicians were sent an anonymous questionnaire regarding erotic contacts with their patients (Kardener et al., 1973); 460 responded, of whom 114 were psychiatrists. Five to 13 percent of all respondents engaged in some kind of erotic behavior with their patients, while between 5 and 7.2 percent had engaged in intercourse with them. For psychiatrists, 5 to 10 percent stated that they had some erotic contact, while 5 percent reported having intercourse.[32]

In still another study, Grunebaum, Nadelson, and Macht (undated) surveyed members of the Massachusetts Psychiatric Society to determine what percentage of the membership knew of other psychiatrists who had engaged in sexual intercourse with their patients. Approximately half of those who returned their questionnaires knew of reported or unreported cases. Twelve instances were cited in which patients reported sexual activities with past psychiatrists to their current psychiatrists. The respondents stated that nine of the complaints were justified; three were probably justified; in no instance was the complaint considered unjustified.

These findings are somewhat impressionistic and do not provide a basis for making firm estimates of how dangerous psychotherapy is.[33] Nonetheless, on the basis of these surveys alone, several conclusions can be drawn. First, psychotherapy obviously has the potential for causing harm. Second, this potential is occasionally realized. Third, the type of danger can range from a minor increase in emotional distress to sexual abuses and therapist-induced suicide.

Empirical Research

In turning to rigorous empirical research it is difficult to find well-conceived studies that examine whether psychotherapy is dangerous. Until the 1950s most research projects simply did not investigate this possibility. The general pattern was to rate patients as cured, improved, or unchanged. The situation has gradually been changing, largely due to the impetus provided by Allen Bergin's continuing examination and discussion of this problem. In 1963 he published an article in the *Journal of Counseling Psychology* on the negative effects of psychotherapy (Bergin, 1963).

Bergin suggested that two lines of evidence existed for concluding that psychotherapy does harm as well as good. First, several studies showed that individuals who had undergone therapy exhibited a good deal more variability in their outcomes than equivalent control groups (*see* Cartwright's [1956] reanalysis of Barron and Leary's [1955] work). In other words, while the average mean score for each group might be the same, the individuals that underwent therapy had a wider range in scores, and evidently some were made worse while others improved. Second, correlations existed between this variability and certain factors that are usually associated with increase in risk. For instance, a number of studies found that change in personality functioning was largely negative under lower conditions of genuineness, nonpossessive warmth, and accurate empathic understanding on the part of the therapist, but positive when these conditions were higher (*see, e.g.*, Rogers and Dymond, 1954: 228; Truax, 1963: 261).

By 1966 Bergin had coined the term "deterioration effect" for those cases in which psychotherapy had apparently harmed the patient (Bergin, 1966). He had accumulated a total of seven studies in which a significant difference in variability existed between individuals in psychotherapy and those who were not.

Problems with this line of reasoning were apparent, however. Critics pointed out that an increase in variability might not be evidence of deterioration caused by psychotherapy (Braucht, 1970). They also raised other objections. Braucht (1970) pointed out that: (1) some of the studies used by Bergin did not actually involve psychotherapy per se (for instance, the *Cambridge-Somerville Youth Study* by Powers and Witmer, 1951); (2) some of the control groups did not actually qualify as control groups; (3) the increase in variability might have been due to factors other than psychotherapy, but these factors were not controlled for; and (4) opposite results on a test do not necessarily imply that one person deteriorated (on a measure of assertiveness, for instance, an overly aggressive, acting-out teenager may achieve more self-control, while a passive housewife may move toward increased aggressiveness).[34]

May (1971) also raised a number of cogent objections to Bergin's findings. He reanalyzed the Powers and Witmer study to demonstrate that the control group was not comparable to the psychotherapy group, and that when experimentals and controls were matched for initial adjustment level, there was a slightly greater variability in the control group. He noted that in the Rogers and Dymond study the greater variability of the experimental group could readily be explained by the fact that the normal group, since it was closer to normal, had less chance of moving widely on the scales that were used. In several of the other studies, he pointed out methodological flaws that may have accounted for the greater variance of change that Bergin attributed to the psychotherapeutic process. Thus, in Barron and Leary's study, patients were not assigned to the experimental and control groups on a random basis, but by a clinic-intake process. This process might very well have affected the composition of the control group, making it a more normal sample of the population. If this were the case, it would have less potential for change, which would account for the increased variance in the experimental group.

In other studies May noted that the method of determining which individuals were to be in the control group was not discussed. He also examined these studies to show that other methodological problems leave Bergin's conclusions open to serious question. He concluded that with the exception of one equivocal study, the statement that psychotherapy may cause harm rests upon a flimsy and poorly controlled or weakly documented base.

Despite these and other criticisms (*see* Eysenck, 1967; Rachman, 1971), Bergin's work received considerable acclaim from some of the most highly respected professionals in the field (*see, e.g.,* Frank, 1967; Matarazzo, 1967). He continued to survey the field for further evidence of deterioration, and by 1971 had added two studies to the seven yielding evidence of increased variability (Bergin, 1971). In addition, he had found more than twenty other studies that provided evidence of harmful effects.

Some of these suggested that psychotherapy was extremely dangerous. In a study by Uhlenhuth and Duncan (1968), 26 percent of those in therapy deteriorated over the course of treatment. Berleman and Steinburn (1967) found evidence that ten of twenty-eight patients (36 percent) had deteriorated from their pre-therapy level at the time of follow-up, while none of the control group had suffered any worsening of their condition. Bergin noted that in only four of the studies where he was able to assess whether deterioration had occurred was there little or no evidence of its presence. According to his subjective reading of the evidence, he concluded that approximately 10 per-

cent of those in therapy deteriorate, while the comparable rate for control groups is less than 5 percent (Bergin, 1971: 248).

Recently Bergin has coauthored a comprehensive review of deterioration effects that completely updates his previous work (Lambert et al., 1977). (See Hadley, Gomes, and Armstrong, 1976, for a good summary of these studies.) While granting that increased variance is not necessarily indicative of deterioration, Bergin and his associates maintain that the nine studies he reported in 1971, when taken together, provide a strong empirical base for this conclusion. Bergin's list of other studies bearing on the deterioration problem has increased to nearly forty. In twenty of these, evidence of deterioration exists for a therapy sample, but no control group exists. Eleven studies do make this comparison. Another eight provide data on deterioration effects for people not receiving therapy, but no corresponding data is provided for a comparable treatment group.

In more than 40 percent of the thirty-one studies examining the dangers of psychotherapy, the percentage of those hurt was greater than 10 percent, at least on some criteria or for part of the sample. This figure is shockingly high, but exactly the same percentage of the control groups experienced a deterioration rate of more than 10 percent. The wide variations in patient populations, criteria, and rigor in design prevented the reviewers from attempting to extrapolate a median deterioration rate for those receiving therapy.

The attempt to establish the percentage of persons who would deteriorate without receiving therapy met with a similar lack of success. As with spontaneous remission (Lambert, 1976) the figures are so variable as to be untrustworthy. Thus, Lambert, Bergin, and Collins (1977) do not even offer a subjective estimate of a median rate, as Bergin had done in 1971.

Conclusion

Drawing definitive conclusions, then, from the data provided by reviewers of the research or from other sources is difficult. The variability of results, the lack of agreement on negative-outcome criteria, and the wide range in the quality of research do not allow meaningful statements to be made about the extensiveness of the risks involved in psychotherapy. Perhaps the soundest conclusions, although few in number, have been made by Strupp and his associates (1976) in their analysis of Lambert, Bergin, and Collins's review. They state emphatically that psychotherapy does occasionally have adverse effects, and that these pose a real and serious problem. On the other hand, according to their analysis, the research literature provides less than convincing evidence that the emotional difficulties of those in therapy are exacerbated by their experience. This is not because these effects do not occur, but because of inadequacies in the available empirical data.[35]

SUMMARY

Although difficult to define clearly, traditional psychotherapy is a process that has roots in religion, science, and magic. Perhaps because of its diverse origins, it is practiced by a wide variety of professionals, including psychologists, psychiatrists, social workers, and nurses. Psychotherapeutic theory and technique is also distinguished by its diversity. Attempts to establish the effectiveness and impact of the therapeutic process, as traditionally conceived, have only recently begun to yield meaningful results. Psychotherapy does appear to have value and to bring about constructive personality changes. At the same time, the potential for negative effects has also been documented, although the extensiveness of these effects has not been adequately determined.

Since traditional psychotherapy has frequently been distinguished from the newer encounter groups and other humanistic therapies, it may be that the above findings do not apply to these latter activities. In this case different regulations may be warranted. The following chapter examines the development of these new methods of therapy, and establishes the extent to which they are efficacious and dangerous.

NOTES

1. *Compare* the definition offered by Curran and Partridge (1955: 353-54):

Psycho-therapy aims at relieving symptoms of psychic origin by adjusting the attitudes that have led to their development.

It is an art rather than a science. . . .

The treatment proceeds by stages which are often referred to as *explanation, suggestion, persuasion* and *re-education.*

with the broad definition recommended by the American Psychological Association (1967: 1099) for use in state legislation:

Psychotherapy . . . means the use of learning, conditioning methods, and emotional reactions, in a professional relationship, to assist a person or persons to modify feelings, attitudes, and behavior which are intellectually, socially, or emotionally maladjustive or ineffectual.

with the very broad definition offered by Lindner (1950: 433):

We can define [psychotherapy] . . . as the art of application of psychological science to the total human organism where experience and experiment establish its theoretical or demonstrated value.

For good summaries of the various definitions in the literature, *see* Eysenck (1966: 6-8) and the American Orthopsychiatric Association (1968 and 1968a). For other definitions, *see* Meltzoff and Kornreich (1970: 3-5), American Psychiatric Association (1975), Wolberg (1967: 1-11), Dollard and Miller (1950), and Pleune (1965). An excellent description of group psychotherapy has been provided by Leonard Horwitz (1971: 249):

In group psychotherapy (1) a relatively small number of patients are involved, the maximum being 8 to 10; (2) the mode of interaction comes as close as possible to being solely verbal, as opposed to various kinds of recreational or other activities; (3) structuring and agenda making are kept to a minimum by the therapist, in contrast to current event groups or other discussion groups; (4) the therapist, with training in psychopathology, psychodynamics, and the technics of individual psychotherapy, is capable of recognizing and interpreting transference phenomena; (5) an objective in all psychotherapy groups is to enhance the patient's self-awareness, particularly his patterns of interacting with others—this aim contrasts with group counseling which emphasizes solutions for reality problems.

2. Hathaway (1951: 259) has stated this problem well:

With the intention of arriving at a working definition of the term psychotherapy, at least two extremes in connotation may help in orientation. The first extreme is illustrated by those few psychoanalysts who affirm that there is only one type of psychotherapy, namely, psychoanalytic therapy, and that any other approach is a covering up or ameliorative procedure not properly so considered. Although the most brash proponents of such an extreme concept of psychotherapy are probably psychoanalytic in persuasion, there are here and there other therapists who hold analogously restricted views. At the other extreme, psychotherapy becomes almost any predominantly psychological procedure, personal or environmental, that is assumed to be contributory to mental hygiene or personal adjustment. With this broader definition, better living conditions, better food, and the like, all become psychotherapeutic procedures insofar as they have psychological implications. One might then cite a music program in a clinic or hospital as an example of psychotherapy and the staff musician as a psychotherapist.

Neither of these extreme positions is here accepted as particularly useful. . . . The former connotation restricts progress by encouraging doctrinal and isolated positions antipathetic to new ideas. It inhibits active experimentation by persons who might not accept the tenets of the particular procedures defined as psychotherapy. The latter is so broad as to constitute almost a statement of the general principle that simply healthy living is therapeutic.

3. Zilboorg and Henry's (1941) *A History of Medical Psychology* is one of the first treatises to deal with the history of psychotherapy. It is a classic text, although somewhat dated. Other good histories can be found in Ackerknecht's (1959) *A Short History of Psychiatry;* Bromberg's (1975) *From Shaman to Psychotherapist;* Ehrenwald's (1976) *The History of Psychotherapy;* Ellenberger's (1970) *The Discovery of the Unconscious;* Freud's (1963) *The History of the Psychoanalytic Movement;* Goshen's (1975) *A Documentary History of Psychiatry;* Janet's (1925) *Psychological Healing;* Kopp's (1971) *Guru: Metaphors from a Psychotherapist;* Murphy and Kovach's (1972) *Historical Introduction to Modern Psychology;* Thompson's (1947) *Magic and Healing;* and Weatherhead's (1951) *Psychology, Religion and Healing.* The discussion in the text is drawn from these various sources.

4. Hippocrates'(in Grimm, 1838: 211) words were:

The position regarding the so-called sacred disease [epilepsy] is as follows: It seems to me to be no more divine and no more sacred than other diseases, but, like other affections, it springs from natural causes. . . . Those who first connected this illness with demons and described it as sacred seem to me no different from the conjurors, purificators, mountebanks and charlatans of our day, who pretend to great piety and superior knowledge. But such persons are merely concealing, under the cloak of godliness, their perplexity and their inability to afford any assistance.

5. In the postscript to his book, *The Question of Lay Analysis*, Freud (1950: 103) argued:

> It will not have escaped my readers that in what I have said I have assumed as axiomatic something that is still violently disputed in the discussion. I have assumed, that is to say, that psychoanalysis is not a specialized branch of medicine. I cannot see how it is possible to dispute this. . . . The possibility of its application to medical purposes must not lead us astray.

Also, in a letter to Paul Federn (1967: 269-70), written in 1927, Freud wrote:

> The battle for lay analysis must, at one time or another, be fought to the finish. Better now than later. As long as I live I shall resist that psychoanalysis be swallowed up by medicine.

6. Excellent basic texts on psychiatry, psychotherapeutic theory and technique (including group psychotherapy) include Arbuckle's (1970) *Counseling: Philosophy, Theory and Practice;* Arieti's (1974-75) *American Handbook of Psychiatry;* Frank's (1973) *Persuasion and Healing;* Kubie's (1950) *Practical and Theoretical Aspects of Psychoanalysis;* Menninger's (1963) *The Vital Balance;* Powdermaker and Frank's (1953) *Group Psychotherapy;* Redlich and Freedman's (1966) *The Theory and Practice of Psychiatry;* and Yalom's (1975) *The Theory and Practice of Group Psychotherapy.*

7. For an excellent history and exposition of Mesmerism, which also examines its relation to the political events of the times, *see* Darnton's (1968) *Mesmerism and the End of the Enlightenment in France.*

8. The most concise explanations of Freud's original theories are contained in his *An Outline of Psycho-analysis* (1969), first published in Germany in 1940, and *A General Introduction to Psychoanalysis* (1920), originally published by Liveright Publishing Company of London.

9. Ernest Nagel (1959: 39-40) has eloquently explicated the problems of psychoanalytic theory:

> [Freudian] theory does not seem to me to satisfy two requirements which any theory must satisfy if it is to be capable of empirical validation. . . . In the first place, it must be possible to deduce determinate consequences from the assumptions of theory, so that one can decide on the basis of logical considerations, and prior to the examination of any empirical data, whether or not an alleged consequence of the theory is indeed implied by the latter. For unless this requirement is fulfilled, the theory has no definite content, and questions as to what the theory asserts cannot be settled except by recourse to some privileged authority or arbitrary caprice. In the second place, even though the theoretical notions are not explicitly defined by way of overt empirical procedures and observable traits of things, nevertheless at least *some* theoretical notions must be tied down to *fairly definite and unambiguously specified* observable materials, by way of rules of procedure variously called "correspondence rules," "coordinating definitions," and "operational definitions." For if this condition is not satisfied, the theory can have no determinate consequences about *empirical* subject matter. An immediate corollary to these requirements is that since a consistent theory cannot imply two incompatible consequences, a credible theory must not only be *confirmed* by observational evidence, but it must also be capable of being *negated* by such evidence. In short, a theory must not be formulated in such a manner that it can always be construed and manipulated so as to explain whatever the actual facts are, no matter whether controlled observation show one state of affairs to obtain or its opposite. In respect to both of these requirements, however, Freudian theory in general, and the metapsychology in particular, seem to me to suffer from serious shortcomings.

10. There is voluminous literature on behavior therapy. For two good overviews, see the American Psychiatric Association Task Force Report (1973) on *Behavior Therapy in Psychiatry;* and Wolpe, Salter, and Reyna's (1964) *The Conditioning Therapies.*

11. The American Psychiatric Association's Task Force (1973: 35–36) on *Behavior Therapy in Psychiatry*, for instance, conducted an extensive review of the research and concluded:

> To summarize the literature as a whole, we conclude that individual subject designs have demonstrated that therapies based on reinforcement principles do produce more improvements than no treatment at all. . . . Review of the numerous studies of desensitization suggests that this procedure produces measurable benefits for patients across a wide range of problems.

For further discussion and evaluation of the research on behavior therapy, see Bergin and Suinn (1975); Glass (1976); Luborsky, Singer, and Luborsky (1975); and Sloane, Staples, Cristol, Yorkston, and Whipple (1975).

12. Another major group that has had a significant effect on psychotherapy has been the European existentialists (*see* Binswanger, 1956; Jaspers, 1964; Ruitenbeek, 1962; Sartre, 1953). Developed by philosophers arguing the importance and consequences of freedom of choice for the human being, existentialism lays great stress on the meaning of anxiety and despair—seeing these as reactions to the meaninglessness of life unless human beings establish their own meaning for it. Existential therapy views its primary task as helping patients deal with these problems in order to confront their own existential abyss.

13. The following books provide a sampling of some of the more popular therapeutic theories and techniques abounding today: Hart and Tomlinson (1970) (client-centered therapy); Janov (1972, 1971, 1970) (primal therapy); Polster and Polster (1974) (Gestalt therapy); Lowen (1969) (bio-energetics); and Berne (1961) (transactional analysis).

14. Roy Grinker (1964) has aptly summed up the current state of affairs in his article "Psychiatry Rides Madly in All Directions."

15. Glass (1976) estimates that roughly 1,000 controlled therapy outcome studies have been conducted.

16. Bergin (1971: 217, references omitted) has commented that "professor Hans Eysenck is still agreed and disagreed with more than any single critic on the psychotherapy scene."

17. Eysenck's update was first published in 1965 in the *International Journal of Psychiatry* and reprinted the following year in book form, from which the citation was taken (Eysenck, 1966).

18. Meltzoff and Kornreich (1970: 175–77) have criticized Truax and Carkhuff's conclusions on a variety of grounds. First, they maintain that the research base was incomplete. They point out that a disproportionate number of the studies yielding negative or null results were of educational counseling, not psychotherapy. Meltzoff and Kornreich would also interpret the studies differently. In fact, limiting themselves to the research that Truax and Carkhuff used, they would find the positive evidence outweighing the neutral and negative by a ratio of seven to one.

19. For an excellent critique of Meltzoff and Kornreich's work, see Malan (1973).

20. After classifying each study as good, fair, or poor on adequacy of design, Bergin declared an outcome positive if change was either greater than in the control group or (where no control group was used) substantially higher than the 30 percent spontaneous-remission rate that he had established as a baseline figure.

21. A placebo has been defined by Shapiro (1971: 440) as "any therapy, or that component of any therapy, that is deliberately used for its nonspecific, psychologic, or psychophysiologic effect, or that is used for its presumed specific effect on a patient symptom, or illness, but which, unknown to patient and therapist, is without specific activity for the condition being treated." Malan is pointing out that the positive studies that Meltzoff and Kornreich have cited may simply be measuring the effects of giving somebody attention, and that the results have nothing to do with the effectiveness of psychotherapy per se.

22. Most reviewers assume that poorly designed studies should be excluded from consideration, whereas Glass's research found no significant differences in validity between

the best- and worst-designed studies. Glass also criticizes the tendency of reviewers to tabulate significant versus insignificant studies, since this creates a bias in favor of large-sample studies that may have only weak findings, and does not attack the problem of how large an effect a particular psychotherapeutic procedure had.

23. He estimated that this amounts to about half of what exists in the way of controlled therapy-outcome studies.

24. Her own conclusion was that, "Looking back over this year's literature we seem now to have reached some consensus that the quality of the psychotherapeutic relationship is important in all treatments" (R.D. Cartwright, 1968: 412).

25. In an unpublished report of the Kennecott Copper Corporation (1972), for instance, discussed by Dörken and his associates (1976: 339-40), 150 employees who received counseling were compared with another group, with similar jobs, who were thought to need treatment but did not. On a per-person, per-month basis, absenteeism for those receiving therapy declined 52 percent, while weekly indemnity costs declined 75 percent, and health, medical, and surgical costs decreased 55 percent. The control group had much lower rates to begin with than those seeking therapy, and absenteeism and health care costs actually showed a slight increase over the period of the study.

26. Cummings and Follette (1976) found that users of the outpatient psychiatric services of the Kaiser Foundation Health Plan significantly decreased their use of medical services over a five-year period following the termination of therapy. Even one session alone could reduce utilization by as much as 60 percent over the following five years, and a 75 percent reduction occurred for those patients who received two to eight psychotherapy sessions.

27. A related problem is establishing how often a therapist must bring about a negative result to be considered harmful. See the relevant sections of chapter 4.

28. No attempt is made here to determine what causes the danger. This matter is considered in the chapter on qualifications for psychotherapists and group leaders.

29. An examination of the history of psychotherapy reveals that in earlier times psychoanalysis aroused many of the very same fears that have been raised about encounter groups today. During Freud's life, for instance, psychoanalysts, as well as other psychotherapists, were constantly accused of sexually abusing their patients, of promoting licentiousness, and of believing in absurd theories (Freud, 1963).

30. Most therapists would dispute this, since increasing a person's capacity and freedom to choose is generally considered a primary value of psychotherapy (see, e.g., Strupp, 1973).

31. Interestingly, 21 percent of the relationships reportedly had a positive effect.

32. Recent research by Perry (1976) has followed up the Kardener, Fuller, and Mensh (1973) study to determine the erotic and nonerotic physical involvement of female physicians with their patients. In a survey of 164 female physicians, Perry found that more female physicians believe in and engage in nonerotic touching, but fewer believe in and engage in erotic touching. None of the female physicians reported sexual intercourse with patients, as compared with the high-percentage figure for male physicians in the Kardener study.

33. A final survey worthy of mention involved a follow-up of 2,500 functional psychoses that were treated at Gaustad Hospital in Oslo, Norway (Astrup, in Eysenck, 1966: 54). According to the findings, a considerable number of psychotic breakdowns were precipitated by intensive analytically oriented therapy.

34. For a response to these criticisms, see Bergin (1970).

35. Among other factors, Strupp, Hadley, Gomes, and Armstrong (1976: 83-86) list the following major problems with the research: (1) inclusion of a broad spectrum of interventions under the label "psychotherapy"; (2) extensive use of inexperienced therapists or inadequate specification of therapist characteristics; (3) inappropriate selection of patient samples; and (4) flaws in the design and methodology of the research, including lack of control groups, inadequate or questionable outcome criteria, and failure to distinguish deterioration from relapse.

REFERENCES

Ackerknecht, E.H. *A Short History of Psychiatry.* (Translated by S. Wolff) New York: Hafner Publishing Co., 1959.

Alder, A. *The Practice and Theory of Individual Psychology.* New York: Harcourt, Brace, 1932.

American Orthopsychiatric Association. "Documents Pertaining to Licensing Feasibility Study of Psychotherapy." Unpublished document, New York, 1968.

American Orthopsychiatric Association. "Psychotherapy Licensing Feasibility Study," Unpublished document, New York, 1968a.

American Psychiatric Association. *A Psychiatric Glossary: The Meaning of Terms Frequently Used in Psychiatry.* (4th ed.) Washington, D.C.: American Psychiatric Association, 1975.

American Psychiatric Association. *The Present and Future Importance of Private Psychiatric Practice in the Delivery of Mental Health Services.* (Task Force Report No. 6.) Washington, D.C.: American Psychiatric Association, 1973.

American Psychological Association. *Casebook on Ethical Standards of Psychologists.* Washington, D.C.: American Psychological Association, 1967.

Arbuckle, D.S. *Counseling: Philosophy, Therapy and Practice.* (2nd ed.) Boston: Allyn and Bacon, 1970.

Arieti, S. (Ed.) *American Handbook of Psychiatry.* (2nd ed.) New York: Basic Books, 1974-75.

Barron, F., and Leary, T. "Changes in Psychoneurotic Patients With and Without Psychotherapy." *Journal of Consulting Psychology,* 1955, v. 19, pp. 239-45.

Berleman, W.C., and Steinburn, T.W. "The Execution and Evaluation of a Delinquency Prevention Program." *Social Problems,* 1967, v. 14, pp. 413-23.

Bergin, A.E. "The Evaluation of Therapeutic Outcomes." In A.E. Bergin and S.L. Garfield (Eds.), *Handbook of Psychotherapy and Behavior Change: An Empirical Analysis.* New York: John Wiley, 1971, pp. 217-70.

Bergin, A.E. "The Deterioration Effect: A Reply to Braucht." *Journal of Abnormal Psychology,* 1970, v. 75, pp. 300-302.

Bergin, A.E. "Some Implications of Psychotherapy Research for Therapeutic Practice." *Journal of Abnormal Psychology,* 1966, v. 71, pp. 235-46.

Bergin, A.E. "The Effects of Psychotherapy: Negative Results Revisited." *Journal of Counseling Psychology,* 1963, v. 10, pp. 244-50.

Bergin, A.E., and Garfield, S.L. (Eds.) *Handbook of Psychotherapy and Behavior Change: An Empirical Analysis.* New York: John Wiley, 1971.

Bergin, A.E., and Suinn, R.M. "Individual Psychotherapy and Behavior Therapy." *Annual Review of Psychology,* 1975, v. 25, pp. 509-56.

Berne, E. *Transactional Analysis in Psychotherapy.* New York: Grove Press, 1961.

Binswanger, L. "Existential Analysis and Psychotherapy." In F. Fromm-Reichmann and J.L. Moreno (Eds.), *Progress in Psychotherapy.* (Vol. 1.) New York: Grune and Stratton, 1956, pp. 144-48.

Bordin, E. *Research Strategies in Psychotherapy.* New York: John Wiley, 1974.

Braucht, G.N. "The Deterioration Effect: A Reply to Bergin." *Journal of Abnormal Psychology,* 1970, v. 75, pp. 293-99.

Bromberg, W. *From Shaman to Psychotherapist: A History of the Treatment of Mental Illness.* Chicago: Henry Regnery, 1975.

Cartwright, D.S. "Note on 'Changes in Psychoneurotic Patients With and Without Psychotherapy.'" *Journal of Consulting Psychology,* 1956, v. 20, pp. 403-4.

Cartwright, R.D. "Psychotherapeutic Processes." *Annual Review of Psychology,* 1968, v. 19, pp. 387-416.

Chapman, A.H. "Iatrogenic Problems in Psychotherapy." *Psychiatry Digest,* 1964, v. 25, pp. 23-29.

Conley, R.W.; Conwell, M; and Arrill, M.B. "An Approach to Measuring the Cost of Mental Illness." *American Journal of Psychiatry*, 1967, v. 124, pp. 755-62.

Cummings, N.A., and Follette, W.T. "Brief Psychotherapy and Medical Utilization." In H. Dörken and Associates, *The Professional Psychologist Today*. San Francisco: Jossey-Bass, 1976, pp. 165-74.

Curran, D., and Partridge, M. *Psychological Medicine: A Short Introduction to Psychiatry*. London: E. & S. Livingstone, 1955.

Darnton, R. *Mesmerism and the End of The Enlightenment in France*. Cambridge, Mass.: Harvard University Press, 1968.

Dittman, A.T. "Psychotherapeutic Processes." *Annual Review of Psychology*, 1966, v. 17, pp. 51-78.

Dollard, J., and Miller, N.E. *Personality and Psychotherapy: An Analysis in Terms of Learning, Thinking, and Culture*. New York: McGraw-Hill, 1950.

Dörken, H., and Rodgers, D.A. "Issues Facing Professional Psychology." In H. Dörken and Associates, *The Professional Psychologist Today: New Developments in Law, Health Insurance, and Health Practice*. San Francisco: Jossey-Bass, 1976, pp. 264-92.

Ehrenwald, J. (Ed.) *The History of Psychotherapy: From Healing Magic to Encounter*. New York: Jason Aronson, 1976.

Ellenberger, H.F. *The Discovery of the Unconscious: The History and Evolution of Dynamic Psychiatry*. New York: Basic Books, 1970.

Eysenck, H.J. "The Non-Professional Psychotherapist." *International Journal of Psychiatry*, 1967, v. 3(3), pp. 150-53.

Eysenck, H.J. *The Effects of Psychotherapy*. New York: International Science Press, 1966.

Eysenck, H.J. "The Effects of Psychotherapy." *International Journal of Psychiatry*, 1965, v. 1(1), pp. 97-142.

Eysenck, H.J. "The Effects of Psychotherapy: An Evaluation." *Journal of Consulting Psychology*, 1952, v. 16, pp. 319-24.

Federn, E. "How Freudian Are the Freudians? Some Remarks to an Unpublished Letter." *Journal of the History of the Behavioral Sciences*, 1967, v. 3, pp. 269-81.

Frank, J.D. *Persuasion and Healing: A Comparative Study of Psychotherapy*. (Rev. ed.) Baltimore, Md.: Johns Hopkins Press, 1973.

Frank, J.D. "Does Psychotherapy Work?" *International Journal of Psychiatry*, 1967, v. 3(3), pp. 153-55.

Freud, S. *The History of the Psychoanalytic Movement*. (Editorial and Introduction by P. Rieff.) New York: Collier Books, 1963.

Freud, S. *An Outline of Psychoanalysis*. 1940. Reprint. (Translated and edited by J. Strachey.) New York: W.W. Norton, 1969.

Freud, S. *The Question of Lay Analysis: Conversations with an Impartial Person*. (Translated and edited by J. Strachey.) New York: W.W. Norton, 1950.

Freud, S. *General Introduction to Psychoanalysis*. (Translated by G.S. Hall.) New York: Boni and Liveright, 1920.

Glass, G.V. "Primary, Secondary, and Meta-Analysis of Research." Paper presented as presidential address to the 1976 Annual Meeting of the American Educational Research Association, San Francisco, Calif., April 21, 1976.

Goshen, C.E. (Ed.) *A Documentary History of Psychiatry*. New York: Jason Aronson, 1975.

Grimm, J.F.C. *The Works of Hippocrates*. (Vol. 2.) Publisher unknown, 1838. Cited in E.H. Ackerknecht, *A Short History of Psychiatry*. (Translated by S. Wolff.) New York: Hafner Publishing Co., 1959, p. 11.

Grinker, R.R., Sr. "Psychiatry Rides Madly in All Directions." *Archives of General Psychiatry*, 1964, v. 10, pp. 228-37.

Grenebaum, H.; Nadelson, C.C.; and Macht, L.B. "Sexual Activity with the Psychiatrist: A District Branch Dilemma." Unpublished manuscript draft, Boston, undated.

Gurin, G.; Veroff, J.; and Feld, S. *Americans View Their Mental Health.* New York: Basic Books, 1960.

Hadley, S.W., and Strupp, H.H. "Contemporary Views of Negative Effects in Psychotherapy." *Archives of General Psychiatry*, 1976, v. 33, pp. 1291-1302.

Hammer v. Rosen, 7 App. Div. 2d 216, 181 N.Y.S.2d 805 (1959), modified, 7 N.Y.2d 376, 198 N.Y.S.2d 65 (1960).

Harrison, S.I.; Bordin, E.S.; Holt, R.R.; Linford, A.A.; Mudd, E.H.; Slovenko, R.; and Visotsky, H. "The Feasibility of a Model Statute Licensing the Practice of Psychotherapy." *American Journal of Orthopsychiatry*, 1970, v. 40, p. 558.

Hart, J.T., and Tomlinson, T.M. (Eds.) *New Directions in Client-Centered Therapy.* Boston: Houghton Mifflin, 1970.

Hathaway, S.R. "Clinical Methods: Psychotherapy." *Annual Review of Psychology*, 1951, v. 2, pp. 259-80.

Horney, K. *Neurosis and Human Growth: The Struggle Toward Self-Realization.* New York: W.W. Norton, 1950.

Horwitz, L. "Training Issues in Group Psychotherapy." *Bulletin of the Menninger Clinic*, 1971, v. 35, pp. 249-61.

Janet, P. *Psychological Healing.* (Translated by E. Paul and C. Paul.) New York: Macmillan, 1925. (2 vols.)

Janov, A. *The Primal Revolution: Toward a Real World.* New York: Simon and Schuster, Touchstone, 1972.

Janov, A. *The Anatomy of Mental Illness.* New York: G.P. Putnam, Berkley Medallion Books, 1971.

Janov, A. *The Primal Scream.* New York: Dell Publishing Co., 1970.

Jaspers K. *The Nature of Psychotherapy: A Critical Appraisal.* (Translated by J. Hoenig and M.W. Hamilton.) Chicago: University of Chicago Press, Phoenix Books, 1964.

Jonckheere, P. "Considérations sur la Psychothérapie." *Acta Neurologica et Psychiatrica Belgica*, 1965, v. 65, pp. 667-84.

Jung, C.G. *Modern Man in Search of a Soul.* (Translated by W.S. Dell and C.F. Baynes.) New York: Harcourt, Brace, 1933.

Jones, E. *The Life and Work of Sigmund Freud.* New York: Basic Books, 1953, 1955, and 1957. (3 vols.)

Jung, C.G. *The Practice of Psychotherapy.* (2nd ed.) (Translated by R.F.C. Hull.) New York: Pantheon, 1966.

Kardener, S.H.; Fuller, M.; and Mensh, I.N. "A Survey of Physicians' Attitudes and Practices Regarding Erotic and Noneerotic Contact with Patients." *American Journal of Psychiatry*, 1973, v. 130, pp. 1077-81.

Kellner, R. "The Evidence in Favour of Psychotherapy." *British Journal of Medical Psychology*, 1967, v. 40, pp. 341-58.

Kellner, R. "The Efficacy of Psychotherapy: The Results of Some Controlled Investigations." *Psychiatria et Neurologia*, 1965, v. 149, pp. 333-40.

Kennecott Cooper Corporation. "Performance Outcome Data." Unpublished document, Utah Copper Division, Salt Lake City, 1972. Cited in H. Dörken and Associates, *The Professional Psychologist Today.* San Francisco: Jossey-Bass, 1976, pp. 339-40.

Kiesler, D.J. "Some Myths of Psychotherapy Research and the Search for a Paradigm." *Psychological Bulletin*, 1966, v. 65, pp. 110-36.

Kopp, S. *Guru: Metaphors from a Psychotherapist.* Palo Alto, Calif.: Science and Behavior Books, 1971.

Kubie, L.S. *Practical and Theoretical Aspects of Psychoanalysis.* New York: International Universities Press, 1950.

Kuhn, T.S. *The Structure of Scientific Revolutions.* Chicago: University of Chicago Press, 1962.

Lambert, M.J. "Spontaneous Remission in Adult Neurotic Disorders: A Revision and Summary." *Psychological Bulletin*, 1976, v. 83, pp. 107-19.

Lambert, M.J.; Bergin, A.E.; and Collins, J.L. "Therapist-Induced Deterioration in

Psychotherapy." In A.S. Gurman and A.M. Razin (Eds.), *Effective Psychotherapy: A Handbook of Research.* New York: Pergamon Press, 1977, pp. 452-81.

Lindner, R.M. "The Problem of Medical and Lay Psychotherapy: Who Shall Practice Psychotherapy?" *American Journal of Psychotherapy*, 1950, v. 4, pp. 432-42.

Lowen, A. "Bio-energetic Group Therapy." In H.M. Ruitenbeek (Ed.), *Group Therapy Today: Styles, Methods and Techniques.* New York: Atherton, 1969, pp. 279-90.

Luborsky, L. "A Note on Eysenck's Article, 'The Effects of Psychotherapy: An Evaluation.'" *British Journal of Psychology*, 1954, v. 45, pp. 129-31.

Luborsky, L.; Singer, B.; and Luborsky, L. "Comparative Studies of Psychotherapies: Is It True That 'Everyone Has Won and All Must Have Prizes?'" *Archives of General Psychiatry*, 1975, v. 32, pp. 995-1008.

Macklin, R. "The Medical Model in Psychoanalysis and Psychotherapy." *Comprehensive Psychiatry*, 1973, v. 14, pp. 49-69.

Malan, D.H. "The Outcome Problem in Psychotherapy Research: A Historical Review." *Archives of General Psychiatry*, 1973, v. 29, pp. 719-29.

Matarazzo, J.D. "Some Psychotherapists Make Patients Worse!" *International Journal of Psychiatry*, 1967, v. 3, pp. 156-57.

May, P.R.A. "For Better or for Worse? Psychotherapy and Variance Change: A Critical Review of the Literature." *Journal of Nervous and Mental Disease*, 1971, v. 152, pp. 184-92.

Meehl, P.E. "Psychotherapy." *Annual Review of Psychology*, 1955, v. 6, pp. 357-78.

Meltzoff, J., and Kornreich, M. *Research in Psychotherapy.* New York: Atherton Press, 1970.

Menninger, K. (In collaboration with M. Mayman and P. Pruyser.) *The Vital Balance: The Life Process in Mental Health and Illness.* New York: Viking Press, 1963.

Murphy, G., and Kovach, J.K. *Historical Introduction to Modern Psychology.* (3rd ed.) New York: Harcourt Brace Jovanovich, 1972.

Nagel, E. "Methodological Issues in Psychoanalytic Theory." In S. Hook (Ed.), *Psychoanalysis, Scientific Method, and Philosophy.* New York: University Press, 1959, pp. 38-56.

New York State. *Hearing on Abuses by Unregulated Therapists in the Mental Health Field.* (Before Louis J. Lefkowitz, Attorney General of the State of New York.) December 15, 1972.

Panzetta, A.F. "Cost-Benefit Studies in Psychiatry." *Comprehensive Psychiatry*, 1973, v. 14, pp. 451-55.

Perry, J.A. "Physicians' Erotic and Nonerotic Physical Involvement with Patients." *American Journal of Psychiatry*, 1976, v. 133, pp. 838-40.

Pleune, F.G. "All Dis-ease Is Not Disease: A Consideration of Psychoanalysis, Psychotherapy and Psycho-social Engineering." *International Journal of Psychoanalysis*, 1965, v. 46, pp. 358-66.

Polster, E., and Polster, M. *Gestalt Therapy Integrated: Contours of Theory and Practice.* New York: Vintage Books, 1974.

Powdermaker, F.B., and Frank, J.D. *Group Psychotherapy Studies in Methodology of Research and Therapy.* (Report of a Group Psychotherapy Research Project of the U.S. Veterans Administration.) Cambridge, Mass.: Harvard University Press, 1953.

Powers. E., and Whitmer, H. *An Experiment in the Prevention of Delinquency: The Cambridge-Somerville Youth Study.* New York: Columbia University Press, 1951.

Rachman, S. *The Effects of Psychotherapy.* New York: Pergamon Press, 1971.

Raimy, V.C. (Ed.) *Training in Clinical Psychology.* New York: Prentice-Hall, 1950.

Redlich, F.C., and Freedman, D.X. *The Theory and Practice of Psychiatry.* New York: Basic Books, 1966.

Rogers, C.R., and Dymond, R.F. (Eds.) *Psychotherapy and Personality Change.* Chicago: University of Chicago Press, 1954.

Rosenzweig, S. "A Transvaluation of Psychotherapy—A Reply to Hans Eysenck." *Journal of Abnormal and Social Psychology*, 1954, v. 49, pp. 298-304.

Ruitenbeek, H.M. (Ed.) *Psychoanalysis and Existential Philosophy.* New York: E.P. Dutton, 1962.

Sarason, I.G., and Ganzer, V.J. "Concerning the Medical Model." *American Psychologist,* 1968, v. 23, pp. 507-10.

Sartre, J. *Existential Psychoanalysis.* (Translated and with an Introduction by H.E. Barnes.) New York: Philosophical Library, 1953.

Schillinger, M. Executive Director, New York State Psychological Association. Personal communication, September 5, 1974.

Schmideberg, M. "Iatrogenic Disturbance." *American Journal of Psychiatry,* 1963, v. 119, p. 899.

Shapiro, A.K. "Placebo Effects in Medicine, Psychotherapy, and Psychoanalysis." In A.E. Bergin and S.L. Garfield (Eds.), *Handbook of Psychotherapy and Behavior Change: An Empirical Analysis.* New York: John Wiley, 1971, pp. 439-73.

Siegler, M., and Osmond, H. *Models of Madness, Models of Medicine.* New York: Macmillan Publishing Co., 1974.

Sloane, R.B.; Staples, F.R.; Cristol, A.H.; Yorkston, N.J.; and Whipple, K. *Psychotherapy versus Behavior Therapy.* Cambridge, Mass.: Harvard University Press, 1975.

Strupp, H.H. "On the Basic Ingredients of Psychotherapy." *Journal of Counsulting and Clinical Psychology,* 1973, v. 41, pp. 1-8.

Strupp, H.H., and Bergin, A.E. "Some Empirical and Conceptual Bases for Coordinated Research in Psychotherapy: A Critical Review of Issues, Trends, and Evidence." *International Journal of Psychiatry,* 1969, v. 7, pp. 18-90.

Strupp, H.H.; Hadley, S.W.; Gomes, B.; and Armstrong, S.H. "Negative Effects in Psychotherapy: A Review of Clinical and Theoretical Issues Together with Recommendations for a Program of Research." Unpublished document, Vanderbilt University, Nashville, Tenn., May 1976.

Taylor, B.J., and Wagner, N.N. "Sex Between Therapists and Clients: A Review and Analysis." *Professional Psychology,* 1976, v. 7, pp. 593-601.

Thompson, C.J.S. *Magic and Healing.* New York: Rider, 1947.

Truax, C.B. "Effective Ingredients in Psychotherapy: An Approach to Unraveling the Patient-Therapist Interaction." *Journal of Counseling Psychology,* 1963, v. 10, pp. 256-63.

Truax, C.B., and Carkhuff, R.R. *Toward Effective Counseling and Psychotherapy: Training and Practice.* Chicago, Ill.: Aldine Publishing Co., 1967.

Uhlenhuth, E.H., and Duncan, D.B. "Subjective Change in Psychoneurotic Outpatients with Medical Students: I. The Kind, Amount, and Course of Change." Unpublished manuscript, Johns Hopkins University, Baltimore, Md., 1968. Referenced in A.E. Bergin and S.L. Garfield (Eds.), *Handbook of Psychotherapy and Behavior Change: An Empirical Analysis.* New York: John Wiley, 1971, p. 249.

Veith, I. "Glimpses into the History of Psychotherapy." In J.H. Masserman and J.L. Moreno (Eds.), *Progress in Psychotherapy: Techniques of Psychotherapy.* (Vol. 3.) New York: Grune and Stratton, 1958, pp. 1-19.

Weatherhead, L.D. *Psychology, Religion and Healing.* New York: Abingdon Press, 1951.

Wolberg, L.R. *The Technique of Psychotherapy.* (2nd ed.) New York: Grune and Stratton, 1967. (2 vols.)

Wolpe, J.; Salter, A.; and Reyna, L.J. (Eds.) *The Conditioning Therapies: The Challenge in Psychotherapy.* New York: Holt, Rinehart and Winston, 1964.

Yalom, I.D. *The Theory and Practice of Group Psychotherapy.* (2nd ed.) New York: Basic Books, 1975.

Zilboorg, G., and Henry, G.W. *A History of Medical Psychology.* New York: W.W. Norton, 1941.

Zipkin v. Freeman, 436 S.W.2d 753 (Mo. 1968).

Chapter 3

An Overview of Psychotherapy, II: Encounter Groups and Other Humanistic Therapies

Regulation through such restrictive means as licensure works most effectively when a field of practice is well established, when a consensus exists on which methods, techniques, and theories are correct, and when the limits of practice are clearly defined. An examination of the many new psychotherapies that have come into existence in the past twenty years, especially encounter groups, will help demonstrate that these conditions do not yet exist in the psychotherapeutic field.

Encounter groups pose more difficulties for understanding than traditional psychotherapy.[1] These difficulties stem from the fact that encounter groups are more recent in origin, the range of practices so labeled are more varied, and the furor surrounding the spread of encounter groups has increased distortions and misperceptions concerning them.

DEFINITIONS AND DESCRIPTIONS

Attempting to define encounter groups is problematical. The range of practices is wide and an endless number of terms are used to describe the variations. Terms such as T-group, encounter group, sensitivity-training group, experiential

group, and the human potential movement have been used to refer to the encounter field in general. Within the field an array of groups exists, including the following:[2]

Gestalt groups
bio-energetic
   groups
Weight Watchers
Synanon
nude encounter
   groups
sensory awareness
   groups
marathons
consciousness-
   raising groups
transactional
   analysis
conflict-manage-
   ment labs
confrontation
   groups
primal therapy
   groups
movement groups
sociodrama
life-planning labs
psychodrama

A number of approaches are open for defining an encounter group. It may be identified according to its goals, purposes, and objectives. Sensitivity groups, sensory awareness groups, and authenticity groups derive their labels from this mode of definition. On the other hand, groups may be defined according to the basic process employed and the results achieved, regardless of stated goals. By this method of defining groups one plunges into arguments about their therapeutic or educational nature.[3]

Groups may also be defined by the particular methods employed (Gestalt groups, Synanon groups), or they may be defined by the theory on which they are based (transactional analysis groups, psychoanalytic groups). Again, definitions may be based on the specific structure or format of the group experience, such as microexperience groups, which are very brief; marathon groups, which are time-extended; or "tape" groups, which are leaderless and in which participants follow tape-recorded programmed instructions.

None of these methods is especially satisfying for developing an overall definition of the encounter group process. In fact a precise definition is impossible unless arbitrary bounds are established. Rather than attempt this, encounter groups will be defined broadly and comprehensively.

A distinctive feature of the encounter experience is that a group is always involved. The meaning of the term "group," however, is subject to significant differences of opinion. Cartwright and Zander (1968: 46) have provided a useful definition of a group as a "collection of individuals who have relations to one another that make them interdependent to some significant degree."[4] Typically, members of such a group define themselves and are defined by others as members of that group; they share norms concerning matters of common interest; they participate in a system of interlocking roles; they tend to act in a unitary manner toward the environment; and they engage in frequent interaction (Cartwright and Zander, 1968: 48).

Since the predominant format for the encounter group is the small-group experience, it is useful to adopt Bales's (1950) criteria for this type of group. He defines a small group as one in which the members engage in single face-to-face meetings to a sufficient degree so that each member receives an impression or perception of every other member distinct enough to allow him or her to have some reaction to each other member, even if only to recall that the other members were present (Bales, 1950: 33).

The range of small groups that are appropriately referred to as encounter groups is large. At one end of the spectrum is the traditional T-group, where the focus is on understanding and influencing group dynamics, exploring how leadership is exerted, how decisions are made, and how groups function. The following report of one participant's experience in a two-week T-group provides a picture of typical events.

On Tuesday, Maurice tried to stop the drifting by proposing the election of a committee that would be charged with drafting a set of group goals. Bradford [the group leader] indicated that he thought this was escapism. "What I see," he said, peering down at the table with his head between his hands, as though he were looking into a crystal ball, "is people trying to have something logical, rational, something not part of *me* to talk about—something to avoid the discomfort of discussing our feelings." A vote on appointing a goals committee was nevertheless taken, and carried. But the majority then found, somewhat to its surprise, that it had no stomach for imposing its will on the minority, and so no committee was appointed after all.

The question of organization, which had been the almost exclusive subject of discussion for two days, was finally settled on Wednesday. Another vote on the issue was called for, and this time half the members, apparently unwilling to vote either for or against Maurice's proposal, didn't vote at all. One of the abstainers, a bald, rough-voiced chemical engineer named Pete, said that although he had started out supporting Maurice, he had now changed his mind. He said that if some people in the group didn't want organization, then the others shouldn't try to ram it down their throats. He added that he suspected many people in the group felt this way.

Bradford nodded. "I think Pete has verbalized one of the most important statements yet," he said solemnly. "If the group is not going to drive anybody out, then we have concern about its members, and we can begin to help one another." Maurice said skeptically that he didn't see that the group, simply by refusing to organize, was in a better position to get down to *his* inner self. But the consensus seemed to be that the group would just have to get on as best it could without a chairman, an agenda, or rules of order. [Klaw, 1970: 28–29.]

Of the many who have outlined the essential features of the T-group, Buchanan (1964) has provided one of the clearest definitions of the process. He states that training approaches that merit the name of T-group employ face-to-face, largely unstructured groups as the primary vehicle for learning. Generally, planned activities encourage group interaction, and this interaction is analyzed in the process of giving feedback to the individual group members. The group members are encouraged to explore new ways of behaving in those situations where their past behavior has proved ineffective or dissatisfying. Finally, an attempt is made to generalize what has been learned in the group, to reformulate old concepts and values, and to determine how these learnings might be applied outside of the T-group setting.[5]

Distinct from the T-group is the personal growth group. Lieberman, Yalom, and Miles (1973: 4) have summarized the essential features of this type of group as follows. It attempts to provide an intensive, high-contact experience through the use of a group ranging in size from six to twenty people. Openness, honesty, interpersonal confrontation, self-disclosure, and strong emotional expression are stressed. Ordinarily the participants are

not referred to as "patients," and the experience is considered educational, not therapeutic, although the groups strive for increased self- and social-awareness and behavior change. Usually personal growth groups involve some type of personal change, especially in the area of behavior, attitudes, values, and life-style, although they occasionally seek only to "turn-on" or entertain.[6]

A participant's description of his experience in such a group will highlight the differences between personal growth groups and T-groups:

Then, a girl lost patience with me and said she didn't feel she could give any more. She said I looked like a bottomless well, and she wondered how many times I had to be told that I *was* cared for. By this time I was feeling panicky, and I was saying to myself, "God, can it be true that I can't be satisfied and that I'm somehow compelled to pester people for attention until I drive them away!"

At this point while I was really worried, a nun in the group spoke up. She said that I had not alienated her with some negative things I had said to her. She said she liked me, and she couldn't understand why I couldn't see that. She said she felt concerned for me and wanted to help me. With that, something began to really dawn on me and I voiced it somewhat like the following. "You mean you are still sitting there feeling for me what I say I want you to feel and that somewhere down inside me I'm stopping it from touching me?" I relaxed appreciably and began really to wonder why I had shut their caring out so much. I couldn't find the answer, and one woman said: "It looks like you are trying to stay continuously as deep in your feelings as you were this afternoon. It would make sense to me for you to draw back and assimilate it. Maybe if you don't push so hard, you can rest a while and then move back into your feelings more naturally."

Her making the last suggestion really took effect. I saw the sense in it, and almost immediately I settled back very relaxed with something of a feeling of a bright, warm day dawning inside me. In addition to taking the pressure off of myself, I was for the first time really warmed by the friendly feelings which I felt they had for me. It is difficult to say why I felt liked only just then, but as opposed to the earlier sessions I really *believed* they cared for me. I never have fully understood why I stood their affection off for so long, but at that point I almost abruptly began to trust that they did care. The measure of the effectiveness of this change lies in what I said next. I said, "Well, that really takes care of me. I'm really ready to listen to someone else now." I *meant* that, too. [Hall, 1965, cited in Rogers, 1970: pp. 31–31.]

The difference between T-groups and personal growth groups should be apparent. Buchanan talks about using "systematic and frequent feedback," while personal growth groups focus on the exploration of feelings. Personal growth groups are only secondarily concerned with the study of small-group dynamics. Instead, intrapsychic processes become of primary importance. Weschler, Massarik, and Tannenbaum (1962: 34) state that the basic change is from focusing on the improvement of group functioning to the development of interpersonal skills and tht total enhancement of the individual. Increasingly, encounter groups are concerning themselves with strengthening individuals in their desires to experience people and events more fully, to know themselves more intimately and accurately, and to find greater meaning in life (Weschler et al., 1962: 34).

Despite the difference in focus, T-groups and personal growth groups still have much in common. They are typically quite small, generally ranging in size from six to eighteen. They are informal. Both types of groups usually have little formal structure and generally no agenda. Participants almost inevitably receive comments on how other members of the group view them, and they learn how to give this information in a constructive fashion. In both the T-group and the personal growth group, the expression of feeling is considered important and new ways of behaving are encouraged.

The question will inevitably arise as to whether particular types of groups are included or excluded from this study. Where a group is advertised explicitly as an encounter group and where the structure, activities, purposes, and methods all conform to the basic outline provided in this chapter, little argument will exist. A vast gray area can be anticipated, however, in which no simple answer is available. Erhard Seminars Training (EST), for instance, is usually conducted in large groups, often with more than fifty people. Its structure, at least in the initial sessions, is more like a classroom, with the tradiional teacher providing information and asking questions. Yet much of the follow-up is conducted in small groups. Research may reveal that the leaders of this type of experience require very different skills and personality characteristics to function effectively than do leaders of a small encounter group or group therapy. Should this prove to be so, then such types of training ought to receive separate treatment with regard to regulatory proposals. The likelihood is that no such differences will be found.

PURPOSES AND GOALS

Several avenues can be used to determine the purposes and goals of encounter groups. The most obvious method is to read what theoreticians and practitioners have to say. In addition, reviews of the research provide information as to what results most often occur.[7] Finally, research examining why participants join encounter groups may be viewed as an indicator of the actual purposes that encounter groups serve. Each of these avenues will be explored.[8]

Goals and purposes can be examined at a number of levels. The highest level concerns the broad thrust of encounter groups and their fundamental values. Warren Bennis (1962) has used the term "meta-goal" to describe this level. Meta-goals are highly general, and they are often not explicitly stated. Nonetheless they shape and give substance to the more specific goals of encounter groups. The next level of goals is the specific outcome desired from encounter groups: increased openness, sensitivity, skill in sharing leadership, and the like. These are much more amenable to operational definition. Finally, goals emerge regarding what happens inside an encounter group. These "process" goals involve such matters as level of group cohesiveness and trust.

Schein and Bennis (1965) have put forth a clear explication of the meta-goals of encounter groups.[9] In their view two sets of values are implicit in the encounter group experience. The first set arises out of science and is related to the orientation a scientist has toward truth and discovery. One such goal is a *spirit of inquiry:* being cautious about making final judgments; being open to new ideas and ways of looking at the world; and having the willingness to experiment with one's own behaviors and ways of doing things. A second goal is *expanded consciousness and choice:* a greater awareness of one's self and the world, and greater freedom in choosing what one will do and who one will be. The final meta-goal connected with science is *authenticity in interpersonal relations:* feeling free to be oneself, as opposed to what others would like one to be.

The second set of values centers around democracy, with specific meta-goals being related to those values essential in making a democracy work. *Collaboration* is extremely important—that is, the ability to work cooperatively with peers, superiors, and subordinates in an interdependent fashion, rather than through authoritarian means. Related to this is the ability to conduct *conflict resolution through rational means*, which involves a problem-solving orientation and the desire to avoid approaches such as power plays, brute force, or suppression.

Schein and Bennis (1965) make it clear

that these values are not absolutes. At times conflicts cannot be resolved through rational means; the critical matter is determining when and under what conditions rational means can be used. Schein and Bennis (1965: 35) stress the importance of freedom of choice, and conclude: *"Choice, regarding the implementation of . . . values, is the overarching and fundamental value."*

Bradford, Gibb, and Benne (1964b: 16–19) have enumerated seven specific outcomes that emanate from the general meta-goals outlined by Schein and Bennis (1965).[10] These include an increased awareness of and sensitivity to emotional reactions and expressions in both oneself and others; greater ability to perceive feelings; increased clarity and development of personal values consonant with the ideals of a democratic society; the development of concepts and theoretical insights that will prove useful in implementing the above values; an increased ability to deal effectively with one's environment; the ability to apply appropriately what is learned in the encounter group experience to situations outside that setting; and "learning how to learn" so that each person becomes an analyst of his or her own learning processes.

The process goals of encounter groups are quite similar to the outcomes described above. Egan (1970: 85–96), for instance, states that the following five process goals must be achieved if an encounter group is to be successful: (1) all participant concerns must become group concerns; (2) participants must accept the fact that theirs is a laboratory experience and hence they will be expected to try out new ways of behaving in certain situations; (3) the group must establish a cooperative, as opposed to competitive, goal structure; (4) the principal focus of the group must be on the here-and-now— what is happening within the group presently, not in the past; and (5) the encouragement of "immediacy" and "specificity," such as using the word "I," speaking to a particular person, and being concrete and specific in describing another's behavior.

Distilling the essence of the encounter group process, Bebout (undated: 8, emphasis omitted) has concluded that the new concept offered by encounter groups (and ignored or minimized in other forms of helping and growth) is that "the overlapping and reciprocal sharing of momentary emotional experience is an event which in itself generates growth and change." It is this event that must transpire in the successful group, and this becomes a process goal of the experience.

In reviewing outcome research, Campbell and Dunnette (1968) found six major outcomes that most practitioners agreed upon as desirable, although various practitioners would emphasize some more than others. First was increased self-insight or self-awareness regarding one's own behavior. Second was increased sensitivity to the behavior of others, which included a greater awareness of the ways in which people communicate and a fuller understanding of the meaning of that communication. Third, encounter groups were meant to enhance a person's awareness and understanding of those processes that facilitate or inhibit group functioning. Fourth, practitioners advocated heightened diagnostic skill in social and interpersonal situations. Fifth, participants were expected to increase their action skill—that is, to become more effective at intervening in inter- or intragroup situations so as to increase member satisfaction, effectiveness, or output. Finally, as Bradford, Gibb, and Benne (1964b: 18–19) have suggested, the encounter group was to be a place where participants "learn how to learn."

In a more current review of the research, Gibb (1971) lists six objectives he believes recur most frequently in the training literature. These six—increased sensitivity; better ability to manage feelings; increased ability to manage motiva-

tion; improved functional attitudes toward oneself; improved functional attitudes toward others; and increased interdependent behavior—are similar to the goals outlined by Campbell and Dunnette. In addition, as Gibb points out, they are very much like the goals of professional psychotherapists and are closely correlated with the dimensions of positive mental health posited by Jahoda (1958).

That group leaders vary in the emphasis they give to the different aims posited above is borne out by the research of Lomranz, Lakin, and Schiffman (1972). The authors investigated the degree of homogeneity of encounter groups. They were specifically interested in whether encounter group leaders had diverse goals, techniques, values, and practices. They found that encounter group leaders could be divided into three distinct groups. In the first, the leaders were primarily concerned with learning, their goal was increased social effectiveness, and they attempted to highlight group and interpersonal conflicts rather than intrapersonal conflicts. Leaders in the second group were interested in remediation or therapy; their central aim was personality integration, and their closest referent was group psychotherapy. The third group was oriented to expanded experiencing, in which the leaders aimed at expressiveness through modeling sensory awareness and expressiveness exercises. These positions were associated with corresponding social values. In terms of absolute percentages, Lomranz, Lakin, and Schiffman found that 39.9 percent of the group leaders fell into the learning-centered category, 35.5 percent were committed to expanded experiencing; and 24.6 percent were concerned with remediation (Shiffman, 1974). Other practitioners and commentators have found just such a division of encounter group goals and commented upon it (Back, 1972; Clark, 1971).

Just as important as the group leader's goals are the expectations of the participants in an encounter group, and these, too, vary widely. Sometimes they are in line with the explicit goals of a particular group; at other times they are not. Some prospective participants expect the group to function as a therapeutic vehicle, while others are simply curious. Yet little is really known about actual participant expectation. Olch and Snow (1970) compared the personality traits of college students volunteering for sensitivity groups with those who did not. Their results indicated that the volunteers were less socially and emotionally adjusted. This may mean that encounter groups are serving a therapeutic function, not the educational function that most people, including the participants, assume. A subsequent study by Seldman and McBrearty (1975) on marathon volunteers confirmed these findings, but research by Gilligan supports the traditional assumption that encounter groups are composed of well-functioning individuals.

Bebout and Gordon (1972: 87) also found that over 70 percent of a sample of 500 participants indicated prominent expectations that were in accord with the pre-set goals of their encounter groups.[11] Lieberman and Gardner (1976) have conducted the most extensive research on this subject, and their findings are more in accord with those of Olch and Snow. They compared those who attended growth centers and NTL laboratories with psychotherapy clinic patients. Using a variety of measures they found that most who attend such activities do so for "psychotherapeutic purposes." Some of the participants did so with the hope of obtaining therapeutic benefits without experiencing the painful elements they associated with the psychotherapeutic process. Others were looking for a more direct, immediate, and intense experience than they believed traditional psychotherapy offered.

Based on these studies, perhaps the safest conclusion is that many participants enter encounter groups with expectations generally in accord with the goals of en-

counter groups as established by group leaders and in informational literature. Often, however, these expectations are not substantially different from those of psychotherapy patients.

This has significant implications for regulatory proposals. Under many licensing laws, for instance, it does not matter what the express purpose or goal of an activity is. As long as an activity is functioning in a certain fashion or having a certain effect, regardless of intent, it comes within the purview of the law. Thus, although unlicensed encounter group leaders might argue that their approach is educational in nature, if the effect of their intervention is therapeutic, they might still be considered in violation of the psychology laws or other relevant professional licensing legislation. More important, the diversity of expectations parallels the diversity that exists in the general goals of both encounter groups and more traditional therapies. This creates serious problems for restrictive forms of regulation such as licensing, since it becomes difficult to identify for what practices one is requiring a license.

HISTORICAL AND THEORETICAL PERSPECTIVES

The history of encounter groups reveals that they are not a unitary phenomenon. Unlike psychoanalysis or Gestalt therapy, encounter groups have no single originator. Nor did encounter groups develop from the collaborative efforts of practitioners and theoreticians. Instead, encounter groups are a potpourri resulting from a number of different and sometimes antithetical conceptual frameworks, theories, practices, roots and people. This fact makes it difficult to understand and organize theoretical and historical statements about them.

Perhaps the most useful perspective on encounter groups is to view them as arising out of four distinct concerns. The first involves the professional use of small groups to facilitate the growth of persons who participate in them. Encounter groups may also be viewed as an extension of the scientific study of small groups—how they work, how they influence their individual members, and how they can be changed and altered (Benne, in Howard, 1970: 113). Through this conceptual lens, encounter groups become an action-research method for scientifically understanding groups. Third, encounter groups may manifest a concern for democracy and an interest in developing educational methods that will train citizens to effectively implement democratic beliefs and methods (Bradford et al., 1964c: 9-10). Finally, encounter groups may represent an outgrowth of the human concern for the religious and social dimension of living (Oden, 1972a, 1972b).

Encounter Groups as Facilitators of Personal Growth

Encounter groups represent one of the most recent developments in the use of small groups to facilitate personal growth. Historically they are a direct descendant of the psychotherapy group. More specifically, within the field of group psychotherapy several major schools have contributed most to the growth of encounter groups.

Historians generally agree that the turn of this century marks the initial appearance of groups specifically and intentionally designed to ameliorate emotional distress.[12] The first such groups were organized to combat social conditions, such as poor settlement housing. They took the form of self-help groups, including those organized through Jane Addams's Hull House, which opened in 1889. Very quickly the psychological potential of small-group methods came to be used to combat physical illnesses as well, including tuberculosis and consumption (Pratt, 1907). Finally, in 1918 Edward Lazell (1921) became the first American to use group methods for problems that were primarily psychological in nature.[13]

It was not until the late twenties with the work of Trigant Burrow (1927) that people in the United States began to apply psychoanalytic ideas to the treatment of individuals in group settings.[14] But Burrow and those who came after him, such as Wender (1936), Schilder (1939), Wolf (1950, 1949), and Slavson (1943), were very strict in their application of Freudian principles. Because of Freud's (1960) theories as expressed in *Group Psychology and the Analysis of the Ego*, they did not take an interest in group dynamics per se, but concentrated on the relationship between the participants and the group leader.

Shortly after World War II, however, England saw the forging of a different application of psychoanalytic theory. Strongly influenced by the field theory of Kurt Lewin (1951), Foulkes and Anthony (1965), Bion (1961), and Ezriel (1950) realized that significant therapeutic gains could be made through attention to group-level phenomena. They found that interpretations made about what was happening in the group as a whole, as opposed to interpretations made only about transactions between the therapist and a particular group member, had powerful therapeutic potential. In the United States, Whitaker and Lieberman (1964) became strong proponents of this approach to groups.

Paralleling these developments was the work of Jacob Moreno (1969, 1954, 1953; Moreno and Moreno, 1960) in Vienna. As early as 1910 he had systematically formulated the process of group psychotherapy. The technique he eventually developed came to be known as psychodrama, and has provided valuable methodological tools for many encounter group leaders. Moreno noticed that children could work through emotionally troublesome events by reenacting them or by allowing their fantasy to deal with them. It seemed logical that such an approach would work with adults, and he began to have his patients act out in the group the life problems they were having. He had other patients play various roles, and the whole affair took on the appearance of a dramatic production. Moreno's theories have had a tremendous impact on encounter groups, especially his ideas of acting out problems, the value of empathic identification as a vehicle for allowing nonparticipants in a role play to receive help from it, and his emphasis on the value of catharsis. It was Moreno who first coined the term "group psychotherapy" in 1932.

Another important theoretical strand in the development of encounter groups was Gestalt therapy. The efforts of Fritz Perls were instrumental in this regard.[15] He had studied with and been strongly influenced by the German Gestalt psychologists Koehler, Wertheimer, and Koffka. The major premise of Gestalt therapy is that the whole is both greater than and different from the sum of its parts. The way in which one perceives something is determined by the total context in which the perception takes place. This applies to one's self as well.

Perls's chief interest lay in helping people become aware of their whole selves and their environment through participation in group therapy. He saw self-awareness as therapeutic and encouraged patients to take responsibility for initiating changes in themselves. Like Moreno, Perls encouraged patients to act out their problems in a group, but he went further than Moreno in encouraging the physical representation and acting out of emotions, attitudes, and fantasies. Whereas Moreno was interested in helping the patient discover more effective ways of dealing with reality, Perls was more interested in helping people perceive reality clearly. To accomplish this Perls used such techniques as exaggerating mannerisms to help patients become more aware of both the mannerism itself and its significance.

Initially, Perls and other group psychotherapists confined their innovations to therapy groups. Over time, however, it became apparent that their methods were equally powerful in promoting growth in relatively normal individuals. It also became apparent that long analysis of past conflicts was not the only means of curing patients of their emotional problems. Therapists began to realize that focusing on strengths could be as helpful as focusing on weaknesses. These realizations hastened the development of encounter groups and allowed the techniques and theories of psychotherapy to be directly applied in the encounter group situation.

Perhaps the person most influential in the development of encounter groups has been Carl Rogers (1970). He argued that meaningful distinctions could not be drawn between reparative psychotherapy and self-actualizing personal growth. He maintained that the exploration of a patient's unconscious was not especially helpful in promoting growth; he also had a strong faith in a patient's ability to learn from fellow patients. Even in the case of severely disturbed individuals, Rogers and his associates (1967) did not believe that complex techniques were necessary for their cure so much as warmly human therapists.

These beliefs led Rogers to experiment with small groups as a vehicle for learning and personal growth as early as the late 1940s, when he was training psychological counselors for the Veterans Administration. The program Rogers developed relied on small and intensive group experiences with considerable emphasis on examining how people in the group felt about each other and how they were behaving. A significant feature of the program was its focus on personal growth through a small-group experience—something that is the hallmark of an encounter group. After this initial experiment with small groups, Rogers's interest lay dormant while he pursued his exploration of individual therapy. In 1964, after becoming a Resident Fellow at the Western Behavioral Science Institute in La Jolla, California, he began working again in the area of intensive group experiences, and shortly thereafter coined the term "encounter group" for the type of group with which he was working (Rogers, 1970).

Another individual who has played a large role in the development of encounter groups is William Schutz (1967). Through the publication of his book *Joy* and his move to Esalen Institute, both of which occurred in 1967, Schutz probably popularized groups more than any individual in the field. The theoretical base for Schutz's work is embedded in a psychoanalytic framework, although he has made a number of significant departures from traditional Freudian theory. Of primary importance is his focus on sensory awareness and physical touching, both of which are prominent components of many of today's encounter groups. An emphasis on sensory awareness and the belief that analysis of bodily tensions can provide a leverage point for relief of emotional distress is also emphasized in Alexander Lowen's (1969) bioenergetic group therapy and Paul Bindrim's (1968) nude encounter groups.

A final develpment that deserves mention is the marathon encounter group. Stoller (1968) and Bach (1967a, 1967b, 1967c, 1966) were among the first to use this technique. Both these men were psychoanalytically oriented, but were dissatisfied with existing modes of group therapy. They began exploring time-extended formats and found the results highly successful. They reasoned that people would more easily let down their defenses when they became tired, that being unable to escape from the presence of the group would ensure that conflicts had to be faced, and that the lack of interruptions in meetings would result in less time wasted getting back together. The marathon group has now become one of the more popular forms of encounter, especially as a result of the work of Mintz (1971).[16]

This view of encounter groups as facilitators of personal growth clearly reveals the profusion of techniques, meth-ods, and goals, stemming from a variety of therapeutic theories and practices—including psychoanalysis, field theory, psychodrama, Gestalt therapy, and client-centered therapy—that have shaped their history. In this sense the encounter field is a true potpourri, with very few organizing principles or unifying theories.

Encounter Groups as a Method and Subject of Scientific and Theoretical Inquiry

Scientific interest in groups, both at the theoretical and practical level, has played a role in the evolution of the encounter group. Small groups have not been subjected to scientific scrutiny until relatively recently, although writers have propounded various theories of how and why groups work.

The dearth of research was partially a consequence of the lack of effective and accurate methodologies and techniques, and it was also due to lack of interest. The sociologists of the nineteenth century, for instance, were more concerned with society and its development. The German sociologist Toennies (1957), for instance, believed that small groups such as the family were an impediment to the development of society. Theoretical analysis focused on large groups and mob psychology (*see, e.g.,* Alexander, in Arnhoff, 1971: 24; McDougall, 1920; Trotter, 1919).

Sigmund Freud (1960) was one of the first to undertake a comprehensive theoretical explanation of small-group behavior. While sociologists had offered reasonable explanations of why some groups could turn into unruly mobs, Freud determined that adequate explanations did not exist for a variety of other behaviors, including the cohesiveness that groups often exhibit, their moral behavior, and the emotional attachments that frequently develop among group members, especially in the family. Freud offered an explanation based on psychoanalytic theory. In essence he stated that group behavior was the result of the group members' sexual attachment to the leader and consequent dependence on her or him. Mutual bonds between group members were based on their common relationship to the leader. This analysis presented a beginning theoretical base on which to develop group therapy, but most psychotherapists, including Freud himself, ignored these implications of his work.

At roughly the same time that Freud was developing his theories, several social psychologists were conducting some of the earliest scientific experiments on groups. The work of Triplett[17] at the end of the nineteenth century, which compared a person's athletic performance alone or when paced by others, and Moede,[18] in 1920, who studied the effects of taking psychological examinations in groups, demonstrated that group forces could be studied scientifically as well as providing some simple techniques for such study (Bonner, 1959). Nonetheless, small-group research lagged until the 1930s and 1940s, when instruments, methods, and techniques became more refined. Then the famous Western Electric researchers of Mayo (1945) and his coworkers Roethlisberger and Dickson (1956) provided the basis for the work of Kurt Lewin, who revolutionized the study of small groups.

Lewin's contribution to encounter groups is worthy of extended treatment because of its scope and brilliance. As a great figure in the history of psychology, Lewin has been compared with Freud.[19] Coming out of a background in Gestalt psychology, Lewin had been one of the first to apply field theory in the psychological realm.[20] Field theory had already revolutionized physics and allowed for the development of quantum mechanics and Einstein's theory of relativity. Lewin believed that such a theory could and should be applied in social psychology. In simplified terms, Lewin argued that behavior was the result of all the existing forces within a field. Any change in one part of a field would have a greater or lesser overall systemic effect. Only present forces

were capable of influence, and past events were of significance only because of the existence of current forces (such as memory).

This theory had important implications for the study and conduct of groups—implications that were soon to be drawn out. It was first of all influential with the psychoanalytically oriented British psychiatrists, giving rise to both group-dynamic psychotherapy and the Tavistock model of encounter groups. More important, Lewin's ideas were directly responsible for the development of the T-group. One implication of field theory was that the very conduct of research would alter, in some way, what was being researched. Attempts to have a wholly neutral observer were fruitless. Recognizing this, Lewin sought to maximize the role that an observer might play in bringing about change in a social system, and developed the notion of the "participant-observer." From this the T-group emerged as a result of some fortuitous circumstances that occurred shortly after the war.[21]

During the summer of 1946 Lewin was working with Kenneth Benne, Leland Bradford, and Ronald Lippitt on a project to train community leaders for the Connecticut Interracial Commission. An additional staff of researchers had been hired to observe the project. In the evenings the research and training staff met to discuss the former's observations. One evening a few of the participants asked to attend the staff meeting. The resulting interchange, as the participants heard how the observers perceived their behavior, was dramatic. Lewin realized three things. First, the participants' perceptions of what had occurred was a valuable research tool that had been neglected. Second, the data resulting from the interchange between the observers and the participants was in itself valuable. And third, the participants found this meeting exciting and valuable as a learning experience.

Lewin and the rest of the staff realized immediately that they had discovered a powerful learning device, and they set about planning a laboratory for its further development the next summer. Unfortunately, Lewin died, but Bradford, Benne, and Lippitt carried out Lewin's intentions by developing the now prestigious National Training Laboratories. Since that time the concept of the T-group has been developed and refined. In the late forties and early fifties the primary emphasis was placed on understanding group dynamics. As time went by, however, and psychiatrists and psychologists were asked to participate in the training, the focus turned more and more to personal growth. The T-group still retains, nonetheless, the notion of the participant-observer and its importance as a learning and research methodology.

Encounter Groups as a Method for Educating Effective Members of a Democratic Society

The effectiveness of a democracy in achieving the goals of society depends directly on the ability of its citizens to participate meaningfully in important decisions. Benne (1975: 43), quoting the Faculty of the Training Laboratory in Group Development (1947: 476), has put the matter well:

Democracy is an ideology which above all others demands that its practitioners be masters of skills of human relationship adequate to help groups of people make intelligent decisions concerning the changing problems that confront them.... Without appropriate and experimentally tested skills and methods for building effective cooperative relationships, democracy has no hands and feet.

Encounter groups, especially the traditional T-group, represent one attempt to educate people so that they might be effective members of society. The search for such a method has a long history, but the efforts of John Dewey in the early 1900s (1959) were especially instrumental and have had a direct impact on encounter groups. Dewey saw education as relevant to the needs of society and responsive to

the individual, as well. According to him education was meant to be an active process involving a continuing reconstruction of experience. The process and goal of education were one and the same. Education was not merely the passing on of knowledge, but experiencing and learning from that experience. Proper education involved a person's values, and ultimately behavioral change was implicit in any form of learning. In other words, education should be both normative and reeducative. In addition, education should "strive to educate with social change in view by producing individuals not complacent about what already exists, and equipped with desires and abilities to assist in transforming it" (Dewey, 1959: 119). Unfortunately, according to Dewey, traditional schooling was ill-equipped and inadequate to develop people capable of bringing about such changes, and he believed that "quite a different method and content is indicated for educational science" (Dewey, 1959: 119).[22]

This quest for an educational science of "quite a different method and content" was continued by the social philosophers of the thirties and forties. The question had become how to pursue the implications of Dewey's philosophy of education and what type of educational methodology would best fulfill the goals Dewey had formulated. The task was phrased most succinctly by Raup, Axtelle, Benne, and Smith (1950: 266) in *The Improvement of Practical Intelligence:* "The central educational problem of today is that of developing in people the kind of characters which we have maintained are necessary if democratic living is to be realized."

At the time an answer was unavailable. Certain guidelines and criteria existed, certain ideas and hypotheses had been formulated, but the vehicle for developing this kind of character had not yet been developed. Fortuitously, two of Dewey's followers, Benne and Bradford, who were prominent men in their own right in education, were also involved with Kurt

Lewin and his research. Their participation in the summer workshop that engendered the T-group ensured that this form of encounter group would have strong attachments and roots in educational and democratic philosophy.

Encounter Groups as a Religious and Social Movement

The rapid growth of encounter groups in the 1960s needs explanation. It is clear that the roots of encounter groups in personal growth, science, and democratic educational philosophy could not, in themselves, provide the spark for the tremendous expansion that took place. Some writers have opined that encounter groups were simply a passing fad or game (Maliver, 1973), or that they might be radical psychological experimentation (Stone, 1970). An alternative explanation, as the following considerations suggest, is that the encounter field has strong religious overtones and, at least in part, has aspects of a social movement.

The developments in U.S. society that have brought about the proliferation of small groups are not difficult to identify. Commentators on the social scene stress the alienation that humanity is experiencing as a result of increasing technocratization, especially the breakdown of the extended family. The loneliness of urban living, the increased social mobility, and the rigidity of traditional social institutions have been partial causes of the increasing interest in encounter groups. Rogers (1970), Lakin (1972), and Stone (1970) point out that increasing dehumanization in our culture has caused people to lose their sense of belongingness, their sense of stability, and their sense of intimacy. A pressing hunger exists for interpersonal relationships that are both close and real. Many participants see the encounter experience as a response to and relief from these problems.

That such problems may have created conditions ripe for the spawning of a social movement like encounter groups is

a thesis that Jerome Frank (1975: 276) has seriously considered in his classic work *Persuasion and Healing:*

Political scientists have noted that small, face-to-face groups flourish whenever a society is in transition, as in pre-revolutionary France, America, and Russia. At such junctures, they perform at least three functions relevant to psychotherapy. They form oases of the like-minded against the buffetings of the outside world, forums in which members feel that they have some power to influence each other, and nuclei of a counter-culture which hammers out the new values and political forms that eventually supersede the old ones. Perhaps the current popularity of encounter groups implies that we are in a pre-revolutionary stage.

And Rosenthal (in Blank *et al.*, 1971: 460) has commented:

Indeed, both Toynbee and Spengler point out that such movements have often appeared in other Western societies when there has been a malaise of spirit, a deterioration of social institutions and collective purpose, an eruption of internal conflict and social violence, a compensated excitement to despair, and, in general, a decay of vital forces. Whether the encounter movement is a modern symptom of this decline or is an omen of a general renewal, only the long run of the future will tell.

Beyond simply being a social movement, encounter groups clearly have religious overtones. An insightful analogy concerning encounter groups as a religious quest has been drawn by Thomas Oden.[23] In his work, *The Intensive Group Experience: The New Pietism*, Oden (1972a) argues that encounter groups follow a long tradition of pietism. In reviewing the history of Christianity and Judaism, Oden found several counterparts to today's encounter groups among the radical groups of Jewish Hasidism and Protestant Pietism. Pietism was a reform movement in the German Lutheran Church during the seventeenth and eighteenth centuries that strove to renew the devotional ideal in the Protestant religion. Hasidism was a sect of Jewish mystics founded in Poland about 1750 in opposition to the formalistic Judaism of the period.

These religious sects emphasized discussions of the here-and-now, and placed a high value on the expression of feeling. They used the small group as a primary vehicle of religious expression, and stressed the importance of mutual trust, immediate confrontation, marathon-like experiences, the sharing of highly personal matters, and honest and direct feedback of people's perceptions of each other. Hasidism and Pietism both maintained that lay leadership needed to be expanded. All these characteristics are equally a part of the encounter group movement.

The similarities between frontier American pietism and encounter groups is even more striking. During the exploration of the early American frontier, ministers were typically quite charismatic. As Oden (1972a: 60–61) writes: "These itinerant charismatic leaders moved constantly on horseback from small lay group to small lay group, facilitating their growth. Energized by visions of vast and rapid human change, armed with eclectic resources, and fascinated by experimental social interaction, they were accustomed to brutally honest feedback procedures." Encounter groups, like Pietism and Hasidism, are highly syncretistic; that is, their theory is a conglomeration and amalgam of many previous theories mixed together in broadly eclectic fashion (Oden, 1972b: 24). Even the social conditions that existed in Pietist times are similar to current conditions (Oden, 1972b: 29). Oden notes a number of other similarities, and presents verbatim descriptions of encounter groups side-by-side with early meetings of these Pietist groups. He concludes that encounter groups are a "demythologized, secularized Judeo-Christian theology" (Oden, 1972a: 89).

The Current Range of Encounter Group Theory and Practice

After thirty years of development, encounter group theory and practice is still a potpourri. In 1964 Bradford, Gibb, and Benne (1964a) ventured some predictions about the development of encounter groups. They suspected that encounter group theory would run a poor third behind technological invention and empirical research. Eleven years later they concluded that their prediction had been borne out (Benne et al., 1975: Ch. 24).

The reasons for this are not hard to find. Theoretical understanding of the field of personal growth and group dynamics is still at a primitive stage. The variety of theories that prevail in the psychotherapeutic literature is impressive testimony on this score. Little is still known about how change and growth take place. In addition, research methodologies and techniques of measurement, although considerably advanced, are still incapable of isolating many of the important variables in the encounter group process.

The range of theories existing today to explain the encounter process is wide and highly varied. Psychoanalytic formulations have been offered by Stone (1970), Freundlich (1972), and Whitman (1964). Houts and Serber (1972), Apfelbaum and Apfelbaum (1973), and Koch (1971) have analyzed the learning processes in groups in terms of behavioral theories of reciprocal inhibition, reinforcement, and other stimulus-response explanations of behavior. Hampden-Turner's (1970) analysis of the research on groups has led to an existential learning theory, while Schein and Bennis (1965: 271–276) offer a learning theory originating from the T-group practitioner's point of view.

Older theories continue to be modified and updated. Mintz (1971), for instance, has reformulated the marathon group concepts of Stoller (1968) and Bach (1966); and Benne (1975) has continued his efforts at providing an adequate conceptual framework for understanding T-groups.[24] In an excellent theoretical piece, Bebout (undated) has reformulated Rogers' (1970) client-centered theories with reference to the encounter experience.[25] These efforts to develop a systematic theory about the encounter group process point to and parallel the growth of encounter groups in general. They also illustrate the diversity, confusion, and lack of knowledge that still exist.

Applications, Impact, and Use of Encounter Groups

The fact that millions of people are responding [to the offerings of human relations trainers] validates the *need* for the kind of education and re-education which human relations training at its best does provide. Men and women, young and old, do need help in gaining more valid understandings of themselves and others, in developing experientially grounded images of integral and autonomous functioning as persons within a community of persons, in developing skills for transforming the relationships through which their lives are lived into more personally fulfilling forms. The response of people to human relations training as it offers and in some measure provides such help shows the "facticity" of the human needs to which it is addressed and the deficiencies of established institutions, industrial, religious and educational, which are now failing to meet these needs. [Kenneth D. Benne (1970) in "The Tearing Down of Walls."]

The large number of people participating in intensive group experiences, the appearance of hundreds of "personal growth centers" across the country, and the significant sums of money spent on encounter groups attest to the relevance of such an experience for a variety of people. At least to some, encounter groups have provided an answer for the increasing problems of alienation and lack of humanness created by a society that humanists argue has not been adequately responsive to the needs of its members. In a world in which sensory awareness, being in touch with and able to express one's feelings, and fulfilling one's human potential are increasingly valued, encounter groups may offer a highly effective method of realizing these goals (Krieger, 1971). Encounter groups may also provide a valuable vehicle to learn to adapt to change (Rogers, 1970).[26]

Perhaps the most direct value and contribution of encounter groups to society, however, has been in the field of psychotherapy. An American Psychiatric Association Task Force (1970: 19) has declared that most of what is known of the basic science of group psychotherapy stems from the research on task groups and T-groups, and that psychotherapy is deeply indebted to T-groups for its understanding of group development, group pressure, leadership, and group norms and values. In addition, many of the techniques and practices that have been developed in the encounter group field have been directly incorporated into psychotherapy—both group and individual.[27]

The extent to which encounter groups have been used in a wide variety of settings suggests that the public believes encounter groups are worthwhile. Several examples will illustrate their potential value. One of the most important applications of encounter groups has been in the professional training of mental health workers. In the training of psychotherapists encounter groups have been effectively used to facilitate physical contact and the expression of feeling, to increase skills in perceiving nuances of meaning, and to develop skills in communicating understanding—skills generally recognized as important to success as a therapist but often ignored in psychiatric residency training programs (Lakin, 1972: 213).[28] Although not extensive, empirical research has borne out the value of this approach, especially in comparison with more traditional discussion groups (*see, e.g.*, Shapiro, 1971).

Encounter groups have also been used to train various professional groups not directly associated with mental health care. The value of this training tends to correlate with the degree to which interpersonal sensitivity is a prerequisite to success on the job. Thus the training of physicians and nurses through encounter techniques has proved especially fruitful.[29] Another frequent application has been in the training of teachers (*see* Lett 1973;

Lindenauer and Caine, 1973) and paraprofessionals in key community positions requiring human relation skills (Sheriden et al., 1973a; Sheridan et al., 1973b). Police officers have also been involved in sensitivity training (Sata, 1975).

One of the most natural uses of encounter groups is as an educational tool for students. Unfortunately, traditional academic institutions have few courses designed to increase emotional sensitivity, self-awareness, or the ability to share one's perceptions of another person with that person. Although this application has met with stiff resistance,[30] its potential value appears significant, as documented by the reports of Carl Rogers (1969) and others (Bessell, 1970; Valine and Amos, 1973).

Business and industry have made considerable use of encounter groups, especially T-groups and transactional analysis groups. In addition to increased sensitivity, the purpose of encounter training has generally focused on understanding group dynamics and increasing group leadership skills. The mid-sixties marked the high point of this particular application. Subsequently, serious questions began to be raised about the value of this form of training in industry (Calame, 1969; Gomberg, 1967, 1966; Jacobs, 1972; Joure et al., 1971; Schrank and Stein, 1970). It became apparent that its potential had been oversold and that it was often used uncritically. A general retrenchment occurred, as many companies concluded that increased sensitivity on the part of their employees was not doing much for productivity. The occasional use of encounter-type experiences in specific industrial situations is probably useful and may even be worthwhile on a cost-benefit basis.[31]

Related to this has been the use of encounter groups, especially the T-group, in community development settings. In a small, one-industry New England village, for instance, citizens, town officials, and the management of the only industry

were involved in such a program (Klein, 1965).[32] The results were largely positive. Evidence indicated that the groups helped to reduce mistrust and apathy, to increase participation in town government and community affairs, and to broaden the perspective of the villagers so that they saw their own needs and interests within the larger geographic region of which they were a part.[33]

Encounter groups have also been used in mental health settings as an adjunct to therapy.[34] In most cases empirical research reveals that patients involved in encounter groups are helped as much as those involved in traditional psychotherapy (*see, e.g.*, Hanson et al., 1969; Johnson et al., 1965). The mental health field has also witnessed encounter groups used in resolving problems in race relations (*see, e.g.*, Anderson and Love, 1973; Cobbs, 1972; Jones and Harris, 1971; McLean, 1974; Rogers, 1970; Schutz, 1967; Walker and Hamilton, 1973; White, 1973), as a form of drug treatment (*see* Casriel, 1971; Enright, 1971; *Newsweek*, 1971), in improving family relations (*see* Golembiewski, 1970; Pilder, 1972), and in women and men's consciousness-raising groups (*see* Brodsky, 1973; Clark, 1972; Halas, 1973; Meador et al., 1972).

Most major systems and institutions in the United States have been involved with encounter groups in one way or another. The legal system, for instance, has used human relations groups to train judges (*see* Lakin, 1972: 221–32). Religious institutions, including seminaries, groups of religious leaders, and parishioners, have found them valuable in building a sense of community and improving communication (Rogers, 1970: 138).

The wide application of encounter groups is not just a phenomenon of the United States.[35] The reach of various international organizations such as the Protestant Episcopal Church has brought encounter groups to countries as far off as New Zealand (Miles, 1962: 6). Japan has become heavily involved in human relations training of various sorts (Massarik, 1974/75). In Europe the European Institute for Trans-national Studies in Group and Organization Development was formed in 1964 and has since expanded considerably, while the Australian Institute of Human Relations has been in operation since 1968 (Benne et al., 1975: 7).

Conclusion

While encounter groups were something of a national fad in the 1960s, they have matured into a process of substantial impact and of considerable potential value for society. Through the social conditions that first generated the popularity of encounter groups may disappear, their roots in the scientific tradition, their value as a vehicle for personal growth, and their potential for educating citizens as effective members of a democratic society appear strong enough to ensure their continued presence. Since their impact is likely to be significant and long-lasting, their regulation deserves careful thought. As with the more traditional forms of psychotherapy, the diversity that exists in the field means that traditional forms of regulation may not be appropriate.

VALUE AND EFFECTIVENESS OF ENCOUNTER GROUPS

Proponents of encounter groups claim that the encounter experience is of considerable societal and individual value. They also maintain that encounter groups are an effective means of bringing about certain behavioral and attitudinal changes in people. Establishing the degree of truth to these assertions is difficult because of the methodological problems involved in conducting social science research. The following assessment relies on a variety of evidentiary sources, including an examination of two large-scale research projects and a study of the most significant reviews of the existing research.

An Examination of Two Research Projects

Two research projects on encounter groups have been conducted that are on such a large scale, are so thorough in their inquiry, and have so many implications for professional practice and regulation that they deserve separate and special consideration. Both were conducted on the West Coast and were oriented strongly toward the personal-growth end of the encounter group spectrum. Each received massive funding from both private and governmental sources. These two projects have yielded by far the most valuable data on groups, and have received considerable attention in numerous journals and books.

The Group Experience Project: A Comparison of Ten Encounter Technologies.[36] The Group Experience Project (GEP), begun in the fall of 1968, took place at Stanford University under the direction of Morton Lieberman, Irvin Yalom, and Matthew Miles—three of the leading practitioners in the encounter field. Its broad purpose was to examine various types of encounter groups to determine: (1) the effectiveness of the different groups; (2) the ways and degree to which people changed as a result of participation; (3) the risks involved in participation; and (4) the conditions that were instrumental in bringing about either the desired or undesirable effects. The definition of what constituted an encounter group was broad, and ten different types were represented[37] in the seventeen groups that were compared. The sixteen group leaders were all highly experienced, and several were nationally known.

The 206 participants were students at the university who had enrolled in a course on race and prejudice. They were thoroughly informed of the nature of the course and warned of its potential dangers. In order to compare the effects of the experience with students who did not participate, a control group was established consisting of 38 students who had enrolled but could not take the course, and an additional 31 demographically matched students.

Testing was conducted before, immediately after, and six to eight months following the encounter group experience. Change was measured from the leader's viewpoint, the participants' own perceptions, the perceptions of significant people in the participants' social networks, the judgments of co-participants from the same group, and a variety of other test instruments.

The areas of change that were assessed included: (1) religious experience (the type of experience that Maslow has termed a "peak experience" and which is reflected in "oceanic, enthusiastic, conversion-like" feelings); (2) interpersonal construct system (the way one views and deals with others); (3) self-issues (concerned with one's self-concept); (4) value reorientation (differences in what behaviors are valued and how one's life goals have changed); (5) life decisions (whether the group helped resolve any major decisions or crises that the participant was faced with during or close to the group experience); (6) meta-learning or learning to learn (whether the participants developed new mechanisms for helping resolve personal dilemmas); and (7) interpersonal changes (dealing with expression of affection and anger, spontaneity, and similar issues) (Lieberman et al., 1971: 480–82).

The results were mixed. From the leaders' perspective the changes for participants were remarkably positive, and this opinion was shared by the participants themselves. On the other hand, friends of the participants did not report significantly more changes in behavior on the part of the participants than did friends of members of the control group. The participants' self-ratings differed significantly from the control group, however. They became more interested in changing the ways they related to people and how they were perceived by others. They became more interested in psychological growth, viewing encounter groups as a safe environment for learning. They decreased the discrepancy between their actual self-image and their ideal self-image, and saw their own interpersonal behavior as more adequate.

The degree of difference from the control group diminished at the time of follow-up, however. After reviewing all the data, Lieberman, Yalom, and Miles (1973) believed that the main changes that occurred for participants were in the area of values and attitudes, which changes may or may not be noticed by outside observers. They concluded that "overall, encounter groups show a modest positive impact" (Lieberman et al., 1973: 130).

The conclusion that encounter groups are only modestly helpful, in conjunction with another conclusion of these researchers that such groups involve substantial risk, has generated significant controversy (Rowan, 1975; Schutz, 1975; Smith, 1975). A major problem is that encounter groups may be such diverse phenomena that broad and all-encompassing conclusions are unwarranted and misleading. Data from GEP itself bear this out, since one of the striking features of the results was their lack of uniformity. Different groups provided different learnings for different types of participants. In one group all members showed a rise in self-esteem, while only 15 percent of another group showed an increase. Drop-out rates ranged from 0 to 40 percent. Some groups had no members who were hurt by the experience. Others were polarized with almost no middle ground, but many high learners and many severely hurt individuals, some of whom suffered severe anxiety and the loss of the ability to function effectively. In still other groups almost no changes were exhibited.

The generalizability of these findings may be seriously limited by a number of other factors. The first is the nature of the population chosen for study. College students, who are undergoing many changes anyway, may be unsuitable because, as one critic put it, research in this environment is very much like "starting an electric fan in a monsoon and measuring the ensuing breeze" (Rowan, 1975: 24). Originally intended as a course on racism, the groups may have attracted a significantly different type of participant from one that was advertised expressly as encounter. That participants were randomly assigned to specific groups may have increased the dangers and minimized the chance of positive outcomes, particularly in attack-oriented groups such as Synanon. Especially damaging to the conclusions is the fact that the group leaders may have been extremely atypical and even dangerous. Schutz (1975) has pointed out that one of the leaders was the only person ever banned from conducting groups at Esalen, while another was excluded for a period of several months. These leaders accounted for five of the sixteen casualties. The Synanon group accounted for two more. The fact that one of the participants committed suicide very early in the group experience, even though his death was not attributable to the groups, may have minimized the potential for learning and for positive change, while increasing the risk of a negative experience by setting a tone for the rest of the group.

Problems also plagued the design of the project. The most severe was the small size of the control group, which was one-third the size of the participant group and which lost one-third of its members by the time of follow-up. Thus, while the researchers did an excellent job of analyzing the process of encounter groups and in determining what brought about specific changes, there is serious question about the generalizability of the overall finding about the value of encounter groups. These criticisms demonstrate the extreme difficulty of conducting research in an area as amorphous as encounter groups and the need for further research to demonstrate whether specific findings can be confirmed by replication.

The Talent in Interpersonal Exploration Groups (TIE) Project. The TIE Project, carried out in Berkeley, California, provides a sharp contrast to the Group Experience Project in its findings and conclusions.[40] It was begun one year after the GEP and took approximately five years to complete. In sheer scope and size, few studies equal it. Major support has come from the National Institute of Mental Health, with total grant monies exceeding $1 million. The principal investigator, James Bebout, is currently analyzing the final research results, but some preliminary findings are available.

The project is attempting to explore three major assumptions (Bebout and Gordon, 1971: 3). First, it postulated that significant positive changes in self-image and interpersonal relationships will result from encounter group participation. The second postulate is that the required leadership skills consist of therapeutic attitudes, interpersonal skills, and personality traits, not theoretical knowledge, diagnostic ability, or technical skills. Third, the assumption is that encounter groups will exhibit regular patterns of group interaction. The project thus focuses on outcomes, leadership, and process.

In contrast to the GEP, the group leaders were nonprofessionals. They usually were recruited from previous groups and tended to be people interested in group process who were also highly recommended by their fellow group members when they were participants. They were then put through an intensive three-month training program involving, in part, ten weekly meetings in a small training group, a weekend retreat, and a minimum of six workshops on encounter theory and technique.

The groups consisted of five males and

five females, who met once a week for ten weeks with a weekend semi-marathon. Total meeting time amounted to roughly seventy to eighty hours. Bebout and Gordon (1972: 85) state that:

They are meant to be supportive, exploratory, and to generate more or less intensive experiences furthering people's personal and social growth. To the extent that personal growth is facilitated the groups are therapeutic. We try for a fail-safe approach. Groups are not problem or attack-oriented by design, and an individual's right to a defense is respected. Responsibility for change rests most with group members, rather than leaders, and dramatic breakthroughs are valued less than lasting increments in emotional growth and sensitivity to others.

Testing was carried out before, during, and after the group experience, and change was measured from a number of different points of view, as with the GEP. Some of the types of changes that TIE was trying to assess included participants' self-perception, self-esteem, interpersonal values, psychosocial alienation, personal and social problems, self-actualization, and role behaviors.

In their discussion of the results, Bebout and Gordon (1972: 117–118) conclude:

We have found significant positive changes in members almost wherever we looked. Self-esteem increases, the self-concept changes in many positive directions, self-actualizing tendencies are greater, alienation is reduced, and individual problems are lessened; interpersonal relations become more empathic and improve; and interpersonal values change perhaps toward a more realistic supportiveness; people become close with each other and feel less lonely.

Our encounter groups do little for productivity, work, or school problems. Since the program does not try to affect these areas, this result is not surprising. Most of our sample are encounter group beginners—they enter the program positively motivated and with appropriate expectations. Under these circumstances people gain the most. Older members and those with more experience gain less. The generally humanistic orientation of our sample does not change, unless

to become more so. Group composition and leader style do make a difference....

Our present conclusion is that encounter groups, when designed to provide a supportive, group-centered climate for personal growth, do produce significant positive changes and have considerable impact.

When group members were asked to rank their experience among eight significant experiences in their lives, a majority of the participants considered it as one of the eight most significant or meaningful such experiences (Bebout and Gordon, 1972: 105), demonstrating the tremendous impact these groups have had on their members.

Reviews of the Research

The task of evaluating the empirical research on encounter groups is enormous.[41] Literally thousands of studies have been executed.[42] Jack Gibb (1975: 59) has identified more than 200 doctoral dissertations dating from 1947 to 1972 that have examined the effects of the laboratory method. Dinges and Weigel (1971) have reviewed more than 250 studies related to marathon groups, which represent only a small part of the total encounter field.

Perhaps the earliest survey of research on encounter groups is that of Dorothy Stock (1964). She reviewed fifty-two studies, focusing on the internal dimensions of groups and their dynamics, but did not examine whether groups made a significant difference in the lives of participants. This emphasis reflected the interest of researchers at the time and mirrored the state of affairs in psychotherapeutic research and its "flight into process." From the few studies that examined group outcomes, she nonetheless cautiously concluded that groups did bring about changes in self-perception, affective behavior, self-insight, sensitivity to the feelings and behavior of others, self-confidence, and ability to diagnose organization problems, stressing that this was only a partial list. On the other hand, she was quite critical of the quality of research in general and strongly emphasized that her findings applied only to *some* participants *some* of the time.

Until the early seventies most of the reviews following Stock's attempted to evaluate the effectiveness of encounter groups in industry. The T-group was the main form investigated. The primary question was whether T-group training made a difference to organizational effectiveness. To answer this question the reviewers necessarily considered the matter of effectiveness related to individual behavior change. Robert House's (1967) "T-group Education and Leadership Effectiveness: A Review of the Empiric Literature and a Critical Evaluation," provides an excellent example of this type of review. He analyzed the findings of fifty of the most important studies on T-groups to determine how participants were changed as a result of their experience.

Certain findings appeared warranted. For example, most participants changed their opinion as to what constituted good leadership and came to believe that environments with less structure than traditional work groups were desirable. They also placed a higher value on being considerate. These conclusions were based on a series of studies of high quality, all of which included control groups and relied on the responses of observers, not the participants themselves. House also concluded that T-groups helped participants to listen better, to be more supportive of others, to be more sensitive, and to be less dependent on authority. Whether these behaviors and attitudes are conducive to increased productivity and efficiency was not demonstrated by the research, however, which contained evidence that T-groups were not effective in increasing organizational productivity.

In conclusion, House (1970: 458) stated that his review offered "ample evidence that the T-group method is a potentially powerful tool for changing behavior which is differentially effective in a wide variety of situations with a wide variety of individuals."

The year following House's review saw the appearance of a thoughtful and often-cited examination of the empirical literature by Campbell and Dunnette (1968). In a comprehensive analysis of nearly 100 studies, they examined the effectiveness of T-group experiences in managerial training and development. The general tone of their article was critical, and the authors stressed the tenuousness of most research conclusions. They fully recognized the difficulties of conducting research, and were sympathetic to the efforts that researchers had made. As academic psychologists, not T-group practitioners, they had little vested interest in positive conclusions. To Campbell and Dunnette the evidence was reasonably convincing that T-groups did induce behavioral changes in people's lives, but the assumption that such changes had positive utility for organizations rested on shaky ground, having been neither confirmed not disconfirmed. The types of changes that seemed to occur most often were increased sensitivity, more open communication, and an increased ability to be flexible in one's organizational role.

The findings of House and Campbell and Dunnette were echoed by Paul Buchanan (1969, 1964) in his two research reviews. In his initial study of research prior to 1964, he had concluded that T-groups were effective in facilitating specifiable changes in individuals in industrial settings. He had also found that T-groups were effective in some programs of organizational development, but not in others. As a result of his analysis of the research between 1964 and 1968, Buchanan found clear evidence that personal growth resulted for most participants. Specifically, they felt better about themselves, achieved new insights, improved their family relations, and became more open, self-aware, and the like. Buchanan found that participants tended to reduce extreme behavior and to become more tolerant of differences. They also improved various operational skills, such as listening and encouraging the participation of others.[43] Buchanan remained unconvinced, however, about the value of encounter groups in improving job performance.

While T-groups generally lead to personal growth, they may only occasionally be valuable in improving organizational effectiveness. This is the basic conclusion of Cooper and Mangham in their 1971 review of the literature. They examined the effectiveness of T-groups in three areas: (1) on-the-job changes; (2) internal changes within the participant, which may not be manifested by any observable behavioral change; and (3) the T-group as a vehicle for organizational change. While recognizing the methodological problems created by the research, Cooper and Mangham believed that empirical studies confirmed that T-groups brought about significantly more changes in on-the-job behavior than other training programs comparable in length and objectives. The types of changes most frequently reported were improved skills in diagnosing individual and group behavior, clearer communication, greater tolerance and consideration, and greater action skill and flexibility. All of these changes lasted some time after training, though reports of fade-out became more common after ten to twelve months. With regard to attitude change, perceptual change, and personality change, the authors reported equivocal results, which they attributed to the inadequacy of the measures used and their inability to distinguish subtle changes. They commonly found inconclusive results as to the effectiveness of T-groups as a vehicle for organizational change, where the methodological problems were even greater.

One of the first efforts that concentrated solely on the efficacy of encounter groups in bringing about personal growth, without regard to on-the-job changes in behavior, was the review of marathon group practice and research by Norman Dinges and Richard Weigel (1971). The authors divided their references into three categories of outcome research, based on the level of sophistication of the studies. Individual testimonials—a form of naturalistic observation of the group by the participants (and the most primitive type of study)—tended to be overwhelmingly positive, whether the testimony was given by the leader or member. Negative accounts were extremely rare, although, as Dinges and Weigel point out, those who might have had a less-than-positive experience might be less likely to respond.

The second category of research, including studies based on consensual anecdotal evidence (derived primarily on data from follow-up questionnaires completed by the participants), was likewise overwhelmingly positive. This finding obtained whether the data were gathered immediately following the group experience or at some later time. When the most sophisticated studies were examined (that is, those that employed objective instruments or behavior-ratings to assess participant change and also compared these changes to a matched control group), the results were not as positive. Dinges and Weigel concluded that these studies did provide some evidence for positive outcome effects, but the results were not consistent and little empirical support existed for *long-term* effects of a single marathon experience. They also warned that most of the studies contained methodological flaws that may have compromised their validity.

Since 1970 Jack Gibb has probably been most active in reviewing the effectiveness of encounter groups. His three reviews (Gibb, 1975, 1974, 1971) are more comprehensive than those of his predecessors, although he does not subject many studies to extensive analysis. Gibb has been involved with encounter groups since the early days of the National Training Laboratories. His earliest review contained 106 studies, and excluded those groups that had a specifically therapeutic orientation or those that would be defined traditionally as educational. Gibb divided encounter groups into eight categories, ranging from creativity-growth groups to inquiry groups. He found that most of the research—in fact nearly 90 percent—was on sensitivity groups: those groups whose central aims were personal competence, group effectiveness, and organizational effectiveness, as opposed to sensory awareness and self-actualization.

Gibb's conclusion about effectiveness was quite favorable. Acknowledging that the evidence was controversial and open to many legitimate interpretations, Gibb maintained that encounter groups brought about changes in sensitivity, feeling management, attitudes toward self and others, directionality of motivation, and interdependence. He noted that these types of changes were very similar to those expected in psychotherapy, but warned that it had not yet been demonstrated whether the magnitude of the effect was comparable to traditional modes of therapy or sufficient to warrant extensive use.

Gibb's (1975, 1974) two more recent reviews have continued his optimism on the value of encounter groups. Both were based on an almost identical list of 344 studies, carefully culled from more than 2,000 documents of a highly diverse nature covering the period 1947 to 1972.[44] Gibb believed a number of conclusions were warranted by the research. First, it was clear that the amount and quality of research had improved dramatically. More than 100 of the studies that he examined employed some form of control group. The range of interdisciplinary sponsorship of research was quite broad, with eighty-seven universities producing doctoral theses on encounter groups. These originated from a wide variety of disciplines, ranging from psychology and counseling to home economics and speech. Gibb found that the research was also becoming more theory-based, with studies

exploring some of the subtler change mechanisms that theory posits as important in encounter groups. The general types of changes he found reported in the literature were similar to those reported by other reviewers, such as warmth, self-acceptance, risk-taking, and expressiveness. The most frequently measured variable was self-acceptance, which occurred in 41 studies, 21 of which showed positive change, and the other 20 of which revealed no change.

Of the 127 studies comparing encounter groups with a no-treatment control, the encounter group participants changed significantly more in 102 of the studies. In 21 other studies no difference existed between the encounter group and control group, while in the remaining 3, the control group obtained superior results. With regard to the long-lasting effects of encounter groups, Gibb found that a third of the studies utilized follow-up measures, mostly between one week and six months after the group experience. The follow-up revealed that the changes brought on by the encounter group tended to persist over time. In fact, 4 studies reported that the positive changes increased with the passage of time—in other words, participants continued to learn and grow as a result of the group experience.

Gibb's reviews are somewhat impressionistic, but most of his conclusions have been borne out in the thorough and detailed review by Peter Smith (1975), whose analysis of the research literature included only those studies that had adequate control groups, repeated-measures design, and training that lasted not less then twenty hours. Because of the rigor of these requirements, most of the studies upon which Campbell and Dunnette (1968) rested their conclusions had to be discarded. Smith's (1975) conclusions were extremely positive. Of 100 studies that measured changes immediately after training, 78 detected positive changes significantly greater than those in control groups. Of 31 studies that followed up these changes more than one month after training, more than two-thirds found that the changes lasted, although some fade-out occurred. Some of the commonly reported changes included more favorable self-concept, reduced prejudice, increased open-mindedness, and changed behavior as perceived by others present during training, and changed organizational behavior.

In some cases nonpositive results seemed best explained on the basis of external problems. For instance, the Tennessee Self-concept Scale obtained significant results in only two of thirteen instances, although semantic differential measures and self-ratings of self-concept consistently revealed significant changes among encounter group participants. Smith argues that this discrepancy is best explained by assuming that the Tennessee Scale does not detect subtle changes in self-concept. The least positive finding of Smith's review is the relative lack of evidence that sensitivity training leads to changes observable immediately after training by persons who are not present during training.[45] On the other hand, where observers have examined participants' behaviors in the group itself, the vast majority of studies indicate significant changes.

In the context of organizational development, encounter groups receive a mixed rating from Smith. Most of the studies indicate some changes, but in several instances the changes were the opposite of those intended, and in others the effects fell somewhat short of the trainer's goals. These organizational studies tended to lack closely matched control groups, which is not surprising because of the methodological difficulties involved. Smith concludes, nonetheless, that sensitivity training can frequently achieve significant effects in this area.

In Smith's opinion the research is significantly conclusive on the value of sensitivity training, and further studies should focus on the mechanisms of change

and other related factors. He believes that adequate documentation exists on a variety of effects caused by encounter groups, one that the documentation is consistent across the entire spectrum of research design.

Conclusion

With a high degree of confidence one can state that encounter groups do bring about significant changes in those who participate in them. The uniformly positive conclusions of the major reviewers seem decisive. Even the most skeptical of the group—Cambell and Dunnette (1968: 98) —granted that "the evidence . . . is reasonably convincing that T-group training does induce behavioral changes in the 'back home' setting." The better-designed and better-executed studies were equally likely to demonstrate that encounter groups are effective (Smith, 1975: 618). Encounter groups also possess potential value in alleviating or giving people the tools to ameliorate much of the alienation that modern society is experiencing (Frank, 1973), as well as providing a means by which persons can learn to adapt to the rapid technological and societal changes that are occurring (Rogers, 1970). The wide use of encounter groups or encounter-type groups in a variety of institutional settings attests to the value that is placed upon them by major segments of the population. Most important has been the value to the field of psychotherapy, where encounter group research and techniques have received wide attention and use.

The types of changes occurring in encounter groups are consistent with those that occur in more traditional psychotherapy. The most frequently mentioned are increased sensitivity, improved communication skills, increased self-confidence and self-acceptance, greater flexibility in interpersonal relations, increased risk-taking, greater genuineness, and improved diagnostic ability. Changes also seem to occur in participants' attitudes, self-concepts, values, and behaviors. On the other hand, the ability of encounter groups to increase organizational effectiveness is open to serious question.

When the research on the effectiveness and value of encounter groups is compared to other psychotherapy research, the results are striking and surprising.[46] Encounter groups bring about many of the same types of changes that are considered desirable in the psychotherapy field as a whole. More important, encounter groups appear remarkably effective in doing this, perhaps as effective as individual psychotherapy. If this should ultimately prove to be the case, future investments in encounter groups may be extremely worthwhile, since they are more economical than the labor-intensive and time-consuming individual psychotherapies.

RISKS AND DANGERS

Although the dangers of traditional psychotherapy have not been deemed especially newsworthy, the risks involved in encounter groups have received frequent media mention.[47] The press has had a strong tendency to focus on the dangers of encounter groups, rather than providing balanced presentations.[48] Since the public is likely to be more interested in sensational stories of harmful encounters than dull reports of successful ones, this emphasis is perhaps understandable. In particular, those groups oriented to personal growth and sensory awareness have aroused fear in many people. Word of grave psychological harm and stories of nude marathons spread rapidly because of their sensationalism, and many become distorted.[49] In 1969 a member of Congress from Louisiana (Rarick, 1969: 15,322) reflected such fears in a speech before the House of Representatives:

Mr. Speaker, the accelerated use of "sensitivity training" as a tool to indoctrinate the masses for a "planned change" in the United States has resulted in confusion, frustration, and wholesale disorientation among our unsuspecting people.

Sensitivity training has been successfully used by the Bolsheviks as a brainwashing technique to erode an individual's will to resist, to destroy moral values, and as a method of controlling enslaved millions.

While Mr. Rarick's warning may leave most people unshaken, if somewhat amazed, more moderate and thoughtful criticism necessitates a serious look at the risks that are involved.[50]

General Risks and Dangers

Nearly all dangers imaginable have been attributed to encounter groups. Jane Howard's (1970: 198–208) collection of the charges most often leveled at such groups in her year-long exploration of them for *Life* magazine provides a representative sample:

1. The groups can be run by charlatans who are corrupt or mediocre or both.
2. The groups are a hotbed of junkies and dope addicts.
3. The groups invade privacy.
4. The groups foster sexual promiscuity.
5. The groups encourage physical violence.
6. Groups can be fatal.
7. Groups do psychological damage.
8. Groups hypnotize their members.
9. Groups are anti-intellectual.
10. The groups cheapen real emotion.
11. The groups themselves are guilty of the failing they most chastise in their members—phoniness.
12. The groups lead to emotional elitism.
13. The groups have ridiculous jargon.
14. The groups may get to be a cult.
15. The groups are pointless.
16. The groups may indeed cause stirring and wonderful things to happen, but these effects aren't valid because they don't last.

A number of critiques have achieved considerable notoriety. Kurt Back (1972) and Bruce Maliver (1973) have thought encounter groups to be a serious enough menace to publish separate books examining and condemning them. Hans Strupp (1973), Sigmund Koch (1971), and George Odiorne (1970) are all well known in the psychology field for their scathing attacks on the encounter culture, which have appeared in professional publications.[51] The focus of these attacks has largely concentrated on the values that encounter groups allegedly propound.

In general, detractors claim that traditional American values are negated, while radically different values are encouraged. Thus, Strupp (1973: 122–123, passim) says that the experiential group movement is "a powerful protest against the values implicitly espoused by individual psychotherapy" and represents "a wholesale rejection of these values." Other damaging features of encounter groups include their anti-intellectual attitude, denigration of reason and rationality, their denial of individuality, depreciation of the inner being, and lack of respect for the privacy of the individual. Not all groups might be guilty of these offenses, but Sigmund Koch (1971: 125) goes so far as to say:

There are certain *generic* characters common to all so-called "encounter" approaches, to all styles and philosophies of leadership, which, when present in some minimal degree, render the group process self-defeating relative to meaningful fulfillment of the stated objectives (I do not deny, of course, that some approaches and/or some leaders of relatively greater sensitivity accomplish results that are less "bad" than do others.)

Most of these critics consider encounter groups to be a response to the prevailing *Zeitgeist* of our time (Strupp, 1972); that is, they compare encounter groups with hula-hoops (Beymer, 1970), seeing them as a response to America's desire for instant intimacy in a sea of turbulence and change. Some view encounter groups as the fast-food chain in the mental health field.

Rowe and Winborn (1973) have analyzed thirty-six selected articles, from the popular and professional literature, that

are critical of encounter groups. Their analysis provides a convenient means of identifying the specific dangers that seem to provoke the most worry. These appear to be the possibility of psychological damage and the problems involved in post-group adjustment. Other frequently mentioned concerns center around commercial abuses, the overemphasis of experiential goals, the anti-intellectual emphasis, and the possibility of home and family being undermined.

Encounter groups have also been accused of thwarting the development of deep and long-lasting emotional bonds because of their emphasis on intense but time-limited relationships. Critics fear that emotions may become merely another commodity in an increasingly alienated and materialistic society. Additional criticisms are based on fears of sexual promiscuity sparked by nude marathons. Yet the actual percentage of such groups and activities appears to be small and to be confined largely to the West Coast.

The use of encounter groups in business has also been seriously questioned (Calame, 1969; Gomberg, 1967, 1966; Odiorne, 1970). According to critics, making people more sensitive may actually lead to a decrease in productivity, while attending groups with co-workers may jeopardize promotions, encourage hostility, and otherwise lead to a deterioration in working relationships. Similarly, revealing important information in a group may prove unwise because of the use to which it is put after the experience is over.

Evidence

Each of the above criticisms contains at least a kernel of truth. Undoubtedly some groups conform to the images painted by those who oppose them. Whether their fears are exaggerated or based on fact, however, is difficult to ascertain, since conclusions are frequently stated without evidence of the degree of danger involved. Critics frequently assume that what is true of the worst encounter groups is also true of the best.[52] Thus, the faddish elements of encounter may be emphasized, while those groups that have complex roots in Lewinian field theory, Rogerian client-centered therapy, and the Deweyian concern for democracy are ignored. The problem has been the tendency to consider encounter groups as a unitary phenomenon. Broad generalizations are inappropriate in a field where diversity is the touchstone (Hogan, 1976). Lomranz, Lakin, and Schiffman (1972), for instance, have found that encounter groups are divisible into three distinct types according to the goals of the leader. Some are concerned with learning and social effectiveness; others with healing and personality integration; a final type strives for expanded experiencing and expressiveness. It is this last group that represents many of the less-desirable characteristics outlined by critics, but these may represent the goals of only a third of the total number of practicing group leaders (Schiffman, 1974).

The available evidence bearing on the dangers of encounter groups and the degree to which they occur comes in a variety of forms and serves a variety of purposes. Anecdotal reports provide documentation that harm does occur, while informed estimates and informal surveys allow conclusions to be drawn as to the level of danger. Although neither provides rigorous proof—which ultimately depends on well-designed and well-conducted scientific research—each of these forms of evidence will be reviewed to provide as sound a base as is presently possible for making these judgments.

Anecdotal Reports. The evidence of deleterious effects of encounter experiences comes from several sources. One is the anecdotal report or case study in which somebody describes how a particular encounter group precipitated harm. These reports appear frequently in research journals and the popular media, and have done much to color people's perceptions of the value of encounter groups. Typical of such reports are four anecdotes described by Everett Shostrom (1969) in *Psychology Today*. He first tells of the case of Joan, who had impetuously entered a group in which, it turned out, she knew several of the participants. She was subjected to cruel attack, exposing many of the most painful aspects of her life. Initially she felt much improved, but soon began believing other people were constantly talking about her problems. Shortly thereafter she drove her heretofore sluggish sedan into a bridge abutment at eighty miles an hour. Shostrom also describes a young man who became a "screaming queen," a reasonably happy married couple who separated with great bitterness, and a rising young corporate star who lost his job—all attributed to irresponsibly run groups.[53]

Determining the value and utility of anecdotal reports is problematic. The number of cases described in the encounter field is sufficiently large, and enough of these are thoroughly documented, to warrant the conclusion that encounter groups can and do cause harm in certain instances. The frequency with which harm occurs, however, remains open to question. Unfortunately the tendency has been to use anecdotal reports as proof that encounter groups are so dangerous that rigid regulation is needed. Yet a similar array of horror stories could easily be assembled about highly credentialed psychiatrists and psychologists, all of them licensed.

A further problem of the anecdotal report is whether it allows documentation of causation. Without extensive data that has been thoroughly analyzed, it is often questionable to infer that the encounter group experience brought about whatever harm occurred. In the case of Joan, described above, for instance, Shostrom assumes that Joan committed suicide. Given the available information, however, any number of other explanations make as good sense. Joan may have been a habitually reckless driver who had just repaired her old sedan. She may have been extremely paranoid prior to the group and might well have committed suicide anyway. Other negative experiences unrelated to the group might have been the precipitating factor. Perhaps Shostrom's analysis is correct, but the data are equivocal.

The complexity of determining causation has been documented by Yalom and Lieberman (1971). A participant in one of the encounter groups they were researching committed suicide shortly after the group's second meeting. He had left a note angrily condemning those people who did not take his problems seriously and who did not appreciate his pain, and holding them responsible for his final act. Though it would have been simple and plausible to blame the group experience for this suicide, additional data gathered by the directors of the project made it unlikely that the group was responsible. In brief, the subject had a long history of psychological problems; he had been in a number of local encounter groups, and was in two forms of psychotherapy; and at the time of the incident he was also in another encounter group. A review of the taperecordings of those first two sessions indicated that the meetings were very low-key and dull. The subject had been constructive in his comments, and was actually optimistic about the group. To establish causality, then, is not an easy matter.

Informed Estimates and Survey Studies. Of more value in establishing the true extent of these dangers are field surveys, especially those conducted by professional associations, and the informed estimates of experts. Even these sources do not generally represent rigorous scientific research. Instead they consist of task force studies or the rough estimates of people who have observed, led, or been part of a variety of group experiences.

Informed individual estimates of the level of risk involved in encounter groups are uniformly low. Jane Howard (1970: 203) spent a year as a participant in a wide variety of groups, and talked with many of the leaders in the encounter group field. She saw only one instance where, in her opinion, somebody might be considered as having had a psychotic break, and this instance ended as a positive experience according to her. Donald Clark (1971) recently completed a year-long study of sensitivity training and its implications for education, sponsored by the Carnegie Corporation. He had an opportunity to observe a variety of encounter groups and found almost no reliable evidence or documentation that group leaders precipitated harm. On the contrary, he found that most inept leaders were simply guilty of wasting the participants' time.

Encounter group leaders themselves believe that the experience does not involve a high level of risk. For instance, John Weir, one of the better-known leaders in the United States, estimated that over a fifteen-year period of leading groups, he had only seen twenty-five or thirty people "dramatically, floridly disturbed" (Howard, 1970: 203). Michael Murphy (1971), the head of Esalen Institute, supports this conclusion; he reported little evidence of psychic damage in the nine years that Esalen had been offering groups as of 1971.[54]

Reviewers of the nonempirical literature on encounter groups report low levels of harm. Dinges and Weigel (1971: 397), for instance, found that individual testimonials about marathon groups were overwhelmingly positive and that negative accounts were almost nonexistent. Easton, Carr, and Whitely (1972: 111) declared that most of the concrete evidence indicated that incidents of psychological harm were comparatively rare and usually involved people with some previous history of psychological difficulty.

Survey studies have reached similar conclusions about the negative effects of encounter groups. The American Psychological Association (APA) has made a substantial effort in this area, but concluded that the dangers were overstated. After two years of study its Task Force on Evaluation of Therapeutic Procedures could not find documentable evidence of harm done by encounter groups, despite an extensive search (Strassburger, 1971). The APA's Committee on Scientific and Professional Ethics and Conduct has likewise found little evidence of harm. A former chairperson stated that "except for two questions of poor taste at APA convention-sponsored affairs the only complaints concerning [encounter groups] brought to the APA ethics committee in recent years were about advertising" (Boring, 1971: 11).

This lack of complaints continued until the issuance of the APA's guidelines for the conduct of encounter groups in October 1973 (Gurel, 1974). Since then the incidence has risen, due mainly to students protesting sensitivity training as a compulsory course in graduate school (Gurel, 1974). Brownfain (1971) notes that in the American Psychological Association's professional liability insurance program there has been a recent surge of cases involving injuries received in encounter groups of various types, although the total number is quite small. Over the four-year period 1967 to 1971, four cases were reported in which physical injuries were alleged as a consequence of certain therapeutic procedures in encounter groups. The Committee on Mental Health of the Michigan State Medical Society (Wille, 1970) reported instances of psychotic breakdowns, the exacerbation of preexisting marital disharmonies, and increases in life tensions following encounter group experiences, but no evidence was offered as to how often these occurred.

The American Psychiatric Association (APA Task Force, 1970) also commissioned a task force to study encounter groups. Specific areas of inquiry were the rapid growth of encounter groups, their relevance to the field of psychiatry, their dangers, and their promise. The APA Task Force (1970: 17) concluded its discussion of the dangers of groups in this way: "In summary, although there are apparent dangers in the encounter group experience, no generalization may be made save that, in the hands of some leaders, the group experience can be dangerous for some participants."

The low incidence rate reported by survey studies and informed estimates should not be lightly dismissed. Most of the sources involved are in positions in which they are likely to hear of any untoward consequences to participants. On the other hand, their conclusions must be kept in perspective. None of the results was derived from controlled scientific studies, and a variety of factors may equally well explain the lack of evidence of negative effects. In the case of the Ethics Committee of the American Psychological Association, to take one example, harmed individuals may never think to report their injury to the committee, or they may not know it exists. Where group leaders or enthusiastic participants report that few dangers are involved, their lack of objectivity may explain their findings. Even if it is true that one group leader has seen few casualties, this finding may not be generalizable to other leaders.

Reviews of the Empirical Research. Reviews of empirical research can be broken into two types. In one the reviewer's task has been to assess the overall impact of encounter groups on participants. The issue of danger is not central, but is discussed in passing. The specific studies that have led the authors to their conclusions are often not mentioned. The second type of review, fewer in number, focuses its analysis expressly on the dangers of encounter groups. Neither of these types has furnished a thorough investigation of the dangers involved, but they do offer a more objective and scientifically sound basis for drawing conclusions than anecdotal reports or informal surveys and estimates.

When reviewers conduct a comprehensive analysis of outcome studies in the encounter field, they generally find little evidence of a high level of risk. Parloff (1970) was one of the first to comment on this fact. His careful perusal of more than fifty references found reports of mild to moderate emotional disturbances during the group experience ranging from 0.5 to 28 percent, while enduring negative reactions occurred in 0.6 to about 6 percent of the cases. Based on this evidence he concluded: "The circumspect clinician who wishes to advise prospective group participants regarding possible dangers can, with confidence, offer only the following kind of advice: participation in most encounter groups is likely to be more dangerous than attending an office Christmas party and somewhat less dangerous than skiing" (Parloff, 1970: 289).

Other reviewers have reached similar conclusions. Fiman and Conner (1973) declared that although inconsistent data did not permit any meaningful statement about the level of risk involved, it was clear that the potential for severe emotional distress had been overemphasized. Jack Gibb (1971) went even further. Basing his conclusion on a review of 106 outcome studies, he argued that the reputed dangers of sensitivity training were greatly exaggerated. Eddy and Lubin (1971) found that the majority of studies reported an incidence of harm between 0.2 and 0.5 percent, although some reported higher proportions of negative results.[55]

Few reviewers have focused exclusively on the dangers of encounter groups. Those that have generally cited only a handful of studies in support of whatever conclusions they draw. Reddy (1972) undertook an investigation of negative effects in encounter groups to determine the need for adequate screening of participants. According to his view, when the available data were analyzed objectively, one had to be impressed by the low incidence of harm reported. Especially when encounter groups were conducted by reputable, competent organizations, the fear of a high casualty rate was simply not warranted. Cooper (1972), who has himself conducted research on the dangers of sensitivity groups, argued from his review of the literature that danger had definitely not been proved, and that some evidence existed that encounter groups were less stressful than university examinations. This finding has been echoed by Hartley, Roback, and Abramowitz (1976), who concluded that the variation in findings and the lack of consensus in the field made definitive statements impossible. Perhaps the most accurate view about the current state of affairs is summarized by Peter Smith (1975: 45) in what is probably the most thorough and analytical review of the literature to date:

The research . . . makes it clear that there is a small incidence of adverse effects appearing after sensitivity training. This incidence varies considerably from one population to another. At present we have no studies at all which shed any light on whether sensitivity training enhances or reduces this incidence of adverse effects in a given population.

An Original Review of the Empirical Research. Because the published reviews of the research have not been comprehensive in scope, it was essential to conduct an original review of the empirical evidence on the dangers of encounter groups.[56] Allegations of harm caused in such groups is probably the most important justification for strict regulation of psychotherapy, and if these allegations are not well founded, then regulatory measures such as licensure may not be necessary.

A careful culling of the literature found thirty-nine studies that examined the question of whether encounter groups are dangerous. These varied widely in quality; some had control groups, others did not; some used objective measures, others relied on subjective reports; and some examined their subjects immediately after the group experience, while others followed them up six or more months later.

Overall these studies reported a variable but relatively low incidence of harm. High incidence levels of harm were generally a result of broad definitions of what constituted injury, which in such cases usually included even relatively minor instances of negative change. The types of harm caused ranged from decreases in self-concept and personality disorientation to acute pathological reactions.

Conclusion
Unfortunately, the analysis of the research presented above and the discussion of the general risks and dangers of encounter groups do not allow comprehensive and definitive conclusions. One may say with reasonable certainty that encounter groups do cause harm to at least some individuals in certain circumstances. Depending upon one's value system a certain percentage of group leaders probably foster life styles and ways of interacting that would be considered harmful or undesirable. Thus, some encounter groups undoubtedly elevate feelings over intellect, while others ignore what happens to participants once they leave the encounter environment.

In the area of psychological damage, encounter groups can and do precipitate psychoses in certain cases, but the evidence indicates that this does not happen very often. In fact, one cannot help but be struck by the number of studies that have found encounter groups to pose only minimal dangers.

It is obvious, however, that more and better-designed research studies are needed. It is especially important to begin comparing the casualties that occur in the encounter setting with those that occur in other settings. Perhaps one of the most serious drawbacks to current research efforts is that they do not examine those groups generally conceded to be the most dangerous—those conducted on a fly-by-night basis by somebody with little or no

training and advertised in underground newspapers. The very fact that a group is being researched may significantly decrease the amount of risk involved.

The concluding comments of the American Psychiatric Association's Task Force Report on *Encounter Groups and Psychiatry* (1970: 17) best describe the current state of affairs in the field:

In summary, although there are apparent dangers in the encounter group experience, no generalization may be made save that, in the hands of some leaders, the group experience can be dangerous for some participants. The more powerful the emotions evoked, the less clinically perspicacious and responsible the leader, the more psychologically troubled the group member, then the greater the risk of adverse outcome. We must especially exercise caution in our evaluation of the overall encounter group field. It is, after all, a very diversified one; there are perhaps as many differences amongst various types of encounter groups as there are between the encounter group and the therapy group. Some groups may be led by competent, responsible leaders who provide a constructive learning experience for the participants; others may be led by wild, untrained leaders who may produce untoward emotional reactions in the participants. Above all we must note that there is distressingly little data; the casualties come to our attention, but the size of the universe from which they arise is unknown: the group participants who have an important, constructive experience are rarely seen by psychiatrists. It is important that psychiatrists study the available evidence, generate new data through research inquiry, and not take the position of responding with a primitive territoriality reflex to the movement as an unmitigated danger which must be curbed or condemned. We must not fail to note that the encounter group field has been a highly innovative one, that it has created techniques for harnessing powerful group forces in the service of education and behavioral change. In a number of ways psychiatry has been enriched by insights and techniques stemming from some parts of the encounter group field; we must not describe the dangers without also noting the promise of the new group approaches.

This has important implications for regulation. The fact that encounter groups may not be as dangerous as previously thought may mean that restrictive licensing is unnecessary and might create more problems than it resolves. As the American Psychiatric Association Task Force has pointed out, encounter groups have a potentially valuable contribution to make to society. The chance for this to occur might be seriously diminished if restrictive laws are passed that prevent innovative practitioners from continuing their work.

NOTES

1. For a thorough examination of encounter group theory and practice, the following texts are recommended: Benne, Bradford, Gibb, and Lippitt (1975), *The Laboratory Method of Changing and Learning: Theory and Application;* Blank, Gottsegen, and Gottsegen (1971), *Confrontation;* Bradford, Gibb, and Benne (1964b), *T-Group Theory and Laboratory Method;* Diedrich and Dye (1972), *Group Procedures;* Egan (1970), *Encounter;* Gibbard, Hartman, and Mann (1974), *Analysis of Groups;* Golembiewski and Blumberg (1970), *Sensitivity Training and the Laboratory Approach;* Lakin (1972), *Interpersonal Encounter;* Mintz (1971), *Marathon Groups;* Oden (1972a), *The Intensive Group Experience;* Rogers (1970), *Carl Rogers on Encounter Groups;* Schein and Bennis (1965), *Personal and Organizational Change Through Group Methods;* Schutz (1973), *Elements of Encounter;* Shaffer and Galinsky (1974), *Models of Group Therapy and Sensitivity Training;* Siroka, Siroka, and Schloss (1971), *Sensitivity Training and Group Encounter;* And Solomon and Berzon (1972), *New Perspectives on Encounter Groups.*

2. See Massarik (1972: 68-69).

3. See Ch. 5 for a fuller explication of the questions involved in this issue.

4. For other definitions of what constitutes a group, see the review of definitions provided by Cartwright and Zander (1963: 46-48). For further definitions, see Knowles and Knowles (1972) and Mills (1967).

5. Compare this definition with Bradford, Gibb, and Benne (1964c: 1):

> A T Group is a relatively unstructured group in which individuals participate as learners. The data for learning are not outside these individuals or remote from their immediate experience within the T Group. The data are the transactions among members, their own behavior in the group, as they struggle to create a productive and viable organization, a miniature society; and as they work to stimulate and support one another's learning within that society.

or Schein and Bennis (1965: 4), who define the T-group as:

> an educational strategy which is based primarily on the experiences generated in various social encounters *by the learners themselves,* and which aims to influence attitudes and develop competencies toward learning about human interactions. So, essentially, laboratory training attempts to induce changes with regard to the learning process itself and to communicate a particular method of learning and inquiry. It has to do with "learning how to learn."

For other definitions of the term T-group, see Lakin (1972: 20-22), Egan (1970: 4-11), and Gibb (in Bradford et al., 1964b: 277-78).

6. The Committee on Standards and Admissions and the Task Force on Personal Growth Group Consultation of the International Association of Applied Social Scientists (1974: 1) have adopted the following definition of the personal growth group:

> Personal Growth Groups are seen by IAASS as a new and expanding form of professional practice and service to the public which has been emerging over the last two decades. The primary focus of attention in these groups is on the dynamics and growth of the individual members, and secondarily on the study of small-group dynamics. This practice and service falls in the gray area between adult learning and therapy. . . .

The distinguishing features of Personal Growth Groups are: (a) utilization of the interaction among group members as the medium for personal growth, as opposed to individual therapy in the presence of the group; (b) convening of the group for purposes of learning and growth, rather than treatment or remediation of personal crisis.

Other definitions abound. See especially those of Massarik (1972: 73), Schutz (1967: 23-24), and Howard (1970: 3) (this definition is half humorous and gives an excellent description and sense of what groups can be like); Koch (1971) (Koch's definition is derived from a very narrow and distorted view of encounter groups, based on his negative image of the human potential movement); American Psychiatric Association (1970); Oden (1972a: 23); and Seashore (1970: 14). The common elements of encounter groups are described in Rogers (1970) and Schutz (1973).

7. Only a cursory examination of the research on encounter group results will be presented here. A thorough review of the literature appears on pages 55-70.

8. Advertisements and informational brochures also provide indications of the purposes of encounter groups. Unfortunately, they are usually not as complete in their descriptions, and they tend to paint a one-sided, somewhat idealistic picture of what encounter groups are designed to do. Many advertisements do not make the goals of the group explicit at all. Occasionally, extravagant claims are made. In some instances the term "encounter" is used when nothing remotely resembling an encounter group is to take place. In other instances, however, the goals are clearly, fairly, and completely stated. On the whole, advertising in the last few years has become less exaggerated as the faddishness of encounter groups has run its course.

9. Other explications of the meta-goals of encounter groups are in accord with those of Schein and Bennis. See Bradford, Gibb, and Benne (1964c: 4-12), and Benne (1975: 52-54).

10. Other descriptions of the goals of encounter groups abound. The descriptions by the following are in basic agreement with those provided herein: Lakin (1972), Rogers (1970), Egan (1970), Golembiewski and Blumberg (1970), Solomon and Berzon (1972), and Schein and Bennis (1965).

11. In an earlier report they felt that they were "dealing with a 'normal' range of students and community members with a 'normal' range of problems for a modern urban setting" (Bebout and Gordon, 1971: 14).

12. Historical accounts of the use of small groups for psychotherapeutic purposes and for personal growth may be found in Appley and Winder (1973), Bradford, Gibb, and Benne (1964b), Bromberg (1975), Durkin (1964), Ehrenwald (1976), National Training Laboratory in Group Development (undated), Oden (1972), Rogers (1970), Schutz (1973), and Shaffer and Galinsky (1974).

13. Lazell (1921), a psychiatrist, used an approach revolving around lectures to deal with the emotional problems of war veterans who had been diagnosed as schizophrenic.

14. The earlier approaches used by Lazell, Pratt, and others developed largely from a social work orientation. Little emphasis was placed on formal theory, and practitioners evolved their methods through trial and error.

15. Perls's major statements on Gastalt therapy appears in Perls (1969a), and Perls, Hefferline, and Goodman (1951). His life is self-chronicled in Perls (1969b). An excellent update and reformulation of his theories can be found in Polster and Polster (1974).

16. Operating out of a strongly psychoanalytic background, Mintz (1971) has adopted many of the techniques of William Schutz and other group leaders, including Gastalt therapy techniques.

17. Discussed in Bonner (1959: 14-15).

18. Bonner (1959: 16 n. 26).

19. Edward C. Tolman said of Lewin in a memorial address at the 1947 convention of the American Psychological Association:

Freud the clinician and Lewis the experimentalist—these are the two men whose names will stand out before all others in the history of our psychological era. For it is their contrasting but complementary insights which first made psychology a science applicable to real human beings and to real human society. [Quoted in Marrow, 1969: ix.]

20. Lewin's theories and concepts are most clearly articulated in the following works: Lewis (1939), "Field Theory and Experiment in Social Psychology: Concepts and Methods"; (1951) *Field Theory in Social Science;* (1947) "Group Decision and Social Change"; and (1948) *Resolving Social Conflicts.* An excellent overview of both his life and work can be found in Marrow (1969). For a concise statement of his theories and a critical evaluation of his work, *see* Hall and Lindzey (1970: 209-58).

21. For a fuller account of the development of the T-group than appears in the text, see Benne (1964), Bradford (1967), and Marrow (1967).

22. For a fuller formulation of Dewey's views, see Dewey (1966, 1929, 1959, 1938, 1935).

23. See also Levine and Bunker (1975).

24. In his latest work Benne (1975) has reformulated the theoretical foundations of T-groups, viewing them, in multiple perspective, as: (1) a way of learning; (2) a way of examining the process of group development; (3) a way of planned change; (4) a process of cooperative action research; (5) a process of knowledge utilization; and (6) a way of resocialization and re-enculturation.

25. In brief, Bebout (undated: 8) argues that *"the overlapping and reciprocal sharing of momentary emotional experience is an event which in itself generates growth and change."* Where earlier Rogerian theory had posited the importance of an empathy that basically was one way (therapist to client), Bebout (undated: 8) stresses a "doubling of empathic and expressive components in interpersonal interaction, rendering a fuller and a more authentic, two-way relationship." Bebout draws heavily from Martin Buber's existential philosophy, in which Buber (1965) emphasized that man's being is contained only in community.

26. The ability to adapt to change is becoming increasingly important as technological developments bring about radical changes in our society. Social and physical mobility have been dramatically increased by the development of rapid communication and transportation systems and the breakdown of the nuclear family. Bennis and Slater (1968: 86) have commented on this state of affairs in their thought-provoking book *The Temporary Society:* "It seems clear that one of the unintended functions of 'sensitivity training' or 'basic encounter' groups is anticipating a world of temporary systems, since these groups emphasize openness, feedback, immediacy, communication at a feeling level, the here-and-now, more awareness of and ability to express deeper feelings, and so on."

27. Forer (1972), for instance, has discussed the importance of physical contact to emotional health, pointing out that encounter groups have been the primary force in helping therapists overcome the long-held belief that no form of physical contact with patients is advisable. Schutz and Seashore (1972) have likewise argued that encounter groups have made psychotherapists more aware of the importance of nonverbal communication, while Steele (1970: 214) maintains that encounter groups have brought about a significant expansion of that part of society that is comfortable in thinking and talking in psychological process terms.

28. For examples and descriptions of encounter groups and their use in training mental health professionals, see Spitz and Sadock (1973) (psychiatric training of graduate nursing students), Berger (1969) (incorporation of experiential groups into the training program at the New York State Psychiatric Institute), and Lumpkin (1972) (student therapists).

29. Cadden et al. (1969) describe a successful application of encounter groups in the training of first-year medical students at Cornell Medical College, while Selvini (1973) describes an internist's experience in a Balint group. Discussions of the application of encounter groups to the nursing profession can be found in Lakin (1972: 218-21) and Henderson (1973).

30. John Steinbacher's *The Child Seducers* (1971) provides a vivid example of how

strongly encounter groups can be resisted, especially when the basis for resistance is irrational.

31. For an excellent description of a successful application of encounter groups, see the discussion by Rogers (1970: 135-37) of TRW's use of it in attempting to work through some of the potential problems being caused by a merger. Rettig and Amano (1976) surveyed personnel managers and professors and found that most felt that sensitivity training programs were moderately successful in improving employee development, manager-subordinate relationships, and productivity, although they were unsure whether the benefits justified the costs.

32. For other descriptions of the use of encounter groups or encounter-like groups in community development settings, see Schindler-Rainman (1975) and Page (1975).

33. There were also improvements in the economic, governmental, educational, and housing situation of the town, although it is difficult to determine whether these changes were attributable to the T-group training or other extraneous factors (Klein, 1965).

34. Encounter groups as adjuncts to individual therapy are described in Johnson et al. (1965), Hanson et al. (1969), Goldberg and Goodman (1973), and Mandelbaum (1973).

35. For a more complete picture of the expansion of encounter-type groups into the international scene, see Miles (1962) and Benne et al. (1975: 7-8).

36. A comprehensive description and analysis of this project can be found in Lieberman et al. (1973). Various aspects of the project have been reviewed in journal articles as well (see Lieberman, 1975, 1972; Lieberman et al., 1972, 1971; Miles, 1975; Yalom, 1975, Yalom and Lieberman, 1971).

37. The ten types were: (1) sensitivity training after the tradition of the NTL model (Basic Human Relations Group, T-group); (2) a similar type, but with a Rogerian, personal-growth orientation; (3) Synanon; (4) transactional analysis; (5) Gestalt; (6) psychodrama; (7) marathon; (8) leaderless tapes (using the Bell and Howell tapes developed by Berzon); (9) Esalen eclectic (a sensory-awareness approach patterned after groups at Esalen); and (10) psychoanalytically oriented (Lieberman et al., 1973: 10-13).

38. They were selected from a list of sixty professionals by asking professionals familiar with each approach to name the two best leaders in the Bay Area.

39. The following data and conclusions are taken from Lieberman et al. (1973: 93-133).

40. Research on the TIE Project is reported in Bebout (1973), and Bebout and Gordon (1972, 1971, 1971-1972).

41. Since the argument of this book is that distinctions between encounter groups and psychotherapy are largely matters of semantic distinctions and professional narrowness, rather than substantive differences (Lieberman, 1976), evidence drawn from the group-psychotherapy literature may also be relevant in determining the effectiveness of encounter groups.

Surprisingly, less research has been done on group psychotherapy than encounter groups, and for this reason a comparative analysis has been omitted here. As recently as 1974 a thoughtful reviewer concluded that adequately designed studies were sparse and that it was premature to answer the question of whether group therapy was effective at this stage in its development (Black, 1974). Where reviewers have been willing to be conclusive about the effects of group psychotherapy, it has often been because research from other change-inducing groups has been included, as in Lieberman's (1976) recent analysis of research on group psychotherapy, encounter groups, self-help groups, and consciousness-raising activities, or because the reviewer has been "soft-hearted" (Grunebaum, 1975). Perhaps the most thorough review of the literature to date has been that of Bednar and Lawlis (1971), which was prepared for inclusion in Bergin and Garfield's *Handbook of Psychotherapy and Behavior Change*. On the basis of thirty-eight outcome studies, they put forth the view that "what was once intuitive confirmation in the mind of many clinicians is now on the road to experimental verification" (Bednar and Lawlis, 1971: 814). That is, Bednar and Lawlis found that the results of most research were positive, but this conclusion generally rested on a very shaky foundation. If studies directly comparing individual versus group psychotherapy is at least as effective (Luborsky et al., 1975: 1001; Meltzoff and Korneich, 1970: 178-184). Unfortunately, few of the better experiments have been replicated, and follow-up investigations suggest that positive treatment effects tend to dissipate over time. Bednar and Lawlis (1971: 814) point out that methodological limitations such as biased sampling, rater contamination, and spontaneous remissions further dilute confidence in the meaning of the data.

42. Many exellent bibliographies on encounter groups exist. Some focus strictly on research, while others are more general. Among the best are Cooper (1973-74, 1971-72), Durham et al. (1967), and Hare (1972).

Other reviews of the encounter group literature exist, but they are not included, either because their scope is too narrow (some focus on a particular type of group only) or their quality is poor. Anderson and Slocum (1973), provide a good review of the leadership characteristics important to running groups. Eddy and Lubin (1971) have written an excellent brief analysis of the literature that also examines most of the major research reviews prior to 1971. Helmreich et al. (1973) review the literature on small groups from 1967-1972. Their focus is on group dynamics, especially influence, conformity, and reactions to stress. They have a brief section on encounter groups. Luke and Seashore (1970) have also conducted a brief evaluation of the encounter group literautre. Saretsky, in Mintz (1971: 218-47), provides an overview of the research on marathon groups, and includes much of the research that has been conducted within the T-group setting. Eitington (1971) reviews the literature using psychology of learning concepts.

For an annual update of the research on encounter groups, an excellent source is the October 1976 issue of the *International Journal of Group Psychotherapy*. A nonevaluative article within the issue discusses the research of the prior year in group psychotherapy and intensive small-group experiences.

43. It is interesting to note that these changes occurred for the most part in groups whose purpose was to increase organizational effectiveness, rather than to help participants in their personal growth.

44. Included within the scope of Gibb's review were sensitivity training, process-oriented organizational development, encounter groups, and programs of which the primary element was a T-group. Gibb limited his analysis to those pieces of research that were available in English. He also excluded studies that focused on group processes and that ignored training outcomes, groups with a therapeutic focus, master's theses, and studies in journals not readily available.

45. Only five of the thirteen revelant studies showed such change.

46. It is difficult to explain away the positive conclusions with regard to the general effectiveness of encounter groups solely on the basis of sloppy research. Most of those who have examined the research on psychotherapy have found that the quality of the encounter group research, especially at the T-group end of the spectrum, is comparable, if not superior, to research on individual psychotherapy research. See American Psychiatric Association Task Force on Recent Developments in the Use of Small Groups, (1970: 19); Durkin (1964: 126). In addition, both Smith (1975) in the encounter group field and Glass (1976) in more traditional psychotherapy have found that positiveness of results is not affected by quality of research.

47. For a sample of the popular media articles on the dangers of encounter groups, see Beldoch (1971), Calame (1969), Chesler (1969), Gorner (1973), Johnson (1976), Maliver (1973, 1971a, 1971b), Stumbo (1973), and Wysor (1971).

48. In constructing a survey questionnaire from newspaper clippings, Kegan (1976), for instance, found many more negative or harmful phrases about encounter groups than positive ones.

49. Empirical research by Batchelder and Hardy (1968) and Bunker and Singer (undated) document the degree to which stories of danger can become exaggerated. In both cases concerted efforts to track down extensive rumors of harm caused in two large encounter group projects eventually found little, if any, substantiation.

50. For balanced discussions of the dangers of encounter groups published in the popular media, see Birnbaum (1969), Black (1970), and *Time* (1973).

51. Other critiques in professional journals include Gomberg (1967, 1966), Lakin (1969), Peters (1973), and Rowe and Winborn (1973). Responses to these critiques and defenses of encounter groups appear in Arbuckle (1973), Benne (1970), Dublin (1972), Haigh (1971), and Hogan (1976).

52. Arbuckle (1976: 49-50) has put the matter most succinctly in responding to Koch's (1971) criticisms of encounter groups:

> His reading material has obviously been somewhat different than mine. By using a similarly skewed and biased reading list, I could conclude that religion consists of meetings where (for a price) psychotic evangelists deliver a group of fearful ignorant people from the clutches of the devil.

53. Other anecdotal reports are contained in Beymer (1970) (four cases: one participant became psychotic participating in an encounter group at a Midwest university, three participants committed suicide in various groups run by one leader over a one-year period); Crawshaw (1969) (three cases: one participant had self-doubts reinforced by the group and dropped out of school; another lost his job and was admitted to a state hospital; a third left a group feeling like the "worst kind of chicken"); Jaffe and Scherl (1969) (three cases: psychotic reaction followed by hospitalization; transient psychosis with three weeks hospitalization; extreme anxiety reaction necessitating departure from the group); Maliver (1971a) (two cases: suicide after sexual affair with group leader, and transient psychotic episode during day-long minilab); Maliver (1973) (one case: suicide at a growth center); Odiorne (1970) (five cases: ranging from damaging effects of encounter groups on a whole company to the effects on a woman who went berserk and required intensive psychiatric treatment); Valpy (1966) (one case: hospitalization for psychiatric treatment); Wysor (1971) (one case: hospitalization for acute psychotic breakdown because of sexual touching in a group).

54. Stoller (1968), one of the originators of the marathon group, claims on the basis of subjective observation that roughly 20 percent of all participants do not get the kind of gain they seek and about 1 or 2 percent undergo actual harm. Van Stone and Gilbert (1972), who have been involved with peer confrontation groups, declare that their use has caused no psychotic breakdowns on an open psychiatric ward, except where there was a previous history of it.

55. The finding of a low rate of casualities is fairly uniform among those who have conducted an overall anlaysis of outcome studies in the encounter field. For reviews other than those discussed in the text see Eitington (1971) (trauma, even in a quasi-clinical sense, is hardly a fact of T group life); Gibb (1975, 1974) (negative effects definitely exist, but it is difficult to determine in what percent of the cases it occurs; studies are cited indicating that encounter groups may increase irritability on the job and in the family, exacerbate rebellious attitudes toward authority, heighten unrealistic expectations, and increase defensiveness); Lambert, Bergin, and Collins (in press) (in general, groups are often less deleterious but can produce more deterioration than therapy); Phares and Campbell (1971) (documented cases of harmful outcome exist for variants of sensitivity training, but they are few and more often stem from those groups focusing on personal growth and sensory awareness); Seashore (1970) (the incidence of serious stress and mental disturbance is less than 1 percent, and most of these occur in persons with a history of prior disturbances); Easton, Carr, and Whiteley (1972) (most of the concrete evidence available indicates that casualties are comparatively rare and usually involve people with some previous history of psychological difficulty); Strandbygaard and Jensen (1973) (psychoses caused by sensitivity training are slight and usually of short duration).

56. The thirty-nine studies mentioned herein were originally cited and analyzed in an appendix for this volume, but they have since been deleted. The unpublished material constituting this appendix is available from the author.

REFERENCES.

American Psychiatric Association, Task Force on Recent Developments in the Use of Small Groups. *Encounter Groups and Psychiatry.* Washington, D.C.: American Psychiatric Association, 1970.

Anderson, C., and Slocum, J.W., Jr. "Personality Traits and Their Impact on T-Group Training Success." *Training and Development Journal,* 1973, v. 27(12), pp. 18-25.

Anderson, N.J., and Love, B. "Psychological Education for Racial Awareness." *Personnel and Guidance Journal,* 1973, v. 51, pp. 666-70.

Apfelbaum, B., and Apfelbaum, C. "Encountering Encounter Groups: A Reply to Koch and Haigh." *Journal of Humanistic Psychology,* 1973, v. 13(1), pp. 53-67.

Appley, D.G., and Winder, A.E. *T-groups and Therapy Groups in a Changing Society.* San Francisco: Jossey-Bass, 1973.

Arbuckle, D.S. "Koch's Distortion of Encounter Group Theory." *Journal of Humanistic Psychology,* 1973, v. 13(1), pp. 47-51.

Archer, D. "Power in Groups: Self-concept Changes of Powerful and Powerless Group Members." *Journal of Applied Behavioral Science,* 1974, v. 10, pp. 208-20.

Arnhoff, F.N. "Psychiatry, Manpower, and Mental Health." (Working Paper of the American Psychological Association, Division of Manpower Research and Development.) Mimeographed. University of Virginia School of Medicine, Charlottesville, Va., 1971.

Bach, G.R. "Discussion." *International Journal of Group Psychotherapy,* 1968, v. 18, pp. 244-49.

Bach, G.R. "Marathon Group Dynamics: I. Some Functions of the Professional Group Facilitator." *Psychological Reports,* 1967a, v. 20, pp. 995-99.

Bach, G.R. "Marathon Group Dynamics: II. Dimensions of Helpfulness: Therapeutic Aggression." *Psychological Reports,* 1967b, v. 20, pp. 1147-58.

Bach, G.R. "Marathon Group Dynamics: III. Disjunctive Contacts." *Psychological Reports,* 1967c, v. 20, pp. 1163-72.

Bach, G.R. "The Marathon Group: Intensive Practice of Intimate Interaction." *Psychological Reports,* 1966, v. 18, pp. 995-1002.

Back, K.W. *Beyond Words: The Story of Sensitivity Training and the Encounter Movement.* New York: Russell Sage Foundation, 1972.

Bales, R.F. *Interaction Process Analysis: A Method for the Study of Small Groups.* Cambridge, Mass.: Addison-Wesley, 1950.

Batchelder, R.L., and Hardy, J.M. *Using Sensitivity Training and the Laboratory Method.* (Foreword by R.O. Lippitt.) New York: Association Press, 1968.

Bebout, J. "Toward a Definition of Encounter Groups." Mimeographed. Berkeley, Calif., undated.

Bebout, J. "A Study of Group Encounter in Higher Education." In J. Vriend and W.W. Dyer (Eds.), *Counseling Effectively in Groups.* Englewood Cliffs, N.J.: Educational Technology Publications, 1973, pp. 281-92.

Bebout, J., and Gordon, B. "The Value of Encounter." In L.N. Solomon and B. Berzon (Eds.), *New Perspectives on Encounter Groups.* San Francisco: Jossey-Bass, 1972, pp. 83-118.

Bebout, J., and Gordon, B. "Progress Report: A Four-Year Research Study of Encounter Groups." Mimeographed. Berkeley, Calif., 1971.

Bebout, J. (In collaboration with B. Gordon.) "The Use of Encounter Groups for Interpersonal Growth: Initial Results of the TIE Project." *Interpersonal Development,* 1971-72, v. 2, pp. 91-104.

Bednar, R.L., and Lawlis, G.F. "Empirical Research in Group Psychotherapy." In A.E. Bergin and S.L. Garfield (Eds.), *Handbook of Psychotherapy and Behavior Change: An Empirical Analysis.* New York: John Wiley, 1971, pp. 812-38.

Beldoch, M. "The False Psychology of Encounter Groups." *Intellectual Digest,* October 1971, pp. 85-88.

Benne, K.D. "Conceptual and Moral Foundations of Laboratory Method." In K.D. Benne, L.P. Bradford, J.R. Gibb, and R.O. Lippitt (Eds.), *The Laboratory Method of Changing and Learning: Theory and Application.* Palo Alto, Calif.: Science and Behavior Books, 1975, pp. 24-55.

Benne, K.D. "The Tearing Down of Walls." *Boston University Literary Currents*, December 3, 1970, pp. 14-16.

Benne, K.D. "History of the T Group in the Laboratory Setting." In L.P. Bradford, J.R. Gibb, and K.D. Benne (Eds.), *T-Group Theory and Laboratory Method.* New York: John Wiley, 1964, pp. 80-135.

Benne, K.D.; Bradford, L.P.; Gibb, J.R.; and Lippitt, R.O. (Eds.) *The Laboratory Method of Changing and Learning: Theory and Application.* Palo Alto, Calif.: Science and Behavior Books, 1975.

Bennis, W.G. "Goals and Meta-Goals of Laboratory Training." *Human Relations Training News*, 1962, v. 6 (3), pp. 1-4. Reprinted in R.T. Golembiewski and A. Blumberg (Eds.), *Sensitivity Training and the Laboratory Approach: Readings About Concepts and Applications.* Itasca, Ill.: F.E. Peacock, 1970, pp. 18-24.

Bennis, W.G., and Slater, P.E. *The Temporary Society.* New York: Harper and Row, 1968.

Berger, M.M. "Experiential and Didactic Aspects of Training in Therapeutic Group Approaches." *American Journal of Psychiatry*, 1969, v. 126, pp. 845-50.

Bessell, H. "Magic Circles in the Classroom: Developing Mastery and Healthy Self-Concepts to Support Cognitive and Motor Learning." In R.T. Golembiewski and A. Blumberg (Eds.), *Sensitivity Training and the Laboratory Approach: Readings About Concepts and Applications.* Itasca, Ill.: F.E. Peacock, 1970, pp. 349-52.

Beymer, L. "Confrontation Groups: Hula Hoops?" *Counselor Education and Supervision*, 1970, v. 9, pp. 75-86.

Bindrim, P. "A Report on a Nude Marathon." *Psychotherapy: Theory, Research and Practice*, 1968, v. 5, pp. 180-88. Reprinted in R.W. Siroka, E.K. Siroka, and G.A. Schloss (Eds.), *Sensitivity Training and Group Encounter: An Introduction.* New York: Grosset and Dunlap, 1971, pp. 149-63.

Bion, W.R. *Experiences in Groups.* New York: Basic Books, 1961.

Birnbaum, M. "Sense About Sensitivity Training." *Saturday Review*, November 15, 1969, pp. 82-85.

Black, D.R. "Current Status of Outcome in Group Psychotherapy." *Group Psychotherapy and Psychodrama*, 1974, v. 27, pp. 110-18.

Black, J.D. "Encounter Groups." *Mademoiselle*, May 1970, pp. 33, 36, 56.

Blank, L.; Gottsegen, G.B.; and Gottsegen, M.G. (Eds.) *Confrontation: Encounters in Self and Interpersonal Awareness.* New York: Macmillan Publishing Co., 1971.

Bonner, H. *Group Dynamics: Principles and Application.* New York: Ronald Press, 1959.

Boring, F. "An Ethical Perspective on Growth Groups." *Massachusetts Psychological Association Newsletter*, April 1971, p. 5.

Boyd, J.B., and Elliss, J.D. *Findings of Research into Senior Management Seminars.* Toronto: Hydro-Electric Power Commission of Ontario, 1962. Cited in J.P. Campbell and M.D. Dunnette, "Effectiveness of T-Group Experiences in Managerial Training and Development." *Psychological Bulletin*, 1968, v. 70, pp. 73-104.

Bradford, L.P. "Biography of an Institution." *Journal of Applied Behavioral Science*, 1967, v. 3, pp. 121-43.

Bradford, L.P.; Gibb, J.R.; and Benne, K.D. "A Look to the Future." In L.P. Bradford, J.R. Gibb, and K.D. Benne (Eds.), *T-Group Theory and Laboratory Method: Innovation and Re-education.* New York: John Wiley, 1964a, pp. 477-86.

Bradford, L.P.; Gibb, J.R.; and Benne, K.D. (Eds.) *T-Group Theory and Laboratory Method: Innovation in Re-education.* New York: John Wiley, 1964b.

Bradford, L.P.; Gibb, J.R.; and Benne, K.D. "Two Educational Innovations." In L.P.

Bradford, J.R. Gibb, and K.D. Benne (Eds.), *T-Group Theory and Laboratory Method: Innovation and Re-education.* New York: John Wiley, 1964c, pp. 1–14.

Brodsky, A.M. "The Consciousness-raising Group as a Model for Therapy with Women." *Psychotherapy: Theory, Research and Practice,* 1973, v. 10, pp. 24–29.

Bromberg, W. *From Shaman to Psychotherapist: A History of the Treatment of Mental Illness.* Chicago: Henry Regnery, 1975.

Brownfain, J.J. "The APA Professional Liability Insurance Program." *American Psychologist,* 1971, v. 26, pp. 648–52.

Buber, M. *Between Man and Man.* (Introduction by M. Friedman; translated by R.G. Smith; afterword translated by M. Friedman.) New York: Macmillan, 1965.

Buchanan, P.C. "Laboratory Training and Organization Development." *Administrative Science Quarterly,* 1969, v. 14, pp. 466–80.

Buchanan, P.C. "Innovative Organizations—A Study in Organization Development." In Industrial Relations Counselors, *Applying Behavioral Science Research in Industry.* (Monograph No. 23.) New York: Industrial Relations Counselors, 1964, pp. 85–107.

Bunker, B.B., and Singer, D.L. "Independent Nonprofessionals in a Community Setting: A Case History Analysis." Unpublished manuscript, undated.

Burrow, T. "The Group Method of Analysis." *Psychoanalytic Review,* 1927, v. 14, pp. 268–80.

Cadden, J.J.; Flach, F.F.; Blakeslee, S.; and Charlton, R., Jr. "Growth in Medical Students Through Group Process." *American Journal of Psychiatry,* 1969, v. 126, pp. 862–68.

Calame, B.E. "The Truth Hurts: Some Companies See More Harm Than Good in Sensitivity Training." *Wall Street Journal,* July 14, 1969.

Campbell, J.P., and Dunnette, M.D. "Effectiveness of T-Group Experiences in Managerial Training and Development." *Psychological Bulletin,* 1968, v. 70, pp. 73–104.

Cartwright, D., and Zander, A. "Groups and Group Membership: Introduction." In D. Cartwright and A. Zander (Eds.), *Group Dynamics.* (3rd ed.) New York: Harper and Row, 1968, pp. 45–62.

Casriel, D.H. "The Daytop Story and the Casriel Method." In L. Blank, G.B. Gottsegen, and M.G. Gottsegen (Eds.), *Confrontation: Encounters in Self and Interpersonal Awareness.* New York: Macmillan Publishing Co., 1971, pp. 179–93.

Chambers, W.M., and Ficek, D.E. "An Evaluation of Marathon Counseling." *International Journal of Group Psychotherapy,* 1970, v. 20, pp. 372–79.

Chesler, P. "Playing Instant Joy in the Lonely Crowd." *Village Voice,* December 25, 1969.

Clark, D.H. "Homosexual Encounter in All-Male Groups." In L.N. Solomon and B. Berzon (Eds.), *New Perspectives on Encounter Groups.* San Francisco: Jossey-Bass, 1972, pp. 368–82.

Clark, D.H. "Encounter in Education." In L. Blank, G.B. Gottsegen, and M.G. Gottsegen (Eds.), *Confrontation: Encounters in Self and Interpersonal Awareness.* New York: Macmillan Publishing Co., 1971, pp. 345–68.

Cobbs, P.M. "Ethnotherapy in Groups." In L.N. Solomon and B. Berzon (Eds.), *New Perspectives on Encounter Groups.* San Francisco: Jossey-Bass, 1972, pp. 383–403.

Cooper, C.L. "How Psychologically Dangerous Are T-groups and Encounter Groups?" *Human Relations,* 1975, v. 28, pp. 249–60.

Cooper, C.L. "Psychological Disturbance Following T-Groups: Relationship Between Eysenck Personality Inventory and Family/Friends Perceptions." *British Journal of Social Work,* 1974, v. 4, pp. 39–49.

Cooper, C.L. "A Bibliography of Current Encounter and T-Group Research: 1971–1973." *Interpersonal Development,* 1973–74, v. 4, pp. 65–68.

Cooper, C.L. "Coping with Life Stress After Sensitivity Training." *Psychological Reports,* 1972, v. 31, p. 602.

Cooper, C.L., and Mangham, I.L. *T-groups, A Survey of Research.* London: Wiley Interscience, 1971.

Crawshaw, R. "How Sensitive Is Sensitivity Training?" *American Journal of Psychiatry*, 1969, v. 126, pp. 868-73.

De Michele, J.H. "The Measurement of Rated Training Changes Resulting from a Sensitivity Training Laboratory of an Overall Program in Organization Development." Ph.D. dissertation, New York University, 1966. Abstracted in *Dissertation Abstracts*, 1966, v. 27A, pp. 3578-79.

Dewey, J. *Democracy and Education.* 1916. Reprint. New York: Free Press, 1966.

Dewey, J. *Dewey on Education: Selections.* (Edited by M.S. Dworkin.) New York: Columbia University Teachers College, 1959.

Dewey, J. *Experience and Education.* New York: Macmillan Publishing Co., Collier Books, 1938.

Dewey, J. *Liberalism and Social Action.* New York: Capricorn Books, 1935.

Dewey, J. *Experience and Nature.* (2nd ed.) Chicago: Open Court, 1929.

Dinges, N.G., and Weigel, R.G. "The Marathon Group: A Review of Practice and Research." *Comparative Group Studies*, 1971, v. 2, pp. 339-458.

Dublin, J.E. "Whose Image of What?: Open Letter to Sigmund Koch." *Journal of Humanistic Psychology*, 1972, v. 12(2), pp. 79-85.

Durham, L.E.; Gibb, J.R.; and Knowles, E.S. "A Bibliography of Research." In NTL Institute for Applied Behavioral Science, *Explorations in Applied Behavioral Science.* (No. 2.) New York: Renaissance Editions, 1967, pp. 25-71.

Durkin, H.E. *The Group in Depth.* New York: International Universities Press, 1964.

Easton, R.H.; Carr, R.J.; and Whiteley, J.M. "Issues in the Encounter Group Movement." *Counseling Psychologist*, 1972, v. 3(2), pp. 89-120.

Eddy, W.B., and Lubin, B. "Laboratory Training and Encounter Groups." *Personnel and Guidance Journal*, 1971, v. 49, pp. 625-35.

Egan, G. *Encounter: Group Processes for Interpersonal Growth.* Belmont, Calif.: Brooks/Cole Publishing Co., 1970.

Ehrenwald, J. (Ed.) *The History of Psychotherapy: From Healing Magic to Encounter.* New York: Jason Aronson, 1976.

Eitington, J.E. "Assessing Laboratory Training Using Psychology of Learning Concepts." *Training and Development Journal*, 1971, v. 25(2), pp. 2-7.

Enright, J.B. "On the Playing Fields of Synanon." In L. Blank, G.B. Gottsegen, and M.G. Gottsegen (Eds.), *Confrontation: Encounters in Self and Interpersonal Awareness.* New York: Macmillan, 1971, pp. 147-77.

Ezriel, H. "A Psychoanalytic Approach to Group Treatment." *British Journal of Medical Psychology*, 1950, v. 23, pp. 59-74.

Faculty of the Training Laboratory in Group Development. "A Laboratory of Educational Dynamics." *School and Society*, 1947, v. 66, pp. 475-79.

Fiman, B.G., and Conner, D.R. "Laboratory Training: A Review of Problem Areas." *Group Psychotherapy and Psychodrama*, 1973, v. 26(1-2), pp. 72-91.

Forer, B.R. "Use of Physical Contact." In L.N. Solomon and B. Berzon (Eds.), *New Perspectives on Encounter Groups.* San Francisco: Jossey-Bass, 1972, pp. 195-210.

Foulkes, S.H., and Anthony, E.J. *Group Psychotherapy: The Psychoanalytic Approach.* (2nd ed.) Baltimore, Md.: Penguin Books, 1965.

Frank, J.D. *Persuasion and Healing: A Comparative Study of Psychotherapy.* (Rev. ed.) Baltimore, Md.: Johns Hopkins Press, 1973.

Freud, S. *Group Psychology and the Analysis of the Ego.* 1922. Reprint. (Introduction by F. Alexander and translated by J. Strachey.) New York: Bantam Books, 1960.

Freundlich, D. "A Psychoanalytic Hypothesis of Change Mechanisms in Encounter Groups." *International Journal of Group Psychotherapy*, 1972, v. 22, pp. 42-53.

Fromme, D.K.; Jones, W.H.; and Davis, J.O. "Experiential Group Training with Conservative Populations: A Potential for Negative Effects." *Journal of Clinical Psychology*, 1974, v. 39, pp. 290-96.

Gibb, J.R. "A Research Perspective on the Laboratory Method." In K.D. Benne, L.P. Bradford, J.R. Gibb, and R.O. Lippitt (Eds.), *The Laboratory Method of Changing and*

Learning: Theory and Application. Palo Alto, Calif.: Science and Behavior Books, 1975, pp. 56-71, 551-69.

Gibb, J.R. "The Message from Research." In J.W. Pfeiffer and J.E. Jones (Eds.), *The 1974 Annual Handbook for Group Facilitators.* La Jolla, Calif.: University Associates, 1974.

Gibb, J.R. "The Effects of Human Relations Training." In A.E. Bergin and S.L. Garfield (Eds.), *Handbook of Psychotherapy and Behavior Change: An Empirical Analysis.* New York: John Wiley, 1971, pp. 839-62.

Gibbard, G.S.; Hartman, J.J.; and Mann, R.D. (Eds.) *Analysis of Groups: Contributions to Theory, Research, and Practice.* San Francisco: Jossey-Bass, 1974.

Glass, G.V. "Primary, Secondary, and Meta-Analysis of Research." Paper presented as presidential address to the 1976 Annual Meeting of the American Educational Research Association, San Francisco, Calif., April 21, 1976.

Goldberg, D.A., and Goodman, B. "The Small-Group System and Training on an Acute Psychiatric Ward." *International Journal of Psychiatry in Medicine,* 1973, v. 4, pp. 173-81.

Golembiewski, R.T. "Enriching Marriages Through the Laboratory Approach: Tentative Steps Toward the 'Open Couple.'" In R.T. Golembiewski and A. Blumberg (Eds.), *Sensitivity Training and the Laboratory Approach: Readings About Concepts and Applications.* Itasca, Ill.: F.E. Peacock, 1970, pp. 345-49.

Golembiewski, R.T., and Blumberg, A. (Eds.) *Sensitivity Training and the Laboratory Approach: Readings About Concepts and Applications.* Itasca, Ill.: F.E. Peacock, 1970.

Gomberg, W. "'Titillating Therapy': Management Development's Most Fashionable Toy." *Personnel Administrator,* 1967, v. 12 (issue unknown), pp. 30-33.

Gomberg, W. "The Trouble with Democratic Management." *Trans-Action,* 1966, v. 3 (5), pp. 30-35.

Gorner, P. "Encounter Groupies, Beware!" *Chicago Tribune,* April 28, 1973.

Gottschalk, L.A. "Psychoanalytic Notes on T-Groups at the Human Relations Laboratory, Bethel, Maine." *Comprehensive Psychiatry,* 1966, v. 7, pp. 472-87.

Grunebaum, H. "A Soft-hearted Review of Hard-nosed Research on Groups." *International Journal of Group Psychotherapy,* 1975, v. 25, pp. 185-97.

Gurel, B.D. Secretary, Committee on Scientific and Professional Ethics and Conduct, American Psychological Association. Personal communication, June 3, 1974.

Haigh, G.V. "Response to Koch's Assumptions about Group Process." *Journal of Humanistic Psychology,* 1971, v. 11(2), pp. 129-32.

Halas, C. "All-Women's Groups: A View from Inside." *Personnel and Guidance Journal,* 1973, v. 52, pp. 91-95.

Hall, C.S., and Lindzey, G. *Theories of Personality.* New York: John Wiley, 1970.

Hall, G.F. "A Participant's Experience in a Basic Encounter Group." Unpublished manuscript, 1965. Cited in C.R. Rogers, *Carl Rogers on Encounter Groups.* New York: Harper and Row, 1970, pp. 30-31.

Hampden-Turner, C.M. "An Existential 'Learning Theory' and the Integration of T-Group Research." In R.T. Golembiewski and A. Blumberg (Eds.), *Sensitivity Training and the Laboratory Approach: Readings about Concepts and Applications.* Itasca, Ill.: F.E. Peacock, 1970, pp. 38-54.

Hanson, P.G.; Rothaus, P.; O'Connell, W.E.; and Wiggins, G. "Training Patients for Effective Participation in Back-Home Groups." *American Journal of Psychiatry,* 1969, v. 126, pp. 857-62.

Hardy, J.M. Personal communication, July 1, 1976a.

Hardy, J.M. Personal communication, June 22, 1976b.

Hardy, J.M. Personal Communication, April 19, 1976c.

Hare, A.P. "Bibliography of Small Group Research: 1959-69." *Sociometry,* 1972, v. 35, pp. 1-150.

Hartley, D.; Roback, H.B.; and Abramowitz, S.I. "Deterioration Effects in Encounter Groups." *American Psychologist,* 1976, v. 31, pp. 247-55.

Helmreich, R.; Bakeman, R.; and Scherwitz, L. "The Study of Small Groups." *Annual Review of Psychology*, 1973, v. 24, pp. 337-54.

Henderson, J. "Training Groups for Public Helath Nurses." *Canada's Mental Health*, 1973, v. 21 (5), pp. 12-14.

Hogan, D.B. "The Experiential Group and the Psychotherapeutic Enterprise Revisited: A Response to Strupp." *International Journal of Group Psychotherapy*, 1976, v. 26, pp. 321-33.

House, R.J. "T-Group Education and Leadership Effectiveness: A Review of the Empiric Literature and a Critical Evaluation." In R.T. Golembiewski and A. Blumberg (Eds.), *Sensitivity Training and the Laboratory Approach: Readings about Concepts and Applications.* Itasca, Ill.: F.E. Peacock, 1970, pp. 435-62. Reprinted from *Personnel Psychology*, 1967, v. 20, pp. 1-32.

Houts, P.S., and Serber, M. (Eds.) *After the Turn on, What? Learning Perspectives on Humanistic Groups.* Champaign, Ill.: Research Press, 1972.

Howard, J. *Please Touch: A Guided Tour of the Human Potential Movement.* New York: Dell, 1970.

Hurley, J.R., and Force, E.J. "T-Group Gains in Acceptance of Self and Others." *International Journal of Group Psychotherapy*, 1973, v. 23, pp. 166-76.

International Association of Applied Social Scientists, Committee on Standards and Admissions. "Recommendation for Accreditation Procedures." Mimeographed. Washington, D.C., 1974.

Jacobs, P.D. "Human Relations Hucksters." *Advanced Management Journal*, 1972, v. 37, pp. 52-55.

Jaffe, L.S., and Scheri, D.J. "Acute Psychosis Precipitated by T-Group Experiences." *Archives of General Psychiatry*, 1969, v. 21, pp. 443-48.

Jahoda, M. *Current Concepts of Positive Mental Health.* New York: Basic Books, 1958.

Johnson, D.L.; Hanson, P.G.; Rothaus, P.; Morton, R.B.; Lyle, F.A.; and Moyer, R. "Follow-up Evaluation of Human Relations Training for Psychiatric Patients." In E.H. Schein and W.G. Bennis, *Personal and Organizational Change through Group Methods: The Laboratory Approach.* New York: John Wiley, 1965, pp. 152-69.

Johnson, J.G. "Albermarle Paper Company v. Moody: The Aftermath of Griggs and the Death of Employee Testing." *Hastings Law Journal*, 1976, v. 27(6), pp. 1239-62.

Jones, F., and Harris, M.W. "The Development of Interracial Awareness in Small Groups." In L. Blank, G.B. Gottsegen, and M.G. Gottsegen (Eds.), *Confrontation: Encounters in Self and Interpersonal Awareness.* New York: Macmillan, 1971, pp. 409-32.

Joure, S.A.; Frye, R.L.; Green, P.C.; and Cassens, F.P. "Examples of Over-Use of Sensitivity Training." *Training and Development Journal*, 1971, v. 25(12), pp. 24-26.

Kane, F.J.; Wallace, C.D., and Lipton, M.A. "Emotional Disturbance Related to T-Group Experience." *American Journal of Psychiatry*, 1971, v. 127, pp. 954-57.

Kegan, D.L. "Perceived Effects of Sensitivity Training: Samples of Police Officers, College Students, and a Group Dynamics Class." *Small Group Behavior*, 1976, v. 7(2), pp. 131-46.

Klaw, S. "Two Weeks in a T-Group." In R.T. Golembiewski and A. Blumberg (Eds.), *Sensitivity Training and the Laboratory Approach: Readings about Concepts and Applications.* Itasca, Ill.: F.E. Peacock, 1970, pp. 24-38.

Klein, D.C. "Sensitivity Training and Community Development." In E.H. Schein and W.G. Bennis, *Personal and Organizational Change through Group Methods: The Laboratory Approach.* New York: John Wiley, 1965, pp. 184-200.

Knowles, M.S., and Knowles, H. *Introduction to Group Dynamics.* New York: Association Press, 1972.

Koch, S. "The Image of Man Implicit in Encounter Group Theory." *Journal of Humanistic Psychology*, 1971, v. 11(2), pp. 109-28.

Krieger, M.H. "Planning for an Affect Based Society: Prediction, Indicators and Structure." (Working Paper 144B.) Mimeographed. Institute of Urban and Regional Development, University of California, Berkeley, 1971.

Lakin, M. *Interpersonal Encounter: Theory and Practice in Sensitivity Training.* New York: McGraw-Hill, 1972.

Lakin, M. "Some Ethical Issues in Sensitivity Training." *American Psychologist,* 1969, v. 24, pp. 923-28.

Lambert, M.J.; Bergin, A.E.; and Collins, J.L. "Therapist-Induced Deterioration in Psychotherapy." In A.S. Gurman and A.M. Razin (Eds.), *Effective Psychotherapy: A Handbook of Research.* New York: Pergamon Press, 1977, pp. 452-81.

Lazell, E.W. "The Group Treatment of Dementia Praecox." *Psychoanalytic Review,* 1921, v. 8, pp. 168-79.

Lett, W.R. "The Relevance and Structure of Human Relations Training in Teacher Education." *Australian Psychologist,* 1973, v. 8(1), pp. 17-27.

Levine, M., and Bunker, B.B. *Mutual Criticism.* Syracuse, N.Y.: Syracuse University Press, 1975.

Lewin, K. *Field Theory in Social Science.* (Edited by D. Cartwright.) New York: Harper, 1951.

Lewin, K. *Resolving Social Conflicts: Selected Papers on Group Dynamics.* (Edited by G.W. Lewin.) New York: Harper and Row, 1948.

Lewin, K. "Group Decision and Social Change." In T.M. Newcomb and E.L. Hartley (Eds.), *Readings in Social Psychology.* New York: Henry Holt, 1947, pp. 330-44.

Lewin, K. "Field Theory and Experiment in Social Psychology: Concepts and Methods." *American Journal of Sociology,* 1939, v. 44, pp. 868-96.

Lieberman, M.A. "Change Induction in Small Groups." *Annual Review of Psychology,* 1976, v. 27, pp. 217-50.

Lieberman, M.A. "Joy Less Facts? A Response to Schutz, Smith, and Rowan." *Journal of Humanistic Psychology,* 1975, v. 15(2), pp. 49-54.

Lieberman, M.A. "Behavior and Impact of Leaders." In L.N. Solomon and B. Berzon (Eds.), *New Perspectives on Encounter Groups.* San Francisco, Calif.: Jossey-Bass, 1972, pp. 135-70.

Lieberman, M.A., and Gardner, J.R. "Institutional Alternatives to Psychotherapy: A Study of Growth Center Users." *Archives of General Psychiatry,* 1976, v. 33, pp. 157-62.

Lieberman, M.A.; Yalom, I.D.; and Miles, M.B. *Encounter Groups: First Facts.* New York: Basic Books, 1973.

Lieberman, M.A.; Yalom, I.D.; and Miles, M.B. "Impact on Participants." In L.N. Solomon and B. Berson (Eds.), *New Perspectives on Encounter Groups.* San Francisco, Calif.: Jossey-Bass, 1972, pp. 119-34.

Lieberman, M.A.; Yalom, I.D.; and Miles, M.B. "The Group Experience Project: A Comparison of Ten Encounter Technologies." In L. Blank, G.B. Gottsegen, and M.G. Gottsegen (Eds.), *Confrontation: Encounters in Self and Interpersonal Awareness.* New York: Macmillan, 1971, pp. 469-97.

Lindenauer, G.G., and Caine, E. "Human Relations Training in Teacher Education." *Journal of Emotional Education,* 1973, v. 13(1), pp. 27-37.

Lomranz, J.; Lakin, M.; and Schiffman, H. "Variants of Sensitivity Training and Encounter: Diversity or Fragmentation?" *Journal of Applied Behavioral Science,* 1972, v. 8, pp. 399-420.

Lowen, A. "Bio-energetic Group Therapy." In H.M. Ruitenbeek (Ed.), *Group Therapy Today: Styles, Methods and Techniques.* New York: Atherton, 1969, pp. 279-90.

Lubin, B., and Lubin, A.W. "Laboratory Training Stress Compared with College Examination Stress." *Journal of Applied Behavioral Science,* 1971, v. 7, pp. 502-7.

Lubin, B., and Zuckerman, M. "Level of Emotional Arousal in Laboratory Training." *Journal of Applied Behavioral Science,* 1969, v. 5, pp. 483-90.

Luborsky. L.; Singer, B.; and Luborsky, L. "Comparative Studies of Psychotherapies: Is It True That 'Everyone Has Won and All Must Have Prizes?'" *Archives of General Psychiatry,* 1975, v. 32, pp. 995-1008.

Luke, B., and Seashore, C. "Generalizations on Research and Speculations from Experience Related to Laboratory Training Design." In R.T. Golembiewski and A.

Blumberg (Eds.), *Sensitivity Training and the Laboratory Approach.* Itasca, Ill.: F.E. Peacock, 1970, pp. 430–35.

Lumpkin, M.A. "The Effect of An Encounter Group Experience on the Role Anxiety and Therapeutic Competence of Student Therapists." Ph.D. dissertation, Texas Tech University, 1971. Abstracted in *Dissertation Abstracts International*, 1972, v. 32(9-B), pp. 5448–49.

McDougall, W. *The Group Mind.* Cambridge, England: Cambridge University Press, 1920.

McLean, R.A. "WBZ 'Encounter Session'—Frank Talk on Busing." *Boston Globe*, November 6, 1974.

Maliver, B.L. *The Encounter Game.* New York: Stein and Day, 1973.

Maliver, B.L. "Encounter Groupers Up Against the Wall." *New York Times Magazine*, January 3, 1971a, pp. 4–5, 37–41, 43.

Maliver, B.L. "Encounter Groups: A Dangerous Game?" *Current*, February 1971b, pp. 3–12.

Mandelbaum, A. "Intergenerational Groups in a Drop-in Mental Health Center." *Social Casework*, 1973, v. 54, pp. 154–61.

Marrow, A.J. *The Practical Theorist: The Life and Work of Kurt Lewin.* New York: Basic Books, 1969.

Marrow, A.J. "Events Leading to the Establishment of the National Training Laboratories." *Journal of Applied Behavioral Science*, 1967, v. 3, pp. 144–50.

Massarik, F. "Human Relations Training in Japan." *Interpersonal Development.* (Special issue.) 1974–75, v. 5(3).

Massarik, F. "Standards for Group Leadership." In L.N. Solomon and B. Berzon (Eds.), *New Perspectives on Encounter Groups.* San Francisco: Jossey-Bass, 1972, pp. 68–82.

Mayo, E. *The Social Problems of An Industrial Civilization.* Boston: Division of Research, Harvard Business School, 1945.

Meador, B.; Solomon, E.; and Bowen, M. "Encounter Groups for Women Only." In L.N. Solomon and B. Berzon (Eds.), *New Perspectives on Encounter Groups.* San Francisco: Jossey-Bass, 1972, pp. 335–48.

Meltzoff, J., and Kornreich, M. *Research in Psychotherapy.* New York: Atherton Press, 1970.

Miles, M.B. "Rejoinder to Schutz, Smith, and Rowan." *Journal of Humanistic Psychology*, 1975, v. 15 (2), pp. 55–58.

Miles, M.B. "Human Relations Training: Current Status." (Revised version of a paper presented at the Fourteenth International Congress of Applied Psychology, Copenhagen, August 1961.) In I.R. Weschler and E.H. Schein (Eds.), *Issues in Human Relations Training.* Washington, D.C.: National Training Laboratories, 1962, pp. 3–13.

Mills, T.M. *The Sociology of Small Groups.* (Edited by A. Inkeles.) Englewood Cliffs, N.J.: Prentice-Hall, Foundations of Modern Sociology Series, 1967.

Mintz, E.E. *Marathon Groups: Reality and Symbol.* New York: Avon Books, 1971.

Mintz, E.E. "Marathon Groups: A Preliminary Evaluation." *Journal of Contemporary Psychotherapy*, 1969, v. 1, pp. 91–94.

Moreno, J.L. "The Viennese Origins of the Encounter Movement, Paving the Way for Existentialism, Group Psychotherapy and Psychodrama." *Group Psychotherapy*, 1969, v. 22, pp. 7–16.

Moreno, J.L. "Interpersonal Therapy, Group Psychotherapy and the Function of the Unconscious." *Group Psychotherapy*, 1954, v. 7, pp. 191–204.

Moreno, J.L. *Who Shall Survive?* Beacon, N.Y.: Beacon House, 1953.

Moreno, J.L., and Moreno, Z.T. "An Objective Analysis of the Group Psychotherapy Movement." *Group Psychotherapy*, 1960, v. 13, pp. 233–37.

Moscow, D. "T-Group Training in the Netherlands: An Evaluation and Cross-Cultural Comparison." *Journal of Applied Behavioral Science*, 1971, v. 7, pp. 427–48.

Murphy, M. President, Esalen Institute. Personal communication, November 23, 1971.

National Training Laboratories. "Commonly Asked Questions About Sensitivity Training." *News and Reports, NTL Institute*, 1969, v. 3 (4). Cited in American Psychiatric Association Task Force on Recent Developments in the Use of Small Groups, *Encounter Groups and Psychiatry.* Washington, D.C.: American Psychiatric Association, April 1970, p. 13.

National Training Laboratory in Group Development. *Explorations In Human Relations Training: An Assessment of Experience, 1947–1953.* Washington, D.C.: National Training Laboratory in Group Development, 1953.

Newsweek Magazine, "The House on 92nd Street." *Newsweek Magazine*, November 22, 1971, p. 115.

Oden, T.C. *The Intensive Group Experience: The New Pietism.* Philadelphia: Westminster Press, 1972a.

Oden, T.C. "The New Pietism." *Journal of Humanistic Psychology*, 1972b, v. 12 (1), pp. 24–41.

Odiorne, G.S. "The Trouble with Sensitivity Training." In R.T. Golembiewski and A. Blumberg (Eds.), *Sensitivity Training and the Laboratory Approach: Readings About Concepts and Applications.* Itasca, Ill.: F.E. Peacock, 1970, pp. 273–87. Reprinted from *Training Directors Journal*, 1963, v. 17 (10), pp. 9–20.

Olch, D., and Snow, D.L. "Personality Characteristics of Sensitivity Group Volunteers." *Personnel and Guidance Journal*, 1970, v. 48, pp. 848–50.

Page, B.B. "Who Owns the Professions?: *Hastings Center Report*, 1975, v. 5 (5), pp. 7–8.

Parloff, M.B. "Group Therapy and the Small-Group Field—An Encounter." *International Journal of Group Psychotherapy*, 1970, v. 20, pp. 267–304.

Perls, F.S. *Gestalt Therapy Verbatim.* New York: Bantam Books, 1969a.

Perls, F.S. *In and Out of the Garbage Pail.* NewYork: Bantam Books, 1969b.

Perls, F.; Hefferline, R.E.; and Goodman, P. *Gestalt Therapy: Excitement and Growth in the Human Personality.* New York: Dell Publishing Co., 1951.

Peters, J.J. "Do Encounter Groups Hurt People?" *Psychotherapy: Theory, Research and Practice*, 1973, v. 10, pp. 33–35.

Phares, L.G., and Campbell, J.P. "Sensitivity Training in Industry: Issues and Research." In L.E. Abt and B.F. Riess (Eds.), *Clinical Psychology in Industrial Organization.* New York: Grune and Stratton, 1971, pp. 176–90.

Pilder, R. "Encounter Groups for Married Couples." In L.N. Solomon and B. Berzon (Eds.), *New Perspectives on Encounter Groups.* San Francisco: Jossey-Bass, 1972, pp. 303–12.

Pollack, D., and Stanley, G. "Coping and Marathon Sensitivity Training." *Psychological Reports*, 1971, v. 29, pp. 379–85.

Polster, E., and Polster, M. *Gestalt Therapy Integrated: Contours of Theory and Practice.* New York: Vintage Books, 1974.

Posthuma, A.B., and Posthuma, B.W. "Some Observations on Encounter Group Casualties." *Journal of Applied Behavioral Science*, 1973, v. 9, pp. 595–608.

Pratt, J.H. "The Class Method of Treating Consumption in the Homes of the Poor." *Journal of the American Medical Association*, 1907, v. 49, pp. 755–59.

Rarick, J.R. "Sensitivity Training." *Congressional Record*, June 10, 1969 (H4667), pp. 15322–35.

Raup, R.B.; Axtelle, G.E.; Benne, K.D.; and Smith, B.O. *The Improvement of Practical Intelligence.* New York: Bureau of Publications, Teachers College, Columbia University, 1950.

Reddy, W.B. "Screening and Selection of Participants." In L.N. Solomon and B. Berzon (Eds.), *New Perspectives on Encounter Groups.* San Francisco: Jossey-Bass, 1972, pp. 53–67.

Reddy, W.B. "Sensitivity Training or Group Psychotherapy—The Need for Adequate Screening." *International Journal of Group Psychotherapy*, 1970, v. 20, pp. 366–71.

Rettig, J.L., and Amano, M.M. "A Survey of ASPA Experience with Management by Objectives, Sensitivity Training and Transactional Analysis." *Personnel Journal*, 1976, v. 55, pp. 26–29.

Roethlisberger, F.J., and Dickson, W.J. *Management and the Worker*. Cambridge, Mass.: Harvard University Press, 1956.

Rogers, C.R. *Carl Rogers on Encounter Groups*. New York: Harper and Row, 1970.

Rogers, C.R. *Freedom to Learn*. Columbus, Ohio: Charles E. Merrill, 1969.

Rogers, C.R. "The Process of the Basic Encounter Group." In J.F.T. Bugental (Ed.), *Challenges of Humanistic Psychology*. New York: McGraw-Hill, 1967, pp. 261–76.

Rogers, C.R.; Gendlin, E.T.; Kiesler, D.J.; and Truax, C.B. (Eds.) *The Therapeutic Relationship and Its Impact: A Study of Psychotherapy with Schizophrenics*. Madison: Wisconsin University Press, 1967.

Rosenthal, B.G. *The Images of Man*. New York: Basic Books, 1971.

Ross, W.D.; Kligfeld, M.; and Whitman, R.W. "Psychiatrists, Patients, and Sensitivity Groups." *Archives of General Psychiatry*, 1971, v. 25, pp. 178–80.

Rowan, J. "Encounter Group Research: No Joy?" *Journal of Humanistic Psychology*, 1975, v. 15 (2), pp. 19–28.

Rowe, W., and Winborn, R.B. "What People Fear About Group Work: An Analysis of 36 Selected Critical Articles." *Educational Technology*, 1973, v. 13 (1), pp. 53–57.

Sata, L.S. "Laboratory Training for Police Officers." *Journal of Social Issues*, 1975, v. 31, pp. 107–14.

Sata, L.S. Unpublished study, 1967. Cited in American Psychiatric Association, Task Force on Recent Developments in the Use of Small Groups, *Encounter Groups and Psychiatry*. Washington, D.C.: American Psychiatric Association, 1970, p. 13.

Sata, L.S., and MacLean, G. "Sensitivity Training: Issues and Responses." Unpublished manuscript, Seattle, Washington, undated.

Schein, E.H., and Bennis, W.G. *Personal and Organizational Change Through Group Methods: The Laboratory Approach*. New York: John Wiley, 1965.

Schiffman, H. Personal Communication, September 13, 1974.

Schilder, P. "Results and Problems of Group Psychotherapy in Severe Neuroses." *Mental Hygiene*, 1939, v. 23, pp. 87–98.

Schindler-Rainman, E. "Community Development Through Laboratory Methods." In K.D. Benne, L.P. Bradford, J.R. Gibb, and R. Lippitt (Eds.), *The Laboratory Method of Changing and Learning: Theory and Application*. Palo Alto, Calif.: Science and Behavior Books, 1975, pp. 445–63.

Schrank, R., and Stein, S. "Sensitivity Training: Uses and Abuses." *Manpower*, 1970 v. 2 (7), pp. 2–7.

Schutz, W.C. "Not Encounter and Certainly Not Facts." *Journal of Humanistic Psychology*, 1975, v. 15 (2), pp. 7–18.

Schutz, W.C. *Elements of Encounter: A Bodymind Approach*. Big Sur, Calif.: Joy Press, 1973.

Schutz, W.C. *Joy: Expanding Human Awareness*. New York: Grove Press, 1967.

Schutz, W.C., and Allen, V.L. "The Effects of a T-group Laboratory on Interpersonal Behavior." *Journal of Applied Behavioral Science*, 1966, v. 2, pp. 265–86.

Schutz, W.C., and Seashore, C. "Promoting Growth with Nonverbal Exercises." In L.N. Solomon and B. Berzon (Eds.), *New Perspectives on Encounter Groups*. San Francisco: Jossey-Bass, 1972, pp. 188–94.

Seashore, C. "What Is Sensitivity Training?" In R.T. Golembiewski and A. Blumberg (Eds.), *Sensitivity Training and the Laboratory Approach: Readings About Concepts and Applications*. Itasca, Ill.: F.E. Peacock, 1970, pp. 14–18.

Seldman, M.L., and McBrearty, J.F. "Characteristics of Marathon Volunteers." *Psychological Reports*, 1975, v. 36, pp. 555–60.

Selvini, A. "An Internist's Experience in a Doctor-Patient Relationship Training Group (Balint Group)." *Psychotherapy and Psychosomatics*, 1973, v. 22, pp. 1–18.

Shaffer, J.B., and Galinsky, M.D. *Models of Group Therapy and Sensitivity Training.* Englewood Cliffs, N.J.: Prentice-Hall, 1974.

Shapiro, J.L. "An Investigation Into the Effects of Sensitivity Training Procedures." Ph.D. dissertation, University of Waterloo, 1970. Abstracted in *Dissertation Abstracts International*, 1971, v. 32 (2-A), p. 799.

Sheridan, E.P.; Shack, J.; Walker, R.E.; Sheridan, K.; Egan, G.; and Lavigne, J. "A Training Program for Small Group Leaders: II. Evaluation." *Journal of Community Psychology*, 1973a, v. 1, pp. 8-12.

Sheridan, K.; Sheridan, E.P.; Shack, J.; Walker, R.E.; Egan, G.; and Lavigne, J. "A Training Program for Small-Group Leaders: I. Overview." *Journal of Community Psychology*, 1973b, v. 1, pp. 3-7.

Shostrom, E.L. "Group Therapy: Let the Buyer Beware." *Psychology Today*, May 1969, pp. 37-40.

Siroka, R.W.; Siroka, E.K.; and Schloss, G.A. (Eds.) *Sensitivity Training and Group Encounter: An Introduction.* New York: Grosset and Dunlop, 1971.

Slavson, S.R. *Introduction to Group Therapy.* New York: International Universities Press, 1943.

Smith, P.B. "Are There Adverse Effects of Sensitivity Training?" *Journal of Humanistic Psychology*, 1975a, v. 15 (2), pp. 29-48.

Smith, P.B. "Controlled Studies of the Outcome of Sensitivity Training." *Psychological Bulletin*, 1975b, v. 82, pp. 597-622.

Solomon, S.N., and Berzon, B. (Eds.) *New Perspectives on Encounter Groups.* San Francisco: Jossey-Bass, 1972.

Spitz, H., and Sadock, B.J. "Small Interactional Groups in the Psychiatric Training of Graduate Nursing Students." *Journal of Nursing Education*, 1973, v. 12, pp. 6-13.

Steele, F.I. "The Socket Wrench Saga." *International Journal of Psychiatry*, 1970-71, v. 9, pp. 212-18.

Steinbacher, J. *The Child Seducers.* Fullerton, Calif.: Educator Publications, 1971.

Stock, D. "A Survey of Research on T Groups." In L.P. Bradford, J.R. Gibb, and K.D. Benne (Eds.), *T-Group Theory and Laboratory Method: Innovation in Re-education.* New York: John Wiley, 1964, pp. 395-441.

Stoller, F.H. "Accelerated Interaction: A Time-Limited Approach Based on the Brief, Intensive Group." *International Journal of Group Psychotherapy*, 1968, v. 18, pp. 220-35.

Stone, A.A. "The Quest of the Counterculture." *International Journal of Psychiatry*, 1970, v. 9, pp. 219-26.

Stone, W.N., and Tieger, M.E. "Screening for T-Groups: The Myth of Healthy Candidates." *American Journal of Psychiatry*, 1971, v. 127, pp. 1485-90.

Strandbygaard, N., and Jensen, K. "Psychiatric Complications Following Intensive Encounter Group Courses." *Ugeskrift for Laeger*, 1973, v. 135, pp. 515-21.

Strassburger, F. "Ethical Guidelines for Encounter Groups." *APA Monitor*, July 1971, pp. 3, 32.

Strupp, H.H. "The Experiential Group and the Psychotherapeutic Enterprise." *International Journal of Group Psychotherapy*, 1973, v. 23, pp. 115-24.

Strupp, H.H. "On the Technology of Psychotherapy." *Archives of General Psychiatry*, 1972, v. 26, pp. 270-78.

Stumbo, B. "Encounter Group Therapy—A Warning." *Los Angeles Times*, February 27, 1973.

Time Magazine. "Hazardous Encounters." *Time Magazine*, April 30, 1973, p. 65.

Toennies, F. *Community and Society.* (Translated and edited by C.P. Loomis.) East Lansing, Mich.: Michigan State University Press, 1957.

Trotter, W. *Instincts of the Herd in Peace and War.* (2nd ed.) London: T. Fisher Unwin, 1919.

Underwood, W.J. "Evaluation of Laboratory Method Training." *Journal of the American Society of Training Directors*, 1965, v. 19, pp. 34-40. Cited in J.P. Campbell and M.D. Dunnette, "Effectiveness of T-Group Experiences in Managerial Training and Development." *Psychological Bulletin*, 1968, v. 70, pp. 73-104.

Valine, W.J., and Amos, L.C. "High School Transfer Students: A Group Approach." *Personnel and Guidance Journal*, 1973, v. 52, pp. 40-42.

Van Stone, W.W., and Gilbert, R. "Peer Confrontation Groups: What, Why, and Whether." *American Journal of Psychiatry*, 1972, v. 129, pp. 583-88.

Vosen, L. "The Relationship Between Self-disclosure and Self-esteem." Ph.D. dissertation, University of California, Los Angeles, 1966. Abstracted in *Dissertation Abstracts*, 1967, v. 27 (B), p. 2882.

Walker, J.R., and Hamilton, L.S. "A Chicano/Black/White Encounter." *Personnel and Guidance Journal*, 1973, v. 51, pp. 471-77.

Walker, R.E.; Shock, J.R.; Egan, G.; Sheridan, K.; and Sheridan, E.P. "Changes in Self-judgments of Self-disclosure After Group Experience." *Journal of Applied Behavioral Science*, 1972, v. 8, pp. 248-51.

Wender, L. "The Dynamics of Group Psychotherapy and Its Application." *Journal of Nervous and Mental Disease*, 1936, v. 84, pp. 54-60.

Weschler, I.R.; Massarik, F.; and Tannenbaum, R. "The Self in Process: A Sensitivity Training Emphasis." In I.R. Weschler and E.H. Schein (Eds.), *Issues in Human Relations Training*. Washington, D.C.: National Training Laboratories, 1962, pp. 33-46.

Whitaker, D.S., and Lieberman, M.A. "Assessing Interpersonal Behavior in Group Therapy." *Perceptual and Motor Skills*, 1964, v. 18, pp. 763-64.

White, L.A. "The Effects of Leader Personality on Group Outcomes in Interracial Encounter Groups." Ed.D. dissertation, East Texas State University, 1972. Abstracted in *Dissertation Abstracts International*, 1973, v. 33A, pp. 4107-8.

Whitman, R.M. "Psychodynamic Principles Underlying T-Group Processes." In L.P. Bradford, J.R. Gibb, and K.D. Benne (Eds), *T-Group Theory and Laboratory Method: Innovation in Re-education*. New York: John Wiley, 1964, pp. 310-35.

Wille, W.S. "Sensitivity Training Programs in Industry." *Industrial Medicine*, 1970, v. 39, pp. 103-4.

Wolf, A. "The Psychoanalysis of Groups." *American Journal of Psychotherapy*, 1950, v. 4, pp. 16-50.

Wolf, A. "The Psychoanalysis of Groups." *American Journal of Psychotherapy*, 1949, v. 3, pp. 525-58.

Wysor, B. "Encounter Games: A Dangerous New Trend." *Harper's Bazaar*, June 1971, pp. 60-61.

Yalom, I.D. *The Theory and Practice of Group Psychotherapy*. (2nd ed.) New York: Basic Books, 1975.

Yalom, I.D. Unpublished data. Cited in American Psychiatric Association, Task Force on Recent Developments in the Use of Small Groups, *Encounter Groups and Psychiatry*. Washington, D.C.: American Psychiatric Association, 1970, p. 13.

Yalom, I.D., and Lieberman, M.A. "A Study of Encounter Group Casualties." *Archives of General Psychiatry*, 1971, v. 25, pp. 16-30.

Yalom, I.D.; Parloff, M.; and Rosenbaum, C.P. Unpublished data. Cited in American Psychiatric Association, Task Force on Recent Developments in the Use of Small Groups, *Encounter Groups and Psychiatry*. Washington, D.C.: American Psychiatric Association, 1970, p. 13.

✳ *Chapter 4*

The Psychotherapist

The previous two chapters focused on psychotherapy as a broad field of inquiry. It was defined, goals and purposes were enumerated, histories and theoretical bases examined, and research evidence presented to determine value, effectiveness, and the risks involved. Painting this broad picture was necessary to provide the context within which to examine the specific role of the traditional psychotherapist and the encounter group leader. What this role is and how it affects clients and participants is perhaps the critical question that must be answered in developing a sound regulatory framework for the mental health field.

Attempts at professional regulation must inevitably resolve certain problems, whether the field in question is law, medicine, carpentry, plumbing, or psychotherapy. What constitutes competency and what skills are necessary to protect the public from harm is the first area of concern. It involves, among other things, a definition of exactly what psychotherapists and encounter group leaders should do. The next task involves a determination of standards and criteria that establish whether a practitioner is competent or dangerous, and the development of training programs that will ensure competency. Assuming that each of these issues is successfully resolved, there remains the task of developing adequate methods of evaluating and choosing those who are qualified.

Unfortunately, methods of resolving these issues have become established without adequate examination in most professional fields, and the mental health field is following suit. Assumptions that are open to empirical examination are made, but not questioned. It is assumed, for instance, that a doctorate in psychology, satisfactory completion of several years of supervised experience, and successful passage of a written examination are necessary to practice psychotherapy. Similarly, three years of law school and completion of the bar examination are assumed to be necessary for competency as a lawyer, and plumbers cannot be licensed unless they have completed lengthy apprenticeships. Although social science research has explored some of these assumptions, those responsible for developing regulatory proposals have rarely consulted this research. An inquiry into the value of these traditional means of identifying the competent practitioner, along with an examination of proposed alternatives, forms the subject matter of this chapter.

ROLES AND FUNCTIONS

Redlich and Freedman (1966: 197-220, 268-305) have presented an excellent analysis of the gradual change in the role and function of the traditional psychotherapist over the past seventy-five years.[1] Historically, psychotherapy was the primary province of the psychiatrist. Because of psychiatry's ties to the medical field, the initial psychotherapeutic interview became patterned after the medical anamnesis and physical examination. This consisted of an examination of what the patient remembered, including the chief complaint, the present illness, past illness, and a review of symptoms. History-taking was followed by a physical examination, a variety of clinical procedures, and laboratory tests.

This rigid approach to the early stages of the therapeutic process has now been largely abandoned. There is a growing belief that the treatment of mental illness is distinctly different from physical illness. A significant number of practitioners believe that the function of diagnosis is generally to identify problems in living, rather than specific disease entities. Many also downplay the importance of biological data, and believe that treatments such as psychoanalysis are not applied in the same way as physical treatments.

The role that the psychotherapist plays in the treatment process can be conveniently divided according to the nature of that process. In discussing the psychosocial therapies, Redlich and Freedman (1966: 273) distinguish the dynamic-analytic therapies from those that use directive-supportive techniques. The former include most forms of analysis and those other therapies that rely on the development of insight and self-awareness as curative factors. The latter consists of those approaches that attempt to change attitudes and behavior by inducing the patient to accept the world view of the therapist. In the former, interpretation and clarification are primary vehicles for change, while in the latter, advice and suggestion, active praise, and direct help are relied upon. Because of these varia-

tions, the role of the therapist in each system is dramatically different.

In dynamic psychotherapy, patients are usually seen for a fifty-minute hour in the private office of the therapist. One to three sessions per week is the norm. Generally the patient and therapist sit opposite each other and talk. The focus of the conversation is on the emotions of the patient, expecially anxiety, depressive feelings, guilt, and shame. Depending on theoretical predilection and personality, the therapist maintains either an aloof and neutral posture or relates to the patient in an empathic and supportive manner.

The primary task of the dynamic therapist is to help the patient become more aware of and to understand her or his behavior. This is achieved through psychoanalytic interpretation of dreams, accurate empathic identification, or other systems of interpretation. At one time or another, most dynamic therapists employ permissiveness, support, a liberating relationship, and other factors in their attempt to foster patient growth. Which of these factors is primarily responsible for the positive changes that take place remains open to question, but Redlich and Freedman (1966: 285) believe that sensitive accepting, listening, and timely interpretation are the main tools.

The directive and supportive therapies rely more heavily on therapist control. Essential to the success of these forms of therapy is absolute confidence in the therapist on the part of the person who is seeking help. Redlich and Freedman (1966: 286–88) have identified four fundamental techniques that such therapists employ. The first is direct suggestion, persuasion, advice, and intellectual guidance. Second is a variety of "magical" procedures that have been carried over from more primitive practices. The third technique is praise and exhortation, which is especially powerful in the group setting, and which has been effectively employed in Alcoholics Anonymous and at Synanon. The final method is manipulation of the physical and social environment, especially those members of the person's family or social group in a position to influence the patient.

Included in this group are the conditioning therapies and other forms of behavior modification, in which patients are taught relaxation exercises and are put through a variety of exercises designed to extinguish the undesired behaviors. Today these therapies have occasionally been taken to the extreme, as in Martin Shepard's (1971) "love treatment," which advocates sexual intercourse with the therapist; or Abraham Zaslow's (*APA Monitor*, 1973, 1972) "rage-reduction therapy," which relies upon physical assaults upon tied-down patients.

The diversity of roles and functions is far greater at the encounter group end of the spectrum.[2] Depending upon theoretical orientation or technical practice, group leaders frequently take diametrically opposed viewpoints on a variety of issues, although certain core functions are almost universally acknowledged. Among the areas of agreement, virtually all group leaders share the view that being the leader of an encounter group is different from such other roles as traditional classroom teaching or chairing a meeting. Group leaders generally do very little lecturing, although short talks are not uncommon. The encounter group meeting is not highly structured, and the purpose of the group leader is to facilitate, as opposed to structure, the flow of communication among participants.

Most groups practitioners stress the importance of creating an environment where learning and growth are facilitated. This reflects the emphasis on not directing activities, the faith in the group's potential to actualize itself, and the idea that the group leader is a catalytic, rather than causative, agent. Group leaders frequently vary their role depending upon the particular group they are dealing with. Thus, extremely passive participants may require more initial structure and direction than a group of self-motivated learners. Concomitantly, high value is placed on the ability to improvise exercises or to devise specialized techniques on the spur of the moment.

Golembiewski and Blumberg (1970: 132–33) state that encounter group leaders must manage three major polarities if they are to be successful. First, group leaders must function as experts, while at the same time projecting themselves as persons. Second, they must function as outsiders by bringing skills and knowledge to bear in encouraging some learning opportunities while discouraging others, yet at the same time they must function as insiders in order to participate meaningfully in the life of the group. Finally, encounter group leaders will be viewed as central to the group and will be greatly depended upon because of their skill and the fact that they have been through the experience before, yet each group leader must work hard to help a group increasingly trust and rely on its own resources.

Whether a group leader should attempt to behave like any other group, relinquishing her or his leadership role, has been the source of considerable argument. Writers such as Lakin (1972: 109) insist that the encounter group leader can never function as an ordinary member, while Rogers (1970: 45) claims that his goal is to gradually become as much a participant in the group as a facilitator. Related to this issue is the extent to which a group leader feels free to share personal problems with the group. The opinion of Carl Rogers is that severe problems should be dealt with elsewhere, while Sidney Jourard (1971) advocates the open sharing of oneself.

Most group leaders have greater experience in dealing with groups than the typical group member. In addition, most group leaders possess greater skills and expertise in working with groups and a more sophisticated conceptual knowledge of how groups function. How group leaders handle this "expertness" varies. In the Tavistock model of groups, for instance, the leader remains quite remote and does not participate at a personal level. Comments are restricted to interpretations of group phenomena, and the manner in which this is done leaves no doubt that the group leader is the expert and, therefore, the authority. This perception is encouraged, in fact, in order to highlight the problems that group members may have in dealing with real-life authority figures.

A different type of expertise is frequently exhibited by leaders of sensory awareness groups. There, the use of specific techniques and exercises that generate powerful emotional reactions cast the group leader as a different type of, but equally revered, expert. Carl Rogers (1970) believes that the use of any such techniques contributes to the leader being placed in an expert role, which he views as unnecessarily fostering dependence and decreasing spontaneity. Rogers (1970: 57) even eschews making comments on what is transpiring in the group, feeling that this leads to self-consciousness and creates the impression that the group is under scrutiny.

Whether group leaders have physical contact with participants varies with the type of group and the particular group leader. On the whole, encounter groups encourage physical contact far more than traditional therapy groups, although T-group leaders tend to emphasize verbal interaction. Leaders of sensory awareness groups explicitly encourage contact, especially through the use of exercises such as arm-wrestling and blind milling.[3]

Another dimension of the leader role deserves mention. The responsibility of the encounter group leader for what happens in a group has been subject to much debate. Schutz (1971: 152) and others argue that the leader has no responsibility for the members in an encounter group. If a participant under-

goes psychotic decompensation, that is her or his responsibility and choice. This extreme is not advocated by many other leaders (Shaffer and Galinsky, 1974: 205), and generally the leader is expected to protect participants from an overload of negative feedback or other verbal attacks (Bradford, Gibb, and Benne, 1964: 364). The differences that exist usually arise from the practitioner's theory of learning. Some leaders feel that the best way to help participants take control of their lives is to give them absolute responsibility immediately. Others are less sanguine and believe that some protection is needed, at least for a specified period. This question of responsibility intertwines with the problem of how much control a group leader should exert over what happens in a group and how much structure should be provided.

The above discussion focuses on the behaviors exhibited by the group leader and the way in which he or she intervenes to affect the life of the group. Several practitioners take a slightly different view of what the role of the leader should be. They state, in effect, that it is not so much what one does as who one is that makes the difference. Carl Rogers (1970: 43–68) has been one of the strongest proponents of this view, stressing the ability to empathize, to be honest and congruent about how one feels, and to feel an unconditional positive regard for each group member. Sidney Jourard (1971) has stressed the idea of simply "being" in a group as the way of best encouraging and facilitating growth.[4]

In reflecting on the many permutations of the role of the encounter group leader, it is apparent that this role correlates strongly with the goals that a group leader has for the group. Lomranz, Lakin, and Schiffman (1972) found, for instance, that group leaders could be classified as (1) learning-oriented; (2) remediation-oriented; or (3) expanded-experiencing-oriented. Their research indicated that the first classification—

learning-centered trainers—focused on group processes and attempted to clarify and analyze group developmental properties. They encouraged all members to participate and did not favor leader-member confrontations.

Remedial leaders resembled group therapists and encouraged emotional expression to alleviate emotional distress, but not as an end in itself. They used the ambiguity of the unstructured group situation to focus on intrapersonal problems, and looked for repeated behavior patterns that might be indicative of pathology. They were quite flexible in using modeling procedures, and would engage in self-disclosure if it would facilitate the group process.

The expanded-experience leaders did not focus on group process at all. Instead they used many nonverbal techniques and other strategies designed to heighten the emotional intensiveness of the experience. They stressed confrontation and challenge, and encouraged self-exploration through the use of individual and group fantasies.[5]

The role of the encounter group leader can be clarified by a brief contrast with the traditional description of the functions of the group psychotherapist.[6] Rogers (1970: 57) points out that most encounter group leaders do not make use of psychoanalytic forms of interpretation; that is, they do not explain behavior as a function or result of early childhood experiences, nor do they typically attempt to formulate an explanation of that behavior in terms of underlying or unconscious motivation. Therapy-group leaders are much more hesitant about physical contact with participants, and many ban any form of contact at all. By restricting interventions to interpretations and observations of individual and group conflicts and resistances, group therapists precipitate the development of a transference relationship with group members. In such a relationship the members conceive of the group leader as

an authority figure and attach irrational and unconscious fantasies to her or him. In the encounter group, purposive steps are taken to minimize this development. Specifically, the group leader often participates as a member (through modeling behavior, willingness to share feelings and problems, and so on and thereby decreases the preoccupation of the group members with the leader, decreases regressive reactions and increases the interaction among and interdependence of the group members (Horwitz, 1964). These differences, while accurate as recently as the early 1960s, have today been substantially blurred as encounter group practice has more and more merged with psychotherapy.

The role of the encounter group leader can be summarized as follows. Certain core elements are common to virtually all group leaders, such as the lack of emphasis on the lecture method, the desire to create an environment that will facilitate growth and learning, and the faith in the ability of a group to actualize itself given certain minimal structural conditions. Wide variations exist on other dimensions, however, such as the extent to which a leader participates as a group member, takes responsibility for what happens in a group, acts as an expert, and uses structured exercises.

Research indicates that these differences in role are directly related to the particular goals that group leaders have for their groups. Specifically, whether a group is learning-centered, concerned with the alleviation of emotional distress and behavioral functioning, or interested in expanded experiencing will largely determine the techniques the group leader will employ and the role he or she will play.

The role of the encounter group leader has traditionally been thought of as different from therapeutic group leaders in many respects (especially with regard to the use of interpretation, participation as a group member, and encouragement of the development of a transference relationship), but this difference has been attenuated in recent years as both encounter groups and therapy groups have become more alike.

STANDARDS AND CRITERIA

Most direct efforts to regulate the professions have attempted to establish specific qualifications that must be met before a practitioner is granted the right to practice. Such attempts constitute the regulation of input, as opposed to output, and rely on the development of professional standards and criteria that are presumably related to competent practice. Obviously, any set of regulations will only be as good as the particular standards and criteria that have been adopted.

A preliminary question that deserves careful attention is whether the therapist is a significant factor in what happens to people in traditional therapy or encounter groups. The therapist may be irrelevant or may only play a minor role. The self-concept of the patient may be the critical factor, in which case professional regulation is irrelevant. On the other hand, the professional may make all the difference. If the practitioner does play a significant role, then the second task is to determine what constitutes competence and the level of competence desired.

Although most regulations do not do so, it is essential to specify precisely what professionals can be expected to do, given their particular competencies. In the mental health field, this translates into whether a therapist can be relied upon to cure neuroses or psychoses, improve communication ability, increase self-confidence, and the like. Since governmental and judicial regulation have generally not required maximum levels of competence, an important task is to establish standards and criteria that ensure either minimal competence or the prevention of actual harm.

A wide range of factors determine how a professional performs and whether one is effective. Technical skills, theoretical knowledge, personal qualities, and personality characteristics are commonly assumed to be relevant. What the expert has to say and what the social science research leads one to conclude must be studied with care. An examination of the empirical evidence reveals some surprising findings about the actual skills that are needed if the public is to be guaranteed a minimal level of competence or protected from harm. It challenges the traditional assumptions about the importance of such factors as diagnostic ability, technical skill, and theoretical knowledge.

The Importance of the Psychotherapist in Determining Outcome.

Five different lines of evidence indicate that the therapist may not be as instrumental in bringing about change as is frequently supposed. First, there is evidence indicating that much of what happens in therapy and in medicine in general is due to the placebo effect, in which people are helped because they believe the treatment they are receiving is effective, not because of its inherent effectiveness. Second is the evidence of the efficacy of faith healing. Third, there is evidence of "spontaneous remission," in which sick people are cured without any form of treatment. Fourth, research has shown that leaderless therapy groups and encounter groups are as effective in achieving positive results as professionally-led groups. Fifth, it has been shown that factors external to the practitioner, such as the mental health of the client or the composition of an encounter group, are more determinative of results than the level of practitioner skill.

The Placebo Effect. "The history of both physiologic and psychologic treatment is largely the history of the placebo effect."—Arthur Shapiro (1971: 463).

Shapiro (1971: 440) has defined a placebo as "any therapy, or that component of any therapy, that is deliberately used for its nonspecific, psychologic, or psychophysiologic effect, or that is used for its presumed specific effect on a patient, symptom, or illness, but which, unknown to patient and therapist, is without specific activity for the condition being treated." While most psychotherapists attribute their effectiveness to their own skills and knowledge or to their use of effective treatment processes, what actually makes a difference may be the influence of this placebo effect.

Research on placebos indicates that they may be a predominant factor in bringing about therapeutic change. Lorr, McNair, and Weinstein (1962), for instance, conducted a double-blind study of 150 male outpatients who had recently been accepted into individual psychotherapy. A wait-list group received no treatment whatever, another group received only individual psychotherapy, a third group received psychotherapy and drug treatment (librium), a fourth group received psychotherapy and a placebo (capsules containing only inert substances), a fifth group received drug treatment only, and a final group was administered the placebo alone. Based on the patients' point of view the researchers found that the placebos brought about as much improvement as the use of tranquilizers with but one exception. This exception was that patients receiving drugs showed greater changes after one week, reporting less anxiety, greater vigor and more overall improvement. However, these effects washed out after four weeks. Based on therapist reports, the groups receiving the placebo alone showed significantly greater reduction in anxiety, self-blame, and physical complaints, and also showed greater overall improvement than those receiving only psychotherapy.[7]

Jerome Frank (1973) has cited a variety of interesting studies that portray the powerful effects of a placebo. In one, patients with warts were treated by painting the warts with a brightly colored but inactive dye and telling the patients that they would be cured as soon as the dye wore off. This treatment was as effective as any other form of treatment, including surgery (Frank, 1973: 140). Other studies indicate that more than half of all patients who receive a placebo will show significant symptomatic improvement (Gliedman et al., 1958).[8]

Perhaps most convincing of the effectiveness of placebos is the fact that until recently most medical treatments, despite their curative effects, had no objective value whatever (Shapiro, 1971: 442).[9] Of Galen's collection of 820 medicines, all were worthless (Shapiro, 1971: 441). Many famous treatments were positively dangerous, such as the use of bloodletting, purging, puking, poisoning, blistering, freezing, and leeching.

Shapiro (1971) has done an extensive study of how the placebo operates.[10] He found that it has more effect on people who are anxious and depressed than on those without such symptoms. People who tend not to react to placebos are rigid, authoritarian, and stereotypic. They tend to use the mechanism of denial and lack a psychological orientation. The arousal of faith and hope are extremely important for the placebo effect to operate, since they help patients feel and function better. Other important patient factors that increase the effectiveness of placebos include the anticipation of relief. Situational factors include the attitude of the placebo-giver toward the patients and her or his belief in the efficacy of the placebo.

This evidence suggests that perhaps a significant part of the psychotherapist's effectiveness can be attributed to their role as a placebo. As such, effectiveness is not determined by skills, treatment techniques, or theoretical knowledge. Rather, it is the result of the participant or patient's belief in the efficacy of the process, which is aroused by the faith that the therapist or group leader has in his or her techniques. This is enhanced by the use of rituals and by inducing the patient or participant to believe that the practitioner is all-powerful

The current proliferation of therapeutic techniques and encounter groups makes it easy to believe that their effectiveness is due more to placebogenic effects than any other factor. A well-recognized admonition in the medical field is to "treat as many patients with the new remedies while they still have the power to heal" (Shapiro, 1971: 442). And Garrison (1921; in Shapiro, 1971: 463) has observed that "whenever many different remedies are used for a disease, it usually means that we know very little about treating the disease, which is also true of a remedy when it is vaunted as a panacea or cure-all for many diseases."

The psychotherapy field fits these admonitions and descriptions. Techniques experience a meteoric rise, and an equally dramatic and rapid decline. Primal therapy, resembling as it so closely does the primitive practices of the shaman with its ritual-like flavor and emphasis on the creation of strong affect, is a prime example of this.[11] The effectiveness of many therapists who lack any of the qualifications that empirical research has found important to success, may well be explained by the operation of the placebo (Oden, 1974: 15).

Even supposedly well-proven techniques such as behavior modification may lose their efficacy with the passage of time. Jerome Kagan (1970: 112) makes a speculative prediction that behavioral therapy techniques will work for some symptoms for about twenty years only. He notes that the power of psychoanalytic techniques started to wane when the public began to understand the psychoanalytic process and learned many of the analysts's secrets (Kagan, 1970: 112).

The conclusion to be drawn from this data is not necessarily that the effective-ness of psychotherapy is due solely to placebo effects. It does argue that much of their perceived effectiveness may be due to factors other than those generally propounded. It certainly calls into serious question the importance of particular techniques and treatment processes, and raises the possibility that professional regulation based on academic degrees may not be focusing on relevant criteria.

Faith Healing. The efficacy of faith healing and other forms of nonmedical treatment indicate that the curative powers of the traditional therapist and the growth-inducing powers of the encounter group leader may stem from sources quite different from those traditionally assumed to be operative.[12] The apparent power of the springs of Lourdes to heal the sick and infirm, the personality changes wrought by religious conversion, the healing power of prayer, the success of quacks and other pedlars of worthless nostrums, and the feats of psychic healing performed by seers and mystics all illustrate the ways in which faith healing is performed. Evidence of faith healing and its variants is sufficient to justify the conclusion that it does occur, although most evidence consists of anecdotal reports and testimonials and few attempts have been made to isolate causative factors.[13] A particularly vivid and re-markable example of faith healing that allows some theoretical speculation as to causative factors has been reported by Frank (1973: 74, footnotes omitted):

The apparent success of healing methods based on various ideologies and methods compels the conclusion that the healing power of faith resides in the patient's state of mind, not in the validity of its object. At the risk of laboring this point, an experimental demonstration of it with three severely ill, bedridden women may be reported. One had chronic inflammation of the gall baldder with stones, the second had failed to recuperate from a major abdominal operation and was practically a skeleton, and the third was dying of wide-spread cancer. The physician first permitted a prominent local faith healer to try to cure them by absent treatment without the patients' knowledge. Nothing happened. Then he told the patients about the faith healer, built up their expectations over several days, and finally assured them that he would be treating them from a distance at a certain time the next day. This was a time in which he was sure that the healer did *not* work. At the suggested time all three patients improved quickly and dramatically. The second was permanently cured. The other two were not, but showed striking temporary responses. The cancer patient, who was severely anemic and whose tissues had become waterlogged, promptly excreted all the accumulated fluid, recovered from her anemia, and regained sufficient strength to go home and resume her household duties. She remained virtually symptom-free until her death. The gall baldder patient lost her symptoms, went home, and had no recurrence for several years. These three patients were greatly helped by a belief that was false—that the faith healer was treating them from a distance—suggesting that "expectant trust" in itself can be a powerful healing force.

Generally speaking, theories of psychic healing explain this phenomenon on the basis of normal or paranormal psychology. Under normal psychological theory, faith healing may be viewed as a striking example of the placebo effect. This seems to be Frank's line of reasoning in the example above. On the other hand, psychic healing may be seen as an example of paranormal phenomena, such as telepathy, extrasensory perception, clairvoyance, and other events not explicable by present-day "natural" laws.[14]

Explanatory theories based on parapsychological arguments generally fall into three categories (LeShan, 1974: 103-5). The first explains faith healing as an intervention of God brought about by prayer. Research on the power of prayer has frequently been negative, however (see, for example, Joyce and Welldon, 1965). The second attributes the positive results to the work of spirits carried out through special linkages with the patient. The final explanation asserts that healing occurs through the transmission or origination of some special form of energy, frequently through the "laying on of hands." This last theory is the most frequently discussed in parapsychological circles, since it is the theory most susceptible to empirical verification. Research on the "Kirlian aura" (see Ostrander and Schroeder, 1970), attempts to provide photographic evidence of healing energy in plants and people (see Academy of Parapsychology and Medicine, 1972: 121-31), and theoretical explanations of the effectiveness of acupuncture (see Academy of Parapsychology and Medicine, 1972: 93-102) have stressed this special form of energy as the logical explanation for psychic phenomena, especially faith healing.

Current theoretical formulations of faith healing are still rather primitive and lack a solid research base. The existence of the phenomenon, however, and the fact that explanations have emphasized criteria widely divergent from criteria traditionally associated with therapeutic success, challenges the reliance that has been placed on these latter criteria in most efforts at regulation. Frank's documentation of the fact that the faith healer may not be necessary for therapeutic results to be achieved even challenges the assumption that any form of expertise is needed at all.

Spontaneous Remission. The phenomenon of emotionally ill persons recovering from their illness without professional treatment has been termed spontaneous remission. If it turns out that most such illnesses are self-limiting, the role of the therapist or group leader in the healing process would not appear to be essential. The apparent effectiveness of psychotherapy and encounter groups, then, would be an artifact resulting from the fact that the patients or participants would have improved in any event.

Precisely this argument was made by Eysenck (1952) in his initial assault on the therapeutic establishment. He argued that approximately 70 percent of all mentally ill people improve significantly within two years whether or not they receive psychotherapy. He cited two early studies in support of his contention. One by Landis (1937) showed that between 1917 and 1934, 72 percent of all hospitalized neurotics in New York State were discharged without receiving psychotherapy. Another study by Denker (1946) indicated that untreated life-insurance disability claimants improved at a similar rate. These figures and the research on which they were based have been seriously criticized (see Luborsky, 1954; Rosenzweig, 1954; Strupp, 1964). In summarizing these criticisms Kiesler (1966) has argued that the research of Landis and Denker suffered from three main problems: (1) the patient groups were not comparable to traditional psychotherapy; (2) it was questionable whether both groups did not receive psychotherapy; and (3) the criteria for improvement or recovery were not comparable to those used in evaluating traditional psychotherapy.

Citing additional studies that offer lower figures, Bergin (1971) has concluded that Eysenck's spontaneous remission rate is out of line with reality. He proposes a median rate in the vicinity of 30 percent. This may very well mean that mental illness is often self-limiting and that many individuals will recover of their own accord. The 30 percent figure may, however, simply represent the results of poor research designs since, as Bergin readily acknowledges, most of the studies on spontaneous remission are seriously flawed.

An alternative theory has been proposed by Bergin (1963), however, in which he argues that spontaneous remission is the result of people in distress seeking help from friends and other help-giving sources. By 1971 he was fairly convinced of this theory. Excellent evidence of its validity was provided by

Gurin, Veroff, and Feld (1960) in their nationwide survey under the auspices of the Joint Commission on Mental Illness and Health. In examining the source of help chosen by people with a personal problem they found that the majority used non–mental-health professionals, and on the whole they were more satisfied with the help they received than those who chose psychiatrists and psychologists (Gurin et al., 1960: 307–9). Bergin notes a study demonstrating that approximately half of those that seek psychotherapy also seek other forms of help from non-professionals, and he discusses detailed reports of significantly helpful non-professionals such as housewives.

The concept of spontaneous remission, then, raises at least two interesting theoretical possibilities. First, studies supposedly demonstrating that therapists are effective may actually be examples of self-limiting neuroses. Second, spontaneous remission may be a consequence of receiving non-professional help that is essentially psychotherapeutic in nature. If this type of help is effective, the clear implication is that academic credentials, traditional diagnostic and technical skills, and theoretical knowledge may not be necessary to practice competently.[15]

Leaderless Groups. In society in general, although particularly prevalent in the psychotherapy and encounter group field, so-called leaderless groups[16] have been gaining increasing acceptance (*Journal of Applied Behavioral Science*, 1976; Seligman and Desmond, 1975; Yalom, 1975). These are groups in which no formal or informal leader exists, and where the main purpose is frequently similar to the goals of psychotherapy or encounter groups.

Leaderless groups may take a variety of forms. In the encounter field, for instance, typical examples include groups of women intent upon consciousness-raising, couples at a party playing the game "Group Therapy," or participants using programmed tapes such as those developed by Berzon, Solomon, and Reisel (1972). These tapes employ a variety of structured exercises to encourage participants to interact with each other in specific ways (such as having the participants tell each other one positive and one negative reaction that each has had of the other). Other forms of leaderless groups use self-administered evaluation forms and instruments as a source of feedback, with consultants working with group members outside of it (Gibb, 1964: 301–2).

Although research on this type of group has not been extensive, reviews of the empirical literature are generally favorable in their assessment of its effect.[17] Gibb (1975: 66), for instance, examined thirty-eight studies, twenty-one of which utilized programmed tapes. He found that although leader-led groups performed better in a majority of studies, there were frequent instances in which leaderless groups produced significantly better results. He was impressed with the fact that the leaderless groups usually showed less evidence of negative effects. Seligman and Desmond (1973: 82) were equivocal in their conclusion, finding that some groups functioned productively without a leader, while others did not.

One of the most instructive findings from the research stems from the Group Experience Project (Lieberman, Yalom, and Miles, 1973) discussed earlier. The directors of that project compared the effectiveness of ten different types of encounter technologies, including two tape-led leaderless groups. They found that one of the tape-led groups was the second most productive of any of the seventeen groups, fifteen of which had highly credentialled leaders (Lieberman, Yalom, and Miles, 1973: 119). In this group, members increased their sense of adequate or active coping strategies, viewed themselves as more lenient, saw more opportunities for open communication among their peers, and increased those values that focused on

the self (Lieberman, Yalom, and Miles, 1973. 128). Both tape-led groups in the project had extremely low levels of negative outcome.

If further research demonstrates that leaderless groups are equally or nearly as productive as those with professional leadership, the case for licensing the encounter group leader is considerably weakened, since their skills would not appear to be essential to positive outcomes and since leaderless groups are generally less dangerous. This line of reasoning follows that based on spontaneous remission for individual psychotherapy. It theorizes that the changes that are brought about in patients of therapy groups or participants of encounter groups are more a consequence of certain group properties than the activities of the group leader or therapist. Although the extant data is by no means dispositive of the issue, it is sufficient to justify resisting the conclusion that the therapist or group leader is all-important in bringing about positive results.

Other Influential Nonpractitioner-Related Variables. The psychotherapy literature provides other theory and research indicating that the traditional therapist and group leader are by no means the only important sources of influence in the therapeutic and growth process. In a comprehensive review of the quantitative research on psychotherapy, which covered 166 studies, Luborsky and his associates (1971), for instance, examined all factors influencing the outcome of psychotherapy. They found a high proportion of studies that emphasized the role of the patient in determining success or failure. Various studies showed that the patient's adequacy of personality functioning, motivation, expectation, intelligence, degree of anxiety, age, social class, education, and student status were all predictive of final outcome. The authors remarked that "possibly, as Astrup believes, . . . the patient's qualities are even more important for his improvement than the psychotherapy or other treatment he receives" (Luborsky et al., 1971: 149). In addition, Frank (1973: 199) has pointed out that therapist-patient similarity, especially with regard to values, is important to success.

Other studies indicate that group atmosphere may be more potent than the therapist in its effects on intrapersonal exploration, a process generally assumed to be strongly correlated with therapeutic outcome (Truax, 1961: 21–22). Numerous other researchers have commented on the variety of factors that are important to the psychotherapeutic process (see, for example, Bergin, 1971; Carkhuff, 1969; Garfield, 1971; Redlich and Freedman, 1966).[18]

Evidence from the encounter group field offers similar findings. In Gibb's (1975: 62) latest review of the literature, the following nonleader-related variables were identified as making major contributions to outcome variance: the macro-environment of the individual or group; the time-length of the group; the group state; the amount of functional feedback; and the amount of affective experiencing. In discussing the macro-environmental factors, Gibb (1975a: 287) argued that "there is increasing evidence that these factors are more powerful in determining change-maintenance than the within-training factors." He also observed that ecological factors such as geography, architecture, space, and seating arrangements may play a much more important role than group leaders have previously thought (Gibb, 1975a: 287–88).

The most persuasive evidence that other sources of influence besides the group leader have a strong impact comes from the extensive research on the influence of group pressure and norms. In the 1940s, Sherif (1947) documented the fact that group norms can significantly alter an individual's interpretation of visual perceptions; and in his now well-known and oft-cited experiments, Asch (1952) demonstrated that group pressure definitely had an effect upon people's willingness to stand by their judgment. Asch (1956) also showed that normal subjects would frequently falsify their visual perceptions of lines of different sizes in order to conform to a unanimously held group opinion. Hovland, Janis, and Kelley (1953) extended these findings to show that interpersonal and social judgments were similarly affected by group norms.

The idea that group norms may have a significant effect on encounter group outcomes was explored by Lieberman, Yalom, and Miles (1973) in the Group Experience Project. They found that final group norms were as accurate in predicting outcome as was the type of leadership, and that differing normative patterns were crucial to whether a group succeeded or not (Lieberman et al, 1973: 294). Interestingly, the creation of group norms did not appear to be strongly affected by the group leader. Lieberman and his associates found that group norms were associated with the expectations that group members had for their groups. Only rarely and with difficulty could these norms be reversed by a group leader.[19]

Related to the impact of group norms and pressure is the simple fact that group members may have a tremendous impact on each other in an encounter group. In exploring the sources of influence in a sensitivity training laboratory composed of six T-groups, Smith (1976) found that participants rated members of their own T-group as a more important source of influence than their trainers. In addition, he found that sources external to the member's group (other T-group members and trainers) were also a significant influence. He concluded that no single source could account for the changes that occur within encounter groups, stressing the fact that the average participant identified nine sources of influence. This conclusion is echoed by Bebout (1976: 5), whose research on the Talent in Interpersonal Explorations Project at Berkeley indicates that "group composition has as powerful an influence as does the style of leadership."

Conclusion. Evidence of the effectiveness of placebos, faith healing, spontaneous remission, leaderless groups, and other variables apart from the practitioner does not necessarily indicate that the professional has no influence. Rather, it raises two significant issues. First, psychotherapists may play a far smaller role than previously thought in determining whether clients improve. In statistical terminology, practitioners may account for only a small percentage of the variance. If so, regulations focusing on the practitioner will have only minimal impact. The public might be better protected by controlling who participates in traditional psychotherapy or encounter groups. Second, even if the practitioner is important, the evidence of the influence of such factors as the placebo should generate inquiry into whether traditional measures of therapeutic competence are valid.

Definitions of Competence
Few people have examined what is meant by the statement that a professional is qualified to practice. The typical assumption is that the practitioner is competent, although vagueness surrounds precisely what "competence" means. A person is usually assumed to be competent because he or she has had a specified amount of academic training and supervised experience, although why this should ensure competence is not specified. Ignored are the subtle questions of what precisely it is that professionals are supposed to do, and how well they do it. These two issues are more complex than is often realized and deserve further elaboration.

A determination must be made of what kind of outcomes will result when the services of a given practitioner are used. In the medical field these outcomes can be fairly specific, as in the case of performing appendectomies or removing tumors.

They may also be somewhat difficult to operationalize, as in assuring that a physician will be able to identify what is wrong with a patient. In the mental health field, outcome measures are very difficult to define and operationalize, though no less necessary if regulations are to be meaningful. Thus, it is essential to identify whether psychotherapists or encounter group leaders are likely to increase a person's level of self-confidence, self-awareness, ability to work effectively with subordinates, happiness, marital satisfaction, or whether and what other changes might be expected.

Significant disagreement is liable to result in choosing any set of outcomes as desirable, since the determination of mental health and illness is highly subjective and open to considerable variation. Without this delineation of potential outcomes, however, the possibility of informed choice for clients becomes meaningless. Without a clear picture of expected outcomes, a determination of what skills the practitioner needs to ensure them is also inherently impossible. Yet licensing laws, academic training programs, and professional associations have rarely, if ever, identified the outcomes they consider desirable.

A second problem that is generally ignored in discussions of competence is what level of competence is being established. Licensing laws are meant to protect the public from harm. A reasonable interpretation of this policy would be that even minimal competence need not be shown, so long as a practitioner could guarantee that no client would be hurt or injured. Given this interpretation, a licensing board would be concerned with whether an applicant for a license knew the limitations of his or her ability and whether highly dangerous procedures would be employed. On the other hand, licensing laws have generally been interpreted as requiring at least minimal competence. On this policy basis, the questions of a licensing board to its applicants would be somewhat different. As well as preventing harm, it would want to know whether an applicant can reasonably be relied upon to produce at least some positive impact in at least some situations. The areas of competence might vary from individual to individual, but each person would be required to have several areas of competence. The actual policy of most licensing laws—especially in psychology and medicine—is aimed at the guarantee of maximal competence; that is, the requirements are meant to ensure that the public is served by practitioners who are highly competent in many areas and who can provide excellent, as opposed to mediocre, results. On this basis, professional associations have argued for doctoral degrees as a prerequisite to practice. It is clear, then, that the standards required for practice will vary radically, depending on one's interpretation of what level of competence is being mandated.

The third and final issue in defining the term competence is difficult to frame as a concise question. There are many ways in which even minimal competence can be defined:

1. Minimal competence is always bringing about at least a modestly positive result in any area of practice without ever risking harm to anybody.
2. Minimal competence is bringing about at least modestly positive results in some areas with at least half of one's clients, without ever harming anybody seriously, although several clients might endure some minor negative effects.
3. Minimal competence is, on average, bringing about modestly positive results in most areas. A modestly positive average might be obtained through helping all clients somewhat, or it might result from helping some clients tremendously, while doing severe damage to a small percentage of others.

Each definition carries a significantly different implication about who is deemed qualified. Under the first or second, for instance, many exceptionally brilliant therapists, who achieved cures where the average practitioner failed completely, would not be licensed if they occasionally made a few serious errors. Researchers and theorists might be denied a license, despite potentially significant contributions to the field. Several internationally known psychotherapists have had the reputation of being high-risk, high-gain, and yet these individuals would be forbidden the right to practice.

These aspects of defining competency have been almost totally ignored in the literature, yet upon them hinges the soundness of all regulatory procedures. Before any decision can be made on appropriate standards and criteria, prior clarification must exist on the policy considerations underlying the definition of competence. Without this clarification, one will not know what it is that practitioners are meant to do, how well they actually do it, what level of competence they have achieved, or the percentage of clients who will be the beneficiaries of competent practice.

Standards and Criteria for Minimal Competence

No matter how small or large a role psychotherapists play, undoubtedly there are certain skills, personal qualities, and other characteristics that will enhance their effectiveness. Identifying these competencies is important in the regulatory process, especially in the professional field, even though the fact of competence may not ensure effectiveness in specific instances. Since the concern of licensing boards has been to identify minimal competence, an attempt will be made first to isolate those skills necessary for successfully performing at some minimal level. Two primary sources of information will be relied upon. First is the opinion of theoreticians and practitioners. Second is the findings of the social science research.

Until recently professional opinion has been heavily relied upon in framing regulations. To some extent this has been necessary, since adequate empirical research has been lacking. Today the situation is changing. The tools and sophistication of research have improved, and the amount of research is now extensive enough to warrant some degree of reliance upon it.[20] Where research and professional opinion are in accord concerning required competencies, considerable faith may be placed in their findings. Where opposite conclusions are reached, caution is advisable.

The types of skills and other qualifications necessary for minimally competent practice may conveniently be broken down into several distinct categories. Obviously critical are certain personal qualities and characteristics, such as empathy and psychological-mindedness. Equally important, at least in the eyes of most theorists, are the possession of certain technical and theoretical knowledge. Finally, diagnostic ability, though variously defined, is generally considered essential.[21]

Personal Qualities and Characteristics. Personal qualities and characteristics include interpersonal skills, such as the ability to empathize or handle conflict, and internal states, such as level of self-confidence and degree of self-acceptance. Virtually all theorists and practitioners agree that at least some of these qualities and characteristics are essential for competence and success.

The psychotherapeutic relationship is replete with statements about the importance of personality characteristics. The Rogerian qualities of empathy, warmth, and genuineness have been stressed in particular. These three traits are regarded as extremely important in the writings of Freud, Fromm-Reichmann, Rank, Adler,

and most of the phenomenologically-oriented psychoanalysts (Truax and Mitchell, 1971: 314). In addition, many behaviorists agree that these qualities are essential as reinforcers or in other capacities (Truax and Mitchell, 1971: 314). A study involving 83 practicing therapists of at least eight different therapeutic approaches found that empathy was rated as the most important of twelve variables (Raskin, 1974).

Holt and Luborsky's (1958, vol. 2,: 328–66) national survey of expert opinion on the personality requisites for psychotherapists indicates that psychological-mindedness, empathy, objectivity, sensitivity, flexibility, tact, and vitality are considered important characteristics for success. Holt and Luborsky have stated that three primary factors are necessary for competent practice: (1) an introspective orientation that allows therapists to understand and empathize with their patients; (2) an intellectual predisposition that allows and encourages intellectual examination of one's self, feelings, and behavior, as well as aiding insight; and (3) a relativistic perspective that accepts and values individual as well as cultural differences.[22]

An excellent overall picture of the ideal personality of the psychotherapist is provided by Jerome Frank (1973: 184–85, footnotes omitted) in his summary of the judgments of practitioners in general:[23]

The good therapist emerges . . . as a good person in general—he is intelligent and responsible, has good judgment, and is creative. He is also judged to be sincere, energetic, and able to display controlled warmth to his patients, that is, to let himself become somewhat emotionally involved without losing his objectivity. Moreover, the type of relationship he offers his patients probably is consistent with his general pattern of social behavior.[24]

The importance attached to personality is borne out in scientific surveys of practitioner opinion. Meehl (1960: 120), for instance, found that 43 percent of more than 150 therapists considered warmth and sympathy more important than an "accurate causal understanding of the client's difficulty." Over three quarters also believed that the personality of the therapist was more important than theoretical beliefs and knowledge. Reviews of the theoretical literature (Truax and Carkhuff, 1967: 25) and questionnaire surveys of practitioners (Raskin, 1974) indicate that personality characteristics such as empathy, especially accurate empathy, are important no matter what particular theory a practitioner subscribes to.

In the encounter field, the primary importance of personality characteristics is also evident. Batchelder and Hardy (1968: 113–14), Rogers (1970), Massarik (1972), Bebout (1974), and Benne and his associates (1975), for instance, all stress such factors as personal warmth, empathy, self-insight and awareness, creativity, caring, confrontational ability, and nondefensiveness. The primacy of these attributes over technical skills and diagnostic ability is especially stressed by Rogers (1970).

Empirical Evidence from Traditional Psychotherapy. Extensive research exists on the relationship of personal qualities and interpersonal skills to psychotherapeutic outcome. One of the initial and most brilliant studies in this area was that of Fiedler (1950 and 1950a), who explored the concept of an ideal therapeutic relationship and then compared therapists of three different schools of thought (psychoanalytic, nondirective, and Adlerian) to determine how well they approximated this ideal. The definition of the ideal relationship posited by experts in the field was very similar to any good interpersonal relationship (Fiedler, 1950: 244). Fiedler (1950a: 442–43) found that experienced therapists could not be distinguished on the basis of their techniques, although they did resemble the ideal more

than inexperienced therapists. He also argued that his data supported the contention that evaluation and diagnosis were not essential to successful psychotherapy.

Carl Rogers (1957) has been the strongest proponent of the notion that the necessary and sufficient conditions of psychotherapy may only involve personal qualities. In his view the therapist must be congruent, genuine, and integrated over a period of time in the therapeutic relationship, must experience an unconditional positive regard and nonpossessive warmth for the client, and must also be able to empathically understand the client's internal frame of reference and to communicate that understanding to some minimal degree. If these criteria are met, the therapist need not possess other skills for effective therapy to occur. In other words, Rogers is in agreement with Fiedler on the lack of necessity of evaluation and diagnosis, and he also asserts that theoretical knowledge and technical skills are superfluous.

Shortly after Rogers first expounded his theory on the core characteristics of the good psychotherapist, Whitehorn and Betz (see, for example, Whitehorn and Betz, 1960; Betz, 1962) began publishing a series of studies at Johns Hopkins on psychiatrists who were successful in their work with schizophrenic patients. They found that the more successful psychiatrists were very warm and sought to understand their patients in their own uniquenesses, whereas the less successful therapists tended to relate impersonally to their patients and focused upon psychopathology. Further studies suggested that the more successful psychiatrists had characteristics very similar to the Rogerian ideal.

The work of Rogers, Whitehorn, and Betz has precipitated a veritable deluge of research and commentary. Truax and Mitchell (1971) analyzed fourteen studies that examined all three of Rogers's hypothesized characteristics, another fourteen that specifically examined empathy, eight that examined genuineness, and thirteen that examined nonpossessive warmth. Based on their analysis of these studies, they concluded that Rogers's and Whitehorn and Betz's theses held up with a wide variety of therapists and counselors, patients, illnesses, and settings (Truax and Mitchell, 1971: 310).[25]

A number of people have issued sharp challenges to these conclusions.[26] Meltzoff and Kornreich (1970: 330–35) in particular do not believe that the client-centered research justifies such definitive conclusions. They argue that the research simply does not allow conclusive interpretation, that many of the studies involved counseling and guidance—not psychotherapy—and that a variety of measures were used, especially of empathy, a number of which were of questionable validity. They also point out that many of the therapists used in the studies were fairly young, frequently of student status, and had worked with very few patients.

Poor research designs posed further limitations on the making of conclusions, claimed Meltzoff and Kornreich, since many of the studies did not control for the length of training, experience, and other factors that might have proved equally powerful predictors of outcome in their own right. In recent years one of the central measures involved in many of these studies (the Truax Accurate Empathy Scale) has come under attack, and an increasing number of studies have been conducted that do not show any correlations between Rogerian conditions and positive outcome.[27] On the other hand, proponents of empathy as an essential criterion cite an ever-increasing body of research that does support their position,[28] and it seems fairly indisputable that empathy is a most critical variable in the therapeutic process, though various researchers may choose to measure it in different ways.

Apart from these core personality characteristics, which are widely regarded as important to the therapeutic process, a number of other traits and personal qualities have received attention from researchers. On the whole, a review of the findings yields mixed results. Meltzoff and Kornreich (1970: 294–98) conclude that the sex of the therapist makes little difference. Likewise, the hypothesis that specific vocational interest patterns would discriminate effective therapists from ineffective remains but a hypothesis because of conflicting research findings (Meltzoff and Kornreich, 1970: 306). Typical variables such as extroversion, mental health, relaxedness, and enthusiasm are far too generalized, subject to multiple interpretations, and have mixed empirical findings with regard to their importance (Meltzoff and Kornreich, 1970: 306–11). Even patient-therapist similarity has not been a useful predictor, no matter what personality dimensions are chosen, and the null hypothesis is probably the most tenable, according to Meltzoff and Kornreich (1970: 325). Similarly, research on the relationship of therapist-liking-of-the-patient as a variable has yielded weak results, largely because of the difficulty in establishing a common definition of the word "liking" (Meltzoff and Kornreich, 1970: 329).

While Meltzoff and Kornreich are pessimistic about the research findings, other reviewers believe that more definitive conclusions are warranted, at least in some areas. For example, Lester Luborsky and his associates (1971), who have had a long-term interest in establishing therapist factors related to change in psychotherapy, believe that level of experience, particular skills, and interest patterns are all directly related to effectiveness. In opposition to Meltzoff and Kornreich, they argue that empathy and other related qualities, as well as therapist-patient similarity in values, attitudes, interests, and social class are critical factors.

It is difficult to reconcile these conflicting points of view, especially because the quality and quantity of research lends itself to multiple interpretations. Nonetheless, the comparison of competent psychiatric residents with poorer functioning residents portrayed by Holt and Luborsky (1958: 283) represents a good summary of what the empirical research has to say about the effective versus ineffective therapist:

The main differences between the two groups may be summmarized in a thumbnail sketch: The better residents were more intelligent, sensitive, and independent in thinking and judgment. They could be warmer but also more self-contained and even-tempered, and they expressed themselves more appropriately. Their relationships with patients and others with whom they worked were better; interest in their work and learning to do it came more easily to them. Through greater stability, maturity, and self-insight, they were self-developing people.

Empirical Evidence from the Encounter Group Literature. The amount of research investigating the relationship between leader characteristics and behavior in a group with resultant participant change is not great. As recently as 1971 Cooper and Mangham (1971: 122–123) had concluded that little attempt had been made to establish what role the group leader played in bringing about change. Gibb's (1975) recent review, which found eighteen studies examining leadership style, indicates that the paucity of research is slowly disappearing. According to his analysis, the amount of warmth, support, and caring exhibited by the leader was critical to learning and positive change. Gibb notes that this provides corroboration of the research on therapist behavior. Beside these main variables, Gibb found additional studies relating self-concept (Mates, 1972), tendency to reward and punish (Bolman, 1971), attractiveness (Cooper, 1969), being process-oriented versus member-oriented (Pino, 1969), and level of self-disclosure (Culbert, 1968) with outcome.

An analysis of the two most important studies of encounter groups and several other individual studies adds flesh to the outline provided by Gibb. In the Group Experience Project (Lieberman, Yalom, and Miles, 1973: 226–67) the most effective leadership style consisted of a combination of factors. Most important, the research indicated that the successful leader must be a highly caring person— the more caring, the better. Similarly, the more a leader provided a conceptual framework or some other way of making sense out of what was happening in the group ("meaning attribution"), the better off the group was. In addition, a moderate amount of "emotional stimulation," in which the group leader confronts participants, shares personal values and feelings, and actively exhorts them to change, is valuable. Finally, a moderate amount of "executive function," which involves setting limits, establishing schedules, and suggesting procedures, is optimum for positive outcomes. Conversely, less effective leadership resulted from very low or high stimulation and executive behavior, and from too little caring and meaning-attribution.

Obviously these four leadership qualities can be combined differently, resulting in a variety of leadership styles. Lieberman, Yalom, and Miles (1973) found that particular styles led to differing outcomes. Thus, "aggressive-stimulators," who were characterized by high charisma, frequent challenging and confrontation, and authoritarian control, had groups in which more peak experiences occurred, but participants in these groups also endured the most casualties and showed a general decrease in self-esteem. Such leaders were forceful, impatient, and did not hesitate to apply considerable pressure on a person to make a breakthrough. They did not seem to differentiate individuals in a group, apparently believing that the same methods were appropriate for everybody. "Love leaders," on the other hand, produced almost the opposite results through a combination of high caring and changing their behavior on the basis of the needs of the individual group members.

The findings from the Talent in Interpersonal Explorations (TIE) Project are remarkably similar. Bebout (1976) concluded that the most successful leaders were a combination of a number of styles, which he characterized as "warm energizers," "heavy workers," and "soft protectors." The warm energizers were emotionally involved with group members, flexible, playful as well as serious, able to express anger as well as warmth, and when they confronted participants, demonstrated caring rather than abrasiveness. The heavy workers saw themselves as therapists, focused on problems, and took their work seriously. The soft protectors were very warm, maternally nurturant, and not hostile. According to Bebout (1976: 5) the worst leaders had exactly the opposite configuration of leadership styles.[29]

Technical Skills and Methods of Treatment.

Experience has taught me to keep away from therapeutic 'methods' as much as from diagnoses. The enormous variation among individuals and their neuroses has set before me the ideal of approaching each case with a minimum of prior assumptions. . . . In reality, everything depends on the man and little or nothing on the method. [Jung, 1970: 81-82.]

Although the literature is replete with therapeutic recipes, very few attempts have been made to find out if they truly have any bearing on outcome. . . . Paracelsus, the eminent Renaissance alchemist and physician, recommended the following salve for burns: "It consisted of the fat of very old wild hogs and bears heated half an hour in red wine, then dropped into cold water, which was next skimmed and the fat rubbed up with roasted angle worms and moss from the skull of a person hung, scraped off during the increase of the moon, to which were added bloodstone, the dried brain the wild hog, red sandal-wood and a portion of a genuine mummy." . . . If this concoction now sounds quaint to us, how will descriptions of psychotherapy, as it is now prac-

ticed, sound four centuries from now? We are now at the point where we can begin to separate out the bear grease from the roasted angle worms of psychotherapy. [Meltzoff and Kornreich, 1970: 203, footnotes omitted.]

Technical skills and methods of treatment cover a wide range in psychotherapy. Technical skills vary from the highly specific, as illustrated by the relaxation techniques of the behaviorists, to the generalized and ill-defined, as in psychoanalytic free association. Most major systems of psychotherapy employ at least ten different techniques, including counter-conditioning, extinction, reward and punishment, social learning, and interpretation (Bergin and Strupp, 1972: 13). The encounter field has a similar array of techniques oriented to group process, such as the use of the "hot seat." Methods of treatment include all schools of psychotherapy that have developed methods based on their particular school, such as traditional psychoanalysis, logotherapy, rational-emotive therapy, and the more recent existential psychotherapies. In the encounter field the number of methods is even larger, since schools of thought are still more fragmented.

The major treatises on psychotherapy and psychiatry emphasize the importance of mastering various techincal skills and methods of treatment (see, for example, Kubie, 1950; Redlich and Freedman, 1966; Wolberg, 1967; Yalom, 1975). Professional associations and certifying bodies generally assume that such skills are necessary for therapeutic effectiveness.[30] Within the psychotherapeutic field most practitioners believe that technical and methodological skills are crucial. The number of different treatment modalities is perhaps the strongest testimony for this, although Garrison (1921) has argued that "whenever many different remedies are used for a disease, it usually means that we know very little about treating the disease, which is also true of a remedy when it is vaunted as a panacea or cure-all for many diseases." Psychoanalysts stress the importance of their competency in analytic techniques, such as the ability to help a person free associate and the ability to make depth interpretations. Gestalt therapists stress the importance of reflecting and exaggerating mannerisms. Behavior modifiers attribute their success to techniques such as reciprocal inhibition or selective reinforcement.

In the field of encounter groups a variety of opinions exists as to what skills are necessary for competency. To some extent the variations depend upon the end of the encounter group spectrum being examined. At the T-group end, theoretical knowledge and technical skills are assumed to be more important. Perhaps the clearest explication of competencies in this area has been presented by Lippitt and his associates (1975), who have isolated seven areas in which professionals need to be competent: (1) diagnosis, including a variety of abilities from that of taking a system point of view to having a broad view of multiple levels and kinds of data; (2) entry and contract development, ranging from the ability to assess one's own strengths and weaknesses to the ability to reject nonviable contracts; (3) design, implying a knowledge of a variety of designs and their likely effects, as well as the ability to develop designs spontaneously; (4) intervention, involving flexibility in utilizing various styles and tools, patience, and the ability to handle hostility; (5) ethical decision-making, ranging from awareness of one's own values to insight on how these values affect others; (6) continuity, follow-up support, and termination, including the ability to terminate relationships appropriately and other abilities such as helping participants transfer learnings; and (7) peer team-building, having to do with working collaboratively with others.

At the personal growth end of the psychotherapy spectrum, certain skills are generally regarded as necessary, while others arouse strong debate. Rogers (1970: 43–68) has attempted to delineate the essential features of what is important in facilitating personal growth in a group. He stresses first the climate-setting function, which involves attentive listening, creating psychologically safe environment, and attempting to "be with" each participant. Accepting the group where it is and having a high degree of empathy with individual members are also critical. Rogers finds that confrontation of discrepant behaviors and feedback of perceptions and feelings is useful. He tends to avoid using exercises and does not make interpretive or process comments.

Rogers regards the following types of behavior as nonfacilitative: (1) pushing a group or otherwise manipulating and making rules for it; (2) judging failure or success by dramatics (how many people have cried); (3) advocating one and only one approach to change (such as Synanon with its dogma of unrelenting attack); (4) having inordinate personal problems; and (5) being highly interpretive.

While the majority of theorists and practitioners believe that technical skills constitute an important source of therapeutic effectiveness, several claim that they are largely irrelevant. Carl Rogers (1973, 1965, 1962, 1957) has been the most outspoken in this regard, arguing that "the techniques of the various therapies are relatively unimportant except to the extent that they serve as channels for fulfilling one of the conditions [of empathy, warmth, and unconditional positive regard]" (Rogers, 1957: 1020). He also asserts that there is no essential value in such techniques as interpretation, free association, analysis of dreams, and the use of hypnosis (Rogers, 1957: 103).

In the empirical literature on traditional psychotherapy, considerable evidence exists that the use of techniques and methodologies based on ideological schools of thought are relatively unimportant to therapeutic effectiveness, at least for minimal levels of competence. Initial evidence for this view comes from the classic studies of Fiedler (1950 and 1950a) at mid-century. He found that therapists of various schools and who use different techniques did not differ in their description of the ideal therapeutic relationship. In addition, the ability to portray accurately that relationship was more a function of "expertness" than of particular theoretical allegiance. When judges examined tape-recorded therapy interviews of novices and experts in three widely differing modes of therapy, Fiedler found that expert therapists of all three schools created a relationship more closely approximating the ideal than relationships created by novices. The relationship created by experts of one school resembled the relationship created by experts of the other schools more nearly than it did the relationship created by novices from the same school.

A study by Strupp (1955) five years later provided added confirmation of this finding. Strupp attempted to determine whether professional affiliation and experience level were important determinants of treatment technique. Using Bales's system of interaction process analysis, he examined the responses of twenty-five psychiatrists, seven psychologists, and nine psychiatric social workers of varying levels of experience. The resultant profiles were remarkably similar. The only statistically significant difference was the psychiatric social workers' predilection for reassurance. Strupp concluded that professional affiliation exerted a relatively minor influence upon the treatment techniques of the different professional groups.

When practitioners are asked to describe their actual practice, as opposed to stating what they believe is important in effective therapy, therapeutic technique loses much of its claimed importance. Interesting confirmation of this assertion comes from a recent study by Henry, Sims, and Spray (1971: 119–23) of the public and private lives of more than 200 psychotherapists of widely differing orientations and training backgrounds. The authors wanted to determine whether the techniques of the practitioners corresponded with the techniques they were exposed to during training. Of eight different types of professionals few agreed that therapists rely primarily on their formally learned skills and techniques (Henry, Sims, and Spray, 1973: 122). The group that agreed most was the psychoanalytically oriented social workers, but their rate of agreement was only 17 percent (Henry, Sims, and Spray, 1973: 128). Since very few items were agreed with by more than a majority of practitioners, the authors concluded that psychotherapists do not rely upon any basic technique or set of techniques (Henry, Sims, and Spray, 1973: 122). They also conclude that considerable similarity exists among the practices of professionals of widely differing persuasions, and that therapeutic ideology makes no difference in the actual behavior of traditional psychotherapists.

Research on encounter groups has come to a similar conclusion. In the Group Experience Project, Lieberman, Yalom, and Miles (1973) found that the theoretical orientation and school of the group leader was unrelated to productivity. Of ten different encounter technologies, a Gestalt leader facilitated one of the most productive groups, while the least productive group was conducted by another Gestalt leader. Similarly, a group led by a transactional analyst ranked next to last. Lieberman, Yalom, and Miles (1973: 242) concluded that "whatever the labels of the diverse encounter leaders, the findings are indisputable that conventional categories of leader orientation are poor predictors of leader behavior."

The extent of use of structured exercises[31] also did not differentiate among outcome classifications, except for the fact that the more exercises a group leader used, the more likely there would be fewer high learners in the group. All groups that employed relatively few exercises produced some gain, while greater variability existed in the outcomes of those groups that used many exercises. The authors' conservative interpretation of the data is that "exercises are irrelevant to producing positive change . . . and . . . may be counterproductive" (Lieberman, Yalom, and Miles, 1973: 412).

The findings from these studies are not unique, according to those who have conducted extensive reviews of the research. Meltzoff and Kornreich's (1970) monumental review of the empiric literature found little evidence of systematic differences in effectiveness of most schools of psychotherapy, except that recent research had indicated that systematic desensitization was superior to various verbal therapies whose goals were insight and self-understanding. Even there, however, they noted that the comparative utility of behavior therapy was only evident in highly specialized cases such as phobias and focalized anxieties. They conclude that "there is no current evidence that one traditional method is more successful than another in modifying psychopathology, alleviating symptoms, or improving general adjustment" (Meltzoff and Kornreich, 1970: 200). Likewise with therapist style and technique, Meltzoff and Kornreich (1970: 203) note that few studies have examined whether these relate to therapeutic outcome.

Lester Luborsky and his associates have conducted several excellent reviews of the research to determine the impact of technique and method on outcome. Their findings are negative. In examining the research on psychoanalytic therapy, Luborsky and Spence (1971) discovered that analytic technique varied considerably from analyst to analyst, which one would not expect if techniques such as free association and analysis of the transference were critical to effectiveness. In a review of the quantitative research on factors influencing therapeutic outcome,

Luborsky and several other associates (1971: 154–56) found that schools of treatment usually made no measurable difference and were likely to be less potent than patient and therapist factors, although the research in this area was generally insufficient.

In a more recent review (Luborsky et al., 1975), the number of studies examining the effectiveness of various schools and types of psychotherapy had increased substantially, but the conclusions to be drawn from the research had not changed significantly. When individual psychotherapy was compared with group psychotherapy, when time-limited therapy was compared with unlimited therapy, when client-centered therapy was compared to other traditional therapies, and even when behavior therapy was compared with other therapies, a large majority of the studies showed no significant difference in effectiveness.

Two recent reviews suggest that the one treatment that was believed to be more effective than others—at least in some situations—namely behavior therapy, may not be more effective after all. Bergin and Suinn (1975) discuss several recent studies that compared behavior therapy with psychoanalytic therapy and found no differences between them on any of a variety of target symptoms rated by an independent assessor, on estimates of more general social and work functioning, and on global ratings of outcome (Sloane et al., 1975). The reviewers suggest that "the supposed major differences between the behavioral and traditional insight therapies are not as great as was once believed, either in outcome or process" (Bergin and Suinn, 1975: 512). In explanation the authors theorize that the earlier zeal in favor of behavior therapy was based upon misleading studies with minimally disturbed volunteers.

Perhaps the most interesting review of therapeutic techniques has been conducted by Gene Glass (1976). Rather than focusing on significant differences alone, he also tried to determine the magnitude of the effect that different types of therapy had. "Effect size" was defined as the "mean difference between the treated and control subjects divided by the standard deviation of the control group" (Glass, 1976: 13). Thus, an effect size of +1 indicates that a person at the mean of the control group would be expected to rise to the eighty-fourth percentile of the control group after treatment.

Using this method, Glass compared ten different types of therapy. The most effective type of therapy was systematic desensitization, which had an effect size of 0.91, based on approximately 100 studies. Next was rational-emotive therapy at 0.77, followed quite closely by behavior modification at 0.76. Psychodynamic therapy (that is, Freudian-like therapy, excluding psychoanalysis) averaged approximately 0.6 of a standard deviation. The last-place finisher was Gestalt therapy, with an average effect size of only 0.25 standard deviation, which Glass (1976: 22) noted was roughly equal to his estimate of the size of the placebo effect.

These differences in effect sizes seemingly argue for the greater effectiveness of particular types of therapy, but Glass is careful to note that duration, severity of problem, type of outcome, and other variables of potential influence were not controlled for. When Glass (1976: 31) grouped the ten therapy types into two broad classes—differentiating between "behavioral" and "nonbehavioral" therapies—and controlled for such factors as the time the outcome measures were made (long- or short-term follow-up), he came to some extremely provocative conclusions:

Despite the fact that libraries can be filled with volumes in which the theoretical and technical differences between behavioral and nonbehavioral therapies are meticulously detailed, despite the fervor with which each side of the controversy praises its own position and denounces the opposition, despite the fact that most academic psychologists believe that "research" has proven the superiority of behavioral therapies, the evidence shows no difference in effectiveness when we sum across the board.

Theoretical and Technical Knowledge. The possession of specific theoretical and technical knowledge is generally considered necessary for effective functioning as a psychotherapist. In traditional psychotherapy this is especially evident from reading basic texts in the field (see, for example, Kubie, 1950; Redlich and Freedman, 1966; Wolberg, 1967; Yalom, 1975). It is also reflected in the demand of mental health professionals that practitioners be required to possess advanced academic degrees. The type of knowledge thought to be essential varies. For traditional psychotherapy, psychiatrists stress an understanding of human biology, neurology, and psychopharmacology; psychologists stress personality dynamics and interpersonal behavior; and social workers believe that a theoretical understanding of environmental influences on behavior is essential. In the encounter group field leading practitioners have been especially adamant about the importance of group dynamics, relevant theory, and an adequate understanding of human behavior and group processes (see, for example, IAASS Task Force, 1974; Lakin, 1969; Massarik, 1972; Mintz, 1971: 273–80). In addition, each school of therapy usually insists that its adherents possess a thorough grounding in the particular theory espoused by that school.

The number of theorists and practitioners who believe that theoretical and technical knowledge are unimportant is not great. Carl Rogers (1957) is one of the few. He argues that "intellectual training and the acquiring of information has . . . many valuable results—but becoming a therapist is not one of those results" (Rogers, 1957: 101). According to Rogers (1970), such knowledge is also not useful for encounter group leaders. Many of the client-centered therapists and group leaders subscribe to this view (see, for example, Clark, 1970: 881–82).

A review of the empirical literature on this subject yields virtually no research directly in point. Surprisingly, comparisons of the effectiveness of therapists with a knowledge of personality theory and without, with an understanding of neurology and without, or studies of the importance of other areas of knowledge are conspicuously absent. Indirectly, however, evidence exists indicating that theoretical and technical knowledge is largely irrelevant to effectiveness, at least for minimal levels of competence, and perhaps for higher levels as well.

There is, first of all, the fact that most of the psychological theories relevant to therapeutic practice have not yet been shown to be valid, let alone to be of value (see, for example, Nagel, 1959, on psychoanalysis). A considerable body of research, discussed later in this chapter, demonstrates that paraprofessionals and laypeople are highly effective and that their levels of competence compare favorably with highly trained experts. In roughly half the studies, in fact, nonprofessionals achieve superior results on a variety of outcome measures, despite their lack of education and despite their lack of knowledge in the field of personality dynamics.

Further evidence, also discussed at a later point in this chapter, indicates that possession of academic degrees is not especially helpful in improving therapeutic competence. The fact that certain and that others can be trained in a minimum of time to function effectively provides additional support for the notion that theoretical and technical knowledge is not a crucial variable in the psychotheranot a crucial variable in the psychotherapeutic or encounter group process.

These arguments do not mean that theoretical and technical knowledge is totally irrelevant. It seems clear that therapeutic effectiveness can be improved for some people at some level through an increase in their theoretical or technical understanding. If for no other reason this is true because as long as both therapist and patient believe a theory to be true, it may help, even if essentially incorrect (Frank, 1962). Which specific areas of knowledge are most important remains an unexamined issue, however. On the other hand, there is strong reason to doubt whether theoretical and technical knowledge is essential to minimal levels of competence. Even at the highest levels, it may be helpful, but not critical. Unfortunately the paucity of research exploring the broad question of the relevance of theory to practice prevents definitive conclusions about these issues.

Diagnostic Ability. The assumed importance of diagnostic ability as part of the psychotherapist's armamentarium hardly needs substantiation.[32] Historically accurate diagnosis has been assumed to be necessary.[33] Menninger (1963: 333) states that "diagnostic assessment *is* treatment," and Redlich and Freedman (1966: 247) comment that "diagnosis . . . provides the necessary focus for therapeutic intervention."

Whether diagnostic skills are in fact essential for the effectively functioning therapist, however, is currently a hotly contested issue. While traditionalists assert that diagnosis is critical, and the American Psychiatric Association touts the value of its revised nomenclature, practitioners such as Rogers (1957: 101) assert that effective therapy does not depend upon an accurate psychological diagnosis of the client, and philosophers such as Niebuhr (1955: 47) maintain that scientific investigations of past behavior cannot become the basis of prediction of future behavior.

Much of the problem and much of the argument over the value of diagnosis stems from misunderstandings and disagreements over the meaning of the term itself. There is no agreement as to how to properly define the word. There is argument over the purpose of diagnosis—what it is supposed to accomplish. There is confusion about the subject matter and methods of diagnosis. And there is confusion over the different stages of diagnosis.

Menninger (1963: 9–35) points out that a large part of the history of the use of the word diagnosis has consisted of its being considered a naming process—that is, to diagnose is to name something. Specifically, it is to name the disease from which a patient is suffering. According to Menninger, this represents a narrow and misleading view of the word and fails to elucidate the heart of the diagnostic process. Preferable is a broader and more basic definition:

To diagnose is to differentiate, to distinguish, to designate. It is to recognize, to have knowledge of, or to come to an understanding of. [Menninger, 1963: 36.][34]

Diagnosis may have many purposes and uses. Meehl (1973: 91) states that diagnosis is important in three broad areas. First, there is formal diagnosis. This corresponds to the naming process that Menninger has argued constitutes a too narrow view of the term. The purpose of formal diagnosis is to attach a nosological label to the patient's symptoms. A patient's behaviors and inner states are measured and analyzed, and the presenting symptoms are classified as "schizophrenic," "involutional melancholia," or some other category within a classification scheme such as the American Psychiatric Association's *Diagnostic and Statistical Manual of Mental Disorders* (APA Comm. on Nomen. and Stats., 1968).

A second purpose is prognosis. Here the aim is to determine what will happen to the patient over the course of time. In addition, prognosis attempts to establish the proper form of therapy and to ascertain how the patient should be treated. Finally, there is personality assessment, which may be phenotypic or genotypic. The former involves a description of the surface features of a patient's behaviors, while the latter attempts to discover the underlying psychodynamics of this overt behavior.[35]

These uses of diagnosis for psychotherapeutic purposes have their encounter group equivalents. Thus, diagnostic ability is said to be important in selecting participants for a group. Leaders are concerned about identifying those types of people who are likely to have an injurious or harmful experience in a group. Some leaders believe that personality assessment is important in constructing a group that will be of maximum utility. The ability to assess and understand group dynamics is also considered a necessary skill.

The methods and tools for performing psychodiagnosis have considerable variability. Projective tests such as the Rorschach, Draw-a-Person, or the Thematic Apperception Test may be used. Inventories such as the Minnesota Multiphasic Personality Inventory, and intelligence tests such as the Wechsler-Bellevue, are also available. Observer ratings of various behaviors constitute yet another method. Perhaps most common, however, is the individual judgment of the clinician using an internal frame of reference based on some standard psychiatric nomenclature. Since it is the clinician's judgment that is most at issue, the ensuing analysis will focus on the extent to which this type of diagnostic ability is necessary to perform as a competent therapist or group leader.[36]

A Note on Reliability and Validity. In evaluating whether diagnostic skill is necessary to therapeutic effectiveness, the concepts of validity and reliability come into play. Whether a diagnostic system is valid is perhaps the most important question that can be asked of it (Lyman, 1971: 21). Of the different types of validity that the American Psychological Association and others recognize (see American Psychological Association et al., 1974), those that are criterion-related are critical to this discussion. These include "concurrent" validity, which determines whether a given test or diagnosis is able to predict other sets of observations or scores about the person at the same time; and "predictive" validity, which concerns the ability of a test or diagnosis to predict future performance, behavior, or events. Translated into common parlance, one wants to know whether mental health professionals are able to identify who are mentally ill (and who are healthy), and from what illnesses they suffer. If diagnosis is to be meaningful, diagnosticians must be able to predict at least something about a patient's future behavior and the course of the illness. Finally, diagnosis is generally thought to provide a basis for deciding what treatment a person will receive, and which treatment is supposed to represent the best choice available.

The reliability of psychiatric or psychological diagnoses is also critical in determining the relationship of diagnostic ability to performance.[37] Psychiatric classifications are meant to measure enduring personality patterns. If a therapist diagnoses a patient as paranoid schizophrenic at one point in time, then rediagnosis a short time later should yield the same diagnostic classification. The degree to which this occurs is known as test-retest reliability. Low reliability indicates that a therapist is being arbitrary in his or her determination, which implies that diagnostic ability is not important.

Similarly, two different therapists who diagnose the same patient should theoretically arrive at the same conclusions as to what the patient is suffering from, what type of therapy is recommended, and what the prognosis of the patient is. If the chances of this happening are low, then the diagnostic system is said to have low interobserver reliability, and again the value of the diagnostic system is called

into question. A further indication of low reliability occurs if the diagnoses of different samples drawn from the same population are not in substantial agreement. Thus, the percentage of patients diagnosed as psychotic at similar mental hospitals should be roughly equal. Wide variations would indicate diagnostic unreliability.

A Review of the Empirical Research. As Menninger (1963) has pointed out, the history of diagnosis has vacillated between the desire to classify and the desire to understand. Research on the reliability and validity of diagnosis as understanding is subsumed under the research on empathy. Its importance is reasonably well documented. Research on diagnosis as classification presents somewhat different findings.

Attempts to classify may use phenotypic or genotypic methods. That is, they may describe surface behaviors, or they may be concerned with explanations of that behavior in terms of underlying dynamics. Phenotypic classifications stress what a person does, while genotypic stress what a person is. Genotypic classification is inferential in nature—causes of behavior are inferred whose existence may not be definitively proved. The existence of the Oedipus complex, for instance, cannot be empirically demonstrated, although various hypotheses following from its assumed existence may strengthen belief in the concept. It is the research on genotypic diagnosis that has stirred the most controversy and put the value of diagnosis for therapeutic purposes most in doubt.

Much of the research, which is discussed below, has centered around the value of the nosological system of the American Psychiatric Association and the ability of psychiatrists and psychologists to distinguish from which, if any, emotional illness a person is suffering. On the whole, the results are quite disappointing: the typical therapist is not very reliable in making fine distinctions, and is only moderately reliable in making gross distinctions (normal versus neurotic versus psychotic). The entire system has serious validity problems. Further, lay people and other nonprofessionals with minimal training are as good or better judges of people than highly trained and experienced clinicians (see the next subsection for a discussion of the evidence).

Empirical research has examined how reliably psychotherapists can classify people based on a standard nomenclature such as the American Psychiatric Association's *Diagnostic and Statistical Manual* (APA Comm. on Nomen. and Stat. 1968). An early study by Ash (1949), for instance, compared classifications given to 52 white males by three psychiatrists at a psychiatric clinic associated with a government agency. Using a conference method, in which the psychiatrists jointly interviewed each patient, the three psychiatrists agreed only 32 percent of the time on specific syndromes and 64 percent of the time for the major categories (psychotic, neurotic, and three other categories). They totally disagreed 31 percent of the time on which specific category a patient should be classified in. A study by Hunt and his associates (1953) four years later arrived at a similar rate of disagreement on the diagnoses given 794 naval enlisted men at precommission and at a later time upon preparation for separation from service. These findings are not atypical,[38] as has been pointed out by other reviewers (for example, Beck, 1962; Ennis and Litwack, 1974; Frank, 1975, 1969; Rotter, 1954).

The reasons for the low levels of reliability reported are numerous. By analyzing the process whereby diagnosticians came to their decisions, Ward and his associates (1962) concluded that 62.5 percent of the disagreements were due to inadequacies of the American Psychiatric Association's *Diagnostic and Statistical Manual*, which lacked clear criteria for determining what illness existed. Another

32.5 percent were due to inconsistencies on the part of the diagnosticians. Least important were inconsistencies on the part of the patients, who accounted for only 5 percent of the variance.

Beck's (1962) review of the literature on the reliability of psychiatric diagnoses cites a variety of factors as potentially significant sources of the variations in reliability of different studies. In particular it made a significant difference: (1) whether the same nosological system was used; (2) whether the background and experience of the diagnosticians were similar; (3) whether the diagnoses were made under the same conditions, controlling for such factors as depth of interviewing, physical location and whether test reports were available; (4) whether a time interval existed between interviews, which might have resulted in genuine patient change; and (5) whether administrative influences might have played a role (in the military a definite bias exists against labeling higher-ranking officers as severely ill, while enlisted men frequently receive such designations). Most of the extant studies have failed to control for these sources of influence, although they may be largely responsible for the poor results.

Beck also points out that several studies have shown that the personality characteristics of judges affects their diagnostic judgment (see, for example, Raines and Rohrer, 1955). An interesting study by Vingoe and Antonoff (1968) adds further support to this conclusion. Based on a comparison of self- and other-ratings with the results of objective tests, the authors found that good raters were significantly less neurotic, were more introverted, tolerant, self-controlled, and better adjusted, and tended to minimize their worries more than their less competent counterparts.

Complex and unproved classification schemes, such as the *Diagnostic and Statistical Manual* of the American Psychiatric Association cited above, probably are responsible for much of the lack of reliability that is demonstrated in study after study (Zigler and Phillips, 1961). Stuart (1970: 75-78) has given a four-pronged argument to explain this. First, he criticizes the fact that such systems are derived from hypotheses about mental illness that cannot be proved or disproved. Second, the American Psychiatric Association's system is extremely complicated and contains more than a hundred categories in an attempt to list every possible illness, rather than focusing on the most commonly observed or most clearly defined. Third, even some of the more general APA categories such as schizophrenia are subject to serious disagreement as to symptomatology, etiology, prognosis, and general definition. Fourth, the APA system has been designed so that the presence of one disease entity excludes the possibility of others, but the presence of a specific set of symptoms for each disease category, marking it off from all others, has not been demonstrated; in fact it appears that many sets of symptoms apply equally well to a number of categories.

In addition, there are studies indicating that simply providing more information may not increase the accuracy of judgment (for example, Huff and Friedman, 1967; Miller, 1956). Research has also shown that being able to use highly sophisticated conceptual schemes to judge people (such as the American Psychiatric Association's *Diagnostic Manual*) does not necessarily lead to significantly more accurate predications about people than do judgments based on undifferentiated interpersonal constructs (Leventhal, 1957).[39] Taken together, all of these problems cited provide a reasonable explanation of why traditional diagnostic processes have proved unreliable, and why reliability is not likely to improve in the near future.

While genotypic diagnosis may be relatively unreliable, there remains the further question of its validity. This can be broken down into three questions. First,

are the various diagnoses made by psychiatrists, psychologists, and other mental health professionals correct? Second, given a specific diagnostic judgment, does that judgment make a difference in terms of the treatment received? Third, even if it does not, does that judgment enable the future behavior of the patient to be predicted reasonably well, especially the outcome of the patient's illness?

Turning to the first question, the very lack of reliability of psychotherapeutic diagnoses severely calls into question their validity. If diagnosticians only agree 50 percent of the time, then they are mistaken at least 50 percent of the time. This means that their judgments are invalid at least half the time. In his now-famous article "On Being Sane in Insane Places," Rosenhan (1973) vividly illustrates the difficulties that even highly trained psychiatrists have in determining so simple a matter as whether a person is normal or insane. Since the details of his study are so striking, it bears extended treatment.[40]

Rosenhan wanted to determine whether psychiatrists and other mental health professionals could distinguish normal individuals from those who were seriously ill. He also wanted to determine the extent to which a diagnosis of insanity was based on contextual and environmental variables. To investigate these questions, Rosenhan had eight pseudopatients who were in reality quite healthy and normal, voluntarily seek admission into twelve different hospitals. During the intake interview they answered all questions truthfully, except for name, vocation, and employment, and except that each person reported one presenting symptom that did not in fact exist.[41] Upon admittance to the psychiatric ward, the pseudopatient ceased to simulate any symptoms of abnormality at all.

What happened to these normal individuals was extraordinary. All of them were hospitalized with the diagnosis of schizophrenia, except for one person who was diagnosed as a manic-depressive psychotic. The total length of hospitalization varied from seven to fifty-two days, with an average of nineteen. The diagnosis at discharge was schizophrenia "in remission." During the pseudopatients' entire hospital stay, none of the psychiatrists, nurses, or other professionals suspected that these people might be normal. Interestingly, the ward patients were quite suspicious, with 35 of a total of 118 patients voicing their doubts about the first three admittees alone.

Rosenhan realized that the diagnosis of insanity seemed to depend heavily on the context in which patients found themselves, that psychiatrists appeared especially open to suggestion effects, and that nonprofessionals were possibly more astute in identifying who is normal and who is not. Further research has added credence to these suppositions. To test psychiatric suggestibility, Rosenhan (1973: 252) informed the staff at a research and teaching hospital that one or more pseudopatients would attempt to be admitted to the hospital during a three-month period. Of 193 patients admitted during that period, 41 were strongly believed to be pseudopatients by at least one staff member, 23 were suspected by at least one psychiatrist, and 19 were suspected by both one psychiatrist and an additional staff member. In fact, no pseudopatients presented themselves during the three months.

The degree to which psychiatrists and other psychotherapists are influenced by irrelevant factors is marked. Using a sophisticated research design, Temerlin (1968) studied the suggestibility of lay jurors randomly selected from a regular jury wheel compared to psychiatrists, practicing clinical psychologists, and graduate students in clinical psychology. These groups were asked to diagnose a sound-recorded interview with a normal, healthy male. Immediately prior to the interview, the professional diagnosticians overheard a confederate of the experimenter say that

"he found the recording interesting because the patient looked neurotic but actually was quite psychotic" (Temerlin, 1968: 349). After listening to the interview, none of the lay jurors felt that the interviewed person was psychotic.[42] On the other hand, 11 percent of the graduate students, 28 percent of the clinical psychologists, and an amazing 60 percent of the psychiatrists stated that this normal individual was, in fact, quite psychotic.

Another strong factor influencing clinician judgment is the race and socioeconomic class of the patient. One of the more publicized findings of Hollingshead and Redlich's *Social Class and Mental Illness* (1958) was that lower-class patients were far more likely to receive severely pathological diagnoses for about the same conditions diagnosed as less severe in middle-class patients. More recent research indicates that this is still the case. Cole and Pilisuk (1976), for instance, found that the diagnostic category, type of psychiatric treatment, and the quality of service offered clients at a clinic depended largely on race. Another study (McDermott et al., 1965) demonstrated that more pessimistic diagnoses were attached to children of blue-collar workers than to children of white-collar families. On the basis of an analysis of all the research, Meehl (1973: 104) has concluded that the power of current diagnostic techniques is seriously in doubt, and that even the most widely used clinical instruments are not very accurate.

A number of interesting studies exist that demonstrate that lay people, paraprofessionals, and professionals with very little experience are equal or superior to highly trained and expert clinicians in their ability to judge people. Taft's (1955) review of the empirical literature more than twenty years ago was one of the first to establish this fact. He concluded that physical scientists, other nonpsychologists (such as personnel workers), and beginning psychology graduate students were as good or better at judging people as experienced clinical psychologists. A subsequent review of the research (Sarbin, Taft, and Bailey, 1960: 262–64) came to a similar conclusion. It found fourteen studies bearing on the issue. In three of them nonpsychologists were more accurate than psychologists; in six instances they were equal; and in five the psychologist was superior. In each of the last five cases, however, there were technical factors or biases that probably accounted for the superior results of the psychologists. Of ten studies comparing students with little training in psychology with students or graduates of considerable training, Sarbin, Taft, and Bailey (1960: 263) found only two in which the more experienced psychologists were superior to their lesser trained counterparts. In the remaining eight, six revealed no differences and two favored the beginners.

An important consideration in determining the value of clinical diagnosis is whether and to what extent tests provide more accurate data than are routinely and more quickly available at far less expense from other sources (Meehl, 1973: 104–6). Kostlan (1954) found that when clinicians were able to use three widely used tests (the Rorschach, MMPI, and a sentence-completion test), their inferences were no more accurate than had somebody made up a description based on that person's basic statistics: that is, knowing only the age, marital status, occupation, education, and source of referral, diagnosticians performed almost as well as clinicians who had all the test information plus a social case history; without the case history the accuracy of their judgments was almost exactly equal.[43]

Expert psychotherapists, then, do not appear particularly adept at determining whether people are sick or well, let alone the finer determinations of what type of illness exists. The reasons for this are varied but not hard to find. As Rosenhan (1975; 1973) has pointed out, psychiatrists operate with a strong bias toward diagnosing illness, which stems from their background as physicians. In the medical profession the general rule is to diagnose somebody as sick rather than well. This may make sense in the medical field, where the harmful consequences of misdiagnosing somebody as ill may be fewer (or "less severe") than the misdiagnosis of health. In the psychotherapeutic field, the consequences of misdiagnosing somebody as mentally ill are more severe.

Other reasons exist for the lack of ability of experts to distinguish illness from health. The bases for this determination are notoriously subjective and involve substantial value judgments, for the signs of mental illness are often not observable and are difficult to measure. Besides, determining the etiology of insanity is exceedingly complex—far more so than in the physical arena. Finally, what is known about mental illness does not begin to equal what is known about physical illness.

If diagnostic judgments are not accurate guides to the mental health of an individual, perhaps they are useful tools in determining what treatment a person receives. Historically this is supposedly so (Breger, 1968). A careful examination of professional opinion, however, reveals that many practitioners believe diagnosis makes no difference.[44] Meehl (1960: 19) surveyed more than 150 medical and nonmedical psychotherapists of various persuasions to determine whether prior knowledge of the client's dynamics and content from such tests as the Rorschach greatly speeded treatment. Only 17 percent believed that such knowledge was useful, 80 percent felt that therapist personality characteristics were more important determinants of the nature of treatment offered and its outcome than theory of personality. Student therapist attitudes toward psychodiagnostic reports are equally pessimistic, with as many as three-fourths believing that they have no relevance for therapeutic decision-making (Mintz, 1968).

Empirical research on the relationship of diagnosis to treatment is scarce. A basic question is whether and to what extent added information obtained in advance from a diagnosis helps in treating the patient. Unfortunately, no published research existed on this matter as of 1973 (Meehl, 1973: 107). In fact, few studies have examined whether diagnosis makes a difference in what treatment is chosen, irrespective of the value of the particular choice.

One of the few studies to do so, although it is usually cited because of its findings correlating social class with severity of diagnosed illness, is that of Hollingshead and Redlich (1958). The primary purpose of their research was to investigate whether diagnosis was related to method of treatment. They studied all persons receiving psychiatric treatment in New Haven, Connecticut during a specified period, and found that the type of treatment received was unrelated to diagnosis. The one variable that did correlate strongly was socioeconomic status; low-status patients received types of mechanical, inexpensive, and quick therapies such as electro-convulsive therapy, while high-status patients received extended and expensive verbal therapies. This relationship manifested itself in both private practice and publicly supported agencies.

Another excellent study was conducted by Bannister, Salmon, and Leiberman (1964). They examined the type of treatment received by 1,000 patients at a large psychiatric hospital. Despite the fact that various physical and drug treatments were included (electro-convulsive therapy, antidepressants, phenothiazines), and "psychotherapy" was considered as one treatment modality without further subdivision, the authors found that habitual or logical links were very limited in extent, although some significant relationships existed.[45]

A study that did examine the practical utility of diagnoses for verbal therapies found that clinical reports did not make a clear and useful difference in treatment decisions 74 percent of the time (Dailey, 1953). On the other hand, several studies of the relationship of diagnostic judgments to the choice of drug treatments in combination with psychotherapy support the contention that these judgments do make a difference in some circumstances (see, for example, Klein and Davis, 1969; Klett and Moseley, 1965).

The final validational concern centers around the capacity of diagnostic judgments and classifications to predict future behavior—that is, the outcome of treatment.[46] Meehl's (1973: 88) review of the literature covered twenty-seven studies comparing the predictive ability of the clinician with a statistician working only from actuarial data such as age, occupation, and education. These studies attempted to predict such matters as parole violations, recovery from psychosis, and the outcome of psychotherapy. In seventeen instances the statistical method proved significantly superior; in ten, both clinicians and statisticians performed about equally; in none did the clinician outperform the statistician.[47]

Other studies indicate that demographic data are better predictors of methods of treatment (for example, Arthur and Gunderson, 1966). A variable that is known to correlate quite well with various aspects of the treatment process, such as type and length of treatment, is the race and socioeconomic class of the patient (Cole and Pilisuk, 1976; Hollingshead and Redlich, 1958; Maas et al., 1955). Paul Meehl (1973: 89) came to the following conclusion about the value of clinical diagnosis in general: "It is highly probable that current predictive methods are costly to taxpayers and harmful to the welfare of patients."

The severe problems inherent in traditional psychodiagnosis have encouraged clinicians to develop alternative and more effective procedures for classifying the mentally ill, especially phenotypic diagnosis. These procedures are characterized by their objectivity and systematization. They have generally been constructed with a specific end in mind, whether classification of illness, determination of ultimate treatment, or prediction of future behavior. Although still in their infant stages, some of these newer methods appear to have a high degree of reliability and validity.

Illustrative of these newer processes is the computer-based program for psychiatric diagnosis known as Diagno II, which was developed by Robert Spitzer and the scientists at Biometrics Research (Spitzer and Endicott, 1969). Dividing up the diagnostic process into three stages, they have developed interview schedules for information-gathering, rating scales for evaluation, and computer programs for organizing and analyzing the data. The basic tenet of Spitzer's work is that systematic procedures are better for making differential diagnoses than unsystematic ones. In commenting on the advantages of this methodology, Conover (1972: 172) declares that nonprofessionals with only a moderate amount of training will soon be able to use it to produce a psychiatric diagnosis better than that produced using traditional clinical procedures.[48]

An excellent example of phenotypic diagnosis is the system developed by Lindsley (1963, 1960, 1956). Through significant long-term work he has demonstrated that psychotics can be distinguished from nonpsychotics using only the measurement of overt behavior. By counting the number of specific responses and examining the situations in which these responses occurred, he was able to obtain a high degree of validity. This type of diagnosis has been successfully used with autistic children (Ferster, 1961) and retarded children (Barrett and Lindsley, 1962). The initial reserarch results indicate that these forms of phenotypic diag-

nosis have greater reliability and validity than genotypic diagnosis.[49] In addition, the amount of training involved and level of skill required are far less.

The Significance of the Effectiveness of Paraprofessionals and Laypersons. A long history documents the effective use of paraprofessionals and laypersons in psychotherapy. An early forerunner of the modern paraprofessional developed toward the end of the eighteenth century in Europe as a result of the rise of "moral treatment."[50] Not a simple treatment technique, moral treatment attempted to create a favorable and comprehensive therapeutic environment for patients. Involved in providing treatment were nurses and doctors, but most were nonprofessionals: attendants, clerks, kitchen personnel, and ward staff. The focus of treatment was the assets and capabilities of patients. Positive thinking was emphasized. The therapeutic program consisted in part of lectures, recreational activities, and discussion groups. Underlying this form of treatment was a high valuation of the individual and a strong belief in the power of self-healing. Moral treatment rapidly took hold in America, most notably at the Worcester State Hospital in Massachusetts, where it enjoyed significant success. In fact, over a twenty-year period the recovery rate reached 71 percent for patients with illnesses of less than a year's duration prior to admission. For all patients, the recovery rate was 59 percent. Even many years later, a follow-up study (cited in Durlak, 1971: 3) found that approximately half of all patients never suffered a relapse.

While this type of treatment died out largely because of the death of its founders, nonprofessional mental health workers have continued to provide services to those with emotional and other behavioral disorders. If it can be demonstrated that these laypersons and minimally trained paraprofessionals can provide effective psychotherapeutic and encounter group services, then many of the traditional standards and criteria used to determine competence as a therapist or group leader are called into question. In particular, the value of theoretical and technical knowledge, the need for technical skills, and the importance of the diagnostic function are seriously challenged. Research on these issues has been gaining momentum.

Several strands of direct and indirect empirical evidence argue that paraprofessionals and laypersons are, in fact, effective as therapists and group leaders. Although not definitive, a number of studies document the fact that people with emotional problems often receive meaningful help from sources outside the mental health field. LeMay and Christensen (1968), for instance, discovered that more than half of all control group members in a study on the effectiveness of a college psychotherapy program received meaningful counseling and help from a variety of outside sources, including the campus minister, a resident-hall study group, and the offices of the Dean of Men.

Further research has found that college students, whether in therapy or not, will seek out an intimate friend or their parents for help with emotional problems, and will find this help more useful than that provided by psychotherapists (Armstrong, 1969). A study by Zolik and Stotsky (1966) sheds light on this finding. The authors asked a group of students what they would do with a person who was characterized as suffering from "mental illness," "emotional disturbance," or a "nervous breakdown." The students had recently completed a psychology course that explained mental illness, described mental health professionals, and recommended prompt and early treatment for emotional problems. Interestingly, the students would only refer somebody to a professional when that person was a relative stranger. When the disturbed person was a close friend or relative, the students responded that they would sit down and discuss the problem as a friend, give reassurance, and try to offer helpful advice and counseling. The majority definitely would not refer this friend or relative to a professional therapist.

This coincides with the findings of Gurin, Veroff, and Feld (1960) in their nationwide survey for the Joint Commission on Mental Illness and Health on how Americans view their mental health. The survey data[51] showed that friends, nurses, lawyers, clergy, and other professional and nonprofessional groups outside the mental health sphere were significant sources of therapeutic help. In fact, such sources were sought out more often than those with a specifically psychological function, such as psychiatrists, clinical psychologists, and social workers. More importantly, those who used these alternative sources were more satisfied with the help they received than those who looked to psychiatrists and psychologists.

The existence of the phenomenon of "spontaneous remission" in psychotherapy has recently been interpreted as providing additional evidence of nonprofessional effectiveness. As previously mentioned, spontaneous remission occurs when patients recover from their illness without any apparent professional help. While early baseline figures for the percentage of people who recovered in this fashion ran as high as 66 percent (Eysenck, 1952), later estimates have lowered it to approximately 30 percent (Bergin, 1971: 240–41). Explanations of this phenomenon ranged from theories that the psychoneuroses were self-limiting, to theories that the data were in error, but Bergin (1971, 1963) argues that spontaneous remission is due to people in distress seeking help from friends and other help-giving others. In support of his thesis he cites the nationwide survey by Gurin, Veroff, and Feld (1960). He also cites the finding of Jerome Frank that approximately half of those who had sought professional psychotherapeutic services had also sought help from a variety of nonmental-health sources. Finally, in further support of his argument Bergin presents case studies of significantly helpful nonprofessionals such as housewives.

Bergin (1971: 245) concludes that certain people are inherently helpful or have developed natural talents in this area (see also Truax and Mitchell, 1971: 326). In a sense, people who receive such help can be considered as receiving a type of "natural" therapy, which may be more effective than professional efforts. These natural therapists are chosen because their ability to form therapeutic relationships and provide significant help is known by word of mouth. Bergin (1971: 245) points out that "these lay therapists may well be a more select group with regard to dimensions relevant to the actual work of therapy than are professionals." Studies of the effectiveness of "companionship therapy," in which untrained volunteers serve as companions and friends to hospitalized mental patients (see, for example, Beck et al., 1963; Goodman, 1972, 1970), and "filial therapy," in which close friends and relations act as therapeutic agents (see, for example, Hawkins et al., 1966; Wahler, 1965; and the studies reported in Guerney, 1969), provide additional evidence that the relatively untrained may function effectively in therapeutic capacities.

Perhaps the best known of the early studies on paraprofessional effectiveness is the "Pilot Project in Training Mental Health Counselors," conducted by Margaret Rioch and her associates (1965). Begun in 1960 under sponsorship from the National Institute of Mental Health, this project investigated the results of a two-year program to train eight college-educated housewives to provide psychiatric help with only a minimum of supervision. The women trainees were approximately forty years old, and their children were all in school. The criteria for selection were congeniality with the

staff and each other, minimal defensiveness and pretentiousness, sensitivity to psychological subtleties, reliability, and good general intelligence. Their training was largely practical; listening to patients as unique individuals rather than diagnosing them was stressed; and theory was not taught systematically until the second year.

This program was evaluated from many points of view and by various methods, ranging from outside observer ratings, staff observation of the progress of the trainee's patients, supervisor ratings, and the impressions of the teachers of the trainees, as well as objective tests. The results were uniformly positive. For instance, four senior psychotherapists judged the trainee's performance to be comparable to that of more highly trained therapists, and 61 percent of the patients were reported to be improved. While it is difficult to compare this group in any sort of objective fashion to experienced therapists, the conclusion of the study was that these women would perform effective therapy with adolescents and adults in mental health agencies, and could also work in less well-controlled situations with supervision.[52]

A very interesting aspect of this study was the authors' evaluations of the risks involved in allowing inexperienced and untrained therapists to work with disturbed patients. They found that the risk was actually in the opposite direction of what they expected. According to the researchers, the counselors unconsciously but surely prevented the outburst of irrational behavior or talk by subtly communicating that they did not want to hear it (Rioch et al., 1965: 12).

The findings of this study sparked considerable interest in paraprofessionals, and resulted in an increasing number of studies on this subject throughout the sixties (Durlak, 1971: 11). One of the prime questions was whether a college education was necessary to effective functioning.

Another was whether a two-year training program was essential. Considerable research indicates that the answer to both these questions is negative.

An excellent example can be found in a solidly conceived study by Carkhuff and Truax (1965). After a training program of less than 100 hours, which involved less than 65 hours of supervisor time, five lay hospital personnel (only one of whom had a college degree), were assigned as leaders of eight therapy groups. Each group was made up of ten patients, whose average age was fifty and who had, on average, been hospitalized 13.6 years. The control group consisted of seventy patients similar in age, length of hospitalization, and other relevant factors. Treatment lasted three months and involved twice-weekly sessions. Change was determined by pre- and post-measures of ward behavior.

The patients in the lay therapists' groups improved significantly more than the control group in the following ways: overall general improvement was better, psychological disturbance decreased, constructive intrapersonal concern rose, as did constructive interpersonal behavior. With regard to total numbers, more than 50 percent of the patients treated by the lay therapists evidenced overall improvement, with just under 50 percent showing no change. Only one patient deteriorated. In the control group, on the other hand, less than 30 percent improved, approximately 50 percent remained unchanged, and 20 percent deteriorated. Hospital discharge rates also favored the group receiving lay therapy, but the difference did not reach statistical significance.

Another example can be found in a frequently cited study by Poser (1966). He examined whether extensive training was required for effectiveness in group therapy leadership. He examined three different types of groups: (1) therapy groups consisting of chronic schizophrenics and conducted by highly trained psychiatrists, social workers, and occupa-tional therapists; (2) similar groups conducted by undergraduate students with no prior training or experience with mental patients; and (3) a control group of untreated patients.

Six different tests were administered to determine whether patients treated by either lay or professional therapists would improve, and by how much. On three tests the lay therapists significantly outperformed the professionals. On the remaining three the professionals were outperformed, but the difference was not significant. A follow-up study three years later indicated that the change was lasting. The only negative implication of this study was that lay therapists may have both helped some patients *and* hurt other patients more than the professionals, who tended to have more consistent results. Poser's (1966: 289) basic finding was that "traditional training in the mental health professions may be neither optimal nor even necessary for the promotion of therapeutic behavior change in mental hospital patients."[53]

Both these studies, as well as virtually all other research on paraprofessionals and nonprofessionals through 1970, have been reviewed by Joseph Durlak (1971), in what is probably the most incisive analysis of the literature available. After a thorough search he found thirteen studies comparing the effectiveness of nonprofessionals with professionals. Surprisingly, in six of these thirteen studies, the lay individuals achieved significantly superior therapeutic results. In the remaining studies the results for both groups were similar. As Durlak (1971: 72) emphatically points out: *"In no study have lay persons been found to be significantly inferior to professional workers."* Various criterion measures were used to assess therapeutic effectiveness, such as self-report by the nonprofessionals themselves, supervisor reports, and hospital discharge rates. The overall results, especially when studies employed a variety of measures, "strongly suggest that extended training, technical expertise and long professional experience are not a *sine qua non* for producing positive therapeutic results" (Durlak, 1971: 73).

In addition to these thirteen studies, Durlak found another thirty-five examples of outcome research that evaluated the general effectiveness of paraprofessionals as psychotherapists without direct comparison to a professional group. His analysis of these studies led him to conclude that workers were not fully trained, some of whom had no formal training whatsoever, had proved effective in a wide range of settings, including individual and group therapy, with psychiatric inpatients and outpatients, with highly disturbed children or chronic schizophrenics, and as residential rehabilitation counselors, college academic adjustment counselors, group leaders in special therapeutic activity programs, and a social counselor, helpers, or aides in special programs for children.

Durlak found only four studies in which paraprofessionals or lay persons did not produce positive results. Although many of the studies lacked methodological rigor and control groups, although evaluation criteria were often weak and subject to rater bias, and although some of the sample sizes were quite small, a number of the studies were comparable to the best of the research on professional psychotherapists. Durlak's (1971: 98-99) conclusion is that "the success and versatility of subprofessional or lay mental health workers has been amply documented. Investigators cannot afford to overlook the implications of these studies since they present a possible solution to the problem of delivering adequate and comprehensive therapeutic services to all segments of the general population."

Conclusion. After reviewing the literature, both theoretical and empirical, it is hard to escape the conclusion that personal qualities and interpersonal skills constitute the basic ingredients of the therapeutic relationship and are important for minimal competence. These are not skills in specific techniques, treatment methodologies, or nosological classification. Rather, they are the ability to empathize, to create warm and genuine relationships, and to otherwise assist a person in self-exploration and growth. Although technical skills and diagnostic ability are undoubtedly important at the highest levels of competence, little evidence can be found suggesting they are necessary for minimal levels of functioning. It is apparent that interpersonal skills and personal characteristics are necessary in some minimal level if therapists are to provide competent help to individuals seeking their services.

The evidence for these conclusions is substantial. Nearly all theoreticians and practitioners agree on the importance of such factors as empathy and caring. Those who believe this range from Freud to Carl Rogers, while all surveys of practitioners have arrived at a consensus on this point. The empirical research bearing on this began with the work of Fiedler (1950 and 1950a) twenty-five years ago, and has been carried on by Rogers (1957) and the client-centered therapists. Although a few reviewers dispute the conclusiveness of these findings (for example, Meltzoff and Kornreich, 1970), hardly any argue that such qualities are unimportant. Other interpersonal skills, such as confrontation ability, persuasive potency, and the ability to focus on patient defense mechanisms, may be important in increasing effectiveness (Truax and Mitchell, 1971: 331-32), but the research results are inconclusive about these factors.

In one very real sense effective psychotherapy may consist largely of the purchase of friendship (Schofield, 1964), in that the necessary qualities are very similar to those one looks for in a good friend. According to Carl Rogers (1962: 422), constructive personality growth and change comes about with the proper creation of a certain psychological climate. He goes on to state that:

The conditions which constitute this climate do not consist of knowledge, intellectual training, orientation in some school of thought, or techniques. They are feelings or attitudes which must be experienced by the counselor and perceived by the client if they are to be effective. Those I have singled out as being essential are: a realness, genuineness, or congruence in the therapist; a sensitive, empathic understanding of the client's feelings and personal meanings; a warm, acceptant prizing of the client; and an unconditionality in this positive regard (Rogers, 1962: 422-23).

Although usually assumed to be critical, little evidence can be marshalled in support of the notion that therapists and group leaders must be in command of various technical skills or be able to use one or more methods of treatment. The available evidence indicates that expert psychotherapists of different schools are more alike than different in their actual practice (see, for example, Fiedler, 1950 and 1950a). Where differences do exist, it is between the novice and the expert within a particular school, and then these differences have to do with interpersonal skills. Research on particular techniques does not indicate that any are differentially more effective. The evidence of paraprofessional and lay person effectiveness suggests that technical skills are not a prerequisite, whether they are skills in a particular treatment modality such as Jungian analysis or utilizing sensory awareness exercises.

The importance of theoretical and technical knowledge for effective psychotherapy, while often believed to be crucial, has received virtually no attention in the empirical literature. The effectiveness of paraprofessionals, however, suggests that traditional conceptual knowledge may be less important than previously believed.

The correlation between diagnostic ability and therapeutic effectiveness or the ability to lead successful encounter groups is a hotly debated issue. Some of the debate stems from confusion about what is being argued, since diagnosis may be viewed as an attempt to understand and make sense of phenomena, or may become an effort to classify these same phenomena according to any one of a number of standard nomenclatures. Confusion and lack of clarity frequently occur over the purposes that diagnosis serves, which ranges from the labeling of illness, to the prediction of future behavior, to providing a means of determining the treatment of choice.

Research on the validity and reliability of genotypic diagnoses yields poor results. Psychiatrists and other mental health professionals find it very hard to agree on even very gross labels such as psychosis, neurosis, or normalcy. For these broad categories, reliability studies typically run between 40 to 70 percent. When asked to make more refined distinctions, professionals do even more poorly. In many instances nonprofessionals possess as good or better ability to classify individuals.

The reasons for this low reliability are varied. Mental health professionals are particularly susceptible to the power of suggestion, especially in making judgments about people. The nosological system of the American Psychiatric Association suffers many defects, which increase the chances of unreliability.

Considerable evidence exists that clinical diagnosis possesses little validity. In Rosenhan's (1973) classic study, psychiatrists in various mental health institutions could not identify perfectly normal individuals, even after repeated contact. Clinical diagnosis does not appear to have much bearing on the type of treatment received, especially if the choice is between competing verbal therapies. Most professionals in the field admit that diagnostic judgments have little influence on how they treat patients. Diagnosis does not help predict the outcome of treatment or what will happen to a particular patient over time. Clinical methods of predicting behavior have not been shown to be superior to simple actuarial methods involving predictions based on age, sex, education, and similar demographic data.

Alternative methods of clinical diagnosis, especially those based on overt behaviors and those which are highly systematized, computerized, and objective, have shown significant promise of overcoming the reliability and validity problems of traditional methods. Even so, the question remains whether a valid and reliable system of diagnosis is necessary for the effective conduct of therapy or the successful leading of an encounter group.[54]

In conclusion, research indicates that certain interpersonal skills and personal qualities are extremely important to the traditional therapeutic process and in leading encounter groups. The traditional assumptions about the importance of diagnostic ability, theoretical knowledge, and technical skills are not borne out by the research, and remain relatively unproved. Unfortunately, definitive statements are difficult to make about any set of standards, because the problems of research design and conflicting empirical results leave room for legitimate dispute.

Standards and Criteria for the Prevention of Harm

Even if definitive standards and criteria for minimal competence as a therapist or group leader could be established, the question remains whether these would be the same as what is necessary to protect the public from harm. No *a priori* reason exists why this should be so. Even total incompetence in all areas but one might not pose a danger to the public, if a practitioner never practiced outside this one area of competence. Since a variety of factors influences the therapeutic and encounter group process, any one of which has the potential of exerting a negative influence, it may be that the

practitioner has little control over the causative agents of harm, no matter how competent. What follows is an attempt to isolate the responsible agents of deterioration, drawing upon rigorous scientific research, expert opinion, case studies, and theoretical analysis.

Traditional Psychotherapy. In traditional psychotherapy Hans Strupp and his associates (1976) have undertaken a thorough survey of expert clinicians, theoreticians, and researchers to determine the prevailing views on the causes of negative effects. Their analysis provides an excellent overview of general opinion in the field,[55] although problems of sexual abuse seem to have been ignored (despite the evidence in volume III of this series that this is a significant problem). First mentioned is the problem of inaccurate or deficient assessment. A comprehensive understanding of the patient by way of a thorough diagnosis is stressed to avoid mismatching of therapist and patient or the use of an inappropriate technique. The functioning of the therapist was one of the most frequently cited sources of negative effects. The major therapist variables responsible for deterioration fell into two broad categories, the first being deficiencies in training and skills, and the second the personality of the therapist. Negative characteristics included coldness, unconscious hostility, seductiveness, and narcissism. On the other hand, certain patient variables were also posited as contributing to deterioration, including lack of motivation and low ego-strength.

The potential for misapplying or deficiently using a specific technique was frequently cited as a significant source of harm. Those surveyed believed that therapists who entertained the false assumption that therapy was a cure-all or that they were omniscient were especially dangerous. Further dangers existed in a therapist choosing inappropriate goals for therapy, including goals that were not in the patient's best interest, that were beyond the capacity of the patient, or that were too vague. Respondents suggested that practitioners might misplace the focus of therapy, concentrating excessively on intrapsychic processes instead of the environment. The clear opinion was expressed that specific techniques might be contraindicated in certain situations. For instance, psychoanalytic techniques might prove especially dangerous with borderline patients, and aversive therapy might be devastating for patients with particularly fragile egos.

The survey by Strupp and his associates (1976) uncovered other explanations of deterioration. Respondents indicated that technical rigidity posed considerable danger, especially when it forced submission to pre-established but inappropriate procedures. Practitioners were concerned with the use of overly intense therapy with unstable patients who might not be able to cope with rapidly uncovered repressed material or strong emotional reactions. The misuse of interpretations or insight therapy was prominently mentioned as a technical factor leading to harm. This misuse could occur in one of two ways. The therapist might unduly focus on interpreting intrapsychic phenomena, diverting critical personality resources and energy from potential growth into wasteful internal investigation. More detrimental, however, the therapist might make destructive or critical interpretations before genuine trust and rapport had been developed. Finally, dangers were seen as arising from therapists who utilized dependency-fostering techniques that encouraged unnecessary and sometimes interminable self-exploration, thereby precluding eventual positive behavioral change.

Further problems identified in the survey by Strupp and his associates included difficulties in the patient-therapist relationship caused by poor rapport, hostile countertransference on the part of the therapist, sexual involvement, and communication breakdowns. Certain problems were viewed as unique to certain forms of therapy. Psychoanalysts voiced concerns that behavioral treatment approaches often failed to deal with the underlying cause of psychological disturbance and resulted only in symptom substitution. The survey revealed the fear that radical therapies involving intensive confrontation or tactile stimulation might precipitate psychotic episodes or other evidence of psychological decompensation.

Theoretical explanations of why and how negative effects occur, along with illustrative case studies, support many of the statements of those responding to the survey by Strupp and his associates. Searles (1958), for instance, has described how the therapist's unconscious processes can be introjected by schizophrenic patients leading to bizarre, grotesque, and destructive behavior. In his own work with severely disturbed individuals, he found examples of patient's setting fires, becoming violent, and engaging in seductive behavior, all of which stemmed from previously unconscious impulses that Searles was experiencing in his relationship with those patients. Bergin (1971) has collected a number of case studies and detailed reports from patients of therapists whose behavior was a significant factor in the patient's deterioration. An analysis of these reports strongly implicates antitherapeutic attitudes and behavior on the part of the therapist, such as overt expressions of hostility, noncaring, or ridicule when patient trust has not been developed.

Professional opinion as to how to prevent harm and what causes it is also expressed through the positions professionals take on the requirements for licensing laws and the certification policies of major professional associations. It is clear that great reliance is placed on the possession of academic credentials, as evidenced by the doctoral prerequisite of most psychology licensing laws, the requirement of an M.D. degree for medical licensure, and the stress on technical and theoretical knowledge evident in the qualifying examination for certification by the American Board of Psychiatry and Neurology or for Diplomate status as a clinical psychologist in the American Psychological Association.

Although professional opinion is quite definite in specifying the causes of danger in psychotherapy, the social science research that can be brought to bear on this matter is very limited. Unfortunately, most of the studies that provide evidence that deterioration occurs do not investigate the reasons for that deterioration. The work of Charles Truax represents one of the few exceptions. His early analysis of the findings from a five-year research project at Wisconsin (Rogers et al., 1967) indicated that high levels of therapist empathy, warmth, and genuineness were related to patient improvement, while low levels led to deterioration (Truax, 1963: 256). This finding was replicated in a study of forty hospitalized mental patients in group psychotherapy (Truax and Carkhuff, 1965). Research at Johns Hopkins (Truax et al., 1966) and related studies by Truax and his associates (summarized in Truax and Carkhuff, 1967: 82–95) all converge in their conclusion that the personality characteristics of the therapist, especially the quality of empathy, are critical in determining whether negative effects will occur.

Apart from the reviews of the research on deterioration effects by Truax (1967; Truax and Carkhuff, 1967; Truax and Mitchell, 1971), Allen Bergin (1971, 1966, 1963; Lambert et al., 1977) is one of the few to have reviewed the evidence on why negative effects occur. His latest review, carried out in collaboration with Lambert and Collins (Lambert et al., 1977), examines the degree to which the personality and behavior of the therapist, experience level, patient variables, therapist-patient interaction, treatment technique, therapeutic school, and various other factors are capable of precipitating harm.

According to Bergin, the behavior and personality of the therapist is probably the most critical factor in patient deterioration. Certainly more research backs up this hypothesis than any other competing explanation. The client-centered therapists have provided most of the evidence on this point, especially the research of Truax, Carkhuff, and Rogers. The most influential personality characteristics, either positively or negatively, appear to be empathy and certain other closely related qualities, which have been summed up by Truax and Mitchell (1971: 312): "Patients seen by therapists low in accurate empathy, nonpossessive warmth, and genuineness account for the vast majority of the deteriorated cases, while therapists high in these conditions account for the majority of the benefited and 'no-change' patients."

Ricks's (1974) analysis of two therapists who achieved strikingly different results in their work with disturbed children provides an excellent case study of the importance of the behavior and personality of the therapist. Ricks found two groups of socially disturbed children who were virtually identical on every variable. One group of fifteen had been in therapy with a practitioner nicknamed Supershrink. Of the fifteen children treated by him, none became chronically schizophrenic, only four (27 percent) had to be temporarily hospitalized, and only another five (33 percent) retained their diagnosis as socially inadequate. The remaining six (40 percent) were adjudged as having attained adequate social adjustment. The other therapist, on the other hand, actually seemed to drive his patients crazy: three (23 percent) became chronic schizophrenics, another eight (61 percent) were temporarily hospitalized, and two (15 percent) remained socially inadequate. None became healthy, at least according to Ricks's criteria.

A close examination of the differences in the therapists' styles revealed that the successful therapist devoted more time to those who were most disturbed, employed outside help, was firm and direct with parents, supported movements toward autonomy, and devoted significant portions of therapy to real-life problem-solving. This was all in the context of a strong therapeutic relationship. Apparently the destructive therapist was frightened by the pathology evident in the sicker children, became depressed over it, and reflected his hopelessness in his interaction with these children. The less successful therapist also spent excessive time exploring and dwelling on intrapsychic material with which the children were simply not capable of dealing.

Several other studies support the observations that Ricks has made. For instance, Feifel and Eells (1963) surveyed therapists and patients who had terminated therapy at a Veterans Administration mental hygiene clinic. In response to the question of what was not helpful in therapy, the therapists' feelings of irritation, anger, boredom, and the like were most frequently given as nonhelpful. In analyzing the counseling provided to delinquents in the famous Cambridge-Somerville Youth Study, Powers and Witmer (1951: 546-76) found two causes of deterioration effects: mistakes on the part of the counselor, such as becoming preoccupied with family members and ignoring the child, and destructive attitudes, such as punitiveness.

A variety of other therapist factors may be influential in causing deterioration, according to Lambert, Bergin, and Collins (1977). The early attempts of Whitehorn and Betz (1960; Betz, 1962) offered evidence that rigid therapists who expected deference and conformity, and who were more authoritarian than their democratic counterparts, produced poorer results with schizophrenic patients.[56] One of the studies reported by Lambert and his associates investigated the degree to which "pathogenic" therapists who consciously or unconsciously utilized dependent individuals to satisfy their own personal needs caused negative effects. They found that the patients of more benign therapists

were functioning at higher levels after six months of treatment regardless of outcome measure. Further anecdotal reports discussed by Lambert and his associates (1977) indicate that such a tendency to exploit can lead to patient deterioration, as well.

A long-standing belief among psychotherapists is that years of therapist experience are important in reducing the risk of harm. Very little research exists on this point. The few studies that examine the effect of experience on positive outcome generally find a positive correlation between these two indices (see the studies reviewed by Lambert et al., 1977; Meltzoff and Kornreich, 1970: 268-72), although Bergin's (1971) review found that experienced therapists also accounted for 71 percent of the cases in which positive results did not occur. Whether inexperience leads to deterioration has not been dealt with in the empirical research, although theories abound as to why it should make a difference (see Lambert et al., 1977).

According to Lambert, Bergin, and Collins (1977), differing schools and types of psychotherapy may have significantly different deterioration rates, but the research is virtually nonexistent on this point. Behavior therapists have been especially remiss in studying deterioration effects. A few anecdotal case studies indicate that relapse or symptom substitution may take place, but the evidence is far from conclusive and the causes of deterioration are unexamined. Client-centered therapy has produced the most evidence of deterioration, but the variables causing harm (the personal qualities of the therapist) may not be school-specific. Instead, they may be important in any type of therapy. The psychoanalytic school is marked by a low frequency of empirical investigations, although several studies indicate that many people may be unsuitable for analytic treatment, which may be the treatment of choice for as few as 5 percent of the patient population.

Unfortunately, comparisons of the deterioration rates among competing schools of therapy are nonexistent (Lambert et al. 1977) Research on marital therapy provides some evidence that deterioration rates are liable to be lower where both spouses are involved in treatment in some way. Areas related to therapy, such as counseling, teaching, and the training of therapists, provide further evidence that personal characteristics are a prime cause of deterioration.

Lambert, Bergin, and Collins explored the question of whether certain patient characteristics could be linked to deterioration. The evidence apparently favors the proposition that the more psychologically disturbed an individual is, the more likely he or she will be to sustain a negative effect. The research of Fairweather and his associates (1960) demonstrates that psychotic subjects deteriorated far more often than any other diagnostic category. Perhaps more meaningful than diagnostic category, however, is the past psychological disturbance of the patient. Kernberg (1973) notes that poor interpersonal relationships are a prognostically bad sign. When these are coupled with low initial anxiety tolerance and low motivation, Kernberg found that outcomes were poor in psychoanalysis and supportive psychotherapies, although better in supportive-expressive treatments.

The possibility exists that the patient-therapist interaction, rather than the therapist alone or the patient alone, is the primary determinant of therapeutic results. According to Lambert, Bergin, and Collins (1977), however, the evidence suggests that the therapist is the most important influence. This is supported by the research of the client-centered school indicating that therapists who are highly empathic and offer a strong amount of unconditional positive regard are relatively unaffected by differing clients, while therapists low in these qualities vary the amount offered depending on the type of client. A number of other factors are undoubtedly operative in producing the negative effects that the research has documented.[57] Lambert, Bergin, and Collins (1977) cite indirect evidence linking race, sex, and class to deterioration.

Encounter Groups. The dangers of encounter groups have received far more attention than the dangers of traditional psychotherapy. The result has been considerably more theoretical speculation about the causes of the dangers involved. Some general charges will be discussed first.

A frequently mentioned criticism is that encounter groups do not adequately integrate what is learned in the group into the remainder of the participant's life. Participants may find that openness and honesty in the special circumstances of a group setting is both enriching and valuable. In the context of a complex business relationship, however, such complete openness may prove harmful. Shostrom's (1969) example of the rising young corporate star who was fired after an open expression of anger illustrates this problem. Where strong emotions are quickly elicited and intense relationships easily entered into and dissolved (so-called "instant intimacy"), the threat may also exist that strong emotional ties of an enduring quality will lose importance. Emotions may then become merely another commodity in an increasingly alienated and materialistic society.

Encounter groups have been severely criticized for stressing the free expression of emotion. Nude marathons have aroused the fear that sexual promiscuity will become endemic. The use of certain group techniques, such as fantasy, is obviously a powerful method of delving into a person's psyche, and may induce psychotic breaks in those participants who are unable to cope with the creations of their imaginations. With some participants the need may be to control feelings rather than to "let it all hang out." The elevation of feeling over thought, emotion over intellect, and experiencing over reflection and analysis, which occurs in some groups, is frequently criticized because of the skewed image of humanity that results.[58]

An overview of what professionals and theoreticians believe are the causes of danger in encounter groups may be gleaned from Rowe and Winborn's (1973) analysis of the objections to groups reported in selected professional journals. Critics who published in professional journals were concerned about leader competence and the lack of standards for leader credentials. They were greatly concerned about the possibility of psychological damage. Many of their fears centered around technical, theoretical, and procedural aspects of encounter groups—those aspects that have a bearing on whether harm ensues. In decreasing order of frequency, the following factors were mentioned:[59] (1) post-group adjustment problems and doubts about the generalization of learning (ten times); (2) lack of ethical standards (seven times); (3) lack of explicit procedures or goals (seven times); (4) and lack of screening procedures, overemphasis on experiential goals, use of involuntary subjects, and an anti-intellectual emphasis (four times each).

Opinions about why encounter groups are dangerous are also reflected in the guidelines that professional associations and other groups have proposed for encounter group leaders (see American Medical Association, Council on Mental Health, 1971; American Psychological Association, 1973; American Group Psychotherapy Association, 1971). Very frequently the stress is on the possession of cognitive knowledge and academic degrees (see, for example, Lakin, 1969; Morris and Cinnamon, 1976).

Opinions about what makes encounter groups dangerous, even though from professionals, has rarely been based on social science research. In some ways this is readily understandable, since so little research has examined this problem. On the other hand, given the magnitude of the problem, it is surprising that professionals have chosen to do so little research in this area. Those who have reviewed the research, however, and who have attempted to determine what factors most frequently and powerfully determine positive and negative results, have come to conclusions that differ from expert opinion. On the whole, researchers and reviewers do not stress academic credentials. Instead, the personal characteristics of both participant and group leader appear paramount.

Fiman and Conner (1973), for instance, endorse Easton, Carr, and Whitely's (1972: 111) conclusion that "most of the concrete evidence available indicates that [casualties] are comparatively rare, and that they usually involve people with some previous history of psychological difficulty." A more recent review by Gibb (1975: 64), acknowledging that the evidence is far from clear, suggests that negative effects may be due to the following factors: "intensive feedback at inappropriate early stages of the group, a training period that is too brief, too little structure especially at early stages of the group, a leader style that is too tightly controlling, or certain dysfunctional compositional groupings." Hartley, Roback, and Abramovitz (1976) suggest three variables that account for deterioration. The first is the type of group member, where the factor most clearly associated with negative effects is previous psychological disturbance. Second, various group techniques and processes may also contribute to deterioration, including lack of structure, lack of group norms, and lack of a task orientation. The third area is leader behavior, where Hartley and her associates (1976) rely heavily on the findings of the Group Experience Project (Lieberman, Yalom, and Miles, 1973; Yalom and Lieberman, 1971) in concluding that insufficient leader restraint and vigilence may be conducive to casualties. This conclusion is also echoed in Lambert, Bergin, and Collins's (1977) review of the literature, which cites the encouragement of confrontation, expression of anger, rejection by either the group or the leader, feedback overload, and coercive group norms as primary factors in producing harmful effects.

These reviews are based on a comparative handful of studies. In large part the analysis of the reviewers has been based on the conjecture of researchers who have explored the degree to which encounter groups are dangerous, but who have not specifically researched what causes danger.[60] Few of these studies can properly be said to provide direct empirical evidence on what causes deterioration, although many offer excellent theoretical formulations. To provide a clear picture of what these studies actually say and to what extent they constitute objective research, it is necessary to discuss each in turn.

Studies Identifying a Variety of Harmful Factors. The most important, comprehensive, and definitive research on dangers is that of Lieberman, Yalom, and Miles (1973; Lieberman, 1975; Miles, 1975; Yalom, 1975; Yalom and Lieberman, 1971) on the Group Experience Project, which has been discussed in earlier portions of this book. Their research found that 16 of the original 206 participants had become casualties, which they define as "sustain[ing] psychological harm as a direct consequence of the group experience" (1973: 174). In closely studying these casualties, Lieberman and his associates identified five main paths that eventually led to harm: (1) attack by the leader or by the group; (2) rejection by the leader or by the group; (3) failure to attain unrealistic goals; (4) coercive expectations; and (5) input overload or "value shuffle."

Ten of the sixteen casualties resulted from attacks by either the leader or the group. In six of the cases the leader was attacking. Attack took various forms and was described by the participants as "I was treated as the lowest thing on earth," or "The leader said I was on the verge of schizophrenia." Rejection was a factor with six of the casualties, and was often closely related with attack. In three instances, however, it was experienced as simply being ignored or left out. Failure to achieve unrealistic goals precipitated casualties in four cases, where individuals felt that the encounter group was magically going to solve their life problems or provide other benefits that the groups could not possibly fulfill. Coercive expectations occurred as a result of group pressure and the norms that became established during the life of the group. Two casualties were dramatically affected by this phenomenon. In both cases the norm of the group was intense emotional displays of feeling. Since the casualties did not experience these strong feelings, they came to feel that they were somehow "less good," "hollow," and "without substance." The final route by which participants became casualties was through "input overload." This is not an easy term to define, according to the authors, but involved an intense overstimulation, such as stirring up unresolved conflicts which the participant is not able to work through during the life of the group. Four casualties were precipitated at least partially through input overload.

It is interesting to note why some people were not hurt by attacks or rejections. Several factors seemed to serve as protective mechanism. One of the most common was lack of substantial involvement in the group. A high level of self-esteem also made casualty status unlikely. A third factor was the use of people outside the group to question whether the group's evaluations were accurate and valid. A final method was to simply maintain one's defenses.

Lieberman, Yalom, and Miles (1973:

233–39) also attempted to determine what role the leader played in bringing about harmful results. They found that the ideological school of the leader was not related to the leader's actual behavior and also could not be considered as the cause of psychological injuries. For example, one of the Gestalt groups produced the most casualties, while a second was among the most beneficial. The type of leader behavior, on the other hand, was significantly related to casualty status.

The researchers found that four basic leadership functions accounted for most of the positive and negative behavior of the leaders in the Group Experience Project: (1) emotional stimulation; (2) caring; (3) meaning-attribution; and (4) executive function. Emotional stimulation consisted of revealed feelings, challenging, confrontation, self-revelation, and the like. Caring involved protecting, offering friendship and love, and the giving of support, praise, and encouragement. Meaning-attribution consisted of providing concepts for understanding groups, explaining, clarifying, interpreting, and providing methods for how to change. It involved helping participants make sense of what was happening. Executive function took the form of management, and involved such behaviors as limit-setting, establishing rules and norms, managing time, questioning, suggesting procedures, and dealing with decision making.

An empirical typology of leaders was derived by examining the profiles of each group leader's four leadership dimensions. From this emerged a seven-category classification system for leadership styles: (1) aggressive stimulators; (2) love leaders; (3) social engineers; (4) laissez-faire leaders; (5) cool, aggressive stimulators; (6) high-structure leaders; and (7) leaderless groups.[61] Yalom and Lieberman (1971) found that the aggressive stimulators accounted for 44 percent of the casualties. These casualties tended, in addition, to be more severe. On the other hand, the love leaders (providers) produced only one casualty. In comparing the percentage of groups these types worked with, the aggressive stimulators conducted 27.8 percent of the eighteen groups while accounting for 44 percent of the casualties. The love leaders, on the other hand, were involved with 16.7 percent of the participants but only accounted for 6.2 percent of the casualties. The encounter tapes (leaderless groups) had no casualties. In addition, the aggressive stimulators, the impersonals, and the laissez-faire leaders accounted for most of the dropouts.

Each participant in the study was eventually classified as a high-learner, moderate changer, unchanged, negative changer, dropout, or casualty. In arriving at a final score on effectiveness for each type of group leader, the love leaders (providers) clearly were superior to any other leadership style, with the tape groups in second place. Interestingly enough, while the love leaders were the most effective in producing positive and constructive changes, they also minimized the number of negative outcomes. After examining the data, Lieberman, Yalom, and Miles (1973: 246) concluded that "the data lend little credence to the notion that high risk is necessary in order to achieve a high level of growth."

In the Group Experience Project, considerable effort went into an attempt to identify the special characteristics of those who went on to learn or falter. Five aspects of each participant's make-up that might have had some bearing on how beneficial or harmful the group had been were investigated: (1) expectations and attitudes; (2) values; (3) psychological adequacy; (4) personality traits; and (5) interpersonal conceptions (Lieberman, Yalom, and Miles 1973: 315). The two most powerful predictors were the values that participants were guided by, and their conceptions of others. Casualties tended to have a unique emphasis on growth, hoping and expecting that the group would be a form of salvation, without recognizing the potential dangers involved. They also tended to have a low interest in sensuality or pleasurable sensory activities (p. 325). In their conceptions of others the casualties came to the encounter group with an extremely negative picture of their best friend and significant other people in their lives.

Yalom and Lieberman (1971) examined a number of other variables and found that levels of self-esteem and self-concept were especially sensitive predictors of casualties. Low level of either increased the likelihood of becoming a casualty:

The entire picture is a consistent one: individuals with generally less favorable mental health with greater growth needs and higher anticipations for their group experience and yet who lacked self-esteem and the interpersonal skills to operate effectively in the group situation were more likely to become casualties. [Yalom and Lieberman, 1971: 28].

Three other studies offer comprehensive explanations on the causes of encounter group dangers. In two of them the results of a survey were used to develop a theoretical formulation of the antecedents of harm. Ross, Kligfeld, and Whitman (1971) sent an open-ended questionnaire to those psychiatrists in the greater Cincinnati area who had seen patients that had been harmed by encounter groups. Details were requested about the causes of harm. Ross and his associates analyzed the responses of the psychiatrists. The most common psychodynamic formulation offered involved some form of attack on the patient's habitual modes of coping. There were several instances of assaults on compulsive defenses, two cases in which the patient's self-esteem was attacked by a verbal diatribe from the group, three instances of homosexual panic resulting from the physical intimacy of the group, and two instances in which women were hetero-

sexually overstimulated by the group situation. These examples confirm Lieberman, Yalom, and Miles's (1973) conclusion that casualties are often caused by attack or rejection by the leader or the group and from what is termed "input overload."[62]

Kane, Wallace, and Lipton (1971) conducted a questionnaire survey of the North Carolina Neuropsychiatric Association asking psychiatrists for information similar to that requested by Ross, Kligfeld, and Whitman (1971). The responses made clear that where T-group participants experienced harm, coercion was frequently used to ensure attendance. In addition, 34 percent of those hurt did not have a clear understanding of what they were about to enter, 80 percent had not been screened, 70 percent had no clear limits set regarding acceptable behavior, and follow-up was not provided in 65 percent of the cases. In the authors' estimation each of these factors contributed heavily to the risks involved (Kane et al., 1971: 956). The authors (p. 956) theorized that inexperience and lack of training is a critical factor, "since almost all those in any discipline trained to care for the ill or disturbed realize that psychopathological reactions may occur during the course of therapy." Whether the factors identified by Kane, Wallace, and Lipton actually are a factor in precipitating harm is not answered, however, since their theory and conclusions are neither proved nor disproved by the data provided.

In a third study, Jaffe and Scherl (1969) carefully analyzed several instances in which participants were hurt through their encounter group experience. A variety of factors are implicated as responsible. First, Jaffe and Scherl point out that screening might have identified the fact that the casualties were particularly vulnerable to severe reactions. In addition, they note that T-groups promote anxiety in order to lower defenses. If compensating supportive mechanisms are not available, the chances of psycho-pathological reactions increase. They stress the importance of developing trust before increased self-awareness is possible. Five guidelines are suggested to minimize the chances of harm: (1) voluntary as opposed to coerced participation; (2) participation based on an informed consent of purposes, goals, and methods; (3) screening by questionnaire and preferably by interview; (4) guidelines as to what behaviors are permissible; and (5) follow-up interviews and help, especially to identify adverse reactions occurring subsequent to the group.

Studies Identifying Individual Factors as Harmful.

Leadership Characteristics. In the Group Experience Project, highly experienced, trained, credentialed, and respected professionals were used, yet the casualty rate was 9.4 percent. By comparison, the casualty rate of the Talent in Interpersonal Explorations (TIE) Project (see pages 57–58) was less than 0.1 percent, despite the almost exclusive use of nonprofessionals with no formal diagnostic skills and very little formal training. It is unlikely that this striking variation can be accounted for by differences in measurement criteria or the adequacy of measurement. Rather, two obvious differences appear to be responsible. The TIE Project employed a fail-safe approach of not taking chances with raising anxiety levels, not making attacks on people, and using program consultants with problem personalities or situations. In the Group Experience Project some of the leaders appeared to be taking almost the opposite approach, although the approach of the "love leaders" seemed fairly close to the TIE approach, and, not surprisingly, the casualty rate was lower with these leaders.

The second difference was the almost exclusive use of nonprofessionals as group leaders in the TIE Project. Group members may tend to place trust in professionals because they are credentialed, even where their actions are destructive. Rather than trusting one's own instincts, a participant may feel that the professional is right and hence the participant must be wrong. This can easily lead to self-doubts and a decrease in self-confidence and self-esteem. It can also mean opening oneself up in a situation where remaining defended would be wiser. Carl Rogers (1970: 156) considers this a possibility. In attempting to explain the success of groups run by nonprofessionals, he hypothesized that people are intimidated by someone they perceive as an expert. Where nonexperts are used, group members will take more responsibility for the group and feel freer to disagree with the group leader.

Bebout (personal communication, November 15, 1971) has not ignored this possibility, and the TIE Project will be utilizing highly skilled professionals to determine whether there is any validity in such an hypothesis:

The question of course is: will recognized professionals produce better outcomes than nonprofessionals in measurable terms? My hypothesis is that our best "non-pros" will compare . . . favorably with the best pros we can recruit, but further that "negative experiences," if any occur, will be more marked with "poor" professionals than with "poor" nonprofessionals.

A second study bearing on the matter of causation is that of George Bach (1967). In developing the dimensions of helpfulness in marathon groups, he found five discrete activities that group members considered least helpful in the group. This was determined from an analysis of post-group protocols by members of therapeutic groups as to what and who was most and least helpful in various group meetings. By analyzing and coding the responses, Bach determined that five clusters of least-helpful behaviors existed: (1) strangeness or being unlike other participants; (2) noncaring, or indifference to what happens to other group members (alienation); (3) narcissism, or being autistically preoccupied with oneself; (4) disjunctive communication, or derailing and confusing communication; and (5) aggression-phobia, or avoidance of conflict.

White (1973) studied the effects of leader personality on group outcomes in interracial encounter groups, and came to definite conclusions as to helpful and harmful leader behaviors. She did pre- and post-testing on a group of forty-nine participants in six encounter groups and one control group using a variety of test instruments. Her conclusions were that: (1) self-directed groups were as effective as groups led by professionals; (2) rigid leaders encouraged the characteristics of frustration, tension, irritability, and an absence of a clear sense of a socially-approved self; and (3) flexible leaders encouraged the characteristics of responsibility, maturity, practicality, composure, consideration of others, and a clear sense of socially approved self.

Although the above studies do not provide evidence of the importance of academic credentials, several of the researchers maintain that they are important. Kane, Wallace, and Lipton (1971), for instance, strongly believe that academic training is necessary, especially to provide necessary diagnostic skill. Hurley and Force (1973) note that in their study of five T-groups, only those led by Diplomates in Clinical Psychology made significant gains in self-acceptance and other-acceptance, while two groups without Diplomates as leaders had participants who deteriorated. The Diplomates were more self-disclosing, they asked for more feedback, and they had considerably more experience as group psychotherapists and in the general mental health sector. Whether possession of academic credentials and Diplomate status, however, produces these effects remains an open question.

Participant Factors. In addition to the studies that provide comprehensive explanations for the causes of encounter group dangers, several studies have focused specifically on potential participant factors. Archer (1974) investigated 102 members of six self-analytic groups at Harvard University. The purpose of the groups was to increase member understanding of issues in personality and interpersonal behavior. The leadership was relatively nondirective. Archer measured self-concept change both before and after the group. Using Bales's measure of dominance, he found that the most powerful group members generally changed positively, while the more powerless participants underwent negative changes. These oppositional changes occurred for a number of other variables, including openness, leadership, and attractiveness.

Archer speculates that powerfulness in a group may be a causal factor in whether people undergo constructive changes. He found that the more powerful group members received significantly more attention in the group and also more group support. In addition, there was a significant correlation between powerfulness and whether participants felt close to others. These factors of attention, support, and closeness may be a direct result of powerfulness, Archer hypothesized. He notes that Lieberman, Yalom, and Miles (1973) found that group members who were low in the VCIA (value congruence, influence and activity) role were more likely to be "negative changers" or "casualties." This role has a great deal of similarity to Bales's "measure of dominance," and reinforces the notion that powerfulness in a group may be an important criterion in determining who shall benefit and who shall be harmed by an encounter group experience.

Several other studies add credence to the theory that participant factors are extremely important in determining whether harm will occur. Fromme, Jones, and Davis (1974) concluded that highly conservative populations are likely to find the encounter experience disruptive and destructive. In their study county extension agents were given an intensive, one-week course in human relations. As a result they became more inhibited, cautious, defensive, disorganized, and emotionally upset. In his doctoral thesis at UCLA Vosen (1966) explored the relationship between self-disclosure, self-esteeem, and how these variables would be affected by encounter group training. In seeking an explanation for the average decrease in self-esteem that occurred in the experimental group, Vosen found that participants who were low self-disclosers decreased significantly in self-esteem as a result of the encounter group experience. Gottschalk's (1966) analysis of NTL T-groups at Bethel, Maine, suggests that participant factors play a definite role in bringing about untoward experiences, especially among the less secure and less well integrated participants.

Group Factors. The potential for psychological damage from undue group pressure or from being scapegoated by a group has been mentioned by a number of commentators (Apfelbaum and Apfelbaum, 1973; Back, 1972; Shaffer and Galinsky, 1974). In his well-known and often-cited experiments, Asch (1952) demonstrated that group pressure definitely had an effect upon a person's willingness to stand by or relinquish her or his judgment. He also showed that normal subjects would frequently falsify their visual perceptions of lines of different sizes in order to conform to a unanimously-held group opinion (Asch, 1956). Hovland, Janis, and Kelley (1953) extended Asch's findings to show that interpersonal and social judgments were similarly affected by group norms. Thus, an encounter group may exert considerable pressure on participants, especially when most of the group members have a commonly-held opinion. In this situation participants may be coerced into changing behavior, thoughts, values, or attitudes when they are not truly ready to or do not want to.

Another common and related criticism is that harmful results can be engendered when the group leader and/or several participants band together to attack another participant's way of behaving or thinking. Empirical evidence within the encounter group literature exists on this point and is discussed below, but several writers have given insightful theoretical explanations of this danger.[63] Stone (1970), for instance, is concerned with the potential danger of attacking ego defenses in an attempt to force participants out of role-playing in the name of "saying what one really feels." This tendency is part of what he considers the anti-intellectual disposition of the Esalen-style group in particular:

This intense assault on the abiding configurations of the mental apparatus must surely be a powerful disruption, if not a catalyst for change. One can only hope that of those subjected to such an assault there are none who are allowed to remain as outsiders. Such disruption without the concomitant opportunity for intimacy and group support would surely be one of the most dangerous psychotherapeutic contexts yet devised. Dangerous because at the same time an assault has been mounted on ego defenses and superego introjects, there is an obvious mobilization of object hunger. [Stone, 1970: 224.]

Lack of Screening. Many studies have suggested that lack of screening may be a direct cause of casualties (for example, Fromme et al., 1974; Kane et al., 1971; Lieberman, Yalom, and Miles, 1973; Ross et al., 1971). Stone and Tieger (1971) have conducted research on this question. They attempted to minimize the dangers of encounter groups by screening out participants who were likely to undergo harm or were otherwise high-risk candidates. Using psychological tests, a written application, and a small-group experience, they screened 105 applicants to a week-long T-group conducted by nonprofessionals. Over a three-year period during which six sensitivity groups conducted, twenty-three people were screened out.

Fifteen were told that they should not attend. Of these, four had difficulties with reality testing (although none was psychotic) and paranoid thinking; eight evidenced marked acute or chronic neurotic reactions such as intense anxiety; and three had difficulties in controlling their impulses. In addition, six decided of their own accord not to attend, and two were excluded by administrative decision (close relatives of the T-group staff). In their follow-up study only two participants experienced severe and disruptive psychological reactions while attending the laboratory: one became psychotic and was removed from the group, while the other became progressively anxious, left the group for a day, but returned for the remainder of the lab.

Stone and Tieger were able to compare their screening procedures with no screening. At a T-group laboratory including seventy-five participants, forty-one of which had not been screened, four of the unscreened left prematurely. Only one woman left from the screened group, and she did so only temporarily. Stone and Tieger conclude that while they originally attempted to screen out only psychotic or prepsychotic applicants, or those who were severely anxious, they concluded that it was important to screen out those with a possibility of worsening a psychosomatic illness, or those with a difficulty with impulse control.

They note several problems with the screening process. First, it is quite long and laborious. Second, it is possible that many of those who were screened out might have had a valuable experience, and their study was unable to measure this. Third, it is a delicate matter to inform somebody that the T-group experience would not be appropriate for them. On the other hand, a surprising value of the process was increasing the confidence of the nonprofessional group leaders, who felt that care had been taken to minimize the risks involved.

Specific Applications. Encounter groups may be particularly dangerous or have a greater degree of negative impact when applied in inappropriate settings. Although no conclusive research exists to document this thesis, the frequently negative results that occur when encounter groups are used in industrial and organizational settings provide reasonably persuasive evidence of this danger. Thus, Boyd and Ellis (1962), investigating the effects of T-groups on managers, found that T-group participants underwent eleven times more negative changes than a control group. A similar study by Underwood (1965) analyzed the changes undergone by fifteen T-group participants and fifteen matched controls. In the control group the ratio of changes judged to be productive in terms of job effectiveness to those judged unproductive was 4:1, while the ratio for the experimental group was 2:1. It may have been that these negative changes were due to poor leadership or other factors. Nonetheless, these findings are suggestive.

Summary. A number of factors appear to interrrelate and contribute to harmfulness in groups. While significantly more research needs to be conducted before conclusive results are likely, reasonable evidence exists in support of the following propositions. Lieberman, Yalom, and Miles (1973, Yalom and Lieberman, 1971) have shown that attack or rejection by either the group leader or the group itself can cause significant psychological injury. Ross, Kligfeld, and Whitman's (1971) analysis of their survey questionnaire supports this conclusion, as do the writings of a number of theoreticians such as Stone (1970). Coercion, both in the initial decision to attend an encounter group and within the group through pressuring group members to change or alter their behavior, is also an important factor. Input overload, such as being confronted with too much feedback at once, too much physical closeness, or a set of group values too discrepant from one's own, can likewise produce harm.

The personal qualities of the group leader appear to be especially critical to how dangerous an encounter group is. In the Group Experience Project "love leaders" produced virtually no casualties, while highly charismatic types accounted for a large percentage, as did the impersonals, and the laissez-faires. Bach's (1967) study indicates that lack of caring, narcissism, and being unlike other participants is considered least helpful by group members. White's (1972) study concludes that rigid leaders were counterproductive. The ideological school of the leader, however, does not appear to be related to risk of harm, nor have the specific techniques employed by group leaders. While Kane, Wallace, and Lipton (1971) and Hurley and Force (1973) maintain that professional training minimizes harm, the high rate of casualties in the Group Experience Project (conducted by highly-credentialed professionals) versus the extremely low rate in the TIE Project (where most of the groups were run by nonprofessionals) argues against such a conclusion.

With regard to participants, a number of factors tend to increase the risk that they will become casualties or will otherwise be harmed by the encounter group experience. The results of the Group Experience Proejct indicate that people with poor mental health, especially those with high anticipations and expectations, where there is no recognition of potential dangers, are likely to be injured. Stone and Tieger (1971) recommend screening out individuals who are psychotic or prepsychotic, the severely anxious, psychosomatics, or those with impulse control. Archer's (1974) study throws a slightly different light on the matter and suggests that those low in "power" are likely to deteriorate in a group, especially with regard to self-concept. On the whole,

however, the research on participant characteristics and its relation to negative outcome is extremely poor, although opinions abound.

Virtually all writers are agreed that certain basic precautions can do much to minimize harm. Making participation voluntary, making sure that consent is informed and that the participant is fully aware of what is expected and involved, establishing clear procedural guidelines, especially with regard to specific behaviors such as physical touching, and the provision of follow-up interviews are generally considered wise guidelines. In addition, screening of candidates has been suggested by a large number of writers, together with concrete proposals as to screening methods. On this matter, however, there is considerable argument due to many factors. Among the arguments against screening are: (1) the lack of reliability and validity of most testing procedures; (2) the lack of evidence and the contradictory results of what evidence exists that a certain type of individual will tend to have negative reactions to encounter group experiences; (3) the expense involved; and (4) the possibility of negative and harmful effects occurring because of screening an individual out.

In terms of identifying who is a casualty, any number of methods have been used. By and large, studies have generally relied on the opinion of a professional, and it is usually the judgment of the professional who has conducted the group. Lieberman, Yalom, and Miles (1973: 175–77) point out that the judgment of the group leader is highly suspect with regard to casualties, and the best method of identification is through fellow group members. Apart from this method, whether somebody has entered psychotherapy during or within six to eight months after an encounter group is a reasonably reliable method, with self-report of the participant somewhat less reliable.

It can be seen that many factors account for the harm that may be produced in an encounter group experience. While the group leader plays an important role, many factors over which she or he has little control also operate to produce harm. These include the personality characteristics of the participants, the type of group norms that get established, and the particular quality and interaction of group members. The fact that the group leader accounts for less than 100 percent of the variance in determining whether a casualty will occur in a group is extremely important in dealing with regulatory issues, since it indicates that regulation of the professional group leader may not eliminate or even significantly decrease the harm that occurs in groups.

Conclusion

A careful examination of empirical research on the roles and functions of traditional psychotherapists and encounter group leaders reveals that traditional assumptions about standards and criteria for practice are seriously open to question. Various strands of evidence suggest that the extent to which therapists are able to influence participant and patient outcomes may be far less than previously imagined. Although the processes are not well understood, documentation of the existence of the placebo effect and faith healing indicates that therapeutic effectiveness may rest in large part on the fact that patients simply believe that their therapists are going to help them. The ability of the therapist to create the impression of expertise and to instill confidence, rather than actual possession of particular technical skills, may be the critical factor. The fact that emotionally ill individuals often recover without any formal treatment and the documented effectiveness of leaderless groups in bringing about constructive growth and personality change suggest that formal training, theoretical knowl-

edge, and technical abilities are far less important than specific personality characteristics and interpersonal skills. The evidence suggests that participant and patient outcomes are strongly affected by some variables having nothing to do with professional expertise (such as the initial level of patient mental health or the member composition of an encounter group). Regulations, then, should focus less on control of the professional than other elements in the encounter group or therapeutic process (such as who qualifies for traditional therapy or how encounter groups are composed).

Although the above arguments suggest that practitioners are not a totally dominating influence, other evidence indicates that they do account for a significant part of the outcome variance. Contrary to much professional opinion, however, the effectiveness of therapists is more determined by the presence or absence of certain personality characteristics and interpersonal skills than technical abilities and theoretical knowledge. Specifically, a therapist's ability to empathize, be warm and caring, and to be genuine in the therapeutic relationship appear important for successful work.

While diagnostic ability (as traditionally defined), technical skills, ability to use various methods of treatment, and theoretical knowledge are most certainly relevant to high levels of competence, little evidence exists that they are essential for minimal competence or that their absence will lead to significant harm. Interestingly, the empirical data on what makes for competent practice and what prevents harm converge: those people who are competent have the same skills and qualifications as those who do not precipitate harm.

If it is true that the personal qualities and interpersonal skills of the therapist constitute the core on which minimal competence and protection of the public are based, this has wide implications for attempts at regulation, for training programs, and for the certification process. It means that traditional criteria in the form of academic credentials are generally inappropriate measures of effectiveness. It means that many people might function as effective therapists with a minimum of training and experience. At the very least, it is sufficient to require rethinking what it means to be competent as either a traditional therapist or group leader.

Perhaps the soundest conclusion that can be drawn is that legitimate grounds for disagreement exist as to the particular ingredients that go into being a successful psychotherapist. The amount of disagreement in the field is extensive and provides an indication that little is still really known. Combs's (1953: 559) warning of twenty-five years ago remains true:

Unfortunately we have a great deal more feeling than fact about what training and experience are required for effective practice in our profession. Almost everyone has his private opinion about what kinds of standards are needed to engage in practice, but we have very little clear-cut evidence of what are really prerequisite to effective service. We need a great deal more systematic exploration of this problem. Meanwhile we need to examine the requirements we write into law with great care.

THE EFFECTIVENESS OF TRAINING PROGRAMS

The problem of graduate training, too little known, too little studied, too superficially dealt with, too potent in its final effects upon world culture to be left to technologists and specialists, must be studied by thoughtful Americans.—Howard Mumford Jones (1946).

From existing data it would appear that only one out of three people entering professional training [has] the requisite interpersonal skills to prove helpful to patients. Further, there is no evidence that the usual traditional graduate training program has any positive value in producing therapists who are more helpful than nonprofessionals. In short, current procedures for . . . training are indefensible. Out of habit we still cling to them and perpetuate them even when the

evidence is clear. Moreover, the chances that a trainee will be taught by a therapist who is himself either ineffective or harmful are two out of three. In this light it is not surprising that nonprofessionals in all studies to date appear to be as effective or more effective than the average trained professional.—Charles Truax and Kevin Mitchell (1971: 337).

Academic credentials constitute the single most important criterion in statutory regulation through licensure laws. This is true for the professions of law, medicine, architecture, dentistry, and even some of the more common occupations such as cosmetology and embalming. It is also true for psychotherapy, the practice of which is regulated through most psychology and social work licensing laws, many medical practice acts, and a variety of other laws, including those regulating marriage and family counseling.[64] It may also prove true for encounter group leaders, since definitions of practice of many professions are broad enough to subsume the practice of leading encounter groups within them.

The pervasive reliance on academic credentials and training in regulating most professions raises several issues. The most critical and obvious is whether academic training contributes to and is a valid sign of professional competence. Closely related is whether academic training is actually necessary for public protection, and whether apprenticeships, field experience, and other modes of nonacademic education might serve the same purpose. A problem underlying all of the above is determining what particular methods of training are effective.

Recently the value of academic credentials and professional training in general has been called into question. In the field of teacher education, for instance, John G. Merrow, Jr.'s (1975) review of the research led him to conclude that no good evidence existed relating any kind of teacher training with subsequent teacher or student performance. Similarly, the

Citizens Commission on Graduate Medical Education (1966) is critical of significant aspects of graduate medical education as it relates to future professional competence. Recent work by Douglas Heath (1977) at Haverford College provides evidence that high academic achievement in one's undergraduate years is negatively correlated with later work competence in general.

The dissatisfaction with academic training has been quite evident in the mental health field. Margaret Rioch (1966), for instance, notes that a fairly large group of mental health professionals do not believe that long years of academic training are necessary for much of the work that professionals do. Surveys of practitioners, discussed below, indicate that much of the content of traditional programs, as well as the manner of teaching that content, are not particularly useful and may even lead to a decrease in effectiveness. Truax and Mitchell (1971: 337), as quoted above, emphatically state that current methods of training for psychotherapists are indefensible and lack any positive value. The fact that so few practicing clinicians meet minimally facilitative levels of competence (Carkhuff and Berenson 1967: 10-11; Truax and Mitchell 1971: 338) is a good indication that academic credentials are not the best measure of competence in the mental health field.

To establish the degree of validity of these contentions it is necessary to take a close look at the relevant social science research. Unfortunately, professional training has proceeded largely without attempts to prove its effectiveness. Even in psychology, which has a strong research orientation and where as many as a third of those in the field practice psychotherapy, little research has been conducted (Mattarazzo 1971: 915-16). As Carl Rogers (1956: 76) succinctly puts it, "For the most part this field is characterized by a rarity of research and a plenitude of platitudes." The situation is no different in the medical or social work professions. Likewise, the research on training encounter group leaders is exceedingly sparce (Gibb 1974). It seems that only three groups of researchers have been systematically concerned with the effectiveness of training procedures: Margaret Rioch's staff at the National Institute of Mental Health; Truax, Carkhuff, and their client-centered associates; and the investigators of the filial therapy techniques of Guerney (Durlak 1971: 249).

Psychiatry

Training the psychotherapist through medical education is a long and involved process. Typically a student attends four years of medical school, with the first two being devoted to the basic sciences and the last two to the clinical sciences (Curran and Shapiro 1970: 513). After a year's internship, most students go on to at least three years of residency training in the process of becoming a full-fledged psychiatrist. The amount of time devoted to psychiatry in the first four years of medical school is quite meager. An analysis of a typical curriculum reveals that psychiatry involves less than 5 percent of the total student hours devoted to medical subjects (see the curriculum in Curran and Shapiro 1970: 514), and very few hours are devoted to the behavioral sciences.

Although this situation has changed somewhat, and although specialization is possible somewhat earlier, there have been escalating criticisms of medical school as a place to train psychotherapists. As far back as the 1940s, Jules Coleman (1947) argued that medical schools fostered authoritarian and directive attitudes inimical to helping patients. He recommended the teaching of psychotherapeutic skills, if only to overcome this tendency. Lester, Gussen, Yamamoto, and West (1962) believe that traditional teaching methods result in students feeling helpless, anxious, and hostile—all of which they consider antitherapeutic. This opinion is reflected in a symposium of all major professions involved in psychotherapy, in which frequent comments were voiced that traditional training fosters a method of dealing with patients that is authoritative, mechanistic, and emotionally distant (Welsch et al. 1956; see also Shakow 1949: 382; Strupp 1972: 273).

The criticism of psychiatric training is not limited to isolated individuals. General surveys of practitioners, schools, and teachers indicate a deep-seated and pervasive dissatisfaction. The American Psychiatric Association and the Association of American Medical Colleges, for instance, sponsored an NIMH-funded conference in 1967 on psychiatry and medical education (Earley, 1969). As part of the conference report, the heads of departments of psychiatry at U.S. medical schools were surveyed. More than 60 percent felt that the number of hours allotted to psychiatry was insufficient (Earley, 1969: 70). Almost half felt that it would be impossible to achieve their own curriculum objectives within the existing structure of medical school (Earley, 1969: 70). Only five chairpeople in the entire country were satisfied with the adequacy of courses on the psychological and behavioral science aspects of medicine.

Henry, Sims, and Spray (9171) conducted a large-scale study to determine the origins and practices of the four core mental health professions. Interesting data on the relevance of professional training were generated through intensive interviews with nearly 300 therapists from Chicago, Los Angeles, and New York City, as well as questionnaries mailed to more than 6,000 other professionals in these three cities (of whom nearly 4,000 responded). When asked how relevant medical school course work was, a third of all psychoanalysts and a quarter of all psychiatrists replied that such work was totally irrelevant (Henry, Sims, and Spray 1971: 162). The idea that a medical background was useful for diagnosing neurological disorders did not impress many physicians practicing psychiatry.

In another survey, Castlenuovo-Tedesco (1969, 1967) reviewed the literature on psychiatric training and concluded that most reports were quite sketchy and hardly qualified as adequate research. To obtain a better picture of how medical training was evaluated by its recipients, he surveyed both nonpsychiatric and psychiatric residents from forty different medical schools throughout the country. The results proved disquieting: 65 percent of the psychiatric residents thought their preparation for psychiatry was either indifferent or poor (Castlenuovo-Tedesco 1969: 477). Nearly half of the nonpsychiatric physicians believed that they had not been taught the amount of psychiatry they would need to practice medicine. Almost a third of all psychiatric residents had never treated a patient in psychotherapy (Castlenuovo-Tedesco 1969: 477). Most clinical work consisted of lectures, diagnostic evaluations, and observations of therapy conducted by an instructor. Of those who had actually conducted some therapy, few had treated more than a handful of patients, nearly a third stated that they had received little or no supervision, and approximately a fifth reported that their instruction had been mainly to "play it by ear."

Few surveys report positive findings. A study commissioned by the California Office of Planning found that two-thirds of all training directors of psychiatric residency programs in the state believed medical education to be ineffective, and nearly a third felt that too much emphasis was placed on somatic medicine (California Department of Mental Hygiene, vol. 2, 1967: 151–54). In terms of practical knowledge gained from medical school, another survey of five medical schools in Philadelphia revealed that the typical graduate lacked even the most basic knowledge of psychiatric practice

(Greenbank 1961). For instance, half of all students believed that a person who talked about suicide would not go through with it, and another half believed that masturbation frequently caused mental illness.

After reviewing the critical literature on medical training, Light (1975) pointed out that psychiatry has put itself in an awkward position by letting another profession (the medical profession) determine the pool of candidates it has to choose from, doing so on different if not counterproductive grounds. He concluded that medical school emerged as a "pathological institution which selects students on the wrong criteria and downplays the qualities long esteemed in clinical work" (Light, 1975: 610).

While these surveys are of distinct value in assessing general professional opinion, they do not meet many of the criteria of rigorous social science research. In particular, no attempt has been made to assess the actual effects of training or to isolate the specific factors in training that make a difference. In the field of traditional psychiatric training, such efforts are conspicuously absent. The only two that come close to qualifying are a study by Khajavi and Hekmat (1971) and another by Klein (1965). Khajavi and Hekmat compared psychiatrists, psychiatric social workers, psychiatric nurses, activity therapists, and psychologists for level of empathy. Based on Hogan's Empathy Scale (1969), the psychologists scored highest, follwed by social workers, psychiatric nurses, activity therapists, and finally psychiatrists, although none of the differences was statistically significant. When first-year psychiatric residents were compared with second-year and third-year residents, graduates, and staff psychiatrists, Khajavi and Hekmat found that first-year residents scored significantly higher on the empathy scale than second-year residents. Third-year residents, graduates, and staff did not score significantly higher on this scale. According to their interpretation of the data, the research confirms that academic competency is not a significant factor influencing the growth of empathy. Although specifically oriented only toward psychoanalytic training, Klein's (1965) excellent research on the selection and evaluation of analysts-in-training found that those who failed to meet the requirements at the psychoanalytic clinic at Columbia University were not easily identified from their previous performance in medical school, internship, or residency.

Despite the lack of objective evidence on the efficacy of psychiatric training, the rising tide of criticism has prompted attempts to change medical school curricula and residency training to achieve greater relevance. The increase in the number of electives in psychiatry, the possibility of greater specialization at an earlier level, and the rise in the number of behavioral science courses bodes well (Curran and Shapiro 1970: 513). Innovative programs have been developed to teach empathy (see, e.g., Muslin and Schlessinger 1971; Truax and Carkhuff 1967). More and more thought is being given as to how psychiatry is best taught (see, e.g., Ekstein and Wallerstein 1972; Lidz and Edelson 1970), including psychoanalysis (see Ornstein, Ornstein, and Lindy 1976). Serious attempts have been made to develop competency-based residency programs for psychiatrists (see Weinstein and Russell 1976). As could be predicted, there has been considerably more research on these innovations in teaching methods (see the research discussed in Matarazzo 1971; Matarazzo, Wiens, and Saslow 1966), in comparison with traditional programs.

Psychology

After World War II the need for psychotherapy rose as a result of the tremendous numbers of veterans returning with severe emotional problems and suffering from "shellshock." The limited numbers of psychiatrists available necessitated the use of the psychologist as a psychotherapist. Training programs developed, especially in clinical and counseling psychology. Since then, training as a psychologist has become one of the principal routes to professional status as a therapist.

Unlike other programs for training mental health professionals, clinical psychology developed from an academic base. As a result, typical programs place far greater emphasis on research, in adherence to the "scientist-practitioner" model advocated by the American Psychological Association and many of its leading members (see, especially, American Psychological Association, Committee on Training in Clinical Psychology, 1947; Shakow 1969; Stayer 1970).

Traditional clinical psychology programs have been widely criticized. Bakan states categorically that "there are today no adequate training facilities for psychotherapists and . . . no 'decent' clinical psychology program exists in North America" (in Bergin and Strupp 1972: 378). George Albee, former President of the American Psychological Association, has long felt that the scientist-practitioner model should be abandoned and that clinical psychology must distinguish between the training of professionals and scientists (Albee and Loeffler 1971). Robert Holt (in Snyder 1962), one of the founders of clinical psychology in this country, believes that a paradox exists in the inadequacy of doctoral-level training programs that produce graduates barely capable of diagnostic testing, let alone psychotherapy. The recent Vail conference of the American Psychological Association (1973a) saw the conferees vote to follow Albee's advice and abandon the scientist-practitioner model.

A number of surveys indicate that the opinions voiced above are shared by a majority of practitioners in the field. In 1960 Kelly questioned members of the Division of Clinical Psychology of the American Psychological Association (Kelly 1961). He found that many of the division's members did not regard clinical training as adequate preparation for clinical practice. In addition, just about half of all clinical psychologists no longer believed in what they were doing and were sorry that they had chosen clinical psychology as a profession. Several years later Lubin (1962) surveyed this same membership and found that 41 percent of the respondents spent at least half their time conducting therapy. In terms of their training, 20 percent had had no supervision in adult therapy. Of those who had received such training, more than half had obtained most of it at the postdoctoral level, often through informal programs.

A study of New York State clinical psychologists at about the same time found that only 7 percent of a total of 696 respondents believed their academic training had prepared them for private practice in psychotherapy, and nearly half stated that doctoral studies had little or nothing to do with preparation for private practice (Kalinowitz 1971: 128–29, citing a survey by Goldman).[65] The more recent work of Henry, Sims, and Spray (1971) reveals that the dissatisfaction of clinical psychologists with their training has continued. Seventeen percent found it completely irrelevant and less than 50 percent believed that it was generally or very relevant.

The opinion of many practitioners that clinical psychology training is less than ideal for developing competent therapists is borne out through an analysis of the purpose and course content of most academic programs. In the early 1960s, Blanck (1963) studied all academic programs in clinical psychology approved by the American Psychological Association. No university program expressly trained psychotherapists for practice, much less for private practice (Blanck 1963: 176–77). As a result, academic courses in psychotherapy do not have a

primary place within any of these programs, and in some cases do not exist
at all. Many departments were strongly
against any professional program, prefer-
ring to view the clinical psychologist as
a scientist.

To determine the type of training
received, Blanck divided all courses into
one of four categories (Blanck 1963: 174-
80). In the theoretical area, which was the
most emphasized, the number of courses
taught varied from one to thirty-four,
with a mean of nearly twelve. Practical
training ranged from no courses to eleven,
with a mean between three and four.
The amount of experiential training—
defined as field work, internships, and
other supervised experience in psychotherapy—was more difficult to determine.
In accordance with the guidelines of the
American Psychological Association, each
program provided one year of internship,
but the traditional emphasis was on
psychodiagnostic testing. The number
of such courses varied from none to seven,
with a mean of approximately two. The
final area, labeled "personal training,"
which Blanck defined as a psychotherapeutic experience, was almost wholly
lacking. This analysis suggests that the
type of training being provided in traditional programs is not geared to training
practitioners.

The very few examples of controlled
research on the effectiveness of academic
training in psychology add empirical
support to the subjective opinion of
practitioners and to the conclusions
drawn from Blanck's analysis presented
above. In one study, Carkhuff, Kratochvil,
and Friel (1968) evaluated the effectiveness of two clinical training programs
approved by the American Psychological
Association. Through tape ratings of fifty-
four therapeutic interviews conducted by
beginning to advance graduate students,
the authors found a general decline in
the levels of empathy, regard, genuineness, concreteness, self-disclosure, and

overall level of conditions communicated
by the more advanced students as compared with beginning students. While
the amount of decline did not reach a
significant level, the fact that declines
occurred on nearly every dimension is
an indication that the more advanced
students were not as effective therapists
as the beginning students.

The authors suggest that the declines
are attributable to the training program.
An extremely interesting aspect of this
study was an examination of the drop-
out rates. They found that in every case
those students who left the program were
rated higher in their levels of empathy,
regard, and other relevant characteristics
than those who remained in the program.
In other words, it appeared that the best
potential counselors left the program. In
another study by Carkhuff (1968),
essentially the same conclusion was
reached. He compared the differential
functioning of lay and professional
helpers and found that therapists in
professional programs exhibited a drop
in the level of functioning over the course
of graduate training, with the largest
drop occurring between the first and
second year.

Another pair of studies by Bergin and
his associates provides further evidence
that psychology students are not particularly empathic. Bergin and Solomon
(1970) explored the relation of empathic
ability to selection criteria for graduate
students in clinical and counseling psychology. The results were depressing.
Rather than an even slightly positive
relationship, they found that empathy
had a negative correlation of -0.30
with verbal intelligence, and -0.18 with
the psychology subscale of the Graduate
Record Examination. In other words,
indicators of intelligence or academic
achievement are unrelated to empathy
measures. In another study Carkhuff and
Truax (1965) found that the level of
empathy exhibited by lay personnel was

significantly higher than the level achieved by post-practicum students in traditional clinical and counseling programs.

Several studies have attempted to evaluate the quality of graduate training by examining how valuable or well-conducted patients or others viewed the psychotherapy provided by therapists of varying levels of training. Schmidt and Strong (1970), for instance, presented a videotape of therapeutic interviews to thirty-seven students; they were conducted by six different therapists who ranged in experience from beginning graduated students to a Ph.D. with five years of experience. Surprisingly, the students' mean ratings of "expertness" were almost perfectly inversely related to the amount of training received—that is, the more training someone had, the more likely that person was to be rated as "less expert."

At the University of Texas Testing and Counseling Center, Grigg (1961) asked more than 200 clients to evaluate whether and to what extent counseling had been helpful to them. The counselors were six highly experienced individuals with doctorates, six experienced trainees who had finished a year of internship, and four inexperienced counselors who neither had completed their internship nor had prior experience. There was virtually no distinction in the amount that people felt they had been helped, although the most experienced therapists were viewed as least helpful.[66]

The massive five-year study by Kelly and Fiske (1951), initiated to explore the prediction of performance of clinical psychologists, has also yielded results bearing on the value of traditional psychological training. Through a variety of procedures, Kelly and Fiske evaluated the therapeutic competence of former clinical psychology students five years after graduation. Not suprisingly they found that academic and research competence could be reasonably well predicted by various measures, but therapeutic competence was relatively uncorrelated with academic grades. Kelly and Goldberg (1959), in a later study, found that the criteria used by most universities to select students were often totally irrelevant to those students' aptitudes for becoming effective therapists.

In recent years an increasing number of changes have occurred in the professional training of the clinical psychologist. While most programs have adhered to the traditional model of training the scientist-practitioner, several have decided to deemphasize the research aspect of training in line with the recommendation of the conferees at the Vail conference. The strongest move in this direction has come from the new schools of professional psychology that have been set up in several states.[67] These schools award a Psy.D. degree instead of the traditional Ph.D., and their curricula strongly emphasize experiential learning and coursework relevant to psychotherapy, as opposed to research and diagnostic testing. Although these programs have been criticized (see, e.g., Shakow, 1976; Stayer, 1970; Stricker, 1975), they are becoming well established, and California's program recently received regional accreditation.

Another trend has been the development of post-doctoral training programs, such as at New York University, to make up for the gaps currently existing in the typical graduate program (Fine, 1966). The American Psychological Association has issued guidelines on recommended standards for psychotherapy education in psychology doctoral programs, including recommendations for departmental structure, faculty, practicum settings, and curriculum (Bookbinder, Fox, and Rosenthal 1971).

Paraprofessional Training

Training programs for paraprofessional psychotherapists have employed a wide variety of approaches and methods.[68] Traditional didactic classroom instruction, informal group discussions, intensive and individualized on-the-job training, brief orientations, and various combinations of the above have all been utilized (Durlak 1971: 247–48). Most of these programs involve varying degrees of professional consultation and supervision. On the whole, such programs stress the experiential dimension of training, emphasizing role-playing, on-the-job training, and other methods that directly involve the trainee as a whole person (Sobey 1970: 117).

Concomitantly, courses and experiences that are not clearly relevant to becoming an effective therapist are usually omitted, many times for strictly pragmatic reasons—there is simply not enough money to underwrite courses of dubious value. In Sobey's (1970: 117) study of over 10,000 nonprofessionals working in 185 projects sponsored by the National Institute of Mental Health throughout the United States, she found that very few training programs emphasized didactic methods. The typical program involved on-the-job apprentice-type training along or combined with some didactic instruction.

A description of two contrasting paraprofessional programs will add flesh to the outline provided above. A model of training that is quite well known has been developed by Rioch and her associates (1965) for housewives. It is very intensive and time-consuming. Although originally intended to be half-time for four academic semesters, it became the equivalent of one-and-a-half years of graduate study. During the first year the trainees received no theoretical inputs. Instead the focus was on on-the-job experiences, supervision, group therapy sessions, and case seminars. During the second year, some theory was taught. The goals of training were to teach the trainees to be "professional" rather than "social" in the therapeutic interview, to deal with, rather than avoid, areas of anxiety and discomfort, to recognize their own defensiveness and anxiety, to understand the effects their own feelings had in hindering therapeutic progress, and to listen to what the patient was saying.

Truax and Carkhuff (1967) have developed an alternative model that is far briefer. The basic idea of their program is to concentrate on those skills and competencies that are central to the therapeutic process, which they believe to be empathy, nonpossessive warmth, and genuineness. After selecting candidates who are relatively high in each of these characteristics, Truax and Carkhuff teach the trainees precisely what makes up the core conditions of therapy. This is done by giving them extensive experience in using the rating scales that Truax and Carkhuff have developed to measure these core conditions, by having them view and evaluate psychotherapeutic interviews of varying degrees of quality, and by giving them practice in making responses that exhibit high levels of the three core conditions. The trainees then begin practicing psychotherapy through pairing off with each other and role-playing various situations that are recorded and later analyzed in the classroom. Following this comes a series of live interviews with actual patients, which are then rated, evaluated, and discussed. In addition, the trainees participate in weekly group therapy experiences that focus on emotional or other problems that might interfere with the trainee's effective therapeutic functioning. The program requires less than 100 hours. According to Truax and Carkhuff (1967: 242), the crucial elements of their program are as follows:

(1) a therapeutic context in which the supervisor himself provides high levels of therapeutic conditions; (2) a highly specific didactic training in the implementation of the therapeutic conditions; and (3) a quasi-group therapy experience where the trainee can explore his own existence, and his own individual self can emerge.

Evidence of the effectiveness of paraprofessional training programs is more abundant than for professional training. Both indirect and direct empirical research exist. First, numerous studies indicate that minimally trained paraprofessionals compare favorably with highly credentialed professionals. Such studies at the very least demonstrate that long years of academic training are not a prerequisite for competence (see pages 120–24 above). Second, the body of research indicating that paraprofessionals are effective, even though no direct comparison is made with professionals, provides additional support for this argument.

Third, a number of studies demonstrating paraprofessional effectiveness have been conducted on people whose only training and experience as practitioners has come through brief programs designed for paraprofessionals. Typical of these is a study by Carkhuff and Truax (1965) that found that trainees who completed less than 100 hours of training over a four-month period were functioning at levels not significantly different in empathy and nonpossessive warmth from a group of well-known and highly experienced therapists, including Carl Rogers, Albert Ellis, and Rollo May.

Unfortunately, on the basis of this type of research it remains an open question whether the effectiveness results from the training or is due to other factors, since the studies do not provide for an equivalent control group, and many provide measures of effectiveness only after the training, precluding pre-training comparisons. These problems are overcome in several studies (see, e.g., Demos 1964; Demos and Zuwaylif 1963), an example of which is Martin and Carkhuff's (1968) research on the changes in personality and interpersonal functioning of counselors-in-training. Using a matched control group, Martin and Carkhuff found that a summer counseling practicum that met five days a week for approximately one and a half hours each day brought about significant changes in personality as measured by the MMPI, in levels of interpersonal functioning, in various therapeutic dimensions, such as empathy, and in the level to which clients underwent self-exploration.

Even more impressive than this type of research have been the numerous studies that not only document a significant increase in effectiveness after training, but also attempt to isolate through careful controls the specific factors that were responsible for the changes that took place. The reasonably extensive research on this point is discussed below in the special section on factors important to the effectiveness of training programs. Since most of it has been conducted on paraprofessional training programs, the positive results are an indication that such programs are, in fact, efficacious.

The Training of Encounter Group Leaders

The training of encounter group leaders in many ways parallels that of the paraprofessional psychotherapist. For the most part both programs have developed outside the traditional academic environment and have tended to concentrate on experiential, as opposed to didactic, instruction. Lippitt and his associates (1975: 478–81) have identified five different patterns of training for encounter group leaders: (1) university-based graduate programs; (2) private institutes and organizations; (3) a less formal sequence in which the trainee functions as a co-trainer or intern in a wide variety of groups and receives feedback and training from the senior group leader; (4) on-the-job development of young professionals in consulting firms, growth centers, and private organizations; and (5) self-training (a pattern that the authors do not advocate).

A number of university-based programs currently train practitioners as encounter group leaders. Boston University, for instance, recently created an experimental two-year program designed to train T-group leaders (Knowles, undated). Students first participate in a human relations laboratory for one semester. Following this they observe a similar group for a semester, while at the same time participating in a seminar in which they learn observation skills. The subsequent two semesters are spent co-training and training other groups, with seminars devoted to learning group theory and other aspects of training.

A strong emphasis is placed on developing qualities of acceptance and understanding, with special stress on respecting a participant's defenses. The lecture method of teaching is largely dispensed with, with the focus on group discussion, role plays, and self-study. Students learn according to their mutual interest and needs. An integral part of the program is the feedback that group leaders receive on their effectiveness. This comes from participants, various members of the training team (each group is led by a trainer, co-trainer, and one or more observers), members in one's seminar, and staff. The primary emphasis of the training is to help group leaders become more facilitative, to be more in touch with their own feelings, to become more open and less defensive in group situations, and to be more empathic, warm, and genuine.

Typical of the private institutes and organizations that have developed group leadership programs is the La Jolla Program at the Center for Studies of the Person (described in Rogers, 1970: 149–57). Practitioners from many different professions and widely differing educational backgrounds participate in an intensive three-week program that has three elements: experience as a participant in an encounter group; cognitive learning about different types of groups, group theory, and other relevant areas of knowledge; and co-facilitating two weekend encounter groups. The cognitive aspect of the program is developed in response to the needs of the participants. Much of the learning that takes place is a result of sharing of experiences with others who are co-facilitating groups. No certificate of completion is given and no degree is awarded, since the program directors believe that their goal is the development of better-qualified leaders, not experts.[69]

Varying opinions exist as to what constitutes the ideal training program for the encounter group leader. In general, professionals and theoreticians in this field have taken a performance-based approach to training and have recognized the importance of certain interpersonal skills in becoming effective. This is not to the exclusion of cognitive knowledge or research skills, and Lippitt, Benne, Bradford, and Gibb (1975: 478) state emphatically that professional development as a group leader should include a background in the behavioral sciences, preferably social or clinical psychology, and also include anthropological and philosophical approaches to human behavior. Further, they stress the importance of a commitment to theory-building, research, and scholarship, and recommend direct participation of the self through some form of psychotherapeutic experience and actual experience in working with groups, although the former is not essential.

Some practitioners still insist that extensive academic knowledge is one of the key features of any training program. Martin Lakin (1972, 1969), for instance, requires this of any group leader, and advocates additional prerequisites for what he terms a "trainer-investigator." The latter, in addition to training functions, would be a researcher, conceptualizer, and trainer of trainers, and must have received training leading to a doctoral degree of some sort. Other group leaders would not necessarily have to possess a doctoral degree, but Lakin still advocates extensive training, coursework, and experience. He believes that training programs should provide a background in personality theory, psychopathology, and group dynamics theory.

On the other hand, a significant number of experts believe that rigid and formal requirements such as these serve little purpose. After completing a year's study of sensitivity training and what its implications were for education, Donald Clark (1970) concluded that it would be a mistake to set up a program to train group leaders within a university setting, since that environment is not conducive to training effective group leaders. William Schutz (1971: 241-54), while convinced that nobody knows very much about training group leaders, is convinced that traditional medical training is poor since it fosters authoritarianism, tightness, and constriction, while traditional clinical psychology programs encourage too great a degee of skepticism and caution. His own suggestions include intensive experience in an encounter group run by an expert leader, ample supervision, co-leading groups with experienced practitioners who provide feedback, undergoing a variety of further experiences in different therapeutic and encounter group techniques, and intellectual training in the major schools of therapy, personality theory, group dynamics, group therapy, psychosomatic medicine, anatomy, physiology, and inductive logic (Schutz, 1971: 251-54).

One of the few surveys of professional opinion on the important elements in human relations training programs was conducted by the Canadian Commission on Human Relations Training (1970). A questionnaire directed to group leaders who were generally accepted as experienced by the Canadian training commu-

nity asked the leaders which experiences were important in preparation to function as a group leader for the first time, and which experiences were important in contributing to trainer competence since the date of the first training experience. The responses showed that actual experiences as a participant or co-leader were most important in initial functioning. University study ranked nearly as high, but participation in seminars and reading were mentioned by a relatively small percentage. In developing further competence after the first experience, the value of university study decreased to almost zero. Research and reading were likewise not considered important. On the other hand, continuing experience as a trainer was designated by most people. Further experience in leadership roles, additional experience as a participant, and experience in designing laboratory programs were all mentioned by more than 40 percent of the respondents.

Virtually no research examines whether one type of training program for group leaders is better than another. The opinions above generally substantiate the belief that an integrated program combining didactic and academic instruction with extensive experiential involvement in actual practice is preferable to the more content-oriented programs traditionally offered in academic settings.[70]

Important Variables in the Training Process

Empirical research on what aspects of training make a difference to practitioner competence is rare and rudimentary. Most of it stems from the paraprofessional field. Many of those aspects of training that have been assumed to be essential have received no scrutiny whatever. Thus, few if any studies have examined whether technical and theoretical courses or specific subject areas are critical to the success of a particular program. The only areas to receive more than cursory attention have been the importance of supervisor personality, the methods of teaching empathic skills and other interpersonal abilities, and the value of an integrated didactic-experiential format.

The Rogerians have especially argued that supervisors of therapists-in-training must have certain interpersonal skills if supervision is to result in increased competence. Without such skills, they argue, no amount of theoretical or technical expertise will be helpful. Low levels of empathy and warmth, in fact, are likely to lead to deterioration in the trainee's ability to function effectively. Research from the client-centered school bears these hypotheses out. Pierce, Carkhuff, and Berenson (1967), for instance, studied seventeen volunteers for a mental-health counselor training program by administering pre- and post-tests on Rogers's three therapeutic conditions (empathy, warmth, and genuineness), as well as degree of concreteness and level of self-disclosure. These volunteers were split up and assigned to either a high-functioning supervisor or one who was low-functioning. Those who were supervised by the former all remained in the program and made significant increases in their ability to empathize, as well as other areas of interpersonal functioning. In the low-functioning group, only four remained, five dropped out, and the group did not achieve any significant gains.

Pagell, Carkhuff, and Berenson (1967) found that therapists-in-training who received high levels of therapeutic conditions from their supervisor offered higher levels of conditions to their own patients than a similar group that was supervised by a therapist who offered low levels of empathy, warmth, and genuineness. The best predictor of the therapist-in-training's behavior was the level of empathy offered by the supervisor. In a related study, Matthews (1972) attempted to investigate selected premises of Carkhuff's theory of training therapists—expecially the validity of Carkhuff's Index of Communication, which strongly focuses on empathic skills—as a method of evaluating potential therapeutic ability. Matthews found that trainees supervised by highly empathic trainers achieved virtually the same level of competence as their trainers. The poor trainers had little effect on their trainees.

Hansen and Barker (1964) studied the effect upon trainees of having a supervisory relationship in which they felt understood, accepted and in which their supervisors were genuine, as opposed to a situation in which this was not the case. The trainees in the former relationship were able to experience themselves at a deeper level, while the latter were more remote from their feelings and more likely to be defensive and cautious in their supervisory relationship. The implication is that the poorer supervisors are less effective in increasing the therapeutic competence of their trainees.

Further studies by Carkhuff and his associates indicate that trainees of trainers who are communicating at high levels improve more than those of low-level communicators, who typically demonstrate negative changes in communication ability (see, e.g., Berenson, Carkhuff, and Myrus, 1966; Carkhuff, Kratochvil, and Friel, 1968). After reviewing more than fifteen studies, Carkhuff (1969: vol. 1, 152-57) concluded that most improvements in trainee functioning came from trainers who were more than minimally empathic if that level of empathy was significantly above that of initial trainee level-of-functioning. According to Carkhuff (1969: 157), "the level of the counselor-trainer's functioning appears to be the single most critical aspect of effective training."

Another series of studies indicates that focusing on the development of specific interpersonal skills, such as empathy and genuineness, when combined with a training approach that combines didactic instruction with experiential learning, leads to excellent results. Carkhuff and his associates have developed training programs that utilize these factors (Carkhuff, 1969, vol. 2; Truax and Carkhuff 1967). An analysis of the level of functioning of student therapists both early and late in a typical 100-hour training program found significant increases in the level of accurate empathy and genuineness (Truax and Silber 1966). In another brief program of empathetic communication training, groups of inner-city preschool teachers and family workers significantly increased their capacity to empathize with other people.

From a methodological standpoint, one of the better designed studies was executed by Berenson, Carkhuff, and Myrus (1966). Unlike much research on training programs, this study employed control groups to determine whether or not the positive results were due to training or some other variable. Undergraduate college students were assigned to one of three different training groups. The first was a control group that received no training. The second was a training group that received the same program as the third group, but did not make use of research scales and was not involved in group therapy sessions. The third group took part in the full 100-hour program developed by Carkhuff and Truax. The trainees were given pre- and post-tests on empathy, positive regard, genuineness, concreteness, and degree of resultant patient self-exploration. To measure these factors, tape ratings, inventory reports of standard interviewees and significant others, and inventory self-reports were used. Each group was comparable at the beginning of the study with regard to the variables measured. In addition, the instructors were tested to ensure that they were functioning at similar levels of interpersonal functioning. The findings were as the authors expected: the greatest gain in interpersonal skills was made by the group receiving full training, and the least gain was made by the control group.

The amount of research that Carkhuff, Truax, and their associates have conducted on the effectiveness of training programs is quite extensive, and a full review of the research would be too lengthy. Their basic findings are that trainees move in the direction of their trainers in interpersonal functioning (the level of empathy, nonpossessive warmth, and genuineness they exhibit); that trainees gain the most with high-level trainers, and progress either minimally or even change negatively with low-functioning trainers; and that those trainees who are functioning at the higher levels will show the greatest improvement. They found that training approaches that concentrate almost solely on didactic instruction do not generally lead to positive improvement on the help-giving dimensions relevant to therapeutic change. Instead, an integrated program of didactic and experiential training with feedback is the best format for conducting effective programs.[71]

Several other training approaches have been developed that contain many of the features of Carkhuff and Truax's programs, yet with significant variations. The research on several of these indicates that they, too, are effective. The microcounseling techniques of Allen Ivey and his associates at the University of Massachusetts, and the training of filial therapists by Bernard Guerney, Jr. and his associates, both deserve mention here.

The training program of Ivey and his associates focuses on certain highly specific skills, such as maintaining eye contact, and employs many of the techniques of behavior-modification. They have found that their program can be effective in as brief a period as five hours. In a series of studies (summarized in Ivey et al., 1968), for instance, when results of their training program were compared with a matched control group, they found a significant increase in eye contact, ability to verbally follow clients, and ability to reflect and summarize accurately what clients said. In addition, the client ratings on the Semantic Differential Form improved significantly, there was a significant improvement in how the clients rated the counselors-in-training, and significant positive changes occurred in the students' self-confidence.

Another variant of the didactic-experience approach combined with feedback has been developed by Guerney and his associates.[72] Known as "filial therapy training," it is a method of teaching parents and other people close to an emotionally disturbed person to function as primary therapeutic agents for that person. Like Truax and Carkhuff, Guerney operates from a primarily Rogerian orientation, attempting to help parents become more empathic, warm, and genuine. The research results have strongly supported the effectiveness of his procedures. For instance, in one study, mothers receiving psychological services at a university child clinic were divided into four groups: two control groups and two experimental groups of six to eight mothers each (Stover and Guerney, 1969). Each of the controls and experimentals spent thirty minutes in a tape-recorded play session with their children. After this session the control groups were asked to wait for approximately four months before returning for another session. In the meantime the experimental groups met for ten hour-and-a-half weekly sessions during which experiential learning was combined with didactic instruction, and the mothers were given constant feedback on their behavior.

When all four groups were compared at the end of training, the results were striking. In both experimental groups the mothers showed significant increases in the percentage of total reflective statements, while the control groups showed no such increase. The children in the experimental groups exhibited significant differences in expressive behavior compared with the controls. Both results were considered signs of constructive changes and were attributed to the effectiveness

of the training program. Further research on this approach to training has yielded largely positive results (see, e.g., Hawkins et al., 1966; Stollak, 1968; Wahler et al., 1965).

While most research has yielded essentially positive results, several reviewers conclude that the evidence is sparse and methodologically weak. Shapiro (1969), for instance, argues that most of the studies cited by Carkhuff and his associates provide only correlational data. Even in the study by Berenson, Carkhuff, and Myrus (1966), for instance, it is impossible to determine precisely which aspects of the training are most important. Meltzoff and Kornreich (1970: 273–88) are even harsher in their evaluation. After reviewing ten different studies on the effectiveness of brief training programs (some of which have been described above), they conclude that their efficacy is not only unproved but essentially untested. They maintain that a good controlled comparison of the effectiveness of trained and untrained therapists has yet to be made.[73]

Summary and Conclusions

The problem of adequately training psychotherapists and encounter group leaders is difficult. Until recently, very little was known about what types of training and what sorts of experiences were valuable in increasing competency in either of these areas. Since psychotherapy has not developed as a separate profession, but as a subpart of other professions, various routes have been established whereby a person might be trained as a therapist. Thus, programs exist in psychiatry, clinical psychology, psychiatric social work, and psychiatric nursing. The training of encounter group leaders, although occasionally conducted under university auspices, has taken place largely outside of academia.

Traditional programs have by and large been the subject of increasing criticism. Most psychiatrists and psychologists do not believe that their professional training is very relevant or useful. A surprising percentage state categorically that most of their training was worthless. In medical training many believe that the bias toward somatic illness and the didactic atmosphere of most medical schools militates against the development of effective therapists. In clinical psychology the major problem in training stems from the research orientation of most programs, combined with an antipractitioner attitude that exists in many departments. In both medical school and graduate psychology programs there is very little opportunity for clinical practice, and much of the educational program is filled with courses of dubious relevance in training competent practitioners.

Although the empirical research on traditional training is scanty, in virtually all studies that bear upon it the findings have been uniformly negative. Simply put, traditional academic training programs seldom increase the therapeutic effectiveness of the average student. When the criteria for measuring competence are the interpersonal qualities and skills that research has most often linked with effectiveness, the results are especially depressing. Although a fairly significant number of studies demonstrate the importance of supervisors and teachers who are highly empathic and interpersonally competent, evidence exists that the typical teacher or superviosr is functioning at less than a minimally facilitative level (see Carkhuff and Berenson, 1967: 9–11), and that such functioning produces a deterioration in the quality of therapeutic help rendered by the therapist-in-training (Pagell, Carkhuff, and Berenson, 1967). When the effectiveness of training is measured by the patient's evaluation of the trainee's performance, the results are also negative (see, e.g., Schmidt and Strong, 1970).

This is not to say that traditional programs do not teach anything. It is most likely true that they do give students an excellent knowledge of psychotherapeutic and psychological theory, as well as other relevant conceptual knowledge. But it does not appear that traditional programs do much to increase a student's skills in interpersonal relationships, nor do they develop skills such as the ability to empathize.

Nontraditional training programs for paraprofessionals, which enounter group training has modeled itself after, have received substantially more empirical investigation. The work of Rioch and her associates indicates that intensive one-year to two-year programs are capable of producing competent therapists without focusing heavily on theoretical and conceptual knowledge. The work of Truax, Carkhuff, and the client-centered therapists indicates that even briefer programs can develop competent therapists if the appropriate people are selected for training.

In attempting to isolate the relevant variables in the training process, researchers have found several important factors.[74] An apparently essential aspect of training is the degree to which supervisors and teachers of students are highly empathic, understanding, warm, and genuine. Lack of these qualities may actually lead to a decrease in the therapeutic functioning of trainees. Programs that offer a student opportunities for feedback are more effective than those that do not (Berenson, Carkhuff, and Myrus, 1966). An integrated approach to training, combining lectures and theory with experiential training, appears to be more effective than didactic instruction alone.

These findings have important implications for the training of traditional therapists and group leaders. One of the more important questions facing the field of professional training is whether traditional programs will be able to modify their formats to develop effective and efficient programs. This appears unlikely.[75] Perhaps the best evidence in support of this statement comes from the rising number of pleas for the development of a totally new profession of psychotherapy, with its own professional training program (see, e.g., Henry, Sims, and Spray, 1971; Holt, 1971). Further evidence lies in the development of post-doctoral programs in psychology, and the extension of the length of residency in psychiatry, both of which implicitly recognize that graduate training is not providing the proper education and training.

Several proposals have been made to resolve this problem. Kubie (1964, 1954) has argued for more than twenty years that what is needed is a school of psychological medicine within medical school. Others have proposed and gone on to establish professional schools of psychology. Still others have proposed the creation of a new mental health profession closely linked to, but separate from, both clinical psychology and medicine. The evidence offered by Holt (1971) and Henry, Sims, and Spray (1971) that psychotherapists trained through each of the major professions end up doing the same thing, have similar backgrounds, skills, and personalities, as well as value certain types of training experiences, indicates similarly that a unified and integrated training program is advisable.

The problem with most proposals, such as that of Kubie, is that the length of training continues to be prolonged, despite the evidence that this is unnecessary. Given the personnel shortages in the mental health field, this should be avoided. Rioch (1966: 291) has suggested that the mental health profession would be better off if its highly credentialed professionals identified themselves with the advancement of knowledge instead of the practice of a craft, which would facilitate the entry of other practitioners into the field. It is also possible that the role of fully qualified psychiatrists and clinical psychologists should be defined as consultants to practicing therapists and as

teacher-trainers of student therapists. The important matter is to limit the amount of time required to achieve competency as a therapist and eliminate the useless and irrelevant aspects of current programs.

SELECTION AND CERTIFICATION

The problem of selection and certification of therapists is intertwined with the broad issue of psychotherapeutic regulation. It is especially important because the predominant mode of professional regulation in the United States is state licensure, which requires an advance determination of who is competent to perform services. If the criteria or methods used to make this advance determination are faulty or unreliable, then the public is not protected. Thus, even if psychotherapy can be adequately defined for licensing purposes, and even if a consensus exists as to what skills are necessary to practice competently, traditional methods of regulation will still fail if the selection process is inadequate.

Depending upon initial criteria selection, procedures ideally identify those who are competent to practice or those who will not present a danger to the public, while eliminating all others. Measurement may focus on three different areas. First, selection may emphasize actual results, examining whether those being selected achieve specific outcomes. In this instance the skill of the practitioner is not measured, only performance. A selection process in an organization of real estate brokers that utilized volume of sales as a membership criterion exemplifies this approach. A second method measures a person's actual skills, personality characteristics, and other factors relevant to competent performance. An example would be a test of typing speed for a secretary. A third focuses on antecedent or indirect factors, which, though not a measure of competence in themselves, are predictive or indicative of it. Experience, age, and academic credentials are illustrative of this type.

Each of these approaches has advantages and disadvantages. The first emphasizes results, which are obviously important, but may be due to accident, not practitioner competence. Research on their correlation is necessary before the value of this approach can be assumed. Focusing on practitioner skills is also sensible, but a tendency exists to assume that certain skills make a difference, when, in fact, they may not. The third approach—focusing on indirect factors—often has economy to recommend it, since it is simple, inexpensive, and time-saving to determine whether somebody is twenty-one years old, has at least three years of experience, and possesses a Ph.D. in psychology. The economy of this approach may be negated, however, if no relationship exists between these criteria and the particular skills that are necessary to produce positive results.

In addition to what is measured, a central concern in the selection process as it relates to regulation is the method of measurement actually employed. The range of possibilities is large. The most common method of selection is the use of written tests. These may take various forms, including graded essays, multiple-choice questions, and fill-in-the-blanks. These types of tests have traditionally been used to measure intelligence, conceptual knowledge, analytical ability, and various other cognitive skills. Oral examinations and interviews have likewise been used to measure these factors, and are often used by assessors to evaluate personality characteristics and interpersonal skills.

When information is desired solely on personality characteristics, a number of psychological tests are available. Some of the most common include the use of personality tests, such as the Minnesota Multiphasic Personality Inventory (MMPI). In this type of test a series of multiple-choice questions or open-ended questions are asked of examinees. The purpose is to explore how those being tested feel about themselves, how they react in various situations, what their values are, and other personal matters. The answers are scored and evaluated based on national norms. Another common method of evaluating intrapersonal dynamics is the use of projective methodologies such as the Thematic Apperception Test or Rorschach Ink Blot Test. Such tests allow an individual to freely respond to a standard stimulus. This response is analyzed by experts to determine its implications concerning the individual. Two other methods that also provide data on interpersonal skills are behavioral checklists and the use of rating scales to evaluate tape-recorded or live interviews. In each case certain behaviors are looked for, categorized, and ultimately analyzed to provide information on a variety of interpersonal characteristics.

Another method of obtaining information on practitioner competence is to ask those who are in a position to evaluate the practitioner's services. Teachers, supervisors, peers, clients and practitioners themselves may all be polled. Finally, various external criteria may be utilized, such as whether one has been through psychoanalysis, how many years of experience one has had, and whether one possesses a medical degree. These methods are not mutually exclusive, and very often they are used in conjunction with each other.

Those responsible for selection have generally employed very few of the wide range of alternatives mentioned above. Traditional approaches to professional selection in the mental health field have focused on academic grades and credentials, oral and written examinations, and amount of supervised experience as the best method of establishing who is competent to practice. Acceptance into medical school is determined by undergraduate grade-point average, letters of recommendation, and scores on the Medical College Admission Test. Licensure as a physician, in turn, which confers on one the right to practice as a psychiatrist, typically requires a degree from an accredited medical school, a period of internship, as well as passage of a complex examination given by the state licensing board. Specialty certification as a psychiatrist, which is obtained by passing the written and oral examinations of the American Board of Psychiatry and Neurology, depends upon letters of recommendation and meeting certain other training and experience requirements (Morgenstern, 1970).

Similarly, licensure as a psychologist, which allows one to practice psychotherapy, generally depends upon possession of a doctoral degree issued by an accredited institution, several years of supervised work experience, and passage of an examination administered by the state licensing board. In addition, many state laws also require candidates to meet age, moral character, citizenship, and residency requirements. As in medicine, admission to a doctoral program in psychology is usually based on various combinations of factors, including undergraduate grade-point average, the Miller Analogies Test, and the Graduate Record Examination (Carkhuff, 1969: 135). Diplomate status as a clinical psychologist, which is often thought of as a sign of superior competence as a therapist, requires an applicant to complete a process similar to that involved for specialty certification as a psychiatrist.

The entrance requirements of postdoctoral programs are even more stringent. In the field of group psychotherapy, for instance, the American Group Psychotherapy Association (AGPA) (1970) has presented model criteria to be satisfied before prospective candidates enter training. The minimal acceptable academic degree is a master's in Social Work, but this must be accompanied by two years of qualified, supervised expe-

rience in a psychiatric agency or clinic. Clinical psychologists must posses a doctoral degree in clinical psychology or its equivalent, or state certification as a clinical psychologist. Psychiatrists must have completed at least one year of approved psychiatric residency. In addition the AGPA stipulates that candidates must have conducted at least 200 hours of individual psychotherapy under qualified supervision.

Paraprofessionals, on the other hand, are generally selected with very little emphasis on academic criteria. Most are chosen on the basis of the personal evaluation of an interviewer, who is generally looking for the presence of certain broad personal qualities such as empathic ability, motivation, interest, and the ability to work with others (Durlak, 1971). In many instances the paraprofessional is self-selected, responding to an ad for volunteer mental health workers. Where this occurs, often only the grossly unfit or pathological are excluded.

The question, of course, is whether these criteria and methods of selection accomplish their intended purposes. A rising number of commentators believe that traditional selection procedures in the mental health field are outmoded (see, e.g., Allen, 1967; Lippitt et al., 1975; Nelson, 1973; Taylor and Torrey, 1972; Tempone, 1971). Criticisms range from broad condemnations of the system as a whole, as in Truax and Mitchell's (1971: 337) accusation that current procedures for selection are indefensible and relatively worthless, to more narrow criticisms of specific processes, such as Morgenstern's (1970) critique of the American Board of Psychiatry and Neurology's examination. Empirical research supports the contention that current procedures are badly in need of overhaul.

Academic Credentials
and Grades

In the mental health field, in the major professions generally, and in many of the common occupations, licensure is dependent upon academic credentials. Whether this reliance is well founded is difficult to determine. Most of the direct and indirect empirical evidence suggests that little correlation exists between competence and academic grades or degrees. This evidence stems from several sources: qualitative evidence derived from a careful examination of the purposes of educational programs and the nature of most academic courses; research on the relationship of academic grades, examination procedures, and selection criteria with various measures of professional competence and career success (including studies of the relationship of academic accomplishments to success in blue- and white-collar jobs; and comparisons of the performance of nonacademically trained lay people with highly credentialed professionals.

The fact that educational institutions focus on the development of cognitive skills to the relative neglect of affective and behavioral competence indicates that an academic credential is unlikely to be a sound measure of competence. The research discussed in the previous section, which generally found that academic training programs for psychotherapists did not improve professional performance and were even detrimental to effective functioning in some instances, supports this contention. Likewise, the effectiveness of paraprofessionals and lay people, when compared with highly credentialed practitioners, argues against academic accomplishments as a measure of therapeutic competence (see pages 120–24).

The idea that success in school is a useful predictor of professional performance has been strongly attacked by a number of leading academics and researchers. David McClelland (1973) at Harvard University has found research indicating that academic grades predict nothing but future grades or results on tests similar to those used in establishing grades. Even with the highly intellectual and technically complicated job of

research scientist, superior on-the-job performance is not related to better grades in college (Taylor, Smith, and Ghiselin, 1963). A Labor Department study found that in only three of twenty cases involving ten occupational groups in two labor markets was there any correlation between years of education and job performance (U.S. Department of Labor, 1970). Evidence such as this led the HEW Task Force on Work in America to conclude that "for a large number of jobs, education and job performance appear to be inversely related" (U.S. DHEW, 1973: 135; see also Berg, 1970).

Even where the occupational job is fairly sophisticated, as with managers, a review of empirical studies by Sterling Livingston (1971) at the Harvard Business School found that academic achievement was not a valid predictor of management potential. Research by Holland and Richards (1965) found almost no correlation between measures of academic ability and real-life achievement outside of the classroom, including actual accomplishments in social leadership, the arts, science, music, and drama. In a most interesting study Heath (see Jacobson, 1977) examined the lives of sixty-eight Haverford men over more than ten years and found no significant link between college-level achievement and work competence. In addition, he uncovered a good deal of evidence indicating that high undergraduate achievement directly correlated with increasing interpersonal immaturity. Those graduates who were highly rated by their departmental faculty tended to have less stable identities and to be less well integrated and autonomous.[76]

In the medical profession, grades in medical school appear to be unrelated to later performance as a doctor. Price and his colleagues (1964), for instance, used information obtained from a population of about 500 doctors to determine what constitutes a "good" physician. When the final factors involved were applied to a group of highly competent practitioners, the authors found that "performance in formal education, as measured by grade-point averages, comes out as a factor almost completely independent of all the factors having to do with performance as a physician" (Price et al., 1964: 208).

In the mental health field itself, evidence exists that academic credentials are inappropriate as a means of identifying the competent practitioner. A reasonably large group of practitioners believe that extensive academic and professional training are not essential (Rioch, 1969: 290). Carkhuff (1969: 135-36) concludes that traditional academic criteria in psychology have a quite variable and low ability to predict very much at all. Empirical research tends to bear this out, although the amount of evidence is scanty. Kelly and Fiske (1951) found that academic and research competence could be reasonably well predicted by academic grades and other graduate school measures and evaluations in clinical psychology. On the other hand, assessment ratings, objective tests, and academic performance were not highly correlated with rated therapeutic competence. Grading criteria may be equally unrelated to the clinical student's ability to function as an effective therapist (Kelly and Goldberg, 1959).

When academic grades are correlated with various measures of professional competence, the results are equally discouraging. A general consensus exists that empathic ability is the critical and most important criterion of therapeutic competence. Unfortunately, several studies suggest that this ability is unrelated to traditional graduate school selection and grading criteria. For instance, Bergin and Solomon (1970) found a slightly negative relationship between verbal empathic ability and verbal intelligence scores, the psychology subscale of the Graduate Record Examination, and grade-point averages (whether overall or restricted to practicum grades).

A replication study by Bergin and Jaspers (1969), while not finding a negative correlation, found virtually no relationship at all between empathic ability and student grade-point averages. Meehl (1971) has found considerable evidence that a strong scientific interest, which is emphasized in the selection criteria of most clinical psychology programs, is at best negligibly related to the "helping" interests generally recognized as important in a psychotherapist. Similarly, Kelly and Goldberg (1959) have concluded that academia's criteria for selecting students is often irrelevant to their aptitude for becoming competent therapists.

Traditional Written and Oral Examinations

Perhaps the most common method of selection is the traditional written or oral examination, including standardized national examinations and personal interviews. However, whether these are valid and reliable is highly debatable. Substantial evidence is mounting that these more traditional methods to not provide useful measures of competence.

Written Examinations. General tests of intelligence and aptitude do not appear to be highly correlated with performance and competence in any field. McClelland's (1973) review of the literature pessimistically concluded that most such tests appear to measure nothing but academic grades and scores on similar tests. Thorndike and Hagen (1959), for instance, were not able to find any significant correlations between aptitude test scores and different measures of later occupational success, despite obtaining more than 12,000 correlations on more than 10,000 individuals. After reviewing fifty years of research, Ghiselli (1966: 121) concluded that general intelligence tests correlated less than a quarter of the time with proficiency in a typical job. Even though intelligence tests generally do correlate better with higher status jobs, McClelland (1973: 3) concludes that it may well be a consequence of social status, not intelligence.

In the medical field a variety of written tests are used to select competent practitioners. This begins at medical school with entrance examinations and continues through the examinations administered by the various specialty boards. Research on the validity and reliability of these examinations is remarkably sparse, but the extant studies do not provide a basis for optimism. The typical essay examination given to medical school students is subject to serious marking errors, and considerable variance occurs even when the same examiner regrades the same examination at a later time (Bull, 1959).

Multiple-choice examinations have a far higher degree of reliability (Murphree, 1961), but few of these have ever been subjected to a validation study based on performance criteria. Even the test given by the National Board of Medical Examiners, which is acceptable for licensure by most state boards and which has been subjected to significant study, has not been researched for its relationship to competent practice.[77] The same is also true of most bar examinations, including the multistate.[78]

The lack of validity of written examinations in the medical field extends to the tests given by the various specialty boards. Even when it comes to measuring a variety of cognitive skills, evidence exists that the examinations of medical specialty boards do not measure these skills. Studies have found that fewer than 10 percent of the questions on these examinations measured anything but the ability to recall isolated information (see the studies cited in Masserman, 1964: 221). This was true whether the examination was objective or essay in nature. The ability to recall information, unfortunately, is only minimally related to tests of problem-solving ability, and does not measure such skills as the ability to integrate data, to analyze problems, to develop and test hypotheses, to observe clinical phenomena, or to formulate a plan of management.

In psychology the situation is not significantly different, despite academia's long-term concern with the validity and reliability of testing in general. As previously noted, traditional graduate school selection and grading criteria do not appear to be related to empathic ability. Bergin and Solomon (1970) found a negative relationship (-0.30) between verbal intelligence scores on the Graduate Record Examination and empathic ability, while the psychology subscale produced only slightly better results (-0.21). Patterson (1968: 79) argues that beyond a necessary minimum, academic ability may not be related to counseling potential, citing research indicating a negative correlation between such potential and scores on the Miller Analogy Test. In a test of the reliability of comprehensive written examinations given to doctoral students in psychology, Pressey, Pressey, and Barnes (1932) reported great variances in the scores given by various graders and by the same grader on different halves of the same examination. In fact, one judge graded the first half of a student's examination at 95, while giving the second half a 50 (the examination had been divided in half and the grader did not know that both halves were to the same exam). The researchers found that a brilliant first-year undergraduate performed better than a graduate student who already had his master's degree.

Oral Examinations. Oral examinations generally have even more problems than written examinations. A few empirical studies do indicate that the typical interview examination can demonstrate high reliability among interviewers (see, e.g., Bull, 1959). These results are somewhat misleading, however, since the reliability figures are often spuriously inflated by ratings made with knowledge of other interview ratings. When these factors are controlled for, the results are not nearly so impressive (see the research cited and discussed in McGuire, 1966).

A careful study of the reliability and validity of oral examinations given by a major specialty board in the medical field indicates that such examinations lack any validity (McGuire, 1966). Observational analysis by a team of trained observers, for instance, discovered that nearly 70 percent of all questions asked by the board examiners basically required only the recall of information. Questions requiring interpretive skill constituted only 1 percent of the questions in one discipline, and overall only amounted to 20 percent of all questions asked. Questions related to problem-solving skills occurred only 4 percent of the time in one discipline, and averaged out to 13 percent of all questions. In less than 2 percent of the cases did the person being interviewed document his or her answer with citations from the literature or other authoritative sources, and in only 0.2 percent of the responses was specific data provided in support of the interviewee's answer.

These conclusions are probably applicable in the field of psychiatry and psychology. An evaluation of three annual oral examinations for psychiatric residents, while indicating a moderate degree of agreement in examiner rankings with each other, found that these oral examinations had poor agreement with practical examinations (consisting of a patient interview), and only a fair to poor relationship with supervisor ratings (Pokorny and Frazier, 1966). The authors of this particular study concluded that oral examinations had many disadvantages and were a relatively useless method for ranking residents.

The examinations of the American Board of Psychiatry and Neurology, which strongly emphasize the oral interview (Pokorny and Frazier, 1966), are likewise suspect. Morgenstern (1970) points out that a candidate may actually be asked to name the home town of prominent psychotherapists. He also notes a number of studies indicating that comprehensive oral examinations are not extremely valid and do not offer high levels of interexaminer reliability. The work of Pressey and his associates (1932) suggests that oral examinations in graduate departments of psychology may lack reliability and validity, as well. As an example, in one of their studies, four pairs of faculty members—more than half of whom were full professors—were involved in oral examinations of a master's degree candidate. The faculty could not agree on whether the candidate should pass (two of the examining pairs flunked the candidate, while two others passed her). The faculty also could not agree on what questions to ask (the questions asked differed widely, and not one was asked in all four examinations, while only one appeared in three of the four).

Professional Certification

Membership in professional associations such as the American Psychoanalytic Association is frequently taken to imply at least a minimal level of competence as a practitioner. Where those associations establish specialty boards, certification by a particular board generally denotes an extremely high level of competence. Research on the validity of the selection processes used by these organizations is almost wholly lacking. Since their methods—which typically involve reliance on academic credentials, years of experience, letters of recommendation, and successful passage of written and oral examinations—are seriously open to question, the value of board certification remains unestablished at best, and meaningless at worst. Carl Rogers (1973: 382), a past president of the American Psychological Association and a founder of the American Board of Examiners of Professional Psychologists (as it was then known), states flatly that as many certified charlatans and exploiters of people exist as uncertified. He (Rogers, 1973: 382) queries:

If you had a good friend badly in need of therapeutic help and I gave you the name of a therapist who was a Diplomate in Clinical Psychology, with no other information, would you send your friend to him? Rogers goes on to answer: Of course not. You would want to know what he is like as a person and as a therapist, recognizing that there are many with diplomas on their walls who are not fit to do therapy, lead a group, or help a marriage. So, certification is *not* equivalent to competence.

Morgenstern (1970) raises similar concerns about the examination process used by the American Board of Psychiatry and Neurology. He questions whether psychiatry and neurology belong together, whether the examinations really measure relevant competencies, whether they measure what they are supposed to measure. He provides evidence that much of what is tested for is clearly irrelevant, and cites the series of studies indicating that comprehensive oral examinations are not extremely valid and do not offer high levels of interexaminer reliability (see e.g., McGuire, 1966; Masserman, 1964; Miller, 1968; Pokorny and Frazier, 1966; Pressey, Pressey, and Barnes, 1932).

Psychological Tests

Especially because interpersonal factors and personality characteristics play a central role in the therapeutic process, one would guess that psychological tests should prove fruitful as selection devices. The results to date have been quite meager, however. Bergin (1966) has summarized much of the research in this area. He found several studies providing evidence that a therapist's degree of anxiety and maladjustment, as measured by various instruments, was negatively correlated with supervisor and client ratings of therapist competence (see Arbuckle, 1956; Bandura, 1956; Bergin and Solomon, 1963). A study by Bandura, Lipsher, and Miller (1960) found that the more anxious a therapist was, as determined by professional evaluation, the more likely the therapist was to avoid client expressions of hostility. This generally led to decreased self-exploration and lack of resolution of the conflict, and was taken as a sign of inferior competence. Winder,

Ahmad, and their associates (1962) found the same to be true with regard to dependency anxiety, as measured by trained raters using observable behaviors.

Standardized personality tests such as the Minnesota Multiphasic Personality Inventory (MMPI) and the Edwards Personal Preference Schedule (EPPS) have received considerable attention as predictors of therapeutic competence. Bergin and Solomon's (1970) research indicates that the Depression and Psychasthenia Scales of the MMPI correlate negatively with empathic understanding. They point out that although none of the other scales showed significant correlations, the positive correlations were inevitably associated with variables indicative of personality strength, while negative correlations occurred only for variables associated with personality disturbance. The EPPS had a number of scales that were negatively correlated with empathy, including the Consistency, Order, and Intraception Scale. On the other hand, the Dominance and Change Scales correlated positively at a significant level.[79]

Lynch, Gardner, and Felzer (1968) have conducted a study suggesting that the traditional interview and psychological tests may eliminate some of the most effective therapists. Using interviews, the MMPI, and the Otis IQ Test, the researchers selected a number of indigenous personnel for jobs as clinical therapists, including several high-risk candidates. The personality items that were being sought focused on intelligence, stability, motivation to learn a new role, openness, compassion, and other related factors. After six months on the job, these therapists were evaluated for their competency. If only the interview had been used, six of the therapists would have been rejected, two of whom turned out to be in the top half of their group as far as actual skill was concerned. Three trainees were dropped from the program, although they received high ratings on their initial interviews. Using the MMPI and Otis tests alone would have led to the rejection of three candidates who were rated as competent and one of whom ended up in the top half of his group.

Other studies investigating psychological tests and their relationship to empathy and other skills important in therapy provide mixed and difficult-to-interpret results (see, e.g., Covner, 1969, and the series of studies summarized in Patterson, 1968). A few tentative conclusions appear warranted, nonetheless. As far as the type of testing process goes, projective tests such as the Rorschach and TAT appear to have very little, if any, predictive value when used alone (Holt and Luborsky, 1958: 302). Tests that measure specific behaviors fare better. The conclusion of Holt and Luborsky (1958), based on their massive ten-year research project at the Menninger Foundation, most accurately sums up the current state of affairs for selection of therapists generally:

Our results strongly suggest that, within limits, the nature of the particular tests used matters less than who uses them. But it is not enough simply to get a "good tester"; he may not be any good at this unique task. With interviewers and with psychological test interpreters alike, *one cannot know who can select psychiatrists until they have been tried out at the job itself.* [Holt and Luborsky, 1958: 302.]

The best results have been obtained from measures of specific psychological traits related to well-being or general measures of psychological health. Carkhuff's (1969: vol. 1, 80) review of the research indicates that most psychotherapists score high on nurturant and social service inclinations, friendliness, affiliation, and other characteristics, which he suggests are traditionally equated with feminine personality dispositions (see also the summaries of research in Farson, 1954; McClain, 1968; Patterson, 1968). On the other hand, the therapeutic personality tends to score low on more aggressive, assertive, and achievement-oriented traits.

Evaluation of Work Performance and Abilities

A most important but seldom utilized set of predictors involves evaluations of a person's actual work performance or his or her performance-related skills. One method of accomplishing this task is through reliance on global individual judgments of competence. Supervisor report, peer review, self-evaluation, and client evaluation are examples of this process. Another method is to isolate and measure specific skills important to therapeutic success. Attempts to measure empathic ability illustrate this approach. In addition, a variety of methods ranging from role plays to taped analyses of interviews may attempt to measure other crucial variables. The value of any particular technique will depend on the centrality of the particular variable being measured to the therapeutic process, and the validity and reliability of the mode of measurement. Research on the predominant techniques in use today will help establish which criteria and methods of measurement are most useful.

Global Individual Judgments of Competence. Global judgments of competence may be made by a variety of people who are in direct contact with practitioners, including supervisors, teachers, peers, clients, and the practitioners themselves. Research indicates a substantial degree of variance in how well the judgments of any one group agree with another or with objective measures of performance.

Supervisor/Teacher Report. Very often subjective judgments of therapeutic competence are made by those responsible for practitioner supervision. These generally global ratings of competence are typically made on the basis of intuitive and implicit criteria. A considerable body of research indicates that such judgments have very little validity.

Masserman (1964: 226) points out that even in the medical profession, evidence suggests that supervisor judgments differ markedly from evaluations based on careful observations of the testee in real-life situations or in test situations designed as analogues. In the field of psychiatry results of a test of diagnostic ability (in which students were asked questions based on their analysis of a movie of a patient) showed that performance was not related to independent assessments of the student's therapeutic competence, nor was it related to a variety of personality factors. The only significant relationship was between clinical judgment and academic grades.

In another study Melloh (1964: 59) attempted to determine the relationship of accurate empathy ratings of counselors with a global criterion of counselor effectiveness made by the counselor's supervisor. He found that "accurate empathy as a characteristic of counselor behavior was not included among the operational criteria of counselor effectiveness by the practicum supervisors." This was true despite the fact that virtually all the supervisors adhered to a client-centered Rogerian therapeutic orientation. The implication is that either supervisor ratings or the accurate empathy measure of Truax is invalid as a measure of therapeutic effectiveness.

Luborsky and Spence (1971: 413-14) have reviewed the studies of supervisor ratings of psychoanalysts and their correlation with actual competency as judged from degree of patient improvement. Their main finding was that virtually no research exists on this question, except for one study by Klein (1965), which is discussed below. Typical of the findings from clinical psychology are those of Kelly and Fiske (1951). In their five-year project to assess and predict performance in clinical psychology, they found that assessment ratings by staff were not highly correlated with rated therapeutic competence. In addition, the assessment staff was relatively unsuccessful in predicting therapeutic competence.

Interestingly enough, the best predictions were based on relatively little material and only brief contact with the individual being rated (Kelly and Fiske, 1951: 182). This latter finding was replicated in another study by these same researchers. They comment: "One aspect of our findings is most disconcerting to us: the inverse relationship between the confidence of staff members at the time of making a prediction and the measured validity of that prediction" (Kelly and Fiske, 1950: 406).

A very few studies do indicate a relationship between supervisor or teacher report and other measures of therapeutic competence (see, e.g., Bergin and Solomon, 1970; Demos, 1964; Klein, 1965). Perhaps the most important of these is Henriette Klein's (1965) research at Columbia in which supervisors evaluated psychoanalysts-in-training as "superior," "above average," or "below average." Sixty-three percent of the patients treated by the superior students showed substantial improvement, while only 39 percent of those seen by below-average therapists were comparably improved. To avoid the problem of confounded variables (since the same supervisor evaluated both student competency and patient improvement), Klein also made an independent assessment of patient dependency. She found that twice the percentage of superior students had at least half of their patients improve.

Carkhuff and his associates have provided some tentative explanations as to why global judgments of supervisors are suspect. He distinguishes between the ability to discriminate and the ability to communicate. The former consists of the ability to discern and evaluate how a patient is functioning and what types of treatment are advisable, while the latter consists of skill in facilitating movement toward deeper self-exploration and self-understanding (Carkhuff, 1969: 82). Carkhuff cites a number of studies indicating that therapists rated low in the ability to communicate are apt to be poor discriminators, especially when evaluating themselves.

The idea that only certain types of supervisors are capable of accurately evaluating therapeutic ability is borne out by Holt and Luborsky's (1958) work at the Menninger Foundation. As part of their project they attempted to assess how well clinicians could predict whether psychiatric residents would be successful. These clinicians had more data than typical supervisors. On average, when clinicians made free predictive ratings, they did not achieve remarkably high levels of accuracy. On the other hand, a few individual clinicians were able to predict accurately more than half the time, which Holt and Luborsky (1958: 348) point out is about as good as the best actuarial attempts to predict success in vocational training. They also note that no objective test predictor reached this level of validity.

Peer Review. Closely related to supervisor evaluations are the judgments of peers. Because of interest in PSRO's (Professional Standards Review Organizations), both the government and private associations—such as the International Association of Applied Social Scientists—have been examining methods of competency assessment that rely on the judgments of fellow practitioners. Although not entirely identical to supervisor report, peer review is so closely analogous that research on the value of supervisor reports is obviously relevant. Few attempts have been made to assess the value of peer review per se. An investigation by McWhirter and Marks (1972) compared the relationship between the Rogerian facilitative conditions and peer and group leader ratings of perceived counseling effectiveness. They found no positive correlation except for genuineness. They concluded that peer evaluations of effectiveness were not based on a counselor's empathy or warmth, while supervisor evaluations were based on none

of the three variables. Contrary to this, although not directly in point, Bergin (1971: 263) has cited research indicating that peer ratings are perhaps the best method of predicting how a Peace Corps Volunteer will perform overseas.

Self-Report. Another form of global judgment is that made by practitioners about themselves. If found to be reliable and valid, such a method would obviously be quick and inexpensive. Unfortunately, self-report is obviously subject to a self-interest bias. Even where self-interest is not a factor, however, the validity of self-report does not appear high. Some evidence exists that poor therapists are apt to be poor at evaluation, especially at evaluating themselves (Burstein and Carkhuff, 1969).

A study by Leitner (1972) compared how two different samples of counselors rated other counselors and themselves as to their helpfulness to a client. Half the counselors had received systematic training on the Rogerian facilitative conditions of empathy, warmth, and genuineness, and were functioning at high levels of therapeutic effectiveness. The other half were experienced counselors but had received no such training. The ratings they gave were compared with the ratings of trained, expert raters who were functioning at high levels on the core therapeutic conditions. Leitner found that the trained group was consistently accurate in discriminating the helpfulness of others and themselves. The counselors who had received no systematic training were able to accurately assess the competency of others, but significantly overrated themselves on their own helpfulness.

Client Evaluation. A natural source to consult on practitioner competence are clients. Although the belief exists that clients have a distinct tendency to distort what is happening in the therapeutic relationship, thereby nullifying the value of their opinion, little empirical evidence exists on the subject. Truax and his associates have carried on a series of studies indicating that patients who are not severely disturbed are able to assess accurately the degree to which therapists are empathic, warm, and genuine, as measured by a relationship questionnaire (Truax and Carkhuff, 1967: 137, 139). These findings applied whether the population was juvenile delinquents, outpatients, or a heterogeneous population of vocational rehabilitation clients. Schizophrenic or other severely disturbed patients, however, may not be able to use such a questionnaire.

The idea that clients are a good source of information is disputed by Meltzoff and Kornreich (1970). Several studies in their review indicate that a therapist's evaluation generally does not agree with that of a client's as to the effectiveness of therapy (see Battle et al., 1966; Bellak et al., 1965; Cartwright and Roth, 1957; Nichols and Beck, 1960). In other studies there is only a modest level of agreement (see, e.g., Stieper and Wiener, 1965). The only conclusion that appears warranted is that reliance on client evaluation is at best a somewhat risky selection method, although the risk may be lessened by properly focusing the areas of competence the client is to evaluate.

Comparative Studies. Comparative studies of supervisor-, peer-, self-, and client-evaluations of competency are infrequent. The research comparing these groups evaluation of client progress in therapy is important, since it is also concerned with the validity of global judgments. Storrow (1960) investigated how well judgments of therapeutic change correlated when made by therapists, patients, relatives or friends, and self-ratings. The therapist's evaluation correlated with the patient's more than half the time (57 percent). Cartwright and Roth (1957), on the other hand, found no relationship between therapist and client views of change. A careful perusal of the studies cited by Meltzoff and Kornreich (1970: 40–45) reveals that little consistency is to be expected from study to study.

Conclusion. What is most apparent from a study of the literature is the lack of evidence that global judgments are valid and reliable as a method of selecting competent therapists. Even supervisor evaluations are highly suspect. Moreover, apparently certain types of individuals, whether supervisors, peers, or clients, are quite capable of identifying who is and who is not effective. Unfortunately, the means for identifying who is expert at such a process has not yet been uncovered.

Measures of Empathy. Historically the ability to empathize has been considered the most important therapeutic skill a practitioner can possess. Obtaining a good measure of empathy, then, should be an excellent method of identifying those who are qualified to practice as a therapist and those who are not. This has not proved to be such an easy matter, however.

Quite a number of researchers have developed independent measures of empathy. Kurtz and Grummon (1972), for example, examined six such measures to determine whether they correlated with each other and whether they were related to therapeutic outcome. They found four basic types. The first, termed "situational measures," utilizes standard test situations to elicit therapist responses. Illustrative of this is the Affective Sensitivity Scale developed by Kagan, Krathwohl, and their associates (1967). The second category consists of predictive measures, whereby the therapist anticipates how clients will self-describe themselves on a personality inventory, Q-sort, or other similar test. The third type is the "tape-judged rating," which is distinguished by the use of a trained and independent judge, who rates the level of therapist-empathy using a specially constructed scale. The fourth and final class is perceived empathy, which involves the therapist's or client's perception of the therapist's empathic ability.

Using a variety of outcome measures, including the Tennessee Self-Concept Scale, MMPI, therapist-rating of client progress, client evaluation of therapist help, and a composite score derived from all of the above, Kurtz and Grummon evaluated thirty-one therapists. The results of their study were provocative. Of twenty-one possible correlations between the various empathy measures, only one was significant at the 0.05 level, which was the correlation between client-perceived empathy after both the third and the final therapy interviews. The only other correlation that approached significance was between tape-judged and client-perceived empathy after the third interview. Only tape-judge empathy was significantly related to the client's depth of self-exploration and understanding. Many of the correlations were actually negative.

Client-perceived empathy after the third interview had a strong and mostly significant relationship with most of the outcome measures. Tape-judged empathy and all outcome measures were positively correlated, but only one was statistically significant. This lack of correlation between the many extant empathy measures has been found in other research as well. Astin (1957), for instance, found no relationship between a situational and a predictive measure; and Katz (1962) found none between judged and predictive empathy.

Where certain measures of empathy have been used as a criterion of therapeutic effectiveness, research has shown that such measures are frequently related to other measures, tests, and evaluation instruments. Bergin and Solomon (1963) found that the degree of therapist personal disturbance was negatively related to empathy as measured by ratings of tape-recorded psychotherapy interviews. On the other hand, measures of personality strength were positively related. In addition, empathic ability was slightly negatively related to verbal intelligence and to the psychology subscale of the Graduate Record Exam. It was also negatively related to the psychasthenia and depression scales of the MMPI and positively related to the dominance and change subscales of the Edwards Personal Preference Inventory. A more recent replication by Bergin and Jasper (1969) gave somewhat different results, however, and has led Bergin to conclude that these findings may have been the result of chance.

Truax and Mitchell (1971: 337–38) report that several measures correlate well with empathy as measured by the Truax Accurate Empathy Scale (see also Truax and Carkhuff, 1967: 232–35), including the Welsh Anxiety Index and parts of the Edwards Personal Preference Schedule. These measures are generally assumed to correlate positively with therapeutic ability. In particular, they suggest that the better therapists, as judged by Truax's scale, are "people low in anxiety, depression, and introversion, who are at the same time themselves striving, strong, dominant, active, and autonomous individuals." Although the Truax Accurate Empathy Scale and its close offshoots have been widely used and widely hailed as excellent measures of empathy, serious problems have been raised by critiques (see Bozarth and Krauft, 1972; Chinsky and Rappaport, 1970; Rappaport and Chinsky, 1972; Shapiro, 1969).

What becomes apparent is the difficulty of operationally defining empathy and designing a test instrument to validly and reliably measure the concept. Certainly for purposes of state or federal regulation, it seems unwise at this stage of development to arbitrarily pick one or several of these measures as valid, when so much is still to be learned about their relative merits.

Other Methods of Evaluating Work Performance and Abilities. The testing field has been ingenious in devising various methods of judging a person's competency to practice. Although relatively unresearched, several deserve mention as potentially valuable tools. Most heavily utilized in the industrial setting to evaluate management potential, role-playing may have applications in the therapy field. In a role-play, a practitioner is asked to respond to an actor or actress who plays the part of a patient. The responses can be taped or evaluated on the spot by specially trained observers. Related to this is the Critical Incident Technique, in which a practitioner's written response as to how she or he has handled difficult work situations is evaluated according to preestablished criteria. Finally, Lipp (1973) has proposed the use of problem-oriented medical records as a means of evaluating a therapist's performance (see also Spitzer, 1973, 1975). Each of these methods, and others like them, have great potential value, but remain relatively untested.

Work Experience

By and large, psychotherapists believe that more experienced therapists perform better than less experienced. Operating on this assumption, those who frame licensing laws or other standards for practice frequently require a minimum amount of experience. Such a prerequisite may rest on shaky assumptions, however. First, while experience may be related to competence, the more basic question is whether those with less than a certain amount of experience are able to function at least at some minimum level of competence. Evidence that paraprofessionals are as effective, if not superior to, highly credentialed and experienced practitioners indicates that years of experience may not be necessary to successful functioning.

The second issue is whether experience and competence are, in fact, related. Some studies have concluded that they are not. Schmidt and Strong (1970), for example, conducted a study in which students were asked to rate a therapist's expertness after observing a videotape of an actual interview. The order of mean ratings of expertness were almost the reverse of the order of the interviewers' training and experience.

This finding is rather atypical, however, and most reviewers have found that a practitioner with more experience functions at a higher level than one with less. Luborsky, Chandler, Auerbach, Cohen, and Bachrach (1971), for instance, examined thirteen studies dealing with level of experience. In eight cases a significant positive relationship existed. Four of the remaining studies reported nonsignificant findings, and the last was difficult to classify. Bergin (1971: 237), who approached the problem in a slightly different fashion, found that twenty out of the twenty-two studies that he reviewed involving positive outcomes utilized experienced therapists. In addition, experienced therapists achieved positive results 53 percent of the time, as opposed to 18 percent for inexperienced therapists. Indeed, Bergin notes that experienced therapists also accounted for 71 percent of those studies that did not yield positive findings.

Meltzoff and Kornreich (1970: 272–73), while noting that the studies do not yield a strikingly definitive pattern, concluded that the preponderance of the evidence suggests that experience does make a difference. Where studies conclude with negative findings, Glass (1976) suggests that the explanation lies in the fact that more experienced therapists may deal with more seriously disturbed and intractable patients. Thus, experience does appear to correlate with competence, but virtually nothing is known about whether very little experience is liable to be dangerous. The evidence of paraprofessional effectiveness, however, suggests the opposite (see pages 120–24).

Personal Therapy

Whether a practitioner has undergone therapy is frequently recommended as an indicator of professional competence. In the case of psychoanalysis it is a *sine qua non* for membership in psychoanalytic societies. The actual value of personal therapy, nonetheless, is open to question. Surprisingly little research has examined this question. Holt and Luborsky's (1958) study of psychiatric residents at the Menninger Foundation examined whether those who received therapy during training would improve more in their performance than others who did not. Changes in level of competence as measured by supervisors' ratings was totally unrelated to the amount of therapy any of the 218 residents had had.

Other studies cited by Meltzoff and Kornreich (1970: 267) fail to document the relevance of therapy to competence. A 1950 survey of 70 prominent therapists, for instance, found that these therapists did not believe that the best-adjusted therapists were the most effective. Henry, Sims, and Spray's (1971) survey of more than 4,300 therapists coast-to-coast revealed that this consensus had not changed much in the intervening twenty years: roughly a quarter of the entire sample had not undergone any psychotherapy, including more than a third of all psychiatrists and social workers. About a third of the entire group evaluated their therapy as as unqualifiedly satisfactory, another third expressed a qualified satisfaction, while the final third were not satisfied with their own therapeutic experience at all. Only 14 percent felt that their therapy had been a major influence on their professional life, while 40 percent listed the experience as having a moderate impact, and nearly half stated that it had had little or no influence at all (Henry, Sims, and Spray, 1971: 168–79). To restate the conclusion of Meltzoff and Kornreich (1970: 268), "So far, personal therapy does not seem to make any critical difference."[80]

Conclusion

A survey of the empirical research and an analysis of professional opinion indicates that significant problems exist in establishing valid and reliable methods of selecting psychotherapists. Traditional reliance on academic grades, written and oral examinations, years of experience, and whether practitioners have undergone therapy have little empirical validation. Where an attempt has been made to measure actual competencies, the method of measurement—such as supervisor or client report—may or may not be valid. Empathy, which is generally recognized as important to therapeutic competence, is one of the most difficult variables to measure. The many attempts to develop test instruments, few of which correlate with each other, attest to this. Perhaps because personal qualities such as empathy are so elusive, government organizations and private certifying bodies have generally ignored them.

In recent years a rising chorus of voices has argued that selection methods should emphasize competency-based criteria, whether the field is psychotherapy or not. Such authorities as John Gardner (National Committee for Careers in Medical Technology, 1970: ii–iii) strongly endorse the development of methods that do not rely on academic grades and degrees to determine whether a person is competent.

This dissatisfaction with traditional methods has led to renewed attempts to develop more effective procedures and has resulted in increasing research on their effectiveness. Current efforts have focused on the actual competencies required. For regulatory purposes this may not be necessary, since the primary interest of most state and federal regulation is what impact a person has, irrespective of how that impact is achieved. Thus, if it could be determined that a certain number of years of experience in a particular type of training program were a virtual guarantee of competence, one would not need to examine whether a person possessed specific skills.

The chances of discovering valid and reliable selection methods in the near or even distant future are slim. The disagreement among psychotherapists about basic outcome criteria, the difficulty of operationally defining these criteria, the problem of finding an adequate test methodology, and the difficulty of conducting research to adequately examine whatever methodology is chosen, ensure that no consensus is likely to develop.

This fact has significant implications for all regulatory proposals. It means that attempts at licensing or other restrictive regulations, no matter what process of selection chosen, will be based on a process that has little reliability or validity and about which no consensus exists as to its value. It suggests that if there are to be licensing laws, a variety of methods of selection should be employed in order to be sure that all competent individuals have a chance to qualify. It also means that if traditional academic and experience requirements are relied upon, the public will be receiving very little protection for its money.

NOTES

1. For other descriptions of the role of the traditional psychotherapist, see Frank (1973), Rogers (1951), and Wolberg (1967).

2. For detailed descriptions of the leadership role in encounter groups, see Roger's (1970: 43-68) "Can I Be a Facilitative Person in a Group?"; Bradford's (1964) "Membership and the Learning Process"; Lippit and This's (1970) "Leaders for Laboratory Training: Selected Guidelines for Group Trainers Utilizing the Laboratory Method"; Tannenbaum et al. (1970) "The Role of the Trainer"; Morris and Cinnamon's (1976: 52-62) "Facilitator Roles and Responsibilities"; Easton et al. (1972: 93-96) "What is the Role of an Encounter Group Leader?"; and Egan's (1970: 123-40) "Leadership." One of the best and most comprehensive descriptions can be found in Lakin's (1972: 97-127) "The Trainer." For a very different but quite compelling view about the group leader role, see Jourard's (1971) "A Way to Encounter."

3. In blind-milling, which is often used in the beginning of a group to help participants become acquainted, group members walk with their eyes closed and touch each other with their hands.

4. Jourard (1971: 118) writes:

There are many ways for a person to be. I see myself as engaged in this world, trying with no guarantee of success to make it fit for me to live and grow in. I cannot pursue this goal for long if I am chronically open, in the way of *I and Thou*. Nor will I move far if I am chronically cunning, self-concealing, and self-protective. Nor will I get anywhere without courage, resolve, and, above all, inventiveness. This is the "self" with which I "lead" the other person in groups I conduct. I lead, if at all, by showing, or showing off. There is nothing, that is, *no thing*, to show—just a way of being, and being with, here. I can enter your world, as one who invites your growth or as a strangler of your possibilities, a prophet of stasis. I try to be the former.

5. Interestingly, the research results of Lomranz et al. (1972) correspond quite well with the classification scheme developed by others such as Shaffer and Galinsky (1974). In developing a conceptual model for group therapy and sensitivity training, Shaffer and Galinsky felt that four different variants of sensitivity training existed. The first, the Tavistock approach to groups, is quite similar to the remedial leader. The T-group approach corresponds with the learning-centered, and the expanded experiencing with Shaffer and Galinsky's encounter group. They include a fourth group type, the theme-centered interactional method, which is more highly structured and is typified by the various women's groups and consciousness-raising groups that have developed in recent years.

6. A fuller description and analysis of the differences (or lack thereof) between en-

counter groups and traditional group psychotherapy are made at the end of this chapter. A recent symposium on "Contrasting Models of Leadership in Group Psychotherapy," in the *International Journal of Group Psychotherapy* (1976), provides a good analysis of leadership roles in group psychotherapy.

7. Brill et al. (1964: 594) reported like findings from a similar study and concluded that "the lack of any marked differences would suggest that neither the specific drug nor the length of psychotherapeutic sessions was the crucial factor in producing improvement in this sample of patients."

8. For excellent summaries of the research on the effectiveness of placebos, see Benson and Epstein (1975), Shapiro (1971), Frank (1973), and Lehmann (1964).

9. Brief histories of the use of worthless medicines appear in Koenig (1974) and Shapiro (1959).

10. Jerome Frank's (1973: 136-64) "The Placebo Effect and the Role of Expectations in Medical and Psychological Treatment," and Frederick Evans's (1974) discussion of "The Power of a Sugar Pill," also provide good overviews of how and why placebos operate.

11. Witness also the rapid growth and demise in popularity of other types of encounter groups, especially Gestalt therapy, sensitivity training, and transactional analysis.

12. Good general discussions of faith healing, psychic healing, and other forms of non-medical treatment may be found in a number of standard psychology reference books. See James's (1902) *The Varieties of Religious Experience*, Janet's (1925) *Psychological Healing*, and Murphy and Kovach's (1972) *Historical Introduction to Modern Psychology*.

13. LeShan (1974: 102-3) concludes as follows:

A survey of the literature in this field made it plain that the phenomenon of psychic healing *did* exist. There was enough solid experimental work and enough careful evaluation of reported claims to make this clear. After I discarded the 95 percent of the claims that could have been due to hysterical change, suggestion, bad experimental design, poor memory, and plain chicanery, a solid residue remained. In these, the "healer" usually went through certain behaviors inside of his head, and the "healee" showed positive biological changes which were not to be expected at that time in terms of the usual course of his condition.

Bernard Grad (1965) has conducted an excellent review of the biological effects of the "laying on of hands" on animals and plants. A quite critical, though somewhat biased, muckraking of faith healers appears in William Nolen's (1974) *Healing: A Doctor in Search of a Miracle.*

14. Interest in the field of parapsychology has been burgeoning in recent years. As a result, books devoted to faith healing, extrasensory perception, and psychic healing have been proliferating. For some of the better works, see, Academy of Parapsychology and Medicine (1972), Devereux (1973), Group for the Advancement of Psychiatry (1976), LeShan (1974), Ostrander and Schroeder (1970), Rose (1971), and Walker (1961).

15. This line of argument is pursued further in the discussion related to the effectiveness of paraprofessionels. See pp. 120-24.

16. Gibb (1964) has said that these groups are better categorized as "leaderful," since the leadership function becomes distributed among many of the group members.

17. Other descriptions and evaluations of the value, uses, and methods of various types of leaderless and instrumented groups than those discussed in the text can be found in Egan (1970: 136-39), Berzon et al. (1972), Farson (1972), Vicino et al. (1973), Hurwitz (1970), Johnson et al. (1965), and White (1972).

18. If one assumes that personality characteristics such as warmth and empathy are important therapist variables in producing positive outcomes, and if one assumes that psychotherapy is reasonably effective, an interesting additional argument can be made that factors other than the therapist may bring about many of the positive results experienced in therapy. The argument proceeds as follows.

In dealing with an overall sample of 237 therapists representing all major professional groups, Strupp and his co-workers (1960) found that less than a third of the therapists could be rated overall as having a positive or warm attitude, while more than a third were rated as having a clearly negative, cold, or rejecting attitude. Truax and Carkhuff (1967: 113-14) have interpreted this data as suggesting that less than a third of all practicing psychiatrists and psychologists are providing positive therapeutic conditions. One would, therefore, expect that most therapy would not be effective. If it is, then it only could be if variables other than the therapist were of major significance in determining outcome. This argument does not appear to have been made by any of the theorists and researchers cited in the text.

19. Bond (1975) has found additional evidence of this phenomenon. In a study of group psychotherapy, client expectations about group norms were the single most important influence on the actual norms that developed and governed the system, regardless of the therapists' views.

20. In the encounter group field, research on the trainer role is only beginning. Stock (1964: 436) writes that:

> The issue of the trainer's role is one of the relatively unexplored areas. On a descriptive level, we do not know how much variation there is in the styles of different trainers or the type and range of trainer-interventions likely to be made in a T group. With reference to process, we do not know how different trainer styles influence the functioning of the group and its usefulness to the individual participant.

The reviews of research conducted by Buchanan (1969, 1965), Campbell and Dunnette (1968), and House (1970) all reflect this opinion. Although this situation has recently changed somewhat, research results are still far from conclusive and at best have isolated only a few of the factors that will probably be shown to have an impact on effectiveness and competency. The same is true of psychotherapeutic research, where Redlich and Freedman (1966: 271) caution that "there are very few truly scientific therapies in our field. . . . [C]aution and admission of ignorance . . . must guide the judicious therapist." Combs (1953: 559) sums up the problem well in commenting upon the difficulties of establishing appropriate standards for psychotherapists in the licensing process: "Almost everyone has his private opinion about what kinds of standards are needed to engage in practice, but we have very little clear-cut evidence of what are really prerequisite to effective service."

21. Factors such as amount of experience are not considered here because they are not truly part of a person's competencies. One develops a certain skill as a result of experience, and perhaps experience is necessary fo developing that skill, but is is antecedent to competence. The question of how important experience is to competence is dealt with in the section on selection criteria, since level of experience may be an excellent predictor of competence, and hence a useful guideline to employ by licensing boards and other certification organizations.

22. For a somewhat different and quite clinical perspective on the necessary qualifications for practicing as a psychotherapist, see Blum and Rosenberg (1968). They argue that the crucial elements of what they term the "psychotherapeutic skill system" consists of the following: (1) the ability to be composed in the presence of troublesome people; (2) the ability to conduct the therapeutic relationship so that the patient is regarded as an object of theoretic interest, rather than affective involvement; and (3) the capacity to elicit, manage, and modify the information received in order to formulate rapid and accurate estimates of the patient's mind.

23. Examples of other descriptions of the personality of the ideal therapist can be found in Strupp (1973), Rioch et al. (1965: 6), and Rogers (1957). In the main, the particular attributes considered desirable are remarkably similar to the qualities recommended by Rogers and outlined by Holt and Luborsky. For an example of the qualifications considered desirable in traditional group psychotherapy, as opposed to individual

therapy, Slavson (1943: 174), one of the early pioneers in the field, offers an exhaustive set of criteria:

> As a result of careful observation of successful group therapists, the following personality traits are at present offered as criteria for qualifications for this work. A group therapist must be: (1) sensitive not only to himself and to his own feelings, but also to the feelings and needs of others; (2) fundamentally unhostile—one whose adjustment to life is on the side of masochism rather than sadism (such persons are sometimes characterized as "saintly"); (3) of few words and of good judgment in the use of language; (4) of a placid temperament—one whose manner and speech are relaxed, quiet, and comforting to others, or what is sometimes referred to as a "therapeutic personality"; (5) positive in his approach to life—he cannot be cynical or destructive; (6) objective—though fond of children and interested in them—for he cannot become involved in the emotional stress of his charges or develop favorites in the group; (7) possessed of what is known as "psychological insight," the capacity to recognize and observe the latent content and meaning of what appears to be ordinary behavior; (8) able to meet unusual problems and resourceful in devising psychological and physical conditions to cope with difficult situations; (9) handy with tools and able to learn easily crafts and other art and mechanical occupations to meet the needs of the group; (10) receptive to suggestions, emotionally responsive, and intellectually hospitable, not on the defensive and unable to grow in his work. There is no room in Group Therapy for the compulsive, the paranoidal, the rigid, or the moralistic. The adult must be psychologically free and receptive in his attitude toward his charges and toward conditions that may contribute to his own development and effectiveness.

Other examples of criteria for group psychotherapists can be found in the symposium on "Contrasting Models of Leadership in Group Psychotherapy," *International Journal of Group Psychotherapy* (1976).

24. To obtain an idea of the similarities and differences in the views of various professional groups (psychiatrist, psychologist, social worker, and so on), see the symposium on "Qualifications for Psychotherapists," *American Journal of Orthopsychiatry* (Welsch et al., 1956).

25. Other reviews of this literature that are in fundamental agreement with Truax and Mitchell include Carkhuff (1969: vols. 1 and 2), Carkhuff and Berenson (1967), Truax and Carkhuff (1967), and Shapiro (1969).

26. The debate over whether empirical research has demonstrated that empathy is important to therapeutic conpetence is still being heatedly waged. The basic objections seem to be whether research designs are adequate, whether the quality being measured is actually empathy, and whether other variables are controlled for. For a sampling of the research and commentaries on this subject, see Bozarth and Krauft (1972), "Accurate Empathy Ratings: Some Methodological Considerations"; Kurtz and Grummon (1972), "Different Approaches to the Measurement of Therapist Empathy and their Relationship to Therapy Outcomes"; Rappaport and Chinsky (1972), "Accurate Empathy: Confusion of a Construct"; Rogers (1957), "The Necessary and Sufficient Conditions of Therapeutic Personality Change"; Astin (1957), "A Comparative Study of the Situational and Predictive Approaches to the Measurement of Empathy"; Bachrach (1976), "Empathy: We Know What We Mean, But What Do We Measure?"; Chinsky and Rappaport (1970), "Brief Critique of the Meaning and Reliability of 'Accurate Empathy' Ratings"; Katz (1962), "Predictive and Behavioral Empathy and Client Change in Short-Term Counseling"; Caracena and Vicory (1969), "Correlates of Phenomenological and Judged Empathy"; Lesser (1961), "The Relationship between Counseling Progress and Empathic Understanding."

27. See the discussion in Bergin and Suinn's (1975: 514–16) review of the research literature on individual psychotherapy from 1971 to 1973 in the *Annual Review of Psychology*.

28. See the comprehensive discussion and review of the research on empathy in the special issue of the *Counseling Psychologist* (1975) entitled "Carl Rogers on Empathy."

29. Other studies are in line with these findings. Komins (1972), for instance, studied the effectiveness of group leaders working in pairs. He identified five types of team behavior, listed in decreasing order of effectiveness: (1) complimentary pairs (the leaders had differing styles that meshed well); (2) warm supporters (the leaders gave warmth, support, and empathy and tried to have the group members view them as participants); (3) busy achievers (the leaders worked the group hard and were very intense); (4) warm teachers (very warm leaders who stressed learning about group dynamics); and (5) crippled teams (differing styles did not mesh, lack of awareness of what was happening in the group, and occasionally irrational behavior). The first three groups showed the most changes, while the latter two did not show significant positive changes and in some cases underwent negative changes. Since the complementary pairs all consisted of teams in which at least one member was quite warm and empathic, this study strongly suggests that warmth and empathy are important in positive results. The research of Long and Schultz (1973) also indicates the importance of empathy (highly empathic group leaders produced groups significantly higher in level of self-exploration, which is generally acknowledged as a critical indicator of successful psychotherapeutic outcome). See also White (1972) (rigid leaders encouraged and increased the amount of frustration, tension, and instability in a group and were responsible for the absence of a clear sense of socially approved self; flexible leaders, on the other hand, encouraged responsibility, maturity, practicality, composure, consideration of others, and a clear sense of a socially approved self); and the review of the research by MacLennan (1975).

30. The Task Force on Personal Growth Group Consultants of the International Association of Applied Social Scientists, for instance, recommended as a standard for certification "strong . . . practical . . . competence in one or more therapy methodologies and/or intrapsychic learning technologies" (IAASS Task Force, 1974: 1).

31. A structured exercise was defined as "a leader intervention that includes a set of specific orders or prescriptions for behavior. These orders limit the participant's behavioral alternatives" (Lieberman, Yalom, and Miles, 1973: 409).

32. General references on the diagnostic process and its relation to psychotherapy include Frank (1975), Hoch and Zubin (1953), Katz et al. (1968), Kendell (1975), Sarbin et al. (1960), and Woody and Woody (1972).

33. For an excellent and in-depth account of the history of diagnosis in psychotherapy, see Menninger (1963), *The Vital Balance.*

34. Redlich and Freedman (1966: 247) define diagnosis in the following way:

Any scientific discipline requires systematic observation, recording, and classifying of its pertinent information. In medicine, these procedures are called *diagnosis.* By means of the diagnostic process, physicians attempt to determine the nature of the disease with which they are confronted and also to distinguish one disease from another. The diagnostic process involves stressing relevant data, eliminating irrelevant information, and arriving at a conclusion that is pertinent to the case at hand. In essence, these are scanning, eliminating, and matching procedures in which physicians have developed unusual skills.

For the counselor Arbuckle (1970: 276-77) defines that meaning of diagnosis as:

The analysis of one's difficulties and the causes that have produced them. More clinically, it may be thought of as the determination of the nature, origin, and maintenance of ineffective abnormal modes of behavior. More simply, it might be considered as the development by the counselor, of a deeper and more accurate understanding and appreciation of the client.

35. Thorne (1961: 44) has added a number of other functional categories and elab-

orated those proposed by Meehl. He sees diagnostic judgments as being used for the following purposes:

1. Clinical diagnosis: collecting, identifying, and analyzing all available data from tests, observations, and so on.
2. Pathological diagnosis: the study and identification of the causes of mental disorders.
3. Nosological diagnosis: corresponding to Meehl's formal diagnosis.
4. Personality assessment: equivalent to Meehl's third category of personality assessment.
5. Prognosis.
6. Postdiction: estimating past events from current data.

See also Bannister et al. (1964).

36. Since so little research has focused on the encounter group leader's ability to make diagnoses, the emphasis will lie almost wholly on the psychotherapeutic literature.

37. For discussions of reliability as related to therapeutic diagnoses, see Geertsma (1972) and Stuart (1970: 68-79).

38. See Kaelbing and Volpe (1963) (constancy of psychiatric diagnoses upon readmission not great); Tarter et al. (1975) (agreement rate of only about 50 percent on whether patient being admitted to hospital neurotic, functionally psychotic, or suffering from personality disorder); Wallinga (1956) (agreement on specific diagnoses achieved only 41 percent of the time, while rate increased to only 58.5 percent for the major categories of psychiatric disturbance); Beck et al. (1963) (under ideal conditions using highly trained and expert diagnosticians, agreement rate only 54 percent for specific diagnoses and 70 percent for broad categories); Schmidt and Fonda (1956) (excluding organic cases, agreement rate for specific diagnoses drops to 42 percent); Arthur and Gunderson (1966) (neither diagnosis nor disposition were highly predictable for 473 male, enlisted Navy personnel at two hospitals); Sandifer et al (1969) (presented with identical clinical data, U.S. psychiatrists reported virtually twice as many symptoms as U.K. psychiatrists); Rickels et al. (1970) (correlations between observer and doctor ratings of psychopathology only moderate, ranging from 0.31 percent to 0.55 percent; between-rater correlation for psychopathology of staff-level observer and experienced practicing psychiatrist only 0.16); and Goldfarb (1959) (interjudge agreement of psychologists based on evaluation of modified clinical reports was approximately 60 percent, as was the interjudge agreement based on making repeated evaluations of the same test data, but the percent of cases in which unanimous agreement existed was considerably less than that). But see Foulds (1955) (reliability of psychiatric diagnosis not as poor as current opinion would lead one to suppose), and Kreitman et al. (1961) (agreement on specific diagnoses, using an agreed-upon list of eleven possible diagnoses, occurred 65 percent of the time, and reached 80 percent at a broader or generic level).

39. For further research on the effect of amount, order, and type of information on reliability and accuracy, see Miller and Bieri (1963) (increase in reliable discriminations as a consequence of adding more case information rather slight); Huff (1966) (order of information presented and overall amount of information possessed had no effect on agreement rate); Huff and Friedman (1967) (redundant information reduces reliability, but new and different information increases it); and Tripodi and Bieri (1964) ability of judges to discriminate social stimuli may be relatively limited; no consistently significant increases in information transmission as dimensionality of the social stimulus increases).

40. Rosenhan's (1973) article has been extensively criticized and otherwise commented upon. See, e.g., Lando (1976), Farber (1975), Millon (1975), and Weiner (1975). For Rosenhan's response, see Rosenhan (1975). For an excellent portrayal of how psychiatrists can misdiagnose schizophrenia even with detailed information and extensive

interviews, see Laing (1967). For a critical commentary of Laing's theories and interpretations of schizophrenia, see Wing (1967).

41. This symptom was the complaint of often hearing voices that were usually unclear but sometimes appeared to say "empty," "hollow," and "thud." This choice of symptoms was based on the fact that such complaints were often indicative of perceived meaninglessness in life, and the additional fact that not one case of existential psychosis was known to exist in the empirical literature.

42. The jurors did not overhear a professional making a diagnostic judgment, but instead were making their determination at a mock sanity hearing set up by the researchers.

43. Several other lines of research call the availability of diagnosis into question and deserve brief mention. Crow (1957) has found that educational training decreases a person's accuracy of judgment. Masserman and Carmichael (1938) and Wallinga (1956) have demonstrated that psychiatric diagnoses arbitrarily change over time. There is also the fact that rates of illness-type diagnosed at various hospitals throughout the country are radically different, despite any compelling reason for this state of affairs (Boisen, (1938).

44. Carkhuff (1969: 50), for instance, states emphatically that "there is little evidence to indicate that traditional assessments of levels of functioning are related to differential treatment. *Traditional diagnosis does not make a difference.*" Breger (1968: 178) concludes tersely that "the main reason that testing is not integrally related to treatment is that the central implicit assumption underlying testing—that one will know what to do with the patient, how to 'treat' him, once he has be 'diagnosed' or assessed—is not true."

45. The authors did find that neurotics tended more frequently than chance to receive psychotherapy, as opposed to other forms of psychiatric treatment (ECT, drugs, and so on), but this is hardly surprising. There was no attempt to analyze whether diagnosis make any difference in the type of psychotherapy received. Other studies have compared various treatments, but they, too, do not differentiate between different forms of dynamic or behavioral therapies (see, for example, Kreitman et al., 1961).

46. An interesting, although perhaps somewhat tangential sidelight to the problem of validity, has been pointed out by Meehl (1956: 265). Suppose that a psychotherapist exists who can identify 85 percent of those who are psychotic in a given population, and among those who are nonpsychotic, she or he errs only 15 percent of the time. Especially if incorrect decisions were serious, it would appear wise to use this person's judgment. In fact, the wisdom of employing this individual depends on what percentage of the total population are psychotic. If half of the population is psychotic, use of this psychotherapist's judgment will decrease the number of errors; but if only 10 percent of the population is psychotic, more diagnostic errors will result from using the therapist's judgment than from simply assuming that all people are nonpsychotic. In other words, using a reasonably valid method of measurement may actually increase the number of mistakes made, as opposed to using no test at all.

47. On the basis of his review of the research, Stuart (1970) argues that dispositional diagnosis does not predict the outcome of different forms of treatment, whether the treatment is psychotherapy, psychiatric hospitalization, or incarceration. He cites research that attempted to determine what variables accounted for the length of hospitalization, of mental patients and found that degree of diagnosed psychopathology accounted for less than 10 percent of the variance. For other studies on the usefulness of diagnosis in predicting behavior, see Gough et al. (1965) (parole outcome); Johnston and McNeal (1967) (length of hospitalization); Raines and Rohrer (1955) (military officer success).

48. A group of scientists at Stanford University headed by Richard Stillman (Stillman et al., 1969) are also attempting to develop a similarly systemized system. In this case, however, the entire process has been computerized so that the patient talks directly to a video-display computer terminal, which asks questions via the display.

49. Descriptions and evaluations of other forms of phenotypic and closely related

methods of diagnosis can be found in Katz et al. (1968) (descriptive and phenom-enological approaches, systems based on patterns of psychological test performance, systems based on premorbid history, course of illness, or reactions to treatment, and systems which attempt to encompass variables from several of the significant dimensions of functioning in mental illness); Kanfer and Saslow (1965) (behavioral diagnosis); Luborsky and Bachrach (1974) (review of research on Health-sickness scale); Spitzer (1973) (problem-oriented medical records); and Laforge and Suczek (1955) (interpersonal checklist). Arthur (1969) describes a variety of new methods, including experimental, behavioral, and decision-making models; and a system based on operations research.

50. This thesis has been put forth by Durlak (1971: 2–8), whose analysis is relied upon in the discussion in the text. See also Ellsworth (1968: 9–10).

51. See Gurin et al. (1960: 307–19 *passim*).

52. A subsequent study by Golann et al. (1966) found that diagnostic ability was not rated as high as therapeutic competence, which is not surprising given the focus of the project. (The researchers asked the mental health counselors in Rioch's project to view a filmed interview between a psychiatrist and a patient and to comment on the patient's background, presenting condition, prognosis, and personality dynamics. The counselors performed significantly more poorly compared with a group of advanced psychiatric residents and senior medical students. They were significantly better than a group of first-year students and another group of untrained hospital volunteer workers.)

53. This study has been criticized on a number of grounds. Cartwright (1968) has pointed out that the untrained therapists did not differ from the highly experienced therapists on the critical variable of hospital discharge rate. Rosenbaum (1966) argues that since most of the untrained therapists were women, while most of the trained therapists were men and all the patients were male, much of the effectiveness of the untrained therapists could be attributed to their sex role. Despite these criticisms, this study has been widely cited in the literature and has appeared in a number of edited volumes (see, for example, Guerney, 1969).

54. This is not to say that traditional diagnosis never makes a difference. Several studies indicate that accurate diagnosis is useful in the appropriate prescription of drugs, and Meehl (1973: 276–80) has presented dramatic evidence that in highly circumscribed cases, traditional diagnosis can be highly reliable, highly valid, and extremely important (especially in the prevention of suicide). What needs to be kept in mind, however, is that these instances are relatively rare and generally apply to very few diagnostic categories. The words of Rosenhan (1973: 257) eloquently describe the current situation and point out the dangers arising from it:

> Whenever the ratio of what is known to what needs to be known approaches zero, we tend to invent "knowledge" and assume that we understand more than we actually do. We seem unable to acknowledge that we simply don't know. The needs for diagnosis and remediation of behavioral and emotional problems are enormous. But rather than acknowledge that we are just embarking on understanding, we continue to label patients "schizophrenic," "manic-depressive," and "insane," as if in those words we had captured the essence of understanding. The facts of the matter are that we have known for a long time that diagnoses are often not useful or reliable, but we have nevertheless continued to use them. We now know that we cannot distinguish insanity from sanity. It is depressing to consider how that information will be used.

55. Strupp and his associates sent letters to 150 experts spanning a wide range of theoretical orientations, 70 of whom responded. Unfortunately, in cataloging the various reasons given concerning the dangers of therapy, they did not provide specific information on the frequency with which various factors were mentioned. Thus it is difficult to determine which factors are most generally recognized as significant.

56. Unfortunately, further analysis of this research indicates that the results are ambiguous and equivocal (Bowden, 1972).

57. It may be that the therapist makes very little difference. A careful study by Kahne (1968), for instance, of the psychiatrists who conducted the therapy of patients who committed suicide, mental hospitals found very little difference between those psychiatrists and others who were more successful. Personality characteristics, opinions, and clinical practices were not distinguishing features. The most influential factors appeared to be hospital case assignment policy, the therapist's position in the hospital structure, the opportunities for contact with patients, and the therapist's capacity to relate to patients as reflected in measures of social distance and the attention the psychiatrist pays to the patient's milieu. Unfortunately, these findings are probably of limited generalizability, since the suicides studied were part of an "epidemic" of such suicides at a private mental hospital with a highly homogenous group of psychiatrists.

58. Ken Benne (1970: 13) has eloquently elaborated the danger involved:

> To counter "formal" established education with an education which elevates feeling and puts down thought, which enthrones body over mind—with the claims of the two upon the management of personal and social conduct still dichotomized, which confuses counterdependent acting out with spontaneity, is not to educate for wholeness. It is rather to educate for a new disintegrity by standing established disintegrity on its head. To elevate the gut over the head is still to fragment the potentially whole person.

59. Only those factors that might be regarded as potentially precipitating harm in encounter groups have been abstracted from Rowe and Winborn's list. Thus, the danger of commercial abuses, which was mentioned seven times, was disregarded, as was the concern about substantiating research (mentioned eleven times). The frequency of fears and objections reported in popular journals was ignored, since these articles did not tend to be based on expert opinion.

60. Thus, even the studies of Hurley and Force (1973) and Chambers and Ficek (1970) do not provide statistical evidence as to what causes groups to be dangerous. Both of these studies used statistical techniques to determine that negative effects occurred, but none of their statistics bear on the problem of causation. Where the authors provide theoretical explanations in this regard, they do so on the basis of theory and a detailed understanding of what happened. This, however, does not represent empirical proof.

61. These were defined as follows: (1) aggressive stimulators (or energizers) were intrusive, confrontive, challenging, highly caring, self-revealing, extremely charismatic, authoritarian, and often structured events in the group; (2) love leaders (or providers) were caring, individually focused, gave love as well as information and ideas, and exuded a quality of enlightened paternalism; (3) social engineers focused on group—not individual —behavior, rarely confronted, were low on authoritarianism, and not charismatic; (4) laissez-faire leaders were not challenging, did not confront, offered little support, generally remained distant and cool, and offered little structure; (5) cool, aggressive stimulators (or impersonals) were like the aggressive stimulators, but less extreme; (6) high structure leaders (or managers) were extremely controlling and authoritarian and used a large number of structured exercises; and (7) leaderless groups (tape groups) focused on learning how to give and receive feedback and making emotional contact, and fostered a warm, supportive climate, deemphasizing interpersonal conflict. See Yalom and Lieberman (1971: 20-23 *passim*).

62. The analysis of Chambers and Ficek (1970) agrees with this. In their evaluation of marathon counseling they found two participants who did not benefit from their experience. In both cases the participants were pushed to their limit, becoming exceedingly anxious and fearful. They comment concerning the failure of the group leaders to recognize and head off the particular situation.

63. For additional comments on this problem other than those discussed in the text, see Gottschalk and Pattison's (1969) "psychiatric Perspectives on T-Groups and the Laboratory Movement: An Overview." See also Houts and Serber's (1972) *After the Turn On, What? Learning Perspectives on Humanistic Groups.*

64. Arizona law, for instance, states that a person shall be issued a certificate as a psychologist if, in addition to age, moral character, citizenship, and other requirements, the applicant:

> has received the doctoral degree based on a program of studies the content of which was primarily psychological, or the substantial equivalent thereof in both subject matter and extent of training, obtained from an educational institution having a graduate program accredited by the American psychological association. . . . [Ariz. Code Ann. § 32-2071(d) 1973.]

65. Very interestingly, the data cited by Kalinkowitz, which apparently appeared in the unpublished report of Goldman, did not appear in the version which was eventually published (Goldman 1963). One wonders at this omission, and cannot help but speculate that the New York State Psychological Association, under whose auspices the survey was conducted, did not wish such negative information to be made public.

66. The actual statistics were as follows: 89 percent of the counselors who had just finished their internship were viewed as moderately or considerably helpful; 85 percent of the beginners were so viewed; but only 80 percent of the highly experienced practitioners were considered helpful. Since the case assignment in this study was not completely random, and since the most experienced counselors may have been given the toughest cases, the results of this study must be viewed with circumspection.

67. Illinois, California, Massachusetts, and New Jersey have instituted professional psychology programs on a state level. Baylor, Hahnemann Medical School in Philadelphia, and Adelphi University have begun professional programs at a private university level. These are described in APA Monitor (1973) (Baylor, Hahnemann, and Adelphi); Cummings (1969) (California); Hedberg, Meredith, and Fitts (1973) (Baylor); Peterson (1969, 1968; Peterson and Barron 1974) (Illinois); Pottharst (1970) (California); Webb et al. (1970) (California); and Weitz (1973) (New Jersey).

68. An excellent description of more than 125 paraprofessional training programs can be found in the National Institute of Mental Health's *Explorations in Mental Health Training* (U.S. NIMH, 1974). These include all projects, both ongoing and completed, which have received grants from the Experiment and Special Training Branch of the Division of Manpower and Training Programs of NIMH.

69. Other excellent programs for training encounter group leaders include the Advanced Training Program in the Applied Behavioral Sciences of the New England Training Institute, and the Group Processes and Sensitivity Training Center at Duke University. The Netherlands has developed a program quite similar to that of Boston University (Schroeder 1971).

70. While training in the university setting may not be ideal, one must also be careful about the value of nontraditional programs. Lieberman, Yalom, and Miles (1973: 428-29), for instance, have documented the fact that specific encounter group techniques such as the "hot seat" may have no value whatsoever, despite the fact that a considerable body of experts may ardently believe in them. Unfortunately, practitioners frequently establish training programs for their disciples that are based on these mistaken beliefs. In so doing they fail to pass on the actual intuitive and unconscious factors that are relevant to effectiveness (Lieberman, Yalom, and Miles, 1973: 428-29).

71. Carkhuff's (1969) two-volume series on *Helping and Human Relations* and Truax and Carkhuff's (1967) *Toward Effective Counseling and Psychotherapy* are excellent sources for both the theory and research behind their work, and provide excellent descriptions of the details of their integrated training programs.

72. For an excellent and thorough discussion of this approach, see Guerney (1969: 381-470).

73. As contradictory evidence to the positive studies, Meltzoff and Kornreich (1970: 283-84) review two negative instances. The first, a study by Sines, Silver, and Lucero (1961), indicates that psychiatric aides in a state hospital setting were ineffective as

therapists. Sixty aides met with 117 long-term female schizophrenic patients in individual sessions twice weekly for fifty minutes over a twelve-month period. The purpose of the sessions was to improve the patient's psychiatric and behavioral status. Training consisted of periodic seminars, periodic reviews of the patients' progress, and guidance with treatment plans. Based on criterion measures such as the L–M Behavior Rating Scale and MMPI, as well as an eleven-category Q-sort, the authors could find no significant differences in test results when compared with a carefully matched control group.

In a second study by Eliseo (1964) at the Lebanon Veterans Administration Hospital, psychiatric aides were unable to affect the social interaction habits of chronic schizophrenic patients through the use of remotivation techniques. It is apparent, however, that the training that was received by the aides in these two studies was not nearly commensurate in quality with the programs designed by Carkhuff and his associates, Guerney and his associates, or Rioch and her associates.

74. Based on her extensive review of the research, Matarazzo (1971: 920) has provided an excellent summary of the primary ingredients desirable in an effective training program:

> Some of the important variables in effective teaching programs appear to be *selection* of psychologically healthy individuals and combined *didactic* and *experiential* training for a specific, *well-defined* role. It appears that individuals who are already interpersonally sensitive and skillful can more quickly learn to become therapeutic. In the most effective programs, the desired attitudes and behaviors have been defined; taught singly, in some instances; and the degree of skill measured, with subsequent feedback. Peer observation and feedback seem to be effective in increasing the student-therapist's awareness of himself and motivating him to change. A warm and accepting supervisor relationship is also apparently a very important part of learning—both freeing the student to experiment with new behaviors, and serving as a model for appropriate, therapeutic behavior. Group experiential learning, with discussion of the students' attitudes and difficulties in the role of psychotherapist, also seems to promote learning.

75. Carl Jung (1954: 82–83) has written that "neither our modern medical training nor academic psychology and philosophy can equip the doctor with the necessary education, or with the means, to deal effectively and understandingly with the often very urgent demands of his psychotherapeutic practice."

76. It should be noted that a variety of studies to indicate that educational credentials are related to increased income and job status (see the research discussed in Solmon and Taubman, 1973). However, neither of these indicators has been shown to be related to actual competence, especially in the mental health field, and it is likely that the increased income is due to the academic credential, not actual performance (see the research discussed in Solmon, 1973).

77. Those that claim that the medical boards are valid generally argue that validity has been demonstrated because of the direct participation of outstanding medical educators and test technicians in the construction of the tests, in addition to high correlations with independent ratings of student proficiency (see, e.g., Cowles and Hubbard, 1954). Neither of these rationales provides any basis, however, for assuming that the test is related to physician competence.

78. For an excellent review of the problems with state bar examinations and data on the validity and reliability of the multistate bar examination, see Hirano-Nakanishi (1977).

79. While both Bergin and Truax have found aspects of the EPPS to accurately measure therapeutic effectiveness, Durlak's (1971: 238) review of eight studies found that they were often directly conflicting and sometimes provided completely negative results. His only conclusion is that this instrument is useless as a tool for selecting competent therapists.

80. The descriptions of methods of selection given in this section by no means exhausts what is possible. Although little researched, other selection methodologies exist. A few descriptions will illustrate the range of these methods. Golann, Breiter, and Magoon

(1966) have developed a filmed thirty-minute spontaneous interview of a psychiatrist with a patient that they then use to ask therapists a series of statements related to the patients' background, present status, prognosis, and psychodynamics. John Senior (1972) has developed a computerized method of testing clinical problem-solving ability, which has potential application in the psychotherapy field. Research by Pagell and his associates (1967) and some of the studies described in Carkhuff's various publications suggest that measuring the level of supervisor empathy may be an excellent method of evaluating the competence of a therapist. Lynn and Nordhoff (1975) recommend a four-step procedure in which therapists conduct an interview with a patient, which is observed and evaluated by a team of staff members to assess diagnostic skills. The very number of methods being experimented with is testimony to the lack of consensus that exists on what methods are, in fact, valid and reliable.

REFERENCES

APA Monitor. "Rage Reduction Therapy Pioneer Battles to Keep California License." *APA Monitor*, March 1973, p. 5.

APA Monitor. "Psychologist Faces Malpractice Charges." *APA Monitor*, September-October 1972, p. 16.

Academy of Parapsychology and Medicine. *The Dimensions of Healing: A Symposium*. Los Altos, Calif.: Academy of Parapsychology and Medicine, 1972.

Albee, G.W., and Loeffler, E. "Role Conflicts in Psychology and Their Implications for a Reevaluation of Training Models." *Canadian Psychologist*, 1971, v. 12, pp. 465-81.

Allen, T.W. "Effectiveness of Counselor Trainees as a Function of Psychological Openness." *Journal of Counseling Psychology*, 1967, v. 14, pp. 35-40.

American Group Psychotherapy Association. *Position Statement on "Nontherapy and Therapy Groups."* New York: American Group Psychotherapy Association, 1971.

American Medical Association, Council on Mental Health. "Sensitivity Training." *Journal of the American Medical Association*, 1971, v. 217, pp. 1853-54.

American Psychiatric Association, Committee on Nomenclature and Statistics. *Diagnostic and Statistical Manual of Mental Disorders*. (2nd ed.) Washington, D.C.: American Psychiatric Association, 1968.

American Psychological Association. "Guidelines for Psychologists Conducting Growth Groups." *American Psychologist*, 1973, v. 28, p. 933.

American Psychological Association. *Levels and Patterns of Professional Training in Psychology*. (Edited by Maurice Korman.) Washington, D.C.: American Psychological Association, 1973a.

American Psychological Association, Committee on Training in Clinical Psychology. "Recommended Graduate Training Program in Clinical Psychology." *American Psychologist*, 1947, v. 2, pp. 539-58.

American Psychological Association; American Educational Research Association; and National Council on Measurement in Education. *Standards for Educational and Psychological Tests*. Washington, D.C.: American Psychological Association, 1974.

Apfelbaum, B., and Apfelbaum, C. "Encountering Encounter Groups: A Reply to Koch and Haigh." *Journal of Humanistic Psychology*, 1973, v. 13(1), pp. 53-67.

Arbuckle, D.S. "Client Perception of Counselor Personality." *Journal of Counseling Psychology*, 1956, v. 3, pp. 93-96.

Arbuckle, D.S. *Counseling: Philosophy, Therapy and Practice*. (2nd ed.) Boston: Allyn and Bacon, 1970.

Archer, D. "Power in Groups: Self-concept Changes of Powerful and Powerless Group Members." *Journal of Applied Behavioral Science*, 1974, v. 10, pp. 208-20.

Armstrong, J.C. "Perceived Intimate Friendship as a Quasi-Therapeutic Agent." *Journal of Counseling Psychology*, 1969, v. 16, pp. 137-41.

Arthur, A.Z. "Diagnostic Testing and the New Alternatives." *Psychological Bulletin*, 1969, v. 72, pp. 183-92.

Arthur, R.J., and Gunderson, E.K.E. "The Prediction of Diagnosis and Disposition in Naval Hospitals." *Journal of Clinical Psychology*, 1966, v. 22, pp. 259-64.

Asch, S.E. "Effects of Group Pressure upon the Modification and Distortion of Judgments." In G.E. Swanson, T.M. Newcomb, and E.L. Hartley (Eds.), *Readings in Social Psychology*. (2nd ed.) New York: Holt, Rinehart, and Winston, 1952, pp. 2-11.

Asch, S.E. "Studies of Independence and Conformity: I. A Minority of One Against a Unanimous Majority." *Psychological Monographs*, 1956, v. 70 (9, Whole No. 416).

Ash, P. "The Reliability of Psychiatric Diagnoses." *Journal of Abnormal and Social Psychology*, 1949, v. 44, pp. 272-76.

Astin, H. S. "A Comparative Study of the Situational and Predictive Approaches to the Measurement of Empathy." Ph.D. dissertation, University of Maryland, 1957. Abstracted in *Dissertation Abstracts*, 1958, v. 18(B), pp. 1091-92.

Bach, G.R. "Marathon Group Dynamics: III. Disjunctive Contacts." *Psychological Reports*, 1967, v. 20, pp. 1163-72.

Bachrach, H.M. "Empathy: We Know What We Mean, But What Do We Measure?" *Archives of General Psychiatry*, 1976, v. 33, pp. 35-38.

Back, K.W. *Beyond Words: The Story of Sensitivity Training and the Encounter Movement.* New York: Russell Sage Foundation, 1972.

Bandura, A. "Psychotherapist's Anxiety Level, Self-insight, and Psychotherapeutic Competence." *Journal of Abnormal and Social Psychology*, 1956, v. 52, pp. 333-37.

Bandura, A.; Lipsher, D.H.; and Miller, P.E. "Psychotherapists' Approach-Avoidance Reactions to Patients' Expressions of Hostility." *Journal of Consulting Psychology*, 1960, v. 24, pp. 1-8.

Bannister, D.; Salmon, P.; and Leiberman, D.M. "Diagnosis-Treatment Relationships in Psychiatry: A Statistical Analysis." *British Journal of Psychiatry*, 1964, v. 110, pp. 726-32.

Barrett, B.H., and Lindsley, O.R. "Deficits in Acquisition of Operant Discrimination and Differentiation Shown by Institutionalized Retarded Children." *American Journal of Mental Deficiency*, 1962, v. 67, pp. 424-36.

Batchelder, R.L., and Hardy, J.M. *Using Sensitivity Training and the Laboratory Method.* (Foreword by R.O. Lippitt.) New York: Association Press, 1968.

Battle, C.C.; Imber, S.D.; Hoehn-Saric, R.; Stone, A.R.; Nash, E.R.; and Frank, J.D. "Target Complaints as Criteria of Improvement." *American Journal of Psychotherapy*, 1966, v. 20, pp. 184-92.

Bebout, J. "Leadership Styles, Group Process Types, and Outcomes." (Interview by E. Meller and J. Elliott.) *Group Leader's Workshop*, 1976, v. 22(3), pp. 3-6.

Bebout, J. Personal communication to the International Association of Applied Social Scientists, April 25, 1974.

Bebout, J. Personal communication, November 15, 1971.

Beck, A.T. "Reliability of Psychiatric Diagnoses: 1. A Critique of Systematic Studies." *American Journal of Psychiatry*, 1962, v. 119, pp. 210-16.

Beck, J.C.; Kantor, D.; and Gelineau, V.A. "Follow-up Study of Chronic Psychotic Patients 'Treated' by College Case-aid Volunteers." *American Journal of Psychiatry*, 1963, v. 120, pp. 269-71.

Bellak, L., and Small, L. *Emergency Psychotherapy and Brief Psychotherapy.* New York: Grune and Stratton, 1965.

Benne, K.D. "Authority in Education." *Harvard Educational Review*, 1970, v. 40, pp. 385-410.

Benne, K.D.; Bradford, L.P.; Gibb, J.R.; and Lippitt, R.O. (Eds.) *The Laboratory Method of Changing and Learning: Theory and Application.* Palo Alto, Calif.: Science and Behavior Books, 1975.

Benson, H., and Epstein, M.D. "The Placebo Effect: A Neglected Asset in the Care of Patients." *Journal of the American Medical Association*, 1975, v. 232, pp. 1225-27.

Berenson, B.G.; Carkhuff, R.R.; and Myrus, P. "The Interpersonal Functioning and Training of College Students." *Journal of Counseling Psychology*, 1966, v. 13, pp. 441-46.

Berg, I.E. *Education and Jobs; The Great Training Robbery*. New York: Praeger, 1970.

Bergen, R.P. "Twelve Months of Medicine in Court." *Journal of the American Medical Association*, 1971, v. 217, pp. 1287-88.

Bergin, A.E. "The Evaluation of Therapeutic Outcomes." In A.E. Bergin and S.L. Garfield (Eds.), *Handbook of Psychotherapy and Behavior Change: An Empirical Analysis*. New York: John Wiley, 1971, pp. 217-70.

Bergin, A.E. "Some Implications of Psychotherapy Research for Therapeutic Practice." *Jouranl of Abnormal Psychology*, 1966, v. 71, pp. 235-46.

Bergin, A.E. "The Effects of Psychotherapy: Negative Results Revisited." *Journal of Counseling Psychology*, 1963, v. 10, pp. 244-50.

Bergin, A.E., and Jasper, L.G. "Correlates of Empathy in Psychotherapy: A Replication." *Journal of Abnormal Psychology*, 1969, v. 74, pp. 477-81.

Bergin, A.E., and Solomon, S. "Personality and Performance Correlates of Empathic Understanding in Psychotherapy." In J.T. Hart and T.M. Tomlinson (Eds.), *New Directions in Client-Centered Therapy*. Boston: Houghton Mifflin, 1970, pp. 223-36.

Bergin, A.E., and Strupp, H.H. *Changing Frontiers in the Science of Psychotherapy*. Chicago: Aldine-Atherton, 1972.

Bergin, A.E., and Suinn, R.M. "Individual Psychotherapy and Behavior Therapy." *Annual Review of Psychology*, 1975, v. 25, pp. 509-56.

Berzon, B.; Solomon, L.N.; and Reisel, J. "Audiotape Programs for Self-Directed Groups." In L.N. Solomon and B. Berzon (Eds.), *New Perspectives on Encounter Groups*. San Francisco: Jossey-Bass, 1972, pp. 211-23.

Betz, B.J. "Experiences in Research in Psychotherapy with Schizophrenic Patients." In H.H. Strupp and L. Luborsky (Eds.), *Research in Psychotherapy*. (Vol. 2.) Washington, D.C.: American Psychological Association, 1962, pp. 41-60.

Blanck, G.S. "The Development of Psychotherapy as a Profession: A Study of the Process of Professionalization." Ph.D. dissertation, New York University, 1963. Abstracted in *Dissertation Abstracts*, 1963, v. 24(07), p. 2974.

Blum, A.F., and Rosenberg, L. "Some Problems Involved in Professionalizing Social Interaction: The Case of Psychotherapeutic Training." *Journal of Health and Social Behavior*, 1968, v. 9, pp. 72-85.

Boisen, A.T. "Types of Dementia Praecox—A Study in Psychiatric Classification." *Psychiatry*, 1938, v. 1, pp. 233-36.

Bolman, L. "Some Effects of Trainers on Their T Groups." *Journal of Applied Behavioral Science*, 1971, v. 7, pp. 309-26.

Bond, G. "Norm Formation in Therapy Groups." Ph.D. dissertation, University of Chicago, 1975. Cited in M.A. Lieberman, "Some Limits to Research on T Groups." *Journal of Applied Behavioral Science*, 1975, v. 11, pp. 241-49.

Bookbinder, L.J.; Fox, R.E.; and Rosenthal, V. "Recommended Standards for Psychotherapy Education in Psychology Doctoral Programs." *Professional Psychology*, 1971, v. 2, pp. 148-54.

Bowden, C.S.; Endicott, J.; and Spitzer, R.L. "A-B Therapist Variable and Psychotherapeutic Outcome." *Journal of Nervous Mental Disorders*, 1972, v. 154, pp. 276-88.

Boyd, J.B., and Elliss, J.D. *Findings of Research into Senior Management Seminars*. Toronto: Hydro-Electric Power Commission of Ontario, 1962. Cited in J.P. Campbell and M.D. Dunnette, "Effectiveness of T-Group Experiences in Managerial Training and Development." *Psychological Bulletin*, 1968, v. 70, pp. 73-104.

Bozarth, J.D., and Krauft, C.C. "Accurate Empathy Ratings: Some Methodological Considerations." *Journal of Clinical Psychology*, 1972, v. 28, pp. 408-10.

Bradford, L.P. "Membership and the Learning Process." In L.P. Bradford, J.R. Gibb, and K. D. Benne (Eds.), *T-group Theory and Laboratory Method: Innovation in Re-education.* New York: John Wiley, 1964, pp. 190-215.

Bradford, L.P.; Gibb, J.R.; and Benne, K.D. (Eds.) *T-Group Theory and Laboratory Method: Innovation in Re-education.* New York: John Wiley, 1964.

Breger, L. "Psychological Testing: Treatment and Research Implications." *Journal of Clinical and Counseling Psychology,* 1968, v. 32, pp. 176-81.

Brill, N.Q.; Koegler, R.R.; Epstein, L.J.; and Forgy, E.W. "Controlled Study of Psychiatric Outpatient Treatment." *Archives of General Psychiatry,* 1964, v. 10, pp. 581-95.

Buchanan, P.C. "Laboratory Training and Organization Development." *Administrative Science Quarterly,* 1969, v. 14, pp. 466-80.

Bull, G.M. "Examinations." *Journal of Medical Education,* 1959, v. 34, pp. 1154-58.

Burstein, J.W., and Carkhuff, R.R. "Objective, Therapist and Client Ratings of Therapist-offered Facilitative Conditions of Moderate to Low Functioning Therapists." *Journal of Clinical Psychology,* 1968, v. 24, pp. 240-41.

California, Department of Mental Hygiene. *Mental Health Manpower—Vol. II: Recruitment, Training and Utilization—A Compilation of Articles, Surveys, and a Review of Applicable Literature.* Sacramento, Calif.: Department of Mental Hygiene, 1967.

Campbell, J.P., and Dunnette, M.D. "Effectiveness of T-Group Experiences in Managerial Training and Development." *Psychological Bulletin,* 1968, v. 70, pp. 73-104.

Canadian Commission on Human Relations Training, Training for Trainers Task Group. "Report of the Training for Trainers Task Group." Unpublished document, 1970.

Caracena, P.F., and Vicory, J.R. "Correlates of Phenomenological and Judged Empathy." *Journal of Counseling Psychology,* 1969, v. 16, pp. 510-15.

Carkhuff, R.R. *Helping and Human Relations: A Primer for Lay and Professional Helpers—Practice and Research.* (Vol. 1.) New York: Holt, Rinehart and Winston, 1969.

Carkhuff, R.R. "Differential Functioning of Lay and Professional Helpers." *Journal of Counseling Psychology,* 1968, v. 15, pp. 117-26.

Carkhuff, R.R., and Berenson, B.G. *Beyond Counseling and Therapy.* New York: Holt, Rinehart and Winston, 1967.

Carkhuff, R.R.; Kratochvil, D.; and Friel, T. "Effects of Professional Training: Communication and Discrimination of Facilitative Conditions." *Journal of Counseling Psychology,* 1968, v. 15, pp. 68-74.

Carkhuff, R.R., and Truax, C.B. "Lay Mental Health Counseling: The Effects of Lay Group Counseling." *Journal of Consulting Psychology,* 1965, v. 29, pp. 426-31. Reprinted in B.G. Guerney, Jr. (Ed.), *Psychotherapeutic Agents: New Roles for Non-Professionals, Parents, and Teachers.* New York: Holt, Rinehart and Winston, 1969, pp. 565-74.

Cartwright, R.D. "Psychotherapeutic Processes." *Annual Review of Psychology,* 1968, v. 19, pp. 387-416.

Cartwright, D.S., and Roth, I. "Success and Satisfaction in Psychotherapy." *Journal of Clinical Psychology,* 1957, v. 13, pp. 20-26.

Castelnuovo-Tedesco, P. "Psychiatric Residents' Appraisal of Psychiatric Teaching in Medical Schools." *Comprehensive Psychiatry,* 1969, v. 10, pp. 475-81.

Castelnuovo-Tedesco, P. "How Much Psychiatry are Medical Students Really Learning?" *Archives of General Psychiatry,* 1967, v. 16, pp. 668-75.

Chambers, W.M., and Ficek, D.E. "An Evaluation of Marathon Counseling." *International Journal of Group Psychotherapy,* 1970, v. 20, pp. 372-79.

Chinsky, J.M., and Rappaport, J. "Brief Critique of the Meaning and Reliability of 'Accurate Empathy' Ratings." *Psychological Bulletin,* 1970, v. 73, pp. 379-82.

Citizens Commission on Graduate Medical Education. *The Graduate Education of Physicians.* Chicago: American Medical Association, 1966.

Clark, D.H. "Response to Lakin Comment." *American Psychologist,* 1970, v. 25, pp. 881-82.

Cole, J., and Pilisuk, M. "Differences in the Provision of Mental Health Services by Race." *American Journal of Orthopsychiatry*, 1976, v. 46, pp. 510-25.

Coleman, J.V. "The Teaching of Basic Psychotherapy." *American Journal of Orthopsychiatry*, 1947, v. 17, pp. 622-27.

Combs, A.W. "Problems and Definitions in Legislation." *American Psychologist*, 1953, v. 8, pp. 554-63.

Conover, D. "Psychiatric Distinctions: New and Old Approaches." *Journal of Health and Social Behaviors*, 1972, v. 13, pp. 167-80.

Cooper, C.L., and Mangham, I.L. *T-groups, A Survey of Research.* London: Wiley Interscience, 1971.

Cooper, C.L. "The Influence of the Trainer on Participant Change in T-groups." *Human Relations*, 1969, v. 22, pp. 515-30.

Counseling Psychologist. *Carl Rogers on Empathy.* (Special issue.) 1975, v. 5(2).

Covner, B.J. "Screening Volunteer Alcoholism Counselors." *Quarterly Journal of Studies on Alcohol*, 1969, v. 30, pp. 420-25.

Cowles, J.T., and Hubbard, J.P. "Validity and Reliability of the New Objective Tests." *Journal of Medical Education*, 1954, v. 29(6), pp. 30-34.

Crow, W.J. "The Effect of Training upon Accuracy and Variability in Interpersonal Perception." *Journal of Abnormal and Social Psychology*, 1957, v. 55, pp. 355-59.

Culbert, S.A. "Trainer Self-disclosure and Member Growth in Two T Groups." *Journal of Applied Behavioral Science*, 1968, v. 4, pp. 47-73.

Curran, W.J., and Shapiro, E.D. *Law, Medicine, and Forensic Science.* Boston: Little, Brown, 1970.

Dailey, C.A. "The Practical Utility of the Clinical Report." *Journal of Consulting Psychology*, 1953, v. 17, pp. 297-302.

Demos, G.D. "The Application of Certain Principles of Client-centered Therapy to Short-term Vocational-Educational Counseling." *Journal of Counseling Psychology*, 1964, v. 11, pp. 280-84.

Demos, G.D., and Zuwaylif, F.H. "Counselor Movement as a Result of an Intensive Six-week Training Program in Counseling." *Personnel and Guidance Journal*, 1963, v. 42, pp. 125-28.

Denker, P.G. "Results of Treatment of Psychoneuroses by the General Practitioner." *New York State Journal of Medicine*, 1946, v. 46, pp. 2164-66.

Devereux, G. (Ed.) *Psychoanalysis and the Occult.* New York: International Universities Press, 1973.

Durlak, J.A. "The Use of Nonprofessionals as Therapeutic Agents: Research, Issues, and Implications." Ph.D. dissertation, Vanderbilt University, 1971. Abstracted in *Dissertation Abstracts International*, 1971, v. 32B, pp. 2999-3000.

Earley, L.W. (Ed.) *Psychiatry and Medical Education: II.* Washington, D.C.: American Psychiatric Association, 1969.

Easton, R.H.; Carr, R.J.; and Whiteley, J.M. "Issues in the Encounter Group Movement." *Counseling Psychologist*, 1972, v. 3(2), pp. 89-120.

Egan, G. *Encounter: Group Processes for Interpersonal Growth.* Belmont, Calif.: Brooks/Cole Publishing Co., 1970.

Ekstein, R., and Wallerstein, R.S. *The Teaching and Learning of Psychotherapy.* (2nd ed.) New York: International Universities Press, 1972.

Eliseo, T.S. "Effectiveness of Remotivation Technique with Chronic Psychiatric Patients." *Psychological Reports*, 1964, v. 14, pp. 171-78.

Ellsworth, R.B. *Nonprofessionals in Psychiatric Rehabilitation: The Psychiatric Aide and the Schizophrenic Patient.* New York: Appleton-Century-Crofts, 1968.

Ennis, B.J., and Litwack, T.R. "Psychiatry and the Presumption of Expertise: Flipping Coins in the Courtroom." *California Law Review*, 1974, v. 62, pp. 693-752.

Evans, F.J. "The Power of a Sugar Pill." *Psychology Today*, April 1974, pp. 54-59.

Eysenck, H.J. "The Effects of Psychotherapy: An Evaluation." *Journal of Consulting Psychology*, 1952, v. 16, pp. 319-24.

Fairweather, G.W.; Simon, R.; Gebhard, M.E.; Weingarten, E.; Holland, J.L.; Sanders, R.; Stone, G.B.; and Reahl, J.E. "Relative Effectiveness of Psychotherapeutic Programs: A Multicriteria Comparison of Four Programs for Three Different Patient Groups." *Psychological Monographs*, 1960, v. 74 (5, Whole No. 492).

Farber, I.E. "Sane and Insane: Constructions and Misconstruction." *Journal of Abnormal Psychology*, 1975, v. 84, pp. 589-620.

Farson, R.E. "Self-directed Groups and Community Mental Health." In L.N. Solomon and B. Berzon (Eds.), *New Perspectives on Encounter Groups*. San Francisco: Jossey-Bass, 1972, pp. 224-32.

Farson, R.E. "The Counselor Is a Woman." *Journal of Counseling Psychology*, 1954, v. 1, pp. 221-23.

Feifel, H., and Eells, J. "Patients and Therapists Assess the Same Psychotherapy." *Journal of Consulting Psychology*, 1963, v. 27, pp. 310-18.

Ferster, C.B. "Positive Reinforcement and Behavioral Deficits of Autistic Children." *Child Development*, 1961, v. 32, pp. 437-56.

Fiedler, F.E. "The Concept of an Ideal Therapeutic Relationship." *Journal of Consulting Psychology*, 1950, v. 14, pp. 239-45.

Fiedler, F.E. "A Comparison of Therapeutic Relationships in Psychoanalytic, Nondirective and Adlerian Therapy." *Journal of Consulting Psychology*, 1950a, v. 14, pp. 436-45.

Fiman, B.G., and Conner, D.R. "Laboratory Training: A Review of Problem Areas." *Group Psychotherapy and Psychodrama*, 1973, v. 26(1-2), pp. 72-91.

Fine, R. "Training the Psychologist for Psychotherapy." *Psychotherapy: Theory, Research and Practice*, 1966, v. 3, pp. 184-87.

Foulds, G.A. "The Reliability of Psychiatric, and the Validity of Psychological, Diagnoses." *Journal of Mental Science*, 1955, v. 101, pp. 851-62.

Frank, G.H. *Psychiatric Diagnosis: A Review of Research*. Oxford, England: Pergamon Press, 1975.

Frank, G.H. "Psychiatric Diagnosis: A Review of Research." *Journal of General Psychology*, 1969, v. 81, pp. 157-76.

Frank, J.D. *Persuasion and Healing: A Comparative Study of Psychotherapy*. (Rev. ed.) Baltimore, Md.: Johns Hopkins Press, 1973.

Frank, J.D. "The Role of Cognitions in Illness and Healing." In H. H. Strupp and L. Luborsky (Eds.), *Research in Psychotherapy*. (Vol. 2.) Washington, D.C.: American Psychological Association, 1962, pp. 1-12.

Fromme, D.K.; Jones, W.H.; and Davis, J.O. "Experiential Group Training with Conservative Populations: A Potential for Negative Effects." *Journal of Clinical Psychology*, 1974, v. 39, pp. 290-96.

Garfield, S.L. "Research on Client Variables in Psychotherapy." In A.E. Bergin and S.L. Garfield (Eds.), *Handbook of Psychotherapy and Behavior Change: An Empirical Analysis*. New York: John Wiley, 1971, pp. 271-98.

Garrison, F.H. *An Introduction to the History of Medicine*. Philadelphia, Pa.: W.B. Saunders, 1921. Cited in A.E. Bergin and S.L. Garfield (Eds.), *Handbook of Psychotherapy and Behavior Change: An Empirical Analysis*. New York: John Wiley, 1971, p. 463.

Geertsma, R.H. "Observational Methods." In R.H. Woody and J.D. Woody (Eds.), *Clinical Assessment in Counseling and Psychotherapy*. New York: Appleton-Century-Crofts, 1972, pp. 86-118.

Ghiselli, E.E. *The Validity of Occupational Aptitude Tests*. New York: John Wiley, 1966.

Gibb, J.R. "A Research Perspective on the Laboratory Method." In K.D. Benne, L.P. Bradford, J.R. Gibb, and R.O. Lippitt (Eds.), *The Laboratory Method of Changing and Learning: Theory and Application*. Palo Alto, Calif.: Science and Behavior Books, 1975, pp. 56-71, 551-69.

Gibb, J.R. "The Training Group." In K.D. Benne, L.P. Bradford, J.R. Gibb, and

R.O. Lippitt (Eds.), *The Laboratory Method of Changing and Learning: Theory and Application.* Palo Alto, Calif.: Science and Behavior Books, 1975a, pp. 277-92.

Gibb, J.R. "The Message from Research." In J.W. Pfeiffer and J.E. Jones (Eds.), *The 1974 Annual Handbook for Group Facilitators.* La Jolla, Calif.: University Associates, 1974.

Gibb, J.R. "Climate for Trust Formation." In L.P. Bradford, J.R. Gibb, and K.D. Benne (Eds.), *T-Group Theory and Laboratory Method: Innovation and Re-education.* New York: John Wiley, 1964, pp. 279-309.

Gibb, J.R. "The Present Status of T-Group Theory." In L.P. Bradford, J.R. Gibb, and K.D. Benne (Eds.), *T-Group Theory and Laboratory Method: Innovation and Re-education.* New York: John Wiley, 1964a, pp. 168-90.

Glass, G.V. "Primary, Secondary, and Meta-Analysis of Research." Paper presented as presidential address to the 1976 Annual Meeting of the American Educational Research Association, San Francisco, Calif., April 21, 1976.

Gliedman, L.H.; Nash, E.H., Jr.; Imber, S.D.; Stone, A.R.; and Frank, J.D. "Reduction of Symptoms by Pharmacologically Inert Substances and by Short-Term Psychotherapy." *Archives of Neurology and Psychiatry,* 1958, v. 79, pp. 345-51.

Golann, S.E.; Breiter, D.E.; and Magoon, T.M. "A Filmed Interview Applied to the Evaluation of Mental Health Counselors." *Psychotherapy: Theory, Research and Practice,* 1966, v. 3, pp. 21-24.

Goldfarb, A. "Reliability of Diagnostic Judgments Made by Psychologists." *Journal of Clinical Psychology,* 1959, v. 15, pp. 392-96.

Goldman, G.D. *The Clinical Psychologist in the Private Practice of Psychotherapy in New York State.* (Report of Committee on Private Practice.) New York: Division of Clinical Psychology, New York State Psychological Association, 1963.

Golembiewski, R.T., and Blumberg, A. (Eds.) *Sensitivity Training and the Laboratory Approach: Readings About Concepts and Applications.* Itasca, Ill.: F.E. Peacock, 1970.

Goodman, G. *Companionship Therapy: Studies in Structured Intimacy.* San Francisco: Jossey-Bass, 1972.

Goodman, G. "Companionship as Therapy: The Use of Nonprofessional Talent." In J.T. Hart and T.M. Tomlinson (Eds.), *New Directions in Client-Centered Psychotherapy.* New York: Houghton Mifflin, 1970, pp. 348-71.

Gottschalk, L.A. "Psychoanalytic Notes on T-Groups at the Human Relations Laboratory, Bethel, Maine." *Comprehensive Psychiatry,* 1966, v. 7, pp. 472-87.

Gottschalk, L.A., and Pattison, E.M. "Psychiatric Perspectives on T-Groups and the Laboratory Movement: An Overview." *American Journal of Psychiatry,* 1969, v. 126, pp. 823-39.

Gough, H.G.; Wenk, E.A.; and Rozynko, V.V. "Parole Outcome as Predicted from the CPI, the MMPI, and a Base Expectancy Table." *Journal of Abnormal Psychology,* 1965, v. 70, pp. 432-41.

Grad, B. "Some Biological Effects of the 'Laying on of Hands': A Review of Experiments with Animals and Plants." *Journal of the American Society for Psychical Research,* 1965, v. 59, pp. 95-129.

Greenbank, R.K. "Are Medical Students Learning Psychiatry?" *Pennsylvania Medical Journal,* 1961, v. 64, pp. 989-92.

Grigg, A.E. "Client Response to Counselors at Different Levels of Experience." *Journal of Counseling Psychology,* 1961, v. 8, 217-23.

Group for the Advancement of Psychiatry. *Mysticism: Spiritual Quest or Psychic Disorder?* (Report No. 97.) New York: Group for the Advancement of Psychiatry, 1976.

Guerney, B.G., Jr. (Ed.) *Psychotherapeutic Agents: New Roles for Nonprofessionals, Parents, and Teachers.* New York: Holt, Rinehart and Winston, 1969.

Gurin, G.; Veroff, J.; and Feld, S. *Americans View Their Mental Health.* New York: Basic Books, 1960.

Hansen, J.C., and Barker, E.N. "Experiencing and the Supervisory Relationship." *Journal of Counseling Psychology*, 1964, v. 11, pp. 107-11.

Hartley, D.; Roback, H.B.; and Abramowitz, S.I. "Deterioration Effects in Encounter Groups." *American Psychologist*, 1976, v. 31, pp. 247-55.

Hawkins, R.P.; Peterson, R.F.; Schweid, E.; and Bijou, S.W. "Behavior Therapy in the Home: Amelioration of Problem Parent-Child Relations with the Parent in a Therapeutic Role." *Journal of Experimental Child Psychology*, 1966, v. 4, pp. 99-107.

Heath, D.H. *Maturity and Competence: A Transcultural View.* (Foreword by M.B. Smith.) New York: Garner Press, 1977.

Hedberg, A.G.; Meredith, R.; and Fitts, M. "The Doctor of Psychology Degree: An Alternative Model for Relevant Clinical Training." *Journal of Behavior Therapy and Experimental Psychiatry*, 1973, v. 4, pp. 191-93.

Henry, W.E.; Sims, J.H.; and Spray, S.L. *Public and Private Lives of Psychotherapists.* San Francisco, Calif.: Jossey-Bass, 1973.

Henry, W.E.; Sims, J.H.; and Spray, S.L. *The Fifth Profession: Becoming a Psychotherapist.* San Francisco, Calif.: Jossey-Bass, 1971.

Hirano-Nakanishi, M.J. "Equal Opportunity, Competence, and the Mystery of the Legal Certification System." Paper presented at the Conference on Credentialism, University of California, Berkeley, April 28-30, 1977.

Hoch, P.H., and Zubin, J. (Eds.) *Current Problems in Psychiatric Diagnosis.* New York: Grune and Stratton, 1953.

Hogan, H. "Development of an Empathy Scale." *Journal of Consulting and Clinical Psychology*, 1969, v. 33, pp. 307-16.

Hollingshead, A.B., and Redlich, F.C. *Social Class and Mental Illness: A Community Study.* New York: John Wiley, 1958.

Holt, R.R. (Ed.) *New Horizon for Psychotherapy: Autonomy as a Profession.* New York: International Universities Press, 1971.

Holt, R.R., and Luborsky, L. *Personality Patterns of Psychiatrists.* (Introduction by R.P. Knight.) New York: Basic Books, 1958. (2 vols.).

Horwitz, L. "Transference in Training Groups and Therapy Groups." *International Journal of Group Psychotherapy*, 1964, v. 14, pp. 202-13. Reprinted in R.T. Golembiewski and A. Blumberg (Eds.), *Sensitivity Training and the Laboratory Approach: Readings About Concepts and Applications.* Itasca, Ill.: F.E. Peacock, 1970, pp. 179-91.

House, R.J. "T-Group Education and Leadership Effectiveness: A Review of the Empiric Literature and a Critical Evaluation." In R.T. Golembiewski and A. Blumberg (Eds.), *Sensitivity Training and the Laboratory Approach: Readings about Concepts and Applications.* Itasca, Ill.: F.E. Peacock, 1970, pp. 435-62. Reprinted from *Personnel Psychology*, 1967, v. 20, pp. 1-32.

Houts, P.S., and Serber, M. (Eds.) *After the Turn on, What? Learning Perspectives on Humanistic Groups.* Champaign, Ill.: Research Press, 1972.

Hovland, C.I.; Janis, I.L.; and Kelley, H.H. *Communication and Persuasion.* New Haven, Conn.: Yale University Press, 1953.

Huff, F.W. "Factors Affecting Agreement Among Clinicians." *Journal of General Psychology*, 1966, v. 75, pp. 265-72.

Huff, F.W., and Friedman, H. "A Study of the Effects on Agreement Among Clinicians of Redundant and New Information, Confidence, and Time Available for Assessments." *Journal of General Psychology*, 1967, v. 76, pp. 49-57.

Hunt, W.A.; Wittson, C.L.; and Hunt, E.B. "A Theoretical and Practical Analysis of the Diagnostic Process." In P.H. Hoch and J. Zubin (Eds.), *Current Problems in Psychiatric Diagnosis.* New York: Grune and Stratton, 1953, pp. 53-65.

Hurley, J.R., and Force, E.J. "T-Group Gains in Acceptance of Self and Others." *International Journal of Group Psychotherapy*, 1973, v. 23, pp. 166-76.

Hurvitz, N. "Peer Self-Help Psychotherapy Groups and Their Implications for Psychotherapy." *Psychotherapy: Theory, Research and Practice*, 1970, v. 7, pp. 41-49.

International Association of Applied Social Scientists, Task Force on Personal Growth Group Consultants. "Draft of Accreditation Procedures." Unpublished document, Washington, D.C., 1974.

International Journal of Group Psychotherapy. "Symposium: Contrasting Models of Leadership In Group Psychotherapy." *International Journal of Group Psychotherapy*, 1976, v. 26, pp. 135-72.

Ivey, A.E.; Normington, C.J.; Miller, C.D.; Morrill, W.H.; and Haase, R.F. "Microcounseling and Attending Behavior: An Approach to Prepracticum Counselor Training." *Journal of Counseling Psychology*, 1968, v. 5(2). (Monograph Supp.)

Jacobson, R.L. "Does High Academic Achievement Create Problems Later On?" *Chronicle of Higher Education*, May 23, 1977, p. 4.

Jaffe, S.L., and Scherl, D.J. "Acute Psychosis Precipitated by T-group Experiences." *Archives of General Psychiatry*, 1969, v. 21, pp. 443-48.

James, W. *The Varieties of Religious Experience*. New York: Modern Library, 1902.

Janet, P. *Psychological Healing*. (Translated by E. Paul and C. Paul.) New York: Macmillan, 1925. (2 vols.)

Johnson, D.L.; Hanson, P.G.; Rothaus, P.; Morton, R.B.; Lyle, F.A.; and Moyer, R. "Follow-up Evaluation of Human Relations Training for Psychiatric Patients." In E. H. Schein and W. G. Bennis, *Personal and Organizational Change through Group Methods: The Laboratory Approach*. New York: John Wiley, 1965, pp. 152-69.

Johnston, R., and McNeal, B.F. "Statistical versus Clinical Prediction: Length of Neuropsychiatric Hospital Stay." *Journal of Abnormal Psychology*, 1967, v. 72, pp. 335-40.

Jones, H.M. *Education and World Tragedy*. Cambridge, Mass.: Harvard University Press, 1946.

Jourard, S.M. "A Way to Encounter." In L. Blank, G.B. Gottsegen, and M.G. Gottsegen (Eds.), *Confrontation: Encounters in Self and Interpersonal Awareness*. New York: Macmillan, 1971, pp. 107-19.

Journal of Applied Behavioral Science. "Self-help Groups." (Special Issue.) *Journal of Applied Behavioral Science*, 1976, v. 12.

Joyce, C.R.B., and Welldon, R.M.C. "The Objective Efficacy of Prayer: A Double-Blind Clinical Trial." *Journal of Chronic Diseases*, 1965, v. 18, pp. 367-77.

Jung, C.G. *Psychological Reflections: A New Anthology of His Writings: 1905-1961*. (Selected and Edited by J. Jacobi, in collaboration with R.F.C. Hull.) New Jersey: Princeton University Press, 1970.

Kaelbling, R., and Volpe, P.A. "Constancy of Psychiatric Diagnoses in Readmissions." *Comprehensive Psychiatry*, 1963, v. 4(1), pp. 29-39.

Kagan, J. "On the Need for Relativism." In D.P. Schultz (Ed.), *The Science of Psychology: Critical Reflections*. New York: Appleton-Century-Crofts, 1970, pp. 98-114.

Kagan, N.; Krathwohl, D.; Goldberg, A.D.; Campbell, R.J.; Schauble, P.G.; Greenberg, B.S.; Danish, S.J.; Resnikoff, A.; Bowes, J.; and Bondy, S.B. *Studies in Human Interaction: Interpersonal Process Recall Stimulated by Videotape*. Washington, D.C., U.S., DHEW, Office of Education, Bureau of Research, 1967.

Kahne, M.J. "Suicide Among Patients in Mental Hospitals—A Study of the Psychiatrists Who Conducted Their Therapy." *Psychiatry*, 1968, v. 31, pp. 32-43.

Kalinkowitz, B.N. "An Ideal Training Program for Psychotherapists: Contributions from Clinical Psychology." In R.R. Holt (Ed.), *New Horizon for Psychotherapy: Autonomy as a Profession*. New York: International Universities Press, 1971, pp. 124-56.

Kane, F.J.; Wallace, C.D., and Lipton, M.A. "Emotional Disturbance Related to T-Group Experience." *American Journal of Psychiatry*, 1971, v. 127, pp. 954-57.

Kanfer, F.H., and Saslow, G. "Behavioral Analysis: An Alternative to Diagnostic Classification." *Archives of General Psychiatry*, 1965, v. 12, pp. 529-38.

Katz, B. "Predictive and Behavioral Empathy and Client Change in Short-term Counseling." Ph.D. dissertation, New York University, 1962. Abstracted in *Dissertation Abstracts*, 1962, v. 23(6), p. 2206.

Katz, J., and Associates. *No Time for Youth: Growth and Constraint in College Students.* San Francisco: Jossey-Bass, 1968.

Kelly, E.L. "Clinical Psychology—1960: Report of Survey Findings." *Newsletter, Division of Clinical Psychology of the American Psychological Association,* 1961, v. 14(1), pp. 1-11.

Kelly, E.L., and Fiske, D.W. *The Prediction of Performance in Clinical Psychology.* Ann Arbor, Mich.: University of Michigan Press, 1951.

Kelly, E.L., and Fiske, D.W. "The Prediction of Success in the VA Training Program in Clinical Psychology." *American Psychologist,* 1950, v. 5, pp. 395-406.

Kelly, E.L., and Goldberg, L.R. "Correlates of Later Performance and Specialization in Psychology." *Psychological Monographs,* 1959, v. 73 (12, Whole No. 482).

Kendell, R.E. *The Role of Diagnosis in Psychiatry.* Oxford, England: Blackwell Scientific Publications, 1975.

Kernberg, O.F. "Summary and Conclusions of 'Psychotherapy and Psychoanalysis, Final Report of the Menninger Foundation's Psychotherapy Research Project.'" *International Journal of Psychiatry,* 1973, v. 11, pp. 62-77.

Khajavi, F., and Hekmat, H. "A Comparative Study of Empathy: The Effects of Psychiatric Training." *Archives of General Psychiatry,* 1971, v. 25, pp. 490-93.

Kiesler, D.J. "Some Myths of Psychotherapy Research and the Search for a Paradigm." *Psychological Bulletin,* 1966, v. 65, pp. 110-36.

Klein, D.F., and Davis, J.M. *Diagnosis and Drug Treatment of Psychiatric Disorders.* Baltimore, Md.: Williams and Wilkins, 1969.

Klein, H.R. *Psychoanalysts in Training: Selection and Evaluation.* New York: Columbia University College of Physicians and Surgeons, 1965.

Klett, C.J., and Moseley, E.C. "The Right Drug for the Right Patient." *Journal of Consulting Psychology,* 1965, v. 29, pp. 546-51.

Knowles, M.S. "Group Process Training Sequence: Curriculum Outline 1969-71." Unpublished manuscript, Boston University School of Education, Department of Administration and Supervision, Boston, undated.

Koenig, P. "Lee's Bilious Pills: The Placebo Effect in Patent Medicine." *Psychology Today,* April 1974, pp. 60-61.

Komins, A.S. "An Analysis of Trainer Influence in T-group Learning." Ed.D. dissertation, Boston University, 1972. Abstracted in *Dissertation Abstracts International,* 1972, v. 33(4-A), p. 1403.

Kostlan, A. "A Method for the Empirical Study of Psychodiagnosis." *Journal of Consulting Psychology,* 1954, v. 18, pp. 83-88.

Kreitman, N.; Sainsbury, P.; Morrissey, J.; Towers, J.; and Scrivener, J. "The Reliability of Psychiatric Assessment: An Analysis." *Journal of Mental Science,* 1961, v. 107, pp. 887-908.

Kubie, L.S. "A School of Psychological Medicine Within the Framework of a Medical School and University." *Journal of Medical Education,* 1964, v. 39, pp. 476-80.

Kubie, L.S. "The Pros and Cons of a New Profession: A Doctorate in Medical Psychology." *Texas Report on Biology and Medicine,* 1954, v. 12, pp. 692-737. Reprinted in M. Harrower (Ed.), *Medical and Psychological Teamwork in the Care of the Chronically Ill.* Springfield, Ill.: Charles C. Thomas, 1955, pp. 125-70.

Kubie, L.S. *Practical and Theoretical Aspects of Psychoanalysis.* New York: International Universities Press, 1950.

Kurtz, R.R., and Grummon, D.L. "Different Approaches to the Measurement of Therapist Empathy and Their Relationship to Therapy Outcome." *Journal of Consulting and Clinical Psychology,* 1972, v. 39, pp. 106-15.

LaForge, R., and Suczek, R.F. "The Interpersonal Dimension of Personality: An Interpersonal Check List." *Journal of Personality,* 1955, v. 24, pp. 94-112.

Laing, R.D., and Esterson, A. "The Abbotts." In T.J. Scheff (Ed.), *Mental Illness and Social Processes.* New York: Harper and Row, 1967, pp. 130-48. Reprinted from *Sanity, Madness, and the Family.* London: Tavistock Publications, 1964, pp. 15-34.

Lakin, M. *Interpersonal Encounter: Theory and Practice in Sensitivity Training.* New York: McGraw-Hill, 1972.

Lakin, M. "Some Ethical Issues in Sensitivity Training." *American Psychologist,* 1969, v. 24, pp. 923-28.

Lambert, M.J.; Bergin, A.E.; and Collins, J.L. "Therapist-Induced Deterioration in Psychotherapy." In A.S. Gurman and A.M. Razin (Eds.), *Effective Psychotherapy: A Handbook of Research.* New York: Pergamon Press, 1977, pp. 452-81.

Landis, C.A. "A Statistical Evaluation of Psychotherapeutic Methods." In L.E. Hinsie, *Concepts and Problems of Psychotherapy.* New York: Columbia University Press, 1937, pp. 155-69.

Lehmann, H.E. "The Placebo Response and the Double-Blind Study." In P.H. Hoch and J. Zubin (Eds.), *The Evaluation of Psychiatric Treatment.* New York: Grune and Stratton, 1964, pp. 75-93.

Leitner, L.A. "Discrimination of Counselor Interpersonal Skills in Self and Others." *Journal of Counseling Psychology,* 1972, v. 19, pp. 509-11.

LeMay, M.L., and Christensen, O.C., Jr. "The Uncontrollable Nature of Control Groups." *Journal of Counseling Psychology,* 1968, v. 15, pp. 63-67.

LeShan, L.L. *The Medium, the Mystic, and the Physicist: Toward a General Theory of the Paranormal.* New York: Viking Press, 1974.

Lesser, W.M. "The Relationship Between Counseling Progress and Empathic Understanding." *Journal of Counseling Psychology,* 1961, v. 8, pp. 330-36.

Lester, B.K.; Gussen, J.; Yamamoto, J.; and West, L.J. "Teaching Psychotherapy in a Longitudinal Curriculum." *Journal of Medical Education,* 1962, v. 37, pp. 28-32.

Leventhal, H. "Cognitive Processes and Interpersonal Predictions." *Journal of Abnormal and Social Psychology,* 1957, v. 55, pp. 176-80.

Lidz, T., and Edelson, M. (Eds.) *Training Tomorrow's Psychiatrist: The Crisis in Curriculum.* New Haven, Conn.: Yale University Press, 1970.

Lieberman, M.A. "Joy Less Facts? A Response to Schutz, Smith, and Rowan." *Journal of Humanistic Psychology,* 1975, v. 15(2), pp. 49-54.

Lieberman, M.A.; Yalom, I.D.; and Miles, M.B. *Encounter Groups: First Facts.* New York: Basic Books, 1973.

Lieberman, M.A.; Yalom, I.D.; and Miles, M.B. "The Group Experience Project: A Comparison of Ten Encounter Technologies." In L. Blank, G.B. Gottsegen, and M.G. Gottsegen (Eds.), *Confrontation: Encounters in Self and Interpersonal Awareness.* New York: Macmillan, 1971, pp. 469-97.

Light, D., Jr. "The Impact of Medical School on Future Psychiatrists." *American Journal of Psychiatry,* 1975, v. 132, pp. 607-10.

Lindsley, O.R. "Direct Measurement and Functional Definition of Vocal Hallucinatory Symptoms." *Journal of Nervous and Mental Disease,* 1963, v. 136, pp. 293-97.

Lindsley, O.R. "Characteristics of the Behavior of Chronic Psychotics as Revealed by Free-operant Conditioning Methods." *Diseases of the Nervous System,* 1960, v. 21(2) (Supp.), pp. 66-78.

Lindsley, O.R. "Operant Conditioning Methods Applied to Research in Chronic Schizophrenia." *Psychiatric Research Reports,* 1956, v. 5, pp. 118-39.

Lipp, M. "Quality Control in Psychiatry and the Problem Oriented System." *International Journal of Psychiatry,* 1973, v. 11, pp. 355-65.

Lippitt, R.L.; Benne, K.D.; Bradford, L.; and Gibb, J. "The Professionalization of Laboratory Practice." In K.D. Benne, L.P. Bradford, J.R. Gibb, and R.L. Lippitt (Eds.), *The Laboratory Method of Changing and Learning: Theory and Applications.* Palo Alto, Calif.: Science and Behavior Books, 1975, pp. 471-90.

Lippitt, G.L., and This, L.E. "Leaders for Laboratory Training: Selected Guidelines for Group Trainers Utilizing the Laboratory Method." In R.T. Golembiewski and A. Blumberg (Eds.), *Sensitivity Training and the Laboratory Approach: Readings About Concepts and Applications.* Itasca, Ill.: F.E. Peacock, 1970, pp. 167-79.

Livingston, J.S. "Myth of the Well-educated Manager." *Harvard Business Review*, 1971, v. 49, pp. 79-89.

Lomranz, J.; Lakin, M.; and Schiffman, H. "Variants of Sensitivity Training and Encounter: Diversity or Fragmentation?" *Jouranl of Applied Behavioral Science*, 1972, v. 8, pp. 399-420.

Long, T.J., and Schultz, E.W. "Empathy: A Quality of an Effective Group Leader." *Psychological Reports*, 1973, v. 32, pp. 699-705.

Lorr, M.; McNair, D.M.; and Weinstein, G.J. "Early Effects of Chlordiazepoxide (Librium) Used with Psychotherapy." *Journal of Psychiatric Research*, 1962, v. 1, pp. 257-270.

Lubin, B. "Survey of Psychotherapy Training and Activities of Psychologists." *Journal of Clinical Psychology*, 1962, v. 18, pp. 252-55.

Luborsky. L. "A Note on Eysenck's Article, 'The Effects of Psychotherapy: An Evaluation.'" *British Journal of Psychology*, 1954, v. 45, pp. 129-31.

Luborsky, L., and Bachrach, H. "Factors Influencing Clinician's Judgments of Mental Health: Eighteen Experiences with the Health-Sickness Rating Scale." *Archives of General Psychiatry*, 1974, v. 31, pp. 292-99.

Luborsky, L.; Chandler, M.; Auerbach, A.H.; Cohen, J.; and Bachrach, H.M. "Factors Influencing the Outcome of Psychotherapy: A Review of the Quantitative Research." *Psychological Bulletin*, 1971, v. 75, pp. 145-85.

Luborsky, L.; Singer, B.; and Luborsky, L. "Comparative Studies of Psychotherapies: Is It True That 'Everyone Has Won and All Must Have Prizes?'" *Archives of General Psychiatry*, 1975, v. 32, pp. 995-1008.

Luborsky, L., and Spence, D.P. "Quantitative Research on Psychoanalytic Therapy." In A.E. Bergin and S.L. Garfield (Eds.), *Handbook of Psychotherapy and Behavior Change: An Empirical Analysis.* New York: John Wiley, 1971, pp. 408-38.

Lyman, H.B. *Test Scores and What They Mean.* Englewood Cliffs, N.J.: Prentice-Hall, 1971.

Lynch, M.; Gardner, E.A.; and Felzer, S.B. "The Role of Indigenous Personnel as Clinical Therapists." *Archives of General Psychiatry*, 1968, v. 19, pp. 428-34.

Lynn, E.J., and Nordhoff, J.A. "Evaluation of Therapist Candidates." *American Journal of Psychiatry*, 1975, v. 132, pp. 656-58.

McClain, E.W. "Is the Counselor a Woman?" *Personnel and Guidance Journal*, 1968, v. 46, pp. 444-48.

McClelland, D.C. "Testing for Competence Rather than for 'Intelligence.'" *American Psychologist*, 1973, v. 28, pp. 1-14.

McDermott, J.F.; Harrison, S.I.; Schrager, J.; and Wilson, P. "Social Class and Mental Illness in Children: Observations of Blue-Collar Families." *American Journal of Orthopsychiatry*, 1965, v. 35, pp. 500-508.

McGuire, C.H. "The Oral Examination as a Measure of Professional Competence." *Journal of Medical Education*, 1966, v. 41, pp. 267-74.

MacLennan, B.W. "The Personalities of Group Leaders: Implications for Selection and Training." *International Journal of Group Psychotherapy*, 1975, v. 25, pp. 177-83.

McWhirter, J.J., and Marks, S.E. "An Investigation of the Relationship Between the Facilitative Conditions and Peer and Group Leader Ratings of Perceived Counseling Effectiveness." *Journal of Clinical Psychology*, 1972, v. 28, pp. 116-17.

Maas, H.S.; Kahn, A.J.; Stein, H.D.; and Sumner, D. "Sociocultural Factors in Psychiatric Clinic Services for Children." *Smith College Studies in Social Work*, 1955, v. 25(2), pp. 1-90.

Martin, J.C., and Carkhuff, R.R. "Changes in Personality and Interpersonal Functions of Counselors-in-Training." *Journal of Clinical Psychology*, 1968, v. 24, pp. 109-10.

Massarik, F. "Standards for Group Leadership." In L.N. Solomon and B. Berzon (Eds.), *New Perspectives on Encounter Groups.* San Francisco: Jossey-Bass, 1972, pp. 68-82.

Masserman, C.M. "Teaching vs. Learning." *American Journal of Psychiatry*, 1964, v. 121, pp. 221-27.

Masserman, J.H., and Carmichael, H.T. "Diagnosis and Prognosis in Psychiatry: With a Follow-up Study of the Results of Short-Term General Hospital Therapy of Psychiatric Cases." *Journal of Mental Science*, 1938, v. 84, pp. 893-946.

Matarazzo, R.G. "Research on the Teaching and Learning of Psychotherapeutic Skills." In A.E. Bergin and S.L. Garfield (Eds.), *Handbook of Psychotherapy and Behavior Change: An Empirical Analysis.* New York: John Wiley, 1971, pp. 895-924.

Matarazzo, R.G.; Wiens, A.N.; and Saslow, G. "Experimentation in the Teaching and Learning of Psychotherapy Skills." In L.A. Gottschalk and A.H. Auerbach (Eds.), *Methods of Research in Psychotherapy.* New York: Appleton-Century-Crofts, 1966, pp. 597-635.

Mates, M.E. "The Effects of Trainer Personality on Trainer Behavior and on Participant Personality Change in a Sensitivity Training Experience." Ph.D. dissertation, George Peabody College for Teachers, 1972. Abstracted in *Dissertation Abstracts International*, 1972, v. 33(B), p. 1767.

Matthews, S.R. "An Investigation of Selected Premises of Carkhuff's Theory of Training Psychological Helpers." Ph.D. dissertation, Michigan State University, 1972. Abstracted in *Dissertation Abstracts International*, 1973, v. 33(9-A), pp. 4843-44.

Meehl, P.E. *Psychodiagnosis: Selected Papers.* St. Paul, Minn.: University of Minnesota Press, 1973.

Meehl, P.E. "The Cognitive Activity of the Clinician." *American Psychologist*, 1960, v. 15, pp. 19-27.

Meehl, P.E. "Wanted—A Good Cookbook." *American Psychologist*, 1956, v. 11, pp. 263-72.

Melloh, R.A. "Accurate Empathy and Counselor Effectiveness." Ed.D. dissertation, University of Florida, 1964. Abstracted in *Dissertation Abstracts*, 1965, v. 12, p. 7110.

Meltzoff, J., and Kornreich, M. *Research in Psychotherapy.* New York: Atherton Press, 1970.

Menninger, K. (In collaboration with M. Mayman and P. Pruyser.) *The Vital Balance: The Life Process in Mental Health and Illness.* New York: Viking Press, 1963.

Merrow, J.G., II. *The Politics of Competence: A Review of Competency-Based Teacher Education.* (Report from the Basic Skills Program on Teaching.) Washington, D.C.: National Institute of Education, 1975.

Miles, M.B. "Rejoinder to Schutz, Smith, and Rowan." *Journal of Humanistic Psychology*, 1975, v. 15(2), p. 55-58.

Miller, G.A. "The Magical Number Seven, Plus or Minus Two: Some Limits on Our Capacity for Processing Information." *Psychological Review*, 1956, v. 63, pp. 81-97.

Miller, G.E. "The Orthopaedic Training Study." *Journal of the American Medical Association*, 1968, v. 206, pp. 601-6.

Miller, H., and Bieri, J. "An Informational Analysis of Clinical Judgment." *Journal of Abnormal and Social Psychology*, 1963, v. 67, pp. 317-25.

Millon, T. "Reflections on Rosenhan's 'On Being Sane in Insane Places.'" *Journal of Abnormal Psychology*, 1975, v. 84, pp. 456-61.

Mintz, E.E. *Marathon Groups: Reality and Symbol.* New York: Avon Books, 1971.

Mintz, J. "Survey of Student Therapists' Attitudes Toward Psychodiagnostic Reports." *Journal of Consulting and Clinical Psychology*, 1968, v. 32, p. 500.

Morgenstern, A.L. "A Criticism of Psychiatry's Board Examinations." *American Journal of Psychiatry*, 1970, v. 127, pp. 33-42.

Morris, K.T., and Cinnamon, K.M. (Eds.) *Controversial Issues in Human Relations Training Groups.* Springfield, Ill.: Charles C. Thomas, 1976.

Murphree, H.B. "Studies on the Reliability and Validity of Objective Examinations." *Journal of Medical Education*, 1961, v. 36, pp. 813-18.

Murphy, G., and Kovach, J.K. *Historical Introduction to Modern Psychology.* (3rd ed.) New York: Harcourt Brace Jovanovich, 1972.

Muslin, H.L., and Schlessinger, N. "Toward the Teaching and Learning of Empathy." *Bulletin of the Menninger Clinic*, 1971, v. 35, pp. 262-71.

Nagel, E. "Methodological Issues in Psychoanalytic Theory." In S. Hook (Ed.), *Psychoanalysis, Scientific Method, and Philosophy.* New York: University Press, 1959, pp. 38-56.

National Committee for Careers in Medical Technology. *Equivalency and Proficiency Testing Related to the Medical Laboratory Field.* Bethesda, Md.: National Committee for Careers in Medical Technology, 1970.

Nelson, S.H. "A New Look at National Insurance for Mental Health." *American Journal of Orthopsychiatry*, 1973, v. 43, pp. 622-28.

Nichols, R.C., and Beck, K.W. "Factors in Psychotherapy Change." *Journal of Consulting Psychology*, 1960, v. 24, pp. 388-99.

Niebuhr, R. *The Self and the Dramas of History.* New York: Charles Scribner, 1955.

Nolen W.A. *Healing: A Doctor in Search of a Miracle.* New York: Random House, 1974.

Oden, T.C. "A Populist's View of Psychotherapeutic Deprofessionalization." *Journal of Humanistic Psychology*, 1974, v. 14(2), pp. 3-18.

Ornstein, P.H.; Ornstein, A.; and Lindy, J.D. "On the Process of Becoming a Psychotherapist: An Outline of a Core-Curriculum for the Teaching and Learning of Psychoanalytic Psychotherapy." *Comprehensive Psychiatry*, 1976, v. 17, pp. 177-90.

Ostrander, S., and Schroeder, L. *Psychic Discoveries Behind the Iron Curtain.* (Introduction by I.T. Sanderson.) New York: Bantam Books, 1970.

Pagell, W.A.; Carkhuff, R.R.; and Berenson, B.G. "The Predicted Differential Effects of the Level of Counselor Functioning Upon the Level of Functioning of Outpatients." *Journal of Clinical Psychology*, 1967, v. 23, pp. 510-12.

Patterson, C.H. "The Selection of Counselors." Paper presented at the Conference on Research Problems in Counseling, Washington University, St. Louis, Mo., 1967. Reprinted in J.M. Whiteley (Ed.), *Research in Counseling.* Columbus, Ohio: Charles E. Merrill, 1968, pp. 69-101.

Peterson, D.R. "Attitudes Concerning the Doctor of Psychology Program." *Professional Psychology*, 1969, v. 1, pp. 44-47.

Peterson, D.R. "The Doctor of Psychology Program at the University of Illinois." *American Psychologist*, 1968, v. 23, pp. 511-16.

Peterson, D.R., and Baron, A., Jr. "Status of the University of Illinois Doctor of Psychology Program, 1974." *Professional Psychology*, 1975, v. 6, pp. 88-95.

Pierce, R.; Carkhuff, R.R.; and Berenson, B.G. "The Differential Effects of High and Low Functioning Counselors Upon Counselors-In-Training." *Journal of Clinical Psychology*, 1967, v. 23, pp. 212-15.

Pino, C.J. "Illinois Institute of Technology Interaction in Sensitivity Training Groups." Ph.D. dissertation, Illinois Institute of Technology, 1969. Abstracted in *Dissertation Abstracts International*, 1969, v. 30(6-B), p. 2915.

Pokorny, A.D., and Frazier, S.H., Jr. "An Evaluation of Oral Examinations." *Journal of Medical Education*, 1966, v. 41, pp. 28-40.

Poser, E.G. "The Effect of Therapists' Training on Group Therapeutic Outcome." *Journal of Consulting Psychology*, 1966, v. 30, pp. 283-89.

Pottharst, K.E. "To Renew Vitality and Provide a Challenge in Training—The California School of Professional Psychology." *Professional Psychology*, 1970, v. 1, 123-30.

Powers, E., and Whitmer, H. *An Experiment in the Prevention of Delinquency: The Cambridge-Somerville Youth Study.* New York: Columbia University Press, 1951.

Pressey, S.L.; Pressey, L.C.; and Barnes, E.J. "The Final Ordeal." *Journal of Higher Education*, 1932, v. 3, pp. 261-64.

Raines, G.N., and Rohrer, J.H. "The Operational Matrix of Psychiatric Practice: I. Consistency and Variability in Interview Impressions of Different Psychiatrists." *American Journal of Psychiatry*, 1955, v. 111, pp. 721-33.

Rappaport, J., and Chinsky, J.M. "Accurate Empathy: Confusion of a Construct." *Psychological Bulletin*, 1972, v. 77, pp. 400-404.

Raskin, N.J. *Studies of Psychotherapeutic Orientation: Ideology and Practice.* (Research Monograph No. 1.) Orlando, Fla.: American Academy of Psychotherapists, 1974.

Redlich, F.C., and Freedman, D.X. *The Theory and Practice of Psychiatry.* New York: Basic Books, 1966.

Rickels, K.; Howard, K.; Lipman, R.S.; Covi, L.; Park, L.C.; and Uhlenhuth, E.H. "Differential Reliability in Rating Psychopathology and Global Improvement." *Journal of Clinical Psychology*, 1970, v. 26, pp. 320-23.

Ricks, D.F. "Supershrink: Methods of a Therapist Judged Successful on the Basis of Adult Outcomes of Adolescent Patients." In D.F. Ricks, A. Thomas, and M. Roff (Eds.), *Life History Research in Psychopathology.* (Vol. 3.) Minneapolis, Minn.: University of Minnesota Press, 1974.

Rioch, M.J. "Changing Concepts in the Training of Therapists." *Journal of Consulting Psychology*, 1966, v. 30, pp. 290-92.

Rioch, M.J.; Elkes, C.; and Flint, A.A. *Pilot Project in Training Mental Health Counselors.* Washington, D.C.: U.S. Department of Health, Education, and Welfare, 1965.

Rogers, C.R. "Some New Challenges." *American Psychologist*, 1973, v. 28, pp. 379-87.

Rogers, C.R. *Carl Rogers on Encounter Groups.* New York: Harper and Row, 1970.

Rogers, C.R. "The Therapeutic Relationship: Recent Theory and Research." *Australian Journal of Psychology*, 1965, v. 17, pp. 95-108.

Rogers, C.R. "The Interpersonal Relationship: The Core of Guidance." *Harvard Educational Review*, 1962, v. 32, pp. 416-29.

Rogers, C.R. "The Necessary and Sufficient Conditions of Therapeutic Personality Change." *Journal of Consulting Psychology*, 1957, v. 21, pp. 95-103.

Rogers, C.R. "Training Individuals to Engage in the Therapeutic Process." In C.R. Strother (Ed.), *Psychology and Mental Health.* Washington, D.C.: American Psychological Association, 1956, pp. 79-92.

Rogers, C.R. *Client-centered Therapy.* Boston: Houghton Mifflin, 1951.

Rogers, C.R.; Gendlin, E.T.; Kiesler, D.J.; and Truax, C.B. (Eds.) *The Therapeutic Relationship and Its Impact: A Study of Psychotherapy with Schizophrenics.* Madison: Wisconsin University Press, 1967.

Rose, A.L. "Do Encounter Groups Hurt People? A Question of Misplaced Responsibility." Symposium on *The Encounter Movement in Psychiatry: Psychotherapy or Encounter*, Hahnemann Medical College and Hospital of Philadelphia, June 16, 1971.

Rosenbaum, M. "Some Comments on the Use of Untrained Therapists." *Journal of Consulting Psychology*, 1966, v. 30, pp. 292-94.

Rosenhan, D.L. "The Contextual Nature of Psychiatric Diagnosis." *Journal of Abnormal Psychology*, 1975, v. 84, pp. 462-74.

Rosenhan, D.L. "On Being Sane in Insane Places." *Science*, 1973, v. 179, pp. 250-58.

Rosenzweig, S. "A Transvaluation of Psychotherapy—A Reply to Hans Eysenck." *Journal of Abnormal and Social Psychology*, 1954, v. 49, pp. 298-304.

Ross, W.D.; Kligfeld, M.; and Whitman, R.W. "Psychiatrists, Patients, and Sensitivity Groups." *Archives of General Psychiatry*, 1971, v. 25, pp. 178-80.

Rotter, J.B. *Social Learning and Clinical Psychology.* New Jersey: Prentice-Hall, 1954.

Rowe, W., and Winborn, R.B. "What People Fear About Group Work: An Analysis of 36 Selected Critical Articles." *Educational Technology*, 1973, v. 13(1), pp. 53-57.

Sarbin, T.R.; Taft, R.; and Bailey, D.E. *Clinical Inference and Cognitive Theory.* New York: Holt, Rinehart and Winston, 1960.

Schmidt, H.O., and Fonda, C.P. "The Reliability of Psychiatric Diagnosis: A New Look." *Journal of Abnormal and Social Psychology*, 1956, v. 52, pp. 262-67.

Schmidt, L.D., and Strong, S.R. "'Expert' and 'Inexpert' Counselors." *Journal of Counseling Psychology*, 1970, v. 17, pp. 115-18.

Schofield, W. *Psychotherapy: The Purchase of Friendship*. Englewood Cliffs, N.J.: Prentice-Hall, 1964.

Schröder, M. Personal communication, November 8, 1971.

Schutz, W.C. *Here Comes Everybody*. New York: Harper and Row, 1971.

Schutz, W.C. *Joy: Expanding Human Awareness*. New York: Grove Press, 1967.

Searles, H.F. "The Schizophrenic's Vulnerability to the Therapist's Unconscious Processes." *Journal of Nervous and Mental Disease*, 1958, v. 127, pp. 247-62.

Seligman, M., and Desmond, R.E. "The Leaderless Group Phenomenon: A Historical Perspective." *International Journal of Group Psychotherapy*, 1975, v. 25, pp. 277-90.

Seligman, M., and Desmond, R.E. "Leaderless Groups: A Review." *Counseling Psychologist*, 1973, v. 4(2), pp. 70-87.

Senior, J.R. "Evaluation of Clinical Competence—The Crux of FLEX." *Federation Bulletin*, 1972, v. 59, pp. 303-19.

Shaffer, J.B., and Galinsky, M.D. *Models of Group Therapy and Sensitivity Training*. Englewood Cliffs, N.J.: Prentice-Hall, 1974.

Shakow, D. "What *Is* Clinical Psychology?" *American Psychologist*, 1976, v. 31, pp. 553-60.

Shakow, D. *Clinical Psychology as Science and Profession: A 40-Year Odyssey*. Chicago: Aldine, 1969.

Shakow, D. "Psychology and Psychiatry: A Dialogue." *American Journal of Orthopsychiatry*, 1949, v. 19, pp. 191-208, 381-96.

Shapiro, A.K. "Placebo Effects in Medicine, Psychotherapy, and Psychoanalysis." In A.E. Bergin and S.L. Garfield (Eds.), *Handbook of Psychotherapy and Behavior Change: An Empirical Analysis*. New York: John Wiley, 1971, pp. 439-73.

Shapiro, A.K. "The Placebo Effect in the History of Medical Treatment: Implications for Psychiatry." *American Journal of Psychiatry*, 1959, v. 116, pp. 298-304.

Shapiro, D.A. "Empathy, Warmth and Genuineness in Psychotherapy." *British Journal of Social and Clinical Psychology*, 1969, v. 8, pp. 350-61.

Shepard, M. *the Love Treatment: Sexual Intimacy Between Patients and Psychotherapists*. New York: Peter H. Wyden, 1971.

Sherif, M. "Group Influences Upon the Formation of Norms and Attitudes." In T.M. Newcomb and E.L. Hartley (Eds.), *Reading in Social Psychology*. New York: Holt, Rinehart and Winston, 1947, pp. 77-90.

Shostrom, E.L. "Group Therapy: Let the Buyer Beware." *Psychology Today*, May 1969, pp. 37-40.

Sines, L.K.; Silver, R.J.; and Lucero, R.J. "The Effect of Therapeutic Intervention by Untrained 'Therapists.'" *Journal of Clinical Psychology*, 1961, v. 17, pp. 394-96.

Slavson, S.R. *Introduction to Group Therapy*. New York: International Universities Press, 1943.

Sloane, R.B.; Staples, F.R.; Cristol, A.H.; Yorkston, N.J.; and Whipple, K. *Psychotherapy versus Behavior Therapy*. Cambridge, Mass.: Harvard University Press, 1975.

Smith, P.B. "Sources of Influence in the Sensitivity Training Laboratory." *Small Group Behavior*, 1976, v. 7, pp. 331-48.

Snyder, W.U. "Professional Training for Clinical Psychologists: A Synthesis of a Symposium." *Journal of Clinical Psychology*, 1962, v. 18, pp. 243-48.

Sobey, F. *The Nonprofessional Revolution in Mental Health*. New York: Columbia University Press, 1970.

Solmon, L.C. "Schooling and Subsequent Success." In L.C. Solmon and P.J. Taubman (Eds.), *Does College Matter?—Some Evidence on the Impacts of Higher Education*. New York: Academic Press, 1973, pp. 13-34.

Solmon, L.C., and Taubman, P.J. (Eds.) *Does College Matter?—Some Evidence on the Impacts of Higher Education.* New York: Academic Press, 1973.

Spitzer, R.L. "Problem Oriented Medical Records: Some Reservations." *International Journal of Psychiatry,* 1973, v. 11, pp. 376-81.

Spitzer, R.L., and Endicott, J. "DIAGNO II: Further Developments in a Computer Program for Psychiatric Diagnosis." *American Journal of Psychiatry,* 1969, v. 125 (Supp.), pp. 12-21.

Stayer, S.J. "The Clinical Psychologist of the Seventies: A Unique Identity or Role Fragmentation." *Clinical Psychologist,* 1970, v. 22 (issue unknown), pp. 4 and 10.

Stieper, D.R., and Wiener, D.N. *Dimensions of Psychotherapy: An Experimental and Clinical Approach.* Chicago: Aldine Publishing Co., 1965.

Stillman, R.; Roth, W.T.; Colby, K.M.; and Roesenbaum, C.P. "An On-line Computer System for Initial Psychiatric Inventory." *American Journal of Psychiatry,* 1969, v. 125 (Jan. Supp.), pp. 8-11.

Stock, D. "A Survey of Research on T Groups." In L.P. Bradford, J.R. Gibb, and K.D. Benne (Eds.), *T-Group Theory and Laboratory Method: Innovation in Re-education.* New York: John Wiley, 1964, pp. 395-441.

Stollak, G.E. "The Experimental Effects of Training College Students as Play Therapists." *Psychotherapy: Theory, Research and Practice,* 1968, v. 5, pp. 77-80. Reprinted in B.G. Guerney, Jr. (Ed.), *Psychotherapeutic Agents: New Roles for Nonprofessionals, Parents, and Teachers.* New York: Holt, Rinehart and Winston, 1969, pp. 510-18.

Stone, A.A. "The Quest of the Counterculture." *International Journal of Psychiatry,* 1970, v. 9, pp. 219-26.

Stone, W.N., and Tieger, M.E. "Screening for T-Groups: The Myth of Healthy Candidates." *American Journal of Psychiatry,* 1971, v. 127, pp. 1485-90.

Storrow, H.A. "The Measurement of Outcome in Psychotherapy: A Study in Method." *Archives of General Psychiatry,* 1960, v. 2, pp. 142-46.

Stover, L., and Guerney, B.G., Jr. "The Efficacy of Training Procedures for Mothers in Filial Therapy." *Psychotherapy: Theory, Research and Practice,* 1967, v. 4, pp. 110-15.

Stricker, G. "On Professional Schools and Professional Degrees." *American Psychologist,* 1975, v. 30, pp. 1062-66.

Strupp, H.H. "On the Technology of Psychotherapy." *Archives of General Psychiatry,* 1972, v. 26, pp. 270-78.

Strupp, H.H. "The Outcome Problem in Psychotherapy: A Rejoinder." *Psychotherapy: Theory, Research, and Practice,* 1964, v. 1, p. 101.

Strupp, H.H. "Psychotherapeutic Technique, Professional Affiliation, and Experience Level." *Journal of Consulting Psychology,* 1955, v. 19, pp. 97-102.

Strupp, H.H.; Hadley, S.W.; Gomes, B.; and Armstrong, S.H. "Negative Effects in Psychotherapy: A Review of Clinical and Theoretical Issues Together with Recommendations for a Program of Research." Unpublished document, Vanderbilt University, Nashville, Tenn., May 1976.

Stuart, R.B. *Trick or Treatment: How and When Psychotherapy Fails.* Champaign, Ill.: Research Press, 1970.

Taft, R. "The Ability to Judge People." *Psychological Bulletin,* 1955, v. 52, pp. 1-23.

Tannenbaum, R.; Weschler, I.R.; and Massarik, F. "The Role of the Trainer." In R.T. Golembiewski and A. Blumberg (Eds.), *Sensitivity Training and the Laboratory Approach: Readings About Concepts and Applications.* Itasca, Ill.: F.E. Peacock, 1970, pp. 139-40.

Tarter, R.E.; Templer, D.I.; and Hardy, C. "Reliability of the Psychiatric Diagnosis." *Diseases of the Nervous System,* 1975, v. 36, pp. 30-31.

Taylor, C.W.; Smith, W.R.; and Ghiselin, B. "The Creative and Other Contributions of One Sample of Research Scientists." In C.W. Taylor and F. Barron (Eds.), *Scientific Creativity: Its Recognition and Development.* New York: John Wiley, 1963, pp. 53-76.

Taylor, R.L., and Torrey, E.F. "The Pseudo-Regulation of American Psychiatry." *American Journal of Psychiatry*, 1972, v. 129, pp. 658-63.

Temerlin, M.K. "Suggestion Effects in Psychiatric Diagnosis." *Journal of Nursing and Mental Disease*, 1968, v. 147, pp. 349-53.

Tempone, V.J. "The American Board of Professional Psychology's Examination Procedure: A Time for Change." *Professional Psychology*, 1971, v. 2, pp. 177-82.

Thorndike, R.L., and Hagen, E. *Ten Thousand Careers.* New York: John Wiley, 1959.

Thorne, F.C. *Clinical Judgment: A Study of Clinical Error.* Brandon, Vt.: Clinical Psychology Publishing Co., 1961.

Tripodi, T., and Bieri, J. "Information Transmission in Clinical Judgments as a Function of Stimulus Dimensionality and Cognitive Complexity." *Journal of Personality*, 1964, v. 32, pp. 119-37.

Truax, C.B. "Research Findings: Translations and Premature Translations into Practice." *International Journal of Psychiatry*, 1967, v. 3, pp. 158-60.

Truax, C.B. "Effective Ingredients in Psychotherapy: An Approach to Unraveling the Patient-Therapist Interaction." *Journal of Counseling Psychology*, 1963, v. 10, pp. 256-63.

Truax, C.B. "The Process of Group Psychotherapy: Relationships Between Hypothesized Therapeutic Conditions and Interpersonal Exploration." *Psychological Monographs*, 1961, v. 75 (7, Whole No. 511).

Truax, C.B., and Carkhuff, R.R. *Toward Effective Counseling and Psychotherapy: Training and Practice.* Chicago, Ill.: Aldine Publishing Co., 1967.

Truax, C.B., and Carkhuff, R.R. "Personality Change in Hospitalized Mental Patients During Group Psychotherapy as a Function of the Use of Alternate Sessions and Vicarious Therapy Pretraining." *Journal of Clinical Psychology*, 1965, v. 21, pp. 225-28.

Truax, C.B., and Mitchell, K.M. "Research on Certain Therapist Interpersonal Skills in Relation to Process and Outcome." In A.E. Bergin and S.L. Garfield (Eds.), *Handbook of Psychotherapy and Behavior Change: An Empirical Analysis.* New York: John Wiley, 1971, pp. 299-344.

Truax, C.B. and Silber, L.D. "Personality and Psychotherapeutic Skills." Unpublished manuscript, University of Arkansas, Fayetteville, 1966. Cited in C.B. Truax and R.R. Carkhuff, *Toward Effective Counseling and Psychotherapy: Training and Practice.* Chicago: Aldine Publishing Co., 1967, p. 109.

Truax, C.B.; Wargo, D.G.; Frank, J.D.; Imber, S.D.; Battle, C.C.; Hoehn-Saric, R.; Nash, E.H.; and Stone, A.R. "Therapist Empathy, Genuineness, and Warmth and Patient Therapeutic Outcome." *Journal of Consulting Psychology*, 1966, v. 30, pp. 395-401.

U.S. Department of Health, Education, and Welfare. *Work in America.* Washington, D.C.: U.S. Government Printing Office, 1972.

U.S. Department of Labor. *Hiring Standards and Job Performance.* (Manpower Research Monograph No. 18, prepared by D. Diamond and F. Bedrosian.) Washington, D.C.: U.S. Government Printing Office, 1970.

U.S. National Institute of Mental Health. *Explorations in Mental Health Training.* (DHEW Publication No. ADM 74-109, Stock No. 1724-00400.) Washington, D.C.: U.S. Government Printing Office, 1974.

Underwood, W.J. "Evaluation of Laboratory Method Training." *Journal of the American Society of Training Directors*, 1965, v. 19, pp. 34-40. Cited in J.P. Campbell and M.D. Dunnette, "Effectiveness of T-Group Experiences in Managerial Training and Development." *Psychological Bulletin*, 1968, v. 70, pp. 73-104.

Vicino, F.L; Krusell, J.; Bass, B.M., Deci, E.L.; and Landy, D.A. "The Impact of PROCESS: Self-Administered Exercises for Personal and Interpersonal Development." *Journal of Applied Behavioral Science*, 1973, v. 9, pp. 737-56.

Vingoe, F.J., and Antonoff, S.R. "Personality characteristics of Good Judges of Others." *Journal of Counseling Psychology*, 1968, v. 15, pp. 91-93.

Vosen, L. "The Relationship Between Self-disclosure and Self-esteem." Ph.D. dissertation, University of California, Los Angeles, 1966. Abstracted in *Dissertation Abstracts*, 1967, v. 27(B), p. 2882.

Wahler, R.G.; Winkel, G.H.; Peterson, R.F.; and Morrison, D.C. "Mothers as Behavior Therapists for Their Own Children." *Behaviour Research and Therapy*, 1965, v. 3, pp. 113-24.

Walker, K. *The Extra-sensory Mind.* New York: Emerson Books, 1961.

Wallinga, J.V. "Variability of Psychiatric Diagnoses." *United States Armed Forces Medical Journal*, 1956, v. 7, pp. 1305-12.

Ward, C.H.; Beck, A.T.; Mendelson, M.; Mock, J.E.; and Erbaugh, J.K. "The Psychiatric Nomenclature: Reasons for Diagnostic Disagreement." *A.M.A. Archives of General Psychiatry*, 1962, v. 7, pp. 198-205.

Webb, W.B.; Goldstein, S.G.; Burdin, E.S. and Bard, M. "Viewpoints on the New California School of Professional Psychology." *Professional Psychology*, 1970, v. 1, pp. 253-64.

Weiner, B. "'On Being Sane in Insane Places': A Process (Attributional) Analysis and Critique." *Journal of Abnormal Psychology*, 1975, v. 84, pp. 433-41.

Weinstein, H.M. and Russell, M.L. "Competency-Based Psychiatric Education." *American Journal of Psychiatry*, 1976, v. 133, pp. 935-39.

Weitz, R.D. "A College of Professional Psychology for New Jersey: The Need, Plan, Development, and Progress." *Professional Psychology*, 1973, v. 4, pp. 462-67.

Welsch, E.E.; Bernard, V.W.; Austin, L.N.; and Schlesinger, H.J. "Qualifications for Psychotherapists: Symposium, 1954." *American Journal of Orthopsychiatry*, 1956, v. 26, pp. 35-65.

White, D.J. "Participant Governmental Action Immunity from the Anit-trust Laws: Fact or Fiction?" *Texas Law Review*, 1972, v. 50, pp. 474-99.

White, L.A. "The Effects of Leader Personality on Group Outcomes in Interracial Encounter Groups." Ed.D. dissertation, East Texas State University, 1972. Abstracted in *Dissertation Abstracts International*, 1973, v. 33A, pp. 4107-8.

Whitehorn, J.C., and Betz, B.J. "Further Studies of the Doctor as a Crucial Variable in the Outcome of Treatment with Schizophrenic Patients." *American Journal of Psychiatry*, 1960, v. 117, pp. 215-23.

Winder, C.L.; Ahmad, F.Z.; Bandura, A.; and Rau, L.C. "Dependency of Patients, Psychotherapists' Responses, and Aspects of Psychotherapy." *Journal of Consulting Psychology*, 1962, v. 26, pp. 129-34.

Wing, J.K. "A Review of *Sanity, Madness, and the Family.*" In T.J. Scheff (Ed.), *Mental Illness and Social Processes.* New York: Harper and Row, 1967, pp. 149-53.

Wolberg, L.R. *The Technique of Psychotherapy.* (2nd ed.) New York: Grune and Stratton, 1967. (2 vols.)

Woody, R.H., and Woody, J.D. (Eds.) *Clinical Assessment in Counseling and Psychotherapy.* New York: Appleton-Century-Crofts, 1972.

Yalom, I.D. *The Theory and Practice of Group Psychotherapy.* (2nd ed.) New York: Basic Books, 1975.

Yalom, I.D., and Lieberman, M.A. "A Study of Encounter Group Casualties." *Archives of General Psychiatry*, 1971, v. 25, pp. 16-30.

Zigler, E., and Phillips. L. "Psychiatric Diagnosis: A Critique." *Journal of Abnormal and Social Psychology*, 1961, v. 63, pp. 607-18.

Zolik, E.S., and Stotsky, B. "Relationships Between Problem Labelling and Treatment Referrals by Laymen." *Community Mental Health Journal*, 1966, v. 2, pp. 114-20.

Chapter 5

The Nature of Psychotherapy:
A Recapitulation and Synthesis

The content of any set of regulatory proposals for the mental health field will be strongly shaped by the way in which the psychotherapeutic process is conceptualized. The clarity with which psychotherapy can be defined, the degree to which it is dangerous, the extent to which it is useful and valuable, the types of qualifications one must have to practice competently—all have significant implications for the types of regulations that will best serve both the profession and the public. The preceding chapters have presented both empirical evidence and theoretical argument bearing on these issues. This chapter recapitulates the major points previously made, synthesizing them through a discussion of whether psychotherapy should be considered a medical process.

The initial point to be made is that psychotherapy is almost impossible to define, especially for legal purposes. Most definitions involve the terms "treatment,"[1] "health"[2] and "illness,"[2] and "mental."[3] The vagueness that inevitably surrounds each of these terms gives rise to the very real danger that the boundaries of psychotherapy will encroach upon related disciplines and result in misapplied regulations.

Apart from the definitional quagmire, there is the problem of whether psycho-therapy is to be conceived of as a medical, educational, or other type of process. This has important implications for the types of treatment considered legitimate, the types of problems and illnesses considered the target of therapy, the types of professional skills needed to deal with those problems, and the particular qualifications such a professional should have.

The most commonly held concept of psychotherapy explains it as a medical process, based on the medical model. This model, articulated in various ways by different people,[4] has several components. In the first place it is generally viewed as offering an explanation of the etiology of mental illness based primarily on physiological, neurological, biological, and hereditary causes. The medical model suggests that mental illness involves discrete disease entities, each with a separate cause, prognosis, and potential treatment. Treatment is a medical procedure, carried out by physicians or under their supervision. Patients are expected to conform to the diseased role. This role exempts them from some or all social responsibilities and absolves patients from personal responsibility for their illness, although requiring them to cooperate with their attending physician (Parsons, 1958: 182).

Until recently the medical model provided the most widely accepted explanation for mental illness. Emil Kraepelin's system for classifying mental illnesses,[5] Freud's medical orientation and background,[6] and the efforts of U.S. psychoanalysts to ally psychoanalysis with medicine[7] have been largely responsible for this state of affairs.

The idea that the medical model is the best vehicle for conceptualizing the psychotherapeutic process has been increasingly open to attack, however, whether viewed as a theoretical model for diagnosing mental illness, a method of conducting psychotherapy, or a sociological framework within which the medical profession is seen to control the social and legal aspects of mental health institutions and practices (Macklin, 1973: 68). The argument has been put forth that the medical model "undermines the principle of personal responsibility, upon which a democratic political system is necessarily based" (Szasz, 1961: 297). Uncritical acceptance of this argument has resulted in the neglect of group and community forces as being partially responsible for the creation of mental illness. It has also allowed psychiatry to be abused as a method of social action disguised as medical treatment (Albee and Loeffler, 1971; Leifer, 1969: 25, and 1970-71).

The argument for medical control of the psychotherapeutic process is often based on the belief that most illnesses will eventually be shown to have a biological or organic basis (see, e.g., Rimland, 1969: 704-05). Even where this eventually proves to be untrue, proponents of the medical model argue that medical practitioners should have ultimate responsibility for all forms of psychotherapy, since the possibility always exists that a given case of mental illness is somatically caused, and therefore requires medical treatment.

This thesis has been vehemently criticized. Opponents argue that determining causation is rarely a simple matter, and it is generally acknowledged that most illnesses have multiple etiologies.[8] While organic factors, such as traumatic brain damage or paresis, are known to cause some forms of mental illness, and empirical research indicates that heredity plays a definite role in schizophrenia (see Murray and Hirsch, 1969), little conclusive evidence exists as to the causes of most other mental diseases. In opposition to this somatic point of view, however, theorists such as Sarbin (1969) propose that failure to establish acceptable social identities is the cause of mental illness, and this failure is a consequence of being denied status, being prevented from holding valued jobs and the performance of useful roles, and lack of involvement in those decisions that most vitally affect the course of one's life.

Anthropologists and social psychologists have provided evidence that one's culture plays a definite role in both the forms and extent of mental illness that exists in a society.[9] William Ryan's (1969) well-known study of mental health problems in Boston documents the importance of money and opportunity in the onset of mental illness, while Scheff (1966) and others (see Becker, 1963; Erikson, 1957; Schur, 1969) provide the thesis that stabilized deviant behavior is primarily a consequence of the reactions of others to that behavior when it initially occurs.[10] Given the disparate opinions that exist and the fact that conclusive evidence is unavailable, the proper stance seems to be to acknowledge that most mental illnesses have multiple causes.[11]

Interestingly, a commonly held view among physicians is that at least half of all patients who see a general practitioner are suffering from symptoms of emotional rather than physical origin.[12] In addition, health programs that utilize psychological examinations and brief psychotherapy as part of the overall examination and treatment given to patients entering the health care system have brought about substantial savings and far fewer subsequent visits to medical doctors (Cummings and Follette, 1976: 167). These two facts suggest that supervision of medical doctors by psychologists is as sensible as the traditional relationship requiring non-M.D.s to be supervised by physicians.

Another argument made for medical control of psychotherapy is that only doctors have the requisite diagnostic and treatment skills to minister safely to patients on an independent basis. Most of what constitutes psychotherapeutic treatment, however, would appear to require very little training. As detailed in Chapter 4, paraprofessionals have obtained results equal or superior to highly credentialed practitioners. Even with regard to the prescription and administration of drugs, Mariner (1967: 279) argues that all the relevant information could be effectively learned in two weeks. If one looks for the effective agent in the therapeutic process, the evidence for nonspecific factors—such as empathy—is quite convincing, yet these factors are not specifically cultivated in the typical medical school curriculum. As for diagnostic ability, the evidence that psychiatrists are quite poor in identifying specific forms of mental illness and have only moderate success in agreeing on gross distinctions (such as neurotic versus psychotic) (see pages 114–18), together with the evidence that diagnosis usually has little impact on treatment plans (see pages 119–20), makes it more difficult to defend the need for medical supervision of all psychotherapy.

Those opposed to the medical model believe that psychotherapeutic skills can be taught relatively quickly to people with the appropriate interpersonal skills. According to them, even the ability to identify those relatively rare instances in which emotional problems are organically based or the ability to prescribe drugs does not require considerable training. As a result of all these criticisms, Torrey (1974: 4) has concluded:

The medical model is equivalent to the model of the sun revolving around the earth. More and more anomalies are being perceived and we are furiously bending the medical model to try and make it accommodate them. But the data are square and the holes are round.[13]

Siegler and Osmond (1974) have identified seven alternative models, which some proponents argue are better ways of conceptualizing the therapeutic process.[14] These include (1) the moral model (in which deviant behavior is classified as wrong, evil, bad); (2) the impaired (in which the individual is thought to be incurable and is considered handicapped); (3) the psychoanalytic (in which mental illness is seen as resulting from childhood conflicts and traumas); (4) the social (in which mental illness is a symptom of a "sick" society and arises because of various environmental and social deprivations such as racism and poverty); (5) the psychedelic (in which madness is considered a potentially healthy and mind-expanding experience); (6) the conspiratorial (in which mental illness is considered to result from society's labeling people mentally ill); and (7) the family interaction model (in which the family is considered the sick unit and psychotherapy must involve the whole family). Each of these models deals with the twelve dimensions outlined by Siegler and Osmond (1974: 16–18) in different fashion.

The most frequently mentioned alternative, however, is psychotherapy as an educational process, in which therapists are not seen as curing neuroses or eliminating symptoms so much as teaching personal and interpersonal skills to be applied to solve emotional problems and to promote self-actualization (Guerney, Stollak, and Guerney, 1971: 277).[15] Proponents of this approach argue that it has numerous potential benefits, including the fact that practitioners will have to become more explicit about what they do, while responsibility for growth and change will rest squarely in the hands of the patient, who is more appropriately referred to as a client or student.[16]

Although opinions differ as to what exactly constitutes the educational model, most proponents agree that it leads to a conception of mental illness as a "problem-in-living," the etiology of which is related to improper learning. Rather than treating mental illness through drugs and various techniques such as electro-convulsive therapy, the emphasis changes to teaching interpersonal skills and increasing awareness.

Boundary problems are then created, however, and it becomes difficult to determine where psychotherapy ends and traditional educational processes begin. The classical distinctions drawn between psychotherapy and encounter groups no longer apply.[17] Historically, differences have been asserted in goals (education and self-actualization versus healing and restoration), the participant's reason for joining (to seek growth versus amelioration of illness), the depth and type of changes instigated (surface behavior versus underlying dynamics), the type of leadership given (participation and involvement versus detached neutrality), and the material examined (present behavior and feelings versus past events and the unconscious).

As should be apparent, more people are conceiving of psychotherapy as precisely the type of process that encounter groups represent. The empirical evidence from previous chapters suggests that the types of learnings and help received -from encounter groups are not substantially different from those received in therapy. The types of leadership skills required also appear to be similar, with interpersonal skills and personal qualities being largely responsible for whatever growth and healing that occurs. Thus, encounter groups become one form of psychotherapy, rather than something different from it.

The problems created by defining psychotherapy as a medical or educational process, and the profound disagreements that exist in the field today about the nature of that process, are unlikely to disappear in the near future. This has important implications for regulatory proposals. First, attempts to limit independent practice to a particular group, such as psychologists or psychiatrists, are premature. Not enough is known about minimal standards and criteria, and a consensus is lacking as to appropriate training programs. Second, the idea that extensive training is required to provide practitioners with the relevant diagnostic and treatment skills is seriously open to question. The evidence of paraprofessional effectiveness and the lack of evidence that nonprofessionals are dangerous (despite theoretical arguments to the contrary) may mean that only minimal training and experience are required, provided certain personality types are chosen. This raises the third major issue—that of selection. The technique of selection is still primitive, and despite the existence of a variety of methods, no consensus exists and little empirical evidence can be found to support any one method as valid and reliable.

This lack of clarity and consensus has important implications. Those who argue the validity of one model over another do so with little empirical support. Only rudimentary knowledge exists about the causes of mental illness, how it is to be defined and identified, what treatment processes are most effective in curing it, what skills are necessary so that treatment is effective, and what selection processes will identify the competent therapist. What is needed is a regulatory framework that will allow these questions, issues, and problems to be explored and effectively resolved, while at the same time protecting the public from significant and demonstrable dangers.

NOTES

1. Psychotherapy has traditionally been thought of as a procedure or treatment that restores the mentally ill person to health. Just as the surgeon treats a patient by performing an operation or the general practitioner prescribes appropriate medication for a burn, so, too, the psychotherapist is said to provide treatment. Attempts to specify precisely what this treatment consists of have proved elusive, however. Ordinary medical treatment involves doing something to a person. In this sense very little of what constitutes normal psychotherapy can properly be considered treatment. Only the use of medication, drugs, chemotherapy, electro-convulsive therapy, or psychosurgery approaches traditional forms of treatment.

The application of therapeutic techniques such as psychoanalysis, rational-emotive therapy, or Gestalt therapy is often spoken of as treatment. But the meaning of the word treatment includes the notion that it is the cause of a patient's being cured. Evidence that therapeutic techniques are the causative factor in a patient recovery are less than convincing. Based on the empirical literature, personal qualities such as empathy appear to make the critical difference. Yet these qualities are not something that one administers in the traditional sense. One *is* empathic, one does not administer empathy.

One alternative is to expand the notion of what is legitimately considered treatment. In the above instance of personal qualities, treatment might very well be considered the creation of a certain type of relationship in which one behaved in a specific fashion without administering anything to the patient. While this represents a departure from the traditional medical model, it also represents a return to the earliest meaning of the word, which the *Oxford English Dictionary* says is "conduct, behavior; action or behavior towards a person." Another possibility is to decide that psychotherapy does not involve treatment at all. This is the view of Thomas Szasz (1965: 30), who writes that "the psychotherapist does not 'treat' mental illness, but relates to and communicates with a fellow human being." In any event, it should be apparent that the term treatment is difficult to define, and that this difficulty poses obvious problems for defining psychotherapy.

2. The primary definition given by the *Oxford English Dictionary* for the word health is "soundness of body; that condition in which its functions are duly and efficiently discharged," and by extension, "The general condition of the body with respect to the efficient of inefficient discharge of functions: usually qualified as *good*, *bad*, *weak*, *delicate*, etc. Illness is defined as "bad or unhealthy conditions of the body (or formerly, of some part of it); the condition of being ill; disease, ailment, sickness, malady." Interestingly enough the *Oxford English Dictionary* also notes that although the word ill is not etymologically related to evil, "the two words have from the 12th c. been synonymous, and *ill* has been often viewed as a mere variant or reduced form of *evil*."

Romano (1950): 411) has pointed out that health and disease are not static entities, but phases of life, and that the maintenance of health depends on the capacity of the organism to maintain a careful balance. Based on this definition, Engel (1960: 459) defines disease as corresponding to "failures or disturbances in the growth, development, functions, and adjustments of the organism as a whole or of any of its systems." The vagueness of the above definitions should be readily apparent.

3. The problem of concisely defining psychotherapy is compounded by attempting to specify what constitutes the mental illness psychotherapy is purported to treat. This has proved even more difficult than defining the broader terms "health" and "illness." Critics are increasingly stating that mental illness is a myth (see Leifer, 1969; Pleune, 1965; Sarbin, 1967, 1969; Szasz, 1961; Torrey, 1974). Sarbin (1969) and Szasz (1961), for instance, point out that the use of the word "illness" in its original application to people with deviant behavior was metaphorical. To save people from being labeled witches, Sarbin (1969: 15) they were looked at *as if* they were ill. With the passage of time, and the development of a psychiatric nosology that equated behavioral with somatic symptoms, the "as if" component became lost, and people were simply considered mentally ill.

Writers have also pointed out that the term "mental" in the phrase "mental illness" simply does not refer to anything. Its literal meaning is "of the mind," but the mind does not exist except as an abstract symbol. Sarbin (1969: 17-19) has traced use of the terms "mind" and "mental" to three developments: (1) the existence of terms such as "courage" and "bravery," which can be reduced to a set of concrete behaviors, but which have mistakenly been thought to exist somewhere within the body as a special state; (2) the transformation in religion from a concern with outward matters of ritual and ceremony to inward problems of faith; and (3) the development of science, which could no longer feel comfortable with the term "soul," but because of the mind-body dichotomy begun by Descartes, decided to conceptualize a "mind" that would be the seat of knowing and thinking. Sarbin concludes that since the mind is a fictional entity, mental illness does not exist.

Szasz (1961: 41-42) has summed up this argument succinctly:

> The adjectives "mental," "emotional," and "neurotic" are simply devices to codify— and at the same time obscure—the differences between two classes of disabilities or "problems" in meeting life. One category consists of bodily diseases—say, leprosy, tuberculosis, or cancer—which, by rendering imperfect the functioning of the human body as a machine, produce difficulties in social adaptation. In contrast to the first, the second category is characterized by difficulties in social adaptation not attributable to malfunctioning machinery but "caused" rather by the purposes the machine was made to serve. . . .

Cogent and articulate responses have appeared to counter the notion that mental illness is a myth. Macklin (1973: 56) states that the proper strategy is to demonstrate that the concept of illness has been enlarged, and that such an enlargement is justified and legitimate. Margolis (1966: 73) agrees:

> In fact, this enlargement of the concept of illness does not obscure the differences between physical and mental illness—and the differences themselves are quite gradual, as psychosomatic disorder and hysterical conversion attest. On the contrary, these differences are preserved and respected in the very idea of an *enlargement* of the concept of illness.

Ausubel (1961: 72) has argued that "the plausibility of subsuming abnormal behavioral reactions to stress under the general rubric of disease is further enhanced by the fact that these reactions include the same three principal categories of symptoms found in physical illness." These three principal categories include manifestations of impaired functioning (depression and catastrophic impairment of self-esteem as comparable to heart failure—in both cases the symptoms indicate underlying pathology but are neither adaptive nor adjustive); adaptive compensation (such as compulsively striving toward unrealistically high-achievement goals, which is not unlike the elevated white blood cell count in acute infections); and defensive overreaction (such as delusions and phobias, which are akin to instances when the human physical system overreacts to an external invasion). For this reason Ausubel states that it makes good sense to consider such psychological signs as symptoms of illness, and that the concept of illness need not be restricted to physical ills. He concludes that Szasz is accurate in stating that mental illness is a reflection of "problems in living," but argues that there is no contradiction involved in considering such problems as illnesses, as well.

Karl Menninger (1963) has been a strong believer in the existence of mental illness and the meaningfulness of the concept. He supports the arguments of Ausubel and Margolis. He believes in a unitary concept of mental illness:

> We disagree with Szasz on technical and epistemological grounds. We insist that there are conditions best described as mental illness. But instead of putting so much emphasis on different kinds and clinical pictures of illness, we propose to think of all

forms of mental illness as being essentially the same in quality, and differing quantitatively. [Menninger, 1963: 32.]

Many critics of the concept of mental illness comment that the definition of whether an act is a sign of mental illness depends on one's values and preferences, whereas sickness in medicine is an objective fact. Engel (1960: 462-70) has effectively refuted this argument, demonstrating that the determination of physical illness is also a matter of personal values. Because of this subjective element, many fear that all behavior that is deviant from societal norms will soon be construed as a sign of mental illness. Macklin (1973: 62) has pointed out that, while society may choose this option, it does not follow logically from admitting the existence of mental illness.

One of the best definitions of what constitutes mental health has been proposed by Marie Jahoda (1958: 23). She recommends using six major concepts, culled from an extensive review of the literature, as aspects of mental health:

1. There are several proposals suggesting that indicators of positive mental health should be sought in the *attitudes of an individual toward his own self*. Various distinctions in the manner of perceiving oneself are regarded as demonstrating higher or lower degrees of health.
2. Another group of criteria designates the individual's style and degree of *growth, development, or self-actualization* as expressions of mental health. This group of criteria, in contrast to the first, is concerned not with self-perception but with what a person does with his self over a period of time.
3. Various proposals place the emphasis on a central synthesizing psychological function, incorporating some of the suggested criteria defined in (1) and (2) above. This function will here be called *integration*. The following three groups of criteria concentrate more exclusively than the preceding ones on the individual's relation to reality.
4. *Autonomy* singles out the individual's degree of independence from social influences as most revealing of the state of his mental health.
5. A number of proposals suggest that mental health is manifested in the adequacy of an individual's *perception of reality*.
6. Finally, there are suggestions that *environmental mastery* be regarded as a criterion for mental health.

According to Jahoda, people exhibit varying degrees of mental health at different times and in different situations. Some are self-actualized in terms of their job, but might be considered mentally ill in their relationship with their family. Mental health and disease become poles on a continuum that has no cut-off point. Instead of defining mental health as the absence of disease, Jahoda has reversed the process. She has, in addition, treated mental health as a multifaceted phenomenon.

For further discussions of the problems involved in ascertaining whether mental illness is a myth, and if not, how to define it, see the following: *Columbia Law Review* (1958); Dollard and Miller (1950); Fabrega (1975); Funkenstein (1962); Grinker, Grinker, and Timberlake (1962); Gursslin, Raymond, and Roach (1964); Leighton, Clausen, and Wilson (1957); Maslow and Mittelmann (1941); Mechanic (1967); Menninger (1963); Moore (1975); Parsons (1958); Patrick, Bush, and Chen (1973); Redlich (1952, 1956, 1957); Scheff (1967, 1974); Seiler (1973); Shagass (1975); Stafford-Clark (1964); Stone (1973); and Wing (1967).

4. Siegler and Osmond (1974: 16-18) have isolated twelve dimensions as comprising the different parts of any model that attempts to provide an explanation for mental

illness, including what and who defines it, its etiology, explanations of mentally ill behavior, methods of treatment, and what influences prognosis.

According to their model, the physician determines what disease a patient has, and this diagnosis determines treatment and prognosis. The etiology of a disease is considered important, although the cause of disease is not always known. A patient's behavior indicates the nature of the patient's illness and may be of significant help in formulating a diagnosis. Treatment consists of medical and surgical treatments, as well as nursing care. The goal of the medical model is to provide treatment to patients for illness, thereby restoring them to health, if possible, or otherwise preventing an illness from becoming worse. In addition, the medical model aims at reducing blame through conferring the "sick" role on patients.

A number of writers have offered different definitions of the medical model. Sahakian (cited in Macklin 1973: 50), for instance, has stated:

> In the medical or disease model, psychopathological states are likened to ailments found in physical maladies with clusters of symptoms termed syndromes, each syndrome associated with its technical nomenclature identifying it. Research is then conducted in order to ascertain the etiology of the syndrome, since hopefully the cause of the ailment puts the researcher well on the way to detecting a cure.

Albee (1969: 870) has provided the following definition:

> Attempts to explain the origins of neurotic and psychotic behavior, addiction to alcohol, juvenile delinquency, mental deficiency, and even such peripheral problems as marital maladjustment and school learning difficulties as sicknesses inside the person make them discontinuous with normal behavior. The sickness model suggests that these conditions are among a number of separate, discrete mental illnesses, each with a separate cause, prognosis, and potential treatment. . . .
>
> The sickness model further suggests that the treatment of these "illnesses" is properly the function of a physician specially trained in their diagnosis and in known methods of intervention. While other professionals may play various useful roles, they will be ancillary to the physician, who is charged with the clinical responsibility for the welfare of the "patient" (who must be "treated" in a hospital or clinic or in the physician's private office). Even the so-called personality disturbances, and all the agonies deriving from a dehumanized and hostile environment, are diagnosed as various kinds of sicknesses or intrapersonal illnesses.

Szasz (cited in Macklin, 1973: 51) offers still another version:

> The assumption is made that some neurological defect, perhaps a very subtle one, will ultimately be found for all the disorders of thinking and behavior. . . . All problems in living are attributed to physicochemical processes which in due time will be discovered by medical research.
>
> "Mental illnesses" are thus regarded as basically no different than all other diseases (that is, of the body). The only difference, in this view, between mental and bodily diseases is that the former, affecting the brain, manifest themselves by means of mental symptoms: whereas the latter, affecting other organ systems (for example, the skin, liver, etc.), manifest themselves by means of symptoms referable to those parts of the body.

For further discussions of the medical model, see Albee (1968); Blaney (1975); Chapanis (1961); Cowen (1967); Fabrega (1975); Halleck (1976); Parsons (1964); Shagass (1975); Stone (1973); and Taylor (1976).

5. Late in the nineteenth century and early in the twentieth, Kraepelin devised a classification system with more than 100 diagnostic categories based on dominant symptom patterns. He believed that the causes of mental illness were hereditary and organic in nature. Kraepelin's work culminated years of interest in classification that had begun with

William Cullen's attempts to explain behavioral disorders based on defects in the central nervous system (Sarason and Ganzer, 1968: 508).

6. Freud's contribution toward legitimating the medical model is two-edged. On the one hand, general agreement exists that "the introduction and entrenchment of the concept of mental health as part of a general health-disease model is due to Freud" (Macklin, 1973: 53). Freud's background was in medicine, he conducted his psychoanalytic practice in his doctor's office, and he was strongly attracted to the objectiveness of medical science. Most important, however, was his belief that physiological and biological causes underlay all psychic energy (Sarason & Ganzer, 1968: 508), despite his fervent explanations of neurotic and psychotic disorders as being precipitated by early childhood conflicts and traumas.

At the same time, Freud maintained that psychoanalysis as a method constituted an educational process, not treatment. In a postcript to his book on lay analysis he argued that "psychoanalysis is not a specialized branch of medicine" (Freud, 1950: 103). And in a letter to Paul Federn in 1927, he wrote that "the battle for lay analysis must, at one time or the other, be fought to the finish. Better now than later. As long as I live I shall resist that psychoanalysis be swallowed up by medicine" (Federn, 1967: 269-70).

Freud apparently distinguished psychoanalysis as an explanatory theory of human behavior from psychoanalysis as a technique. His attempts to keep the technique of psychoanalysis separate from the medical profession, however, were defeated.

7. In large measure, the entrenchment of psychoanalysis within the medical field resulted from the efforts of the American branch of the International Psychoanalytic Association. In 1926 the New York legislature passed a bill making the practice of analysis illegal; and in 1927 the New York Society of Psychoanalysis issued a resolution condemning lay analysis (Siegler and Osmond, 1974: 49). The result has been that virtually all forms of psychotherapy are now considered through the lens of the medical model.

8. Engel (1960: 473) has identified a number of factors that may be considered in the etiology of illness:

> . . . *factors which either place a burden on or limit the capacity of systems concerned with growth, development, or adaptation; or . . . factors which, by virtue of their physical or chemical properties, have the capacity to damage cells or parts of the body.* They may operate through the impact of something added to or impinging on the system as well as by virtue of a deficiency, as when something required is inadequate or unavailable. They may originate within the organism as well as in the environment.

Engel points out that there is never a single cause for any disease state, although different factors may be more important than others. Engel (1960: 474) suggests differentiating types of causes as "permissive," "precipitating," "conditioning," "predisposing," or "specific," or differentiating on the basis of its mode of action, such as "genic," "biochemical," "physiological," "psychological," or "social."

9. See Chapter 2 in Plog and Edgerton (1969: 78) "Does Culture Make a Difference?" for an excellent series of articles reviewing the evidence that, indeed, culture does make a difference.

10. For the research and theory as to the causes of mental illness, see Selzer (1971) (empirical data on how psychological stress causes physical illness); Cowen and Zax (1967); Eisenberg (1962) (emphasizes the sociocultural and psychological origins of mental illness); Galdston (1950) (represents the biological point of view); Engel (1962); Hollingshead and Redlich (1958); Kaplan (1972) (sociology of mental illness); Reed, Alexander, and Tomkins (1963); Dunbar (1955); Maslow and Mittelmann (1941); Leighton, Clausen, and Wilson (1957), Parsons (1964); Redlich (1956, 1957); Seiler (1973); Gottesman and Shields (1972) (genetic etiology of schizophrenia); Gruenberg and Huxley (1961); Clausen and Huffine (1975) (social factors); Dohrenwend (1975) (social factors); Lipowski (1975) (review of epidemiological data on how physical illness causes mental

disease); Mechanic (1975) (review of literature on sociocultural factors); and Freud (1896) (heredity).

11. Some would disagree. Rimland (1969: 704), for instance, predicts that "research will ultimately show psychosocial influences to have minor—if any—relevance in causing the limited disorders called 'neuroses,' and even less relevance in causing the severe disorders known as psychoses." On the other hand, Sarbin (1969: 29) counters that "the search for 'causes' will be in social systems, not in mythic internal entities."

12. Shapiro (1971: 441) has pointed out that more than 2,000 years ago Galen estimated that 60 percent of all people visiting a doctor had symptoms that were emotionally, rather than physically, caused. Shapiro also states that the contemporary estimate is 50 to 80 percent. Citing other documents, the Minister of National Health and Welfare of Canada (1974: 61) estimates that mental disorders play a role in half of all patients seen in general medical practice. Granatir (1971: 269) cites estimates that "up to 75 percent of the people visiting physicians either have complaints of psychic origin or have difficulties that have been aggravated by emotional factors."

13. Other typical comments on the medical model include George Albee (1966: 17), former president of the American Psychological Association, who emphatically states that "we must abandon the illness model and develop a viable alternative. . . . So long as we acquiesce to the fiction that people with neurotic and psychotic behavioral disturbances are sick, our field will keep itself in bondage." Thomas Szasz (1961: 296), the well-known critic of the concept of mental illness, has commented:

> It is customary to define psychiatry as a medical specialty concerned with the study, diagnosis, and treatment of mental illnesses. This is a worthless and misleading definition. Mental illness is a myth. Psychiatrists are not concerned with mental illnesses and their treatments. In actual practice they deal with personal, social, and ethical problems in living.

The noted humanistic psychologist Abraham Maslow (1971: 51) has tersely stated:

> I have used the words "therapy," "psychotherapy," and "patient." Actually, I hate all these words, and I hate the medical model that they imply. . . .

14. Sahakian (in Macklin, 1973: 69) has provided another classification for the various models, which he identifies as follows: (1) the unitary concept of disease and mental illness (represented by Menninger); (2) the moral model (subscribed to by O.H. Mowrer); (3) the dynamic model (as postulated by Freud, Fromm-Reichmann, Adler, and Jung); (4) the behavioral and learning theory model; (5) the statistical model; (6) the ontoanalytic or existential model (represented by Viktor Frankl and Rollo May); (7) the endocrinological model; (8) the psychopharmaceutical model; and (9) the genetic model.

15. So strongly do some feel about the negative effects of a medical conception of psychotherapy that they recommend the complete elimination of the word psychotherapy from usage. Maslow (1971: 51) has recommended "psychogogy," Bugental "ontogogy" (in Maslow, 1971: 51), and Rioch (1970: 141) has suggested "psychological counselor."

16. Torrey (1974: 121) believes that an educational model will help the behavioral sciences to attain their proper place in the medical school curriculum and establish the importance of the therapist's personality.

17. See, for instance, Appley and Winder (1973); Berger (1968); Egan (1970); Frank (1964); Gertz (1969); Gibbard, Hartman, and Mann (1974); Lakin (1972); and Teicher, de Freitas, and Osherson (1974).

REFERENCES

Albee, G.W. "Conceptual Models and Manpower Requirements in Psychology." *American Psychologist*, 1968, v. 23, pp. 317–20.

Albee, G.W. "Give Us a Place to Stand and We Will Move the Earth." In J.G. Harris (Ed.), *Mental Health Manpower Needs in Psychology: Proceedings of a Conference*. Lexington, Ky.: University of Kentucky Press, 1966, pp. 15-27.

Albee, G.W., and Loeffler, E. "Role Conflicts in Psychology and Their Implications for a Reevaluation of Training Models." *Canadian Psychologist*, 1971, v. 12, pp. 465-81.

Appley, D.G., and Winder, A.E. *T-groups and Therapy Groups in a Changing Society*. San Francisco: Jossey-Bass, 1973.

Ausubel, D. "Personality Disorder *Is* Disease." *American Psychologist*, 1961, v. 16, pp. 69-74. Reprinted in T.J. Scheff (Ed.), *Mental Illness and Social Processes*. New York: Harper and Row, 1967, pp. 254-66.

Becker, H.S. *Outsiders; Studies in the Sociology of Deviance*. New York: Free Press of Glencoe, 1963.

Berger, M.M. "Similarities and Differences Between Group Psychotherapy and Intensive Short Term Group Process Experiences—Clinical Impressions." *Journal of Group Psychoanalysis and Process*, 1968, v. 1, pp. 11-30.

Blaney, P.H. "Implications of the Medical Model and Its Alternatives." *American Journal of Psychiatry*, 1975, v. 132, pp. 911-14.

Bugental, J.F.T. (Ed.) *Challenges of Humanistic Psychology*. New York: McGraw-Hill, 1967.

Canada, Health and Welfare Department. *A New Perspective on the Health of Canadians*. Ottawa, Ontario: Government of Canada, 1974.

Chapanis, A. "Men, Machines, and Models." *American Psychologist*, 1961, v. 16, pp. 113-31.

Clausen, J.A., and Huffine, C.L. "Sociocultural and Social-Psychological Factors Affecting Social Responses to Mental Disorder." *Journal of Health and Social Behavior*, 1975, v. 16, pp. 405-20.

Columbia Law Review. "Implementation and Clarification of the Durham Criterion of Criminal Responsibility." *Columbia Law Review*, 1958, v. 58, pp. 1253-68.

Cowen, E.L., and Zax, M. "The Mental Health Fields Today: Issues and Problems." In E.L. Cowen, E.A. Gardner, and M. Zax, *Emergent Approaches to Mental Health Problems*. New York: Appleton-Century-Crofts, 1967, pp. 3-29.

Cummings, N.A., and Follette, W.T. "Brief Psychotherapy and Medical Utilization." In H. Dörken and Associates, *The Professional Psychologist Today*. San Francisco: Jossey-Bass, 1976, pp. 165-74.

Dohrenwend, B.P. "Sociocultural and Social-Psychological Factors in the Genesis of Mental Disorders." *Journal of Health and Social Behavior*, 1975, v. 16, pp. 365-92.

Dollard, J., and Miller, N.E. *Personality and Psychotherapy: An Analysis in Terms of Learning, Thinking, and Culture*. New York: McGraw-Hill, 1950.

Dunbar, F. *Mind and Body: Psychosomatic Medicine*. New York: Random House, 1955.

Egan, G. *Encounter: Group Processes for Interpersonal Growth*. Belmont, Calif.: Brooks/Cole Publishing Co., 1970.

Eisenberg, L. "Discussion." In P.H. Hoch and J. Zubin (Eds.) *The Future of Psychiatry*. New York: Grune and Stratton, 1962, pp. 251-55.

Engel, G.L. *Psychological Development in Health and Disease*. Philadelphia: W.B. Saunders, 1962.

Engel, G.L. "A Unified Concept of Health and Disease." *Perspectives in Biology and Medicine*, 1960, v. 3, pp. 459-85.

Erikson, K.T. "Patient Role and Social Uncertainty: A Dilemma of the Mentally Ill." *Psychiatry*, 1957, v. 20, pp. 263-74.

Fabrega, H., Jr. "The Need for an Ethnomedical Science." *Science*, 1975, v. 189, pp. 969-75.

Federn, E. "How Freudian Are the Freudians? Some Remarks to an Unpublished Letter." *Journal of the History of the Behavioral Sciences*, 1967, v. 3, pp. 269-81.

Frank, J.D. "Training and Therapy." In L.P. Bradford, J.R. Gibb, and K.D. Benne (Eds.), *T-Group Theory and Laboratory Method: Innovation and Re-education.* New York: John Wiley, 1964, pp. 442-51.

Freud, S. *The Question of Lay Analysis: Conversations with an Impartial Person.* (Translated and edited by J. Strachey.) New York: W.W. Norton, 1950.

Freud, S., "Heredity and the Aetiology of the Neuroses." *Revue Neurologique,* 1896, v. 4, pp. 161-70. Reprinted in S. Freud, *Collected Papers.* (Vol. 1.) (Translated by M. Meyer.) New York: Basic Books, 1959, pp. 138-54.

Funkenstein, D.H., and Farmsworth, D.L. "The Future Contributions of Psychitary to Education." In P.H. Hoch and J. Zubin (Eds.), *The Future of Psychiatry.* New York: Grune and Stratton, 1962, pp. 70-82.

Galdston, I. "The Problem of Medical and Lay Psychotherapy: The Medical View." *American Journal of Psychotherapy,* 1950, v. 4, pp. 419-31.

Gertz, B. "Trainer Role vs. Therapist Role." In C.R. Mill (Ed.), *Selections from Human Relations Training News.* Washington, D.C.: NTL Institute for Applied Behavioral Science, 1969, pp. 35-37.

Gibbard, G.S.; Hartman, J.J.; and Mann, R.D. (Eds.) *Analysis of Groups: Contributions to Theory, Research, and Practice.* San Francisco: Jossey-Bass, 1974.

Gottesman, I.I., and Shields, J. *Schizophrenia and Genetics: A Twin Study Vantage Point.* New York: Academic Press, 1972.

Granatir, W.L. "Psychotherapy and National Health Insurance." *American Journal of Psychiatry,* 1974, v. 131, pp. 267-70.

Grinker, R.R., Sr.; Grinker, R.R., Jr.; and Timberlake, J. "'Mentally Healthy' Young Males (Homoclites)." *Archives of General Psychiatry,* 1962, v. 6, pp. 405-53.

Gruenberg, E.M., and Huxley, M. "The Conference on Causes of Mental Disorders: A Review of Epidemiological Knowledge, 1959." *Milbank Memorial Fund Quarterly,* 1961, v. 39, pp. 7-13.

Guerney, B.G., Jr.; Stollak, G.; and Guerney, L.F. "The Practicing Psychologist as Educator—an Alternative to the Medical Practitioner Model." *Professional Psychology,* 1971, v. 2, pp. 276-82.

Gursslin, O.R.; Hunt, R.G.; and Roach, J.L. "Social Class and the Mental Health Movement." In F. Riessman, J. Cohen, and A. Pearl (Eds.), *Mental Health of the Poor: New Treatment Approaches for Low Income People.* New York: Free Press, 1964, pp. 57-67.

Halleck, S.L. "The Medical Model and Psychiatric Training." *American Journal of Psychotherapy,* 1976, v. 30, pp. 218-35.

Hollingshead, A.B., and Redlich, F.C. *Social Class and Mental Illness: A Community Study.* New York: John Wiley, 1958.

Jahoda, M. *Current Concepts of Positive Mental Health.* New York: Basic Books, 1958.

Kaplan, H.B. *The Sociology of Mental Illness.* New Haven, Conn.: College and University Press, 1972.

Lakin, M. *Interpersonal Encounter: Theory and Practice in Sensitivity Training.* New York: McGraw-Hill, 1972.

Leifer, R. "The Medical Model as Ideology." *International Journal of Psychiatry,* 1970-71, v. 9, pp. 13-21.

Leifer, R. *In the Name of Mental Health: Social Functions of Psychiatry.* New York: Science House, 1969.

Leighton, A.H.; Clausen, J.A.; and Wilson, R.N. (Eds.) *Explorations in Social Psychiatry.* New York: Basic Books, 1957.

Lipowski, Z.J. "Psychiatry of Somatic Diseases: Epidemiology, Pathogenesis, Classification." *Comprehensive Psychiatry,* 1975, v. 16(2), pp. 105-24.

Macklin, R. "The Medical Model in Psychoanalysis and Psychotherapy." *Comprehensive Psychiatry,* 1973, v. 14, pp. 49-69.

Margolis, J.Z. *Psychotherapy and Morality: A Study of Two Concepts.* New York: Random House, 1966.

Mariner, A.S. "A Critical Look at Professional Education in the Mental Health Field." *American Psychologist*, 1967, v. 22, pp. 271-81.

Maslow, A.H. *The Farther Reaches of Human Nature.* New York: Viking Press, 1971.

Maslow, A.H., and Mittelmann, B. *Principles of Abnormal Psychology.* New York: Harper, 1941.

Mechanic, D. "Sociocultural and Social-Psychological Factors Affecting Personal Responses to Psychological Disorder." *Journal of Health and Social Behavior*, 1975, v. 16, pp. 393-404.

Mechanic, D. "Some Factors in Identifying and Defining Mental Illness." In T.J. Scheff (Ed.), *Mental Illness and Social Processes.* New York: Harper and Row, 1967, pp. 23-32. Reprinted from *Mental Hygiene*, 1962, v. 46, pp. 66-74.

Menninger, K. (In collaboration with M. Mayman and P. Pruyser.) *The Vital Balance: The Life Process in Mental Health and Illness.* New York: Viking Press, 1963.

Moore, M.S. "Some Myths About 'Mental Illness.'" *Archives of General Psychiatry*, 1975, v. 32, pp. 1483-97.

Murray, H.G., and Hirsch, J. "Heredity, Individual Differences, and Psychopathology." In S.C. Plog and R.B. Edgerton (Eds.), *Changing Perspectives in Mental Illness.* New York: Holt, Rinehart and Winston, 1969, pp. 596-627.

Parsons, T. "Mental Illness and 'Spiritual Malaise': The Role of the Psychiatrist and of the Minister of Religion." In T. Parsons, *Social Structure and Personality.* New York: Free Press, 1964, pp. 292-324.

Parsons, T. "Definitions of Health and Illness in the Light of American Values and Social Structure." In E.G. Jaco (Ed.), *Patients, Physicians, and Illness.* New York: Free Press, 1958, pp. 165-87.

Patrick, D.L.; Bush, J.W.; and Chen, M.M. "Toward an Operational Definition of Health." *Journal of Health and Social Behavior*, 1973, v. 14, pp. 6-23.

Pleune, F.G. "All Dis-ease Is Not Disease: A Consideration of Psychoanalysis, Psychotherapy and Psycho-social Engineering." *International Journal of Psychoanalysis*, 1965, v. 46, pp. 358-66.

Plog, S.C., and Edgerton, R.B. (Eds.) *Changing Perspectives in Mental Illness.* New York: Holt, Rinehart and Winston, 1969.

Redlich, F.C. "The Concept of Health in Psychiatry." In A.H. Leighton, J.A. Clausen, and R.N. Wilson (Eds.), *Explorations in Social Psychiatry.* New York: Basic Books, 1957, pp. 138-64.

Redlich, F.C. "Some Sociological Aspects of the Psychoses." (Paper presented at the dedication of the Renard Hospital, St. Louis, Mo., October 1955.) In *Theory and Treatment of the Psychoses: Some Newer Aspects.* St. Louis, Mo.: Washington University Studies, 1956, pp. 59-75.

Redlich, F.C. "The Concept of Normality." *American Journal of Psychotherapy*, 1952, v. 6, pp. 551-69.

Reed, C.F.; Alexander, I.E.; and Tomkins, S.S. (Eds.) *Psychopathology: A Source Book.* (Introduction by R.W. White.) Cambridge, Mass.: Harvard University Press, 1963.

Rimland, B. "Psychogenesis versus Biogenesis: The Issues and the Evidence." In S.C. Plog and R.B. Edgerton (Eds.), *Changing Perspectives in Mental Illness.* New York: Holt, Rinehart and Winston, 1969, pp. 702-35.

Rioch, M.J. "Should Psychotherapists Do Therapy?" *Professional Psychology*, 1970, v. 1, pp. 139-42.

Romano, J. "Basic Orientation and Education of the Medical Student." *Journal of the American Medical Association*, 1950, v. 143, pp. 409-12.

Ryan, W. (Ed.) *Distress in the City.* Cleveland, Ohio: Case Western Reserve University Press, 1969.

Sarason, I.G., and Ganzer, V.J. "Concerning the Medical Model." *American Psychologist*, 1968, v. 23, pp. 507–10.

Sarbin, T.R. "The Scientific Status of the Mental Illness Metaphor." In S.C. Plog and R.B. Edgerton (Eds.), *Changing Perspectives in Mental Illness*. New York: Holt, Rinehart and Winston, 1969, pp. 9–31.

Sarbin, T.R. "On the Futility of the Proposition that Some People be Labelled 'Mentally Ill.'" *Journal of Consulting Psychology*, 1967, v. 31, pp. 447–53.

Scheff, T.J. "The Labelling Theory of Mental Illness." *American Sociological Review*, 1974, v. 39, pp. 444–52.

Scheff, T.J. (Ed.) *Mental Illness and Social Processes*. New York: Harper and Row, 1967.

Scheff, T.J. *Being Mentally Ill: A Sociological Theory*. Chicago: Aldine Publishing Co., 1966.

Schur, E.M. "Reactions to Deviance: A Critical Assessment." *American Journal of Sociology*, 1969, v. 75, pp. 309–22.

Seiler, L.H. "The 22-Item Scale Used in Field Studies of Mental Illness: A Question of Method, A Question of Substance, and A Question of Theory." *Journal of Health and Social Behavior*, 1973, v. 14, pp. 252–64.

Selzer, M.L. "Psychological Stress and Legal Concepts of Disease Causation." *Cornell Law Review*, 1971, v. 56, pp. 951–61.

Shagass, C. "The Medical Model in Psychiatry." *Comprehensive Psychiatry*, 1975, v. 16, pp. 405–13.

Shapiro, A.K. "Placebo Effects in Medicine, Psychotherapy, and Psychoanalysis." In A.E. Bergin and S.L. Garfield (Eds.), *Handbook of Psychotherapy and Behavior Change: An Empirical Analysis*. New York: John Wiley, 1971, pp. 439–73.

Siegler, M., and Osmond, H. *Models of Madness, Models of Medicine*. New York: Macmillan Publishing Co., 1974.

Stafford-Clark, D. Review of T.S. Szasz, *Law, Liberty and Psychiatry*. *Yale Law Journal*, 1964, v. 74, pp. 392–99.

Stone, A.A. "Psychiatry Kills: A Critical Evaluation of Dr. Thomas Szasz." *Journal of Psychiatry and Law*, 1973, v. 1, pp. 23–37.

Szasz, T.S. *The Ethics of Psychoanalysis: The Theory and Method of Autonomous Psychotherapy*. New York: Dell Publishing Co., 1965.

Szasz, T.S. *The Myth of Mental Illness: Foundations of a Theory of Personal Conduct*. New York: Dell Publishing Co., 1961.

Taylor, F.K. "The Medical Model of the Disease Concept." *British Journal of Psychiatry*, 1976, v. 128, pp. 588–94.

Teicher, A.; de Freitas, L.; and Osherson, A. "Group Psychotherapy and the Intense Group Experience: A Preliminary Rationale for Encounter as a Therapeutic Agent in the Mental Health Field." *International Journal of Group Psychotherapy*, 1974, v. 24, pp. 159–73.

Torrey, E.F. *The Death of Psychiatry*. Radnor, Pa.: Chilton, 1974.

Wing, J.K. "A Review of *Sanity, Madness, and the Family*." In T.J. Scheff (Ed.), *Mental Illness and Social Processes*. New York: Harper and Row, 1967, pp. 149–53.

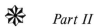 *Part II*

Regulation in Perspective

 *Chapter 6*

An Overview of Professional Regulation

The regulation of psychotherapists involves many of the same issues that occur in regulating any professional group, from physicians to plumbers. Some preliminary comments, therefore, about the history, purposes, and different methods of professional regulation will provide a context within which to evaluate current efforts to regulate this newly developing profession.[1]

THE PURPOSE OF REGULATION

The purpose of regulation may be viewed in at least two ways. The prevailing conception defines regulation as a form of social control that comes into being through an exercise of authority.[2] Regulatory laws are seen as a means of implementing restrictions that are enforced by sanctions.[3] This focus on control is a logical outgrowth of the positivistic philosophy of law advocated by Austin (1954), Kelsen (1945), and H.L.A. Hart (1961). In the field of professional regulation, which has adopted this legal philosophy, the result has been an emphasis on control, discipline, the elimination of quackery and charlatans, and the protection of the public from incompetent practice.

Another broader conception of the regulatory process is advisable, however. Lon Fuller (1969) of the Harvard Law School argues that the basic purpose of laws is to provide a framework for, and method of facilitating, human interaction.[4] Thus, regulations are designed not only to protect the public, but they must be framed in such a way that they meet the needs of that public. When the purpose of professional regulation is conceived of in this fashion, issues arise that are normally ignored. For instance, an interactional stance draws attention to the possibility that licensing laws may create personnel shortages and increase the cost of professional services to such an extent that the value of any increased quality of services is lost. An interactional view helps focus attention on unanticipated, negative side effects that may occur as a result of various regulatory proposals. Thus, the effect of professional regulation on the organization and administration of mental health services must be considered in evaluating any set of proposals, no matter how much they ensure that incompetent practitioners are prevented from practicing. The overarching purpose of regulation, then, becomes not so much protecting the public from harm as ensuring that the quality, quantity, and cost of mental health services in this country is improved.

METHODS OF PROFESSIONAL REGULATION

The most common reaction to the need for professional regulation is to suggest the enactment of stiff licensing laws—laws that would eliminate quacks and incompetents from the field and would enforce and ensure high standards of practice (see, for instance, the American Psychological Association and Conference of State Psychological Associations, 1955: 729). It is often thought that statutory regulation through licensing laws is the only method available. Nonetheless, positive regulation may be achieved through any of a variety of means, both direct and indirect.

There are, first of all, many agencies, systems, and institutions that have a substantial impact on the quality and type of professional services. At the federal level intervention does not take the form of licensing laws, because of the doctrine of states rights, under which all powers not specifically conferred on the federal government by the Constitution are reserved to the states or the people (U.S. Constitution, Article X). On the other hand, the federal government exerts considerable control through its right to prescribe qualifying and performance standards that must be adhered to if psychotherapists are to receive reimbursement for services rendered under various federal employee benefit programs.

The impact of such regulations depends directly on the size of the federal program involved. State regulation may take many forms, but the most common are licensing, certifying, or registration laws. Through these, the state regulates who is allowed to practice by prescribing standards for admission to the profession and by disciplining professionals who practice in an immoral or otherwise prohibited fashion. Only occasionally have municipal laws been used to regulate therapists, as when the city of San Diego prohibited the practice of psychology except for those who had registered with the city. Instead, municipal ordinances are generally used to regulate where certain activities take place, giving rise to ordinances licensing taverns, restaurants, and dance halls.

Nongovernmental organizations constitute regulatory bodies of considerable power and scope (see Moore, 1970: 113–30). Professional associations exert power through standards for membership, accreditation of facilities, certification of specialties, and approval of training programs. They exert indirect influence through formal or informal control of licensing boards.[5] Health insurance companies are another major source of influence through their right to decide who is to be reimbursed for providing professional services, including psychotherapy.

The judicial system represents another institution affecting the quality of care provided by psychotherapists. The courts are responsible for determining whether unlicensed practitioners are illegally practicing. Through malpractice suits the courts exercise control over the standard of care provided by typical practitioners in a community.

Another powerful means of exerting regulatory control, although frequently underestimated and almost always ineffectively utilized, is consumer education. Although professional associations have by and large taken the position that the general public does not have the ability to make delicate judgments about the qualifications and competence of professionals, Ralph Nader and other consumer advocates have argued that consumers are not so inept as once thought. A movement has begun to educate the consumer as to the state of the art within various professional fields, and to provide the consumer with the information necessary to evaluate the quality of professional services.

Efforts to control the quality of care provided by professionals in this country have generally rested on directly influencing professional standards and practices. The belief has been that high quality is best ensured by competent professionals who meet certain educational and experiential requirements and are possessed of certain moral and ethical qualities. Milton Roemer (1970) has pointed out that the achievement of quality in medical care is dependent upon many factors quite apart from the competency of the health practitioner. For instance, he notes that six underlying conditions may drastically affect the quality of health care, including the maintenance of a safe and hygienic environment, the requirement of an educated people, an adequate supply of physical and human resources, financial access to medical care resources, spatial or geographic accessibility, and a continuing flow of new knowledge (Roemer, 1970: 284–86).

In a warning that has direct applicability to the mental health field, Roemer concludes that "it is not uncommon for deficiencies in medical care quality to be naively attributed to failures in the 'control' mechanisms . . . , when the root cause is simply a quantitative lack of medical or financial resources or transportation or some other basic requirement . . . . (1970: 286). He goes on to outline nine points at which one may intervene in the health field to influence the quality of care: (1) personnel standards; (2) facility standards; (3) control of drugs and appliances; (4) organizational frameworks; (5) disciplinary incentives; (6) continuing education; (7) judicial controls; (8) geographic regionalization; and (9) comprehensive health planning. In addition, regulations in the mental health field may regulate specific techniques such as Gestalt therapy or psychoanalysis, or they may control the consumer of services, if it can be demonstrated that certain types of clients are liable to be hurt by specific types of experiences.

Another perspective through which to view methods of regulation is provided by systems analysis. Regulations may be seen as controlling input, process, or outcome. The licensing requirements that profes-sionals must meet before being allowed to practice provide perhaps the clearest example of regulation of input measures, since they establish what inputs are allowed into the system. Regulation of process is illustrated by peer review organizations that attempt to assess whether proper procedures were followed. Professional liability suits provide the most clear-cut example of attempts to regulate outcome, since the primary concern is with results.

Historically, the greatest emphasis has been placed on regulating input measures through licensing and other forms of professional standard-setting. The value and efficacy of input regulation (or process regulation, for that matter) ultimately depends on the relationship of input measures to outcome. If it turns out that the standards and criteria used in measuring input bear no relation to outcome, then regulation will not achieve its purpose. Until recently, however, even in the medical field, it has been difficult to adequately define outcomes or to design methods of measuring them.[6]

A detailed examination of the value and potential of each method of regulation and an analysis of the effects on the mental health field of regulating the various aspects of psychotherapy or encounter groups is beyond the scope of this book. The focus will, therefore, rest on professional regulation. Since psychiatrists, clinical psychologists, and other professionals practice as therapists, their competency to practice will be considered and the methods currently being used to evaluate and regulate their practice will be examined. The purpose will be to determine whether adequate methods can be developed to regulate the practitioner in such a way that the quality of professional practice is improved in specifiable ways without significant negative side effects. The most important and salient methods in current use will be examined in detail, including statutory regulation through licensure, judicial regulation through professional liability suits, and nongovernmental regulation through professional associations.

WHAT CONSTITUTES A PROFESSION

Throughout this book psychotherapists, including encounter group leaders, have been referred to as professionals. For two reasons it is now time to examine this term to determine whether it is appropriately applied. First, as previously mentioned, if psychotherapists are properly considered professionals, then the formulation of recommendations for regulation takes on added importance because of the increasingly central position of the professions in our society and the potential applicability of these recommendations for other professional groups. Second, there are pragmatic considerations, such as a determination of the applicability of antitrust laws, which have generally been considered inapplicable to the "learned professions," as opposed to the more common occupations.

The matter of defining a profession is not simple. Most lexicographers and sociologists agree that no absolute definition can be found (*Corpus Juris Secundum*, 1956: 1215–16). There is further agreement that the extent to which a given occupation can be said to be a profession is a matter of degree (see, e.g., Moore, 1970). Morris Cogan (1955, 1953) believes that many of the problems of defining a profession can be resolved if it is recognized that three levels of definition are necessary, and that most definitions cover only one level. Illustrative of one level is Carr-Saunders and Wilson (1933), who use an historical and lexicological approach; that is, they study the professions as they have existed throughout history to arrive at a definition that incorporates the essential features that seem always to exist. A second level is made up of persuasive

definitions in which professions are defined in an ideal sense, the purpose of which is to redirect people's attitudes. Finally, there are operational definitions, which provide guidelines for the professional in making day-to-day decisions. The definition that Cogan (1953: 48–49) offers, which is a synthesis of the definitions provided by the major theoreticians in the field, states:

A profession is a vocation whose practice is founded upon an understanding of the theoretical structure of some department of learning or science, and upon the abilities accompanying such understanding. This understanding and these abilities are applied to the vital practical affairs of man. The practices of the profession are modified by knowledge of a generalized nature and by the accumulated wisdom and experience of mankind, which serve to correct the errors of specialism. The profession, serving the vital needs of man, considers its first ethical imperative to be altruistic service to the client.[7]

Another method by which to determine whether a given occupation is highly professionalized and justifiably referred to as a profession is to examine the current stage of its development. Sociologists and historians have found that professions tend to develop in and through similar stages. Barber (1965), for instance, notes a number of characteristics of a newly emerging or marginal profession. Typically its members have widely differing backgrounds in their levels of education and community orientation. Its leaders will often be found making statements that acknowledge that the profession is still in its infancy, but adding that this is not unlike medicine and law when they first began to emerge as professions. The construction of a professional code of ethics will be one of the first and most important tasks of the profession, as will be the task of building a strong professional association. Attempts at licensure will often take place in order to add prestige, but such attempts will usually be resisted by the less professional members.

Attempts will be made to establish or strengthen university professional schools. An effort will be made to inform the public about the services that the profession has to offer.[8]

Other scholars have developed prescriptive models of what constitutes a "good" profession. For instance, Paul Freund (1965) argues that professions should be measured by three standards: (1) independence; (2) availability; and (3) learning. Independence includes loyalty to one's client, independence from government control, and authority over professional standards and discipline. Availability involves the degree to which professional services are available on a wide basis to all income groups. Finally, learning is the degree to which a profession is capable of using available information and the degree to which that information is up to date. Sanford (1951: 668–70) argues that a good profession, among other things, is motivated by a sense of social responsibility, has perspective on its place in society, renders services only within its area of demonstrable competence, devotes relatively little energy to guild functions, is free of nonfunctional entrance requirements, and has a code of ethics designed mainly to protect the public, and only secondarily the profession.

Lippitt and his associates (1975) have approached the problems of what constitutes a good profession by identifying the pathologies in professionalism as it has developed historically. According to their analysis, professions have had a tendency to confuse credentials with competence. They have tended to define credentials more and more in terms of external badges of schooling and degrees, which are only obtainable through a rigid educational route. They have acted at times solely to protect the vested economic interests of their members, including resisting expansion of membership. Professions have also tended to resist the development and use of paraprofessionals, and have been tardy in recruiting and training volunteers. They have tended to cultivate in the public the myth that the professional is all knowing and all-powerful, rather than educating the public as to the profession's strengths and weaknesses. Finally, the professions have tended to coalesce with and be responsive to established institutions, rather than those lacking power.

PSYCHOTHERAPY AS A PROFESSION

Talcott Parsons (1968) sees the field of psychotherapy as an important profession that has recently emerged as a part of a group of professions concerned with the problems of the individual as a member of society. He believes that the basic discipline in this field is psychology, which provides the intellectual undergirding of three fields of professionalization, one of which is psychotherapy.

The degree to which psychotherapy is a developed profession is debatable.[9] Blanck (1963) argues that psychotherapy is relatively well developed, since it possesses, to varying degrees, a body of knowledge, standards of professional responsibility, its own training programs, and is largely founded upon the general system of education. According to her, it only lacks integration within the university system of education and has not yet achieved licensure. On the other hand, Blanck argues that psychotherapy has not yet clearly defined itself or differentiated itself from other professions. In fact, several professions, including psychology, social work, and medicine, have incorporated psychotherapy within their own boundaries.

The work of Henry, Sims, and Spray (1971: 182) documents the fact that while many training routes exist to becoming a therapist, and while many disparate and often antagonistic organizations claim to represent psychotherapy as a profession, the final product in terms of the professional that emerges is remarkably similar. Although differences in ideologies and specific techniques exist, these are minimal. The typical social work professional, for instance, tends to have a similar background, belief system, set of attitudes, and work habits as those educated as psychotherapists through other systems.

Whether psychotherapy is developing in sound fashion as a profession is open to serious question. Using some of Sanford's (1951) criteria, the field appears to have overestimated its ability to provide competent services to the community. The amount of time spent in politicking and guild functions by the various professional associations concerned with psychotherapy (such as the American Psychological Association and the American Psychiatric Association) is far greater than would be found in Sanford's picture of the ideal profession. The evidence from previous chapters indicates that the entrance requirements to the various professions are largely irrelevant and nonfunctional. Finally, therapeutic services are still relatively expensive and unavailable to the poor and disadvantaged, indicating that the profession's efforts to become more service-oriented have not been successful. Given the fact that the myriad professional groups fighting for a piece of the therapeutic pie are not likely to join together to resolve their problems, many of the major problems that plague the profession will probably continue, seriously undermining its development.

Whether or not psychotherapy constitutes a developed profession, its relationship to encounter groups is problematical. As pointed out above, traditional distinctions between psychotherapy and encounter may be arbitrary, and such distinctions are becoming blurred. Considered as a separate entity, however, encounter groups have tended to proliferate outside of academic settings.[10] Encounter group leaders have lacked strong professional associations, and

theory and research development has been relatively lacking (Bradford, Gibb, and Benne, 1964: 478; Schein and Bennis, 1965: 322-27). In the 1970s this picture has been changing. Fred Massarik (1972) comments favorably on the formation of organizations such as the International Association of Applied Social Scientists, the Association for Creative Change, and the International Transactional Analysis Association, whose purposes have been to establish standards of practice and ethical codes for practitioners in the field. Nonetheless, the field is obviously a long way from maturity, since these associations have had only minor impact on the field as a whole (Benne et al., 1975).

A basic question is whether encounter groups should remain distinct from psychotherapy. The evidence discussed above indicates that traditional distinctions do not provide a proper basis for their separation. Furthermore, Inglis (1964), in his book on unorthodox medicine, has made an argument that has direct applicability to the mental health field. He notes that the traditional distinction between accepted medical practice and fringe medicine is that "orthodox treatment relies mainly on fighting disease with the help of drugs and surgery, whereas unorthodox treatment concentrates on stimulating the patient's constitution to fight on its own behalf, on the assumption that this is safer and more effective" (Inglis, 1964: 264).

The parallel with psychotherapy and encounter groups is obvious. Encounter groups constitute the fringe, wherein practitioners attempt to release the growth-promoting qualities and energies of human beings. Encounter group leaders attempt to ameliorate illness by focusing on a participant's positive capacities. Inglis argues that "fringe medicine" has an important contribution to make and should be incorporated within the mainstream of the medical profession. Similarly, it may be argued that the positive aspects of encounter groups should be incorporated within the realm of psycho-therapy, and that both should be considered part of a larger mental health profession.

A BRIEF HISTORY OF THE PROFESSIONS AND THEIR REGULATION, WITH A SPECIAL EMPHASIS ON MEDICINE

Early History

The origins of the professions, at least as known in the Western world, are subject to considerable debate.[11] Whitehead (1933) has argued that they have their roots in the academies of early Greece during the time of Plato and Aristotle, while Carr-Saunders and Wilson (1933: 289) maintain that the basic prototype for the modern professions originated much later in time—during the eleventh century—when occupations began to organize as a result of a rising movement toward association.

If one agrees with Whitehead, then the first attempt to regulate the professions may have been the tarriff imposed on medical practitioners by the Code of Hammurabi in 2000 B.C. (Sigerist, 1960: 5). Under this code, surgeon's fees were determined and penalties were established for what was considered malpractice, including the severing of a surgeon's right hand when an operation resulted in a patient's death. Julius Caesar instituted a form of licensing containing provisions such as tax exemptions designed to attract Greek doctors, but which eventually came to be used to limit the number of doctors practicing in a given community, much as has happened today.

In the thirteenth century, Frederick II, king of Sicily, established regulations remarkably similar to current licensing laws to control the medical profession (Derbyshire, 1969: 1-2). His laws required extensive educational training (three years of philosophy, five of medicine, and one of practical experience), and made provisions for candidates to be tested by a medical faculty (the Masters of Salerno). Practicing without a license was forbidden, a feature of the law quite unusual for its time. In addition, Frederick II's code established fee schedules, made free service for indigents mandatory, established ethical codes with strong penalties, and made it unlawful for a physician to own an apothecary. By the mid-fourteenth century similar laws were enacted in Spain, Germany, and Naples.

The Guilds and Their Downfall

The early professions were considered to be law, medicine, and theology. These were largely under the aegis of the church, but as they became secularized, new professions arose as the power of the medieval guilds increased. The three basic types of guilds—merchant, craft, and professional—although distinguishing themselves from each other, had similar features.[12] They were established and encouraged by local government as a means of regulating the cost and quality of goods and services, they were to be responsible for the poor, and they were to give service to the sick and indigent. In many ways guild regulation resembles that of modern-day professional associations in conjunction with licensing laws.

The basic elements of the early guilds consisted first and foremost of the requirement of compulsory membership. This ensured that all practitioners would be subject to the guild's mandate and effectively established a monopoly. Second, the guilds generally set high entrance fees and required the consent of the guild membership before new members were admitted. Third, a period of apprenticeship was required that became longer with time, until by the sixteenth century seven years of experience was commonly required. Fourth, the guilds generally limited the number of apprentices that a given member might have. This served to curtail their abuse, but with the passage of time it became an additional means of limiting the number of potential members. Finally, medieval guilds generally established minimum prices for services and goods, as well as maximum wages for workers. The guilds fit perfectly into medieval conceptions of society, which included a belief in a hierarchical organization of authority, the importance of status versus contract, and a fusion of governmental authority with nongovernmental bodies.

The debilitating effects of the guild system were not immediately apparent. In the thirteenth century, guild membership was fairly open and restrictions were minimal. By the mid-fourteenth century, signs existed that the guilds were beginning to limit competition, and by the mid-fifteenth century there were flagrant and gross efforts to artificially restrict the number of guild members. The guilds wielded virtually monopolistic power over the vocations and professions in which they existed. Eventually the high entry requirements, the inordinately long periods of apprenticeship, the practice of dismissing apprentices just prior to completion of their apprenticeships, and the establishment of irrelevant membership requirements began to severely curtail economic growth.

The demise of most guilds came shortly after the fifteenth century. The philosophy of laissez-faire, the increase in the size of the economic market (Carr-Saunders and Wilson, 1933: 294), the accumulation of capital, the rise of strong nation states (Webb and Webb, 1917), and the rise of mercantilism (Gilb, 1966: 8-9) all worked toward the rapid disintegration of the guilds. Although certain professional guilds remained intact throughout this period, such as the apothecaries and surgeons, who dealt in personal services, their disintegration was considered a "welcome release from what had become an unreasonable interference with the free play of economic forces, and their demise generally is accounted one of the principal elements in our vaunted advance from 'status' to 'contract'" (Grant, 1942: 303).

The Regulation of Medicine in England Since 1500

Since the Middle Ages, statutory regulation of the professions in Europe has been used sporadically and with varying degrees of success. An examination of this history will demonstrate that many of the same problems and negative side effects that current methods have engendered have occurred repeatedly throughout the last four centuries. English legislation in the medical field provides an excellent case in point. The first law to provide for the licensing of physicians was enacted in 1511 (Shindel, 1965). Powers were granted to the bishop of each diocese to administer an examination to any physician who desired to practice. Seven years later the medical profession was also granted the power to license, with a charter given to the Royal College of Physicians. The three professions in the medical field consisted of an elite group of physicians; the surgeons—who were originally barbers and who were looked down upon by the physicians for practicing a menial craft; and the apothecaries, who both sold and prescribed drugs and who were originally a part of the vocation of grocers, but who achieved autonomous status and a separate charter in 1617 (Carr-Saunders and Wilson, 1933: 72).

In much the same way that psychiatrists are currently attempting to restrict the right to practice of psychologists and social workers, the Royal College of Physicians constantly attempted to keep the surgeons and apothecaries in check, while paying little attention to eliminating the real quacks and charlatans present in nearly every marketplace. According to Carr-Saunders and Wilson (1933: 72):

In its earlier days the College harried both the apothecaries and the surgeons; it would be more proper to charge it with not harrying the real quacks. The campaign against the apothecaries did not succeed, primarily because the exclusion policy resulted in keeping the number of physicians so low that an inferior body, catering to the needs of the general public, was bound by the mere logic of the situation to force its way sooner or later to a form of recognition.

During this period administration of licensing physician laws was exercised by both the medical corporations and the universities. The church, at least officially, still had the right to license in certain instances. The Apothecaries Act of 1815 gave the Society of Apothecaries the right to examine and establish standards for those who wished to become apothecaries, and also the right to prosecute those who illegally practiced medicine. The powers of enforcement were generally inadequate, however, and the demand for medical services was simply too great. On the whole, regulatory efforts during this period were not very sophisticated and were often more of an encumbrance than help (Carr-Saunders and Wilson, 1933: 305).

The constant jurisdictional battles were finally put to an end with the passage of the historic Medical Act of 1858. This act merged the three separate professions of physicians, surgeons, and apothecaries, and led to an enforcement of uniform standards in the examinations of the licensing bodies. It made provisions for a public register listing all legally qualified medical practitioners and only allowing those on the list to sue for medical fees or hold public office. Interestingly, the law did not (and still does not) forbid the practice of medicine by laypeople.[13]

The Regulation of Medicine in the United States: 1600 to 1850

While England overturned the guild method of regulating the professions and moved toward a socialized system, especially in medicine, the United States has taken an opposite tack.[14] In the early days of colonial America the guilds did not take hold. The guild system was already beginning to deteriorate in Europe. Mercantile regulations placed on the colonies created numerous restrictions upon the manufacture of raw materials that competed with those manufac-

tured by English craftspeople, and the guilds depended a great deal on an urban setting for their effective functioning (Council of State Governments, 1952). Together with the tremendous need for different services and crafts in America at the time, these factors successfully dampened the desire of the early settlers for such a system of government.

Thus, licensing laws as currently known were almost nonexistent. In the medical profession the lack of educational institutions and formalized systems of apprenticeship made attempts at regulation most difficult.[15] For a solid education, Americans returned to Europe; yet, since so few were able to do so, most practitioners simply apprenticed themselves informally to an already practicing professional.

The earliest laws to directly regulate the medical profession were enacted in Virginia in 1639 (Derbyshire, 1969: 2). Their purpose, however, was to control the amount charged by practitioners, since so many complaints had been voiced about excessive fees. Ten years later Massachusetts passed a law regulating "Chirurgeons, Midwives, Physicians or others" who were "employed at any time about the body of men, women or children, for preservation of life, or health" (Derbyshire, in Shryock, 1967: vii). This law marked the first attempt to control quackery in the New World. Those included within its ambit were not to practice "without the advice and consent of such as are skillful in the same Art (if such may be had) or at least some of the wisest and gravest then present." Violators were to be subjected to "such severe punishment as the nature of the fact may deserve." This law was copied by New York in 1665, but neither was enforced, and virtually no further regulation of quackery occurred before 1760.

During the last half of the eighteenth century and the first part of the nineteenth, the newly created states passed a variety of laws licensing physicians and surgeons. One of the prototypes of current legislation was a Maryland law passed in 1798 creating a Medical Board of Examiners, whose principal function was to examine prospective physicians and surgeons (Derbyshire, 1969: 4). As state medical societies gradually came into existence, they began taking over the licensing function. At the same time the number of proprietary schools increased precipitously. Between 1830 and 1845 the number of medical colleges in the United States more than doubled (Blanck, 1963: 96; see also Young, 1970).

The question arose whether graduation from a chartered school should not be sufficient in itself to allow one to practice. The matter was first put to the test in 1803 in Massachusetts (Shryock, 1967: 25–26). Harvard's medical school, which had been established in 1783, maintained that its students were as well qualified to practice as those licensed through the Massachusetts Medical Society. Because of public pressure, both groups took an examination, and the Harvard students performed far better than their Medical Society counterparts. As a result the law was amended to allow the Harvard diploma, as well as the traditional society examination, to qualify one for practice. Similar amendments were soon passed in other states, allowing anybody to qualify for a license who possessed a diploma from a chartered school.

Such charters were easy to garner at this time. The prevailing philosophy of Jacksonian democracy emphasized minority groups, the underprivileged, the poor, and the needy. It advocated a laissez-faire policy that allowed citizens to do whatever they wanted. The doctrine was one of *caveat emptor*. The practical application of this philosophy to the professions was made with a vengeance. Proprietary medical schools were established that offered only the lowest quality of education and granted degrees with impunity. Since the populace had become upset with the restrictive practices and attitudes prevalent in the medical societies, a strong movement was made to abolish

or amend many of the licensing acts that had been passed. This movement met nearly complete success. By 1845 eight states had never enacted any licensing laws whatever, and ten others had repealed earlier legislation. By 1849 only New Jersey and the District of Columbia had laws that even hinted at adequate regulatory arrangements. Thus, by 1850 the practice of medicine was open to virtually anyone who desired to hang out a shingle. A similar deterioration in licensing laws was exhibited in the legal profession as well, where two-thirds of the states had abolished all regulations for admission to the bar by 1840, and many were advocating the abolishment of the legal profession altogether (Shryock, 1967: 30–31).

Many historians have evaluated this period as marking one of the low points in U.S. medicine. At a time when educational standards were low, when so many quacks were allowed to practice, and when regulatory controls were so ineffective, arguments supporting such an evaluation are fairly persuasive. Nonetheless, several prominent authorities, particularly Kett (1968) and Shryock (1967), make an excellent case for the opposite point of view. Shryock points out that, bad as much of the education was, most regular practitioners in the towns, and close to 50 percent of all rural practitioners, had received some sort of formal training by 1850. This compares with an estimate for Virginia in the eighteenth century of about 11 percent (Shryock, 1967: 107), and is rather remarkable in light of the fact that most doctors had received no formal training whatever only fifty years previously. Shryock cites comments made by leading practitioners and medical school faculty of the time that suggest that the average medical practitioner of 1830–1850 was actually better off than before.

Kett (1968: 69) points out another valuable effect of the lack of licensure laws during this period. The fact that all one had to do to practice medicine was to obtain a diploma from a chartered medical school meant that the diploma came to have a far greater importance than previously. When licensure laws were abolished, people began to look for those who had some medical education, no matter how inferior. The result was two-fold. First, the importance of medical education was reinforced and became established. Second, as Kett (1968: 69) describes it: "The facility with which degrees could be obtained ensured that a fairly high percentage of practitioners was brought into the organized medical fraternity. While the state of their preparation left much to be desired, this was still a vast improvement over conditions before 1760 when the establishment of an identifiable profession outside of a few large cities had been extremely difficult."

Even more convincing evidence supports the thesis that the lack of licensing during this era was sound policy. This period in the development of medicine as a science was marked by a large number of different schools of thought explaining what caused disease and how to cure it. Allopathy, homeopathy, osteopathy, naturopathy, Thomsonianism, and chiropractic, among others, all vied for public attention. Each claimed instances of success, and each had an elaborate, if unproved, theory as to how illness developed and how health was restored. No group could marshal evidence that would overwhelmingly prove its case, nor could evidence be effectively marshaled to rebut competing theories. It would have been unwise and premature to establish one school as the only legally permissible one. Thus, despite the existence of so little statutory regulation, Kett (1968: 179–80) argues that the medical profession in the United States was better regulated at this time than any other in its previous history:

Medical institutions either did not serve their original purpose or they accomplished results almost by accident. Medical societies, designed to distinguish regular from empirical practitioners and extinguish the latter, came to grief. Medical schools, designed to raise professional standards, multiplied so rapidly that they frustrated this object and, in addition, damaged the position of the medical societies. But precisely because there were so many schools, the medical degree in effect accomplished the separation of regular from empirical practitioners. At the same time a subtle change in popular attitudes which produced a demand for medical advisors versed in scientific terminology brought about a tightening of requirements for entering the profession where innumerable laws and organizations had failed. The medical profession on the eve of the Civil War was thus better regulated than it had been at any other time in American history, not because of institutions but in spite of them.

The Regulation of Medicine in the United States: 1850 to 1915

State medical societies became increasingly distressed at the lack of standards that existed and the poor quality of many proprietary schools. Their attempts at securing effective state regulation had failed, but they had not given up hope. Largely out of this concern with standards and regulation, the various state societies formed the American Medical Association in 1847 (see Garceau, 1941; Hyde and Wolff, 1954; Rayack, 1967; for a detailed history of the formation of the AMA). At first its efforts were notably unsuccessful. The AMA misjudged the strength of various vested interests and set standards far higher than warranted, given the shortage of physicians and the lack of sufficient high-quality educational institutions.[16] Reform was also made more difficult because of internal disagreements within the profession itself, especially since many members served on the faculties of proprietary schools and had a vested interest in maintaining low standards.

Eventually, however, the AMA began to have an impact. In 1873 Texas passed a law establishing a state examining board, and by 1895 nearly all states had such legislation (Derbyshire, 1969: 6). During the twenty-five-year period from 1875 to 1900, a gradual effort was made to improve standards. As opposed to early regulatory arrangements, state laws did not vest direct control of licensing in either the societies or the medical schools, but restricted it to the examining board. The medical societies, however, continued to wield significant influence through their sometimes legislatively mandated power to nominate or select those who were to serve on the board.

The turn of the century marked an important period in the development of licensure laws. National associations of all sorts had begun to rise in this country during the mid-nineteenth century (see Gilb, 1966: 17). The power of such organizations was greatly enhanced by the rapid expansion of the railroad and the improved means of communication brought about by the telephone and telegraph. Through their state and local societies they were able to push through licensure laws at an ever-increasing rate. Between 1911 and 1915 alone, 110 statutes licensing twenty-four occupations were enacted. In medicine licensing became mandatory in every state by 1900, and twenty-two required both a diploma from a medical school and successful passage of an exam (Shryock, 1967: 54–55).

CONCLUSIONS

The purpose of this chapter has been to lay the groundwork for an analysis of how best to regulate the profession of psychotherapy. To do this it has been important (1) to isolate the characteristics of a profession; (2) to determine to what extent psychotherapy fulfills those characteristics; (3) to determine the limits of psychotherapy and whether encounter groups should be included within its scope; (4) to define carefully what constitutes regulation; and (5) to explore the various methods available to bring about the proper purposes of regulation.

It should be clear that psychotherapy is a rapidly growing profession, even though its development may not be complete, and even though its limits are almost impossible to articulate. Talcott Parsons (1968), for one, argues that psychotherapy is crucial to society because of its concern with the problems of the individual as a member of it.

How psychotherapy is best regulated is problematical. Traditional conceptions of the regulatory process are too narrow. Lon Fuller's (1969) broader view of the interactive and facilitative nature of the legal process helps focus on whether a given set of regulations not only protects the public, but meets the needs of that public. In the past fifty years the United States has come to rely increasingly on licensing laws as the primary vehicle for regulation. Relatively ignored have been a host of other mechanisms that may accomplish the purposes of licensing with fewer negative consequences.

Conceptually, the problem may be that regulation of input is rarely as effective or efficient as regulation of output. History suggests that alternative means of regulation may be as effective as licensing. In the ensuing chapter a closer look will be made of the actual extent of licensing in the United States with an attempt to evaluate its effectiveness.

NOTES

1. The following books and articles provide an excellent analysis of the role, structure, and influence of modern professions: Gilb (1966) (an excellent analysis of most aspects of the professions in detail and with a strongly historical perspective using a Hegelian theoretical framework); Goode (1957) (discusses the formation of professions,

their reward system, and who controls what aspects); Laski (1935) (Laski would like to see most of the professions organized as a public service, much in the way Russia has); Lieberman (1970) (excellent in its portrayal of the guild aspects of modern professions and its study of licensure laws); Lynn and the Editors of *Daedalus* (1965) (most of the chapters are devoted to descriptions of different professions; only a few are devoted to analyzing the professions and their role); Moore (1970) (represents an excellent sociological analysis of the professions, especially with regard to how they are different from other aspects of our society); Parsons (1939, 1968) (concludes that the professions constitute the institutional framework in which many of our most important social functions are carried on—notably science, liberal learning, and the practical application of medicine, technology, law, and teaching); Pound (1949) (takes an opposite point of view from Laski and is against an extreme service state and government control of the professions); Grant (1942 and 1942a) (excellent analysis of how modern professional organizations have adopted the guild structure to achieve virtually complete self-regulation); Reiff (1974) (fine theoretical article positing the basis of professional power not in knowledge itself, but the control of knowledge, and arguing that this power must be shared with consumer groups and the public).

2. *Black's Law Dictionary* (1968: 1451) defines "to regulate" as "to fix, establish, or control; . . . to direct by rule or restriction; to subject to governing principles or laws." The popular *American Heritage Dictionary* (1973: 1096) says that a regulation is "a principle, rule, or law designed to control or govern behavior."

3. Kelsen (1945: 45, 61), for instance, writes that "law is the primary norm, which stipulates the sanction," and "the norms which form a legal order must be norms stipulating a coercive act, i.e., a sanction."

4. In agreement with this is Paul Freund (1965: 38), who comments: "To define law, as sociologists frequently do, as rules with sanctions is to obscure the essentially facilitative role of a good deal of law." This represents an interactional view in which the reciprocal expectancies between lawmaker and subject become important, as opposed to the stance of logical positivists, who are concerned solely about the expectations of the lawmaker.

5. Illustrative of the power of professional associations is the American Medical Association. Most state licensing agencies are composed of American Medical Association members, and in many instances it is a matter of law that board members be members of the AMA or chosen from a list submitted by the state medical society. Apart from control of the licensing function, the AMA and its various state constituents exercise control of personnel standards through their codes of medical ethics, and the more than thirty specialty boards recognized by the AMA. These specialty boards establish standards for training and for examinations. Their influence stems from the fact that participation in various programs and the ability to practice in certain hospital settings is dependent on board certification. Further regulation by the AMA takes place through its influence on the accreditation of hospitals, which is made possible by its participation in the Joint Commission on Accreditation of Hospitals formed in 1952 (Roemer, 1970: 290). In the field of psychology and psychotherapy the American Psychological Association is attempting to play a similar role. For an excellent discussion and analysis of the AMA's power, see Hyde and Wolff (1954).

6. Several writers have stressed the importance of regulation through outcome monitoring. See Carlson (1970) and Tancredi and Woods (1972).

7. Illustrative of other definitions is Talcott Parson's (1968). He states that three core criteria are crucial to determining whether an occupation constitutes a profession. First, formal technical training must be a requirement, and there must be an institutionalized means of assessing the quality of the training and the competence of the person trained. It is important that this training be concerned with something culturally vital, and further that the intellectual aspect of the training be essential for effective performance. The development of skills in the use and application of the cultural tradition

that has been mastered constitutes a second criterion. Finally, an institutional means must exist to ensure that professionals put their skills to uses that are responsive to the needs of society.

Justice Louis D. Brandeis (1914) has argued that three characteristics distinguish a profession. Like Parsons, he believed that the necessary preliminary training must be intellectual in character and the profession must be pursued mainly for the benefit of others, not for egotistic reasons. In addition, Brandeis emphasized the fact that the amount of monetary reward is not the accepted measure of success. Brandeis did not place great stress on whether the profession is organized.

The former dean of the Harvard Law School, Roscoe Pound (1949), largely agrees with Parsons and stresses the importance of organization as an aspect of being a profession. Other writers in the legal field have stressed the presence or absence of special attributes in determining whether a field should be considered professional. De Lancey (1938: 14), for instance, limits her definition to "vocation[s] in which individuals are licensed by the state after a period of formal academic education and training in an approved professional school." Carr-Saunders and Wilson (1933: 4), in their classic work on the professions, state that any attempt at defining precisely what a profession is is fraught with difficulty: "Indeed, the drawing of a boundary line would be an arbitrary procedure, and we shall not offer, either now or later, a definition of professionalism." They go on to say, however, that "it will emerge that the typical profession exhibits a complex of characteristics, and that other vocations approach this condition more or less closely, owing to the possession of some of these characteristics fully or partially developed."

Most writers believe that one of the distinguishing features of the professions is that their members are motivated by altruistic considerations—the desire to help their compatriots. Parsons (1968) argues, nonetheless, that this may be a false dichotomy. It is more in keeping with the facts, according to him, that the professional has much the same motivation as the businessperson. What is different is the institutional structure: the professions are explicitly designed to serve society, and the structure of the profession is such as to encourage this. Thus, virtually all professions have codes of ethics that emphasize public service.

For further definitions of the term "profession" and for analyses of the problems and implications of various definitions, see Barber (1966: 18), Blanck (1963: 31), Cogan (1955), Gilb (1966: 27), Goode (1966), Greenwood (1966), Laski (1935), Lippitt and This (1962), Massarik (1972), Moore (1970), and Peterson (1976).

8. Several other descriptions of how professions develop are worthy of note. Massarik (1972), in his analysis of whether encounter group leaders constitute a distinct professional group, has borrowed a paradigm from Friedrichs. He posits six stages of professional growth. In Stage 1, *inchoate origins*, the professional is practicing something that he or she is not sure of. The practice is quite experimental, there may be some risk involved, and there is no definitive explanation or knowledge of why practitioners are effective. The number of people involved in practice is extremely small. In the second stage, *initial, limited expansion*, the profession begins to attract more followers and becomes more visible, gaining a sense of identity. Stage 3, the *developing struggle*, continues this process, but now there are definite attacks upon the profession, and other threatened professions take pains to denigrate it. The attacks take the form of law suits, critical articles in the press pointing out certain instances of harm, charlatanry, and the like, and the breaking away of small groups or sects within the newly developing profession. This stage is followed by a fourth, *forced maturity*, in which the profession becomes concerned with normative, self-regulatory issues. This concern eventually leads to Stage 5, *responsible maturity*, in which there is a continuing concern with effectiveness and an effort to develop and maintain standards of practice and ethics. The profession is highly and strongly organized. Finally, there comes a sixth stage of *decline and demise*, in which the profession disintegrates because of challenges from newly created profes-

sions or from other external causes, such as the changing needs and aspirations of the public the profession is serving. Massarik cites examples of this evolution in the rise of Freudian psychoanalysis as a challenge to traditional turn-of-the-century medicine and neurology, and the subsequent rise of humanistic psychotherapy as an alternative to psychoanalytic therapy.

Blanck (1963: 160–61) has conducted a sociological study of the development of medicine as a profession and found a series of phases with fairly concrete identifying characteristics. The first phase involved medicine's differentiation from other professions: first from theology after the Reformation, and lately from other such rivals as chiropody and optometry. The second phase is concerned with the system of education for the profession. Blanck divides this into the following stages:

a. The practice of the craft or profession on the basis of inheritance, aptitude, or propensity.
b. The establishment of an apprentice system.
c. The seeking of more complete education in Europe.
d. The private seminar as a transitional form of education.
e. The formalization of the private seminar into a more institutional type of education, in the case of medicine, giving rise to the proprietary school.
f. Integration with the university system of education.

The third phase of professional development involves the creation and emergence of professional organizations, centralized and on a national level. Finally, there comes legal recognition of the profession, with licensure the ultimate symbol of highest recognition. Blanck argues that each profession must pass through these stages sequentially; according to her, the attempt to seek licensure or other legal recognition prematurely is detrimental to the development of a profession.

Goode (1960: 903) has also reviewed the most commonly cited definitions of what constitutes a profession to determine its essential attributes. He concludes that the two most important characteristics are a "prolonged specialized training in a body of abstract knowledge, and a collectivity or service orientation" (Goode, 1960: 903). In addition, as occupations become more professionalized they tend to possess more and more of the following highly specific traits:

1. The profession determines its own standards of education and training.
2. The student professional goes through a more far-reaching adult socialization experience than the learner in other occupations.
3. Professional practice is often legally recognized by some form of licensure.
4. Licensing and admission boards are made up of members of the profession.
5. Most legislation concerned with the profession is shaped by that profession.
6. The occupation gains in income, power, and prestige ranking, and can demand higher caliber students.
7. The practitioner is relatively free of lay evaluation and control.
8. The norms of practice enforced by the profession are more stringent than legal controls.
9. Members are more strongly identified and affiliated with the profession than are members of other occupations with theirs.

10. The profession is more likely to be a terminal occupation. Members do not care to leave it, and a higher proportion assert that if they had it to do over again, they would again choose that type of work.

9. For references other than those discussed in the text concerning the development of psychotherapy as a profession, see Henry, Sims, and Spray (1971) (discusses and analyzes research results from personal interviews and survey responses of more than 4,000 practicing professionals); Henry, Sims, and Spray (1973) (advocates the formation of a single profession of psychotherapy with its own training program); Kubie (1971, 1964, 1954) (Kubie has written extensively on this subject and for years has advocated the formation of a new profession of "medical psychology" that would be set within the framework of the modern medical school); Shakow (1969) (the author has played a major role in the development of psychology as a profession); see also Abroms and Greenfield (1973); Armstrong (1947); Goode (1960); Zinberg (1965); and Peterson (1976).

10. Several exceptions to this exist. For a long time the Sloan School of Management at M.I.T. sponsored sequences of courses to develop competency as a group leader. Other centers, such as the well-known and well-respected Boston University Human Relation Center, have offered courses to improve group leadership skills. One of the more innovative programs in the country was developed by Dr. Malcolm Knowles within the Boston University Adult Education Program in the Department of Administration and Supervision of the School of Education. This consisted of a two-year sequence of courses, both theoretical and practical, designed to develop competency as a leader of T-groups. Unfortunately the program has not been continued. One of the few programs designed to train group leaders within a psychology department has been developed by Dr. Martin Lakin at Duke, where he is coordinator of the Group Processes and Sensitivity Training Center.

11. The history of professions in Western society has received very little extended treatment. The best histories to date have been provided by Carr-Saunders (1928); Carr-Saunders and Wilson (1933); Schlesinger (1944); and Webb and Webb (1917). The writings of Sigerist (1960, 1934) provide an excellent source of information on the early history of the medical profession and form the basis for much of the material contained in this section.

12. For descriptions of these features and comparisons with modern professional groups, see De Lancey (1938); Friedman (1962); Gellhorn (1956); Gilb (1966); Grant (1942, 1942a); Levin (1974, 1971, 1970); and Lieberman (1970).

13. The only medically related group that is barred from the practice of medicine are nonlicensed midwives, since the Midwives Registration Act forbids "any woman, not being a certified midwife, from habitually and for gain attending women in childbirth otherwise than under the direction of a qualified medical practitioner" (Webb and Webb, 1917: 42). England also has laws against the prescribing of certain narcotic drugs except by those on the Medical Register. The fact that a layperson has the right to perform surgery, however, does not mean that this happens often. The socialized nature of British medicine and the fact that only those patients who are treated by a practitioner on the Medical Register receive these services at the expense of the government ensure that only the very rich are likely to visit a nonregistered doctor.

14. The following books and articles give a good overview of medical regulation in the United States: Derbyshire (1973) (builds on the monumental work of Richard Shryock and takes up where his work ended, covering the period from 1965 to the present); Caldwell (1923); Kett (1968) (a very insightful analysis of the early developments in the regulation of U.S. medicine, with interesting conclusions about the efficacy of licensing, the value of the early proprietary schools, and the impact of medical societies); M. Roemer (1970) (outlines the underlying conditions for medical care quality, such as maintenance of a safe environment, and then looks into the operations of the

medical care system, examining the following regulatory mechanisms: personnel standards, facility standards, control of drugs and appliances, organizational frameworks, geographic regionalization, and comprehensive health planning); R. Roemer (1970) (discusses the multiple means of regulating health personnel, from state and federal licensing to voluntary mechanisms, including professional associations, and examines the problems involved in effectively using paraprofessionals); Shryock (1967) (the most authoritative text on medical regulation through licensing in this country); and Sigerist (1934).

15. The first medical school was not established in America until 1765 (Shryock, 1967: 16), and it was not until the end of the next decade that a law professorship was established at William and Mary (Council of State Governments, 1952: 14).

16. The AMA lauded the strict standards that existed for licensing physicians in European countries, but ignored the fact that the European system relegated the general practice of medicine to apothecaries and barber-surgeons, who had little if any formal training and were certainly no better prepared and no more capable than their American counterparts.

REFERENCES

Abroms, G.M., and Greenfield, N.S. "A New Mental Health Profession." *Psychiatry*, 1973, v. 36, pp. 10-22.

American Heritage Publishing Co. *The American Heritage Dictionary of the English Language.* (Edited by W. Morris.) Boston: American Heritage Publishing Co.; Houghton Mifflin, 1973.

American Psychological Association and Conference of State Psychological Associations, Committees on Legislation. "Joint Report of the APA and CSPA Committees on Legislation." *American Psychologist*, 1955, v. 10, pp. 727-56.

Armstrong, C.P. "On Defining Psychology as a Profession." *American Psychologist*, 1947, v. 2, pp. 446-48.

Austin, J. *The Province of Jurisprudence Determined.* 1832. Reprint. London: Weidenfeld and Nicolson, 1954.

Black, H.C. *Black's Law Dictionary.* (4th ed.) (Revised by Publisher's Editorial Staff.) St. Paul, Minn.: West Publishing Co., 1968.

Barber, B. "Some Problems in the Sociology of the Professions." In K.S. Lynn and the Editors of Daedalus (Eds.), *The Professions in America.* Boston: Houghton Mifflin, 1965, pp. 15-34.

Benne, K.D.; Bradford, L.P.; Gibb, J.R.; and Lippitt, R.O. (Eds.) *The Laboratory Method of Changing and Learning: Theory and Application.* Palo Alto, Calif.: Science and Behavior Books, 1975.

Blanck, G.S. "The Development of Psychotherapy as a Profession: A Study of the Process of Professionalization." Ph.D. dissertation, New York University, 1963. Abstracted in *Dissertation Abstracts*, 1963, v. 24(07), p. 2974.

Bradford, L.P.; Gibb, J.R.; and Benne, K.D. "A Look to the Future." In L.P. Bradford, J.R. Gibb, and K.D. Benne (Eds.), *T-Group Theory and Laboratory Method: Innovation and Re-education.* New York: John Wiley, 1964, pp. 477-86.

Brandeis, L.D. *Business—A Profession.* (Foreword by E. Poole.) Boston: Small, Maynard, 1914.

Business Week. "How Licensing Hurts Consumers." *Business Week*, November 28, 1977, pp. 127-29.

Caldwell, L.G. "Early Legislation Regulating the Practice of Medicine." *Illinois Law Review*, 1923, v. 18, pp. 225-44.

Carlson, R.J. "Health Manpower Licensing and the Emerging Institutional Responsibility for the Quality of Care." *Law and Contemporary Problems*, 1970, v. 35, pp. 849-78.

Carr-Saunders, A.M. "Professionalization in Historical Perspective." In H.M. Vollmer and D.L. Mills (Eds.), *Professionalization*. Englewood Cliffs, N.J.: Prentice-Hall, 1966, pp. 3–9.

Carr-Saunders, A.M., and Wilson, P.A. *The Professions*. 1933. Reprint. London: Cass, 1964.

Cogan, M.L. "The Problem of Defining a Profession." *Annals of the American Academy of Political and Social Science*, 1955, v. 297, pp. 105–11.

Corpus Juris Secundum. "Profession." *Corpus Juris Secundum*, 1956, v. 72, pp. 1215–20.

Council of State Governments. *Occupational Licensing Legislation in the States: A Study of State Legislation Licensing the Practice of Professions and Other Occupations*. Chicago: Council of State Governments, 1952.

De Lancy, F.P. *The Licensing of Professions in West Virginia*. Chicago: Foundation Press, 1938.

Derbyshire, R.C. "Professional Licensure, Organizational Behavior, and the Public Interest: Comment." *Milbank Memorial Fund Quarterly*, 1973, v. 51, pp. 89–93.

Derbyshire, R.C. *Medical Licensure and Discipline in the United States*. Baltimore, Md.: Johns Hopkins Press, 1969.

Freund, P.A. "The Legal Profession." In K.S. Lynn and the Editors of Daedalus (Eds.), *The Professions in America*. Boston: Houghton Mifflin, 1965, pp. 35–46.

Friedman, M. *Capitalism and Freedom*. Chicago: University of Chicago Press, 1962.

Fuller, L.L. "Human Interaction and the Law." *American Journal of Jurisprudence*, 1969, v. 14, pp. 1–36.

Garceau, O. *The Political Life of the American Medical Association*. Cambridge, Mass.: Harvard University Press, 1941.

Gellhorn, W. *Individual Freedom and Governmental Restraints*. Baton Rouge, La.: Louisiana State University Press, 1956.

Gilb, C.L. *Hidden Hierarchies: The Professions and Government*. New York: Harper and Row, 1966.

Goode, W.J. "'Professions' and 'Non-professions.'" In H.M. Vollmer and D.L. Mills (Eds.), *Professionalization*. Englewood Cliffs, N.J.: Prentice-Hall, 1966, pp. 34–43.

Goode, W.J. "Encroachment, Charlatanism, and the Emerging Profession: Psychology, Sociology, and Medicine." *American Sociological Review*, 1960, v. 25, pp. 902–14.

Goode, W.J. "Community Within a Community: The Professions." *American Sociological Review*, 1957, v. 22, pp. 194–200.

Grant, J.A.C. "The Gild Returns to America: Part I." *Journal of Politics*, 1942, v. 4, pp. 303–36.

Grant, J.A.C. "The Gild Returns to America: Part II." *Journal of Politics*, 1942a, v. 4, pp. 458–77.

Greenwood, E. "The Elements of Professionalization." In H.M. Vollmer and D.L. Mills (Eds.), *Professionalization*. Englewood Cliffs, N.N.: Prentice-Hall, 1966, pp. 10–19. Reprinted from "Attributes of a Profession." *Social Work*, 1957, v. 2(3), pp. 44–55.

Hart, H.L.A. *The Concept of Law*. Oxford, England: Clarendon Press, 1961.

Henry, W.E.; Sims, J.H.; and Spray, S.L. *Public and Private Lives of Psychotherapists*. San Francisco, Calif.: Jossey-Bass, 1973.

Henry, W.E.; Sims, J.H.; and Spray, S.L. *The Fifth Profession: Becoming a Psychotherapist*. San Francisco, Calif.: Jossey-Bass, 1971.

Hyde, D.R., and Wolff, P. "The American Medical Association: Power, Purpose, and Politics in Organized Medicine." *Yale Law Journal*, 1954, v. 63, pp. 938–1022.

Inglis, B. *Fringe Medicine*. London: Faber and Faber, 1964.

Kelsen, H. *General Theory of Law and State*. (Translated by A. Wedberg.) Cambridge, Mass.: Harvard University Press, 1945.

Kett, J.F. *The Formation of the American Medical Profession, 1780–1860*. New Haven, Conn.: Yale University Press, 1968.

Kubie, L.S. "A Doctorate in Psychotherapy: The Reasons for a New Profession." In R.R. Holt (Ed.), *New Horizon for Psychotherapy: Autonomy as a Profession.* New York: International Universities Press, 1971, pp. 11-36.

Kubie, L.S. "A School of Psychological Medicine Within the Framework of a Medical School and University." *Journal of Medical Education,* 1964, v. 39, pp. 476-80.

Kubie, L.S. "The Pros and Cons of a New Profession: A Doctorate in Medical Psychology." *Texas Report on Biology and Medicine,* 1954, v. 12, pp. 692-737. Reprinted in M. Harrower (Ed.), *Medical and Psychological Teamwork in the Care of the Chronically Ill.* Springfield, Ill.: Charles C. Thomas, 1955, pp. 125-70.

Laski, H.J. "The Decline of the Professions." *Harper's Magazine,* November 1935, pp. 676-85.

Levin, T. "Humanizing Health Care." *Social Policy,* 1974, v. 4(5), pp. 49-56.

Levin, T. "Professionalism and Guildism in Health Manpower." *Bulletin of the New York Academy of Medicine,* 1971, v. 47, pp. 382-92.

Levin, T. "Social Policy and Guild Policy in Health Manpower." *Bulletin of the New York Academy of Medicine,* 1970, v. 46, pp. 1112-19.

Lieberman, J.K. *The Tyranny of the Experts: How Professionals Are Closing the Open Society.* New York: Walker, 1970.

Lippitt, R.L.; Benne, K.D.; Bradford, L.; and Gibb, J. "The Professionalization of Laboratory Practice." In K.D. Benne, L.P. Bradford, J.R. Gibb, and R.L. Lippitt (Eds.), *The Laboratory Method of Changing and Learning: Theory and Applications.* Palo Alto, Calif.: Science and Behavior Books, 1975, pp. 471-90.

Lippitt, R.L., and This, L.E. "Is Training a Profession?" In I.R. Weschler and E.H. Schein (Eds.), *Issues in Human Relations Training.* Washington, D.C.: National Training Laboratories, 1962, pp. 114-21.

Lynn, K.S., and the Editors of Daedalus. (Eds.) *The Professions in America.* Boston: Houghton Mifflin, 1965.

Massarik, F. "Standards for Group Leadership." In L.N. Solomon and B. Berzon (Eds.), *New Perspectives on Encounter Groups.* San Francisco: Jossey-Bass, 1972, pp. 68-82.

Moore, W.E. *The Professions: Roles and Rules.* New York: Russell Sage, 1970.

Parsons, T. "Professions." In D.L. Sills (Ed.), *International Encyclopedia of the Social Sciences.* (Vol. 12.) New York: Macmillan Publishing Co., 1968, pp. 536-47.

Parsons, T. "The Professions and Social Structure." *Social Forces,* 1939, v. 17, pp. 457-67.

Peterson, I. "Albany Bomb Scare and Party Slow Court-Reform Bill." *New York Times,* June 24, 1976.

Pound, R. "The Professions in the Society of Today." *New England Journal of Medicine,* 1949, v. 241, pp. 351-57.

Rayack, E. *Professional Power and American Medicine: The Economics of the American Medical Association.* Cleveland, Ohio: World Publishing Co., 1967.

Reiff, R. "The Control of Knowledge: The Power of the Helping Professions." *Journal of Applied Behavioral Science,* 1974, v. 10, pp. 451-61.

Roemer, M.I. "Controlling and Promoting Quality in Medical Care." In C.C. Havighurst, "Health Care: Part I." (Special issue.) *Law and Contemporary Problems,* 1970, v. 35, pp. 284-304.

Roemer, R. "Legal and Other Institutional Impediments to Realignment of Health Service Functions." In American Medical Association, National Congress on Health Manpower, *Expanding the Supply of Health Services in the 1970's.* (Sponsored by The Council on Health Manpower.) Chicago: American Medical Association, 1970, pp. 43-64.

Sanford, F.H. "The Criteria of a Good Profession." *American Psychologist,* 1951, v. 6, pp. 668-70.

Schein, E.H., and Bennis, W.G. *Personal and Organizational Change Through Group Methods: The Laboratory Approach.* New York: John Wiley, 1965.

Schlesinger, A.M. "Biography of a Nation of Joiners." *American Historical Review,* 1944, v. 50, pp. 1–25.

Shakow, D. *Clinical Psychology as Science and Profession: A 40-Year Odyssey.* Chicago: Aldine, 1969.

Shindell, S. "A Survey of the Law of Medical Practice." *Journal of the American Medical Association,* 1965, v. 193, pp. 601–6.

Shryock, R.H. *Medical Licensing in America, 1650–1965.* Baltimore, Md.: Johns Hopkins Press, 1967.

Sigerist, H.E. *Henry E. Sigerist on the History of Medicine.* (Edited by F. Marti-Ibanez.) New York: MD Publications, 1960.

Sigerist, H.E. *American Medicine.* New York: W.W. Norton, 1934.

Tancredi, L.R., and Woods, J. "The Social Control of Medical Practice: Licensure Versus Output Monitoring." *Milbank Memorial Fund Quarterly,* 1972, v. 50, pp. 99–125.

Webb, B., and Webb, S. "Special Supplement on Professional Associations." *New Statesman,* April 21, 1917 (Supp.), pp. 1–48.

Whitehead, A.N. *Adventures of Ideas.* 1933. Reprint. New York: Macmillan Publishing Co., 1961.

Young, R.H. "Medical Examining and Licensing." *Federation Bulletin,* 1970, v. 57, pp. 234–50.

Zinberg, N.E. "Psychiatry: A Professional Dilemma." In K.S. Lynn and the Editors of Daedalus (Eds.), *The Professions in America.* Boston: Houghton Mifflin, 1965, pp. 154–69.

Chapter 7

Statutory Regulation through Licensure

Although statutory regulation of the professions may take many forms, licensure has been the basic vehicle used in the United States. The primary purpose of licensing laws has been to protect the public health, morals, safety, and general welfare. (Council of State Governments, 1952:1). Licensing attempts to accomplish this by eliminating quacks, charlatans, incompetents, and unethical practitioners from the field,[1] which is done through strict entrance requirements, enforcing discipline, and preventing unlicensed practice.

Generically, licensure is an example of government control through administrative regulation, as opposed to regulation by the judicial, legislative, or executive branches of government.[2] Administrative law requires government regulatory agencies to carry out its functions. These are created and governed by constitutional law, statutory law, common law, and agency-made law (Davis, 1972: Ch. 1). The importance of administrative bodies and their potential power to achieve regulation is attested to by Mr. Justice Jackson:

The rise of administrative bodies probably has been the most significant legal trend of the last century and perhaps more values today are affected by their decisions than by those of all the courts, review of administrative decisions apart. They also have begun to have important consequences on personal rights. They have become a veritable fourth branch of the Government, which has deranged our three-branch legal theories much as the concept of a fourth dimension unsettles our three-dimensional thinking. [*FTC v. Ruberoid Co.*, 343 U.S. 470 (1952) at 487 (dissenting opinion) (citations omitted).]

SALIENT FEATURES OF LICENSING LAWS

Terminology

Terminology in the field of licensing is confusing. To illustrate the definitional problems involved, laws that forbid people from practicing without a license have been referred to as licensing laws, mandatory licensing, and practice acts, while laws that only forbid the use of titles have been termed certification laws, permissive licenses, or title acts. Both types are frequently referred to as licensing or licensure laws. In addition, laws that do not require a practitioner to meet certain standards but do make registration mandatory are termed registration laws, and are also generally considered a form of licensure.

For the sake of consistency and conceptual clarity, laws that forbid the practice of a profession without a license, and require meeting certain minimum standards, will be termed practice acts. Laws that require meeting certain minimum standards to use certain titles, but which do not restrict the right to practice, will be referred to as title acts. Those laws that only require registration with a state agency and do not demand the successful completion of an examination or the meeting of other minimum requirements will be referred to as registration laws. Licensing and licensure will be used interchangeably and will include both title and practice acts and registration.[3] The term "certification" will be reserved for nongovernment associations and their efforts to determine whether practitioners have met certain standards of competence, which may either be minimal or maximal. Accreditation will be defined as the process a governmental or nongovernmental agency undertakes to determine whether an academic or nonacademic training institution or program meets certain predetermined standards.

The Proper Purposes and Functions of Licensure

As previously mentioned, the basic function of licensing has been to protect the public health, morals, safety, and general welfare. Since licensing laws provide for criminal penalties, a further purpose is to exact societal retribution for undesirable behavior. To carry out these purposes, licensing laws perform three functions: (1) they establish entry requirements that must be met before a person enters the field; (2) they make provisions for disciplining wayward licentiates; and (3) they empower appropriate authorities to prevent unlicensed practice or title usage.

Although not their express purpose and perhaps not in the public interest, licensing laws also serve other functions. It is well recognized, for example, that licensing laws promote the economic well-being of the profession regulated.

In fact, they may have been enacted with that purpose expressly in mind (Gellhorn, 1956; Moore, 1961; Stevens, 1973). The justification for this is that the quality of services would deteriorate otherwise. Related to this is the effort to enhance and protect the reputation of the profession. Professional associations believe that statutory regulation is a symbol of respectability and demonstrates that the profession is well established (Monaghan, 1961). With such recognition, professionals claim that they have less difficulty in attracting high-caliber recruits (see, for instance, the American Psychological Association and Conference of State Psychological Associations, 1955). Some argue that legal regulation helps define a professional field more clearly.[4] Licensing laws may also be used to control the number and geographic distribution of practitioners in a profession (see Rayack, 1975).

Although the clear purpose of licensure is only to protect the public from harm (and a case can be made that anything more is a violation of the Constitution), most licensing laws have entry requirements beyond what is necessary. In the early days of licensing, entry requirements were meant to establish minimal competence. Today, however, most professions have promoted laws or amendments to existing laws that ensure as high a level of competence as possible. The rationale seems to be that the public must be protected from any chance of being harmed by a practitioner *at all*. In addition, such a policy has the advantage of promoting the prestige and economic well-being of a profession.

Despite vigorous assertions to the contrary, it is debatable whether the public is actually being protected, since the harmful side effects of licensing laws usually outweigh their supposed benefits. In fact, a central thesis of this book is that licensing laws are a significant factor in: (1) unnecessarily restricting the supply of practitioners; (2) decreasing their geographic mobility; (3) inflating the cost of services; (4) making it difficult for paraprofessionals to perform effectively; (5) stifling innovations in the education and training of practitioners and in the organization and utilization of services; and (6) discriminating against minorities, women, the poor, and the aged. In addition, licensing laws, as currently conceived, tend to promote unnecessary and harmful consumer dependence, since their implicit philosophy is that the public is incapable of making use of information to decide on practitioner competence.

The attempt to ensure that practitioners will rarely, if ever, cause harm lies at the heart of the problem. This policy needs revision. While it is true that the public needs protection from quacks, it also needs protection from the harmful side effects of licensing. Because of this, the theory that protection from harm is best achieved by allowing only the most highly qualified professionals to practice deserves reconsideration.

Very different standards would be deemed relevant if the goal of licensing were only protection from harm. Instead of long years of training, licensing boards would, among other things, look for whether practitioners knew their limitations. Licenses might be granted to persons who were only competent in one small area, so long as they could be depended upon not to misapply their skill.

An argument can even be made that minimal competence is not a valid standard for licensing boards, since the relevant question is whether a practitioner might cause harm, rather than do the job well. In other words, based on a philosophy of preventing harm, a license might be granted to a person who was not competent at all, as long as the person was not dangerous.

Whether the yardstick for determining licensing standards is defined as non-dangerousness, minimal competence, or maximum competence, the critical factor is the balancing of benefits against unintended, but negative, side effects. Based on Fuller's interactive view of the law, this requires a reformulation of the purpose of licensing. Whereas the current purpose is simply to protect the public from harm caused by practitioners, the preferred policy is to protect the public from harm in general, whether or not incurred by a practitioner. Such a policy requires an examination and weighing of the unintended and potentially deleterious side effects of licensing. The ultimate purpose of licensing, then, is to protect the public from harm, while at the same time making sure that the public has an adequate supply and easy access to reasonably competent and nondiscriminatory services provided at a reasonable cost.[5]

Administration

Since their inception, licensing laws have generally been administered by independent licensing agencies (Council of State Governments, 1952: 29). The typical pattern is for each occupation to establish a separate board for its own regulation. In some cases, as with dental hygienists, another board controls licensure. In the late forties and early fifties the first efforts were made to provide uniformity and coordination in the functioning of licensing boards, especially through the adoption of administrative procedures acts. Nonetheless, in the health field more than half of the almost-800 state licensing boards remained autonomous as of the mid-sixties (U.S. National Center for Health Statistics, 1968: 7). Those that are centralized are generally located within a Department of Registration, Department of Health, or State Department of Education. In a minority of instances, licensing laws are administered through a larger state agency that does not provide for any professional licensing board.

Licensing boards are by and large composed of professionals from within the field licensed, except where a sub-profession (such as licensed practical nurses) is controlled by a more dominant profession (Coleman, 1970, and see U.S. National Center for Health Statistics, 1968: 9). As of mid-century roughly three fourths of all licensing boards were composed *exclusively* of members of the regulated group. Since then the consumer movement has placed some public members on certain boards, so that by the late sixties only half of all licensing boards were composed solely of members of the regulated profession. California has led the way in this regard.

The method by which board members are selected plays an important part in the functioning of the licensing board. Most laws place ultimate responsibility in the hands of the governor of the state. Many laws require a governor to select from a list submitted by the local professional association. Others require the governor to consider such a list, without demanding that the final choice be made from it, although in the earlier part of this century such practices were quite common.[6] In some instances, professional associations have managed to pass legislation allowing the association itself to directly select the board (Grant, 1942: 322).

Either directly or indirectly, associations exert considerable influence on licensing boards.[7] The National Advisory Commission on Health Manpower (U.S. National Advisory Commission on Health Manpower, 1967: II, 296–97) found that state governors must still appoint medical licensing boards from lists submitted by state medical societies in the great majority of states, without giving the society sole power to select board members. Even where no statutory provision exists, many state governors have a policy of consulting the appropriate professional associations before making appointments (U.S. National Center for Health Statistics, 1968: 9), and the professional associations themselves frequently exert political pressure in this regard (Rayack, 1975).

Various justifications for this state of affairs have been offered, including the necessity of preventing political patronage, the importance of ensuring competent, well-qualified board members, the guarantee of expert understanding concerning the problems faced by practitioners, and the importance of developing close cooperation between the state and the profession (Council of State Governments, 1952: 38). On the other hand, arguments have been made that government functions should not be performed by private associations, that professionals may not always find the public interest in their own interest, and that such members have very little accountability to the public (Council of State Governments, 1952: Derbyshire, 1969: 34–5).

For the most part licensing boards are self-sustaining, that is, they receive no funds from the state and generate their income from the fees charged for various licenses and examinations. Each board is authorized to perform certain functions as specified in the enabling legislation, which generally include the development of rules and regulations, the enforcement of discipline, and the prevention of illegal practice. Violations of the licensing laws are usually classified as a misdemeanor, and punishment may consist of a small fine or imprisonment for a period of usually less than a year. Disciplinary violations generally give the board the right to censure practitioners or suspend or revoke their license.

Problems in Definitions of Practice and Delegation of Authority

Perhaps the most critical aspect of a licensing law is its definition of what constitutes professional practice, especially where a law forbids such practice without a license. Typically, statutory language prohibits unlicensed practitioners from performing, offering to perform, or holding themselves out as performing certain functions without the required license. Exemptions are generally made for various groups, such as federal and armed service personnel, and professionals in related fields who perform similar work as part of their own profession.[8]

Definitions of practice are usually both broad and vague. There are several reasons for this. Broad definitions are said to offer the most comprehensive protection to the public. Since the nature of professional practice in many fields tends to change over time, vagueness allows for an expansion of functions without the need for legislative amendments. Perhaps the best explanation for broad and vague definitions, however, is simply the difficulty of framing more precise ones. Even in the medical field, the various states cannot agree on a common definition, with some state's efforts running nearly 200 words and others being as brief as 30.

The difficulties of formulating precise definitions creates serious problems that may rise to constitutional proportions. When a law is broadly defined, determining whether a particular activity falls within its purview can prove extremely difficult. This becomes critical when several professional groups claim the right to perform the same activity, and often the claims of public protection take on economic overtones. The Arizona legal profession provides a case in point (Lieberman, 1970: 31).[9] The Arizona bar claimed that it had the sole right to draft and use a variety of real estate documents, including contracts to purchase property and rental agreements. This claim was made despite the fact that it had long been the practice of real estate and land title companies to perform these functions through the use of standardized printed documents. The Arizona Supreme Court decided in favor of the lawyers, and a constitutional amendment was required to permit the real estate profession to continue their past practices.

Broad licensing laws may also inhibit paraprofessionals from performing various functions that are quite within their capacity. In the health field this has proved to be a particular impediment.

Medical practice acts, for instance, frequently stipulate that only physicians may "prescribe" or "furnish" drugs, while pharmacists are only allowed to "dispense" them, and nurses may only "administer" them. The courts have not hesitated to convict different professional groups in the health field of illegal medical practice, even where such practice is customary in the community (see, e.g., *Barber v. Reinking* [1966]). Naturally, allied health professionals have become hesitant to undertake new responsibilities without legislative clearance.

Prohibitions against practicing without a license in broadly defined fields of practice have created other serious problems, the major one of which is the ability of professionals to delegate various tasks and functions to assistants and paraprofessionals. As of 1967 this was considered the major problem of medical licensure by leading experts in the health field (see Forgotson et al., 1967: 432–33; Willig, 1971: 149). Prior to the 1960s no state had explicit provisions for such delegation. While the doctrine of "custom and usage" supposedly established the right of a physician to delegate, malpractice suits and criminal actions for illegal medical practice, though few in number, discouraged physicians from delegating responsibility without clear legislative approval. As a result of the recommendations of the National Advisory Commission on Health Manpower, many states have since enacted some form of delegation amendment, including the many physician assistant laws of recent vintage.

THE CURRENT EXTENT OF PROFESSIONAL AND OCCUPATIONAL LICENSURE

Licensing laws are now estimated to affect directly a third to a fifth of the work force (*Behavior Today*, 1976). According to the U.S. Department of Labor, 25 percent of the employed labor force in some states is composed of licensed practitioners (*Business Week*, 1977: 127). As of 1969, roughly 10 percent of the national income of the United States originated in occupationally licensed labor markets (Carroll and Gaston, 1977: 2). The number of licensed professions or occupations has reached the 500 mark (see U.S. Department of Labor, 1969: Appendix C), up from the 73 occupations that were licensed in one or more states as of 1950 (Council of State Governments, 1952: 7–8, 28). The passage of legislation has been so rapid that by 1970 the health field alone licensed 30 different occupational groups, with 12 regulated in all states (U.S. DHEW, 1971: 136).

This trend has continued unabated.[10] Despite an HEW moratorium on licensure (U.S. DHEW, 1971: 73), which was supported by a variety of professional associations, nearly thirty new laws were enacted in 1974 in the health field alone (U.S. DHEW, 1975: 6). According to recent study by the Department of Labor (U.S. Department of Labor, 1969), almost 5,000 different licenses are granted across the country, which averages out to 100 per state. California and Illinois are the leaders, licensing more than 175 occupations each.

Seemingly few groups are not licensed in one state or another. The following sampling from a Department of Labor study (U.S. Department of Labor, 1969: Appendix C) illustrates the wide range:

Aerial horsehunters
Athletic exhibition agents
Alligator hunters
Astrologers
Bedding cleaners
Quail breeders
Ice cream buyers
Cactus plant agents
Antifreeze dealers
Junk dealers
Dog training area operators
Fortune-tellers, clairvoyants, and palmists
Handlers of frozen desserts

Installment paper purchasers
Moving picture operators
Photographers
Rainmakers
Cemetery sales people
Toy salespeople
Tattoo artists
Tree experts
Weatherpeople
Wildlife exhibit managers

At least with some of these occupations one can wonder whether a license is necessary to protect the public. In some cases it seems clear that the group seeking licensure is simply attempting to ensure its own economic well-being. An interesting example of this is the "maintenance gardeners" of California (Hetherington, 1958: 249). They introduced a bill into the California assembly that would have required a license of anybody who wanted to mow lawns for money, including the neighbor's son or daughter. The fine for disobeying went as high as $500, with potential imprisonment of six months. Luckily, this bill failed; this, however, is the exception rather than the rule. Until recently most professions have not had a great deal of difficulty in convincing legislatures of the need to protect the public from those without the proper credentials.

Once a law has been passed, it is rarely taken off the statute books, and the courts will only act occasionally to overturn such legislation. This did occur in North Carolina, however, where the legislature passed a law in 1937 requiring all those who wished to lay, set, or install tile, marble, and terrazzo floors and walls to first obtain a license (Hanft and Hamrick, 1938). The law established rigid criteria for admission into the newly created profession. A candidate must have at least two years' experience in tile laying, possess knowledge to specify the proper kind of materials, have the ability to install these materials in accordance with specifications and blueprints, and pass an examination administered by the North Carolina Licensing Board for Tile Contractors. Interestingly enough, those who were practicing tile laying on the date of enactment of the law could receive a license automatically, and the act did not apply to contracts of less than $150 nor to work done in state buildings. The justification for this law was that it was necessary to protect the public health. Twenty years later the state supreme court decided that the law had nothing to do with protecting the public, but everything to do with creating a monopoly:

It is doubtful whether any other licensing agency has been granted the facilities for such tight and absolute control over any profession or business. The licensing board has the power to make a monopoly out of an industry which one of the defendants' witnesses described as having grown "into a major segment of today's construction business." [*Roller v. Allen*, 245 N.C. 516, 96 S.E.2d 851, 857 (1957).]

In commenting upon the entrance requirements and the need for extensive experience, the court said:

Nothing in the record shows that a man of average intelligence and some aptitude for such work cannot learn quickly enough to do average work. Successful tile contracting consists in doing the work rather than describing it in a written examination paper. In all probability the average worker could learn to do acceptable tile work as quickly as he can learn to describe it on paper. [92 S.E.2d at 857.]

Licensure laws can be divided into two categories, depending on whether the law was initiated by the occupation or profession itself ("friendly" licensure) or by a group antagonistic to the group being licensed ("hostile" licensure) (Friedman, 1965: 475–76). Examples of the latter include many of the licensure laws applicable to the allied health professions. In many states, for example, licensed practical nurses are regulated by a board composed solely of registered nurses. Typically, with hostile laws it is either a superior or rival professional group that initiates the law to curtail the development of the rival profession. This usually happens in an occupation that has hazy limits or which overlaps with other related occupations.

In most cases, however, the profession itself is the one to seek legislation. Rarely, if ever, does a legislature license an occupation as a result of complaints raised by the public or specific consumers of the occupation's services (Blanck, 1963: 137; Caldwell, 1923: 228; Davis, 1972: 5; Gilb, 1966: 228; Hanft and Hamrick, 1938: 4, Moore, 1961: 93; U.S. DHEW, 1971: 30). Since few organized groups exist that might be opposed to licensing, it is not difficult for a profession to have itself licensed. Only when another professional group is threatened is there likely to be a legislative fight, as when the New York State psychologists attempted to pass a psychological practice act in the early fifties, thus incurring the wrath of the medical profession, which waged an all-out war to prevent its passage.

Along with the tendency for more laws, several other trends have become apparent with regard to licensure. First, once a specific occupation achieves licensing in several states, it is not long before most states license that occupation.[11] As an example, in 1903 New York and Virginia became the first states to license nurses. Merely thirteen years later forty states had enacted similar laws, eight being passed in the year 1909 alone (Council of State Governments, 1952: Table 1). This process is facilitated if state associations, supported by a well-organized and vigorous national association, exist. A second trend is the tendency of states to amend their original laws from title-protection acts to laws forbidding practice without a license. The licensing laws regulating nurses provide an excellent example of this inclination. While most of the early acts protected only the title "registered nurse," current laws cover both that title and specific practices, as well.

A LEGAL ANALYSIS OF THE APPLICABILITY OF CURRENT LICENSING LAWS TO PSYCHOTHERAPY*

Whether a given licensing law includes the practice of psychotherapy within its definition of practice is often difficult to answer. Even where expressly included, the question remains as to what specific practices are involved. When psychotherapy is not expressly mentioned, the broad language of the statute may still imply it. From a legal standpoint, four vehicles are available to determine individual cases. First, the legislature may clarify a particular law through amendment. Second, the courts may interpret the provisions of the law through decisions in litigated cases. Third, licensing boards may issue rules or regulations further defining what constitutes professional practice. Finally, the office of the attorney general may issue an opinion in response to the request of a petitioner.

Psychotherapy as the Practice of Psychology

In the case of psychology, little doubt exists as to the inclusion of psychotherapy within most statutory law. More than half of all state licensing laws expressly include it, with seven elaborating what constitutes therapy. An additional fifteen states consider counseling as part of the practice of psychology, while the remainder have definitions of practice so broad that psychotherapy would un-

*This section constitutes a condensed summary of the information contained in Chapter 2 of Volume II in this series, *A Handbook of State Licensure Laws.*

doubtedly be included. Kentucky law is illustrative:

A person practices psychology . . . when he renders to individuals, groups, organizations, or the public any service involving the application . . . of principles, methods or procedures of the science and profession of psychology, to include:

. . . .

(b) recommendation for: selection of personnel, arrangement of effective work and learning situations, resolution of interpersonal or social conflicts (c) application of: principles and methods of psychological modification of behavior, including hypnosis, and the results of research on such modification of behavior, to individuals or to groups [Ky. Rev. Stat. Ann. § 319.010 (1).]

Psychotherapy as the Practice of Social Work

Definitions of social work practice are universally so broad that psychotherapy must be considered within their scope. In six of the twenty-one states licensing social workers, the term is expressly used in defining what constitutes practice, with four of these also defining what constitutes psychotherapy. More than half of all laws include counseling. The social work profession currently has bills pending in almost every jurisdiction in this country, and it will not be long before most states have such laws.

Psychotherapy as the Practice of Marriage and Family Counseling

The one other professional group powerful enough to have a significant number of laws passed regulating psychotherapy is the marriage and family counselors. The American Association of Marriage and Family Counselors (AAMFC) have been actively pursuing legislation for a number of years. To date six states regulate its practice, and all expressly include one form or another of psychotherapy within their scope.

Other Relevant Laws Directly Regulating Psychotherapists

Other licensing laws granting the licensee the right to independent and unlimited practice of psychotherapy exist in four states. These include the laws regulating pastoral counselors in New Hampshire, Texas's social psychotherapy law, Utah's laws regulating recreational therapy, and Virginia's law for professional counselors, certified alcoholism counselors, and certified drug counselors.

Arkansas, California, Colorado, and Kansas regulate mental health technicians. These laws are clearly intended to cover therapeutic practice, but since they apply to people who must work under supervision of other licensed health-care professionals, they are not relevant to the independent practice of therapy. They do, however, provide an avenue for noncredentialed people to practice.

The laws licensing drugless healers or healers using drugs and minor surgery were enacted to cover a wide range of practices, including psychotherapy, although the latter is expressly mentioned only in Ohio. While most of these provisions have been repealed, they still exist in the District of Columbia, Illinois, Ohio, South Carolina, Utah, and Washington. Most licensing boards, however, have rarely issued licenses for this category of practitioner.

Psychotherapy as the Practice of the Healing Arts and Medicine

The healing arts statutes and medical practice acts were mostly enacted at the beginning of this century. The early acts were narrower in scope than current laws, covering only the use of drugs, the performance of surgery, and the use of the title "doctor" (Hodgson, 1977: 649). The focus lay on the method of treatment, not the illness treated. Early court decisions tended to interpret medical practice quite broadly (Schoenback and Snider, 1936: 504–5), however, and

with the repeal of many of the drugless healing provisions, the medical practitioner's domain expanded considerably. Apart from Ohio, no state expressly includes psychotherapy or counseling within the definition of medical practice.

The basis for inclusion of psychotherapy within medicine stems from the restrictions relating to the treatment of mental illness or the use of mental techniques in the treatment of illness generally, and from restrictions regarding the treatment of illness generally or prohibitions against the uses of any types of treatment whatsoever. Thirty-seven states forbid unlicensed practitioners from treating either physical or mental illness, while another eight simply forbid the treatment of illness generally. Only five states limit their definition to physical illnesses, and some of these only by implication.

With regard to treatment techniques, a total of thirty-eight states forbid the use of all types of treatment whatsoever, although what constitutes such treatment is rarely spelled out. Another nine prohibit the use of mental forms of treatment, leaving Massachusetts and Minnesota as the only states that expressly allow people to use such methods.[12] In those states expressly prohibiting mental forms of treatment, five do so for all forms, while another nine simply state that such treatment is prohibited, without specifying any particular type and without expressly stating that all types are prohibited.

The vagueness of terms used in the medical practice acts has raised serious questions as to whether psychotherapy is meant to be included, and if so, to what extent and in what circumstances. The courts have reached this question a number of times. In earlier days the issue often centered on faith healers, those healing through the laying-on-of-hands, and others healing through prayer. The predominant trend of judicial decisions exonerated those who healed by faith alone, as part of their religious practice, and where no specific treatment or advice based on special expertise was involved. Thus, in *State v. Mylod* (1898), where the complained-of acts consisted of silent prayer, explaining the principles of Christian Science, and advising patients to think of God and look on the bright side of things, the Rhode Island Supreme Court ruled that the defendant was not practicing medicine. It based its decision on the fact that no examination was made and there was no claim of expertise or understanding of disease and drugs. It did not matter that the practitioner accepted compensation for his services.[13] On the other hand, where a practitioner kept a furnished office with a sign that said "Professor Smith, Healer" on the door, the Supreme Court of Colorado threw out the defendant's contention that he should be exempted as a religious practitioner (*Smith v. People* [1911]).[14]

Where practitioners do not claim to be following the religious tenets of their church, the courts have consistently rendered a guilty verdict if the practitioner was attempting to treat physical illnesses or was using physical means of treatment. Thus, in *Parks v. State* (1902) the defendant was engaged in the practice of "magnetic healing" and had been doing so for about eight years. He did not use medicines or surgery, but called himself "Professor" and diagnosed patients entirely "by the nerves." He was accused of practicing medicine in treating a pateint who came to him with a lame ankle, which he diagnosed as rheumatism, and which he treated through magnetic healing and rubbing the afflicted parts. The Indiana Supreme Court ruled that this constituted the practice of medicine "since he held himself out as a magnetic healer, and his method of treatment was, at least in part, the method that medical practitioners sometimes employ" (64 N.E. 862, at 870).[15]

One of the very few modern cases dealing with this issue is *Evans v. Hoyme*, decided by the Supreme Court of South Dakota in 1960. There, the defendant Hoyme, a "reflexologist," was brought into court to be enjoined from holding himself out as qualified to engage in the diagnosis and treatment of human ills and from engaging in or offering to engage in their treatment. Reflexology was based on theory that the human body had defined nerve zones that had their endings in the feet. Treatment consisted of the judicious rubbing and massaging of the foot. Hoyme never attempted to make a diagnosis of the illness, although he asked each patient what his or her complaint was. There was no evidence that the defendant ever used the word "doctor" or any abbreviation thereof in describing himself or his activities. The court concluded, however, that the defendant was engaged in the practice of medicine and that he had also violated that portion of the law forbidding anybody from calling himself or herself a "doctor" or any designation that would indicate qualification to engage in diagnosis or treatment. This latter violation was based on the fact that he treated people, which activities the court found implied that he was holding himself out as qualified.

This case is important for several reasons. First, "nervousness" is defined as a human ill, indicating that almost any emotional distress might be considered as such. Second, the court considered it of no moment that some of Hoyme's patients were not in fact ill. What apparently mattered is that they thought they were ill. Third, if actual treatment may be interpreted as a "holding oneself out as qualified to treat," which is what the court held, then licensing laws that only forbid the use of certain titles have been transformed into laws forbidding practice as well, since actual practice may be deemed a holding oneself out as competent and qualified.

Even where no touching or physical treatment is involved, the courts may still decide that certain activities constitute the practice of medicine. In one of the few cases to reach the U.S. Supreme Court on this issue, the Justices held the defendant guilty despite the fact that he did "not employ either medicine, drugs or surgery in his practice, nor [was] there anything harmful in it to the individual or dangerous to society, but he [did] employ in practice faith, hope, and the process of mental suggestion and mental adaptation" (*Crane v. Johnson*, 242 U.S. 339, 340 [1916]). The Court distinguished mental suggestion from prayer on the basis that prayer required no ability to distinguish among specific diseases and thereof required no expert knowledge.

The attorneys general of a number of states have ruled on the question of whether types of psychotherapy are within the purview of medical practice acts. Early in the century the attorney general of Louisiana ruled that a psychic, who advertised himself as "Doctor LaZell" and whose advertisement contained the question, "What should you do to get well?" was clearly in violation of the medical practice act (Opinions of the Attorney General, 1918–20, 618 [February 21, 1919]). More recent opinions indicate that the practice of psychotherapy is not strictly in the province of the physician, especially if therapists confine themselves to nonphysical methods for nonphysical illnesses.[16]

This brief review of judicial decisions and attorney general opinions does not resolve the question of how the medical practice acts will be interpreted. The courts and attorneys general have not had sufficient opportunity to face squarely whether unlicensed practitioners conducting various forms of dynamic pshycotherapy with clients who are not physically ill are guilty of practicing medicine. If severe shortages of professionals exist, and if the quality of service rendered by psychologists, psychiatrists, and other licensed groups is perceived as poor, government officials and the courts may be more willing to limit definitions to protect the unlicensed.

Far more likely, however, is a broad interpretation of medical practice definitions. Historically the courts have construed medical practice acts broadly, holding that diagnosis need not be express to be illegal, that prescribing is synonymous with "recommending," that treatment need not involve drugs, surgical instruments, or remuneration, and that mental condition need not be one of "disease" in the ordinary sense (Hodgson, 1977: 650-55). In addition, the medical and psychiatric professions are lobbying for just such a liberal interpretation of the law.[17] Perhaps the most telling precursors of what is likely to happen, however, have been the recent amendments to the medical practice acts. Within the last ten years, six states have amended their licensing laws expressly to include either mental illness or mental forms of treatment within their definition of medical practice.

The Application of Licensing Laws to Encounter Group Leaders

While psychotherapy is clearly within the boundaries of many licensing laws, the issue remains whether encounter groups are, as well. To date no law expressly mentions encounter groups or other forms of nontraditional therapy, although many legislatures have considered such bills. The best-known and certainly the most sustained effort to regulate group leaders has been waged by the New York State Psychological Association (NYSPA). From 1970 to 1975 it engaged in a tremendously bitter, divisive, and expensive battle to amend the N.Y. psychology laws from a title protection act to a law forbidding unlicensed practice. In defining that practice, NYSPA proposed that psychology be statutorily defined to include "sensitivity training, or procedures designed to modify behavior through environmental manipulation or rearrangement of interpersonal networks in or outside of organizational settings'' (H.B. 10654, 1971-72, Reg. Sess.). Despite the support of the attorney general, the State Department of Education, and the professional associations of psychiatrists, psychologists, nurses, and social workers (Glenn, 1974: 80), the bill failed by one vote.

Instead of legislative amendments, a tactic finding increasing use is for various licensing boards to rule that encounter groups are within the realm of their particular field of professional practice. The broad definitions of practice in psychology, social work, marriage and family counseling, and medicine make such a conclusion difficult to contest (see Volume II in this series). The executive directors of the Psychology Examining Boards in Florida and Illinois have stated unequivocally that their laws cover group leaders (Kobler, 1974; Lord, 1974). Several state boards are now considering adopting rules that would explicitly include encounter groups within their definition of psychological practice, and Ohio has already done so (see Ohio State Board of Psychology, Rules, PSY-4-03[4] [May 17, 1976]). The Ohio board is already active in prosecuting unlicensed practitioners under these provisions, and has recently caused the arrest of a clinical member of the International Transactional Analysis Association (*International Transactional Analysis Bulletin*, no date). It intends to proceed against other practitioners, as well (Walke, 1976).

Conclusion

Although the public generally considers the practice of psychotherapy to be unregulated, the licensing laws of many professions either explicitly or implicitly contain it within their field of practice. In fact, many definitions are so broad that it is difficult to know what is not within their purview. Most likely, the future will find more laws enacted and current laws interpreted more broadly. A study of the history of the health field reveals that definitions of what constitutes health and health services have continually expanded (Illich, 1976). It is reasonable to assume that a similar expansion will take place in psychology and other mental health professions.

The fact that so many professional groups are claiming psychotherapy as their territory has been a strong force that in itself has caused further licensing, since all relevant professions want to protect their right to practice. The prospects of national health insurance and the willingness of private insurance carriers to reimburse the treatment of mental illness by psychotherapeutic means has also contributed to the proliferation of licensing, since reimbursement is generally predicated on whether a practitioner possesses a license.

A SUMMARY OF CURRENT LICENSING LAWS REGULATING PSYCHOTHERAPY[18]

As the previous section has made clear, the licensing laws of many professions impinge on the practice of psychotherapy. In fact, more than 150 separate laws must be dealt with (see Volume III of this series). Medical practice acts and psychology licensing laws exist in all states, while social work licensing laws, marriage and family counseling regulations, and several other counseling laws exist in a number of states. In addition, licensing laws regulating psychiatric technicians, limited-practice licenses granted to specialized practitioners in the health field, and other laws that license paraprofessionals practicing under supervision create a further set of relevant regulations.

Psychology

After a long battle with the medical profession and psychiatry, the psychology profession has finally enacted licensing laws in all jurisdictions. In twenty-seven of these it is illegal to practice psychology without a license, while in the remaining states only the use of specified titles and representations is prohibited. The practice of psychology is universally defined in global terms, and psychotherapy is expressly included in more than half the state laws. Restricted titles generally include any term with psychology in it, and some states expressly prohibit people from calling themselves psychotherapists or counselors. Violation of the law is almost always a misdemeanor, with penalties consisting of a fine generally not greater than $500 and/or imprisonment of one year of less.

The typical educational requirement for licensure consists of a doctoral degree from an accredited university or college in a program that is primarily psychological in nature, although four states grant full licensure for those possessing only a master's degree in psychology. Accreditation is generally the responsibility of the board. In addition, applicants must usually have several years of supervised experience and must successfully pass a written examination, the content of which the board is free to specify.

When an applicant is already licensed in another state or has Diplomate status with the American Board of Professional Psychology, an examination is generally excused. Other frequent requirements include good moral character, being twenty-one years of age, having declared one's intent to become a citizen (if a foreigner), and not having failed the licensing examination within a certain past period of time.

Although the American Phychological Association has consistently resisted licensing more than one level of practitioner, seventeen states have multilevel licensing that allows assistants or associates to be licensed without doctoral degrees, as long as they work under supervision. Generally a master's degree is necessary for licensure in this situation. Licensing fees are relatively expensive, with some states having the right to charge as much as $200.

Exemptions to the psychology laws are varied. Nonlicensed psychologists—such as students, interns, nonresidents temporarily practicing in a state, and lecturers—are usually exempted. While various types of counselors and therapists are only occasionally exempted, established professionals, such as physicians, lawyers, and the clergy, are often excused from the operation of the law. When professionals as a general class are exempted, this frequently only applies if the person is a qualified member of a recognized profession. Finally, the employees of accredited academic institutions, government agencies, research laboratories, and business corporations need not be licensed in many states.

Several limitations exist on a psychologist's right to practice, even if licensed. Clauses in licensing laws frequently declare that the practice of medicine is prohibited, and fifteen states require a licensed psychologist to establish some form of collaboration with a physician in specified instances. Various grounds for discipline exist, but laws frequently fail to make incompetence, repeated negligence, unprofessional conduct, and practicing outside one's area of competence a ground for discipline. Few states require demonstrations of continuing education or competence before a practitioner will be relicensed.

As for administration, psychology licensing laws are all operated by boards of professional examiners, although in several instances these boards are only advisory to a regulatory agency within the state. The typical board is composed only of psychologists, although public members are gaining positions on some boards. In general, licensing boards have complete autonomy and are not centralized, giving them complete power in establishing rules and regulations, issuing licenses, and taking action to discipline practitioners. The limited budgets that most boards have prevents much activity, however, and most board members hold other full-time jobs. Appointment to a board is usually the responsibility of the governor, but in nearly half the states the governor must choose from a list submitted by the state psychological association.

Social Work

The organized efforts of social workers to achieve licensure have only recently been successful.[19] Unlike psychology, the attacks on licensure proposals did not come from medicine but from within the profession itself, as lesser-credentialed practitioners resisted attempts to require advanced degrees as a prerequisite for licensure.

Major differences exist in the twenty-one social work laws, when compared with psychology. Public members are much better represented on licensing boards, and only two states require their governor to choose board members solely from a list submitted by the local social work chapter. Social work laws usually provide for multilevel licensing, generally based on academic credentials and experience. In no state need one possess a doctorate for independent practice, and most will license a person with only a bachelor's degree, although that person must work under supervision. Social work laws frequently have provisions for specialty licensing and independent practice licenses. Continuing education requirements are also much more prevalent.

In other respects the social work laws are similar to psychology. Approximately half the states licensing social workers restrict unlicensed practice as well as the use of certain titles, with practice being broadly defined and including psychotherapy and counseling. General requirements for licensure, provisions for exemptions, restrictions on practice, and the structure of licensing boards are all reasonably like the equivalent provisions in psychology laws.

The most significant difference, perhaps, lies in the accreditation provisions, since a person may not be licensed in more than half of all the licensed categories of social workers unless he or she has an academic degree obtained from a program approved by the Council on Social Work Education, which is an arm of the National Association of Social Workers. This gives the profession considerable control over the licensing process.

Marriage and Family Counseling

The profession of marriage and family counseling is relatively young. This is reflected in the fact that only six states license such counselors. Existing laws are modelled after licensing laws in the psychology and medical profession. Four of the six states licensing marriage and family counselors forbid unlicensed practice, while the remaining two only restrict the use of certain titles. Definitions of practice are extremely broad, including psychotherapy and counseling activities.

Requirements for licensure vary, but all states will grant a license to a person who possesses a doctorate or master's degree, as long as it is in a field related to marriage and family counseling, and as long as one has the requisite experience, which may be as much as five years. Exemptions, limitations on licensed practice, and board structure and functioning are all reasonably similar to psychology laws. No states require marriage and family counselors to produce evidence that they are still competent to practice when they apply for license renewal. In contrast to psychology, the licensing boards of marriage and family counselors contain a wide variety of professionals on them.

Other Relevant Laws Directly Regulating Psychotherapists

Several other counseling laws exist that give practitioners the right to practice psychotherapy independently. These include licensing laws for pastoral counseling in New Hampshire, social psychotherapy in Texas, recreational therapy in Utah, and professional counseling in Virginia. None requires a doctorate for licensure. Instead, they rely on the master's degree. Other provisions contained within these laws are similar to existing provisions in psychology and social work licensing statutes.

Another group of relevant laws are those regulating mental health technicians and assistants, which exist in Arkansas, California, Colorado, and Kansas. Except for Kansas, it is illegal to practice as a technician unless licensed. Licensure generally requires a high school diploma and some relevant work experience. Licensed practitioners must usually work under the supervision of a fully licensed doctor or other professional. Responsibility for administering the laws is generally given to the state board of nursing, although California places it in the hands of physicians.

A third set of laws includes those regulating drugless healers or healers using only drugs and minor surgery. Six states still have such laws on their books, which are a vestige from the earliest medical practice acts enacted at the turn of the century. Requirements for licensure vary, although academic degrees are rarely pegged at more than the bachelor's level. On the other hand, examination requirements are quite strict. These laws are administered by licensing boards composed of physicians, who are given broad powers, including the power to establish license requirements and limit the functions that a practitioner may perform.

Healing Arts

Healing arts statutes are generally intended to be broader and more encompassing than medical practice acts, which they often subsume. The earliest were meant to cover practitioners who did not subscribe to established theory and treatment processes, such as chiropractors and osteopaths. Most of these laws have been removed from the statute books, although six states still require practitioners of any healing art to take a basic science examination. The broad definitions of what constitutes a healing art mean that many psychotherapists might be considered in violation of such laws unless properly licensed.

Medicine

All states forbid the practice of medicine without a license, and the definition of what constitutes medical practice is extremely broad, generally including both physical and mental forms of treatment or the treatment of physical or mental ills.[20] Within the last ten years, where the application to psychotherapy was not clear, a number of states have amended their laws to expressly include the treatment of mental illness or the use of mental forms of treatment. Requirements for licensure, exemptions from the operation of the law, limitations on practice, and the structure and functioning of the licensing boards are all similar to the psychology laws.[21]

THE PROBLEMS OF LICENSING AS A VEHICLE FOR ENSURING COMPETENT PRACTICE

Legislative license is sheer humbug—mere abstract paper thunder under which every ignorance and abuse can still go on. Why this mania for more laws?—William James (1920: vol. 2, p. 66)

Licensing laws are intended to protect the public's health, welfare, safety, and morals. Whether they accomplish these laudable goals, and at what cost, is an empirical question only recently the subject of significant research. The results of that research, discussed below, along with accompanying qualitative evidence and argument, have not been particularly salutary.[22]

In the first place, licensing does not appear to accomplish its avowed purposes. As has already been pointed out, licensing laws attempt to assure the public that only competent people are allowed to practice; they provide legal redress if an unlicensed person attempts to practice; and they provide grounds for disciplining licensed practitioners when they perform in a manner detrimental to the public interest, to the consumer, or to their colleagues. Unfortunately, the available evidence suggests that the quality of services has not improved since licensing laws have been instituted, disciplinary actions are woefully inadequate, and the prevention of illegal practice is generally spotty and often aimed at eliminating competition, rather than incompetence.

In the second place, even if licensing laws do assure competent practitioners, an excellent argument can be made that the costs are not worth it. The increased cost of services, the creation of shortages in supply, and the development of maldistributions of professionals resulting from licensing laws lead to direct harm to the public through the inability of the poor and other disadvantaged groups to afford or find any practitioner at all. Frequently such persons resort to injurious self-help, as is documented below. Quite apart from these more obvious costs, the entry requirements of licensing laws have a tendency to discriminate against the poor, the aged, women, and minorities, as well as inhibiting important innovations in the methods of organizing and delivering professional services.

In the third place, even if the net benefits of licensing outweigh the costs, an argument can be made that equally beneficial alternatives are available at less cost. In addition, other factors than licensing are far more influential in determining the quality of service ultimately received by the public, and it is these factors that should be looked to if sound regulation is desired.

Unnecessary or Arbitrary Entry Requirements

I firmly believe that if the whole *materia medica, as now used,* could be sunk to the bottom of the sea, it would be all the better for mankind—and all the worse for the fishes.—Oliver Wendell Holmes (1892: 203)

Licensing laws generally require candidates to meet four types of qualifications: (1) general or personal requirements, such as good moral character, citizenship, and residency; (2) formal educational requirements; (3) experience requirements, such as apprenticeships, internships, and supervised practice; and (4) successful completion of an examination administered by the licensing board or other acceptable body.

The Council of State Governments' (1952) review of occupational practices found the following standards and criteria to be fairly typical of most occupations and professions. As for general requirements an applicant usually had to be at least eighteen or twenty-one. He or she also had to be a citizen or have filed a declaration of intent to become one. Most statutes require good moral character, and prior conviction of a felony is frequently adequate grounds for license denial. Many states require an applicant to be a resident.

Educational qualifications vary widely, but are almost unanimously required of all occupations and professions. This is a dramatic departure from earlier times, when on-the-job training in the form of apprenticeships were the rule. The amount of education required varies according to the nature of the occupation, but even such activities as cosmetology now require years of study in many states. Certain licensing laws specify that particular trade schools must be attended for specific lengths of time. Embalmers, for instance, must be high school graduates and have completed a nine- to twelve-month course in an approved embalming school. In rare instances, although their number is increasing, a candidate for licensure may fulfill her or his educational requirements through alternate routes. Thus, credit may be given for certain types of supervised work experience. Recently, some have advocated eliminating educational prerequisites if an applicant can demonstrate the capability of performing competently by successfully passing a proficiency examination.

Most occupations and professions demand licentiates to have a certain amount of experience before issuance of a license. In the medical profession the internship requirement for physicians is well known. Embalmers and barbers are required to serve apprenticeships of one to three years. Some occupations, however, may require a minimum of ten years, as is the case with master plumbers. Other professions allow candidates to substitute education in lieu of work experience.

Today most states require candidates to take an examination. A notable exception is the teaching profession, which requires only graduation from an approved school. When given, examinations may be written, oral, practical, or a combination of these. In general, however, they are written. Licensing boards usually prepare, administer, and grade all examinations, although there is increasing reliance on national examinations prepared by independent, private testing services. An example is the use by medical boards of the examination prepared by the National Board of Medical Examiners.

The impact of these requirements on the level of practitioner competence has never been demonstrated (Kessel, 1970: 273), and direct empirical research on this question is almost totally unavailable.[23] Substantial indirect evidence exists, however, to indicate that licensing has done little to improve quality. As a starting point, the considered judgments of professionals may be looked to. Forgotson and Cook (1967), who served as consul-

tants to the President's National Advisory Commission on Health Manpower, do not feel that licensure is particularly effective. In the dental field nearly half of all dental school deans and almost 40 percent of all professors believe that licensing boards are not accurate in their assessment of an applicant's ability (American Council on Education, 1961). Even the American Medical Association (AMA Counc. on Med. Ed. and Counc. on Health Manpower, 1971: 30), in a statement approved by the House of Delegates in 1971, concluded:

Possession of a license in itself does not directly bear upon professional competence. . . . In its bureaucratic context, licensure lags well behind the state of current practice . . . [and] [a]s an organizational process, it is costly and difficult to implement and continuous surveillance of standards is negligible.

Roughly a fourth of all medical boards do not believe they adequately screen out inept practioners (Dornette, 1976: 9–10). And a former president of the American Medical Association (Rouse, 1968: 72) has written that most board-prepared examination questions "offer few clues to a physician's competence to practice medicine."

A more objective measure of the quality of practitioner performance is provided by empirical studies. The medical field is one of the few areas in which such studies have been done, despite the enormous difficulties involved in defining and measuring "quality."[24] On the whole, the findings indicate that practitioners are not as competent as the public would think.[25]

Illustrative is the research of Osler Peterson and his associates (1956), who studied the quality of care delivered in the private office of a typical North Carolina general practitioner (GP). Expert evaluators directly observed eighty-eight GPs in their daily practice for an average of three and one-half days each. They found only 9 percent of the physicians took reasonably thorough histories and were adequately skilled at interviewing. In the giving of physical examinations the GPs were seriously deficient: 45 percent did not ask patients to disrobe; 74 percent performed only a cursory examination of the eyes; 38 percent examined only the throat or tonsils, ignoring teeth, gums, and tongue, only 24 percent performed a careful abdominal exam; 64 percent did not generally conduct a vaginal exam; and 86 percent ignored a breast exam.

The GPs were also not adept at employing appropriate tests and techniques. For instance, nearly half did not use an EKG at all, did not use it skillfully, or did not use it when indicated. Nearly a third of all doctors generally did not recognize emotional problems of any sort, while more than half recognized them but did not attempt psychological treatment or treated the physical aspects only. Only 17 percent both recognized and treated emotional problems suitably. In conclusion, less than one physician in thirty carried out an adequate physical examination.[26]

Evaluating the available research, Ralph Nader's study group (McCleery, 1971: 153) on the quality of care provided by physicians concluded:

As a premise for judgment of the present quality of care and of the quality control system, the study asked only whether or not a patient being treated by any physician in his office or hospital can be *reasonably sure:* that his physician is reasonably competent to treat *that ailment* (or that the physician will refer him to another physician whom the first believes to be reasonably competent); that his physician is reasonably up-to-date on diagnostic and treatment techniques, and on drug therapy information; that his physician will keep such records as to afford reasonable assurance that his work can later be effectively evaluated; that his physician's performance, no matter where given, will be monitored with reasonable frequency, objectivity and expertness by his peers.

We are forced to conclude that a patient cannot be reasonably sure.

In this mental health field the competence of the average psychotherapist does not appear to be very high. Strupp (in Bergin and Strupp, 1972: 226) believes that only about 20 percent of all therapists are competent, while Meehl (in Eysenck, 1966: 58-59) places the maximum figure at 25 percent. After a careful analysis of the research, Truax and Mitchell (1971: 340) declare that two out of three therapists are either ineffective or harmful. Carl Rogers (1973: 382) offers the most scathing indictment, concluding that as many certified charlatans and exploiters of people exist as uncertified.[27]

A series of less direct arguments and evidence may be brought to bear on the ability of licensing laws to assure competence. The existence of obviously irrelevant requirements indicates that some of the standards being used are not related to the quality of professional practice. Gellhorn (1956) argues that many of the standards and criteria used by licensing boards are actually designed to exclude specific groups and limit competition, rather than to protect the public. For instance, Georgia enacted a law requiring those seeking a commercial photography license to "submit a certificate from the board of health, showing a negative Wasserman test" (Gellhorn, 1956: 125). Even though the relationship to competence is difficult to discern, chiropodists, tree surgeons, embalmers, and many others must be eligible to vote before a license can be obtained.

Perhaps the most glaring indication that licensing laws are ineffective in protecting the public is their failure to reassess periodically whether a practitioner is still competent. As of 1967 no state in the country required medical doctors to demonstrate evidence of further education or professional growth (U.S. National Advisory Commission on Health Manpower, 1967: II, 501-2). The obvious problem is that a practitioner may have been licensed forty years ago, but has practiced very little since then.

Provided such persons have regularly paid their license renewal fees, their right to practice would be maintained.

Recently, a number of laws that require evidence of continuing education have been adopted to remedy this situation. Typically, such laws allow credit for attending professional conferences and extension course, and for obtaining additional schooling. Yet little evidence exists that continuing education is a good measure of competence; the research on competency assessment indicates that it probably is not.

Two other lines of attack may be used to question licensing requirements. First, there is no evidence that licensing requirements measure significant factors. The emphasis on educational degrees, for instance, assumes that such degrees are a valid and reliable measure of competence. The evidence from previous chapters, however, argues against such an assumption (see also Harshbarger, 1974; Schwitzgebel, 1973).

To recapitulate briefly, a wide range of research indicates that academic grades predict nothing but future grades and results on tests similar to those used in establishing grades (McClelland, 1973). Even ability in highly intellectual and technical jobs such as scientific research cannot be predicted by grades in college (Taylor, Smith, and Ghiselin, 1963). A Labor Department study found correlations between years of education and job performance in only three of twenty cases involving ten occupational groups in two labor markets (U.S. Department of Labor, 1970). In the medical profession, grades in medical school appear unrelated to later performance as a doctor (Price et al., 1964), and in mental health, evidence exists that academic credentials are inappropriate as a means of identifying competent practitioners (see pages 158-60).

A second line of attack has to do with the methods of testing that are currently used to determine competency. Virtually all state boards give examinations to candidates. These tests are usually written, oral, or both. Most occupations such as plumbing and barbering rely on written examinations devised by the state boards themselves. Often they test only the ability to memorize irrelevant facts. Rarely are they a good measure of competency. Shimberg, Esser, and Kruger (1972: 194), who conducted a widely heralded five-year research study sponsored by the Department of Labor, concluded:

The quality of testing found in many occupational licensing programs is so low that one wonders how the revolution in testing—especially the advances in technology that have been made since World War II—could have managed to bypass so completely the field of occupational licensing.

Few boards make use of outside consultants in test development, administration, and interpretation. Other problems also prevent licensing tests from being useful, including a lack of planning, overreliance on essays, and the poor quality of multiple-choice questions (Shimberg, Esser, and Kruger, 1972: 194-95). Some professions have moved toward national examinations developed by nongovernmental organizations, such as the three-part test administered by the National Board of Medical Examiners. These have a tendency to test academic ability or intellectual knowledge, rather than the required competencies for practice (U.S. DHEW, 1971: 8). Few exams, even those administered on a national level, have been validated. The use of proficiency testing and educational equivalency examinations is only in its infant stages.[28]

Even if one grants that licensing laws have increased the level of service provided by individual practitioners, the cost may not be worth it. Subsequent sections present evidence that licensing significantly increases the cost of services and creates shortages of practitioners. When combined with the discriminatory effects of most licensing laws, the inhibitions they impose on methods of training practitioners, and the problems they create in organizing the delivery of professional services, the negative effects of licensing may outweigh any potential benefits.

One of the effects of increasing the cost of services and decreasing the supply of practitioners is that some of those who need services will suffer from lack of treatment or from poorly administered self-treatment.[29] Evidence for this proposition exists. Carroll and Gaston (1977: Appendix V: 8) have found that states with strict licensing laws for plumbers have more people doing their own plumbing, as measured by per-capita retail sales of plumbing supplies. Where entry requirements for real estate brokers are strict, they found that houses tended to stay on the market longer (Carroll and Gaston, 1977: Appendix I). More dramatically, Carroll and Gaston (1977: Appendix V) also discovered that accidental electrocutions were directly related to the restrictiveness of a state's licensing laws for electricians. In fact, in the seven most restrictive states, up to ten times more accidental electrocutions occurred (*Business Week*, 1977: 128).

Even if the net benefits of licensing outweigh the costs, an argument can still be made that it is advisable if an equivalent investment in another method of regulation would achieve superior results or result in less harm. This may very well be so. Milton Roemer (1970) has pointed out that certain factors such as the maintenance of a safe and hygienic environment, an educated public, and an adequate supply of physical and human resources are essential for minimal quality in health services. Without these factors no amount of physician competence makes much difference.

Given this fact, the general level of the public's health may be improved more effectively by spending an equivalent investment in promoting an adequate supply of physicians and paraprofessionals.[30]

Alternatively, other methods of regulation may be available that are equally effective, but result in less harm. Again, Roemer (1970) lists a variety of regulatory mechanisms, including laws regulating hospitals and other facilities, control of drugs and appliances, and comprehensive health planning. In the concluding portions of this book several such models will be proposed.

Inadequate Disciplinary Enforcement

In most licensure laws a provision exists for disciplining practitioners who are not performing in accordance with the stipulations of the law. Typically a state board is responsible for administering disciplinary actions. These boards generally have the power to promulgate rules and regulations, to investigate complaints, to initiate hearings, and to make final dispositions of individual cases. They have the power to censure a practitioner or to suspend or revoke that person's license. Such action is generally justified not on the basis of the board's power to punish, but its duty to protect the public against further harm from incompetent and unethical practice (see *State v. Hays* [1908]; *State v. Shumate* [1900]).

Because professional licenses are considered property rights, due process must be afforded before a license is revoked or suspended (see *Notre Dame Lawyer*, 1968: Tuttrup, 1926–28). Summary revocation is not admissible; written notice and a hearing are generally necessary. Where revocation or suspension occurs, a practitioner may apply for judicial review, even where no such provision exists in the enabling legislation. Several states grant exclusive or concurrent authority to suspend or revoke medical licenses to the courts. In several instances the administrative agency to which the board is attached has this right.

Licensing boards generally do not initiate disciplinary proceedings without a complaint being lodged by a consumer, peer, or somebody from the public at large.[31] Where the licensing function has been centralized, a hearing officer often makes an initial determination of outcome, subject to review by the board or the head of the relevant department. In some of the larger professions, disciplinary subcommittees have been created to act as a screening group for charges of unprofessional conduct (Council of State Governments, 1952: 42). Once a violation has been shown, the board is not required to process the complaint or to assess punishment, and a decision not to act is not subject to judicial review (Hansen, 1962: 12–13).

Legal provisions for disciplining licensed practitioners must balance the public's interest in competent and ethical practice versus the interest of practitioners in operating without undue interference (Forgotson, Roemer, and Newman, 1967: 312). Therefore, statutory grounds for suspension and revocation are usually spelled out in detail, even if only vaguely defined. These may be conveniently categorized into three areas: (1) personal disqualifications such as mental illness or alcoholism; (2) illegal acts, such as conviction of a felony or abetting an unlicensed person in the illegal practice of the profession; and (3) unprofessional conduct such as improper advertising, fee-splitting, or gross malpractice.

Tremendous variability exists in the types of offenses subject to discipline. In the medical profession more than ninety grounds for revocation or suspension exist, with no one group to be found in all states (U.S. Natl. Adv. Comm., 1967: II, 313). A typical list of grounds, as found by the research department of the Oklahoma Legislature (1950: 39–42) in their study of various occupations, includes: conviction of a felony; being guilty of moral turpitude; fraud; violation of the provisions of the licensing law; cause; incompetency; violating sanitary requirements; malpractice; practice when knowingly diseased; false or deceptive advertising; habitual drunkenness; habitual addiction to drugs; willfully betraying a professional secret; using other than one's own name; failure to pay the renewal fee; two or more valid suspensions; splitting fees or compensation; failure to attend short course; violation of the narcotic laws; employing solicitors; violating the rules and regulations of the board; criminal operation; exorbitant charges; employing an unlicensed or nonregistered person; being a fugitive from justice; and failing to display one's certificate properly.

Unfortunately, few statutes contain a comprehensive list of grounds in themselves, and some grounds are conspicuously absent. As of 1965, for instance, no jurisdiction in the medical field made educational obsolescence a ground for discipline (U.S. Natl. Adv. Comm., 1967: II, 317). Incompetency is another ground frequently omitted from a state's licensing law. Derbyshire's (1969: 87) study of the medical practice acts revealed that mental incompetence is a ground for discipline in only twenty-seven states, with physical or professional incompetence a sufficient reason in eighteen.

Data on the Extent of Disciplinary Enforcement. The Medical Disciplinary Committee of the American Medical Association (1961) has suggested that discipline should be the primary responsibility of state boards of medical examiners. Most licensing boards, however, whether within or without the medical field, have been unable to assume this responsibility. In the legal field, for instance, the Special Committee on Evaluation of Disciplinary Enforcement of the American Bar Association (1970: 1) concluded:

After three years of studying lawyer discipline throughout the country, this Committee must report the existence of a scandalous situation that requires the immediate attention of the profession. With few exceptions, the prevailing attitude of lawyers toward disciplinary enforcement ranges from apathy to outright hostility. Disciplinary action is practically nonexistent in many jurisdictions; practices and procedures are antiquated; many disciplinary agencies have little power to take effective steps against malefactors.

In the health field, the Department of Health, Education, and Welfare (U.S. DHEW, 1971: 33) was forced to conclude in its Report to Congress that "disciplinary action by medical boards is almost insignificant in terms of the universe of practicing physicians [and the] data indicate a tendency toward leniency even in the relatively few cases that result in formal board action." These conclusory statements are more than borne out by the available data. For instance, one of the earliest studies to investigate how well licensing boards enforced discipline was conducted over a seventeen-year period by the National Education Association (1938). It examined boards of architecture, law, accountancy, nursing, medicine, and teaching. Its findings were extremely discouraging. In the field of accounting, each state board revoked, on average, less than one license over the entire period covered by the study. In addition, nearly half the states responding reported no hearings whatsoever. In architecture, only eight architects in a total of twenty-one states lost their licenses over the same seventeen-year period, with almost two-thirds of the states reporting no hearings at all. In the legal profession a lawyer was disbarred only once every three years on a state-by-state basis. In the nursing profession more than half of all states reporting held no hearings whatever, and only one nurse per state was likely to lose his or her license over the entire seventeen-year period, despite the existence of nearly 150,000 nurses.[32]

More recent data indicate that the lack of enforcement changed.[33] In Massachusetts, for instance, data from the Office of Consumer Affairs (Rosenbloom, 1973) revealed that the Board of Registration of Hairdressers received 6,250 complaints from 1969–1971, yet it held only one hearing, and revoked or suspended only one license. The State Board of Examiners of Electricians received 6,025 complaints, but felt that only five of them were serious enough to warrant a hearing. Like the hairdressers, they revoked only one license. These statistics are directly in line with the findings of Elton Rayack's (1975) economic analysis of occupational licensure, in which he examined the records of complaints brought before fifteen licensing boards in Massachusetts, Connecticut, and Rhode Island. Based on available evidence (Rayack, 1975: 130), it appeared that more than half of the boards did not receive any consumer complaints, another third had very few, and only the plumbing and electrician boards reported significant numbers of complaints. Nearly two-thirds of the boards had never revoked any licenses in their history. Of those that had, one did so for advertising prices; one revoked four licenses in twenty years; another, three licenses over a sixteen-year period; and no information was available from the other two. Recent reforms did not significantly change the complexion of the situation, which led Rayack (1975: 142) to conclude:

> The review of the activities of fifteen licensing boards, the Division of Professional Regulation in Rhode Island, and the attempts at reform in Massachusetts indicates that dealing with consumer complaints is virtually a nonexistent activity for most boards in the three states and at best a low priority item for others.

The situation is not much different in the major professions. In 1972 only 357 of the nation's 380,000 practicing lawyers were disciplined, which amounts to approximately 0.1 percent (Nader and Green, 1976: 48). Jerome Carlin's (1966) excellent sociological analysis of the New York City Bar attempted to assess the moral integrity of the legal profession. As part of this he examined the extent to which the bar disciplined wayward practice. Carlin (1966: 151) found that between 1951 and 1962 the number of complaints filed averaged 1,450 per year. About two-thirds of these involved a dispute over fees or client neglect. Most were disposed of by a phone call. Only 4 percent ever led to a formal hearing, of which less than half brought a recommendation for prosecution. An average of ten cases per year resulted in disbarment. Carlin (1966: 160–61) was forced to conclude that "the formal machinery of the bar does not, and probably could not, do an effective job of policing the profession. Too few violators are formally charged and punished to suggest that this activity by itself does much to weed out or discipline unethical lawyers." Carlin also concluded that formal sanctions do little to influence or deter potential violators, because the most common violations (fraud and solicitation of clients) receive only mild sanctions and more than half of all disbarments are by consent, in which case the record and charges are not made public.[34]

In the medical field the situation is similar. Derbyshire (1969) reviewed all disciplinary actions from 1963 through 1967, using as his source the files of the Federation of State Medical Boards. Excluding cases dropped for lack of evidence, cases in which prior action was rescinded, and cases arising for technical reasons such as failure to pay registration fees, 938 actions were taken against physicians. These resulted in probation in 375 instances, reprimands in 68 cases, license suspension in 161, and license revocation in 334 cases. Since there were more than 300,000 physicians in the United States in 1967, with more than 265,000 in active practice (Theodore and Sutter, 1967), less than 0.25 percent of all practicing physicians were likely to lose their license. The most common ground for discipline was for narcotics, which accounted for nearly 50 percent of all disciplinary actions. Most of these violations were also actionable under existing criminal law, making board action somewhat redundant.

Further data on discipline in the medical field comes from the American Medical Association's Department of Medical Ethics (1970, 1969). Until 1969 the AMA published an annual medical disciplinary report examining actions by state boards of medical examiners. The data for 1967 indicate only 348 procedures resulting in 61 revocations, which means that a little more than 0.1 percent of all physicians were brought before disciplinary boards, and less than 0.25 percent had their licenses revoked. In 1968 more than half of the states did not revoke any licenses whatsoever. Only one state revoked more than ten licenses, and only two revoked more than five. The state of California alone accounted for almost a quarter of all licenses revoked. Nine states were so lax that they did not institute a single proceeding.

The data for 1969 are even more discouraging. Thirty-three states, as opposed to twenty-six in 1968, did not revoke any licenses. California was the only state to revoke more than five, and it alone accounted for a third of all revocations. Thirteen states did not hold any hearings. An examination of the four- and five-year comparison data provided by the AMA indicates that fewer and fewer physicians are losing their licenses. The year 1969 saw almost 25 percent fewer revocations than 1963. Interestingly, the AMA ceased publishing surveys of disciplinary enforcement in 1969 (AMA, Office of the General Counsel, 1972). A request to the Federation of State Medical Boards to have statistics for subsequent years released met with no success, since the board secretary stated that the information was confidential. (Crabb, 1977).

The argument is often made that disciplinary actions are rare because physician competence and ethics are high. Previous sections have raised the issue of whether this is so, and professional opinion seems to concur. Jervey (1961: 85–90), for instance, estimates that 1 to 3 percent of all physicians constitute a disciplinary problem. If one includes unethical activity as well, the number of physicians involved becomes roughly 15,000 to 20,000.

Jervey believes these figures are conservative, and concludes that between 2 and 10 percent of all physicians are involved in unscrupulous, unethical, delinquent, or incompetent activity. This is certainly nowhere near the number of those disciplined.

In the mental health professions, data from the field of psychology support the proposition that board discipline is virtually nonexistent (see Appendix O in Hogan, 1972). To gather information on this, all state boards were sent questionnaires asking for the following information: (1) how many complaints had been filed with the board since its inception; (2) how many psychologists had had their licenses suspended or revoked; and (3) how many of these suspensions and revocations were specifically for unprofessional or unethical conduct. Twenty-nine states replied, of which twenty-six had state boards. The boards often responded to the questions by stating that they had received few or very few complaints. Since each state's law was passed, it appears that less than 200 complaints of any sort were filed with the boards, which averages out to roughly 1 complaint per year per state board. For the entire period during which these boards had been operative up until 1972, only five licenses or certificates had been revoked. Even in states with large numbers of psychologists, disciplinary action is unlikely. In New Jersey, for instance, where 900 psychologists were licensed, not one psychologist had had his or her license suspended or revoked for unprofessional conduct.

Explanations of the Lack of Enforcement. The above data document the fact that a serious problem exists in enforcing discipline. Whether it can be remedied remains to be seen. Several separate lines of thought, however, converge to indicate that the problem is likely to remain acute unless significant changes take place.

The first comes from the analysis of the legal profession undertaken by Jerome Carlin (1966). The problems that he found are probably typical of all licensing boards, including those regulating psychology, social work, and medicine.

Carlin attempted to establish why some ethical violations led to more severe sanctions than others and why many apparent violations never met with any action. The kind of charge brought proved to be important: lawyers who violated the ordinary ethical standards of the layperson were more likely to be caught and severely punished than lawyers who violated norms unique to the legal profession. In addition, three other factors correlated positively with degree of punishment: (1) the amount of money involved in the offense; (2) the number of acts of misconduct; and (3) the extent to which the violation received publicity or notoriety.

Carlin (1966: 159) combined these factors to obtain an Index of Visibility, which turned out to be more important in determining disbarment than the ethical salience of the charge. His conclusion (Carlin, 1966: 161–62) is worth quoting in detail:

The organized bar through the operation of its formal disciplinary measures seems to be less concerned with scrutinizing the moral integrity of the profession than with forestalling public criticism and control. . . .

Further evidence that the organized bar is responding primarily to a concern for preserving its public image is the considerable importance of the visibility of the offense to the general community. . . . It is consistent . . . with a desire to avoid lay interference and control that the most widely publicized violations would be the most severely and publicly sanctioned. Failure to punish visible violations might result in public criticism of the bar, and the visibility itself offers the profession an opportunity to demonstrate to the public that it can discipline its own members. . . .

Finally, in assessing the significance of formal controls for the integrity of the bar, it should not be forgotten that the few lawyers who are officially disciplined are, for the most part, precisely those whose low status renders them least capable of conforming to the ethical standards of the bar.

Carlin also attempted to determine what sort of lawyers in which situations were likely to act unethically. The formal control of the bar, exercised through its disciplinary mechanism, had little correlation with the degree of ethical behavior exhibited by lawyers. A factor that did prove important to professional ethics was the inner disposition of the lawyer. Unfortunately, no evidence existed that this disposition was significantly influenced by law school, status in the bar, or a lawyer's actual practice.

These findings suggest that the formal disciplinary mechanism exercised by the state is not a significant factor in bringing about adherence to ethical norms and in ensuring minimal competency. Carlin (1966: 181), in fact, argues that other routes ought to be explored, such as government subsidy, prepaid insurance plans, and group legal practice.[35] In the medical field, the Committee on Medical Practices of the American Medical Association (1955: 847) came to roughly the same conclusion.[36] The committee argued that unethical practices in surgery stemmed from the intense competition for such work resulting from various arbitrary restrictions for entering practice. The committee (1955: 850) saw "little hope of curing fee splitting by superimposing more oaths, rules, restrictions, regulations, and inspections," and pointed out that "there is a long human history of broken oaths and regulations, where law does not conform to the realities of a situation." Rather, the committee (1955: 854) recommended informing the public as to the degree to which medicine was an exact science, the degree to which doctors were fallible, and the point at which physicians might be expected to subordinate their patient's interest for their own self-interest.

According to the above argument, even if licensing laws were fully enforced, there is little likelihood that such enforcement would lead to improved practice. The chances of even partial enforcement are unlikely, however, under present methods of administering licensing laws. The amount of money with which most licen-

sing boards operate, the poor methods of administration, the lack of investigative skills, and a host of similar problems appear insurmountable.

The Special Committee on Evaluation of Disciplinary Enforcement of the American Bar Association (1970) found the severity and depth of the problem to be evident everywhere. The committee had difficulty obtaining meaningful statistics from most disciplinary agencies, since many did not bother with adequate records. Decentralization of the disciplinary function hindered the likelihood of any action being taken by an agency, since members of the disciplinary body were often friends of those being complained against and were unlikely to take action. Decentralization also resulted in lack of uniformity in discipline imposed. The lack of communication among state enforcement agencies resulted in lawyers being able to practice in one state, although having been previously disbarred in another.

Most enforcement bodies did not have self-starting grievance machinery to protect the public from illegal collusion between lawyer and client. Often an agency had inadequate alternatives for taking action: minor complaints could not be dealt with appropriately because procedurally a formal proceeding was the minimal action allowed, and it was often considered too severe in relation to the offense. The committee (American Bar Association, 1970: v–x) formulated thirty-six problem areas, including:

1. inadequate financing of disciplinary agencies for investigations and the conduct of proceedings;
2. cumbersome structures that result in an inordinate time gap between the inception and conclusion of disciplinary proceedings;
3. inadequate professional staff;
4. absence of training programs for disciplinary agency staffs;
5. inadequate   provisions   for   dealing

with attorneys incapacitated by reason of mental illness, senility or addiction to drugs or intoxicants;

6. inadequate provisions concerning public disclosure of pending disciplinary proceedings;
7. failure to publish the achievements of disciplinary agencies;
8. disbarred attorney too readily reinstated by the courts;
9. reluctance on the part of lawyers and judges to report instances of professional misconduct;
10. no training courses on ethical standards and disciplinary enforcement for judges responsible for lawyer discipline.

There is no reason to believe that these problems are not equally present in other professional licensing boards, including those involved in the regulation of psychotherapists.

In addition to organization and structural problems, licensing boards face the challenge of vaguely worded and often incomplete grounds for discipline. The vagueness of such phrases as "unprofessional conduct" often gives rise to a question of whether a particular statute is unconstitutional because it lacks specificity. The most famous case in this regard is *Czarra v. Board of Medical Supervisors* (1905). There, the appellate court of the District of Columbia ruled that the term "unprofessional or dishonorable conduct" was too vague and did not provide advance notice to physicians about those acts for which their right to practice might be taken away. Nonetheless, most courts have upheld such statutory terminology by strictly construing the particular term involved (see, for instance, *Sage-Allen Co. v. Wheeler* [1935]). Where the term "unprofessional conduct" is further defined in various subsections, the courts have had little trouble in upholding the constitutionality of the statute (*State Board v. Macy* [1916]).[37]

The net effect, however, has been that

licensing boards have tended to adopt narrow statutory interpretations of grounds for discipline. The result is that the public is only protected from relatively infrequent and extreme offenses (De Lancy, 1938: 92; Hansen, 1962: 11; U.S. Nat'l Adv. Comm. on Mental Health, 1967: II, 315). Together with other judicial decisions requiring licensing agencies to provide due process, the overall impact has been to make licensing boards relatively ineffective as disciplinary enforcers.[38]

Sporadic Prevention of Unlicensed Practice

People do not visit a fringe practitioner because they are gullible, stupid or superstitious, though they may be: they go to him because they think, or hope, they can get something from him that their doctor no longer gives. They are right; often their doctor does not pretend to be able to give it. It is customary for doctors to lament the spread of fringe systems of treatment; but it is the medical profession itself, through its own failure to provide what the community needs, that must take the responsibility—and the consequences. [Inglis 1964: 53–54.]

One of the major functions of practice acts is to prevent unlicensed practitioners from operating. Illegal practice may take several forms, the most blatant of which is the practice of outright charlatans. These are people who recognize they are not qualified to practice and who deliberately dupe the public. Quackery constitutes another form and consists of those who honestly believe they possess the requisite professional knowledge, but in fact do not (see Jameson, 1961: 17–18). Other types of unlicensed and illegal practice are subtler. In those fields that have vague boundaries, including psychotherapy, closely related professions may be engaging in illegal practice, depending on an interpretation of what constitutes professional practice. Finally, paraprofessionals within a profession may be operating illegally if they usurp their limited field of practice, even if this is done with the senior professional's consent.[39]

The extent of unlicensed practice in the professions seems to vary over time and place. In the medical field, Young (1967: vii) asserts that quackery is rampant and has never enjoyed such success as now.[40] He believes that quacks and charlatans make as much as $2 billion per year from innocent clients, which is more than the amount spent on medical research. Many look upon all those who lead encounter groups as quacks, and see this as a major problem for the mental health profession.[41]

It is difficult to determine how effective licensing laws are in curbing illegal practice. The very presence of the law, apart from enforcement activities, may deter some unlicensed practitioners. For practices that are highly visible and easily documentable, such as surgery, this is a safe assumption. For professions in which it may be difficult to prove that somebody is actually practicing illegally, as in the field of psychotherapy, it is unlikely that licensure operates as a deterrent.

Evidence of the effectiveness of licensing laws in this area is scarce, but Derbyshire (1969: 105-17)—one of the leading analysts on licensing laws in the medical field—does not believe that the requirement of a license poses much of an impediment for charlatans. He recounts numerous examples of how imposters have functioned for long periods without being detected, with their eventual exposure frequently a matter of accident. His careful examination of the records of thirty successful imposters found that only eight had bothered to obtain forged or stolen credentials. Carl Rogers (1973: 383), one of the leading psychologists in this country, is another who claims that high professional standards do little to eliminate exploiters and charlatans.

In terms of enforcement it does seem that licensing agencies are more zealous in prosecuting unlicensed practitioners than disciplining those with a license. In New

Jersey (1971), the Batemean Commission found that more than half of all individuals penalized by the Board of Architects were unlicensed. For electrical contractors the figure was slightly less than half, and in addition, nearly half of all disciplinary actions against licensed professionals were for improperly lending their license to unlicensed persons.

If one examines those sued for illegal practice and the situation in which these suits are brought, an interesting pattern is revealed. Rayack's (1975) study of occupational licensure in New England found that complaints against the unlicensed were generally brought by those with a license, and such complaints increased when economic conditions took a turn for the worse. The AMA's (AMA, Law Department, 1967) records of court decisions involving state boards of medical examiners contains reports involving five instances of unlicensed practice. Three of these involved clearly competent practitioners, and all five resulted in a licensed physician being punished for aiding another without a license. In one case the staff director of a hospital had failed to register as interns several doctors who possessed licenses in other states. In a second instance a doctor's license was revoked for utilizing three highly skilled foreign physicians as anesthetists.[42]

Lieberman (1976: 107-11) narrates numerous instances in which bar associations have sought to enjoin real estate brokers and others from performing simple tasks that do not require a great deal of expertise, that are in fact performed competently, but which the bar claims constitute the illegal practice of law. In a recent case a typist who prepared divorce papers for indigents was brought to court for illegal practice (Public Citizen, 1978). It did not matter that the indigents had no other source of legal assistance, and despite her apparent competence, the bar took action, apparently because her charge for services was only one-seventh of what a lawyer would charge.

These instances suggest a pattern in which the licensing boards appear to be more interested in protecting the economic interests of their profession than the public's interest in competent services (Lieberman, 1976, 1970; Public Citizen, 1978). If this is so, then enforcement of the laws against illegal practice will ultimately hurt the very people the law was supposedly designed to protect.

Quite apart from board policies about unlicensed practitioners, the organizational structure and financing of licensing boards create severe enforcement problems. Most boards are financed by licensing fees, which rarely allow a board the opportunity to be proactive in the enforcement area. Board members are also untrained in the art of investigation. Even where a legitimate case is found, district attorneys often display an unwillingness to prosecute because the crime involved is only a misdemeanor (Derbyshire, 1972: 164).[43]

Several other arguments suggest that licensing laws are unlikely to be effective in removing unlicensed practitioners, or that alternative methods are likely to be more effective. In the first place, it may well be that an ill-informed or gullible public is the primary factor in making quackery successful. Cobb's investigation of twenty patients who went to nonmedical sources for the treatment of cancer suggests that miracle-seekers, the uninformed, those who are restless, and strawgraspers are frequent visitors to the unlicensed, with the uninformed being the largest group (see also Barrett and Knight, 1976; Jameson, 1961). On the other hand, a study of health practices and opinions conducted for the Food and Drug Administration (U.S. FDA, 1972) found that many people used unorthodox practitioners on the theory that it was "worth a try," rather than from any degree of gullibility. Although little commonality existed among people's susceptibility to health fallacies, the same study found that those who followed quacks tended to have a general tendency toward the

use of self-medication, accepted advertising claims more readily, were more critical of physicians, and were more worried about their own health (U.S. FDA, 1972: xi–xii). If a certain type of person is more likely to visit a nonlicensed practitioner, then efforts to change consumer behavior may prove more fruitful than the enactment of stiff licensing laws. In particular, efforts to educate the public on how to choose practitioners may be of significant value.[44]

Another set of influences may ultimately prove more pivotal in efforts to eliminate quackery, however. Perhaps the best method of protecting the public is to ensure that enough competent practitioners are available to all people at a reasonable cost. A study of the history of medicine indicates that quacks flourish when physicians are scarce or when their remedies are ineffective. If this is so, then licensing laws may tend to exacerbate the problem, since they further restrict the supply of practitioners.[45]

Any efforts to eliminate the unlicensed should recognize the potential costs involved. Especially where standards of practice are not clearly articulated or proved, as in the field of psychotherapy, attacking the fringe practitioner may be eliminating an important source of information and ideas, as well as competent practice (Carlson, 1975: 224–25). Friedman (1962: 156–57) emphasizes the potential value of the unorthodox, and stresses that restricting it to customary practice will reduce the amount of experimentation and the rate of growth of knowledge in the area. Licensing laws may very well promote the legitimation of quackery (at least as conservatively defined), to the extent that politically powerful fringe practitioners, such as chiropractors, successfully pursue licensure in their own field as protection from rival groups already licensed (Friedman, 1962: 155–56). Finally, the dangers of supposed quacks need to be more thoroughly documented, since some studies suggest that large majorities of those who visit them are satisfied with the services they receive (U.S. FDA, 1972: xi).

THE HARMFUL EFFECTS OF LICENSING

Under any system of regulation a number of side effects will occur, both anticipated and unanticipated, in addition to those intended by the framers of the regulation. In the case of licensing, mounting evidence suggests that licensure has significant negative effects that often outweigh any potential benefits in terms of protecting the public.[46] There are six major areas in which licensing laws have a negative impact: (1) the supply of professional personnel and the availability of their services; (2) the distribution of professionals geographically, institutionally, and in different specialties; (3) the cost of professional services; (4) the use of paraprofessionals; (5) methods of organizing and delivering services, professional training, and professional education; and (6) discrimination due to race, sex, age, and wealth.

In many instances, properly designed and constructed licensing laws might eliminate at least some problems, but political realities make it a near certainty that such changes are unlikely to occur. Furthermore, even the best-designed laws will still produce negative effects that counteract any actual benefits.

Exacerbation of Shortages in the Supply of Practitioners

The impact of licensing on the supply of practitioners would not be a pressing issue if an adequate supply were available. In fact, if an oversupply existed, perhaps even arbitrary licensing restrictions might be viewed as beneficial. Where the supply is less than adequate, however, unnecessary restrictions are bound to have negative effects, and even justifiable curtailments may not be worthwhile.

The determination that a shortage exists is not always an easy matter. The National Manpower Council (1957: 225 et seq.) suggests six useful indicia: (1) upward movement in wages or salaries;[47] (2) existence of a demonstrated social need;[48] (3) existence of unfilled, budgeted positions in public and nonprofit enterprises;[49] (4) training requirements or other qualitative factors;[50] (5) difficulties in filling specialist billets in the armed services;[51] and (6) unfavorable comparisons with other countries.[52]

In the 1950s, U.S. Department of Labor (1957) data provided evidence that shortages would exist in all professional and technical occupations during the 1960s. A more than 33 percent increase in professionals was projected for 1965, while the number of unskilled jobs would decline by 3 percent; the number of farm jobs would decline by 15 percent. This trend has continued in the health field, where most studies conclude that shortages exist at all professional levels. In 1967, for instance, the U.S. National Advisory Commission on Health Manpower (1967: II, 230) pointed out that a physician shortage existed. Four years later the American Medical Association (1971: 3) agreed, citing the fact that most practicing physicians were overworked, many towns and entire counties did not have adequate access to services, and many positions in teaching, administration, research, and practice remain unfilled.[53] Physician income has increased at a faster rate than almost all other occupational groups,[54] indicating that more physicians are needed, or that better use ought to be made of the existing supply. The large number of foreign-trained physicians practicing, and the fact that more than a third of all licenses granted in 1976 were to foreign-trained practitioners (American Medical Association, Center for Health Services Research and Development, 1977: 580), also provide an indication that the United States does not have an adequate supply of physicians.[55]

The situation in allied health fields is not much different. A National Institute of Health study (Pennell, Proffitt, and

Hatch, 1971: 11) estimated that the shortages of allied practitioners would be nearly 25 percent by 1980. The U.S. Public Health Service estimated a deficit of more than 400,000 allied health workers for 1975 (American Medical Association, Council on Health Manpower, 1972: 5). In the dental field the supply of dentists and paraprofessionals is totally inadequate to meet the increasing demand for services (*Yale Law Journal*, 1974). In the nursing profession the U.S. National Center for Health Statistics (1969) projected a shortage of 100,000 nurses by 1975. Even if the figures are overestimated by as much as 50 percent, it is still true that significant shortages exist.

In the mental health field, determining whether practitioner shortages exist is especially difficult. This stems in part from the difficulties involved in defining what constitutes mental health, and hence, what are to be the goals of treatment; the lack of clarity about the essential skills and tasks to be performed by practitioners; the problem of identifying who "needs" mental health services, especially since measuring the amount of demand in terms of use is subject to so many vagaries; and the problem of determining who is currently providing services, since nurses, teachers, encounter group leaders, as well as psychiatrists, psychologists, and social workers, all provide therapeutic-like services (see Arnhoff, 1971).

An overarching problem, however, is the simple fact that basic data are not available, except on a very fragmented and incomplete basis.[56] Rough estimates, however, indicate that there were 28,332 active psychiatrists and neurologists in 1972 (U.S. NCHS, 1974: 178), 17,000 to 18,000 psychologists providing mental health services as of 1976 (Centor, 1976), and 15,700 social workers employed in psychiatric facilities (U.S. NCHS, 1974: 283).

A general consensus exists that this number of mental health professionals is not enough, even if other groups such as psychiatric nurses are included.[57] Typical of the findings is the work of George Albee (1959). He drew together impressive data to demonstrate that the amount of mental illness in this country was tremendous. He provided documentation that between 20 to 25 percent of all positions in state and county hospitals remained unfilled. The number of professionals available came nowhere near the recommended minimum standards established by the American Psychiatric Association. Albee was very pessimistic about changes in this situation. The burgeoning population and the lack of commitment to education (when compared with the efforts of the Soviet Union) would, in his opinion, ensure that only a small pool would be available from which to develop the skilled personnel required in future years:

We must conclude this survey with the prediction that our country will continue to be faced with serious personnel shortages in all fields related to mental illness and mental health for many years to come. Barring the possibility of a massive national effort in all areas of education, with all of the social changes such an effort would imply, or the possibility of a sharp breakthrough in mental health research, the prospects are pessimistic for significant improvements in the quantity or quality of professional services in these fields (Albee, 1959: 259).

Albee's work was published in 1959 as part of the ten-volume series of the Joint Commission on Mental Illness and Health. In the years since nothing has happened to change his dire prediction.

The President's Commission on Mental Health (1978: 8) has concluded that close to 15 percent of this country's citizens are in need of some form of mental health services. Yet 22 percent of all psychiatric residency training positions are unfilled, with a quarter of those that are filled being occupied either by the foreign-born or foreign-trained (Weinstein, 1968). Kubie (1967) has estimated that between 20,000 to 50,000 positions for trained social workers remain empty each year. The recent right-to-treatment cases, such as *Wyatt v. Stickney* (1974), the extremely high and rising cost of therapeutic services, and the current geographic maldistributions of personnel are indicative of significant shortfalls in the supply of practitioners.

The extent to which licensing plays a role in exacerbating this problem is difficult to determine, but it is probably substantial. It is clear that a variety of factors is at work. The National Manpower Council (1957: 255 et seq.) suggested three broad reasons why shortages are likely to occur in all professions and occupations: (1) the demands created by a dynamic economy and a society with a rapidly advancing technology and science; (2) the demand of citizens for more and better services; and (3) the desire to remove all obstacles impeding government efforts to achieve its societal objectives. In the mental health field in particular, critics have pointed out that educational policies have resulted in the overtraining of a small number of practitioners for clinical positions; that clinicians have tended to move into private practice to the neglect of public service, with the result that certain populations find services unavailable; and that little effort has been expended on adequately training paraprofessionals (see, for instance, Ryan, 1969: 250).

That licensing should also play a role in creating shortages seems self-evident.[58] The purpose of licensing laws, especially those restricting the right to practice as well as use of titles, is to limit the number of people practicing. If the qualifications one must meet are in any way arbitrary, or if other aspects of the administration of licensing laws restricts the number of practitioners, then licensing will have a negative impact on supply. Even if standards are not arbitrary, a curtailment will take place, although it may be argued that this is justified. An examination of the provisions of most licensing laws indicates that many provisions are, in point of fact, arbitrarily restrictive. For instance, entrance requirements have had a tendency to become more stringent, and the change is difficult to account for on the basis of changes in the competencies required. Grant (1942a: 460) cites instances in which age limits and general cultural requirements are increased, and it is typical to require ever-increasing periods of schooling, with requirements for accreditation becoming stricter, as well. Although licensing laws are meant to establish minimal competence, most professions talk in terms of amending laws to raise the level of competence and to ensure that practitioners render only the highest quality services.

While a theoretical argument can be made that increasing the period of schooling required is beneficial, many prerequisites for licensure cannot be justified on any basis. Most requirements regarding a person's race, antecedent local residence, and citizenship have very little to do with competent practice, although they frequently appear on the law books. Even requirements of no criminal record[59] or good moral character[60] are of dubious value in protecting the public, and can produce far more injustice than they prevent. The fact that pass rates on licensing examinations in many occupations vary inversely with the level of unemployment suggests that the criteria for passing is, at least in part, based on a desire to insulate those already licensed from competition (Rayack, 1975: 146–48). In the medical field the rigid, idiosyncratic, and hard-to-satisfy requirements for foreign medical students appear not only to be an effort to keep out the incompetent but to keep out the competition.[61]

By far the most convincing argument that licensing laws unnecessarily restrict the supply of practitioners in the mental health field is the evidence from preceding chapters that little, if any, relationship exists between requirements for licensure and competent practice. A fairly large group of professionals agrees that this is the case (Rioch 1966: 290), and the empirical research tends to bear this out (see earlier chapters, and Hogan, 1977). Not only is there little evidence that credentials are related to competence, but academic grades, licensing examinations, intelligence tests, and aptitude tests have not been shown to have any correlation with the skills needed to practice therapy or any other professional endeavor effectively.

While qualifications are meant to test only minimal levels of competence, a comparison of state laws suggests that this is not so. When requirements for related professions were compared by the Council of State Governments (1952), it found that highly similar occupations often had significantly different entrance prerequisites. This was especially true of barbers and beauticians. The well-established professions of law, medicine, and accountancy tended to have a high degree of conformity from state to state, but plumbers and electricians did not. In the mental health field, the widely diverging requirements for becoming a licensed psychologist, social worker, or psychiatrist indicate that some irrelevancies must be entering in, in addition to suggesting that little is known about what criteria are actually important or how to measure them.

The fact that licensing standards in a given profession tend to rise over time, although without demonstration that the standards required for minimally competent practice have risen, also indicates that current standards are higher than necessary, and hence unduly restrictive.[62] The high cost of obtaining the necessary education and training for a license, and the difficulties that practitioners licensed in one state have in being licensed in another, also suggest that licensing operates to restrict the supply of practitioners available.

Another significant way in which licensure laws unnecessarily restrict entry into a profession is somewhat less direct.

Most licensing laws specify that any academic degree required must be obtained from an accredited institution or program. The importance of accreditation in this country is primarily the result of the efforts of the American Medical Association (Selden, 1971: A-1). In the late 1800s the AMA became increasingly interested in weeding out those medical schools of obviously inferior quality, but it lacked the organization and the power to accomplish this task. A few early efforts were made to develop an accreditation process within a state licensing agency, such as the list of acceptable medical shoools developed in 1880 by the Illinois Board of Health (Grimm, 1972: I-12). But it was not until the early twentieth century that accreditation and licensure became firmly interlocked (Grimm, 1972: I-12).

The American Medical Association was completely reorganized shortly after the turn of the century (Garceau, 1941). As part of this reorganization, a Council on Medical Education was created. This council helped organize the first Congress on Medical Education, which published a list of medical schools classified by the percentage of failures of its students in passing state licensing examinations. Soon therafter the council developed a second classification as a guide for state licensing boards, in which all medical schools were listed as approved, on probation, or unapproved (Shryock, 1967: 60-62).

The resentment encountered by the council as a result of its accreditation process led to its seeking support from the Carnegie Foundation for the Advancement of Teaching to carry out a more objective and thorough evaluation of medical education in the United States. The eventual outcome was the publication of the now famous Flexner Report in 1910, the effect of which was nothing less than dramatic: within five years 40 percent of all medical schools had closed (Selden, 1971: A-4).

Soon therafter the standards of accreditation required by the American Medical Association were incorporated into state licensing statutes and board regulations (Grimm, 1972: I–13). Today most state licensing boards in the medical field rely on the accreditation lists of the American Medical Association or the Association of American Medical Colleges (which maintain the same lists). One consequence of this development has been the ceding of considerable power to the American Medical Association over medical education in this country, since removal from its list is tantamount to disaster.

Most other professions have followed this accreditation model (Newman, 1973: 61). It is typically the dominant professional association in a given field that establishes an accreditation process. Accreditation is then made a requirement before a licensing board will accept an applicant's degree. In many statutes this requirement is expressly mentioned. Where it is not, the large majority of statutes specify that the licensing board is responsible for accrediting institutions and programs. In most instances these boards choose to rely on the lists provided by professional associations or regional or national accrediting agencies (which, in turn, often rely on professional associations).

Whether the actual accrediting body is a state agency, professional association, or regional organization, the fundamental issue is whether the process ensures that licensure applicants have had sound training. Little if any social science research has examined this matter. Subjective study of what actually happens, however, gives the impression that the typical accreditation process is not something on which to rely. Most agencies attempt to examine whether sound education is provided, not whether competent practitioners are produced. Typical concerns center around student-faculty ratios, the number of classroom and other facilities, and faculty background and training (Newman, 1973: 62). Little effort has

been made to determine whether any of these factors is related to future professional performance.

These arbitrary criteria of excellence have grave potential for political abuse. The accrediting arm of the American Bar Association, for instance, is generally acknowledged as having driven most night law schools out of business due to its insistence on full-time law school faculties (Newman, 1973: 62). The degree to which professional associations control this process is illustrated by the fact that 39 states require graduation from a law school accredited by the American Bar Association in order to sit for the bar examination (Newman, 1973: 62). Not coincidentally, as the *Newman Report* (1973: 62) points out, the ABA also controls the examination process and evaluates the "moral fitness" of all candidates for the bar. Members of state licensing boards frequently serve on accreditation organizations, and are often officers of the professional associations representing the field. Since the actual purposes of most accreditation is not to ensure competence, and since the accreditation process is easily abused, the chances that such a process actually does ensure competence are minimal.

Equally damaging is the lack of thoroughness that characterizes much of what passes as accreditation. Even the inspection of medical schools carried out by Abraham Flexner in the early part of this century was somewhat cursory. Taylor and Torrey's (1972) study of accreditation in the mental health field further illustrates how casual the accreditation process can become.

In psychiatry, accreditation is the function of the Joint Residency Review Committee for Psychiatry and Neurology, which consists of six psychiatrists. The committee meets only twice a year, and does so in private. It is typical to act upon as many as 100 separate programs. The evidence on which a determination is made consists of written applications and the additional comments of field staff. These field staff usually inspect at least two programs in a normal workday, and sometimes as many as four or five. The written application asks for information that has virtually no relevance to the quality of the training provided, asking for such data as the number of consultants available in tuberculosis, anesthesia, and urology. Taylor and Torrey (1972: 661) conclude:

The most damaging aspect of this current system of training program accreditation is its destructive influence on the evolution of psychiatric education. Training programs, in order to ensure continued approval, must conform to rigid requirements. Experimentation in developing psychiatric manpower that is more relevant to the public need must be curtailed in order to maintain an accreditation upon which federal support is dependent. . . .

The self-regulation of American psychiatry is a facade that hides the absence of meaningful regulation from the public eye. Despite the regulatory activities of the American Board of Psychiatry and Neurology, the Joint Residency Review Committee, and the various state governments, the fact remains: *to practice psychiatry in this country requires nothing other than a medical license. No demonstrated psychiatric competency is required.*

Empirical research on the effects of licensing are difficult to find. Rayack's (1975: 147) careful research on the operations of licensing agencies in southern New England offers evidence that the failure rates on licensing examinations increase significantly during periods of high economic unemployment: "When labor market conditions worsen, licensing boards tend to fail a higher percentage of applicants for licensure, irrespective of the qualifications of the applicants, in order to reduce the flow of new entrants into the market and thereby strengthen the competitive position of the licensed" (see also Maurizi, 1974). Moore's (1961: 93) research on the actual purposes served by licensing led him to conclude that "the

most restrictive types appear to have been established to benefit practitioners of the regulated occupations and businesses." At the same time, Moore (1961: 106) suggests that such laws are also passed to protect the public on the theory that society knows best, especially "when the variance in the quality of the service furnished by the practitioner is high, when the importance of that variance is great, when the amount of training necessary to evaluate the service is large, and when the degree of exposure of the consumer to the practitioner is small" (see also Leffler, 1977). Carroll and Gaston's (1977: 41) careful study of eight diverse professions found that restrictive licensing significantly lowered the number of people licensed, and that such restrictions may actually lower the quality of service received.

Attempts to verify empirically the restrictive effects of regulation in other areas, such as the airlines and electric utilities, may have some generalizability to the field of professional licensing. Jeffrey Pfeffer (1974: 478), of the University of California, Berkeley, has collected and reviewed existing research, including regulation by federal agencies, and concludes:

The role of administrative regulation in the solution of social problems must be called into question. There is evidence that administrative regulation and licensing has actually operated against the public interest; and that rather than protecting the public from the industry, regulation has frequently operated to protect and economically enhance the industry or occupation.

Typical of the studies he reviewed was Stigler and Friedland's (1962) examination of electric utilities, which sought to determine whether regulation curtailed the exercise of monopoly power and the elimination of price discrimination. They found that the laws had no effect whatever, except for one year in which there was some indication that regulation protected the industrial consumers, who were never meant to be the prime benefactors of the law. Demsetz (1968) offers additional evidence that regulation has operated to drastically decrease the number of separate public utilities that exist in this country. Studies by Jackson (1969) and Moore (1970) indicate that regulation does little to reduce rates. Volotta (1967) has found convincing evidence that the impact of federal controls on motor carrier operations has reduced the number of carriers. A study by Peltzman (1965) indicates that legal restrictions in the banking industry have resulted in a 25 to 50 percent decrease in commercial banks in this country. In the airline industry, Jordan (1970: 16–17) notes that the only carriers providing trunk service today are those that existed when the Civil Aeronautics Board was formed in 1938. Where the CAB does not have jurisdiction, however, as in California, sixteen interstate carriers entered the field in the twenty years up to 1965.

Several other facets of licensure operate as an impediment to people entering the field. Most licensing laws, especially in the field of psychotherapy, define professional practice in such broad terms that paraprofessionals are seriously hindered from effective and efficient functioning, and related professions must often worry about infringing upon another profession. Rigid supervisory requirements in the use of paraprofessionals significantly decrease their effectiveness, although little evidence exists for the necessity of such close supervision. When combined with: (1) the existence of entrance criteria of questionable relevance; (2) educational requirements that take long periods to fulfill; (3) the existence of only one method of becoming licensed, as opposed to allowing credit for work experience or demonstrated competence; and (4) the existence of strict accreditation requirements of questionable relevance, licensing laws have operated as a significant deterrent to entry into the field and have helped exacerbate existing shortages.

Exacerbation of Maldistributions in the Supply of Practitioners

The health field as a whole, and the mental health field in particular, has been beset with serious problems in the distribution of practitioners.[63] This problem exists along a number of dimensions. First, health personnel, especially physicians, are not equally distributed on a state-by-state or regional basis (American Medical Association, 1971; Hiestand and Ostow 1976). Physicians tend to be concentrated in urban areas, as opposed to rural settings (Beeson, 1974; Carlson, 1975: 39–40). Health professionals tend to serve the rich rather than the poor (Carlson, 1975: 39–40). Physicians tend to be concentrated in certain types of institutions, to the relative neglect of other institutions (for instance, mental hospitals have a serious problem in finding adequate numbers of psychiatrists). The medical field also has a skewed distribution according to specialty (American Medical Association, 1971; Carlson, 1975: 39–41; Carlson, 1970: 859), with surgery one of the fields most in demand and the role of general practitioner relatively neglected.

A few examples will help bring the nature and extent of the problem into sharper relief. As of 1973 there were 171 physicians per 100,000 population in this country. In West Virginia, however, the equivalent population was served by only 111 physicians (Beeson, 1974). Breaking this down even further, while West Virginia is primarily rural in character, fully two-thirds of all licensed doctors resided in only twelve of fifty-five counties (Beeson, 1974). In 1970, while the more affluent states averaged 160 practicing physicians per 100,000 population, the less affluent had roughly half as many (Carlson, 1975: 39). Even where physicians are not badly distributed, sick or injured persons often do not know how to gain access to appropriate medical help.[64]

In the late sixties, 30 percent of the U.S. population was in rural areas, but only 12 percent of all physicians and 18 percent of all nurses practiced there (Carlson, 1970: 859, m. 33). The problem of specialty maldistribution is also severe and likely to get worse. As of 1970 the AMA recognized sixty-three specialties, but only 21 percent of all physicians classified themselves as general practitioners. Recent predictions are that the percentage of primary-care physicians will drop to 50 percent by 1980, from its current level of 55 percent (Carlson, 1975: 41). The problem of specialty maldistribution is especially complex because specialists tend to practice in urban areas. For instance, only 8 percent of all pediatricians practice outside urban settings (Carlson, 1970: 859, m. 33).

In the mental health field, Albee (1959: 47–61) was one of the first to document the problems of maldistribution. He found that psychologists tended to be quite urban: the ratio in metropolitan and adjacent areas was more than four times as high as rural areas per 100,000 population. The same was true for psychiatrists. As of 1955, 40 percent of all psychiatrists were practicing in the eighteen largest U.S. cities, which contained less than 18 percent of the total population. More than three-fourths of all psychoanalysts in this country were to be found in the ten largest U.S. cities as of 1957, with almost two-thirds in New York, Chicago, Los Angeles, Boston, and Washington. In the ten most urbanized states, Albee found one psychiatrist for every 12,000 people, while in the ten least urbanized, the ratio was one for every 43,800 (Albee, 1959: 60). He noted that the same sort of evidence could be cited for other types of psychotherapists, such as psychiatric social workers (Albee, 1959: 61).

The situation has not changed much in the years since Albee did his original study. In fact, it has probably become worse. As of 1969 more than half of all psychiatrists were located in five states— New York, Pennsylvania, Massachusetts, Illinois, and California (National Association for Mental Health, 1969). The cities of New York, Boston, Washington, and San Francisco contain 28 percent of all psychiatrists, despite the fact that only 10 percent of the population resides in these cities (U.S. National Institute of Mental Health, 1969). Moreover, only 4 percent of all psychiatrists practice outside of an urban setting (Carlson, 1970: 859, m. 33). One of the most provocative statistics is the fact that two adjacent buildings on New York's 96th Street contain the offices of sixty-five psychiatrists—more than the total number of psychiatrists in sixteen different states and as many as the total number in twenty-seven nations (Wykert, 1971). Even within a city, psychiatrists in private practice see a highly skewed sample of the total population.[65]

A variety of factors accounts for this maldistribution of practitioners. Mechanic (1970: 240) has isolated a number of the more significant ones:

Like other professionals, doctors seek to live in areas that provide educational and cultural opportunities, and where they can earn a comfortable living within pleasant surroundings. Many doctors find it more comfortable and less trying to work with patients who share their cultural definitions and understandings. Moreover, . . . medical training in the context of the teaching hospital encourages a pattern of practice that requires the technology of a hospital and considerable colleague cooperation. The isolation of practice in underdoctored areas outside close proximity to an adequate hospital and colleagues is frustrating to the physician who feels he cannot implement the level of scientific training he received. Many rural practices would isolate him from a colleague network, more complex diagnostic and treatment aids, and the ancillary assistance available in more densely populated areas. Practice in impoverished areas also involves other frustrations, such as a high prevalence of drug addiction and alcoholism which may threaten the doctor, shortages of assisting personnel and resources, and the complexity of social and economic problems that affect the care of patients.

Licensure laws are also a contributing factor. The geographic problem has been exacerbated because licensure laws make it difficult for licensed practitioners in one state to obtain a license in another. Florida, for instance, has been notorious for its stringent and arbitrary requirements for out-of-state physicians, which constitute a direct attempt to discourage semiretired practitioners from moving to the state, since they pose an economic threat to those doctors already practicing.[66] Wide variations in licensing examination policies have hampered the movements of practitioners from state to state, especially those attempting to be licensed for the first time, but this problem has diminished as more states adopt national examinations. The National Board of Medical Examiners, for instance, now provides tests for all graduates of U.S. and Canadian schools, while the Federation of State Medical Boards tests foreign graduates. Social work and psychology have only recently begun to experiment with national examinations, but unfortunately none has been tested to determine whether it measures important competencies.

Broad and overly vague definitions of professional practice, when combined with stringent supervisory requirements, also foster maldistributions.[67] Effective use of paraprofessionals in rural areas, for instance, is dependent upon the elimination of "over-the-shoulder" and "on-the-premises" supervision, since such requirements are impractical and eliminate the substantial value of paraprofessionals making house calls or operating clinics under periodic supervision. In addition, definitions of practice need to be narrowed or exemptions provided so that paraprofessionals can undertake certain types of carefully and narrowly prescribed medical diagnoses and treatment. Physicians have been relatively loathe to use physician assistants precisely because of their fear of malpractice suits and technical violations of the law.[68]

Rigorous empirical verification of the impact of licensing on maldistribution is woefully inadequate, but three of four extant studies indicate that the effect is significant. More than ten years ago Arlene Holen (1965) studied the interstate mobility and resource allocation of dentists, lawyers and judges, and physicians and surgeons. In the case of physicians, where reciprocity agreements were common, she found much greater interstate mobility (as reflected by migration rates) and resource allocation (as reflected by differences in professional incomes by state) than for dentists and lawyers. A more recent finding by Holen (1977), however, demonstrates that those states with more stringent requirements have actually had a greater increase in dentists per capita over the last ten years. Holen suggests that this occurs because dentist income is higher in those states with more stringent requirements, which attracts more and better-qualified applicants.

On the other hand, a study by Shepard (undated), to be published in the *Journal of Law and Economics*, documents the various means that licensing boards use to exclude out-of-state practitioners, which he estimates results in a 15 percent increase in dental fees nationwide and an overall cost of approximately $700 million. Shepard cites findings that the 35 dental boards that do not have reciprocity agreements with other states fail an average of 22 percent of recent dental school graduates from out of state, versus a mean figure of 9 percent in reciprocity states. These same states granted significantly fewer dental degrees to students in their own states, as well.

Shepard's study found that fees were significantly higher in states that lacked reciprocity—which he attributes to the differences in state laws, and which is evidence of maldistribution. These conclusions are supported by Boulier (1974), who found that dentists were less mobile than other professionals and that the variance in prices of dental services between states was greater than within-state variance.

Although the above evidence suggests that licensing laws do exacerbate problems of maldistribution in various professional fields, the question remains whether this is true for the field of psychotherapy. On this no evidence exists apart from the logical arguments provided above. It is perhaps true that licensing constitutes less of an impediment because most laws regulating psychologists, social workers, and physicians have adequate reciprocity and endorsement agreements. The existence of maldistribution is probably more a function of therapists being attracted to urban areas where the number of patients is sufficient to earn a reasonable income.

Even though the impact of licensing laws on maldistributions may be less for the therapy field than in other professions, the negative consequences may be greater. For instance, the fact that licensing laws, as well as other factors, may encourage specialists to reside in urban areas may be of little consequence, since specialists do not need to work in the same proximity of their patients. This is especially true where diagnosis and treatment need to be provided on a one-time basis only. On the other hand, psychotherapy is typically provided through a series of contacts extending over a significant period of time, and necessitates a practitioner living in the neighborhood of the client.

Increased Cost of Services

The cost of health care in this country has been spiralling, with much of it due to the rise in cost of professional services. In 1978, Americans will spend close to $200 billion dollars on health care, which is 10 percent of the U.S. Gross National Product (GNP) (Shabecoff, 1978). This amount is more than the entire GNP of all but six other nations; it is more than seven times what is spent on the criminal justice system (including police, the judiciary, and prisons), and it represents a rate of inflation more than three times the annual increase in the cost of living

(Somers, 1977: 962). Health care is now the country's third largest industry, behind only food and construction (Shabecoff, 1978).

The rise in physician fees accounts for a substantial proportion of this increase. Spending on physician services represents the second largest medical expenditure in health care costs, and physician fees rose 13.4 percent between April 1974 and June 1975 alone (U.S. Social Security Administration, 1975: 10, 24). Physician income has been rising at an annual rate of 9 percent, and the average net income of physicians is now approximately $60,000 a year (Claiborne, 1978: 50), up from $37,372 in 1968 and $49,415 in 1973 (U.S. Social Security Administration, 1975: 59). A physician's annual income is now more than 20 percent greater than a lawyer's and 25 percent more than an engineer's (Claiborne, 1978: 50).[69]

Although data are more difficult to locate for the mental health field, fees and income have undergone a somewhat less drastic increase. In 1951 the mean income of psychiatrists was $17,300, which was nearly 50 percent greater than for general practitioners (Albee, 1959: 23-24). More than twenty years later the average psychiatrist was earning $40,027, or more than $2,000 less than a GP (U.S. Social Security Administration, 1975: 59). On the other hand, practicing psychologists have seen their average income rise from $3,572 in 1949 (Albee, 1959: 23-24) to $37,500 in 1973, with more than one-quarter reporting incomes of $50,000 or more (Dörken and Associates, 1976: 11). Thus, practicing psychologists are rapidly achieving parity with their psychiatric counterparts.

It is clear that the rise in health-care costs is due to a variety of factors: (1) the expanded government funding of health care; (2) the growth in per capita visits to physicians; (3) greater utilization of higher-priced specialists; (4) hospital costs; (5) the increase in physician fees; and (6) the relative lack of control that insurance companies have been able to exert on physician and hospital costs. The extent to which the rise in costs is due to licensing laws—especially for physicians' services—is significant. If licensing laws contribute to shortages and maldistributions, as argued above, then the law of supply and demand dictates that prices will rise as a result. Thus, the arguments and evidence presented in the two previous sections apply here. Even the American Medical Association (AMA Council on Health Manpower, 1970: 2), although arguing that no empirical evidence exists, appears to agree:

The effects of licensure on costs of health care have not been documented, and more complete data should be collected before conclusions are drawn. Analysis of increased hospital costs, however, offers some indication of the effect in terms of salary demands when there is legislative recognition of a given health occupation. In addition, if mandatory licensure trends continue in the present era of functional and knowledge specialization, the time may come when an individual will need four or five licenses to perform a limited service, with resulting underutilization of personnel, and concomitantly increased cost to the consumer.

Since 1970, when the AMA made the above statement, a growing body of research supports the thesis that licensure increases the costs of professional goods and services. Benham (1972), for instance, found that in states that prohibited advertising related to eyeglasses and eye examinations, the prices of eyeglasses were 25 to more than 100 percent higher than states with no restrictions. It did not appear that advertising restrictions were a proxy for other restraints on competition, since interstate barriers to mobility were not responsible and qualitative evidence did not implicate any other factors. Most important, Benham was not able to find any evidence that unrestricted advertising affected the quality of eyeglasses. A follow-up to this study three years later came to similar conclusions: prices of

eyeglasses were 25 to 40 percent higher, and the proportion of individuals obtaining eyeglasses in a given year was significantly lower in markets with greater professional control (Benham and Benham, 1975).

An FTC study by Phelan (1974) adds support to the hypothesis that licensing increases the cost of services rendered. The cost of TV repairs in Louisiana—which has a strict licensing law requiring two years of formal training or two years of apprenticeship and successful completion of a written exam for a person to be licensed—was compared with California, which allows anyone to practice so long as she or he is registered with the state, but which also has a very active disciplinary board, and Washington, where no law whatsoever exists. The cost of repairs was significantly higher in New Orleans (Phelan, 1974: 26). The variations in costs were significantly less in San Francisco. In both New Orleans and Washington, one-half of the repair firms made fraudulent repairs, while the rate in California was only 20 percent. To the extent that fraud is an indication of poor quality, this study indicates that strict licensing is no better than no licensing at all, and worse than alternative forms of regulation.

Other studies are largely in agreement with these findings.[70] White (forthcoming, 1978, 1975), for instance, documents the fact that licensing of clinical laboratory personnel has raised wages without any proof that quality has improved. He concludes that licensing is not worth the resultant costs. Shepard's (undated: 7) analysis of licensure restrictions and the cost of dental care revealed that fees for eleven of the twelve most common services were higher in states that lacked reciprocity agreements with other states. These differences were statistically significant at the 5 percent level for seven of the twelve services, even when accounting for regional cost-of-living variations. Although Holen's (1977: 34) research on the same subject found that dentist earnings and the price of services were higher in states with more stringent licensing, she also found that the overall quality of dental care, as measured by the amount of untreated dental disease relative to total dental disease, was better. Contrary to Shepard, she was unable to find any association between reduced dentist mobility or the number of dentists per capita and licensing barriers.

Unfortunately, no studies exist that directly examine the question of whether licensing laws in the psychotherapy field influence the cost of services. It is possible, however, to examine the impact of other forms of regulation in other industries on the price of services. If these are found to be ineffective, especially where their primary purpose is the control of prices, it provides indirect, but suggestive, evidence that regulation through licensure will result in a cost increase. Pfeffer's (1974) review of the empirical literature in the transportation and utilities industries, where federal regulation is expressly designed to protect consumers from unwarranted and monopolistic price increases, indicates that regulation either has no effect or increases the cost of services.[71]

Regulation in the airline industry has been notoriously ineffective. An article in the *Yale Law Journal* (Levine, 1965: 1416–17) concluded:

Government restriction of entry into the industry and the regulation of fares has fostered unnecessarily high fares, encouraged uneconomic practices, and limited the variety of service available to the public. The performance of the largest air transportation market in the world provides convincing evidence that fares are much lower and service more responsive to public needs where restrictions on entry are absent and control over fares is rarely exercised.

The author of the article, Michael Levine, argues that neither traditional economic arguments regarding the dangers of monopolies, nor social objectives such as providing services to out-of-the-way places, nor the fears of increased risks to passenger safety justify present methods. Levine studied the effect of regulation by the Civil Aeronautics Board (CAB) on interstate airlines by comparing air transportation between Los Angeles and the San Francisco Bay area, which involved no regulation since it was wholly intrastate, with the rest of the country, where air traffic was regulated by the CAB. Traffic between San Francisco and Los Angeles increased almost 300 percent between 1959 and 1964, although traffic in the United States as a whole rose only 50 percent. The cost per mile of travel in California was only 3.9 cents, versus 5.5 cents for average jet coach fare in the United States. Air fare between Boston and Washington, which involves interstate traffic and a distance roughly equivalent to the Los Angeles–San Francisco trip, cost more than twice as much ($24.65 versus $11.43).

The problems and horrors of lack of regulation did not occur. No disastrous competition and price wars ensued. Despite the fact of reduced rates, firms were able to operate profitably. Small, local airlines have been able to compete with the larger established airlines. Even the expected increased risk to passenger safety did not materialize. Levine (1965: 1444) notes that Pacific Southwest Airlines had not experienced a fatal accident up to the time of his study, and Trans California, the most recent intrastate entrant, had no safety problems whatever during the two years it was in operation.[73]

In summary, it appears that licensure laws are very likely to play a significant role in increasing the cost of professional services. Qualitative evidence suggests that restrictions on entry into the field, expensive training and education requirements, difficulties in making maximal and effective use of paraprofessionals, and prohibitions on advertising will tend to increase costs. Although empirical evidence on the effects of licensing mental health professionals is absent, evidence from other licensed professions and studies of the impact of regulation in other industries indicates that regulation leads to inflation in the cost of doing business.

Ineffective Utilization of Paraprofessionals

In the field of psychotherapy the issue of paraprofessional utilization has been relatively ignored.[74] Although little empirical research has been done, qualitative evidence from other professional fields, especially the health field, indicates that paraprofessionals are not effectively utilized because of restrictions imposed by licensing laws and that this has had a significant impact on the extent and quality of services rendered to the public.[75] It seems reasonable that the situation in the mental health field is not likely to be substantially different from medicine, since both are dominated by highly trained professionals; both are labor intensive, requiring personal services that cannot be substituted for by machine; and licensing laws in the mental health field have been modeled after those regulating physicians and surgeons. Thus, problems created for paraprofessionals in medicine will most likely exist in psychotherapy.

Few professions make adequate use of paraprofessionals. Several underlying factors are responsible. First, the use of paraprofessionals may be viewed as an economic threat by established practitioners.[76] Even if practitioners are not threatened, they may not be convinced of the efficacy of less than fully trained professional help (Roemer, 1970a: 52-53). Paraprofessionals themselves frequently have attitudes and feelings of inadequacy that militate against their most effective use.[77] The attitude of consumers toward paraprofessionals may also operate as a hindrance, although empirical research indicates that auxiliaries are quickly accepted by those who have dealt with them.[78] Finally, institutional factors such as the economics of solo

practice and the roles that hospitals have historically established for auxiliaries may constrain their maximum utilization (Roemer, 1970: 52). The result of these forces has been the enactment of policies and procedures, especially in licensing laws and the rules and regulations of licensing boards, that seriously restrict the paraprofessional's chance of operating efficiently.

Perhaps the most serious problem with licensing laws has been their tendency to restrict the numbers of auxiliaries available to practice. By defining in extremely broad terms those practices restricted to fully licensed practitioners, and by making no provision or very rigid and narrow provisions for delegating functions to others, licensing laws unnecessarily limit those who can provide auxiliary services. In their report to the National Advisory Commission on Health Manpower, Forgotson, Roemer, and Newman (1967: 332) stated that "among the many problems presented by the medical licensure laws, without question, the issue of delegation of tasks is a highly significant, if not the most significant, problem requiring resolution."

Educational requirements and other prerequisites for obtaining a license seriously restrict the number of paraprofessionals able to practice. Many requirements are unrelated to ability, especially citizenship, residency, age, and other personal requirements. The amount of schooling and experience demanded is often excessive. Many of the laws regulating the paraprofessional do not allow alternative routes to licensure, such as through equivalency or proficiency testing, or through giving credit for related work experience. Often no credit is allowed for formal education in a degree program different from the one licensed, even if the courses are identical—a fact that has serious implications for career mobility. Egelston (1970: 44) comments: "The increasing number of allied health groups seeking licensure ultimately will create job overlap and increase the number of dead-end jobs. Moreover, it appears predictable that a proliferation of licensing laws eventually will require multiple licenses for practitioners."

Data collected by Arnhoff (1971: 73–77) indicate that paraprofessional training programs in the military require far briefer time commitments without necessarily sacrificing quality. For instance, where civilian programs require dental specialists to be trained for 2 years, the military requires only 16 weeks. A similar differential exists for X-ray specialists. Dental assistant programs located in technical institutes and hospitals almost always are less than a year in length, while almost 50 percent of those located in universities and hospitals require more than 71 weeks.

Licensing laws also hinder paraprofessionals once they are on the job. Overly broad definitions of practice for the fully licensed practitioner prevent auxiliaries from performing many tasks of which they are fully capable. Lave and Lave (1970: 257–60) estimate that 80 percent of pediatric practice could be done by personnel with far less training. The typical medical practice act allows only the physician to diagnose, operate, treat, or prescribe for mental or physical illnesses. Paraprofessionals are granted limited and circumscribed fields of practice.

It is difficult to know what the limits of the physician's functions are. The result is that most physicians are hesitant to allow paraprofessionals to perform questionable tasks unless a legal determination has been made that performing a particular task will not be in violation of the law. Roemer's (1970: 48–49, footnotes omitted) analysis of the problem is worth quoting in detail:

As for specific prohibitions in the statutes or regulations, one may take the example of providing medication. The medical practice acts stipulate that only phsyicians may "prescribe" or "furnish" drugs; the pharmacy laws authorize pharmacists to "dispense" drugs; and the nursing practice acts authorize nurses to "administer" them. The question is: what acts constitute "dispensing," and what acts constitute "administering"? This is not a matter of semantics but a practical question affecting behavior of health personnel.

Interpretations of the pharmacy law in some states are so restrictive that nurses refuse to issue routine refills of prescriptions in the absence of standing orders or telephone prescriptions from a physician. Thus, in Los Angeles County, public health nurses were concerned about their authority to provide continuing medication in an isoniazid therapy program of tuberculosis control. A night nurse on duty in a small hospital without a pharmacist at night may be acting in a grey area between medical and nursing practice if she issues medications.

. . . It is significant that the medical licensure laws were enacted in the late 1800's and early 1900's when the provision of medical care was vastly different from that in the current health system. Licensure laws for other health professions and occupations were patterned after the medical model. What may have been proper when medical care was largely provided by solo practitioners in an entrepreneurial fashion may no longer be reasonable when medical care is increasingly a product of team effort in an organized setting, rather than of an individual practitioner. Between 1900 and 1967, physicians declined from 35 percent to 9 percent of the total supply of health manpower. Yet no significant amendment of any state medical practice act has been made in nearly a century, and the definitions of scope of functions in the various licensing laws have now become a straitjacket on delivery of services by a health team.

Until relatively recently no medical practice acts explicitly provided for the delegation of various functions to other allied health personnel. Such delegation was simply a matter of prevailing custom and practice. Cases such as *Barber v. Reinking* (1966), however, have held that professional custom is not a legitimate defense for violating a licensing statute. As a result, many states have enacted amendments to their medical practice acts, which expressly allow delegations of certain functions (Sadler, 1974; Willig, 1971).

These amendments have taken two general forms (Howard and Ball, 1973). The first codifies the legal right of the physician to delegate tasks to certain qualified nonphysicians; the second involves a completely separate licensing law for the auxiliary personnel. As of 1972, fourteen states had enacted the former and eight the latter.

Several problems have arisen from these approaches. In many instances physicians' assistants are not allowed to perform functions they are perfectly capable of doing. Even when they are capable, the degree of supervision required minimizes the freedom of the auxiliary and requires a good deal of the physician's time, which could be better spent elsewhere.[79]

While medicine has been sponsoring legislation that permits delegation of certain functions to assistants, psychology has tended to ignore this problem. Of the twenty-seven states in which practice is restricted to those with a license, only ten have express provisions for delegation to unlicensed assistants. In all of these, supervision is required, and in three cases the type of supervision is specified. Fortunately, only two states restrict the types of function that may be delegated.[80] Where enabling legislation does not exist, or where it is narrowly drawn, the fear of malpractice suits or the fear of noncoverage or cancellation of malpractice insurance will seriously constrict the degree to which the paraprofessional is used.[81]

A final problem of licensing laws with respect to paraprofessionals is their tendency to block horizontal or vertical career mobility.[82] Different licenses are required for a wide variety of allied health fields. Each generally specifies certain educational requirements, including graduation from an approved school. Because the range of approved schools is usually small, graduation from one school frequently does not help in obtaining a license in another field, no matter how closely related. Frequently, relevant course work or experience counts for nothing, making horizontal mobility difficult. Since licensing laws have rarely been constructed with career ladders in mind, most operate as a significant deterrent against vertical mobility, as well. Thus, the enactment of physician assistant laws, which have been widely heralded for their value in increasing paraprofessional utilization, seldom offer nurses credit for any of their education or experience, no matter how extensive and no matter how well qualified they may be.

Inhibition of Important Innovations in Professional Practice, Training, Education, and Organization of Services

There are many different routes to knowledge and learning and the effect of restricting . . . practice . . . and defining it as we tend to do to a particular group, who in the main have to conform to the prevailing orthodoxy, is certain to reduce the amount of experimentation that goes on and hence to reduce the rate of growth of knowledge in the area. [Friedman 1962: 157.]

Licensure laws in virtually all occupations and professions—both within and without the health field—have exerted a negative influence on professional practice, training, education, and the methods by which professional services are organized. The most effective means by which this is accomplished is through the disciplinary provisions of the laws. In his recent books on the professions in general and the legal profession in particular, Lieberman (1978, 1970) describes incident after incident in which licensing laws have been used to curb developments of comprehensive prepaid group medical plans such as those developed by Kaiser, Ross-Loss, Group Health, and HIP (see also Kessell, 1970: 270), as well as the development of low-cost clinics in the legal field.

As a result of the technological break-throughs in the medical field in recent years, many of the tasks that formerly required the unique skills of the physician now can be adequately performed by semiskilled technicians. Because the medical practice acts lag far behind current developments, however, their definitions of what constitutes medical practice frequently block the benefits that would flow from these improvements (Hershey, 1970: 173–74).

Licensing laws also inhibit needed improvements in the education and training of professionals and paraprofessionals, alike. In earlier years it was common for medical practice acts to specify explicitly the number and type of courses required, the number of hours, and even the content of courses that had to be satisfied before a license was granted. Although today this is rarely the case (Leymaster and Mason, 1972: 476), laws frequently specify the duration of medical school training, thereby impeding experiments with three-year programs.

The nature of licensing examinations, the areas in which an examinee will be tested, and the requirement that an applicant have graduated from a program accredited by the American Medical Association ensure that medical education will be quite standardized, although there is little evidence that current teaching methods and programs are superior to other alternatives.[83] Jervey (1971: 91–92) has described the problem well:

What of the laws governing the practice of medicine in the various states? Sir William Osler in 1902 said, "Our medical licensing system is provincialism run riot and is in a pestiferous condition." Unfortunately the libretto may have changed slightly with the passage of time, but the tune has remained essentially the same. The most recent studies done by such prestigious groups as the President's Health Manpower Commission and the Coggeswell Report and others have indicated that the state laws are impeding not only medical education but everything medical including the distribution and delivery of health care.

In the mental health field, professional education and training has not been hindered by licensure laws nearly as much as in medicine, at least within particular professions. Thus, in psychology the basic requirement for licensure is generally a doctorate in a subject that is primarily psychological in nature from a program approved by the state board. To date, boards have not required that programs be APA-approved, and specific courses are not required in most laws. Also on the positive side, most state laws regulating psychology, social work, and marriage and family counseling have not attempted to take a restrictive stance toward organizational developments in the field. Thus, practitioners are not generally subject to legal sanctions for participating in comprehensive prepaid group practices.

On the other hand, licensing laws are heavily implicated in the continued fragmentation of the mental health field. Licenses in psychology, social work, medicine, and marriage and family counseling all confer the right to practice psychotherapy, but only marriage and family counseling has seen fit to honor course work or educational degrees obtained in these related fields. As the lines among these professions are more rigidly drawn in efforts for inclusion in national health insurance, licensing laws will make it difficult, if not impossible, to create a unified psychotherapeutic profession.

Discrimination against Minorities, Women, the Aged, and the Poor

A very serious liability of current licensing laws, especially those that rely on academic credentials, is the resultant discriminatory impact. In the professions generally, and particularly in the mental health field, the poor, the aged, minorities, and women are underrepresented.

For instance, in medicine, women comprise only 8.3 percent of all physicians (AMA, Center for Health Services Research and Development, 1977: 11, 35); 11.4 percent of all psychiatrists (American Psychiatric Association, 1973: 3); and 25 percent of all physician-assistant graduates (Hiestand and Ostow, 1976: 77). In psychology, women constitute only 23.4 percent of the APA membership (Boneau and Cuca, 1974: 823), and have received only 22.5 percent of all doctoral degrees awarded (American Psychological Association, 1973: 51), despite the fact they constitute 51 percent of the population.

For minorities the situation is even worse. Blacks make up only 1.4 percent of all psychiatrists (American Psychiatric Association, 1973: 5); 1.4 percent of the membership of the American Psychological Association (Boneau and Cuca, 1974: 825); and 4.3 percent of all physician assistant graduates (Hiestand and Ostow, 1976: 77). Over nearly half a century, blacks received only eight doctoral degrees in psychology from the ten most prestigious schools in the country, and six of these did not grant any degrees to a black person (American Psychological Association, 1973: 43).

The extent to which licensing laws are responsible for the absence of these groups from the professions is difficult to determine. Only two studies bear even directly on the matter. Dorsey's (Business Week, 1977: 128) research on the Illinois and Missouri licensing examinations for barbers and cosmetologists revealed that black applicants failed 40 percent more often than whites, while high school drop-outs failed 15 percent more often than high school graduates. According to Shepard (undated: 18), H.E. Frech has found a "startling body of evidence indicating that ethnic and sexual discrimination has arisen from . . . entry restrictions imposed by organized medicine." Neither of these studies provides conclusive evidence of licensing's involvement in discrimination, however, and it is necessary to turn to an indirect and somewhat qualitative approach.

In essence the argument for the existence of discrimination is rather simple. It runs as follows. If academic credentials are required for entry into a profession, and if these credentials are not valid or reliable measures of competence, and if minorities, women, the poor, and the aged have greater-than-normal difficulty in obtaining these credentials, then it is reasonable to assume that discrimination has taken place (whether intentional or not). White and Francis (1976) have provided convincing arguments with supporting data to indicate that this is the case. They first point out that a major determinant of who completes high school, who enters college, and who graduates with a college degree is socioeconomic class.[84] Since minority groups constitute an abnormally high percentage of the poor, and more than twice the percentage of blacks than caucasians leave high school without graduating, the prerequisite of academic achievement becomes a powerful force for racial discrimination.

Credentials also operate against women. White and Francis (1976: 1223) point out that in 1968, 14 percent fewer women than men in the eighteen- to twenty-four-year-old age bracket went on to college after high school graduation. The percentage of doctorates awarded to women has not increased substantially since 1900, when it was 9 percent, despite the fact that women receive superior grades in both high school and college. Other evidence indicates that academic admission policies have favored men over women, even when both have identical qualifications.

A final group that White and Francis (1976: 1225-26) argue are discriminated against by credential requirements are older men and women, since earlier generations left school with fewer credentials than the average student today. In fact, by 1980 half of the U.S. labor force will be composed of individuals under thirty-five with at least four years of college. On the other hand, half of the workers with no more than an elementary school education will be over fifty. Most older men and women cannot afford to leave their jobs and go back to school. Thus, the reliance of licensing laws on academic credentials, which are less frequently possesed by the poor, minorities, women, and the elderly, has a deeply pernicious and discriminatory effect, especially when evidence does not exist that these credentials are positively correlated with competence.[85]

CONCLUSION: THE RETURN OF THE GUILDS

It must be concluded that the outcomes of regulation and licensing are frequently not in the interests of the consumers or the general public. It is difficult to find a single empirical study of regulatory effects that does not arrive at essentially this conclusion. . . .

In a review of the outcome of regulation and licensing, we have found that the effect is almost always to enhance the position of the industry or licensed occupation at the expense of the public at large. . . .

In view of these empirical results, accumulated in a series of studies covering both different time periods and different industries, the role of administrative regulation in the solution of social problems must be called into question. There is evidence that administrative regulation and licensing has actually operated against the public interest; and that rather than protecting the public from the industry, regulation has frequently operated to protect and economically enhance the industry or occupation.

. . . Even if quality differences are observed, the question remains as to whether they are worth the cost. [Pfeffer, 1974: 474, 478.]

As a result of recent technological developments and the increase in knowledge, the number of professions in society has proliferated. With this proliferation has come a demand for licensure, and the result has been the licensing of more than 500 occupations as of 1970.

Many political scientists believe that these events mark a return to the guild society of the Middle Ages.[86] Lieberman (1970: 3), for instance, states that "the medieval guild system would not be consciously tolerated in the United States today; yet to a degree greater than most people realize, America is returning to that presumably long-dead institution, as scores of occupations rush to achieve professional status." All the elements of the guild are present. Like the guilds, licensed professions have established the requirement of compulsory membership, creating a monopoly. Like the guilds, licensing standards have become higher and the cost of licensure has increased as educational requirements have lengthened. Like the guilds, periods of apprenticeships have been lengthened, the number of apprentices have been restricted, and in many cases the possibility of obtaining a license through apprenticeship has been eliminated.

De Lancey (1938) has pointed out that this is not the only method of regulating the professions. During the era of Jacksonian democracy, any person who wanted to could practice what he or she wished in a system of extreme laissez-faire. Other countries have adopted socialistic methods of regulation, which, in their most extreme form, give the state absolute authority to hire and fire practitioners, to determine how many practitioners are needed, and to determine the salary, training, function, and location of those practitioners.

Alternatives to the present system of licensing, however, are difficult to conceive of for most Americans, who have come to accept licensure as the major, if not only, means of adequately protecting the public. The mounting evidence that even in established professions licensing may not do a very good job of protecting the public, and may even be causing a significant degree of harm, suggests that the time for developing alternatives is rapidly arriving. More important, the time has come to recognize that the basic issue involved in regulation of any sort is not simply to protect the public, but also to ensure that all members of society have adequate and prompt access to professional services at a reasonable cost.

NOTES

1. Lieberman (1970: 246) has identified six types of activities that licensure laws are designed to cover (whether or not they should be used to cover such matters is another issue):

(1) activity which if negligently performed may lead to death or serious bodily injury (i.e., inherently dangerous injury); (2) activity which may result in deprivation of legal rights; (3) activity resulting in defective craftsmanship of an objective nature (e.g., watchmaking); (4) activity resulting in defective craftsmanship of a subjective nature (e.g., photography); (5) activity by those who receive money in advance or those who do not have a fixed place of business; and (6) activity involving a fiduciary trust the breach of which can lead to a serious psychological or economic injury.

2. For general references to the administrative process, see Davis (1972); Freund (1928); Gellhorn and Byse (1974); and Leiserson (1975).

3. Licensing has been defined as the administrative lifting of a legislative prohibition (Freund, 1928). The Council of State Governments (1952: 5) states that:

[I]t is the granting by some competent authority of a right or permission to carry on a business or do an act which otherwise would be illegal. The essential elements of licensing involve the *stipulation of* circumstances under which permission to perform an otherwise prohibited activity may be granted—largely a legislative function; and the actual granting of the permission in specific cases—generally an administrative responsibility.

Barnett (1953: 15) points out that looking at a license as a privilege is not technically correct, and suggests that "if the wayward courts had only realized that a 'license' is not a *grant* of a *new 'privilege,'* but, on the contrary, a *restriction* upon a *'right' already existing*, all this absurd confusion, with resulting deprivation of constitutional protections, would have been avoided.

4. This was, for instance, one of the purposes behind the Massachusetts legislation regulating psychology (Dr. Stanely Rosenzweig, President, Massachusetts Psychological Association, personal communication, January 28, 1972).

5. Ruth Roemer (1971: 1057–58) has proposed the following list as a summary of the objectives of a sound legal system for regulating health professionals:

1. Eliminate legal barriers to an increased supply of health manpower.
2. Permit lateral and vertical mobility of personnel.
3. Allow maximum productivity of health professionals and optimal use of all members of the health team.
4. Encourage innovations in use of personnel, with protection of practitioners against legal sanctions as a result of such innovations.
5. Facilitate interstate mobility and more equitable geographic distribution of personnel.
6. Require effective controls of the quality of personnel, both with respect to initial entrance into the occupation and continuation in it.

7. Integrate regulation of health personnel with regulation of health facilities and the overall health care system.
8. Provide for public accountability.
9. Protect the public, not the persons licensed.
10. Evolve a system of regulation sufficiently flexible to take account, without undue lag, of new needs, new knowledge, and changed technological and social conditions in health services.

6. In 1934, twenty-two pharmacy boards, eighteen dental boards, sixteen nursing boards, and thirteen medical boards were chosen by governors who were required to choose from lists submitted by state associations. In addition, a lesser number of boards (those regulating embalmers, veterinarians, optometrists, osteopaths, chiropodists, architects, and engineers) had provisions requiring recommendations from professional associations (Lancaster, 1934: 286).

7. An analysis of the statistics provided by the Council of State Governments (1952: 37–38) reveals that many licensure laws require the governor to appoint board members from lists submitted by the local professional association. For pharmacists, twenty-two of forty-eight states had this requirement; for osteopaths the figure was eighteen of forty-eight; and for veterinarians eight of forty-eight. The following statistics, adapted from Appendix B, Table IV, of the Council's report, give a further idea of the extent to which the professions control the choice of board members:

Profession	Require Governor to Use Association List	Allow Direct Appointment by Association
Nursing	32	1
Physicians	16	3
Dentists	26	3
Embalmers	15	1
Pharmacists	22	
Optometrists	14	
Osteopaths	18	

This situation had not changed significantly as of 1965. See the data provided in the 1967 survey by the Public Health Service (U.S. National Center for Health Statistics, 1968).

8. Thus, since lawyers often provide counseling and give advice of a psychological nature, especially in divorce and custody proceedings, they are exempted from the operation of the psychology laws in many states, so long as they do not refer to themselves as psychologists.

9. For other excellent examples of the internecine struggle between professional groups see Friedman (1965: 500–1); Grant (1942a: 463–72); and Rayack (1975).

10. For studies and surveys of licensure laws in individual states, see Akers (1968) (Kentucky); De Lancy (1938) (West Virginia); Florida (1975); Hanft and Hamrick (1938) (North Carolina); Illinois (1949); Knudsen (1949) (Nebraska); Minnesota Law Review (1974); Moore (1961) (Illinois); New Jersey (1971); Oklahoma (1950); Rayack (1975) (Connecticut, Massachusetts, Rhode Island); Rosenbloom (1973) (Massachusetts); Rozovsky (1975) (Quebec); Smith (1976) (Oklahoma); Sucher (1955) (Wisconsin); and Wisconsin (1952).

For studies and surveys of particular occupations, see AMA, Cent. for Health Serv. Research and Devel. (1977) (physicians); Blanck (1963) (psychotherapy and medicine); Caldwell (1923) (the early law regulating medical practice in America); Kikel (1946) (photography); Mizuno (1974) (physician assistants); Morris and Moritz (1971) (medicine); Yale Law Journal (1974) (dental assistants); Shryock (1967) (medicine); U.S. DHEW (1974a) (dental assistants); and Zuckerman and Savedra (1972) (social work). For further studies of individual professions, see the references in the next paragraph.

For detailed statistics on licensure across a number of occupation and professional groups in the United States, see American Medical Association, Council on Medical Education (1973, 1973a) (statistics on medical licentiates for 1972 and 1973); Cohen and Dean (1974) (data on physician assistant laws and board regulations through March 1974); Council of State Governments (1952) (an early classic that covers virtually all the major professions and occupations and includes an excellent analysis with recommendations); Derbyshire (1969) (while not in table form, contains detailed statistics on the medical practice laws); Forgotson, Roemer, and Newman (1967) (an exhaustive national survey of physician licensure as of 1967, undertaken by the authors as part of their panel report to the U.S. National Advisory Commission on Health Manpower; appears in virtually identical form in the Commission's report; Hansen (1962) (critical analysis of the medical practice acts of all the state, with special emphasis on their implications for group practice); Howard and Ball (1973) (good summary of physician assistant laws as of 1972, with details on the availability of professional liability insurance, hospital utilization, professional recognition, and educational requirements); Lurie (1970) (data on the number of physician licentiates each year, with an analysis of the cost of licensing); National Education Association (1938) (national statistics for the professions of accountants, architects, lawyers, nurses, physicians, and teachers, with good data on disciplinary enforcement); Pennell, Proffitt, and Hatch (1971) (data on sixteen allied health professions); Shimberg, Esser, and Kruger (1972) (study of licensing in the health occupations, construction trades, service occupations, and the transportation field); Shindell (1965)(analysis of current medical practice acts, with special attention to definitions of practice and reasons for revocation of license); U.S. DHEW (1975) (analysis of licensing legislation proposed and enacted in the health field in 1974); U.S. DHEW (1974) (analysis of licensing legislation proposed and enacted in the health field in 1973); U.S. DHEW (1973) (provides an update of the 1971 report, with emphasis on recently enacted allied health bills); U.S. DHEW (1971) (good data on current activities in credentialing health personnel); U.S. Department of Labor (1969) (comprehensive list of all occupations licensed in each state); U.S. National Advisory Commission on Health Manpower (1967) (extremely comprehensive study of health personnel in this country as of 1967; Appendix VII in Volume II contains a thorough breakdown of all medical practice acts, as well as other allied health professions such as dentistry, osteopathy, nursing, and practical nursing); and U.S. National Center for Health Statistics (1968) (detailed statistics on twenty-two different health professions, including psychologists and social workers; contains a state-by state analysis as well as a national summary).

11. Moore (1961), for instance, studied fifteen occupations for which data were available and found that it took less than twelve years between the time when 10 percent of the states licensed a particular occupation and the time when half of them had enacted laws.

12. Massachusetts exempts persons practicing hypnotism, magnetic healing, and mind cure (Mass. Gen. Laws Ann. ch. 112, § 7 [1973]), while Minnesota specifically exempts any person who endeavors to prevent or cure disease or suffering exclusively by mental or spiritual means (Minn. Stat. Ann. § 147.10 [West 1970]).

13. See also *People v. Cole* (1916).

14. For other related cases in which the defendant was convicted of practicing medicine illegally, see the three Washington cases of *State v. Pratt* (1916, 1914), and *State v. Verbon* (1932); the New York case of *People v. Hickey* (1935); and the Arizona decision in *State v. Horn* (1966). For examples of practices that were upheld as religious in nature and therefore not subject to prosecution, see the Iowa case of *State v. Miller* (1933) and the Alabama decision in *Fealy v. Birmingham* (1916). For law review articles examining this issue, see Laughran's (1975) "Religious Beliefs and the Criminal Justice System: Some Problems of the Faith Healer," and the early review of Schoenbach and Snider (1936) "Physicians and Surgeons—What Constitutes the Practice of Medicine within Statutes Regulating the Same? *People v. Hickey*, 283 N.Y. Supp. 968."

15. See also *Smith v. State* (1913), *People v. Mulford* (1910), *State v. Evertz* (1918), *People v. Phippin* (1888), and *State v. Maxfield* (1977). For citations to further cases and a cogent analysis of them, see Hodgson (1977: 653 et seq.).

16. See the series of opinions by the Attorneys General of California (Ops. Att'y Gen. No. CV74/37 [March 24, 1975]; 49 Ops. Att'y Gen. 104 [1967]; and 47 Ops. Att'y Gen. 204 [1966]) and Michigan (Ops. Att'y Gen. No. 2359, p. 26 [January 20, 1956] and Ops. Att'y Gen. No. 1645 [April 22, 1953]). For other opinions dealing with psycho-therapy see Massachusetts (2 Ops. Att'y Gen. 1899-1905, p. 270 [May 15, 1901]); New York (New York Ed. Dept., 2 Ed. Dept. Reps. pp. 525-26 [1963]); Kentucky (Ops. Att'y Gen. No. 63-443 [May 13, 1963]); and West Virginia (ops. Att'y Gen. No. 66 [May 19, 1965]). These opinions are more fully discussed in Volume II of this series.

17. See the joint resolution of the American Medical Association, American Psychiatric Association, and America Psychoanalytic Association (1954); the statements of local medical societies (for example, the views of the Medical Society of the State of New York as expressed in Brody, 1965); the statement of the American Psychiatric Association (1973a) on the psychiatrist's relationship with nonmedical mental health professionals; and the most recent definition of psychotherapy in the American Psychiatric Associa-tion's (1975a) latest edition of the *Psychiatric Glossary*, which reaffirms that medical psychotherapy is only to be carried out by a psychiatrically trained physician.

18. See Volume II of this series for full details on these laws.

19. For a useful history of licensing in the social work field, see Zuckerman and Savedra (1972).

20. An excellent history of medical licensure can be found in Shryock's (1967) *Medi-cal Licensing in America, 1650-1965*, as updated by Derbyshire's (1969) *Medical Licen-sure and Discipline in the United States*.

21. Since most professions and occupations have modelled their licensing laws after the medical profession, this is to be expected.

22. For studies and reports analyzing the problems created by licensure in general, and which make specific recommendations regarding statutory changes, see American Hospital Association (1970); American Medical Association Council on Health Manpower (1970); Barron (1966); *Business Week* (1977); Carlson (1970); Carroll and Gaston (1977); Cohen (1973); Council of State Governments (1952); Derbyshire (1969); Engman (1974); Florida (1975); Forgotson, Roemer, and Newman (1967); Gellhorn (1956); Hansen (1962); Lurie (1970); Maurizi (1974); New Jersey (1971); Phelan (1974); Rayack (1975); Selden (1970); Shepard (undated); Shimberg, Esser, and Kruger (1972); Shryock (1967); Tancredi and Woods (1972); U.S. DHEW (1975a); U.S. DHEW (1973); U.S. DHEW (1971); U.S. Nat's Adv. Comm. on Health Manpower (1967II,: Appendix VII); White (1975); and Yale Law Journal (1974).

The literature on licensing psychologists is fairly extensive. Some of the more repre-sentative articles include: American Psychological Association, Committee on Legislation (1967); American Psychological Association, Committee on State Legislation (1975); American Psychological Association and Conference of State Psychological Associations, Committees on Legislation (1955); American Sociological Society (1958); Asher (1973); Beck (1948); Borgatta (1958); Columbia Law Review (1951); Combs (1953); Deutsch (1958); Ellis (1953); Frank (1973); Gerty (1952); Heiser (1950); Kayton (1959); Kelly (1950); May (1954); Mosher (1973); Newfield (1973); Oden (1975); Peatman (1950); Rogers (1973); Saffir (1950); and Wolfe (1950).

For studies of licensing in the field of psychotherapy generally, see American Orthopsychiatric Association (1968, 1968a); Blanck (1963); California, Assembly Com-mittee on Health and Welfare (1976); and Harrison et al. (1970).

23. Only two studies have been found. A doctoral dissertation by Healy (1973) com-pared the proficiency of personnel in the clinical laboratory field in a state with stiff licensing requirements and a state with no requirements. Her finding was that personnel licensure did not significantly improve the quality of output of the laboratory. A study

by Holen (1977), on the other hand, found that dental services were improved in states with stiff licensing requirements.

24. The problems involved in defining and measuring quality and in conducting research on medical care in general are covered in Barro (1973); Cordero (1964); Donabedian (1966); Fessel and Van Brunt (1972); Greene (1976); Klein et al. (1961); Lembcke (1959, 1956); Peterson (1963); Slee (1969); and Williamson (1971).

25. Studies of medical care quality include Barr (1955) (the dangers of medical diagnosis, and so on); Bird (1975) (evidence of substandard care in U.S. hospitals); Brook, Berg, and Schechter (1973) (inadequacy of care provided at a city hospital and large private teaching hospital); Burgess and Burgess (1966) (iatrogenesis from unnecessary hospitalization); Codman (1914) (evidence of low quality of care); Doyle (1953, 1952) (unnecessary hysterectomies); Eisele, Slee, and Hoffman (1956) (evaluation of internal medicine in hospitals); Evans (1968) (unnecessary tonsillectomies); Kohl (1955) (responsible factors in perinatal mortality); Lipworth, Lee, and Morris (1963) (compares fatalities in teaching versus nonteaching hospitals); McLachlan (1976) (research on quality of British health care); Ogra (1971) (unnecessary tonsillectomies and adenoidectomies); Rosenfeld (1957) (unnecessary female pelvic surgery); Schimmel (1964) (dangers of hospitalization); Schimmel (1963) (iatrogenic complications of hospitalized patients; Shapiro, Weiner, and Densen (1958) (mortality rates of patients seen by fee-for-service versus H.I.P. physicians in New York City); Starfield and Scheff (1972) (effectiveness of pediatric care); Trussell (1965); Trussell, Morehead, and Ehrlich (1962) (quantity, quality and costs of medical and hospital care provided to teamster families in the New York area); and U.S. Congress, House Committee on Interstate and Foreign Commerce (1976, 1975) (unnecessary surgery).

26. A companion study conducted by Clute (1963) in Ontario and Nova Scotia yielded remarkably similar results, giving support to the likelihood that the poor quality of practice in North Carolina was not an isolated instance.

27. The situation in the field of psychotherapy is not much different from the early days of U.S. medicine. Most historians agree that the quality of medical practice in the early years of America was less than adequate. In fact, many of the more common and well-accepted practices were downright dangerous. As a result it was questionable whether licensing those who followed acceptable practice was better than attempting to exclude those who were considered quacks. Caldwell (1923: 235–42) writes:

> Undoubtedly there was some suffering caused by quackery and ignorance, although, on the other hand, it may be doubted whether much of the quackery was as harmful to life and health as the recognized practices of physicians of that day. The heroic remedies, mercury, antimony, and copious bleeding, were in vogue. . . .
>
> After all, the regulars were only half right. Granted that the premises of the homeopathic and of the Thomsonian group of schools were untenable, how much of the regular therapeutics of those days has borne the test of time? The time was ripe for a reaction against the heroic remedies of the regular physician; in this and in other respects, the irregulars made many valuable contributions to medicine.

28. One of the more recent developments with regard to licensure qualifications has been the increasing emphasis placed on equivalency and proficiency testing as alternate routes to licensure. The Department of Health, Education, and Welfare has offered the following definition for each type of testing:

> *Equivalency testing* refers to examinations used to equate nonformal learning with learning achieved in academic courses or training programs. Such tests may be designed to enable colleges and universities to grant academic credit for off-campus learning. They also may be used by employers or certifying bodies to qualify individuals whose non-formal study and on-the-job learning is deemed equivalent to that expected from a formal program.
>
> *Proficiency testing* refers to the measurement of an individual's competency to

perform at a certain job level—a competency made up of knowledge and skills, and related to the requirements of the specified job. Such testing is therefore not only a measure of the knowledge gained through didactic instruction but also an assessment of job capabilities. [U.S. DHEW, 1971: 53, n. 98.]

One of the earliest examples of an organization using a proficiency measure is the Red Cross in its life-saving program. It tests candidates through actual demonstrations of swimming ability and ability to rescue somebody from the water. Until recently few licensing statutes made provisions for either method of testing, but with the return of military personnel following termination of U.S. involvement in Vietnam, the states have been faced with a large number of practitioners qualified to perform a variety of medical services but without training or education from an approved school. In addition, recent court decisions, based on Title VII of the Civil Rights laws and using the Equal Employment Opportunities Commission guidelines, have demanded that tests must have a rational relationship with the skills needed on the job. This has exerted indirect effects on licensing boards to develop such tests within their respective profession, especially because of the possibility that EEOC guidelines may eventually be applied to licensure agencies.

To date, however, the number of licensing statutes that provide for equivalency and proficiency testing is miniscule. HEW has been supporting a number of programs designed to develop such measures. For instance, the Bureau of Quality Assurance has administered a contract to develop a proficiency examination in practical nursing. Under the Social Security Amendments of 1972 (P.L. 92-603), there are provisions for proficiency exams of specific health care personnel. Proficiency examinations for physical therapists have been developed and administered for licensed therapists who did not meet Medicare standards (U.S. DHEW 1973: 35). The 1973 HEW update of its 1971 report on licensure discusses Tennessee's plans to use a proficiency examination with former military laboratory specialists in order to license them (U.S. DHEW, 1973: 35). This same report indicates that several other states have integrated proficiency and equivalency testing into their licensure system, at least in part (U.S. DHEW, 1973: 36). This includes California, where qualified medical corpspeople are eligible for licensure as LPNs and RNs. Emergency medical technicians can also become licensed in Florida through proficiency and equivalency examinations.

Cohen and Dean (1974) have conducted a detailed study of the laws regulating physician assistants and found several uses of each type of testing among state licensure boards. They note that Vermont apparently is the only state that uses an equivalency approach without requiring any didactic instruction. Most states require formal training, however, and equivalency is interpreted to be the right to substitute one course of a briefer training program for another. Five states (Alabama, New York, Oklahoma, Virginia, and Wyoming) allow proficiency testing instead of traditional criteria, but the precise standards and form of examination are not spelled out. On the whole, Cohen and Dean (1974: 358) conclude that "the laws and regulations, for the most part, provide relatively broad latitude for employing such mechanisms."

29. Both Kessel (1970) and Friedman (1962) have made this argument. Kessel (1970: 272, footnotes omitted) writes:

It is of course a well-known axiom that an increase in quality requires an increase in price. And an increase in price implies an increase in efforts to economize on a resource that has become more scarce. Hence, an increase in quality implies a greater effort to economize on physicians' services. What this means specifically is that people tend to substitute self-diagnosis and treatment for the services of a physician. This tendency manifests itself at the onset of an illness or suspected illness, and going to a physician is deferred until the symptoms become alarming. Consequently, increasing the quality of physicians does not necessarily imply that the quality of medical care that the public as a whole receives also increases, since the public receives a mixture of professional attention and self-treatment.

Friedman (1962: 156) argues that:

Under the interpretation of the statutes forbidding unauthorized practice of medicine, many things are restricted to licensed physicians that could perfectly well be done by technicians, and other skilled people who do not have a Cadillac medical training. I am not enough of a technician to list the examples at all fully. I only know that those who have looked into the question say that the tendency is to include in "medical practice" a wider and wider range of activities that could perfectly well be performed by technicians. Trained physicians devote a considerable part of their time to things that might well be done by others. The result is to reduce drastically the amount of medical care. The relevant average quality of medical care, if one can at all conceive of the concept, cannot be obtained by simply averaging the quality of care that is given; that would be like judging the effectiveness of a medical treatment by considering only the survivors; one must also allow for the fact that the restrictions reduce the amount of care. The result may well be that the average level of competence in a meaningful sense has been reduced by the restrictions.

Evidence provided by Carroll and Gaston (1977) bears out these fears.

30. Nader's study group on the self-regulation of the medical profession (McCleery et al., 1971: 4) clearly acknowledges the importance of factors other than licensure in determining the level of care provided by physicians to patients:

We wish to acknowledge the importance of many other factors that affect the quality of care, such as: the number and distribution of physicians, the over-dependence on foreign medical school graduates to fill the deficit of an adequate supply of U.S. graduates, the urgent need for a large number of well-trained para-medical personnel, the distribution and variable quality of hospitals, problems of cost and financing of medical care, problems of the quality and availability of care in ghetto and rural areas, the question of quality related to solo practice versus private group practice versus prepaid group practice.

31. The California Board of Medical Examiners provides a distinct exception to this. The board was reorganized in the early sixties, and as a result of increased financial resources has taken a proactive role in regard to discipline. The board subscribes to a newspaper clipping service and makes extensive use of the State Justice Department's Criminal Identification and Investigation Division's computer facilities. For a comprehensive discussion of the California Medical Board, see Marsh (1972).

32. At about the same time, De Lancy (1938) examined the number of licenses revoked over a six-year period for the thirteen licensed professions in West Virginia. On the average, less than two revocations occurred per profession for the entire period. In eight professions, no one lost her or his license during this time. More than half of all revocations were accounted for by the medical profession, but only three of the instances were attributable to malpractice.

Also at about this time Fellman (1941: 235, m. 109) reports that the barbering profession did not show a very active disciplinary arm. In fact, over a twelve-year period Nebraska revoked only one license per year, six of which were for making false statements in the license application process. Of the 25,000 barbers in Pennsylvania in 1937, only forty-five had their licenses revoked.

33. Several other sources of data are available on disciplinary enforcement. The Research Department of the Oklahoma Legislature (1950) studied license revocations for all professions in the state for the ten-year period 1940 through 1949. For nineteen professions, 455 licenses were revoked. More than 85 percent of these revocations, however, were accounted for by three professions, and more than 90 percent derived from

failure to renew licenses. In seven professions no licenses were revoked at all, while another three had only one revocation.

The well-known Bateman Commission in New Jersey (1971), which conducted four public hearings and gathered data directly from licensing boards, concluded that the boards were not very effective in their disciplinary enforcement.

A Federal Trade Commission study (Phelan 1974) compared enforcement policies in the TV-repair industry in California and Louisiana. California's proactive stance toward discipline was reflected in the large number of complaints received over a seven-year period (21,820), and the large number of revocations per year (an average of eleven). During the same time period Louisiana's board revoked only one license for reasons other than nonrenewal (Phelan, 1974: 14).

34. The paucity of action taken against lawyers becomes even more meaningful as an index of disciplinary laxity when the extent of legal incompetence is examined. Supreme Court Chief Justice Warren Burger recently stated that 50 percent of all lawyers who argued their cases before the bar were incompetent (Mintz 1978).

Carlin (1966: 181) writes that:

> Measures such as government subsidy, prepaid insurance plans, and group legal practice would serve to increase and stabilize the demand for legal services, thereby enhancing the economic security of marginal practitioners. If this requires altering certain canons of ethics, then let it be done, since it would permit a *genuine* improvement of ethical conduct in the bar. The effective extension of legal services is thus entirely consistent with, if not an indispensable condition for, strengthening the moral integrity of the legal profession.

36. The report of the Committee on Medical Practices has become widely known as the "Truman Report." The purpose of the report was to study and make recommendations about unethical medical practices. The conclusions were quite controversial. Some held the study as the most important since the Flexner Report of 1909. Considerable evidence exists that the Board of Trustees of the American Medical Association actually tried to suppress it. (See the editorial introduction to the report in *Northwest Medicine*, August 1955.)

37. The courts have had varying reactions to other terms used as grounds for discipline. The Supreme Court of Colorado ruled that "moral turpitude" had a definite meaning and as such had legal currency (*Graeb v. State Board of Medical Examiners* [1913]). On the other hand, the Oklahoma Supreme Court held unconstitutional a Colorado law making "the obtaining of any fee on the assurance that an incurable disease can be permanently cured" a ground for revoking a physician's license. The court considered the statute too indefinite and uncertain (*Freeman v. State Board of Medical Examiners* [1916]). In some instances the courts have used the "delegation of legislative authority" doctrine to nullify portions of professional practice acts. The Kentucky Supreme Court, for instance, struck down vague grounds for discipline on the basis that it gave unlimited discretion to the Board of Health to decide what was unprofessional (*Matthews v. Murphy* [1901]).

38. Two examples will illustrate the difficulties a board faces, even when it desires to take action, and even when the violation of the licensure laws is quite flagrant. The first involves an application of the psychology laws, the details of which have been obtained from the Supreme Court's decision in the case of *Morra v. State Board of Examiners of Psychologists* (1973), personal correspondence with the board's secretary, Paul E. Thetford, March 16, 1972, and an article in *Professional Psychology* by Sinett and Thetford (1975). In July 1971, the Kansas State Board of Examiners of Psychologists held an eleven-hour hearing based on complaints by two patients against a certified psychologist. The plaintiffs, both female, presented evidence that the psychotherapist, a male, had attempted to induce them to "sexual intimacies and/or intercourse." The charge against the psychologist was that he had been guilty of unprofessional conduct as defined by

rules established by the board or, in the alternative, that he had been guilty of negligence of wrongful actions (sexual improprieties) in the performance of his duties.

The plaintiffs were interviewed separately and each narrated a remarkably similar story, despite the fact that neither plaintiff had previously met or talked with the other. This fact in itself was quite persuasive to the board, and in September 1971 it revoked the psychologist's certificate.

The defendant obtained a stay of the board's revocation decision from the district court. He continued to see patients during this time, practicing forty to fifty hours per week according to his own account, and taking on new patients, as well. He hoped to continue practice until his appeal was finally decided, which would have involved a period of three years.

The state supreme court, however, reversed the stay order, and the psychologist agreed to cease his private practice. In the process of conducting the board hearings and the judicial proceedings, the plaintiffs were required to make their clinical records and psychological test reports a matter of public record. Their names were identified. In addition, the therapist's attorney attacked their statements as impeachable because they were in psychotherapy and mentally ill.

Derbyshire (1969: 98–102) narrates another of the more fantastic tales in the annals of attempts to revoke licenses. The incident occurred in Michigan in the medical profession and involved a period of eleven years, beginning on February 28, 1956. On that date the Michigan Board of Registration in Medicine revoked one Dr. Clark's license on the basis of moral turpitude and abortion. A newspaper report stated that the action was also taken because he molested women. Four months later Dr. Clark was arrested for practicing medicine without a license. A little more than a year later the Michigan Board reinstated Dr. Clark's license contingent upon his continuing psychiatric treatment and reporting to the board every six months.

In June of 1958 the board again revoked his license for not complying with the terms previously set up by the board. A circuit court reversed the order of revocation and remanded the case for another hearing. At this subsequent hearing in December the board revoked Dr. Clark's license on the basis of commitment to a state mental hospital and on charges of assault upon a patient. Dr. Clark again brought suit and ten months later the circuit court again reversed the order of revocation and ordered another hearing.

This time the board revoked the doctor's license for unprofessional and dishonest conduct and moral turpitude. Specifically, Dr. Clark was charged with "taking indecent liberties with person of woman [sic] in his office" (Derbyshire, 1969: 99). This order, too, was stayed pending appeal to the circuit court, which allowed Dr. Clark to continue in practice for more than a year, when the circuit court finally affirmed the order of the board.

This did not mark the end of the case. In August of 1961 the board was served with an injunction staying its decision until an appeal had been heard by the Supreme Court of Michigan. Approximately a year later and nearly three years after the October 1959 board order, the supreme court upheld the order of the board. In the next year, however, the board decided to reinstate Dr. Clark's license, perhaps concluding that he had reformed his ways.

Not much was heard about him until four years later, when headlines of the *New York Times* proclaimed "9 Deaths Studied in Doctor's Case" (Derbyshire, 1969: 100). The same Dr. Clark had now moved on to misconduct of a more serious nature. He was charged in the death of a part-time office assistant, who had died from an overdose of sodium pentothal, which he had used to treat her heart disease. He was arrested following a twelve-hour chase through snow in near-zero-degree weather. The prosecutor was investigating a "large incidence of deaths attributed to therapeutic misadventure, cardiac arrest, or an injection of one sort or another" (Derbyshire, 1969: 100).

At long last, in July 1968, Dr. Clark was brought to trial and convicted of manslaughter, with a sentence of from three to fifteen years in prison. Thus, it was ultimately a jail sentence that removed Dr. Clark from medical practice, a feat that was apparently impossible through the disciplinary arm of the licensing board.

For other examples see the *Boston Globe* (1975); Bloom (1968); Layne (undated); and Lieberman (1970: 104 et seq.).

39. In the state of Washington, for instance, it was standard practice for licensed practical nurses to give injections in innoculating patients against various diseases. Although considered accepted practice, the Washington Supreme Court ruled that this constituted the illegal practice of medicine (*Barber v. Reinking* [1966]).

40. An excellent description of the varieties of quacks and charlatans operating in the health field can be found in Barrett and Knight (1976); for the situation in England, see Jameson (1961).

41. In England the number of individuals who visit "faith healers" each year is large. Inglis (1964: 236) cites estimates by Neville Randall in 1961 that a million people consult such healers yearly in Britain, and comments that this figure is probably not much of an exaggeration.

42. In this latter case the court held that the revocation amounted to an abuse of discretion. Instead it stated that probation or suspension of the physician's license would be more appropriate.

43. The severity of this problem is excellently portrayed by Derbyshire (1969: 112).

I remember one instance in which my board of medical examiners discovered a man who was practicing medicine without a license. On two different occasions the investigator for the board obtained receipted bills, copies of prescriptions, and samples of drugs the man had been dispensing, certainly more than sufficient evidence for the conviction of this fraud. But the district attorney showed no interest in prosecuting him. It was not until some two years later, after the impostor had been responsible for the death of a patient, that the state police arrested him on a charge of manslaughter, for which he was convicted and sentenced to five years in prison.

44. Robert Lindner (1950: 440), writing about the value of medical degrees as a prerequisite for the practice of psychotherapy, comments:

You will have noticed, I am sure, that I have paid no attention to the question of psycho-quackery and charlatanry. This is because I, . . . regard this problem as of minimal importance and as one which will decline proportionately with the dissemination of correct education among the public. . . .

45. Justin Miller (1934: 202), former dean of the School of Law at Duke University, believed that problems in regulation are likely to ensue whether a profession establishes low or high standards:

Whether the method of procedure adopted by the particular profession is, as the lawyers have done, to keep the standards for admission so low that the profession is constantly concerned with the problem of eliminating its shysters or, as the physicians have done, to keep the standards so high by educational requirements and basic science boards that the profession is constantly concerned by the activities of quacks and fakers outside—neither method nor any other method will be successful until the members of each profession, individually and collectively, are made acutely aware of their professional obligations and trained to interpret the profession to the public.

46. Forgotson, Roemer, and Newman (U.S. Nat'l Adv. Comm. on Health Manpower, 1967: II, 331-32), in their report to the National Advisory Commission on Health Manpower, present a series of conclusions, typical of most studies, regarding the impact of medical licensure:

This study of licensure laws affecting physicians, osteopaths, and chiropractors indicates, among other things, that:

1. Current statutory provisions impose constraints on medical school curricular innovations;

2. Specific statutory requirements restrain needed developments in graduate medical education, such as elimination of the internship as a separate entity and substitution therefor of appropriate programs of graduate medical education integrated with undergraduate medical education;

3. Initial licensure examination requirements of the States do not measure many of the qualities relevant to fitness to practice and are not necessarily relevant to current goals of undergraduate medical education;

4. Legal requirements for programs in continuing medical education to prevent educational obsolescence are absent;

5. Incomplete interstate recognition of medical licenses results in barriers to geographic mobility of physicians;

6. Licensure requirements for foreign medical graduates are not generally geared specifically to fitness to practice high quality American medicine;

7. Delegation of tasks to allied and auxiliary personnel is governed by statutes which may be restrictive, ambiguous, or unrelated to accepted custom and usage;

8. Statutory interpretations relevant to delegations of tasks by physicians to allied and auxiliary personnel are not always based on the realities of the delivery of modern medical care;

9. Osteopaths cannot, under present laws, be integrated fully into the practice of medicine so as to permit their addition to the pool of physician manpower; and

10. Attempts to control unscientific schools of practice or cultism by licensure cannot give unscientific practices a scientific basis but can endanger the public by giving unscientific schools, such as chiropractic, protection through the sanction of law.

47. This follows from the law of supply and demand, but does not always apply. For instance, nurses are in short supply, but receive poor salaries.

48. This criterion usually appears in the form of a specified minimum number of professionals required in a given population.

49. This is one of the surest signs that a shortage exists, but the absence of unfilled positions is not necessarily indicative of an adequate supply, if those positions are being filled with unqualified people.

50. When professional standard-setting organizations determine that positions are being filled by personnel with inadequate training, the implication is that a professional shortage exists. Thus, the many foreign medical graduates of dubious competency now filling many of the positions in state mental hospitals provide evidence that not enough U.S.-trained psychiatrists are available for such work.

51. This is similar to the third criterion.

52. If most other countries have two or three times the number of practitioners per 100,000 population, this may be an indication that a shortage exists in the United States.

53. Data on the supply of practitioners in the health field are available from the following sources: American Medical Association, Center for Health Services Research and Development (1977); Health Services Research Center (1971); Hiestand and Ostow (1976); U.S. DHEW (1976); U.S. Nat'l. Cent. for Health Statistics (1974, 1968).

54. Rayack (1967: Ch. 4) cites data documenting that between 1939 and 1959 the mean income of physicians increased 434 percent. For the period 1939 to 1959 this

exceeded other occupational classes by as much as 132 percent. His conclusions apply to both specialists and general practitioners.

55. Others who agree that a physician shortage has existed include the Board of Trustees of the American Medical Association (1969); the Carnegie Commission on Higher Education (1970); Fein (1967); and Hyde and Wolff (1954).

Morrow and Edwards (1976) are typical of the few who argue that no shortage exists. They believe that serious consideration should be given to reducing the rates at which the health personnel pool is increasing. In essence, they argue that the current rate of producing practitioners will divert another 4 percent of the U.S. GNP (approximately $50 billion annually) to the health care field over the next 25 years, but with only a marginal rise in the level of care provided.

56. Arnhoff (1971: 18) notes that:

> Despite its preeminent role in training program development and funding, manpower research and evaluation has never been a priority concern for the National Institute of Mental Health. Between 1960 and 1969 the National Institute of Mental Health provided some $700 million for mental health training programs. During this same period approximately $800,000 or about 0.1 of one percent was spent on manpower evaluation studies. The result is a very incomplete and fragmented picture of the total scene and an almost total absence of the basic data for overall monitoring of program development, manpower utilization, etc.

57. Data on the supply of practitioners in the mental health field are available from the following sources: American Psychiatric Association (1973) (survey of the nation's psychiatrists as of 1970); American Psychiatric Association (1973b) (analysis of private psychiatric practice); Boneau and Cuca (1974) (overview of psychology's human resources); California Department of Mental Hygiene (1965) (bibliography of mental health womanpower and manpower); Dörken and Associates (1976) (psychology); Marmor (1975) (national study of private office practice of psychiatrists); U.S. DHEW (undated) (state-by-state analysis of nonfederal psychiatrists); U.S. DHEW (undated [a]) (survey of American Psychological Association members providing psychological services in 1972); U.S. National Institute of Mental Health (1976) (staffing of mental health facilities in the United States in 1974); and U.S. National Institute of Mental Health (1975) (staffing of mental health facilities in the United States in 1972).

For those who argue that a shortage exists, see Albee (1968, 1968a, 1959); American Psychiatric Association (1975); Blain and Robinson (1957); Boneau (1968); Cates (1970); Fink and Oken (1976); Kubie (1967); Wallerstein (1972); and Weinstein (1968).

For further references discussing personnel shortages in the mental health field, or providing data on the number of practitioners available, see Boxley and Wagner (1971) (numbers of minority students in clinical psychology); Clark (1957); Coates (1973) (psychology); Cowen and Zax (1967); Hobbs (1969); Joint Commission on Mental Illness and Health (1961); Knott (1969); Matarazzo (1971); National Association for Mental Health (1969); U.S. National Institute of Mental Health (1969); Wykert (1971); and Yolles (1967).

58. Carlson (1970: 856) is emphatic about the role of licensing laws in contributing to supply shortages:

> Undeniably such shortages are exacerbated by licensure laws. To be employed in the health field, personnel must fit into licensure categories which vary from state to state but are uniformly restrictive in their application. Legal boundaries around manpower categories have led ineluctably to sub-optimal utilization by precluding the matching of skills with tasks to be performed. Entry barriers created by such laws restrict the supply of new manpower in the health field. State-to-state variations in licensure laws restrain interstate mobility, which possibly would alleviate the shortages caused by maldistribution.

Very few disagree with this point of view. Arthur Centor (1976), chairperson of the Board of Professional Affairs of the American Psychological Association, argues that licensing not only does not create a shortage, but actually stimulates supply because licensing allows reimbursement by third-party payers. The obvious response to this is that it is the third-party reimbursement that is sparking interest, not licensure. Franklyn Arnhoff (1976) states that he does not know of any evidence that licensing has been a restrictive influence in the mental health field. The fact that psychology, social work, and other mental health professions have continued to grow appears to argue against such a theory, according to Arnhoff. Again, it seems apparent that the growth of these professions is due to other forces than licensure, and that licensure has limited the extent of growth.

59. While some crimes may definitely make a candidate less fit to practice, it is obvious that other types have no bearing on a person's ability to perform. Revoking a watch-maker's license after conviction of a felony, for instance, where the felony may be statutory rape, makes little sense.

60. The requirement of good moral character is subject to gross abuse. Gellhorn (1956: 130) cites the case of a junior high school teacher of music who was forced to resign after being identified as a Communist and who then had difficulty becoming a piano tuner in the District of Columbia because he was not of good moral character. Even more absurd is a law in the state of Washington about which Gellhorn (1956: 130) wryly comments, "Veterinarians . . . may not minister to an ailing cow or cat unless they have first signed a non-Communist oath, thus assuring that they will not indoctrinate their four-legged patients."

61. Derbyshire (1969a: 180) comments as follows:

The foreign graduate is welcomed with open arms if he has a certificate from the Educational Council for Foreign Medical Graduates, proposes to limit his activities to serving on the house staff of a nonuniversity affiliated hospital, and intends to return to his native land at the conclusion of this training period. But, if the foreign graduate aspires to state licensure with a view to settling down to practice, thus contributing his share of foreign aid in reverse, the situation is entirely different. By studying the State Board Number of the *Journal of the American Medical Association* he will find such a bewildering patchwork of laws, rules, and regulations throughout the various states that I am amazed that he has the courage even to attempt to become licensed.

He reports that as of 1969, three states would not license a foreign medical graduate under any circumstances. Another three states, for all practical purposes, would not allow a foreigner to practice. In all other jurisdictions a foreign graduate will find a bewildering variety of standards that are not required of U.S.-trained doctors. Once licensed, the foreign graduate will find that most states do not accept another state's license, thus forcing the doctor to once again go through the torturous licensing process, although this would not be true of a U.S.-trained physician.

62. For documentation of this, see Grant (1942a: 460) and Council of State Governments (1952: 25-27).

63. See, for instance, the comments and statements to that effect in Carlson (1975); Carlson (1970: 859); Derbyshire (1969); Forgotson, Roemer, and Newman (1967); Mechanic (1970); Roemer (1970: 298); U.S. DHEW (1973: 29-32); U.S. DHEW (1971: 43-48); U.S. Department of Labor (1969: 9, 13 et seq.); U.S. National Advisory Commission on Health Manpower (1967 I + II); and Volpicelli (1972). For data on the geographic distribution of physicians and allied health personnel see U.S. NCHS (1974).

64. Carlson (1975: 40-41, footnotes omitted), for instance, states that:

Today many persons do not know a healer of general competence, or even anyone to advise them where to go or what to do. More than 50 percent of patient visits to emergency rooms do not involve emergencies; people go there because they do not know where else to go. Recent studies have pegged the level of nonemergency use of emergency rooms even higher—in one case at 90 percent. And the volume of demand has greatly increased in recent years. In one study, the percentage of nonemergency visits rose from 45.4 percent in 1960 to 72.5 percent in 1967. These data depict a public that does not know where to go when illness strikes.

65. Ryan's (1969: 15) study of the design and administration of mental health services in Boston, for instance, revealed the following:

> Slightly over half of all Boston residents in private psychiatric treatment live in four contiguous census tracts (out of Boston's 156 census tracts). This area contains less than four per cent of the total Boston population. It is bounded approximately by the Charles River, Boston University, Boylston Street, and the Public Garden. If to this small strip of land is added the rest of Back Bay and the front of Beacon Hill (this enlarged area including about seven per cent of Boston's population), over 70 percent of all Boston patients in private psychiatric treatment will be included.

66. See Volpicelli (1972). For a defense of the Florida Medical Board's policies, see Astler (1974).

67. Carlson (1970: 859) comments as follows:

> Restrictions on entry of paraprofessionals, together with excessive stringency in the specification and regulation of practice spheres, aggravates . . . maldistribution. Recognition must be given to the fact that in a system marked by shortages, the supply will be least in areas least attractive to practitioners; rural areas and low-income pockets in large urban areas suffer the most from distribution patterns. The distributional problems are in part circular. Much of the unattractiveness of underserved areas is attributable to the unreasonable workloads created by manpower shortages. The problem can thus be alleviated in two ways: by modification of licensure barriers to allow entry by paraprofessionals and by change in the law to permit more optimal utilization of currently licensed personnel.

68. A relatively recent nationwide study concluded that 61 percent of all physicians favored the concept of the physicians' assistant, but only 42 percent said they would use one, largely because of the fear of malpractice suits (Coye and Hansen, 1969).

69. This trend in physician fees and income is not a recent matter. Rayack (1967) demonstrates that both have been increasing more rapidly than in other professions and the Consumer Price Index (CPI). For instance, from 1929 to 1965 physician fees increased 43 percent faster than the CPI (Rayack 1967: 39). The income of nonsalaried physicians, who made up more than 80 percent of the profession at the time, rose 218 percent from 1939 to 1951 (Rayack 1967: 109). This was more than 100 percent of the corresponding increase for lawyers, full-time employees, managers, officials, and proprietors.

70. For studies other than those discussed in the text; see Benham, Maurizi, and Reder (1968); Boulier (1976); and Maurizi (1974).

71. Stigler and Friedland (1962), for instance, found that regulation of electric utilities in the early part of the century had no effect on rates whatsoever, except for one year in which industrial consumers were protected. An examination to determine whether price discrimination had been reduced (large industrial users tended to receive lower rates) found more discrimination, instead of less, although a more refined analysis revealed essentially no difference. A continuation of their study by Jackson (1969) found that residential consumers continued to receive no benefits for the 1940s and 1950s. Moore's (1970) recent study of electric utilities found that regulation reduced rates by no more than 5 percent, and concluded that regulation was not worth it.

In other industries, the findings have been the same. For instance, MacAvoy (1965) examined railroad rates after the creation of the Interstate Commerce Commission, and found that prices were significantly higher, though more stable. Sloss's (1970) investigation of motor freight rates in Canada found that regulated provinces actually had rates roughly 10 percent higher than those without regulation.

72. Under subchapter IV of the 1958 CAB Act, the CAB is empowered to exercise supervision and control over entry into the industry, cities to be served, rates, direct subsidies, and terms of mail carriage. In addition, it has the power to approve or prevent mergers, acquisitions, and transfers of control of air carriers.

73. Jordan (1972) has conducted a similar, but more recent, study of airline regulation and come to similar conclusions. He found that coach fares within California on intrastate carriers were consistently lower than fares for similar trips on carriers regulated by the CAB. In California, coach fares were 32 to 47 percent lower than fares for CAB-regulated markets. In another study, Keeler (1972) constructed a theoretical model to predict hypothetical unregulated fares for most of the major domestic carriers. California intrastate rates correlated well with his predictions. When compared with the fares charged on regulated routes for the year 1968, he found these latter fares were 20 to 95 percent higher than they should be. When his results were updated for the year 1972, the regulated fares were 48 to 84 percent higher than they would have been without regulation.

74. One of the only organizations to seriously study this issue has been the American Orthopsychiatric Association. In 1967 it commissioned a task force consisting of some of the leading psychologists and psychiatrists in the field to formulate a model statute for the practice of psychotherapy. The task force (Harrison et al., 1970) concluded that psychotherapy did not require statutory control at the time, partially because "it seemed untimely to run the risk of legislatively freezing the current situation just as nontraditional mental health workers are becoming more active."

The problem is occasionally brought up in arguments concerning the advisability of enacting state licensing laws for psychologists. For instance, see the debates over the Biondo bill in the early 1970s in New York State (Frank, 1973; Johnson, 1973; Newfield, 1973; Riegelman, 1973).

75. The difficulties that paraprofessionals have had in practicing as a result of restrictive licensing laws is discussed in Forgotson, Bradley, and Ballenger (1970); Hapgood (1969); Palomba (1973); Rayack (1967); Tancredi and Woods (1972); Todd (1972); U.S. National Advisory Commission on Mental Health (1967); White (forth-coming, 1978, 1975); and the *Yale Law Journal* (1974). See also Egelston (1970); Egelston and Kinser (1970, 1969); U.S. DHEW 1977, 1973, 1971) (series on credentialing health manpower, developments in health manpower licensure; and report on licensure and related health personnel credentialing); U.S. DHEW (1975a) (credentialing of drug abuse treatment and rehabilitation workers); U.S. DHEW (1975b) (report of the meeting to discuss the feasibility of a national system of certification for allied health personnel); U.S. DHEW (1974a) (legal provisions on expanded functions for dental hygienists and assistants); and U.S. Department of Labor (1969).

76. Interestingly, the evidence indicates that physicians who employ paraprofessional assistance have practices that are more lucrative than those who do not (AMA National Congress on Health Manpower, 1970: 28-42; Roemer and Dubois, 1969).

77. Roemer (1970a: 52-53), for instance, has noted the deep tradition in nursing of subservience to physicians, which results in nurses being reluctant to assume new tasks and functions of which they are perfectly capable.

78. A study by Nelson, Jacobs, and Johnson (1974) indicates that patient acceptance of physician assistants is quite favorable. Lewis and Resnik (1967) compared two groups of similar patients, one of which received care from a physician and the other from a nurse and found that the latter "shifted their preferences in favor of the nurse as a provider of many of the services formerly reserved for the physician. The quality of care and patients' satisfaction with care were higher in the experimental group" (p. 1241). An examination of patient responses to physician assistant care in the state of Washington found that patients were satisfied with their services after experiencing them, although

they were somewhat hesitant at first to be treated by an auxiliary health care professional (James 1970). For other studies, see Coye and Hansen (1969); Estes and Howard (1969); and Silver (1969).

79. Sadler (1974: 36) explains that supervision can take place at least at three levels: (1) over-the-shoulder; (2) on the premises; and (3) remote with regular monitoring and review. In over-the-shoulder supervision the auxiliary is only allowed to practice in the immediate presence of a physician who is overseeing the quality of the paraprofessional's work. This may not be a hindrance in the case of a surgeon using a surgical assistant. It definitely creates problems with other groups, such as dental hygienists. For this type of person, "on the premises" supervision is probably in order, since the doctor or dentist can adequately check on the hygienist from time to time.

Yet even this type of supervision creates significant problems for many allied personnel. For instance, midwives must often perform their jobs in places not in close proximity to a supervising physician. Requiring on-the-premises supervision eliminates the value of midwives. As long as midwives know when to call in a physician, there is really no need for supervision other than "remote with regular monitoring and review." Unfortunately, few statutes are of this type.

80. District of Columbia law states that assistants may not practice psychotherapy, and West Virginia law empowers the board to specify which functions are to be restricted.

81. In the case of *Barber v. Reinking* (1966), for instance, both the supervising physician and a licensed practical nurse were held liable for damages to a child patient when a needle broke off in the child's body while the nurse was giving the child an injection. Despite the fact that nurses acting in this capacity was both common and accepted practice in the medical profession in Washington, the court stated that the two parties were guilty, since giving innoculations constituted the practice of medicine within the meaning of the licensing law, and hence was illegal. In another well-known case, a California court held a neurosurgeon and former army medical corpsperson guilty of violation of the medical practice act because the corpsperson had drilled holes in the patient's head with a Geigle saw, although the neurosurgeon had placed the saw in place and was in the presence of the corpsperson the entire time, and the corpsperson had considerable experience with this procedure (*People v. Whittaker* [1966]).

The well-known case of *Darling v. Charleston Community Memorial Hospital* (1966) has established a broadened responsibility on the part of a voluntary hospital to control the quality of medical care provided by its visiting staff. In this case the court held that the hospital was negligent in failing to enforce its own by-laws, since a physician did not seek consultation in a particularly difficult case. Despite the fact that such suits are relatively rare (Roemer 1970a: 48), threat of them has seriously jeopardized attempts to exact maximal use out of paraprofessionals. Beeson (1974: 173) has written that "the possibility of increased liability, whether real or imagined, presents the greatest obstacle to effective utilization of the [paraprofessional]."

82. For an excellent discussion of the problems created, and documentation that lower-rung professionals are quite capable of performing functions normally reserved to higher-rung professionals, see Goldstein and Horowitz (1977) and U.S. Department of Labor (1975, 1974).

83. Forgotson and Cook (1967: 739) have concluded that "an educational curriculum which because of rigid legal restrictions cannot be made more responsive to new technology, scientific progress, the information explosion, and changing patterns of medical care, is not serving the public's best interests." See also Kessel (1970) and Leymaster and Mason (1972: 58). On the other hand, John Morton (1975), past president of the Federation of State Medical Boards, argues that licensing laws do not inhibit innovations.

84. White and Francis (1976: 1220) cite data demonstrating that "a student who ranks in the top quarter in academic ability but in the lowest quarter socioeconomically has about the same probability of entering college as a student who comes from the top quarter of families socioeconomically but next to the bottom quarter academically."

85. Previous chapters have documented the lack of evidence that academic success is a predictor of professional competence. They have also presented evidence and arguments why such credentials may be invalid as indicators of competence.

86. Gilb (1966: 16) claims that "The dialectic has moved nearly full circle from American individualistic egalitarianism back again to a socioeconomic order bearing some resemblance to medieval corporate society." See also Friedman (1962) and Grant (1942, 1942a).

REFERENCES

Books and Articles

Akers, R. L. "The Professional Association and the Legal Regulation of Practice." *Law and Society Review*, 1968, v. 2, pp. 463-82.

Albee, G. W. "Conceptual Models and Manpower Requirements in Psychology." *American Psychologist*, 1968, v. 23, pp. 317-20.

Albee, G. W. "Models, Myths, and Manpower." *Mental Hygiene*, 1968a, v. 52, pp. 168-80.

Albee, G. W. *Mental Health Manpower Trends.* New York: Basic Books, 1959.

American Bar Association, Special Committee on Evaluation of Disciplinary Enforcement. *Problems and Recommendations in Disciplinary Enforcement.* Chicago: American Bar Association, 1970.

American Council on Education. *Survey of Dentistry in the United States.* Washington, D.C.: American Council on Education, 1961. Cited by L. Shepard, "Licensure Restrictions and the Cost of Dental Care." Mimeographed. Department of Agricultural Economics, University of California, Davis, undated, p. 22.

American Hospital Association, Special Committee on Licensure of Health Personnel. *Statement on Licensure of Health Care Personnel.* (Approved by AHA, November 18, 1970.) Chicago: American Hospital Association, 1971.

American Medical Association, Board of Trustees. *Report I.* (Report of Committee on Planning and Development, "The Himler Report.") Chicago: American Medical Association, 1969.

American Medical Association, Center for Health Services Research and Development. *Physician Distribution and Medical Licensure in the U.S., 1976.* Chicago, Ill.: American Medical Association, 1977.

American Medical Association, Committee on Medical Practices. "Report to the Board of Trustees of the American Medical Association of the Committee on Medical Practices, November 1954." *Northwest Medicine*, 1955, v. 54, pp. 844-59.

American Medical Association, Council on Health Manpower. *Health Manpower Progress Report: 1972.* (Adopted by AMA House of Delegates.) Chicago: American Medical Association, 1972.

American Medical Association, Council on Health Manpower. *Licensure of Health Occupations.* (Adopted by AMA House of Delegates.) Chicago: American Medical Association, 1970.

American Medical Association, Council on Health Manpower. *Guidelines for Development of New Health Occupations.* (Adopted by AMA House of Delegates.) Chicago: American Medical Association, 1969.

American Medical Association, Council on Medical Education. *Medical Licensure Statistics for 1973.* Chicago: American Medical Association, 1973.

American Medical Association, Council on Medical Education. "Medical Licensure 1972, Statistical Review." *Journal of the American Medical Association*, 1973, v. 225, pp. 299-310.

American Medical Association, Council on Medical Education and Council on Health Manpower. *Physician Manpower and Medical Education, A Report.* Chicago: American Medical Association, 1971.

American Medical Association, Department of Medical Ethics. "1969 Medical Disciplinary Report." *Journal of the American Medical Association,* 1970, v. 213, pp. 588-90.

American Medical Association, Department of Medical Ethics. "1968 Medical Disciplinary Report." *Journal of the American Medical Association,* 1969, v. 210, pp. 1092-93.

American Medical Association, Medical Disciplinary Committee. *Report to the Board of Trustees.* Chicago: American Medical Association, 1961.

American Medical Association, National Congress on Health Manpower. *Expanding the Supply of Health Services in the 1970's.* (Sponsored by the Council on Health Manpower.) Chicago: American Medical Association, 1970.

American Medical Association, Office of the General Counsel. Personal communication, February 17, 1972.

American Medical Association; American Psychiatric Association; and American Psychoanalytic Association. "Resolution on Relations of Medicine and Psychology." *American Journal of Psychiatry,* 1954, v. 3, pp. 385-86.

American Orthopsychiatric Association. "Documents Pertaining to Licensing Feasibility Study of Psychotherapy." Unpublished document, New York, 1968.

American Orthopsychiatric Association. "Psychotherapy Licensing Feasibility Study." Unpublished document, New York, 1968a.

American Psychiatric Association. *Delivering Mental Health Services: Needs, Priorities & Strategies.* Washington, D.C.: American Psychiatric Association, 1975.

American Psychiatric Association. *A Psychiatric Glossary: The Meaning of Terms Frequently Used in Psychiatry.* (4th ed.) Washington, D.C.: American Psychiatric Association, 1975a.

American Psychiatric Association. *The Nation's Psychiatrists-1970 Survey.* Washington, D.C.: American Psychiatric Association, 1973.

American Psychiatric Association. "Position Statement on Psychiatrists' Relationships with Nonmedical Mental Health Professionals." *American Journal of Psychiatry,* 1973a, v. 130, pp. 386-90.

American Psychiatric Association. *The Present and Future Importance of Private Psychiatric Practice in the Delivery of Mental Health Services.* (Task Force Report No. 6.) Washington, D.C.: American Psychiatric Association, 1973b.

American Psychological Association. *Levels and Patterns of Professional Training in Psychology.* (Edited by Maurice Korman.) Washington D.C.: American Psychological Association, 1973.

American Psychological Association, Committee on Legislation. "A Model for State Legislation Affecting the Practice of Psychology, 1967: Report of APA Committee on Legislation." *American Psychologist,* 1967, v. 22, pp. 1095-103.

American Psychological Association, Committee on State Legislation. "A Model for State Legislation Affecting the Practice of Psychology, 1975: First Draft." Mimeographed. Washington, D.C., 1975.

American Psychological Association and Conference of State Psychological Associations, Committees on Legislation. "Joint Report of the APA and CSPA Committees on Legislation." *American Psychologist,* 1955, v. 10, pp. 727-56.

American Sociological Society, Committee on the Implications of Certification Legislation. "Legal Certification of Psychology as Viewed by Sociologists." *American Sociological Review,* 1958, v. 23, p. 301.

Arnhoff, F.N. Personal communication, February 25, 1976.

Arnhoff, F.N. "Psychiatry, Manpower, and Mental Health," (Working Paper of the American Psychological Association, Division of Manpower Research and Development.) Mimeographed. University of Virginia School of Medicine, Charlottesville, Va., 1971.

Asher, J. "Opposition Wins Latest Round in Fight over New York Licensing Bill." *APA Monitor*, June 1973, pp. 1 and 12.

Astler, V.B. "Probe of State Licensing Boards." *Journal of the Florida Medical Association*, 1974, v. 61, pp. 176-78.

Barnett, J.D. "Public Licenses and Private Rights." *Oregon Law Review*, 1953, v. 33, pp. 1-16.

Barr, D.P. "Hazards of Modern Diagnosis and Therapy—The Price We Pay." *Journal of the American Medical Association*, 1955, v. 159, pp. 1452-56.

Barrett, S., and Knight, G. (Eds.) *The Health Robbers: How to Protect Your Money and Your Life.* (Foreword by A. Landers.) Philadelphia: George F. Stickley, 1976.

Barro, A.R. "Survey and Evaluation of Approaches to Physician Performance Measurement." *Journal of Medical Education*, 1973, v. 48, pp. 1047-93.

Barron, J.F. "Business and Professional Licensing—California, A Representative Example." *Stanford Law Review*, 1966, v. 18, pp. 640-65.

Beck, S.J. "The Psychologist in the Clinic Setting: Round Table, 1947." *American Journal of Orthopsychiatry*, 1948, v. 18, pp. 492-522.

Beeson, J.S. "Physicians and Surgeons—The Expanding Role of the Physician's Assistant." *West Virginia Law Review*, 1974, v. 76, pp. 162-75.

Behavior Today. "Pressure Builds to Improve Occupational Licensing by States." *Behavior Today*, August 23, 1976, pp. 1-2.

Benham, L. "The Effect of Advertising on the Price of Eyeglasses." *Journal of Law and Economics*, 1972, v. 15, pp. 337-52.

Benham, L., and Benham, A. "Regulating Through the Professions: A Perspective on Information Control." *Journal of Law and Economics*, 1975, v. 18, pp. 421-47.

Benham, L.; Maurizi, A.; and Reder, M.W. "Migration, Location and Remuneration of Medical Personnel: Physicians and Dentists." *Review of Economics and Statistics*, 1968, v. 50, pp. 332-47.

Bird, D. "Substandard Care is Found in the Majority of Hospitals in Federal Spot Check." *New York Times*, March 23, 1975.

Blain, D., and Robinson, R.L. "Personnel Shortages in Psychiatric Services: A Shift of Emphasis." *New York State Journal of Medicine*, 1957, v. 57, pp. 255-60.

Blanck, G.S. "The Development of Psychotherapy as a Profession: A Study of the Process of Professionalization." Ph.D. dissertation, New York University, 1963. Abstracted in *Dissertation Abstracts*, 1963, v. 24(07), p. 2974.

Bloom, M.T. *The Trouble with Lawyers.* New York: Simon and Schuster, 1968.

Boneau, C.A. "The Educational Base: Supply for the Demand." *American Psychologist*, 1968, v. 23, pp. 308-11.

Boneau, C.A., and Cuca, J.M. "An Overview of Psychology's Human Resources." *American Psychologist*, 1974, v. 29, pp. 821-40.

Borgatta, E.F. "The Certification of Academic Professions: The Case of Psychology." *American Sociological Review*, 1958, v. 23, pp. 302-6.

Boston Globe. "Physician, Heal Thyself." (Editorial.) *Boston Globe*, August 24, 1975.

Boulier, B.L. "An Examination of Licensure and Licensure Reform on the Geographical Distribution of Dentists." 1976. Cited in A. Holen, "The Economics of Dental Licensing." Mimeographed. The Public Research Institute of the Center for Naval Analyses, Arlington, Va., November 1977, p. 64.

Boulier, B.L. "Two Essays on the Economics of Dentistry: A Production Function for Dental Services and an Examination of the Effects of Licensure." Ph.D. dissertation, Princeton University, 1974. Abstracted in *Dissertation Abstracts International*, 1975, v. 35(9-A), p. 5630.

Boxley, R., and Wagner, N.N. "Clinical Psychology Training Programs and Minority Groups: A Survey." *Professional Psychology*, 1971, v. 2, pp. 75-81.

Brody, M. "State Medical Society Opposes Unsupervised Lay Psychotherapy." *Bulletin of the New York State District Branches of the American Psychiatric Association*, September 1965, pp. 3-4.

Brook, R.H.; Berg, M.H.; and Schechter, P.A. "Effectiveness of Nonemergency Care via an Emergency Room." *Annals of Internal Medicine*, 1973, v. 78, pp. 333–39.

Burgess, A.M., and Burgess, A.M., Jr. "Caring for the Patient—A Thrice-Told Tale." *New England Journal of Medicine*, 1966, v. 274, pp. 1241-44.

Business Week. "How Licensing Hurts Consumers." *Business Week*, November 28, 1977, pp. 127-29.

Caldwell, L.G. "Early Legislation Regulating the Practice of Medicine." *Illinois Law Review*, 1923, v. 18, pp. 225-44.

California, Assembly Committee on Health and Welfare. "Final Report of Sex Therapy and Counseling Licensure in California." Mimeographed. Sacramento, Calif., July 1976.

California, Department of Mental Hygiene. *Mental Health Manpower-Vol. I: An Annotated Bibliography and Commentary*. Sacramento, Calif.: Department of Mental Hygiene, 1965.

Carlin, J.E., *Lawyers' Ethics: A Survey of the New York City Bar*. New York: Russell Sage Foundation, 1966.

Carlson, R.J. *The End of Medicine*. New York: John Wiley, 1975.

Carlson, R.J. "Health Manpower Licensing and the Emerging Institutional Responsibility for the Quality of Care." *Law and Contemporary Problems*, 1970, v. 35, pp. 849-78.

Carnegie Commission on Higher Education. *Higher Education and the Nation's Health*. New York: McGraw Hill, 1970.

Carroll, S.L., and Gaston, R.J. *Occupational Licensing*. (Final Report to the National Science Foundation.) Knoxville, Tenn.: Department of Economics, University of Tennessee, 1977.

Cates, J. "Psychology's Manpower: Report on the 1968 National Register of Scientific and Technical Personnal." *American Psychologist*, 1970, v. 25, pp. 254-63.

Centor, A. Administrative Officer, Board of Professional Affairs, American Psychological Association. Personal communication, February 11, 1976.

Claiborne, R. "The Great Health Care Rip-off." *Saturday Review*, January 7, 1978, pp. 10-13, 16, 50.

Clark, K.E. *America's Psychiatrists: A Survey of a Growing Profession*. Washington, D.C.: American Psychiatric Association, 1957.

Clute, K.F. *The General Practitioner: A Study of Medical Education and Practice in Ontario and Nova Scotia*. Toronto: University of Toronto Press, 1963.

Coates, B. "National Board of Examiners in Psychology." *American Psychologist*, 1973, v. 28, p. 267.

Codman, E.A. "The Product of a Hospital." *Surgery, Gynecology and Obstetrics*, 1914, v. 18, pp. 491-96.

Cohen, H.S. "State Licensing Boards and Quality Assurance: A New Approach to an Old Problem." In U.S. Department of Health, Education, and Welfare, *Quality Assurance of Medical Care*. (DHEW Publication No. HSM-73-7021.) Washington, D.C.: U.S. Government Printing Office, 1973, pp. 49-65.

Cohen, H.S., and Dean, W.J. "To Practice or Not to Practice: Developing State Law and Policy of Physician's Assistants." *Milbank Memorial Fund Quarterly*, 1974, v. 52, pp. 349-76.

Coleman, F.C. "Licensure Problems of Allied Health Personnel." *Federation Bulletin*, 1970, v. 57, pp. 204-13.

Columbia Law Review. "Regulation of Psychological Counseling and Psychotherapy." *Columbia Law Review*, 1951, v. 51, pp. 474-95.

Combs, A.W. "Problems and Definitions in Legislation." *American Psychologist*, 1953, v. 8, pp. 554-63.

Cordero, A.L. "The Determination of Medical Care Needs in Relation to a Concept of Minimal Adequate Care: An Evaluation of the Curative Outpatient Services of a Rural Health Centre." *Medical Care*, 1964, v. 2, pp. 95-103.

Council of State Governments. *Occupational Licensing Legislation in the States: A Study of State Legislation Licensing the Practice of Professions and Other Occupations.* Chicago: Council of State Governments, 1952.

Cowen, E.L., and Zax, M. "The Mental Health Fields Today: Issues and Problems." In E.L. Cowen, E.A. Gardner, and M. Zax, *Emergent Approaches to Mental Health Problems.* New York: Appleton-Century-Crofts, 1967, pp. 3–29.

Cowen, E.L.; Zax, M.; and Laird, J.D. "A College Student Volunteer Program in the Elementary School Setting." In B.G. Guerney, Jr. (Ed.), *Psychotherapeutic Agents: New Roles for Nonprofessionals, Parents, and Teachers.* New York: Holt, Rinehart and Winston, 1969, pp. 188–204.

Coye, R.D., and Hansen, M.F. "The 'Doctor's Assistant,'" *Journal of the American Medical Association,* 1969, v. 209, pp. 529–33.

Crabb, M.H. Secretary, Federation of State Medical Boards. Personal Communication, January 3, 1977.

Davis, K.C. *Administrative Law Text.* (3rd ed.) St. Paul, Minn.: West Publishing Co., 1972.

DeLancy, F.P. *The Licensing of Professions in West Virginia.* Chicago: Foundation Press, 1938.

Demsetz, H. "Why Regulate Utilities?" *Journal of Law and Economics,* 1968, v. 11, pp. 55–65.

Derbyshire, R.C. "Better Licensure Laws for Better Patient Care." *Hospital Practice,* September 1972, pp. 152 et seq.

Derbyshire, R.C. "Licensing the Foreign Medical Graduate." *Federation Bulletin,* 1969a, v. 56, pp. 178–91.

Derbyshire, R.C. *Medical Licensure and Discipline in the United States.* Baltimore, Md.: Johns Hopkins Press, 1969.

Deutsch, C.P. "After Legislation—What Price Psychology?" *American Psychologist,* 1958, v. 13, pp. 645–52.

Dörken, H. and Associates. *The Professional Psychologist Today: New Developments in Law, Health Insurance, and Health Practice.* San Francisco: Jossey-Bass, 1976.

Donabedian, A. "Evaluating the Quality of Medical Care." *Milbank Memorial Fund Quarterly,* 1966, v. 44, pp. 166–206.

Dornette, W.H.L. "Role of the Healing Arts Licensing Board in the Current Medical Malpractice Crisis." *Journal of Legal Medicine,* 1976, v. 4(3), pp. 9–13.

Doyle, J.C. "Unnecessary Hysterectomies: Study of 6,248 Operations in Thirty-five Hospitals During 1948." *Journal of the American Medical Association,* 1953, v. 151, pp. 360–65.

Doyle, J.C. "Unnecessary Ovariectomies." *Journal of the American Medical Association,* 1952, v. 148, pp. 1105–11.

Egelston, E.M. "Licensure and Career Mobility." *Hospitals,* December 1, 1970, pp. 42–46.

Egelston, E.M., and Kinser, T. "Licensure of Hospital Personnel" *Hospitals,* November 16, 1970, pp. 35–39.

Egelston, E.M., and Kinser, T. *Exploratory Investigation of Licensure of Health Personnel.* Chicago: American Hospital Association, 1969.

Eisele, C.W.; Slee, V.N.; and Hoffmann, R.G. "Can the Practice of Internal Medicine Be Evaluated?" *Annals of Internal Medicine,* 1956, v. 44, pp. 144–61.

Ellis, A. "Pros and Cons of Legislation for Psychologists." *American Psychologist,* 1953, v. 8, pp. 551–53.

Engman, L.A. "A Critical Report on Government Regulation." *U.S. News and World Report,* November 4, 1974, pp. 81–82.

Estes, E.H., Jr., and Howard, D.R. "The Physician's Assistant in the University Center." *Annals of the New York Academy of Sciences,* 1969, v. 166, pp. 903–10.

Evans, H.E. "Tonsillectomy and Adenoidectomy: Review of Published Evidence For and Against the T and A." *Clinical Pediatrics,* 1968, v. 7(2), pp. 71–75.

Eysenck, H.J. *The Effects of Psychotherapy.* New York: International Science Press, 1966.

Fein, R. *The Doctor Shortage: An Economic Diagnosis.* Washington, D.C.: Brookings Institution, 1967.

Fellman, D. "A Case Study in Administrative Law—The Regulation of Barbers." *Washington University Law Quarterly*, 1941, v. 26, pp. 213-42.

Fessell, W.J., and Van Brunt, E.E. "Assessing Quality of Care from the Medical Record." *New England Journal of Medicine*, 1972, v. 286, pp. 134-38.

Fink, P.J., and Oken, D. "The Role of Psychiatry as a Primary Care Specialty." *Archives of General Psychiatry*, 1976, v. 33, pp. 998-1003.

Florida, House of Representatives, Committee on Regulated Industries and Licensing. *Examining the Examiners: An Investigation of the Licensure Examination Practices and Policies for Florida's Boards of Dentistry, Medical Examiners, Podiatry Examiners, and Veterinary Medicine with Recommendations for State and Federal Action.* (Prepared by J.P. Halstead.) Tallahassee, Fla.: Florida House of Representatives, 1975.

Forgotson, E.H.; Bradley, C.R.; and Ballenger, M.D. "Health Services for the Poor—the Manpower Problem: Innovations and the Law." *Wisconsin Law Review*, 1970, v. 1970, pp. 756-89.

Forgotson, E.H., and Cook, J.L. "Innovations and Experiments in the Uses of Health Manpower—the Effect of Licensure Laws." *Law and Contemporary Problems*, 1967, v. 32, pp. 731-50.

Forgotson, E.H.; Roemer, R.; and Newman, R.W. "Licensure of Physicians." *Washington University Law Quarterly*, 1967, v. 1967, pp. 249-331.

Forgotson, E.H.; Roemer, R.; Newman, R.W.; and Cook, J.L. "Licensure of Other Medical Personnel." In U.S. National Advisory Commission on Health Manpower, *Report of the National Advisory Commission on Health Manpower.* (Vol. 2.) Washington, D.C.: U.S. Government Printing Office, 1967, pp. 407-92.

Frank, J.D. *Persuasion and Healing: A Comparative Study of Psychotherapy.* (Rev. ed.) Baltimore, Md.: Johns Hopkins Press, 1973.

Freund, E. *Administrative Powers over Persons and Property: A Comparative Survey.* Chicago: University of Chicago Press, 1928.

Friedman, L.M. "Freedom of Contract and Occupational Licensing 1890-1910: A Legal and Social Study." *California Law Review*, 1965, v. 53, pp. 487-534.

Friedman, M. *Capitalism and Freedom.* Chicago: University of Chicago Press, 1962.

Garceau, O. *The Political Life of the American Medical Association.* Cambridge, Mass.: Harvard University Press, 1941.

Gellhorn, W. *Individual Freedom and Governmental Restraints.* Baton Rouge, La.: Louisiana State University Press, 1956.

Gellhorn, W., and Byse, C. *Administrative Law: Cases and Comments.* (6th ed.) Mineola, N.Y.: Foundation Press, 1974.

Gerty, F.J.; Holloway, J.W.; and MacKay, R.P. "Licensure or Certification of Clinical Psychologists." *Journal of the American Medical Association*, 1952, v. 148, pp. 271-73.

Gilb, C.L. *Hidden Hierarchies: The Professions and Government.* New York: Harper and Row, 1966.

Glenn, R.D. "Standard of Care in Administering Non-traditional Psychotherapy." *University of California, Davis Law Review*, 1974, v. 7, pp. 56-83.

Goldstein, H.M. and Horowitz, M.A. *Entry-Level Health Occupations: Development and Future.* Baltimore, Md.: Johns Hopkins University Press, 1977.

Grant, J.A.C. "The Gild Returns to America: Part I." *Journal of Politics*, 1942, v. 4, pp. 303-36.

Grant, J.A.C. "The Gild Returns to America: Part II." *Journal of Politics*, 1942a, v. 4, pp. 458-77.

Greene, R. *Assuring Quality in Medical Care: The State of the Art.* Cambridge, Mass.: Ballinger Publishing Co., 1976.

Grimm, K.L. "The Relationship of Accreditation to Voluntary Certification and State Licensure." In National Commission on Accreditation, *Accreditation of Health Educational Programs, Part II: Staff Working Papers.* Washington, D.C.: National Commission on Accreditation, 1972, pp. I1-I30.

Hanft, F., and Hamrick, J.N. "Haphazard Regimentation under Licensing Statutes." *North Carolina Law Review,* 1938, v. 12, pp. 1-18.

Hansen, H.R. *Medical Licensure and Consumer Protection: An Analysis and Evaluation of State Medical Licensure.* Washington, D.C.: Group Health Foundation, 1962.

Hapgood, D. "The Health Professionals: Cure or Cause of the Health Crisis?" *Washington Monthly,* June 1969, pp. 60-73.

Harrison, S.I.; Bordin, E.S.; Holt, R.R.; Linford, A.A.; Mudd, E.H.; Slovenko, R.; and Visotsky, H. "The Feasibility of a Model Statute Licensing the Practice of Psychotherapy." *American Journal of Orthopsychiatry,* 1970, v. 40, p. 558.

Harshbarger, D. "Quality Services." *APA Monitor,* July 1974, pp. 2 and 9.

Healey, K. "The Effect of Licensure on Clinical Laboratory Effectiveness (with special reference to its effect on quality of output)." Ph.D. dissertation, University of California, Los Angeles, 1973. Abstracted in *Dissertation Abstracts International,* 1973, v. 34(B), p. 2728.

Health Services Research Center, Institute for Interdisciplinary Studies. "Medical Manpower Specialty Distribution Projections: 1975 and 1980." Mimeographed. Minneapolis, Minn., 1971.

Heiser, K.F. "The Need for Legislation and the Complexities of the Problem." *American Psychologist,* 1950, v. 5, pp. 104 and 108.

Hershey, N. "Inhibiting Effect upon Innovation of the Prevailing Licensure System." *Federation Bulletin,* 1970, v. 57, pp. 165-80.

Hetherington, J.A.C. "State Economic Regulation and Substantive Due Process of Law, Part 2." *Northwestern University Law Review,* 1958, v. 53, pp. 226-51.

Hiestand, D.L., and Ostow, M. (Eds.) *Health Manpower Information for Policy Guidance.* Cambridge, Mass.: Ballinger Publishing Co., 1976.

Hobbs, N. "Mental Health's Third Revolution." In B.G. Guerney, Jr., (Ed.), *Psychotherapeutic Agents: New Roles for Nonprofessionals, Parents, and Teachers.* New York: Holt, Rinehart and Winston, 1969, pp. 14-27.

Hodgson, E.L. "Restrictions on Unorthodox Health Treatment in California: A Legal and Economic Analysis." *UCLA Law Review,* 1977, v. 24, pp. 647-96.

Hogan, D.B. "The Regulation of Human Relations Training: An Examination of Some Assumptions and Some Recommendations." Unpublished third-year manuscript, Harvard Law School, Cambridge, Mass., 1972.

Hogan, D.B. "State Licensing, Academic Credentials and Accreditation: Implications and Recommendations for Postsecondary Educational Institutions." Paper presented at the Conference on Credentialism, University of California, Berkeley, April 28-30, 1977.

Holen, A. "The Economics of Dental Licensing." Mimeographed. The Public Research Institute of the Center for Naval Analyses, Arlington, Va., November 1977.

Holen, A. "Effects of Professional Licensing Arrangements on Interstate Labor Mobility and Resource Allocation." *Journal of Political Economy,* 1965, v. 73(5), pp. 492-98.

Holmes, O.W., Sr. *Medical Essays.* Boston: Houghton Mifflin, 1892.

Howard, D.R., and Ball, J.R. "The Legal and Professional Recognition of Physician's Assistant." *Federation Bulletin,* 1973, v. 60, pp. 7-21.

Hyde, D.R., and Wolff, P. "The American Medical Association: Power, Purpose, and Politics in Organized Medicine." *Yale Law Journal,* 1954, v. 63, pp. 938-1022.

Illich, I. *Medical Nemesis.* London: Calder and Boyars, 1976.

Illinois, Legislative Council. "Licensing of Practical Nurses and Nurses' Aides." (Memorandum report pursuant to Proposal 277, sponsored by Representative B.T. Van de Vries.) Mimeographed. Legislative Council, Springfield, Ill., 1949.

Inglis, B. *Fringe Medicine*. London: Faber and Faber, 1964.

International Transactional Analysis Bulletin. "Ohio Transactional Analysis Association Appeal for Money." *International Transactional Analysis Bulletin*, date and issue unknown.

Jackson, R. "Regulation and Electric Utility Rate Levels." *Land Economics*, 1969, v. 45, pp. 372-76.

James, R.D. "Many Pnysicians Hire 'Assistant Doctors' to Help Ease Burden." *Wall Street Journal*, April 23, 1970.

James, W. *The Letters of William James*. (Vol. 2.) (Edited by H. James.) Boston: Atlantic Monthly Press, 1920.

Jameson, E. *The Natural History of Quackery*. London: Michael Joseph, 1961.

Jervey, H.E., Jr. "Medical Practice Acts: Barriers to Innovation in Medical Education?" *Federation Bulletin*, 1971, v. 58, pp. 90-101.

Jervey, H.E., Jr. "A Survey of Medical Discipline." *Federation Bulletin*, 1961, v. 48, pp. 83-95.

Johnson, M.C. "The Age of Psychotherapy and 'Mental Health' Is Over." *Village Voice*, January 18, 1973.

Joint Commission on Mental Illness and Health. *Action for Mental Health*. (Final Report.) New York: Basic Books, 1961.

Jordan, W.A. "Producer Protection, Prior Market Structure and the Effects of Government Regulation." *Journal of Law and Economics*, 1972, v. 15, pp. 151-76.

Jordan, W.A. *Airline Regulation in America: Effects and Imperfections*. Baltimore, Md.: John Hopkins Press, 1970.

Kayton, I. "Statutory Regulation of Psychologists: Its Scope and Constitutionality." *St. John's Law Review*, 1959, v. 33, pp. 249-63.

Keeler, T.E. "Airline Regulation and Market Performance." *Bell Journal of Economics and Management Science*, 1972, v. 3, pp. 399-424.

Kelly, G.A. "Single Level versus Legislation for Different Levels of Psychological Training and Experience." *American Psychologist*, 1950, v. 5, pp. 109 and 111.

Kessel, R. "The A.M.A. and the Supply of Physicians." *Law and Contemporary Problems*, 1970, v. 35, pp. 267-83.

Kikel, M.J. "Statutory Regulation of Photography." *Rocky Mountain Law Review*, 1946, v. 18, pp. 421-26.

Klein, M.W.; Malone, M.F.; Bennis, W.G.; and Berkowitz, N.H. "Problems of Measuring Patient Care in the Out-Patient Department." *Journal of Health and Human Behavior*, 1961, v. 2, pp. 138-44.

Knott, P.D. "On the Manpower Problem and Graduate Training in Clinical Psychology," *American Psychologist*, 1969, v. 24, pp. 675-79.

Knudsen, R.A. "Licensing of Professions and Occupations in Nebraska." *Nebraska Law Review*, 1949, v. 29, pp. 146-52.

Kobler, F. Chairperson, Illinois Psychologists Examining Committee. Personal communication, June 13, 1974.

Kohl, S.G. *Perinatal Mortality in New York City: Responsible Factors*. Cambridge, Mass.: Harvard University Press, 1955.

Kubie, L.S. "The Overall Manpower Problem in Mental Health Personnel." *Journal of Nervous and Mental Disease*, 1967, v. 144, pp. 466-70.

Lancaster, L.W. "Private Associations and Public Administration." *Social Forces*, 1934, v. 13, pp. 283-91.

Laughran, C.W. "Religious Beliefs and the Criminal Justice System: Some Problems of the Faith Healer." *Loyola University Law Review*, 1975, v. 8, pp. 396-431.

Lave, J.R., and Lave, L.B. "Medical Care and Its Delivery: An Economic Appraisal." *Law and Contemporary Problems*, 1970, v. 35, pp. 252-66.

Layne, B. "Excessive Prescription of Amphetamines: Who Enforces Ethical Norms?"

(Case Study No. 14.) Mimeographed. Kennedy Interfaculty Program in Medical Ethics, Harvard University, Cambridge, Mass., undated.

Leffler, K.B. "Physician Licensure: Competition and Monopoly in American Medicine." (Working Paper Series No. 7620.) University of Rochester, Graduate School of Management, February 1977.

Leiserson, A. *Administrative Regulation: A Study in Representation of Interests.* 1942. Reprint. Westport, Conn.: Greenwood Press, 1975.

Lembcke, P.A. "Professional Practice: A Scientific Method for Medical Auditing: Part I." *Hospitals*, June 16, 1959, pp. 65, 68, 70-71.

Lembcke, P.A. "Medical Auditing by Scientific Methods." *Journal of the American Medical Association*, 1956, v. 162, pp. 646-55.

Levine, M.E. "Is Regulation Necessary? California Air Transportation and National Regulation Policy." *Yale Law Journal*, 1965, v. 74, pp. 1416-47.

Lewis, C.E., and Resnik, B.A. "Nurse Clinics and Progressive Ambulatory Patient Care." *New England Journal of Medicine*, 1967, v. 277, pp. 1236-41.

Leymaster, G.R., and Mason, H.R. "The Impact of Medical Education Changes on Prevailing Licensure Requirements." *Federation Bulletin*, 1972, v. 59, pp. 58-70.

Lieberman, J.K. *Crisis at the Bar: Lawyers' Unethical Ethics and What to Do About It.* New York: W.W. Norton, 1978.

Lieberman, J.K. "How to Avoid Lawyers." In R. Nader and M. Green (Eds.), *Verdicts on Lawyers.* New York: Thomas Y. Crowell, 1976, pp. 105-17.

Lieberman, J.K. *The Tyranny of the Experts: How Professionals Are Closing the Open Society.* New York: Walker, 1970.

Lindner, R.M. "The Problem of Medical and Lay Psychotherapy: Who Shall Practice Psychotherapy?" *American Journal of Psychotherapy*, 1950, v. 4, pp. 432-42.

Lipworth, L.; Lee, J.A.H.; and Morris, J.N. "Case-Fatality in Teaching and Non-teaching Hospitals 1956-59." *Medical Care*, 1963, v. 1, pp. 71-76.

Lord, H. Executive Director, Florida State Board of Examiners of Psychology. Personal Communication, June 20, 1974.

Lurie, M. "Physician Licensing Policy." In American Medical Association, National Congress on Health Manpower, *Expanding the Supply of Health Services in the 1970's.* (Sponsored by The Council on Health Manpower.) Chicago: American Medical Association, 1970.

MacAvoy, P.W. *The Economic Effects of Regulation: The Trunk-Line Railroad Cartels and the Interstate Commerce Commission Before 1900.* Cambridge, Mass.: MIT Press, 1965.

McCleery, R.S.; Keelty, L.T.; Lam, M.; Phillips, R.E.; and Quirin, T.M. *One Life— One Physician: An Inquiry into the Medical Profession's Performance in Self-regulation.* (A Report to the Center for Study of Responsive Law.) Washington, D.C.: Public Affairs Press, 1971.

McClelland, D.C. "Testing for Competence Rather than for 'Intelligence.'" *American Psychologist*, 1973, v. 28, pp. 1-14.

McLachlan, G. (Ed.) *A Question of Quality?—Roads to Assurance in Medical Care.* Oxford, England: Oxford University Press, 1976.

Marmor, J. *Phychiatrists and Their Patients: A National Survey of Private Practice.* Washington, D.C.: American Psychiatric Association, 1975.

Marsh, H.M. "California Board of Medical Examiners." *University of California, Davis Law Review*, 1972, v. 5, pp. 114-29.

Matarazzo, J.D. "Some National Developments in the Utility of Nontraditional Mental Health Manpower." *American Psychologist*, 1971, v. 26, pp. 363-72.

Maurizi, A. "Occupational Licensing and the Public Interest." *Journal of Political Economy*, 1974, v. 82, pp. 399-413.

May, R. "Psychology and Legislation." *American Psychologist*, 1954, v. 9, pp. 585-86.

Mechanic, D. "Problems in the Future Organization of Medical Practice." *Law and Contemporary Problems*, 1970, v. 35, pp. 233-51.

Miller, J. "The Philosophy of Professional Licensure." *Federation Bulletin*, 1934, v. 20, pp. 201-24.

Minnesota Law Review. "The Minnesota Chiropractic Licensing Statutes: A Time for Revision." *Minnesota Law Review*, 1974, v. 58, pp. 1091-123.

Mintz, M. "Burger Again Blasts Unqualified Lawyers." *Washington Post*, February 13, 1978.

Mizuno, B.K. "The Physician's Assistant and the Problem of Statutory Authorization." *University of California, Davis Law Review*, 1974, v. 7, pp. 413-31.

Monaghan, H.P. "The Constitution and Occupational Licensing in Massachusetts." *Boston University Law Review*, 1961, v. 41, pp. 157-82.

Moore, T.G. "The Effectiveness of Regulation of Electric Utility Prices." *Southern Economic Journal*, 1970, v. 36, pp. 365-75.

Moore, T.G. "The Purpose of Licensing." *Journal of Law and Economics*, 1961, v. 4, pp. 93-117.

Morris, R.C.; and Moritz, A. *Doctor and Patient and the Law.* (5th ed., rev.) St. Louis, Mo.: Mosby, 1971.

Morrow, J.H., and Edwards, A.B. "U.S. Health Manpower Policy: Will the Benefits Justify the Costs?" *Journal of Medical Education*, 1976, v. 51, pp. 791-805.

Morton, J.H. "Do Licensing Requirements Inhibit Innovation in Medical Schools?" *Federation Bulletin*, 1975, v. 62, pp. 370-74.

Mosher, L. "A Shell Game in Shrinkdom." *National Observer*, May 5, 1973.

Nader, R., and Green, M. (Eds.) *Verdicts on Lawyers.* New York: Thomas Y. Crowell, 1976.

National Association for Mental Health. *Facts About Mental Illness.* New York: National Association for Mental Health, 1969.

National Education Association. "Statutory Status of Six Professions—Accountancy, Architecture, Law, Medicine, Nursing, Teaching." *Research Bulletin*, 1938, v. 16, pp. 183-233.

National Manpower Council. *Womanpower.* New York: Columbia University Press, 1957.

Nelson, E.C.; Jacobs, A.R.; and Johnson, K.G. "Patients' Acceptance of Physician's Assistants." *Journal of the American Medical Association*, 1974, v. 228, pp. 63-67.

New Jersey, Professional and Occupational Licensing Study Commission. *Regulating Professions and Occupations.* (Reported submitted to the Governor and Legislature, State of New Jersey.) Trenton, N.J., 1971.

Newfield, J. "My Back Pages." *Village Voice*, March 15, 1973.

Newman, F. *The Second Newman Report: National Policy on Higher Education.* (Report of a Special Task Force to the Secretary of Health, Education and Welfare.) Cambridge, Mass.: M.I.T. Press, 1973.

Notre Dame Lawyer. "Occupational Licensing: An Argument for Asserting State Control." *Notre Dame Lawyer*, 1968, v. 44, p. 104.

Oden, T.C. "Consumer Interests in Therapeutic Outcome Studies: A Reply to Herron." *Journal of Humanistic Psychology*, 1975, v. 15(3), pp. 75-84.

Ogra, P.L. "Effect of Tonsillectomy and Adenoidectomy on Nasopharyngeal Antibody Response to Poliovirus." *New England Journal of Medicine*, 1971, v. 284, pp. 59-64.

Oklahoma, Legislative Council Research Department. *The Licensing of Professions in Oklahoma.* Oklahoma City, Okla.: Legislative Council Research Department, 1950.

Palomba, N.A. "The Role of Law in Achieving Efficient Health Care Delivery." *Labor Law Journal*, 1973, v. 24, pp. 733-38.

Peatman, J.G. "The Problem of Protecting the Public by Appropriate Legislation for the Practice of Psychology." *American Psychologist*, 1950, v. 5, pp. 102-3.

Peltzman, S. "Entry in Commercial Banking." *Journal of Law and Economics*, 1965, v. 8, pp. 11-50.

Pennell, M.Y.; Proffitt, J.R.; and Hatch, T.D. *Accreditation and Certification in Relation to Allied Health Manpower.* Washington, D.C.: U.S. Government Printing Office, 1971.

Peterson, O.L. "Evaluation of the Quality of Medical Care." *New England Journal of Medicine*, 1963, v. 269, pp. 1238-45.

Peterson, O.L.; Andrews, L.P.; Spain, R.S.; and Greenberg, B.G. "An Analytical Study of North Carolina General Practice, 1953-1954." *Journal of Medical Education*, 1956, v. 31. (Special Supp., Part II.)

Pfeffer, J. "Administrative Regulation and Licensing: Social Problem or Solution?" *Social Problems*, 1974, v. 21, pp. 468-79.

Phelan, J.J. *Regulation of the Television Repair Industry in Louisiana and California: A Case Study.* (Staff Report to the Federal Trade Commission.) Washington, D.C.: U.S. Government Printing Office, 1974.

President's Commission on Mental Health. *Report to the President.* Washington, D.C.: U.S. Government Printing Office, 1978 (4 vols.)

Price, P.B.; Taylor, C.W.; Richards J.M., Jr.; and Jacobsen, T.L. "Measurement of Physician Performance." *Journal of Medical Education*, 1964, v. 39, pp. 203-11.

Public Citizen. "Unauthorized Practice." *Public Citizen*, Winter 1978, p. 2.

Rayack, E. "An Economic Analysis of Occupational Licensure." Unpublished manuscript, U.S. Department of Labor, Manpower Administration (Grant No. 98-02-6851), 1975.

Rayack E. *Professional Power and American Medicine: The Economics of the American Medical Association.* Cleveland, Ohio: World Publishing Co., 1967.

Riegelman, H. "Toward a Psychologists' Monopoly?" *New York Times*, April 24, 1973.

Rioch, M.J. "Changing Concepts in the Training of Therapists." *Journal of Consulting Psychology*, 1966, v. 30, pp. 290-92.

Roemer, M.I. "Controlling and Promoting Quality in Medical Care." In C.C. Havighurst, "Health Care: Part I." (Special issue.) *Law and Contemporary Problems*, 1970, v. 35, pp. 284-304.

Roemer, M.I., and Dubois, D.M. "Medical Costs in Relation to the Organization of Ambulatory Care." *New England Journal of Medicine*, 1969, v. 280, pp. 988-93.

Roemer, R. "Legal Regulation of Health Manpower in the 1970's." *HSMHA Health Reports*, 1971, v. 86, pp. 1053-63.

Roemer, R. "Legal and Other Institutional Impediments to Realignment of Health Service Functions." In American Medical Association, National Congress on Health Manpower, *Expanding the Supply of Health Services in the 1970's.* (Sponsored by The Council on Health Manpower.) Chicago: American Medical Association, 1970a, pp. 43-64.

Rogers, C.R. "Some New Challenges." *American Psychologist*, 1973, v. 28, pp. 379-87.

Rosenbloom, J. "Who Regulates the Regulator?" *Boston Globe*, December 26, 1973.

Rosenfeld, L.S. "Quality of Medical Care in Hospitals." *American Journal of Public Health*, 1957, v. 47, pp. 856-65.

Rosenzweig, S. President, Massachusetts Psychological Association. Personal Communication, January 28, 1972.

Rouse, M.O. "Walter L. Bierring Lecture." *Federation Bulletin*, 1968, v. 55, pp. 70-78.

Rozovsky, L.E. "Health Professional Licensure: The New Dilemma." *Dimensions in Health Service*, 1975, v. 52(4), pp. 18-20.

Ryan, W. (Ed.) *Distress in the City*. Cleveland, Ohio: Case Western Reserve University Press, 1969.

Sadler, B. "Recent Legal Developments Relative to Physician's Assistants and Nurse Practitioners." *Physician's Assistant Journal*, Winter-Spring 1974, pp. 35-44.

Saffir, M.A. "Certification versus Licensing Legislation." *American Psychologist*, 1950, v. 5, pp. 105-6.

Schimmel, E.M. "The Hazards of Hospitalization." *Annals of Internal Medicine*, 1964, v. 60, pp. 100-110.

Schimmel, E.M. "The Physician as Pathogen." *Journal of Chronic Diseases*, 1963, v. 16, pp. 1-4.

Schoenbach, F.R., and Snider, A. "Physicians and Surgeons—What Constitutes the Practice of Medicine Within Statutes Regulating the Same. *People v. Hickey*, 283 N.Y. Supp. 968." *Boston University Law Review*, 1936, v. 16, pp. 488-506.

Schwitzgebel, R.K. "Right to Treatment for the Mentally Disabled: The Need for Realistic Standards and Objective Criteria." *Harvard Civil Rights—Civil Liberties Law Review*, 1973, v. 8, pp. 513-35.

Selden, W.K. "Historical Introduction to Accreditation of Health Educational Programs." In National Commission on Accreditation, *Accreditation of Health Educational Programs, Part I: Working Papers*. Washington, D.C.: National Commission on Accreditation, 1971, pp. A1-A7.

Selden, W.K. "Licensing Boards Are Archaic." *American Journal of Nursing*, 1970, v. 70, pp. 124-26.

Shabecoff, P. "Soaring Price of Medical Care Puts a Serious Strain on Economy." *New York Times*, May 7, 1978.

Shapiro, S.; Weiner, L.; and Densen, P.M. "Comparison of Prematurity and Perinatal Mortality in a General Population and in the Population of a Prepaid Group Practice, Medical Care Plan." *American Journal of Public Health*, 1958, v. 48, pp. 170-87.

Shepard, L. "Licensure Restrictions and the Cost of Dental Care." Mimeographed. Department of Agricultural Economics, University of California, Davis, undated.

Shimberg, B.; Esser, B.F.; and Kruger, D.H. *Occupational Licensing: Practices and Policies*. (A Report of the Educational Testing Service.) Washington, D.C.: Public Affairs Press, 1972.

Shindell, S. "A Survey of the Law of Medical Practice." *Journal of the American Medical Association*, 1965, v. 193, pp. 601-6.

Shryock, R.H. *Medical Licensing in America, 1650-1965*. Baltimore, Md.: Johns Hopkins Press, 1967.

Silver, H.K. "The Pediatric Nurse Practitioner and the Child Health Associate: New Types of Health Professionals." *Annals of the New York Academy of Sciences*, 1969, v. 166, pp. 927-33.

Sinnett, E.R., and Thetford, P.E. "Protecting Clients and Assessing Malpractice." *Professional Psychology*, 1975, v. 6, pp. 117-28.

Slee, V.N. "Measuring Hospital Effectiveness: Patterns of Medical Practice." *University of Michigan Medical Center Journal*, 1969, v. 35, pp. 112-15.

Sloss, J. "Regulation of Motor Freight Transportation: A Quantitative Evaluation of Policy." *Bell Journal of Economics and Management Science*, 1970, v. 1, pp. 327-66.

Smith, V.S. *Legal Credentialing of Health Personnel in Oklahoma: Licensure and Related Practices*. Oklahoma City, Okla.: Oklahoma University Health Sciences Center, 1976.

Somers, A.R. "Accountability, Public Policy, and Psychiatry." *American Journal of Psychiatry*, 1977, v. 134, pp. 959-65.

Starfield, B., and Scheff, D. "Effectiveness of Pediatric Care: The Relationship Between Processes and Outcome." *Pediatrics*, 1972, v. 49, pp. 547-52.

Stevens, R.A. "Medical Licensing and the Public Interest." *Federation Bulletin*, 1973, v. 60, pp. 218-30.

Stigler, G.J. and Friedland, C. "What Can Regulators Regulate? The Case of Electricity." *Journal of Law and Economics*, 1962, v. 5, pp. 1-16.

Strupp, H.H. "On the Technology of Psychotherapy." *Archives of General Psychiatry*, 1972, v. 26, pp. 270-78.

Sucher, R. LaF. "Licensing of Occupations in Wisconsin." L.L.M. thesis, University of Wisconsin Law School, 1955.

Tancredi, L.R., and Woods, J. "The Social Control of Medical Practice: Licensure Versus Output Monitoring." *Milbank Memorial Fund Quarterly*, 1972, v. 50, pp. 99-125.

Taylor, C.W.; Smith, W.R.; and Ghiselin, B. "The Creative and Other Contributions of One Sample of Research Scientists." In C.W. Taylor and F. Barron (Eds.), *Scientific Creativity: Its Recognition and Development.* New York: John Wiley, 1963, pp. 53-76.

Taylor, R.L., and Torrey, E.F. "The Pseudo-Regulation of American Psychiatry." *American Journal of Psychiatry*, 1972, v. 129, pp. 658-63.

Theodore, C.N., and Sutter, G.E. "A Report on the First Periodic Survey of Physicians." *Journal of the American Medical Association*, 1967, v. 202, pp. 516-24.

Thetford, P.E. Secretary, Kansas State Board of Examiners of Psychologists. Personal communication, March 16, 1972.

Todd, M.C. (Ed.) *Symposium on Distribution of Health Manpower.* Symposium sponsored by the Council on Health Manpower, American Medical Association, Chicago, June 17, 1972.

Truax, C.B., and Mitchell, K.M. "Research on Certain Therapist Interpersonal Skills in Relation to Process and Outcome." In A.E. Bergin and S.L. Garfield (Eds.), *Handbook of Psychotherapy and Behavior Change: An Empirical Analysis.* New York: John Wiley, 1971, pp. 299-344.

Trussell, R.E. *The Quality of Medical Care as a Challenge to Public Health.* New York: American Public Health Association, 1965.

Trussell, R.E.; Morehead, M.A.; and Ehrlich, J. *The Quantity, Quality and Costs of Medical and Hospital Care Secured by a Sample of Teamster Families in the New York Area.* New York: Columbia University School of Public Health and Administrative Medicine, 1962.

Tuttrup, R.R. "Necessity of Notice and Hearing in the Revocation of Occupational Licenses." *Wisconsin Law Review*, 1926-28, v. 4, pp. 180-86.

U.S. Congress, House Committee on Interstate and Foreign Commerce. *Cost and Quality of Health Care: Unnecessary Surgery: Report by the Subcommittee on Oversight and Investigations, January 1976.* Washington, D.C.: U.S. Government Printing Office, 1976.

U.S. Congress, House Committee on Interstate and Foreign Commerce. *Getting Ready for National Health Insurance: Unnecessary Surgery: Hearings Before the Subcommittee on Oversight and Investigations.* (Serial No. 94-37.) Washington, D.C.: U.S. Government Printing Office, 1975.

U.S. Department of Health, Education, and Welfare. *Credentialing Health Manpower.* Washington, D.C.: U.S. Government Printing Office, July 1977.

U.S. Department of Health, Education, and Welfare. *Analysis of 1974 State Health Manpower Licensure Legislation.* (DHEW Publication No. HRA 106-74-125.) Springfield, Va.: National Technical Information Service, March 1975.

U.S. Department of Health, Education, and Welfare. "Credentialing of Drug Abuse Treatment and Rehabilitation Workers." (Discussion draft, prepared by S.S. Steinberg, A.L. Batista, A.S. Bisconti, and I.L. Gomberg,) Mimeographed. University Research Corp., Washington, D.C., February 1975a.

U.S. Department of Health, Education, and Welfare. *Report of the Meeting to Discuss the Feasibility of a National System of Certification for Allied Health Personnal.* (DHEW Publication No. HRA 75-66.) Washington, D.C.: U.S. Government Printing Office, January 1975b.

U.S. Department of Health, Education, and Welfare. *Analysis of 1973 State Health*

Manpower Licensure Legislation. (DHEW Publication No. HSM 110-73-510.) Springfield, Va.: National Technical Information Service, February 1974.

U.S. Department of Health, Education, and Welfare. *Legal Provisions on Expanded Functions for Dental Hygienists and Assistants—Summarized by State.* (2nd ed., rev.) Washington, D.C.: U.S. Government Printing Office, July 1974a.

U.S. Department of Health, Education, and Welfare. *The Supply of Health Manpower: 1970 Profiles and Projections to 1990.* (DHEW Publication No. HRA 75-38.) Washington, D.C.: U.S. Government Printing Office, December 1974b.

U.S. Department of Health, Education, and Welfare. *Developments in Health Manpower Licensure: A Follow-up to the 1971 Report on Licensure and Related Health Personnel Credentialing, June 1973.* (Prepared by H.S. Cohen and L.H. Miike.) Washington, D.C.: U.S. Government Printing Office, 1973.

U.S. Department of Health, Education, and Welfare. *Report on Licensure and Related Health Personnel Credentialing* (to the Congress of the United States). Washington, D.C.: U.S. Government Printing Office, 1971.

U.S. Department of Health, Education, and Welfare. "American Psychological Association Member Respondents to 1972 Survey Who Stated That They Provided Psychological Services." Unpublished document, Washington, D.C., undated.

U.S. Department of Health, Education, and Welfare. "Non Federal Psychiatrists by State, December 31, 1973 (AMA)." Unpublished document, Washington, D.C., undated (a).

U.S. Department of Labor. *Upgrading—Problems and Potentialities: The R&D Experience.* (Manpower R&D Monograph No. 40.) Washington, D.C.: U.S. Government Printing Office, 1975.

U.S. Department of Labor. *Job Analysis for Human Resource Management: A Review of Selected Research and Development.* (Manpower Research Monograph No. 36.) Washington, D.C.: U.S. Government Printing Office, 1974.

U.S. Department of Labor. *Hiring Standards and Job Performance.* (Manpower Research Monograph No. 18, prepared by D. Diamond and F. Bedrosian.) Washington, D.C.: U.S. Government Printing Office, 1970.

U.S. Department of Labor. *Occupational Licensing and the Supply of Nonprofessional Manpower.* (Manpower Research Monograph No. 11.) Washington, D.C.: U.S. Government Printing Office, 1969.

U.S. Department of Labor. *Our Manpower Future—1955-1965.* Washington, D.C.: U.S. Government Printing Office, 1957.

U.S. Food and Drug Administration. *A Study of Health Practices and Opinions.* Springfield, Va.: National Technical Information Service, 1972.

U.S. National Advisory Commission on Health Manpower. *Report of the National Advisory Commission on Health Manpower.* Washington, D.C.: U.S. Government Printing Office, 1967 (2 vols.)

U.S. National Center for Health Statistics. *Health Resources Statistics: Health Manpower and Health Facilities, 1974.* Washington, D.C.: U.S. Government Printing Office, 1974.

U.S. National Center for Health Statistics. *Health Resource Statistics.* Washington, D.C.: National Center for Health Statistics, 1969.

U.S. National Center for Health Statistics. *State Licensing of Health Occupations.* (Prepared by M.Y. Pennell and P.A. Stewart.) Washington, D.C.: U.S. Government Printing Office, 1968.

U.S. National Institute of Mental Health. *Staffing of Mental Health Facilities, United States, 1974.* (DHEW Publication No. ADM 76-308.) Washington, D.C.: U.S. Government Printing Office, 1976.

U.S. National Institute of Mental Health. *Staffing of Mental Health Facilities, United States, 1972.* (DHEW Publication No. ADM 74-28.) Washington, D.C.: U.S. Government Printing Office, 1975.

U.S. National Institute of Mental Health. *The Nation's Psychiatrists.* Washington, D.C.: U.S. Public Health Service, 1969.

U.S. Social Security Administration. *Medical Care Expenditures, Prices, and Costs: Background Book.* Washington, D.C.: U.S. Government Printing Office, 1975.

Volotta, A. *The Impact of Federal Entry Controls on Motor Carrier Operations.* University Park, Pa.: Pennsylvania State University, Center for Research of the College of Business Administration, 1967.

Volpicelli, F.J. "An Open Letter to HEW Secretary Richardson from a Physician Critical of the Medical Licensing System in the United States." *Federation Bulletin,* 1972, v. 59, pp. 246-52.

Walke, V.L. Administrative Assistant, Ohio State Board of Psychology. Personal communication, April 27, 1976.

Wallerstein, R.S. "The Futures of Psychoanalytic Education." *Journal of the American Psychoanalytic Association,* 1972, v. 20, pp. 591-606.

Weinstein, M.R. "Phychiatric Manpower and Women in Psychiatry." *Journal of Nervous and Mental Disease,* 1968, v. 145, pp. 364-70.

White, D.M., and Francis, R.L. "Title VII and the Masters of Reality: Eliminating Credentialism in the American Labor Market." *Georgetown Law Journal,* 1976, v. 64, pp. 1213-44.

White, W.D. *Public Health and Private Gain: The Economics of Licensing Medical Laboratory Personnel.* Chicago: Maaroufa Press, forthcoming.

White, W.D. "The Impact of Occupational Licensure of Clinical Laboratory Personnel." *Journal of Human Resources,* 1978, v. 13(1), pp. 91-102.

White, W.D., "Occupational Licensure and the Labor Market for Clinical Laboratory Personnel 1900-1973." Ph.D. dissertation, Harvard University, 1975.

Williamson, J.W. "Evaluating Quality of Patient Care: A Strategy Relating Outcome and Process Assessment." *Journal of the American Medical Association,* 1971, v. 218, pp. 564-69.

Willig, S.H. "The Medical Board's Role in Physician Assistancy." *Federation Bulletin,* 1971, v. 58, pp. 126-59 and 167-201.

Wisconsin, State of. *Licensing by the State of Wisconsin.* (Research Bulletin No. 108.) Madison, Wis.: Wisconsin Legislative Reference Library, 1952.

Wolfe, D. "Legal Control of Psychological Practice." *American Psychologist,* 1950, v. 5, pp. 651-55.

Wykert, J. "World-wide Survey of Psychiatrists Reported at Congress." *Psychiatric News,* September 15, 1971, pp. 19, 30 and 32.

Yale Law Journal, "Restrictive Licensing of Dental Paraprofessionals." *Yale Law Journal,* 1974, v. 83, pp. 806-26.

Yolles, S.F. "Community Mental Services: The View from 1967." Paper presented to the American Psychiatric Association, Washington, D.C., May 11, 1967.

Young, J.H. *The Medical Messiahs: A Social History of Health Quackery in Twentieth-Century America.* Princeton, N.J.: Princeton University Press, 1967.

Zuckerman, L.T., and Savedra, R.A. "Professional Licensing Legislation in the United States with an Emphasis on Social Work Statutes in California." Mimeographed. Venice, Calif., 1972.

Legal Cases

Barber v. Reinking, 68 Wash. 2d 139, 411 P.2d 861 (1966).

Crane v. Johnson, 242 U.S. 339 (1916).

Czarra v. Board of Medical Supervisors, 25 App. D.C. 443 (1905).

Darling v. Charleston Community Memorial Hospital, 33 Ill. 2d 326, 211 N.E.2d 253 (1965), cert. denied, 383 U.S. 946 (1966).

Evans v. Hoyme, 78 S.D. 509, 105 N.W.2d 71 (1960).

FTC v. Ruberoid Co., 343 U.S. 470 (1952).

Fealy v. Birmingham, 15 Ala. App. 367, 73 So. 296 (1916).

Freeman v. State Board of Medical Examiners, 54 Okla. 531, 154 P. 56 (1916).

Graeb v. State Board of Medical Examiners, 55 Colo. 523, 139 P. 1099 (1913).

Matthews v. Murphy, 23 Ky. 750, 63 S.W. 785 (1901).

Parks v. State, 159 Ind. 211, 64 N.E. 862 (1902).

People v. Cole, 219 N.Y. 98, 113 N.E. 790 (1916).

People v. Hickey, 157 Misc. 592, 283 N.Y.S. 968 (Ct. Spec. Sess. 1935).

People v. Mulford, 202 N.Y. 624, 125 N.Y.S. 680 (1910).

People v. Phippin, 70 Mich. 6, 37 N.W. 888 (1888).

People v. Whittaker, No. 35307 (Cal. Just. Ct., Redding Jud. Dist., Shasta Cty. Dec. 1966). Cited in E.H. Forgotson and J.L. Cook, "Innovations and Experiments in the Uses of Health Manpower—The Effect of Licensure Laws." *Law and Contemporary Problems*, 1967, v. 32, pp. 731-50.

Sage-Allen Co. v. Wheeler, 119 Conn. 667, 179 A. 195 (1935).

Smith v. People, 51 Colo. 270, 117 P. 612 (1911).

Smith v. State, 8 Ala. App. 352, 63 So. 28 (1913), cert. denied sub nom. *Ex parte Smith*, 183 Ala. 116, 63 So. 70 (1913).

State Board of Medical Examiners v. Macy, 92 Wash. 614, 159 P. 801 (1916).

State v. Evertz, 202 S.W. 614 (Mo. App. 1918).

State v. Hays, 64 W. Va. 45, 61 S.E. 355 (1908).

State v. Horn, 4 Ariz. App. 541, 422 P.2d 172 (1966).

State v. Maxfield, 564 P.2d 968 (Idaho 1977).

State v. Miller, 216 Iowa 806, 249 N.W. 141 (1933).

State v. Mylod, 20 R.I. 632, 40 A. 753 (1898).

State v. Pratt, 92 Wash. 200, 158 P. 981 (1916).

State v. Pratt, 80 Wash. 96, 141 P. 318 (1914).

State v. Shumate, 48 W. Va. 359, 37 S.E. 618 (1900).

State v. Verbon, 167 Wash. 140, 8 P.2d 1083 (1932).

Wyatt v. Stickney, 325 F. Supp. 781 (M.D. Ala. 1971), enforced in 344 F. Supp. 373 (M.D. Ala. 1972), enforcement aff'd in part, modified in part sub nom. *Wyatt v. Aderholt*, 503 F.2d 1305 (5th Cir. 1974).

Chapter 8

Judicial Regulation through
Professional Liability Suits

The major form of judicial regulation that has a direct impact on professional practice is professional liability suits. Criminal suits against practitioners for unethical activities are relatively rare, as are cases involving judicial review of decisions by administrative agencies, such as licensing boards. The most frequent form of civil suit is based on tort law, where the plaintiff seeks redress for injuries sustained. These injuries may be economic (for instance, the loss of money spent on therapeutic services), physical (broken bones or physical illnesses suffered as the result of poorly rendered services), or mental (anxiety, depression, distress, and other emotional upset). In addition, a plaintiff may allege denial of constitutional rights (such as the right to liberty or due process).

Until recently it had not been the purpose of tort law to attempt to achieve societal goals. Instead, its main thrust had been "to make a fair adjustment of the conflicting claims of the litigating parties" and "to protect the interest in freedom from various kinds of harm" (Prosser 1964: 14 and 634). Today, however, the courts are responding to a notion of "public policy," recognizing that a case today will affect future litigants. Thus the purpose of tort law has broadened "to make a conscious effort to direct the law along lines which will achieve a desirable social result, both for the present and for the future" (Prosser 1964: 14–15).

The question remains, however, whether malpractice suits have achieved the socially desirable results expected of them. This includes the question of whether they have had a positive impact on the quality of professional services delivered to the public. Overall, the evidence suggests that this has not occurred.

THE INCIDENCE AND TYPES OF SUITS AGAINST PSYCHOTHERAPISTS

Although the total number of suits brought against psychotherapists is still quite small, in recent years a dramatic increase has occurred. The American Psychiatric Association's Professional Liability Program has had the number of claims opened go from zero for the first seven months of the program (ending in May 1973), to seven for the year ending May 1974, to thirty-one for the following year, and seventy-one from May 1975 to April 1976 (Trent, undated: 15). Of the 300 suits discussed in Volume III of this series, only one-sixth were decided prior to 1950, another sixth from 1950 to 1960, and two-thirds of all cases were decided in the last seventeen years (see Table 45, Appendix C, Volume III).

Information on the types of suits brought against psychotherapists is critical to evaluating the impact of such suits on the mental health field. Unfortunately, such information has been lacking. The many law review articles on the subject tend to focus on a relatively narrow set of cases, and there has been no comprehensive attempt to analyze existing decisions, even those limited to reported cases. Much of the problem has been caused by difficulties in gaining access to the relevant cases. Insurance companies rarely reveal information on suits brought against their policyholders, most trial court decisions are not reported, and even reported appellate-level decisions are difficult to track down, since the legal digests and encyclopedias do not conveniently index psychotherapeutic malpractice.

A careful search of the literature, however, has located 300 relevant cases, most of which are reported decisions. These include malpractice in the diagnosis, treatment, or care of mental illness by a therapist, mental hospital, or its staff, as well as the wide variety of cases involving wrongful commitment or inadequate custodial care. Most cases involve a tort suit in negligence, but a number are criminal proceedings or judicial reviews of administrative actions. The major findings appear in Volume III of this series.

Of the 300 cases analyzed, negligent treatment is involved in 32 percent of all suits, many of which are class actions for inadequate treatment. Sexual involvement is alleged only 4 percent of the time, and even the negligent administration of drugs occurs in only thirteen instances. Far more common are suits for negligent diagnosis or care, both of which are alleged in nearly half of all cases. Inadequate supervision (106 cases) and wrongful commitment (70 cases) account for nearly 60 percent of all suits reported. Inadequate supervision generally involves negligence in an understaffed and overcrowded pub-

lic mental hospital, while wrongful commitment suits are most often brought by an involuntarily committed mental patient who alleges that the committing physicians failed to make a proper examination or did not make any examination at all.

The next most common suits all involve custodial care and consist of: failure to provide proper care (such as failing to bar the windows of the rooms of suicidal patients) (30 cases); failing to diagnose the proper type of care needed (such as prescribing open-ward therapy for a suicidal patient) (26 cases); and negligently determining that a patient should be released (26 cases). Most of these negligent activities result in physical injuries or death, either self-inflicted or accidental.

AN EXPLANATION OF THE NUMBER OF MALPRACTICE SUITS AGAINST THERAPISTS

As has been true in other professional fields, malpractice suits against psychotherapists have proliferated. A variety of forces have generated this increase in suits. First, there is growing public awareness of the possibility of suing practitioners. In the psychotherapy field, the publicity given to cases involving sex between therapist and patient has contributed substantially to this awareness. Second, the myth of physician and professional infallibility has eroded over the past two decades, so that people are now more aware that practitioners make mistakes. Third, the rising tide of consumerism has emphasized methods of seeking redress for alleged wrongs and poor service. This has coincided with the growing use of litigation in U.S. society. Fourth, consumers have become increasingly angered over the high cost of professional services. And finally, many of the doctrines that formerly made it difficult to win a malpractice suit have fallen by the wayside.

On the other hand, the total number of

suits against therapists is relatively small, and is likely to remain that way. The overriding explanation for this state of affairs is the extreme difficulty involved in establishing an adequate case. A brief discussion of the essential elements necessary to support a malpractice action will illustrate the problems involved. Ordinarily a plaintiff must demonstrate that four conditions existed before a court will award a verdict in her or his favor: (1) a legal duty existed between the practitioner and the injured party; (2) the practitioner was derelict in that duty (either through an act that should not have occurred or through an omission); (3) the patient or client suffered harm or injury of some sort; and (4) the harm or injury was directly and proximately caused by the doctor's dereliction of duty.

The first element required, that of a legal duty, does not usually create problems for a plaintiff, since evidence of this is generally clear, sufficient, and not debatable. The fact that a practitioner is not a physician is of no great import, since malpractice suits may be brought against any profession. Where a professional-client relationship is not alleged, however, a lawsuit will be dismissed (see, e.g., *Hammer v. Polsky*, 1962).

In determining whether professionals were derelict in their duty, the courts will ask whether the practitioners conformed to the standard of care required. This will be measured by the degree of ability or skill possessed by other practitioners; the degree of care, attention, diligence, or vigilance ordinarily exercised by those practitioners in the application of their skills; and the special or extraordinary skill of specialists, if practitioners have represented themselves as such (U.S. DHEW 1973a: 123).[1]

For psychiatrists this duty has been defined as bringing "to their relationship the skill and the care of a professionally qualified psychiatrist practicing in that community. . . . The concept of skill is one of technical proficiency: knowledge

of and the ability to apply the medically appropriate therapy. Care, on the other hand, imparts a mode of execution, the guidance which the will gives to skill" (Dawidoff 1966: 700–1). More specifically, Saxe (1969: 191) has argued:

The psychiatrist should have some degree of insight into his own motivation in order to control the countertransference. . . . [The patient's interest] may be impeded by a lack of insight by the psychiatrist into his own unconscious motivations.[2]

In determining standard of care, courts until recently would only compare a practitioner's actions with those of professionals from the same community (Holder, 1975: 53–55). This so-called "locality rule" was designed to protect rural practitioners, who would have difficulty keeping abreast of recent developments in the field. This placed an inordinate burden of proof on claimants, since practitioners from the same community were not sanguine about testifying against their professional colleagues (Minnesota Law Review, 1961).[3] Because of improved communications, better systems of transportation, and the increase in available professional journals and postgraduate courses, however, the locality rule has been overturned in many jurisdictions, either by judicial decision or legislative action (see, e.g., *Brune v. Belinkoff* and Mass. Ann. Laws, ch. 233, § 79C [1956]). As a result, courts are increasingly allowing out-of-state physicians to testify as expert witnesses, and judges are allowing the introduction of medical tests as evidence of acceptable professional practice.

One of the more difficult tasks confronting an injured patient is to determine what school of therapy a practitioner adheres to and what standards of care are appropriate for that school. The idea that different standards are permissible developed from nineteenth-century medicine, when physicians adhered to many different schools (Kett, 1968). Each school had its own standards of practice, its own theories as to the causes and cures of disease, and its own modes of treatment. The judiciary refused to accept any one school as necessarily best. Instead, the judicial doctrine developed that where different schools of thought existed, a doctor would ordinarily be judged by the school she or he professed to follow (Prosser, 1964: 166; see also Pope, "Who Shall Decide When Doctors Disagree?" *Moral Essays*, 1754, Epistle III, Line 1; *Force v. Gregory*, 63 Conn. 167, 27 A. 1116 [1893]; *Nelson v. Dahl*, 174 Minn. 574, 219 N.W. 941 [1928]). To constitute a school, Prosser (1964: 166) has said that it "must be a recognized one with definite principles, and it must be the line of thought of at least a respectable minority of the profession." Schools of psychotherapy such as behaviorism, client-centered therapy, and psychoanalysis meet these criteria. Newer schools such as Gestalt therapy, transactional analysis, and rational-emotive therapy probably do, as well. Whether some of the more esoteric therapies qualify, such as the "rage-reduction therapy" advocated by Robert Zaslow (see *Abraham v. Zaslow*, 1972), is a matter of judicial judgment. Stone (1970: 226) argues that the field may reduce itself to radical experimentation unless the newer therapies attempt to validate what works and what does not. On the other hand, the courts do not want to hinder necessary experimentation in an evolving profession.[4] In actually deciding a particular case, a judge may look at whether the particular school in question has developed a professional association, clearly articulated standards of practice, and ethical guidelines.

In determining the standard of care to which a practitioner will be held, two other doctrines must be taken into account. The first has to do with the psychotherapist as specialist. Generally, a practitioner will only be held to the level of performance of the ordinary practitioner in the field. However, when a therapist holds himself or herself out as an expert in a particular field, that person must then meet the standard of care required in that area. Thus, physicians who refer to themselves as psychiatrists will be held to a standard of care that is different from the standard for physicians who make no such claim. Similarly, clinical psychologists will probably be held to higher standards than those who do not profess to have special expertise. Where nonmedical practitioners perform psychotherapy, the courts will not require them to meet the standards of physicians or psychiatrists (see, for instance, *Bogust v. Iverson*, 1960).

In some cases, where a negligent act is so glaring as to constitute sufficient evidence in itself of negligence, the requirement of expert testimony is dispensed with. This doctrine, known as *res ipsa loquitur*, was first enunciated in the British case, *Scott v. London and St. Katherine Docks Co.* (1865). An English customs officer was hit on the head by several sacks of sugar that had fallen out of a warehouse window. The judges reasoned that sacks of sugar do not fall out of second-story windows and hit pedestrians unless negligence is involved. According to Wigmore (1961: vol. 4, § 2509), three elements are essential before the doctrine can be invoked:

1. The apparatus must be such that in the ordinary instance no injurious operation is to be expected unless from a careless construction, inspection, or user.
2. Both inspection and user must have been at the time of the injury in the control of the party charged.
3. The injurious occurrence or condition must have happened irrespective of any voluntary action at the time by the party injured.

In the past this doctrine has had only limited applicability in malpractice suits. It is generally applied when a foreign object is left in a patient's body after surgery or after burns or other injuries are suffered while a patient is under anesthesia (U.S. DHEW, 1973: 28). In California the doctrine has been extended to situations where a rare accident occurs and some evidence of negligence exists. In the field of psychotherapy the doctrine has not been widely used. Public mental hospitals that place known suicidal patients on the fourth story of a building without window bars may find the doctrine invoked against them, as may therapists who engage in unusual and obviously dangerous techniques, such as physically beating patients (cf. *Abraham v. Zaslow*, 1972; *Hammer v. Rosen*, 1960).

After the standard of care required has been established by expert testimony or medical treatise, the plaintiff must demonstrate that the psychotherapist deviated from this standard. Expert testimony is not necessary to establish this deviation, and the plaintiff may demonstrate negligence through written memoranda, letters, and the statements of witnesses (Cassidy 1974: 133–34). Unfortunately, since most treatment consists of one-to-one contact between therapist and client, evidence of negligence is difficult to substantiate. Even allegations of sexual abuse can be denied or explained as the neurotic or psychotic fantasies of a patient. Where the therapist has simply made a mistake in judgment or has employed less skill than others in utilizing a specific method of treatment, the courts will not generally grant a verdict for the plaintiff (Rothblatt and Leroy, 1973: 263). Thus, the court in *Taig v. State* (241 N.Y.S.2d 495, at 496 [1963]) stated:

The decision to release the patient from the hospital and place him on convalescent status was a medical judgment and the decision to continue him on convalescent out-patient status after February, 1955 and to discharge him in June were also matters of professional medical judgment. Although another physician might disagree as to the form and period of treatment to be fol-

lowed, a liability would not arise; nor would it arise if the professional judgment to discharge him was in fact erroneous.

Even where negligent activity occurred, recovery is dependent upon the existence of compensable damages. This does not pose an insuperable hurdle in those suits involving physical injuries or where there has been physical contact of some sort between therapist and client. Historically, however, the judiciary has hesitated to allow an action where the only damages sought are for emotional distress or other impairment of mental functioning, including such factors as loss of self-esteem (Cassidy, 1974: 134). The basis for this position was that determining whether injury had occurred and what dollar value was to be attached to it was too difficult.[5] Today, far less hesitation exists in this regard.[6]

Where it has been demonstrated that a psychotherapist did deviate from the requisite standard of care, and the client has indeed suffered an actionable injury, it still must be proved that the injury was proximately caused by the negligent activity. This is frequently not an easy matter. Declines in mental health may be attributable to other factors, such as loss of job, divorce, or other life changes. Where the plaintiff alleges that his or her job was lost as a result of the negligent treatment, the courts may find that other precipitating factors account for the injuries equally well. In addition, the injury must not be too remotely related to the negligent act, and it must be foreseeable. As Dawidoff (1973: 72) has said, "In short, the injury must be within the risk exposed by the breach, and the person who is injured must be among the group protected by the duty." In most cases it will be expert testimony that determines whether the plaintiff's injury resulted from the defendant's carelessness, except for instances that are clearly within the reach of the average person and where the negligence is so gross and readily apparent that the injury must have been caused by it (Cassidy 1974: 135). The end result is extreme difficulty in proving proximate causation.[7]

Apart from legal problems of proof, several other factors will reduce both the frequency of suits and the chances of an injured patient winning. While the medical field has witnessed a significant decrease in the amount of face-to-face contact with general practitioners and an increased emphasis on seeing medical specialists, psychotherapy generally involves long-term contact with the same practitioner. The fact of continuous contact and the skill of therapists in handling hostility and other negative feelings will reduce the chances of a person suing (Dawidoff 1966: 696, Heller 1957: 401). Since patients often come into therapy with negative self-images, patients are likely to blame themselves for any negative feelings toward their therapists, neglecting the possibility that the therapist might have been at fault. Finally, patients who have been harmed are often loathe to disclose the details surrounding the incident in a court of law (Cassidy, 1974: 131; Dawidoff, 1966: 696; Slovenko, in Dawidoff, 1973: vii).

THE IMPACT OF MALPRACTICE SUITS GENERALLY

Whether intended or not, the rising number of malpractice suits has had a significant impact on the delivery of professional services. Unfortunately, most of this impact appears to be negative, and there is little indication that the consumer has been protected. The recent crisis in medical malpractice insurance illustrates some of the problems involved. Over the past decade the number of suits and the size of awards for physician malpractice have grown exponentially. Malpractice premiums have risen at even steeper rates. The problem became a crisis in the fall of 1974 when the Argonaut Insurance

Company announced its intentions to increase premiums 380 percent and ultimately to cease writing any malpractice policies at all (Aitken 1975: 27). Shortly thereafter, other companies declared their desire to withdraw from the malpractice arena, and recently both psychologists and psychiatrists have had difficulty in obtaining insurance, despite the fact that both have been good risks (see *Behavior Today*, January 17, 1977 and March 8, 1976; Trent, undated; Trent and Muhl, 1975).

This rise in premiums has had a significantly negative impact. First, the increased costs to physicians and other professionals have been passed on to the consumer in the form of a 2 percent yearly increase in medical costs (Trent undated: 2, citing a study by Chase Econometrics). Because the cost of doing business for physicians and other professionals has risen sharply, many have opted for early retirement, and the profitableness of part-time practice has seriously decreased, driving still more practitioners from the field (U.S. DHEW 1973: 20). For the person injured, even if there is final victory in court, a large award may not be worth the cost of bringing suit because of the length of time involved[8] and the relatively small percentage of the premium dollar that eventually ends up in the hands of the patient.[9]

The problems created by the current crisis have been so serious that the federal government recently spent more than $2 million to study the problems involved (U.S. DHEW 1973 and 1973a). Apart from being a constant topic in the news, state legislatures have devoted a substantial amount of time in developing legislative solutions to the problem (Altman 1975; and see various issues of the *State Health Legislation Report* issued by the American Medical Association).

This raises the issue of whether there have been any offsetting benefits. More specifically, is there evidence, qualitative or otherwise, that judicial regulation results in improved practice or a decrease in negligent practice? Also, is there evidence that a reasonable proportion of those who are harmed by professionals are adequately recompensed?

Not only is there a lack of solidly conceived research in this area, but there is also a dearth of data.[10] Insurance companies have not been particularly responsive to requests for information, and no other central data-gathering source has developed. On the basis of qualitative evidence, however, it is generally asserted that the threat of civil suits in the medical field establishes a strong incentive to initiate hospital rules for more thorough work, better record-keeping, increased willingness to obtain consultation in difficult cases, increased willingness to refer difficult cases to specialists, and a general cautiousness and greater attentiveness to the quality of one's work (McDonald 1971: 4; Roemer 1970: 297).

On the other hand, a considerable body of opinion suggests that, on balance, malpractice suits are a negative influence in a variety of areas. There is general agreement that they inhibit the use of paraprofessionals, since physicians do not delegate any but the most clearly allowed functions to assistants (Forgotson and Cook 1967: 744; for examples, see the cases of *People v. Whittaker*, 1966, and *Barber v. Reinking*, 1966) and worry about the potential of suits brought against them for the negligence of their assistants, even where the practice is clearly legal.[11]

R. Crawford Morris (1971: 1211), one of the most respected defendant lawyers in the field of malpractice and a leading authority on medico-legal problems, states that the threat of malpractice suits has seriously interfered with the traditional doctor-patient relationship and undermined much of the trust necessary on the part of both parties. Many physicians simply will not take clients they believe to be litigious or who have previously sued a doctor (U.S. Congress, Committee on Government Operations, 1969: 7). In addition, physicians tend to avoid medical procedures that are known to involve a high risk of suit, and there is a tendency to order unnecessary X-rays, tests, and other medical procedures to defend against possible allegations of negligence (McDonald 1971: 3). These tests in themselves may entail a greater risk than were they left undone. Concludes Morris (1971: 1211): "On balance, I feel that such lawsuits, even the threat of them without their actually being brought, has produced a detrimental effect upon the quality of patient care."

Not only are malpractice suits detrimental to the quality of patient care, but only seldom do they recompense people who have suffered as the result of professional negligence. The many studies of iatrogenic injuries in medicine indicate that the base-line rate for doctor-caused harm is quite high.[12] A study conducted under the auspices of the Commission on Medical Malpractice of HEW found that 7.5 percent of the medical records of the surgical, medical, and gynecological services at two general hospitals showed evidence of iatrogenic injury, nearly a third of which was due to physician negligence (U.S. DHEW 1973a: 63). For a variety of reasons the authors of the study believe that this figure significantly underestimates the true rate of negligence, but even if one assumes a rate of only 2 percent, it is clear that the number of malpractice suits is miniscule in proportion to the overall rate of harm.[13]

In addition to the relative paucity of suits, there is reason to believe that those suits that are initiated do not do a good job of discriminating between the competent and incompetent physician. Senator Ribicoff, chairperson of a congressional committee investigating medical malpractice, has cited evidence that some of the best physicians have more than their share of suits filed against them, while many of the worst doctors escape suit altogether. He concludes that "this would seem to indicate that there is no general statistical relationship between the number of malpractice suits and claims and the competence of physicians involved in malpractice actions (U.S. Congress, Committee on Government Operations, 1969: 6).

THE IMPACT OF MALPRACTICE SUITS IN THE FIELD OF PSYCHOTHERAPY

While a strong argument can be made that malpractice suits have had an overall negative effect on the quality of professional practice in the medical field, the evidence is even more persuasive in the field of psychotherapy. In addition to the many problems described above, which are equally applicable to the psychotherapeutic endeavor, the mental health field has special problems that make judicial regulation especially ineffective and perhaps harmful. There is, first of all, the very difficult task of establishing a case against a therapist. Second, the most frequently brought cases, such as commitment proceedings or complaints about inadequate supervision, are the least likely to have any substantive impact on the general quality of therapeutic practice. They will probably cause physicians to be more careful in committing patients to public mental hospitals, if they do not cause physicians to avoid such proceedings altogether. Hopefully, they will encourage greater safety on the part of mental hospitals. Unfortunately, they do not touch the heart of the therapeutic process, which consists of a therapist engaging in conversation with a patient. In fact, as long as therapists restrict their practice to talk, interpretations, and advice, they will remain relatively immune from suit, no matter how poor their advice, how damaging their comments, or how incorrect their interpretations. Even unsuccessful suits against psychotherapists are difficult to find. It is generally necessary either for some form of physical contact to be involved, as in those suits

alleging sexual (12 cases) or physical (5 cases) assault; failure to obtain informed consent (10 cases); or negligent administration of drugs or convulsive therapy (32 cases). Where these fact situations do not exist, the therapist is reasonably safe from suit. Even where sexual activity takes place, patients have extreme difficulty in proving their case (Stone 1976: 1139).

On the positive side of the ledger the recent rash of malpractice suits will probably have some beneficial results. As previously mentioned, confinement procedures will become more rigorous and the quality of custodial care should improve.[14] Legislatures have enacted a substantial amount of laws controlling informed consent proceedings regarding electro-convulsive therapy (see recent issues of the *State Health Legislation Report* published by the American Medical Association). The exclusion of sexual activity and physical assaults from coverage in professional liability programs is also attributable to the rise in number of suits in these areas. Since therapists are unlikely to risk their personal assets in a suit, such activities should decrease as a result.

On the other hand, the many suits involving a patient's constitutional right to treatment may be having some unexpectedly deleterious consequences. Stone (1977, 1975, 1975a, 1974), in a series of carefully reasoned articles and monographs, suggests that implementation of the right-to-treatment decisions may be driving psychiatrists out of the public sector because of their fear of suit. This may leave the patient with no alternative but nursing homes and other ill-equipped facilities, since society has not taken responsibility for providing adequate halfway homes for released patients. Stone also points out that recent decisions such as *Tarasoff*, which impose a duty on therapists to warn third parties endangered by their patients, will result in a tendency for therapists to overidentify dangerousness and will decrease the degree of trust and rapport between therapist and patient. This will ultimately increase the risk to public safety, since therapists will simply avoid treatment of potentially dangerous patients, leaving them to act out their problems without outside intervention (Stone 1976a).

Worse, those therapists who are most irresponsible and dangerous, and who are the ones that should be brought to court, will rarely, if ever, see an action brought against them. This is so because the large, responsible, and prestigious organizations and the highly educated and credentialed therapists carry professional liability insurance. These institutions and people are worth suing, since a large judgment is more likely. On the other hand, those who are completely unqualified, who advertise in underground papers, and who are considered the most dangerous of all, will not be affected. They are simply not worth suing.

There is perhaps an even larger problem, however. Psychotherapy is a young profession with ill-defined methods, unproved techniques, and a wide variety of schools. The ability of a therapist to diagnose dangerousness, sanity, or type of mental illness is open to serious question (see Chapter 4). Encounter groups and many of the newer humanistic therapies offer strong challenges to the traditional therapist's methods of practice. Little evidence exists that one method is superior to another, and even less of a consensus exists concerning what standards ought to be used to judge therapeutic competence. In such a situation the courts must tread carefully in attempting to establish standards of practice. Arbitrary efforts to do so may result in the unnecessary, premature, and unhealthy rigidification of the profession at a time when the proper posture is one of careful and fully disclosed experimentation.[15]

NOTES

1. This standard of care has been concisely summarized by Chief Justice Tindal in *Lanphier v. Phipos*, 8 Car. & P. 475, at 479, 173 Eng. Rep. 581, at 583, as long ago as 1832:

> Every person who enters into a learned profession undertakes to bring to the exercise of it a reasonable degree of care and skill. He does not undertake, if he is an attorney, that at all events you shall gain your case, nor does a surgeon undertake that he will perform a cure nor does he undertake to use the highest possible degree of skill. There may be persons who have higher education and greater advantages than he has, but he undertakes to bring a fair, reasonable, and competent degree of skill, and you will say whether, in this case, the injury was occasioned by the want of such skill in the defendant. The question is, whether this injury must be referred to the want of a proper degree of skill and care in the defendant or not.

2. Dawidoff (1966: 711) supports this position:

> The question in each case should be whether the doctor has taken undue advantage of the relationship for the pursuit of personal gain; whether he has demonstrated a control of his own motives which falls below the standard of the relevant psychiatric community, not alone whether his treatment was an expression of his unconscious hostility toward the patient.

3. Where the courts have adopted the "locality rule," psychiatrists are afraid that such testimony will result in ostracism from the profession. William Bellamy (cited in Dawidoff, 1973: 62) has written:

> Too many physicians believe that it is unethical to testify against a colleague. If more physicians would only read the Code of Ethics of the American Medical Association—

as adopted, too, by the American Psychiatric Association—they would see that a professional man is expected to speak up in the face of wrong.

Dawidoff (1973: 62) has offered other reasons why expert testimony is difficult to find: "Time, financial deprivation, fear of reprisal and compromise of a reticence to come forth from a realm of privacy and confidence may loom among the motivations contributing to the 'conspiracy of silence.'"

4. William Curran (1959: 541) argues:

One might say that any practice starts out as experimental, then becomes a new procedure, and then becomes commonly accepted. At what stage in this development does its user cease to apply it at his own peril? I would think it is part of legally accepted practice while it is still a "new procedure," as long as a significant number of the profession is now using it in ordinary practice (not with experimental patients or clients). Otherwise, the law would be penalizing intelligent advances in the professions.

5. Although this represented the prevailing opinion as long ago as 1936, MaGruder (1936: 1067) wrote then that "the courts have already given extensive protection to feelings and emotions. . . . No longer is it even approximately true that the law does not pretend to redress mental pain and anguish 'when the unlawful act complained of causes that alone.'"

6. Dawidoff (1973: 75) argues that the courts must be quite careful in allowing recovery:

This raises an important point about any injury dealt a psychiatric patient. In the myriad of psychiatric judgments, not every palpable decline in health is actionable. Perhaps only a congeries of setbacks or the kind of serious reaction which makes further improvement more difficult and costly is or should be the occasion for successful legal recompense. There are declines of even a psychotic nature which will not and should not be compensated for, since they may be unavoidable pitfalls in working through the tangled terrain of one's mental complexion. Research in the traditional therapies as in the encounter therapy may be sparse and the unavoidable concomitants of many treatments may be psychiatric ups and downs multiplied by intensity when compared to the usual struggles of living. Thus temporary psychosis should be separated from chronic schizophrenia in the phenomena being advanced as injury. Similarly, while some psychiatrists may interpret every act of living as being a result of the psychiatrist-patient interaction, car accidents, job or marital failures and even suicide may be difficult of causal link to acts in the therapy, or at least until more ample evidence makes the psychopathology of everyday life of more universal acceptance.

7. Cassidy (1974: 135) has concluded, "It is quite likely that a psychiatrist will be liable only where the injury is substantial and explainable by nothing other than the psychiatrist's negligence."

8. The average length of time from the occurrence of the negligent act to final verdict for the 300 cases reviewed in Volume III was nearly five years. For the winning plaintiff it was 5.4 years. This represents reported decisions involving malpractice in psychotherapy. According to Trent (undated: 4), there is a five-month lapse between the date when negligence occurs and when the claim is reported to the insurance company. He also points out that there is a delay of four to seven years until cases reach trial in large metropolitan areas such as New York and Los Angeles (Trent, undated: 10-11).

9. Aitken (1975: 35) notes that in a successful suit, the patient receives only 34 cents of the premium dollar, while 44 cents goes to the insurance company and 22 cents to the attorney. Cf. U.S. DHEW (1973a: 42) and McDonald (1971: 4).

10. Eli Bernzweig (1970: 15), Special Assistant for Malpractice Research and Prevention at HEW, has written: "At the moment, we are in the midst of an epidemic without statistics."

11. For a contrary opinion, see Marcus (1973) and Bernzweig (in U.S. DHEW 1973a: 168–73).

12. See the studies listed in footnote 19 of Chapter 7.

13. In fact, a malpractice suit is a relatively rare event. The report of the secretary of HEW on medical malpractice (U.S. DHEW 1973: 12) includes the following statistics:

- Despite the publicity resulting from a few large malpractice cases, a medical malpractice incident is a relatively rare event; claims are even rarer and jury trials are rarer still.
- In 1970, a malpractice incident was alleged or reported for one out of every 158,000 patient visits to doctors.
- In 1970 a claim was asserted for one out of every 226,000 patient visits to doctors.
- Fewer than one court trial was held for every 10 claims closed in 1970.
- Most doctors have never had a medical malpractice suit filed against them, and those who have, have rarely been sued more than once.
- In 1970, 6.5 medical malpractice claim files were opened for every 100 active practitioners.
- A 10-year survey, from 1960 to 1970, of the claims experience of 2,045 physicians in Maryland indicated that 84 percent had not been sued, 14 percent were sued once, and 2 percent were sued more than once.
- Most hospitals, no matter how large, go through an entire year without having a single claim filed against them.
- Sixty-nine percent of 4,113 hospitals surveyed from 1971 to June 1972 had not had a malpractice claim, 10 percent had one, and 21 percent had two or more.
- Most patients have never suffered a medical injury due to malpractice and fewer still have made a claim alleging malpractice.
- If the average person lives 70 years, he will have, based on 1970 data, approximately 400 contacts as a patient with doctors and dentists. The chances that he will assert a medical malpractice claim are 1 in 39,500.

Trent and Muhl (1975: 1312) estimate that a lawsuit occurs once every five to seven years against physicians, while the figure for psychiatrists is once every fifty to one hundred years. Aitken (1975: 31) cites data indicating that "30 percent of the patients represented in the claim files [of insurance companies] are potential victims of negligent health care who never become aware of it and never file a claim."

14. In any event, improved supervision and custodial care should occur as a result of the decrease in number of mental patients caused by the ability of many of the newer drugs to allow patients to function outside an institutional setting, and because of the effects of recent right-to-treatment decisions.

15. The problem of prematurely establishing strict standards of what constitutes a psychotherapeutic school has been outlined by Fink (1973: 708):

Psychiatry is not yet at the stage where it can provide the courts with such standards. Unless the psychiatrist's behavior is so exceptional that the court is willing to waive the requirement of expert testimony to establish negligence, a patient injured by psychiatric negligence in the execution of psychotherapy would most likely be without recourse. If courts were to relax the traditional standard of proof for malpractice cases when dealing with psychotherapy, they would, in effect, be shaping the future course of psychotherapy. Before courts will be able to deal effectively with psychiatric negligence, psychiatry will have to develop its theories and procedures so that courts will have some guidelines in setting standards of care. For a court to take a more active role at this point the court would have to be willing to pretend that there is more "order" in psychiatry than there actually exists, or the court would have to disregard psychiatric practice and treat the psychiatrist as it would treat any lay defendant in a negligence case.

REFERENCES

Books and Articles

Aitken, W.A. "Medical Malpractice: The Alleged 'Crisis' in Perspective." *Western State University Law Review*, 1975, v. 3, pp. 27–39.

Altman, L.K. "Malpractice Crisis Overshadows Agenda as A.M.A. Session Opens." *New York Times*, June 15, 1975.

Behavior Today. "Malpractice Insurance and the Psychotherapists." *Behavior Today*, January 17, 1977, pp. 2–4.

Behavior Today. "Malpractice-Insurance Problems for Psychologists." *Behavior Today*, March 8, 1976, pp. 4–5.

Bernzweig, E.P. "Lawsuits: A Symptom, Not a Cause." *Trial*, February-March 1970, pp. 14–15, 22.

Cassidy, P.S. "The Liability of Psychiatrists for Malpractice." *University of Pittsburgh Law Review*, 1974, v. 36, pp. 108–37.

Curran, W.J. "Professional Negligence—Some General Comments." *Vanderbilt Law Review*, 1959, v. 12, pp. 535–47.

Dawidoff, D.J. *The Malpractice of Psychiatrists: Malpractice in Psychoanalysis, Psychotherapy and Psychiatry.* Springfield, Ill.: Charles C. Thomas, 1973.

Dawidoff, D.J. "The Malpractice of Psychiatrists." *Duke Law Journal*, 1966, v. 1966, pp. 696–716.

Fink, V.M. "Medical Malpractice: The Liability of Psychiatrists." *Notre Dame Lawyer*, 1973, v. 48, pp. 693–708.

Forgotson, E.H., and Cook, J.L. "Innovations and Experiments in the Uses of Health Manpower—the Effect of Licensure Laws." *Law and Contemporary Problems*, 1967, v. 32, pp. 731–50.

Heller, M.S. "Some Comments to Lawyers on the Practice of Psychiatry." *Temple Law Quarterly*, 1957, v. 30, pp. 401–7.

Hogan, D.B. *The Regulation of Psychotherapists, Vol. III: A Review of Malpractice Suits in the U.S.* Cambridge, Mass.: Ballinger Publishing Co., 1978.

Holder, A.R. *Medical Malpractice Law.* New York: John Wiley, 1975.

Kett, J.F. *The Formation of the American Medical Profession, 1780-1860.* New Haven, Conn.: Yale University Press, 1968.

McDonald, D. (Ed.) *Medical Malpractice: A Discussion of Alternative Compensation and Quality Control Systems.* Santa Barbara Calif.: Center for the Study of Democratic Institutions, 1971.

MaGruder, C. "Mental and Emotional Disturbance in the Law of Torts." *Harvard Law Review*, 1936, v. 49, pp. 1033–67.

Marcus, H.B. "The Effect of Fear of Litigation on Utilization of Physicians' Assistants." In U.S. Department of Health, Education and Welfare, *Appendix: Report of the Secretary's Commission on Medical Malpractice.* Washington, D.C.: U.S. Government Printing Office, 1973, pp. 173–76.

Minnesota Law Review. "Overcoming the 'Conspiracy of Silence.'" *Minnesota Law Review*, 1961, v. 45, pp. 119–55.

Morris, R.C. "Lawsuits and Quality of Patient Care." *Journal of the American Medical Association*, 1971, v. 215, pp. 1211–12.

Pope, Alexander. "Who Shall Decide When Doctors Disagree?" *Moral Essays*. Glasgow: R. Urie, 1754.

Prosser, W.L. *Handbook of the Law of Torts*. (3rd ed.) St. Paul, Minn.: West Publishing Co., Hornbook Series, 1964.

Roemer, M.I. "Controlling and Promoting Quality in Medical Care." In C.C. Havighurst, "Health Care: Part I." (Special issue.) *Law and Contemporary Problems*, 1970, v. 35, pp. 284-304.

Rothblatt, H.B., and Leroy, D.H. "Avoiding Psychiatric Malpractice." *California Western Law Review*, 1973, v. 9, pp. 260-72.

Saxe, D.B. "Psychiatric Treatment and Malpractice." *Medico-Legal Journal*, 1969, v. 37, pp. 187-96.

Stone, A.A. "Recent Mental Health Litigation: A Critical Perspective." *American Journal of Psychiatry*, 1977, v. 134, pp. 273-79.

Stone, A.A. "The Legal Implications of Sexual Activity Between Psychiatrist and Patient." *American Journal of Psychiatry*, 1976, v. 133, pp. 1138-41.

Stone, A.A. "The *Tarasoff* Decisions: Suing Psychotherapists to Safeguard Society." *Harvard Law Review*, 1976, v. 90, pp. 358-78.

Stone, A.A. *Mental Health and Law: A System in Transition*. Washington, D.C.: National Institute of Mental Health, Center for Studies of Crime and Delinquency, 1975.

Stone, A.A. "Overview: The Right to Treatment—Comments on the Law and Its Impact." *American Journal of Psychiatry*, 1975, v. 132, pp. 1125-34.

Stone, A.A. "The Right to Treatment and the Medical Establishment." *Bulletin of the American Academy of Psychiatry and the Law*, 1974, v. 2, pp. 159-67.

Stone, A.A. "The Quest of the Counterculture." *International Journal of Psychiatry*, 1970, v. 9, pp. 219-26.

Trent, C.L. "Early Claims Experience with the A.P.A. Professional Liability Program." Unpublished manuscript, Ocean, N.J., undated.

Trent, C.L., and Muhl, W.P. "Professional Liability Insurance and the American Psychiatrist." *American Journal of Psychiatry*, 1975, v. 132, pp. 1312-14.

U.S. Congress, Senate Committee on Government Operations. *Medical Malpractice: The Patient versus the Physician*. Washington, D.C.: U.S. Government Printing Office, 1969.

U.S. Department of Health, Education, and Welfare. *Medical Malpractice: Report of the Secretary's Commission on Medical Malpractice*. (DHEW Publication No. OS 73-88.) Washington, D.C.: U.S. Government Printing Office, 1973.

U.S. Department of Health, Education, and Welfare. *Medical Malpractice: Report of the Secretary's Commission on Medical Malpractice: Appendix*. (DHEW Publication No. OS 73-89.) Washington, D.C.: U.S. Government Printing Office, 1973a.

Wigmore, J.H. *Evidence in Trials at Common Law*. (Rev. ed.) Boston: Little, Brown, 1961.

Legal Cases

Abraham v. Zaslow, No. 245862 (Cal. Super. Ct., June 30, 1972).

Barber v. Reinking, 68 Wash. 2d 139, 411 P.2d 861 (1966).

Bogust v. Iverson, 10 Wis. 2d 129, 102 N.W.2d 228 (1960).

Brune v. Belinkoff, 354 Mass. 102, 235 N.E.2d 793 (1968).

Force v. Gregory, 63 Conn. 167, 27 A. 1116 (1893).

Hammer v. Polsky, 36 Misc. 2d 482, 233 N.Y.S.2d 110 (Sup. Ct. 1962).

Hammer v. Rosen, 7 App. Div. 2d 216, 181 N.Y.S.2d 805 (1959), modified, 7 N.Y.2d 376, 198 N.Y.S.2d 65 (1960).

Lanphier v. Phipos, 8 Carrington and Payne's 475, 173 Eng. Rep. 581 (1832).

Nelson v. Dahl, 174 Minn. 574, 219 N.W. 941 (1928).

People v. Whittaker, No. 35307 (Cal. Just. Ct., Redding Jud. Dist., Shasta Cty. Dec. 1966). *Cited in* E.H. Forgotson and J.L. Cook, "Innovations and Experiments in the Uses of Health Manpower—The Effect of Licensure Laws." *Law and Contemporary Problems*, 1967, v. 32, pp. 731-50.

Scott v. London & St. Katherine Docks Co., 3 Hurlestone and Gordon's 596, 159 Eng. Rep. 665 (Exch. Ch. 1865).

Taig v. State, 19 App. Div. 2d 183, 241 N.Y.S.2d 495 (1963).

Chapter 9

Regulation through Nongovernment Professional Associations

Throughout history the professions have consistently insisted on the control of their own affairs, including the establishment and enforcement of standards of practice. Justification for self-regulation has been based on the special expertise and knowledge required. It is argued that only practitioners from the same profession are capable of evaluating each other. Control also reinforces the authority and mystique of the professional, which is said to be critical, if not essential, in establishing optimal working relations with clients.

To date the professions have been notably successful in their efforts to have such control. Even where the state apparently regulates, as with licensing laws, these laws have been largely formulated and are usually administered or indirectly controlled by the professions. Even in the judicial arena, it is "acceptable professional practice in the community" that defines misconduct, not public or government definitions of proper practice.

The potential of professions to adequately regulate their members is considerable. It is obvious that the professions of today are exceedingly powerful, but whether that power will be used for the benefit of the public and consumer is another matter. In addition, whether that power requires control of government

processes, such as licensing, and whether the ability to regulate standards is significantly affected by the professions' control of legal processes, is open to question. The solution to these problems depends in part on an evaluation of the current effectiveness of professional associations. Even if their past record has not been good, it still may be that a restructuring of the professions and a redistribution of professional power might provide an avenue to effective regulation.

THE POWER, IMPORTANCE, AND HISTORICAL TENDENCIES OF PROFESSIONAL ASSOCIATIONS

Alexis de Tocqueville (1966: 177) said in 1835 that "no countries need associations more—to prevent either despotism of parties or the arbitrary rule of a prince—than those with a democratic social state." Arthur Schlesinger (1944: 24) has declared: "Considering the central importance of the voluntary organization in American history there is no doubt it has provided the people with their greatest school of self-government." And Alfred North Whitehead (1943: 56–62) expressed a strong belief that the professions represent one of the bulwarks of society in the support and maintenance of freedom and liberty.

It was not accidental that the Axis dictators insured their rise to power by repressing or abolishing voluntary associations (Schlesinger 1944: 25). They understood only too well that these associations, including professional organizations, were the cornerstone of a democratic government and a threat to totalitarianism. This structural importance of the professions to society perhaps best explains the willingness to cede substantial and relatively unchecked powers to them in the United States. In addition, the professions have followed a course of action designed to ensure that this power remains in their hands.

National associations arose in this country during the mid-nineteenth century (Gilb 1966: 17), and their numbers have increased ever since. Their rise to power was greatly enhanced by the rapid expansion of the railroads and the improved communication brought about by the telephone and telegraph. Early associations were usually structured along federalist lines, with state branches maintaining considerable autonomy. Within state associations there were frequently a number of local societies. In this way they achieved unity of purpose but maintained decentralization of method.

The driving force behind the formation of professional associations has been the desire to protect the public by establishing control of specific areas of practice and by increasing professional prestige and economic security. National associations were quick to realize the potential value of licensing in accomplishing these ends. Because of the danger of fragmentation, however, and to ensure that most practitioners in a given professional field were enlisted, initial licensing efforts involved advocacy of fairly low standards of admission and often restricted only the use of certain titles, not practice. With licensing laws in place and after the professions had become well established, professional associations rapidly began to raise standards and limit practice to the licensed few. Perhaps the most powerful continuing tool of professional associations has been control of the accreditation process, which allows direct or indirect determination of what programs and schools are able to have their graduates licensed by the state.

Professional control of the standard-setting process and general ability to influence a wide range of policy might not be a matter of importance if professional associations did, in fact, serve the public. Growing public resentment toward the professions and the opinions of many political scientists and sociologists suggest that this is not the case, however.[1] In particular, the various negative side effects of licensure laws discussed in the previous chapter may be viewed as an outcome, whether intentional or not, of the policies promoted by professional organizations. Rayack (1967: 287), for instance, writes of the American Medical Association:

Our analysis of the policies and practices of the American Medical Association since the turn of the century demonstrates beyond question that the critics of the A.M.A. are fundamentally correct. Organized medicine has used its power as a professional organization to restrict entrance into medical schools, to oppose the expansion of much-needed training facilities, to restrict the practices of health practitioners in competition with medical doctors, to control staff privileges in hospitals, and to oppose the development of voluntary health insurance. Society has delegated considerable power to organized medicine, and the A.M.A. and its constituent societies have all too frequently used that power in a socially undesirable manner. Furthermore, our brief look into prospective developments in the medical market indicates that organized medicine will often be in the position where it can continue to use its power to protect the economic interests of its members at a very real cost to society.

This viewpoint is not new (see, for example, Webb and Webb 1917: 47), and earlier in the century, Carr-Saunders and Wilson

(1933: 494) warned of the tendency of professions to raise entry requirements until "the ludicrous result [is reached] that teachers in universities, of intellectual eminence and proved teaching capacity, are ineligible to teach in, or at least to gain a high position on the staff of, an elementary school."

Although the professions' attempts to protect the public through the establishment and control of the licensing process has not apparently done so, membership criteria and the disciplinary processes within professional associations may help ensure competence and may, in fact, protect the public. Again, however, the evidence is not very salutary. Since membership criteria in professional associations generally parallel licensing requirements, especially with regard to educational prerequisites, they suffer the same defects previously pointed out, the most serious of which is a lack of demonstrable relationship with competent practice and lack of indication that membership requirements weed out dangerous practitioners.

As with licensing laws, the activities of national organizations probably engender serious negative side effects, with seriousness being directly related to the association's monopolistic position in the field. Evidence collected by Lyons (1971), indicates that associational activities in the health field are responsible for entry restrictions and the inflation of medical-service prices, even where licensing is not involved.[2]

Especially where an association dominates a specific area of professional practice and can successfully lobby government and industry to restrict their use of practitioners to the association's members, the need for licensing decreases. Accordingly, it is probable that the complete dismantling of the licensing system in the medical field, for instance, would not seriously affect the number or quality of practitioners available initially, since the American Medical Association would exert its influence through other means. Substantiating this hypothesis are data from the Federal Trade Commission (U.S. FTC 1975: 45–46) on the amount of advertising in the drug industry in those states where such advertising is a violation of state law versus those states in which no legal restrictions exist:

The more unusual fact, however, is that few instances of price disclosure have been reported . . . in those sixteen jurisdictions where no official restrictions exist. This apparent anomaly is explained by the existence of an intricate network of private restraints which appear to influence both the professional and economic behavior of pharmacists, as well as their employers, in every state in the nation. The facts . . . disclose a web of private restraints directed at preventing the disclosure of prescription drug price information to the general public and aimed specifically at those individuals and organizations which advocate or engage in such activity.

. . . [T]he moving force behind these private restraints appears to be conscious parallel behavior and concerted efforts by the major organizations purporting to represent pharmacists on the national level. The national groups work in cooperation with state and local pharmaceutical associations and state boards of pharmacy to prevent or restrict the disclosure of prescription drug prices to the general public. . . . [T]he motivation underlying such cooperative behavior is not rooted *primarily* in a concern for the public health and welfare, but . . . stems rather from a common interest in insulating the practice of pharmacy from the normal economic pressures and perils of the marketplace. [U.S. Federal Trade Commission, 1975: 45-46.]

Turning to the disciplinary process of national professional associations and their constituent state or local societies, it appears that the lack of action by ethical committees is even more appalling that the dearth of disciplinary activity of state licensing boards. Local medical societies, for instance, have a long history of nonenforcement.

The well-known Truman Report (AMA Committee on Medical Practices, 1955) provided some of the first documentation in this regard. Thorough in-depth interviews with both doctors and patients in a wide range of states, as well as a detailed mail survey of all disciplinary actions over a two-year period by county medical societies, the Committee found that only 21 doctors were expelled: 10 for unspecified reasons, 6 for illegal acts, 4 for offenses against patients, and 1 for an offense against a colleague. Only 100 other doctors were suspended or even censored. The report concluded that the supervision of organized medicine over the technical standards of doctors was "not adequate to protect the public or the good name of the profession" (AMA Committee on Medical Practices, 1955: 859).

In the intervening years the extent of discipline has deteriorated even further. In 1967, when more than 250,000 physicians were in active practice, only four doctors were expelled from all medical societies in this country, while only twelve had their membership suspended (AMA Department of Medical Ethics, 1969: 1093). The average number of expulsions per year from 1963 to 1968 was only seven, while suspensions averaged seventeen. In two of the states with the largest concentrations of physicians in the country—California and New York—the state medical societies did not institute any proceedings against physicians in either 1968 or 1969 (AMA Department of Medical Ethics, 1970, 1969).[3] For unexplained reasons the AMA stopped publishing data on disciplinary enforcement in 1969.

Lieberman (1978, 1970) believes that most professional ethical codes are actually designed to protect the profession more than the public. He suggests that restrictions on such activities as advertising and prepaid group practice serve to protect the financial interests of professionals, who might otherwise be forced by the laws of the marketplace to charge a lower fee. This view is finding increased support, and the

Federal Trade Commission and other federal agencies have taken action against some of the more blatantly restrictive practices and ethical code provisions.

PROFESSIONAL ASSOCIATIONS IN TRADITIONAL PSYCHOTHERAPY

Until 1950 the field of psychotherapy was dominated by two professional organizations: the American Psychiatric Association (APA) and the American Psychoanalytic Association. The American Psychiatric Association is composed of physicians specializing in psychiatry, who may or may not have undergone psychoanalytic training. Most of its members practice psychotherapy, but some do not. It is one of the oldest professional associations in America, dating back to 1844. The objectives of the association are to advance the standards of treatment and care for the mentally ill, to make psychiatric services available to all who need them, to further psychiatric education and research, and to extend psychiatric knowledge to other professions and the public generally (Blanck 1963: 188). The association has and continues to have a great deal of power in the field, where it influences the accreditation of mental hospitals, residency training programs, and internships.

Rivalling the APA in power has been the American Psychoanalytic Association, which has local branches in different areas of the country. Founded in 1911, it became a federation of constituent bodies in 1932. Although having a small membership, psychoanalysts enjoy considerable power and respect, stemming largely from medical acceptance of psychoanalysis as the highest mode of intervention in curing mental illness by psychotherapeutic methods. Many members of the American Psychoanalytic Association are also members of the APA, which provides analysts with considerable political power. The

American Psychoanalytic Association has been opposed to the training of nonmedical analysts, in opposition to the International Psychoanalytic Association, which has caused considerable friction between them. The American Psychoanalytic Association is composed almost exclusively of physicians, although it does have a number of lay members.

In the last twenty-five years the power of the American Psychiatric Association and the American Psychoanalytic Association has been reduced as other professional associations have vied for their place in the mental health arena. Foremost among these organizations has been the American Psychological Association. Founded in 1892 and incorporated in 1925, its purpose has been to advance psychology as a science, as a profession, and as a means of promoting human welfare. It has been active in promoting the rights of psychologists to perform psychotherapy and to be regarded as primary health care providers, to which it has devoted considerable time and money (see Dörken and Associates, 1976). Because of highly effective politicking, its efforts have achieved considerable success, as evidenced by the existence of the psychology licensing laws in every state, the increasing acceptance by insurance companies of psychologists as primary health care providers, and the changes in regulations within hospitals, mental institutions, and other organizations allowing psychologists to hold positions formerly restricted to medically trained psychiatrists.

Even more recently the National Association of Social Workers has become an influential political force in the mental health field. Psychiatric social workers have been attempting to gain parity with psychologists and psychiatrists as deliverers of health services, and in the last decade have launched a highly organized campaign for licensing and for reimbursement by insurance companies for services delivered to clients.

These four organizations dominate the field of psychotherapy. Other associations exist, however, and although their political power is small, they are capable of having a significant impact on the field. In particular, the American Association of Marriage and Family Counselors has been highly active in seeking state licensure. To date it has been successful in six states. The rising divorce rate and easing of divorce laws indicates that interest in such counseling will continue, and the profession will almost certainly have an impact on regulatory issues for some years to come.

Other significant organizations include the American Orthopsychiatric Association (an interdisciplinary group composed of nonprofessionals and a variety of professionals, including psychiatrists, psychologists, and social workers), the American Group Psychotherapy Association, the American Association of Sex Educators and Counselors, the American Association of Pastoral Counselors, the American Association of Psychotherapists, the National Psychological Association for Psychoanalysis, and the American Academy of Psychotherapists. Most of these organizations are cross-disciplinary, but require at least a doctorate or master's degree for membership.

The organizational pattern in the field of psychotherapy, thus, is characterized by multiple associations. There is no particular unity to the field, and over the years the diversity of organizations has been increasing as the power of the stronger associations has decreased. Given the nature of the discipline, this situation is not surprising and will probably continue, unless one of the major associations is able to pass restrictive legislation that gives it a monopoly position. In many respects this state of affairs is similar to somatic medicine in the early to middle 1800s, when any number of schools of medicine claimed that their theories and methods of healing, their methods of training, and their standards of judging physician competence were correct and indisputable.

As with other professional groups, organizations within the mental health field have not done an adequate job of ensuring competent practice, either through admission standards or disciplinary enforcement. Standards for admission have not been shown to relate to professional competence, and the policies and position statements adopted by the major associations on issues related to competence do not appear to promote such standards. In a scathing article entitled "The Pseudo-Regulation of American Psychiatry," Taylor and Torrey (1972) argue that certification of individual psychiatrists by the American Board of Psychiatry and Neurology and accreditation of psychiatric training programs does not ensure competence. This board, which was established under the sponsorship of the American Medical Association, has close ties with both the AMA and the American Psychiatric Association. They point out that no policy exists for recertification and that proficiency standards are ignored in favor of inordinately rigid requirements; furthermore, they point out that training programs are approved without examination of whether the training produces competent practitioners. Taylor and Torrey (1972: 658) conclude:

American psychiatry vividly illustrates the inadequacies of the self-regulation of professionals. Whereas effective regulation should ensure competent service providers, self-regulation tends to evolve into protectionism that focuses on guaranteeing professional advantage and freedom from outside encroachment.

The self-regulation of American psychiatry occurs through a complex organizational arrangement involving the American Medical Association and the American Psychiatric Association. The resulting regulatory structures have a built-in tendency to advance professional interest over public interest when the two come into conflict. We are not implying that there is an active psychiatric conspiracy at work to take advantage of the public. Rather we are suggesting that the process of self-regulation operates with a structural bias that has a way of changing regulation into protectionism.

Discipline is woefully inadequate. The American Psychiatric Association considers disciplinary enforcement a matter for its district branches. Only recently has it instituted a policy, which is not uniformly followed, requiring all complaints to be reported to the central office. A recent study by Zitrin and Klein (1976) provides some of the available data on the problems that the APA faces with regard to discipline. They found that some district branches had no ethics committees whatever, while others were only advisory to the local medical society. From May 1973 to May 1974 only sixty-one complaints of unethical conduct were received by the APA's central office, despite the fact that the APA's membership was more than 20,000.

At the district level, even where ethics committees are quite diligent, it is difficut to take action. Zitrin and Klein (1976) reported on the experience of one branch with a total membership of 1,535 members. From 1970 to 1974 only forty-four complaints were lodged against members, which was four times the number for the previous four years. In only two instances did the ethics committee of the branch take action: once for excessive fees, and once for exerting undue influence on a patient.

The situation is not much different in the field of psychology. The American Psychological Association (AP1A) has a highly developed Code of Ethics (see AP1A 1967) based on the day-to-day decisions made by psychologists (Golann 1969: 454). Action by the disciplinary body of the American Psychological Association, the Committee on Scientific and Professional Ethics and Conduct (CSPEC), can seriously affect a psychologist, since expulsion may lead to loss of license, professional regard, referrals, and professional liability insurance.

Although the disciplinary machinery of the American Psychological Association is viable in theory, the available evidence suggests that enforcement is infrequent. At the national level the American Psychological Association handled 113 cases involving unethical practice in their 1971 reporting year (AP1A, CSPEC 1971). Twenty-eight of these were cases from the prior year that had not yet been closed. Sixty-one were referred to different state psychological associations for action (in accordance with the association's policy of decentralization). Three others were referred to other agencies for adjudicative or other appropriate action. Of the forty-nine remaining cases, no members were suspended and none had membership terminated—except for several cases where membership was based upon forged transcripts and degrees.

Data for state psychological associations is scant, but it also indicates lack of enforcement. A questionnaire distributed to all state associations asked for details on complaints filed against psychologists and what action was taken (see Hogan, 1972: Appendix 0). Fifteen of fifty associations responded, or 30 percent of all associations. A total of only sixty complaints were filed against the approximately 3,700 members of these associations, and in only two cases were psychologists' memberships terminated.

PROFESSIONAL ASSOCIATIONS IN ENCOUNTER GROUPS

The newer humanistic therapies and encounter groups have given birth to a multiplicity of professional organizations that have so far remained unintegrated with the more established professions connected with traditional psychotherapy. Unlike the latter, few of these organizations have been able to exert significant impact on the field as a whole, although any number have attempted to regulate standards and enforce discipline within a narrowly prescribed area.

According to Lippitt, Benne, Bradford, and Gibb (1975), associations in this area have organized themselves on four different bases. First, several are organized geographically, including laboratory trainers in the Canadian Province of Manitoba, the Australian Institute of Human Relations, and the European Institute for Trans-national Studies in Group and Organization Development. Within larger organizations, smaller regional bodies often exist, such as the New England Training Institute (NETI), which is associated with the Association for Creative Change.

A second basis for the setting of professional standards is institutional. The Association for Creative Change (ACC), which focuses on practitioners whose principal place of work is within churches and church-affiliated programs, illustrates this approach. The rationale for this manner of organization is that special skills are often required when working within specific institutions.

A third method of organization is based on the particular methology, technique, or theory employed in the therapeutic process. In the encounter field such associations are quite common. One of the more powerful is the International Transactional Analysis Association (ITAA), which is based on the theories of Eric Berne. ITAA has established a lengthy, complex, and arduous process for an individual to achieve full certification as a T–A practitioner. Other groups, such as the Gestalt therapists, while not having an official certification program, have developed sophisticated training programs designed to give one the required skills in using particular techniques.

A fourth basis for organization discussed by Lippitt and his associates is through the older disciplines, such as the two APAs, who have made efforts to define what constitutes competence as a group leader and to adapt their ethical codes to the particular exigencies of encounter group practice.

A further basis for organization is by type of client system served and the manner in which one works with that system. The International Association of Applied Social Scientists (IAASS), incorporated in 1971, illustrates this approach. It certifies social scientists in several areas, depending upon whether the practitioner works with organizations, communities, or small groups, and depending upon whether the practitioner works as an external consultant or internally within an organization.

Although (perhaps because) these associations have had only limited impact, they have managed to avoid many of the pitfalls connected with traditional professionalism. Unlike many established associations, they tend to emphasize competency-based testing instead of academic credentials and traditional written examinations. Also evident is a willingness to explore a variety of standards and criteria, as well as alternative methods of measuring those criteria. IAASS, for instance, gives applicants the opportunity to develop their own procedures for certification, while reserving the right to disapprove the process. Instead of traditional procedures, IAASS suggests submission of a record of experiences, a statement of philosophy and theory, and an ethical statement, and then requires peer and client evaluations of performance.

The International Transactional Analysis Association, on the other hand, has an extremely rigorous process of certification. Clinical members must successfully complete a number of courses and exams, a written contract, a lengthy period of supervised practice, and an appearance before and approval by an examining board. The examination is heavily weighted toward intellectual knowledge, and personal qualities account for only a sixth of the final score. The Association for Creative Change is much less rigorous than either IAASS or ITAA, and at one point allowed the decision for or against certification to rest with the applicant.

While all these associations have been quite innovative in establishing standards for practice, there is no evidence that they have been any more successful than the major professions in disciplining their membership.

CONCLUSION

Professional associations, as currently constituted and regulated, are unlikely to achieve positive self-regulation to protect the public. The historical trend has been for associations to attempt to establish monopolistic positions in their respective field. This has most effectively been accomplished through control of the licensure process, although control is not absolutely necessary. Where associations achieve power, little evidence exists that they will promote standards of practice that have demonstrable relationship with the skills required for effective performance. Even less evidence exists that discipline will be enforced. At the same time, associational policies tend to promote precisely the same harmful effects of licensure, although their effects are probably not as pervasive.

Certainly in the psychotherapeutic field, regulation as traditionally carried out by professional associations is unlikely to provide adequate public protection. In the first place, little guarantee exists that the professions have a serious commitment to such protection, except to the extent it coincides with their own self-interest. In the second place, even if commitment existed, the lack of consensus about appropriate standards and the lack of valid and reliable methods of measuring those standards make it almost impossible to distinguish the competent from the incompetent. Finally, given budgetary problems, lack of time, and the problem of disciplining one's fellow professionals, who are often personal friends or at least known acquaintances, only a remote possibility exists that the ethical committees of professional associations will do an adequate job of preventing errant or unethical practice.

Professional associations have recently instituted peer review mechanisms as the answer to the public outcry against rising costs and poor service. It is unfortunate, but probably true, that such efforts will fail, especially if they do not involve substantial public and consumer control. The conclusion of Ralph Nader's study group report on the medical profession's performance in self-regulation (McCleery et al., 1971: 93) is probably not only true but applicable to other professions, as well:

It seems clear that AMA interest in peer review is due primarily to a recognition that the American public demands it, and that if they don't express an interest in quality control mechanisms, the Federal government will take the lead to institute such controls. It is questionable that, with motivations such as these, the AMA could initiate and carry out a vital and adequate system of quality control.

Even with the best of motivations, it would still be imprudent for a regulatory mechanism to be completely controlled by the persons being regulated.

This pessimistic view does not imply despair at the possibility of professional associations regulating themselves. It does suggest that adequate safeguards, consumer participation, and government *regulations are needed* to establish the conditions that will allow the professions to achieve positive self-regulation.

NOTES

1. Studies of the sociology of the professions, most of which are highly critical of the restrictivist tendency of professional associations, include Ben-David (1963-64); Bergstrom and Olson (1975); Friedson (1973, 1970); Gilb (1966); Lees (1966); Lieberman (1970); Moore (1970); Parsons (1939); Vollmer and Mills (1966); and Webb and Webb (1917). Specific sociological studies and critiques of the profession of medicine may be found in Berlant (1975); Carlson (1975); Ehrenreich and Ehrenreich (1970); Freeman et al. (1972); Freidson (1970); Garceau (1941); Gross (1966); Howard and Strauss (1975); Hyde and Wolff (1954); Illich (1976); Jaco (1958); Klass (1975); Knowles (1965); Mechanic (1974, 1968); Rayack (1967); and Sigerist (1960).

2. To test this hypothesis, Lyons (1971) examined the rehabilitation industry, which manufactures orthotic (body-brace) and prosthetic (artificial-limb) devices. The industry is two-tiered, with manufacturer-suppliers constituting one group and fitters and fabricators the other, who are responsible for distribution. The American Orthotic and Prosthetic Association (AOPA) and its affiliates, such as the American Board for Certification (ABC), dominate the field. This latter group is responsible for certifying distributors, and attempts to suppress such unethical activities as "unprofessional" pricing, advertising for or soliciting patients, and other competitive activities. It attempts to persuade—and apparently is successful—major buyers to use only certified distributors. Various state agencies and other organizations have made it a policy to buy only from ABC-certified distributors. Lyons found that the cost of orthotic devices had risen 41 percent and prosthetic devices 48 percent from 1957-1969, although the Consumer Price Index had risen only 21 percent and the Wholesale Price Index only 9 percent. He also found that the income level of distributors was $2,500 to $5,000 more per year than for other skilled workers of comparable education and training. Thus, even where licensing is not involved, associations are often able to achieve the same results through a powerful certification or accreditation process.

3. Data on the disciplinary activities of other professional organizations is difficult to gather, but evidence from the architectural profession is similar to the findings in the

medical field. In architecture, ethical and professional practice is mainly enforced through the Standards of Professional Practice of the American Institute of Architects (AIA). Violation of the ethical code can lead to censure, suspension, or termination of membership in the institute. The latter two can lead to revocation of license in those states that have parallel provisions in their statutory regulations.

The disciplinary record of the AIA has not, however, been good. J.W. Rankin (1972), administrator of the Department of Institute Services of the AIA, stated that in the nine-year period from 1963 through 1971, only eighty-nine charges of unprofessional conduct were brought. Of these, 32 percent were withdrawn by the complaining party; 18 percent were dismissed either after a formal hearing or on the basis of lack of evidence; 31 percent resulted in censure; 14 percent were suspended for varying periods of time; and 5 percent ended in expulsion. In any particular charge there may be more than one defendant. If one assumes an average of five members charged per case, and if the cases were evenly distributed over the nine-year period, and based on a total membership in the AIA of 23,000 at the time, then approximately 0.1 percent of all AIA members were disciplined in some way during the year, and 0.01 percent were expelled.

REFERENCES

American Medical Association, Committee on Medical Practices. "Report to the Board of Trustees of the American Medical Association of the Committee on Medical Practices, November 1954." *Northwest Medicine*, 1955, v. 54, pp. 844–59.

American Medical Association, Department of Medical Ethics. "1969 Medical Disciplinary Report." *Journal of the American Medical Association*, 1970, v. 213, pp. 588–90.

American Medical Association, Department of Medical Ethics. "1968 Medical Disciplinary Report." *Journal of the American Medical Association*, 1969, v. 210, pp. 1092–93.

American Psychological Association. *Casebook on Ethical Standards of Psychologists.* Washington, D.C.: American Psychological Association, 1967.

American Psychological Association, Committee on Scientific and Professional Ethics and Conduct. "General Report, 1971." Mimeographed. Washington, D.C., 1971.

Ben-David, J. "Professions in the Class System of Present-day Societies: A Trend Report and Bibliography." *Current Sociology*, 1963-64, v. 12, pp. 247–330.

Bergstrom, R., and Olson, P.A. *A Time Half Dead at the Top: The Professional Societies and the Reform of Schooling in America—1955-75.* Lincoln, Nebr.: Study Commission on Undergraduate Education and the Education of Teachers, 1975.

Berlant, J.L. *Profession and Monopoly: A Study of Medicine in the United States and Great Britain.* Berkeley, Calif.: University of California Press, 1975.

Blanck, G.S. "The Development of Psychotherapy as a Profession: A Study of the Process of Professionalization." Ph.D. dissertation, New York University, 1963. Abstracted in *Dissertation Abstracts*, 1963, v. 24(07), p. 2974.

Carlson, R.J. *The End of Medicine.* New York: John Wiley, 1975.

Carr-Saunders, A.M., and Wilson, P.A. *The Professions.* 1933. Reprint. London: Cass, 1964.

Dörken, H. and Associates. *The Professional Psychologist Today: New Developments in Law, Health Insurance, and Health Practice.* San Francisco: Jossey-Bass, 1976.

Ehrenreich, B., and Ehrenreich, J. *The American Health Empire: Power, Profits and Politics.* New York: Random House, 1970.

Freeman, H.E.; Levine, S.; and Reeder, L.G. (Eds.) *Handbook of Medical Sociology.* (Rev. ed.) Englewood Cliffs, N.J.: Prentice-Hall, 1972.

Freidson, E. (Ed.) *The Professions and Their Prospects.* Beverly Hills, Calif.: Sage, 1973.

Freidson, E. *Professional Dominance: The Social Structure of Medical Care.* Chicago: Aldine Publishing Co., 1970.

Freidson, E. *Profession of Medicine: A Study of the Sociology of Applied Knowledge.* New York: Harper and Row, 1970.

Garceau, O. *The Political Life of the American Medical Association.* Cambridge, Mass.: Harvard University Press, 1941.

Gilb, C.L. *Hidden Hierarchies: The Professions and Government.* New York: Harper and Row, 1966.

Golann, S.E. "Emerging Areas of Ethical Concern." *American Psychologist,* 1969, v. 24, pp. 454-59.

Gross, M.L. *The Doctors.* New York: Random House, 1966.

Hogan, D.B. "The Regulation of Human Relations Training: An Examination of Some Assumptions and Some Recommendations." Unpublished third-year manuscript, Harvard Law School, Cambridge, Mass.: 1972.

Howard, J., and Strauss, A. (Eds.) *Humanizing Health Care.* New York: John Wiley, 1975.

Hyde, D.R., and Wolff, P. "The American Medical Association: Power, Purpose, and Politics in Organized Medicine." *Yale Law Journal,* 1954, v. 63, pp. 938-1022.

Illich, I. *Medical Nemesis.* London: Calder and Boyars, 1976.

Jaco, E.G. (Ed.) *Patients, Physicians, and Illness.* New York: Free Press, 1958.

Klass, A.A. *There's Gold in Them Thar Pills: An Inquiry into the Medical-Industrial Complex.* New York: Penquin Books, 1975.

Knowles, J.H. (Ed.) *Hospitals, Doctors, and the Public Interest.* Cambridge, Mass.: Harvard University Press, 1965.

Lees, D.S. *Economic Consequences of the Professions.* London: Institute of Economic Affairs, 1966.

Lieberman, J.K. *Crisis at the Bar: Lawyers' Unethical Ethics and What to Do About It.* New York: W.W. Norton, 1978.

Lieberman, J.K. *The Tyranny of the Experts: How Professionals Are Closing the Open Society.* New York: Walker, 1970.

Lippitt, R.L.; Benne, K.D.; Bradford, L.; and Gibb, J. "The Professionalization of Laboratory Practice." In K.D. Benne, L.P. Bradford, J.R. Gibb, and R.L. Lippitt (Eds.), *The Laboratory Method of Changing and Learning: Theory and Applications.* Palo Alto, Calif.: Science and Behavior Books, 1975, pp. 471-90.

Lyons, T.L. "Monopoly in the Health Industries: The Role of 'Professional' Associations in the Inflation of Medical-Service Prices." *Antitrust Law and Economics Review,* 1971, v. 5, pp. 95-102.

McCleery, R.S.; Keelty, L.T; Lam, M.: Phillips, R.E.; and Quirin, T.M. *One Life—One Physician: An Inquiry into the Medical Profession's Performance in Self-regulation.* (A Report to the Center for Study of Responsive Law.) Washington, D.C.: Public Affairs Press, 1971.

Mechanic, D. *Politics, Medicine and Social Science.* New York: John Wiley, 1974.

Mechanic, D. *Medical Sociology: A Selective View.* New York: Free Press, 1968.

Moore, W.E. *The Professions: Roles and Rules.* New York: Russell Sage, 1970.

Parsons, T. "The Professions and Social Structure." *Social Forces,* 1939, v. 17, pp. 457-67.

Rankin, J.W. Administrative Officer, Department of Institute Services, American Institute of Architects. Personal Communication, February 14, 1972.

Rayack, E. *Professional Power and American Medicine: The Economics of the American Medical Association.* Cleveland, Ohio: World Publishing Co., 1967.

Schlesinger, A.M. "Biography of a Nation of Joiners." *American Historical Review,* 1944, v. 50, pp. 1-25.

Sigerist, H.E. "Medical Societies Past and Present." *Yale Journal of Biology and Medicine,* 1934, v. 6, p. 358. Reprinted in H.E. Sigerist, *Henry E. Sigerist on the Sociol-*

ogy of Medicine. (Edited by M.I. Roemer.) New York: MD Publications, 1960, pp. 157–68.

Taylor, R.L., and Torrey, E.F. "The Pseudo-Regulation of American Psychiatry." *American Journal of Psychiatry*, 1972, v. 129, pp. 658-63.

Tocqueville, A. de *Democracy in America.* (2 vols.) 1836. Reprint (2 vols. in 1). (Translated by G. Lawrence. Edited by J.P. Mayer and M. Lerner.) New York: Harper and Row, 1966.

U.S. Federal Trade Commission. *Prescription Drug Price Disclosures.* (Staff Report to the Federal Trade Commission.) Washington, D.C.: Federal Trade Commission, 1975.

Vollmer, H.M., and Mills, D.L. (Eds.) *Professionalization.* Englewood Cliffs, N.J.: Prentice-Hall, 1966.

Webb, B., and Webb, S. "Special Supplement on Professional Associations." *New Statesman*, April 21, 1917 (Supp.), pp. 1-48.

Whitehead, A.N. *Adventures of Ideas.* 1933. Reprint. New York: Macmillan Publishing Co., 1954.

Zitrin, A., and Klein, H. "Can Psychiatry Police Itself Effectively? The Experience of One District Branch." *American Journal of Psychiatry*, 1976, v. 133, pp. 653-56.

✳ *Part III*

A Proposal for the Regulation of Psychotherapists and the Professions

Chapter 10

Findings and Conclusions

For some Americans [the mental health services system] presents few problems. They are able to obtain the care they need.

For too many Americans this does not occur. Despite improvements in the system, there are millions who remain unserved, underserved, or inappropriately served.

—Because of where they live or because of financial barriers, far too many Americans have no access to mental health care.

—Because the services available to them are limited or not sufficiently responsive to their individual circumstances, far too many Americans do not receive the kind of care they need.

—Because of their age, sex, race, cultural background, or the nature of their disability, far too many Americans do not have access to personnel trained to respond to their special needs.—President's Commission on Mental Health (1978, vol. 1: 2)

PSYCHOTHERAPY

Efforts so far to regulate psychotherapy, especially through licensure, have encountered significant problems. One of the fundamental explanations for this is the consistent failure of regulators to take into account the difficulties involved in defining and assessing the nature of the therapeutic process. Psychotherapy is a complex, highly amorphous, somewhat artistic, and not well-understood activity. It has roots common to the religious and magical traditions of the shaman and witch doctor and the medical tradition of the physician. Although its history is long, no such thing yet exists as "current psychotherapeutic theory." Rather, a wide variety of theories vie for acceptance, and a seemingly endless succession of techniques and methodologies comes and goes.

Where therapy was once defined as a healing and restorative process entered into by a sick patient to resolve underlying conflicts, today therapy often focuses on self-actualization and growth through an examination of overt behavior, typified by the encounter approach. Where the therapist was once neutral and detached, today the therapist is often highly involved, especially in the newer humanistic therapies. Where psychoanalytic theory once predominated, today therapists employ a panoply of techniques and argue the merits of any number of methods of providing therapeutic care.

Empirical evidence indicates that those

in the helping professions bring about similar results no matter what techniques are used, no matter what the purpose of their methods is, and irrespective of type of academic training. These facts suggest that past distinctions between therapy and other practices, such as encounter groups, may not have heuristic value. They also suggest that psychotherapy does not yet lend itself to easy or precise definition. Unfortunately, difficulties in operationalizing a definition of therapy have not kept proponents of rigid regulations from enacting licensing laws with broad definitions of practice encompassing activities never previously thought of as being therapeutic.

Whether and how one chooses to regulate a profession depends in great part on the potential value of the services offered, as well as the risk of harm entailed. Over the past thirty years psychotherapy research on these questions has progressed considerably. In the 1950s the lack of outcome studies prevented definitive conclusions, although researchers such as Eysenck (1952) maintained that psychotherapy was not effective. By the mid-sixties this situation was changing. Today the consensus of reviewers is that psychotherapy, whether as traditionally defined or including encounter groups, does have positive value and can bring about significant change. Psychotherapy seems to be of help in improving self-concept, ability to function effectively, emotional well-being, and other important areas of mental health.

At the same time it is also true that certain risks are involved. Although the research on dangers is scanty and less comprehensive than on effectiveness, psychotherapy appears to have the potential for serious harm. While there is some disagreement, Bergin's (1971: 248) finding that a very high proportion of therapy samples studied revealed that harm had occurred and his conclusion that the mean rate of deterioration for therapy

cases was approximately 10 percent, versus 5 percent for control, appears reasonable (see also Lambert et al., 1978).

At the encounter end of the therapy spectrum, criticisms have been raised about the values espoused in such groups, sexual abuses, and psychological damage. An examination of anecdotal reports, survey data, and social science research indicates that most of the reported dangers of encounter groups are exaggerated, especially as to their pervasiveness. Most reviewers conclude that the casualty rate is less than 1 percent, although the research relied upon tends to be on those groups least likely to be dangerous. Taken together, these findings indicate the potential need for regulation in the therapy arena, but do little to establish the types of control that might be effective.

The determination of standards and criteria for positive regulation depends upon the causative factors at work in the therapeutic process. Unfortunately, little effort has been put into articulating what professional competence really means. Only rarely is competence defined in relation to specifiable results—such as a patient's increased self-confidence or ability to function in the world. Only rarely is the level of achievement specified that a patient will reach after therapy. And those involved in the determination of competence seldom specify the percentage of people who will be helped by a therapist or whether competence is based on a mean-change score, in which either more people are helped than hurt, or no persons are hurt, or all must achieve some minimal level of growth. Because this clarity makes meaningful measurement difficult, a question remains as to the effectiveness of current modes of regulation.

A careful examination of empirical research on the roles and functions of psychotherapists reveals that traditional assumptions about standards and criteria for practice are seriously open to question. Documentation of the placebo effect and faith healing indicates that therapeutic results may rest in large part on the fact that patients simply believe their therapists are going to help them. The ability of the therapist to create the impression of expertise and to instill confidence, rather than actual possession of particular technical skills, may be the causative factor. The evidence that participant and patient outcomes are strongly affected by variables external to the therapist (such as initial level of patient mental health or composition of an encounter group) argues for regulations that focus less on control of the professional than other elements in the therapeutic process (such as who qualifies for therapy or how encounter groups are composed).

Still, little doubt exists that the therapist does play some role in bringing about change. Contrary to much professional opinion, however, the effectiveness of therapists is more determined by the presence of certain personality characteristics and interpersonal skills than technical abilities, diagnostic skills, and theoretical knowledge. Specifically, a therapist's ability to empathize, to be warm and caring, and to be genuine appear necessary for successful work. While diagnostic ability (as traditionally defined), technical skills, ability to use various methods of treatment, and theoretical knowledge are undoubtedly relevant to the highest levels of competence, little evidence exists that they are essential for minimal competence, or that their absence will lead to significant harm. Highly charismatic, intrusive, and hostile therapists appear to be the most likely to precipitate harm. Interestingly, the empirical data on what constitutes competent practice and what prevents harm converge: The same skills and qualifications are necessary.

If it is true that the personal qualities and interpersonal skills of the therapist constitute the core on which minimal competence and protection of the public are based, this has wide ramifications for attempts at regulation. It means that

traditional criteria in the form of academic credentials are highly suspect, and it means that many people might function as effective therapists with minimum training and experience. At the very least, it necessitates rethinking what it means to be competent as a psychotherapist. Perhaps the fairest conclusion that can be drawn from the data is that legitimate grounds for disagreement still exist as to the particular ingredients that go into successful psychotherapy.

As with standards and criteria of competence, little is really known about what training processes make good therapists. Traditional programs have been the subject of increasing criticism. Psychiatrists and psychologists by and large do not believe that their formal academic training is relevant, and a surprising percentage state categorically that most of their training was worthless. The research on the effectiveness of training has yielded largely negative results, despite the fact that academic training provides students with excellent knowledge of psychotherapeutic theory and technique.

Paraprofessional programs appear to be more effective, largely because selection is more often based on relevant personal qualities and because training programs emphasize the value of supervised experience and are more experientially based. Research indicates that the best training programs combine several important factors. An apparently essential aspect of training is the degree to which supervisors and teachers are highly empathic, understanding, warm, and genuine. Programs that offer opportunities for feedback and criticism of actual functioning are more effective than those that do not. An integrated approach, combining lectures and theory with supervised experiential training, appears to be most effective.

These findings provide substantial support for the proposition that academic training is not particularly helpful in preparing competent practitioners. They also indicate that significant changes must be made before academic training becomes effective in this regard. There are also implications for other areas of regulation. For instance, these findings suggest that traditional criteria for accrediting training programs may be less than helpful. In addition, it does not appear that long years of experience are necessary to become minimally competent.

Even if one knew what standards, criteria, and training programs were relevant to therapeutic competence, strict regulation would be difficult without valid and reliable selection methods. Unfortunately, no consensus exists as to which methods are best. Traditional reliance on academic grades, written and oral examinations, years of experience, and whether practitioners have undergone therapy have little empirical validation. Where an attempt has been made to measure actual skills, the method of measurement, such as supervisor reports, may not be valid. Empathy, which is generally recognized as important to the therapeutic process, is one of the most difficult variables to measure, and few of the measures that have been developed correlate with each other. Only recently has there been an effort to focus on performance-based criteria, and this has led to an exploration of problem-oriented records and other similar methods to determine therapeutic performance.

The disagreement among psychotherapists about basic outcome criteria, the difficulty of operationally defining these criteria, the problem of finding an adequate test methodology, and the difficulty of conducting research to adequately examine whatever methodology is chosen, ensure that no consensus is likely to develop in the near future. This fact has significant implications for all regulatory proposals. It means that attempts at licensing or other restrictive regulations, no matter what method of selection chosen, will be based on a process that has little reliability or validity and about which no consensus exists as to its value. It means that if traditional academic and experience requirements are relied upon, the public is likely to be receiving very little protection for its money.

The lack of clarity and consensus in each of these important domains of psychotherapy must be taken into account in framing regulatory proposals. Only rudimentary knowledge exists as to the causes of mental illness, how it is to be defined and identified, what treatment processes are most effective in curing it, what skills are necessary for effective treatment, and what selection processes are capable of identifying the competent therapist. What is needed is a regulatory framework that will allow these questions, issues, and problems to be explored and effectively resolved, while at the same time protecting the public from significant, demonstrable, and preventable dangers.

REGULATION

Psychotherapy is a relatively young profession that is developing rapidly, though its limits are hazy and its structure quite fragmented. How it is best regulated is problematical. It is a fundamental thesis of this book that traditional modes of professional regulation, typified by licensing laws that focus on control and that depend upon the unilateral exercise of power by an authoritative body, have not been effective and may be harmful.

One means to counter this tendency is to reconceptualize the regulatory process so that it is viewed as an interactive process between lawmaker and citizen, with a concomitant change in purpose from control to the facilitation of interaction (Fuller, 1969). Viewed in this fashion, the value of regulation depends not only on protecting the public, but meeting the needs of that public. More specifically, the choice of regulatory vehicle depends upon a balancing of its protective potential against the negative side effects that regulation generates. On this basis, it becomes important to explore regulatory mechanisms that accomplish the same purposes of more restrictive measures but with less negative impact. Conceptually such an approach suggests an emphasis on the regulation of output as more effective and efficient than the regulation of input.

The primary vehicle for professional regulation in the United States has been licensure, whose stated purpose has been to protect the public health, morals, safety, and general welfare. Licensure does this through the regulation of input by establishing entry requirements that must be met before a person enters the field, by disciplining unethical or incompetent licensed practitioners, and by empowering appropriate authorities to prevent unlicensed practice or title usage.

Licensing also serves several subsidiary purposes. It is well recognized that licensing promotes the economic well-being of the profession regulated, enhances the reputation of the profession, and helps to define more clearly the fields of professional practice. Although licensing is meant to accomplish its task through the enactment of minimum requirements for professional practice, most professions have successfully lobbied for relatively high standards of admission that go well beyond the essentials for minimally competent practice.

The use of licensing to regulate occupations and professions is extensive. Twenty-five percent of the employed labor force in some states is composed of licensed practitioners (*Business Week*, 1977: 127), and roughly 10 percent of the national income of the United States originates in occupationally licensed labor markets (Carroll and Gaston, 1977: 2). The number of licensed professions or occupations has now reached the 500 mark (see U.S. Department of Labor, 1969: Appendix C), up from the 73 occupations licensed in one or more states in 1950 (Council of State Governments, 1952: 7–8, 29). Once

a profession is licensed in several states, it is not long before most states also enact laws. With the passage of time these laws become stricter: title protection acts are amended to prohibit unlicensed practice; academic and experience requirements are raised; exemptions are dropped; and definitions of practice are broadened.

Although it is commonly believed that psychotherapy is unregulated through licensure, in fact more than 150 state licensing laws involving more than six professions expressly or implicitly define psychotherapeutic practice within their scope, including those regulating medicine, psychology, social work, and marriage and family counseling. Licensing laws have been interpreted quite broadly, and many boards are already beginning to construe their laws to include encounter group practices. Given past trends, more laws are to be expected.

As far as the content of existing laws goes, most have extremely rigid entrance requirements. Psychology and medicine both require a doctoral-level degree for independent practice, while social work and marriage and family counseling generally require a master's degree. Only rarely does a licensing law allow alternative routes to licensure, and the use of proficiency or educational equivalency examinations is rare. Few laws make relicensure dependent upon satisfaction of continuing education requirements, and even fewer base renewal on a competency-based examination. Exemptions to the laws often eviscerate the value of licensing by allowing numerous groups to practice without a license. At the same time, the lack of certain exemptions frequently makes it difficult for nontraditionally trained, but nonetheless quite competent, practitioners to work. The frequent absence of provisions allowing licensed practitioners to delegate functions to unlicensed assistants, even if carefully supervised and otherwise qualified, also significantly inhibits the effective utilization of paraprofessionals. As for the administration of the laws, licensing boards are composed almost exclusively of professionals, who must frequently be selected from lists submitted by state associations. Where public members are present, they are such a minority that their potential impact is seriously diminished.

While the professions argue that traditional licensing laws are an effective vehicle for protecting the public, evidence is mounting that this is not so. In the first place, the three primary functions of licensing are not carried out effectively. Where licensing is meant to ensure that only competent professionals are admitted to practice, little evidence exists that current entrance requirements have any bearing on the necessary skills or any relationship to performance. This appears to be true no matter what profession is examined. Furthermore, many requirements are obviously unrelated to competence. In the second place, data on the extent of disciplinary enforcement reveals a woefully inadequate system that rarely takes action against a licensed person. When action is taken, it is frequently to protect the good name of the profession, more than to protect the public. The fact that disciplinary boards lack adequate funds and technical skills, along with other problems, virtually ensures that this situation is unlikely to change. In the third place, even the prevention of unlicensed practice, which is in the economic interest of the professions, tends to be sporadic. When it does occur, it is frequently aimed at curbing economic competition, rather than preventing harmful practices, as when lawyers attempt to prevent real estate brokers from writing contracts for the sale of land.

In addition to not protecting the public, licensing tends to have negative side effects. First, higher than necessary and irrelevant entry requirements restrict the number of persons able to enter the professions, exacerbating shortages in the supply of personnel. Second, through making it unnecessarily difficult for pro-

fessionals licensed in one state to be licensed in another, licensing aggravates problems in the geographical distribution of practitioners. Third, broad definitions of practice, lack of provision for, or overly restrictive regulation of, paraprofessionals, and the absence of alternative routes to licensure, have seriously undermined the effective utilization of paraprofessionals. Each of these three helps produce a fourth problem, which is the significant increase in the cost of professional services resulting from rigid, unnecessarily high, and frequently irrelevant entrance requirements. The fifth problem that licensing creates is to inhibit important innovations in professional practice, training, education, and the organization of services. It does so through disciplinary provisions and ethical standards making it illegal to advertise services and restricting how services may be delivered, through reliance on accreditation agencies whose criteria are not based on whether schools or programs produce competent practitioners, and through defining quality professional practice in terms of what is currently acceptable by the majority, not empirical evidence of effectiveness. Finally, reliance on academic degrees and the imposition of other arbitrary requirements as a prerequisite for licensure results in serious discrimination against minorities, women, the aged, and the poor. This discrimination is two-edged. Licensing makes it more difficult for these groups to enter the profession, and because they are underrepresented, these same groups have difficulties in finding adequate professional services as clients.

According to some political scientists, the pervasiveness of licensing is an indication that the United States is returning to a guild form of society reminiscent of the Middle Ages. Like the guilds, licensed professions have established and enforced compulsory membership, creating a monopoly. Like the guilds, licensing standards have become higher and the cost of licensure has increased. And like the guilds, periods of apprenticeships have been lengthened, the number of apprentices has been restricted, and the possibility of licensure through apprenticeship or work experience has generally been eliminated.

Although legislative regulation of psychotherapy through licensure laws has not proved salutary, perhaps the impact of judicial regulation through professional liability suits has been more positive. Malpractice law is considered an important vehicle for ensuring that the public is protected from incompetent practice, as well as for redressing injuries and injustices. When the negative impact of judicial regulation is weighed against the few positive results, however, the potential value of malpractice suits seems minimal.

On the positive side of the ledger, professional liability suits in the medical field have probably improved hospital procedures and rules, led to better record-keeping, increased consultations and referrals in difficult cases, and provided incentives for caution. In the field of psychotherapy, malpractice suits may be useful in deterring some of the grosser abuses that occur, such as sexual or physical injury, negligent administration of electro-convulsive therapy, wrongful commitments, and inadequate supervision.

On the other hand, where malpractice suits occur with some frequency, as in the medical field, they have a tendency to inhibit the use of paraprofessionals, to undermine client trust, to lead to unnecessary diagnostic procedures and defensive medicine, and to increase the cost of services. At the same time, evidence exists that judicial regulation seldom recompenses those who have suffered as the result of professional negligence. Evidence also exists that malpractice suits are relatively ineffective in discriminating between the competent and incompetent professional.

In the field of psychotherapy the arguments against the value of professional liability suits are even more persuasive.

Unless the negligence of the therapist is extremely gross, it is difficult to prove that any wrong has occurred. There are problems in establishing what standard of care should be applied, that the practitioner was derelict, that the patient suffered harm, and that the harm was directly or proximately caused by the therapist's dereliction of duty. Especially if therapists confine themselves to talking, and if the injury sustained is emotional, cases of malpractice are almost impossible for the plaintiff to win. Stone (1977, 1975, 1975a) has suggested that judicial regulation through the right-to-treatment cases may be driving psychiatrists out of the public sector because of fear of suit, while judicial imposition of a duty to warn relevant parties endangered by a patient may result in therapists avoiding treatment of potentially dangerous patients.

There is perhaps an even larger problem, however. Psychotherapy is a young profession with ill-defined methods, unproved techniques, and a wide variety of schools. Little evidence exists that one method is superior to another, and even less of a consensus exists as to what standards ought to be used to adjudge therapeutic competence. Premature efforts to establish uniform standards may result in the unnecessary and unhealthy rigidification of the profession at a time when the proper posture is one of careful experimentation.

The final traditional mode of professional regulation is through nongovernmental associations. The professions have always maintained that self-regulation is the only viable means of effectively regulating their members. The primary vehicle for ensuring this has been the professional association. Apart from dictating the form of licensure laws and ensuring that licensing boards are controlled by professionals, professional associations also establish their own membership requirements and have their own disciplinary process.

It is clear that professional associations wield great power. This power stems from the prestige and the deference U.S. society has accorded the professions, the control of knowledge that professionals exercise, and their control of the process of evaluation and regulation. Whether this power has been used to protect the public is questionable, however. The activities of professional associations have induced the same problems that licensure laws engender. Standards for membership have not been shown to be related to competent practice in any profession, and the lack of disciplinary enforcement by professional societies is even more lax than for licensing boards.

Even where licensing has not been the tool to achieve monopoly, associations have been successful in achieving the same effect through lobbying government and nongovernment organizations to use their members exclusively. This tendency toward monopoly, in a field where little consensus exists about standards and criteria for competent practice, is likely to create more problems than it resolves. Given the fact that professional associations have not done much historically to protect the public, there is little reason to believe that this will change without adequate safeguards, consumer participation, and government regulation.

CONCLUSION

The fundamental conclusion suggested by the preceding findings is that traditional modes of professional regulation have not done a particularly good job of protecting the public. Licensing boards, the courts, and professional associations are not likely to provide the forum in which effective regulation will take place, at least as traditionally conceived. The difficulties in adequately defining the nature and limits of psychotherapy, the lack of standards and criteria for determining what practices are harmful, and the lack of valid and reliable methods of selection exacerbate all the problems associated with traditional forms of professional regulation. If the public is to be protected—and there is little doubt that it should be—and if regulation is not to have serious negative side effects, then the development of an alternative model and the improvement of existing methods are necessary.

REFERENCES

Bergin, A.E. "The Evaluation of Therapeutic Outcomes." In A.E. Bergin and S.L. Garfield (Eds.), *Handbook of Psychotherapy and Behavior Change: An Empirical Analysis.* New York: John Wiley, 1971, pp. 217-70.

Bergin, A.E. "The Deterioration Effect: A Reply to Braucht." *Journal of Abnormal Psychology*, 1970, v. 75, pp. 300-302.

Bergin, A.E. "The Effects of Psychotherapy: Negative Results Revisited." *Journal of Counseling Psychology*, 1963, v. 10, pp. 244-50.

Business Week. "How Licensing Hurts Consumers." *Business Week*, November 28, 1977, pp. 127-29.

Carroll, S.L., and Gaston, R. J. *Occupational Licensing.* (Final Report to the National Science Foundation.) Knoxville, Tenn.: Department of Economics, University of Tennessee, 1977.

Council of State Governments. *Occupational Licensing Legislation in the States: A Study of State Legislation Licensing the Practice of Professions and Other Occupations.* Chicago: Council of State Governments, 1952.

Eysenck, H.J. "The Effects of Psychotherapy: An Evaluation." *Journal of Consulting Psychology*, 1952, v. 16, pp. 319-24.

Fuller, L.L. *The Morality of Law.* (2nd ed., rev.) New Haven, Conn.: Yale University Press, 1969.

Lambert, M.J.; Bergin, A.E.; and Collins, J.L. "Therapist-Induced Deterioration in Psychotherapy." In A.S. Gurman and A.M. Razin (Eds.), *Effective Psychotherapy: A Handbook of Research.* New York: Pergamon Press, 1977, pp. 452–81.

President's Commission on Mental Health. *Report to the President.* Washington, D.C.: U.S. Government Printing Office, 1978. (4 vols.)

Stone, A.A. "Recent Mental Health Litigation: A Critical Perspective." *American Journal of Psychiatry*, 1977, v. 134, 273–79.

Stone, A.A. *Mental Health and Law: A System in Transition.* Washington, D.C.: National Institute of Mental Health, Center for Studies of Crime and Delinquency, 1975.

Stone, A.A. "Overview: The Right to Treatment—Comments on the Law and Its Impact." *American Journal of Psychiatry*, 1975, v. 132, pp. 1125–34.

U.S. Department of Labor. *Occupational Licensing and the Supply of Nonprofessional Manpower.* (Manpower Research Monograph No. 11.) Washington, D.C.: U.S. Government Printing Office, 1969.

Chapter 11

Toward Positive Regulation: General Principles, Basic Policies, and Goals

Sound regulation depends on a clear picture of what is ultimately to be achieved. The goal of providing high-quality mental health care to all U.S. citizens, no matter what the cost, for instance, has very different implications for regulatory policy than providing minimal care at a reasonable cost. Similarly, the type of relationship to be established between the mental health profession and general medicine has significant implications for regulations governing the relationship between the medical and nonmedical psychotherapist. In this chapter an attempt will be made to articulate the fundamental goals and principles that the final recommendations regarding regulation are meant to embrace.

AN INTEGRATED, INTERDEPENDENT MENTAL HEALTH PROFESSION

An integrated, interdependent mental health profession needs to be created. There is growing agreement that most psychotherapists do the same things and use similar techniques, whether they have been trained as psychologists, psychiatrists, psychiatric nurses, or psychiatric social workers.[1] The work of Holt (1971) and Henry, Sims, and Spray (1973, 1971)

documents the fact that therapists from each of these traditional training programs end up doing the same thing, have similar backgrounds, skills, and personalities, and value similar types of training experiences. Most important, little research indicates any differential effectiveness among these different groups.

Instead of these divergent training tracks, psychotherapists should be united into an integrated mental health profession. This recommendation is not particularly new (see, e.g., Abroms and Greenfield, 1973; Blanck, 1963; Guiora and Harrison, 1973; Henry, Sims, and Spray, 1973, 1971; Holt, 1971; Kubie, 1971, 1964, 1954; Mariner, 1967). This profession would include encounter group leaders and humanistic therapists. Training programs would be unified. Licensing laws, should they continue to exist, would be amended so that therapy was no longer divided among the various professions as it now is. Instead of the current hierarchical structure of the field, in which the medical practitioner has ultimate control and responsibility, responsibility would rest with those persons with the requisite skills and knowledge, regardless of academic training or professional title. This mental health profession would be made up of public mental health practitioners (including preventive medicine and health education), mental health researchers, and therapists.

AN INTEGRATED, INTERDEPENDENT HEALTH PROFESSION

The mental health profession should be integrated into the overall health care system on an equal basis with general medicine. Today only 12 percent of all health care expenditures are for mental health services (President's Commission on Mental Health, I, 1978: 9), despite the fact that more than half of all hospital beds in this country are occupied by mentally ill patients (Fein, 1967: 4), and despite the fact that mental illness is generally considered to be the major health problem that the United States faces (Fein, 1958: 4). This inequity needs to be eliminated.

In addition, although half or more of all patients who see a physician have complaints that are aggravated by emotional factors or are psychological in origin,[2] it is the physician who has been placed in charge of health care. Since even physical illness seems to have a large psychological component, it would make as good sense to have mental health practitioners in charge of medical practice, because a physician is more likely than a psychotherapist to mistake physical illness as physically caused instead of emotionally determined.

The solution is to establish a health care profession in which physical and mental health are integrated.

GOALS AND PRINCIPLES

The health care system of the United States should have the following goals and operate on the following principles:

1. The primary goal should be to improve the overall level of health without drawing critical resources away from other areas of the economy, such as education.

The important aspect of this recommendation is that improvements in health must be balanced against the cost to other segments of society. Also to be noted is the lack of emphasis on maximum health, since such an emphasis would place an undue strain on the economy.

2. The primary focus of the health care profession should be on prevention. In planning an intervention strategy, appropriate recognition should be given to the multiple causes of illness, including life style and environment.

The Canadian government (Canada, 1974: 13) has noted how major advances in health have generally been achieved through limitations of family size, increases in the food supply, and a healthy physical environment. Medical care has been a relatively minor factor. This means that the emphasis on delivery of professional therapeutic services in either the health or mental health field should be transformed into a focus on prevention through influencing the environment and lifestyle factors responsible for health care. It does not mean that no role exists for the professional therapist. It does mean that this role will decrease in importance.

3. The mental health care system should not have as its goal the delivery of the highest quality services to each individual. Instead, the goal should be an optimum health service designed to provide all individuals, regardless of age, sex, race, or wealth, with ready access to adequate and nondiscriminatory services at minimal cost.

The President's Commission on Mental Health (I, 1978: 2) believes that "mental health care of high quality and reasonable cost should be readily available to all who need it." As long as the emphasis is on high quality, it is only the well-to-do who will be well served. As long as the emphasis is on high quality care to each individual, a rationalization is provided for the use of academic credentials in the regulatory process, which serves to exclude minorities, the aged, the poor, and women as deliverers of mental health services. As long as the emphasis is on high quality, inadequate use will be made of the nonprofessional and paraprofessional resources in this country. The large percentage of the U.S. GNP that goes to the health care industry and the highly inflationary yearly increase in the cost of medical services should be sufficient warning that the goal of high quality services for all is unaffordable. Instead, the goal should be the provision of reasonable care of adequate quality within a system of health care that provided such services to all individuals.

This goal of providing reasonably satisfactory services for all, rather than high-level services for a few, has been echoed by a number of people (see, e.g., Cowen, 1967: 431; Hiatt, 1976), and is the policy of the health care systems of Russia (Roemer, 1962: 378) and China (Starfield and Holtzman, 1975: 12-19). Sigmond (in McKinlay, 1973: 125) summarizes this point of view well in arguing that the goal should not be "best patient care," but an "optimum health service."

4. Every effort must be made to demystify the professions and to encourage client independence, responsibility, and control.

The time has come when the patients and clients of professionals should no longer blindly accept what they are told. Especially in the field of psychotherapy, where so little is known, it is essential to have a public that is well informed on the limits of therapeutic theory, knowledge, and ability to heal. The professions should concentrate on making as much information available to the public as possible. Related to this, regulatory policies should encourage clients of professionals to take responsibility for their own health and well-being, and to

be appropriately involved in the development and implementation of regulatory policies governing the professions, including the evaluation of professional effectiveness.

THE PURPOSE OF REGULATION

Regulation must be viewed as an interactive process between lawmaker and citizen. Its purpose must not be merely to control behavior, but to order and facilitate the interactions of those involved.

The above principle is based upon Lon Fuller's (1971) conceptualization of the legal process. It makes apparent the necessity of considering the negative impact that laws have, and it switches the law's negative emphasis on control to a positive emphasis on the facilitation of interaction. In the field of professional regulation this translates itself into a policy of providing protection for the public, while minimizing the likelihood of a negative impact on the supply, distribution, and cost of professional services. It also suggests that regulations must take into account broader issues, such as the tendency of particular laws to foster or inhibit client independence and responsibility.

POLICIES

To achieve the goals of the mental health system, the following specific policies should be implemented:

Client Related

1. The public and consumer of professional services should be educated as to the potential value and dangers involved in the mental health field, the extent of knowledge about professional effectiveness, the points at which professionals are likely to act incompetently, unethically, or illegally, how to identify who is competent, and what to do if one encounters incompetence.

This policy is based upon the belief that clients are far more capable of making sound decisions in their choice of practitioner than is currently believed. To date, the problem has been one of providing adequate information and overcoming professional and public belief that only professionals are capable of evaluating professional services.

2. Regulatory policies should encourage client responsibility and independence.

An example of such a policy can be drawn from the medical profession and its rules surrounding a patient's right to access to or ownership of his or her medical records. To encourage client self-responsibility, all medical records should be owned by and remain in the possession of the patient. Until recently the medical profession has adopted the opposite policy, thereby encouraging client dependence. Over the long run, this creates a self-fulfilling prophecy in which clients become incapable of evaluating professional services and therefore need rigid regulations to protect them.

3. The development and implementation of regulatory proposals should involve a balanced representation of public, client, professional, government, and other relevant interest groups.

The contention of the professions that self-regulation is necessary and the only feasible method of sound regulation is anachronistic. It is clear that self-regulation has not worked, and the analysis presented in this book suggests that it will not work without appropriate involvement of other constituencies. Administrative boards should no longer be composed solely of professionals, but should include members of the public, government officials, and other groups, such as experts in testing and the enforcement of discipline. No one group should have a majority.

Organization Related

4. Because of the lack of consensus on important regulatory and professional

issues, a pluralistic system of mental health care should be developed.

Because psychotherapy is a relatively young profession, and because little is definitively known about standards of practice, methods of training, and methods of selection, regulations must protect innovativeness and encourage responsible experimentation. This recommendation applies not only for professional practice. It also means that diversity of methods should be encouraged in the training and selection of therapists and in the way in which professional services are organized. It means that a variety of methods of regulation should be tried to determine which one truly protects the public and which one does so at the least direct and indirect cost.

This has several important implications, one of which is a movement away from national tests and a policy of uniformity in licensing examination. Instead, the preferable policy is one of diversity, competition, and freedom to innovate in responsible fashion. Eventually, wisdom and social science research will determine whether a more homogeneous system is advisable.

Profession-Related

5. Definitions of what constitutes high-quality services should include such factors as patient satisfaction and the overall quality of the health care system.

In the past, measurement of the quality of health care has been based on the level of service provided by the individual practitioner. This narrowness of approach stems from the fact that professionals have established relevant standards without client input and without adequate concern for the health care system as a whole. Where clients and the public are included, and where the foucs is on the health care system as a whole, different criteria tend to be stressed. Mechanic (1970: 248) has suggested a few for evaluating the health care field as a whole:

Relative mortality and morbidity; patient satisfaction, professional satisfaction; cost;

stimulation of new investments; coordination and integration of elements of care; recruitment and retention of personnel; quality of special services (such as mental health services); capacity for innovation and adaptation; accessibility of services; effectiveness of manpower distribution; quality of controls over professional work; incentives for abuse of services; and continuity of care.

In evaluating the individual practitioner, not only is quality of work important, but so, too, is the speed with which it is done, the cost of performing the services, the usefulness of what was done, and its acceptability.[3]

6. The evaluation of whether a person is qualified to practice should be determined by competency-based or performance-based criteria, not academic credentials and other input measures.

The increasing evidence that academic credentials and other traditional measures of professional performance do not provide proof that somebody is qualified to practice means that other alternatives deserve exploration. The two most important approaches are the attempt to determine what skills, knowledge, and other qualities are important to practice and the attempt to measure whether somebody has actually performed a job well.

7. To the greatest extent possible, direct services to the public should be provided by paraprofessionals. These practitioners should be given responsibility and remuneration in direct proportion to their demonstrated competence. Such responsibility should include the right to make independent judgments regarding treatment and diagnosis.

In the mental health field, paraprofessionals should have the major responsibility for delivering psychotherapeutic services. To this end they should be given a large measure of responsibility and a heavy measure of independence. This increased use of paraprofessionals will be one of the most effective means of stabilizing the cost of professional services, ensuring that shortages of personnel do not arise, and in providing services to those who today are not able to obtain adequate help. The development of paraprofessionals will provide a natural pool from which more fully trained professionals can be developed. Horizontal and vertical career ladders should be constructed so that paraprofessionals have maximum flexibility and mobility in their career development.

Empirical research on the effectiveness of paraprofessionals as therapists provides convincing evidence that this policy will work. In those societies that have made a definite and strong commitment to paraprofessionals, the results have been salutary. For instance, it is generally agreed that the European tradition of using midwives to deliver babies is a major factor in the relatively lower rate of maternal and neonatal mortalities in Europe as compared with the United States.[4]

8. Highly trained professionals should concentrate on training paraprofessionals, providing consultation and supervisory services, conducting research, and performing certain specialized services that require high levels of skills.

This recommendation is a direct corollary of the previous one. From a cost-effectiveness standpoint it obviously represents a much sounder policy than what is currently in force, in which much of the work professionals perform requires little of the specialized background that they possess.

Research-Related

9. Further research on the therapeutic process and the impact of various regulatory policies is essential. Research on the therapeutic process is reasonably abundant, but should continue at an accelerated pace. Further study is necessary to determine the types of changes psychotherapy brings about, the impact of the therapist, the dangers involved, methods of training, and selection procedures. In particular, researchers should examine the

importance of conceptual knowledge, the impact of various techniques, and the value of diagnosis for professional effectiveness.

On the regulatory side of the equation, careful studies need to be conducted of the effectiveness of various regulatory schemes. The value of licensing, judicial regulation, and the impact of professional associations deserve extensive consideration.

Regulation-Related

10. Whenever any set of regulations is considered, it is essential to determine whether less-restrictive alternatives are available that would accomplish the same results, but with less negative consequences and at less cost.

This policy has specific implications for licensing laws, where it suggests exploring the value of registration as opposed to the more rigid regulatory processes of laws restricting the right to practice or use certain titles.

NOTES

1. This excepts the psychiatrist, who by law is the only therapist licensed to administer drugs or perform electroconvulsive therapy and lobotomies.

2. The Canadian government (Canada Health and Welfare Department, 1974: 61) estimates that mental disorders are a factor in 50 percent of the patients seen in general medical practice. Rashi Fein (1958: 4), the noted Harvard economist, has cited congressional testimony stating that "conservative estimates based on incidence studies have shown that approximately 50 percent of patients who are treated in general practice have psychiatric complications." Granatir (1974: 269), president of the Washington Psychoanalytic Society, estimates "that up to 75 percent of the people visiting physicians either have complaints of psychic origin or have difficulties that have been aggravated by emotional factors." Dörken and his associates (1976: 282) comment that "it is generally agreed that 50 to 60 percent of persons seeking health care do so because of emotional or mental disorder either as the primary or a concurrent problem."

Arthur Shapiro (1971), perhaps the leading expert in this country on the placebo effect in medicine, notes that psychological factors have always played a role in physical illness—a fact recognized as far back as the time of Hippocrates. According to Shapiro (1971: 441), Galen estimated that 60 percent of all patients have symptoms of emotional rather than physical origin. Shapiro (1971: 441) states that "this figure is close to the contemporary estimate of 50 to 80 percent."

3. HEW (U.S. DHEW, 1975: 142), in its *Forward Plan for Health*, posits effectiveness, safety, cost, and patient satisfaction as the four most important factors in determining the quality of a given episode of health. Thomas Scheff (1972: 59) has developed an even more elaborate set of criteria to measure the "ideal approach to 'mental health' problems," as follows:

(1) effectiveness; (2) cost; (3) speed; (4) freedom from harmful side effects; (5) applicability to a broad range of problems, and not limited to very specific problems; (6) applicability to a broad range of populations, in terms of social class, race and ethnicity, age, education, etc.; (7) whether the approach had preventive, as well as therapeutic, potential; and (8) whether the approach had implications for social, cultural, and political change, as well as for individual change, so that it did not merely help individuals adjust to the status quo.

4. Milton Roemer (1970: 302, footnotes omitted), a leading analyst of health care policy, comments: "So far as we can tell, the British National Health Service, with its

extensive use of midwives for most deliveries, has a better maternal and neonatal mortality record than the United States with its theoretical desideratum . . . of obstetrical specialists."

REFERENCES

Abroms, G.M., and Greenfield, N.S. "A New Mental Health Profession." *Psychiatry*, 1973, v. 36, pp. 10–22.

Blanck, G.S. "The Development of Psychotherapy as a Profession: A Study of the Process of Professionalization." Ph.D. dissertation, New York University, 1963. Abstracted in *Dissertation Abstracts*, 1963, v. 24(07), p. 2974.

Canada, Health and Welfare Department. *A New Perspective on the Health of Canadians.* Ottawa, Ontario: Government of Canada, 1974.

Cowen, E.L. "Emergent Approaches to Mental Health Problems: An Overview and Directions for Future Work." In E.L. Cowen, E.A. Gardner, and M.Zax (Eds.), *Emergent Approaches to Mental Health Problems.* New York: Appleton-Century-Crofts, 1967, pp. 389–455.

Dörken, H. and Associates. *The Professional Psychologist Today: New Developments in Law, Health Insurance, and Health Practice.* San Francisco: Jossey-Bass, 1976.

Fein, R. *The Doctor Shortage: An Economic Diagnosis.* Washington, D.C.: Brookings Institution, 1967.

Fein, R. *Economics of Mental Illness.* New York: Basic Books, 1958.

Fuller, L.L. "Human Interaction and the Law." In R.P. Wolff (Ed.), *The Rule of Law.* New York: Simon and Schuster, 1971, pp. 171–217.

Granatir, W.L. "Psychotherapy and National Health Insurance." *American Journal of Psychiatry*, 1974, v. 131, pp. 267–70.

Guiora, A.Z., and Harrison, S.I. "What is Psychiatry? A New Model of Service and Education." *American Journal of Psychiatry*, 1973, v. 130, pp. 1275–77.

Henry, W.E.; Sims, J.H.; and Spray, S.L. *Public and Private Lives of Psychotherapists.* San Francisco, Calif.: Jossey-Bass, 1973.

Henry, W.E.; Sims, J.H.; and Spray, S.L. *The Fifth Profession: Becoming a Psychotherapist.* San Francisco, Calif.: Jossey-Bass, 1971.

Hiatt, H.H. "Is Medical Technology Playing Too Big a Role in US Health Care?" *Boston Globe*, August 27, 1976.

Holt, R.R. (Ed.) *New Horizon for Psychotherapy: Autonomy as a Profession.* New York: International Universities Press, 1971.

Kubie, L.S. "A Doctorate in Psychotherapy: The Reasons for a New Profession." In R.R. Holt (Ed.), *New Horizon for Psychotherapy: Autonomy as a Profession.* New York: International Universities Press, 1971, pp. 11–36.

Kubie, L.S. "A School of Psychological Medicine Within the Framework of a Medical School and University." *Journal of Medical Education*, 1964, v. 39, pp. 476–80.

Kubie, L.S. "The Pros and Cons of a New Profession: A Doctorate in Medical Psychology." *Texas Report on Biology and Medicine*, 1954, v. 12, pp. 692–737. Reprinted in M. Harrower (Ed.), *Medical and Psychological Teamwork in the Care of the Chronically Ill.* Springfield, Ill.: Charles C. Thomas, 1955, pp. 125–70.

Mariner, A.S. "A Critical Look at Professional Education in the Mental Health Field." *American Psychologist*, 1967, v. 22, pp. 271–81.

Mechanic, D. "Problems in the Future Organization of Medical Practice." *Law and Contemporary Problems*, 1970, v. 35, pp. 233–51.

President's Commission on Mental Health. *Report to the President.* Washington, D.C.: U.S. Government Printing Office, 1978, (4 vols.)

Roemer, M.I. "Controlling and Promoting Quality in Medical Care." In C.C. Havighurst, "Health Care: Part I." (Special issue.) *Law and Contemporary Problems*, 1970, v. 35, pp. 284-304.

Roemer, M.I. "Highlights of Soviet Health Services." *Milbank Memorial Fund Quarterly*, 1962, v. 40, pp. 373-406.

Scheff, T.J. "Reevaluation Counseling: Social Implications." *Journal of Humanistic Psychology*, 1972, v. 12(1), pp. 58-71.

Shapiro, A.K. "Placebo Effects in Medicine, Psychotherapy, and Psychoanalysis." In A.E. Bergin and S.L. Garfield (Eds.), *Handbook of Psychotherapy and Behavior Change: An Empirical Analysis.* New York: John Wiley, 1971, pp. 439-73.

Starfield, B., and Holtzman, N. "Health Care in China: There's More to It than Acupuncture." *Johns Hopkins Magazine*, July 1975, pp. 12-19.

U.S. Department of Health, Education, and Welfare. *Forward Plan for Health: FY 1977-81.* Washington, D.C.: U.S. Government Printing Office, 1975.

Chapter 12

Recommendations

The regulation of professions in Western society is a matter of importance. It has been the basic contention of this book that traditional methods of regulation, especially licensure, have serious deficiencies. This chapter presents both an alternative model to current methods and a series of recommendations to improve existing laws.

The practical recommendations in this chapter are broken into five parts: (1) an outline of a proposed model of professional regulation; (2) general guidelines applicable for virtually any set of recommendations; (3) specific recommendations for licensure, judicial regulation, education of the public, and other forms of regulation; (4) the implications of these recommendations for other forms of regulation; and (5) possible strategies and tactics to implement these recommendations.

A PROPOSED MODEL FOR PROFESSIONAL REGULATION

The model that follows is meant for the field of psychotherapy, but may have applicability to other professions as well. It presents a brief summary of the more detailed recommendations that appear in subsequent sections,

beginning with methods of regulation that have direct impact on the quality of service rendered to the public and proceeding to methods that affect the quality of service indirectly.

Registration Laws

The most preferable method of regulation is licensing through registration. Any person desiring to practice as a psychotherapist should be required to register with the state. The registration fee should be nominal, and practitioners should not have to meet any educational, experiential, or other prerequisites before being granted the right to practice. They would, however, have to provide the state with their name, address, and other information related to their intended field of practice, such as relevant experience and academic training, the methods they intend to use, the goals of treatment, their fees, and a statement of ethical beliefs. The registration laws would be administered by a board of registration that would also be responsible for disciplinary enforcement (see below).

Laws Requiring Full Disclosure

Because a consensus does not exist on standards of professional practice, a critical method of protecting the public is to provide clients with sufficient information to decide for themselves what services they desire to purchase. To further this, state governments should enact laws requiring practitioners to disclose to any client as exact a description as possible of their practice and background. This would include the information provided to the state, as described above, and might also include other information such as proposed length of treatment and what results are to be expected. This should also include information as to how dissatisfied clients can file complaints with the state registration board.

Client Evaluations

Because at least some aspects of a professional's practice are subject to direct evaluation by a client, such as client satisfaction, laws should be enacted to require practitioners to distribute to clients evaluation forms regarding the services rendered by professionals. These evaluations would be voluntarily made at the termination of the professional-client relationship and would be submitted to the state disciplinary body. Room would be made on the evaluation form for specific criticisms, as well as positive comments. The evaluation form would be designed for computer usage to provide future clients with a concise summary of past client evaluations. A sufficient number of negative comments or ratings would bring about a disciplinary inquiry or hearing (see below). Client anonymity would need to be protected, although some clients might indicate a willingness to discuss their evaluations with either their therapist or potential clients of that therapist. Potential abuses of this system would have to be carefully monitored, expecially with regard to who had access to the data.

Laws Establishing Effective Disciplinary Agencies

To date, licensing boards responsible for administering professional discipline have been notoriously ineffective. A wide variety of factors accounts for this, including lack of funds and the assumption that licensure means that most practitioners will act ethically and competently because they are licensed. Under a system requiring registration with a state government, the role of disciplinary boards would be crucial. Such boards must take a proactive stance toward discipline. They should make use of the client evaluations discussed above. They should actively look for disciplinary violations, rather than waiting for complaints to come to them. This could be accomplished by such procedures as subscribing to newsclipping services and hiring investigators to look into suspect practices. Such disciplinary boards would have to be adequately funded and they should not depend on registration fees for their operation.

Boards should not be dominated by members of the profession, but should reflect a balanced representation of interests, including members of the public, clients, government officers, and practitioners. The administration of disciplinary board activity should be carried out by persons skilled in the tasks to be performed. Thus, board members themselves would not carry out investigative activities, but would rely on skilled personnel, perhaps from the attorney general's office, as in some states.

Enforcement of Existing Laws

Many of the dangers that occur in psychotherapy are capable of being dealt with through existing legal avenues. Fraud statutes and laws requiring truth-in-advertising, both at the state and federal level, could prevent many of the deceptive practices that now occur. Criminal sanctions are also possible for those instances in which physical or sexual abuse takes place. In some cases, laws may need to be amended to take into account the special exigencies of psychotherapeutic practice. In other cases it is simply a matter of more rigorous enforcement.

Judicial Regulation

It is unlikely that judicial regulation will provide a useful vehicle for many of the harmful practices that occur in psychotherapy. Professional liability suits are not well adapted to the psychotherapeutic field, in which most of what occurs is conversation between therapist and patient. On the other hand, such suits still have a place in dealing with the grosser abuses that occur, such as physical and sexual attacks and cases of blatant fraud.

Special Laws for Specific Problems

Where special dangers are identified in the psychotherapeutic process, and where traditional avenues of dealing with them are ineffective, special laws should be enacted. If the legislature, for instance, decides that therapists should not have sexual intercourse with their patients, then a law making such an act criminal should be enacted. In other situations, justification might exist for adopting licensing laws restricting the right to perform certain functions.

This would only occur when a specific practice was known to be dangerous without specialized skills, knowledge, or training; and it should be limited to the very specific practice involved. For instance, if it were demonstrated that the use of certain specialized techniques, such as primal therapy, resulted in significant harm unless practitioners had special training, then the right to use such techniques should be restricted to those with appropriate training.

Education of the Public

Although little used until now as a method of professional regulation, education of the public has the potential as a powerful tool in protecting the public from harm. To be effective, however, considerable effort, money, time, and commitment must be devoted to developing a sound program for public education and the dissemination of information.

Laws requiring full disclosure of relevant information and laws requiring therapists to distribute client evaluation forms provide two sources of significant information. State agencies should undertake programs to help educate potential clients of therapists as to what to look for in a therapist, what questions to ask, and what to do if dissatisfied with therapeutic services. A summary of the information gathered by client evaluations should be available to any person seeking therapeutic services.

State agencies should act as a conduit for information supplied by various professional groups to inform the public as to the state of the art in psychotherapy. This should include what social science research and professional opinion indicate about the effectiveness and dangers of therapy, the reasons for them, and other relevant information.

Professional Associations

Professional associations will continue to have a strong role to play in the regulation of psychotherapists. Because of the lack of consensus on standards of practice, methods of training, and methods of selection, however, it will be important to create a situation in which many professional associations coexist, each advocating different methods and theories for the training and certification of therapists. The goal should be a pluralistic system in which the public can choose any of a variety of therapists.

By carefully monitoring the effectiveness of therapists certified by different associations, long-term research might begin to establish which methods of training and selection produced the most competent or least dangerous therapists. On the other hand, such research might reveal that each method was effective in some situations, while not in others.

Government and Foundation Support

Since the goal of regulation is to produce a pluralistic system in which a variety of services are available, government and foundations should encourage the development of alternative methods of training, selection, and practice. For this reason the use of national tests should be avoided, since they are based on the false assumption that one method of selection is capable of identifying all who are competent to practice.

Research

The potential impact of research on the regulation of psychotherapy should not be ignored. The organized dissemination of the results of social science research is a potentially powerful vehicle for influencing standards of therapeutic practice and methods of regulation. Research on the nature of the therapeutic process, what makes a therapist effective, and what methods of regulation achieve positive results is essential. Dissemination of such information to the public would be useful in dispelling some of the myths perpetrated about the therapeutic process.

GENERAL GUIDELINES FOR REGULATORY PROPOSALS

It is impossible to frame all possible recommendations regarding the regulation of psychotherapists. The basic challenge for this chapter has been to set out what is essential. Apart from the basic policies discussed in the previous chapter, certain guidelines have been used in formulating these recommendations, and they would apply to other attempts at regulation as well.

Definitions of Practice

Definitions of what constitutes psychotherapeutic practice need to be carefully and precisely drawn. Most statutory definitions of practice fall seriously short in this regard. This is especially true of licensing laws. The more a regulation restricts practice to a limited few, the more rigidly this guideline needs to be applied. It suggests that any definition must specify what techniques and methods are considered psychotherapeutic, whether activities that aim to be educational are also to be considered therapeutic, and whether the practice involved must involve remuneration of some sort. All such definitions should be as narrow as possible.

Standards and Criteria

Standards and criteria used to determine whether therapists are competent to practice should be competency-based and related to actual performance. Academic credentials and other noncompetency-based measures should only be used if they have a demonstrable relationship to performance. This becomes increasingly important as regulations become more restrictive.

Definitions of Competence

The determination that a practitioner is worthy of certification or is qualified to practice should be based on a clear idea of what is meant thereby. This involves a determination of whether certification indicates a high level of competence, a minimum level, or that a practitioner will not precipitate significant harm. It also requires specification of what results are to be expected. Within any of these levels there must be a further specification of whether certification indicates that a practitioner will be able to help all clients or only a certain percentage, and whether it is possible that a certain small percentage of people might be harmed. All definitions should be clear about whether a therapist is good at changing behavior or attitudes, increasing sensitivity, changing self-concept, and the like.

Alternative Paths to Certification

The more restrictive a form of regulation is and the more it affects all practitioners, the more important it becomes to provide alternative paths to certification. This stems from the lack of consensus that exists as to what standards should be used to determine therapeutic competence and what methods best measure that competence. Thus, laws restricting practice and title usage should allow practitioners to be licensed through proficiency examinations, educational equivalency exams, apprenticeships, academic training, or certification by any of a number of organizations. Certification organizations should experiment with peer review, client review, written and oral examinations, on-the-job evaluations, and the plethora of other ways of establishing professional competence.

Emphasis on the Paraprofessional

Since it appears that relatively little academic training is necessary for a person to function effectively as a therapist, and since the current emphasis on highly trained professionals is uneconomic, it is essential to develop the potential of the paraprofessional to as great an extent as possible. The general rule should be that persons ought to perform a task with as little training as possible and they should be given as much responsibility as possible, based on their competence. This should include the right to make independent judgments. Regulations should be enacted in such a way that this guideline is not interfered with. Thus, if restrictive licensing laws are to be enacted, they should make adequate provision for licensed practitioners to delegate any and all functions to paraprofessionals, and they should not arbitrarily and unnecessarily restrict who is able to function as a paraprofessional.

Regulation of Output, Not Input and Process

Regulation through licensure constitutes control of input, since it establishes standards and criteria governing entrance into a profession. Because current requirements have not been shown to be related to effective performance, alternatives should be considered. Competency-based measures represent a sounder attempt at regulation, since they attempt to correlate particular skills with effective performance. Regulations that are based on output measures or correlated with them are strongly to be preferred.[1]

Balanced Representation of Interests, Not Professional Control

The design and administration of regulatory policies and programs should not be dominated by professionals, but should be controlled by a balanced representation of appropriate constituencies. These constituencies should normally include the public, professionals, government officials, clients, and other affected parties. No group should have the power to dominate, unless it is to be the members of the public. This is in recognition of the fact that regulation is primarily designed to protect the public. It also recognizes the historical fact that the professions may not act in the best interests of the public when their economic position is threatened.

SPECIFIC RECOMMENDATIONS

The specific recommendations follow the format for the preceding section, but with greater emphasis on the licensing process. An attempt is made not only to give ideal recommendations, but to provide alternatives when the ideal is clearly impossible, for political reasons or otherwise.

Licensing Laws

Whether and When to Use What Form of Licensure. Laws that restrict a person's right to practice a profession should not be enacted unless the following conditions are met.[2]

Profession as Mature and Well Established. The profession or occupation being regulated must be mature and well established. When a profession is young and developing, too early licensure may unduly hamper necessary changes in professional practice, training, and organization of services. Where a lack of consensus exists on important professional issues, licensure is often a divisive force in terms of unifying a profession.

Blanck (1963: 160–61) sees licensing as the final stage in the normal growth of a profession, which is ordinarily preceded by: (1) differentiation from other professions; (2) evolution of a system of education based on an intellectual factor and a body of knowledge; and (3) the development of national associations that represent most practitioners in the field. Curran (1970: 1086) argues that "in general, it is best in the evolution of professional groups to start with registration acts and to move to licensure only after the professional group is fully matured, clearly defined in its responsibilities and capable within its own educational and training programs of meeting the reasonable manpower needs in its field of practice." The fact that a profession is dominated by one professional association and has highly uniform standards of practice is not necessarily a sign that such a profession is mature. The critical factor is whether agreement on uniform standards of practice is warranted by the empirical research.

Clearly Defined Field of Practice. The profession being regulated must have a clearly defined field of practice that is adequately differentiated from other professions. Without clear differentiation, the negative effects caused by impinging upon other professions are not worth the benefits gained through licensure. Forgotson and Cook (1967:

741) summarize the problems involved succinctly:

The difficulty with the present statutory definitions is that they attempt to resolve difficult scope-of-practice issues through the use of vague and ambiguous classifications without establishing guidelines by which the public, the courts, administrative agencies, and the professions themselves can determine scope-of-practice issues not specifically resolved by statute. Without further statutory definitions and standards, such terminology is subject to a variety of inconsistent administrative and judicial interpretations. Even within individual states, considerable judicial and administrative interpretation will be necessary to establish with reasonable certainty the content of the criteria. On the other hand, of course, legislative semantic precision is not necessarily desirable because of the inflexibility it could produce.

Significant Public Impact. The profession must have a significant degree of public impact. This condition is designed to ensure that only important professions are regulated. This criterion suggests that the profession must have substantial dealings with the public. "Substantial" may take the form of size and numbers, as with the nursing profession, or may result from the degree of public impact, as with architects.

New Benefits Outweigh Negative Side Effects. The benefits of licensing must outweigh the negative impact in terms of increased cost of services, lack of availability of professional help, inhibitory effect on the organization of services, and discriminatory impact. This criterion forces lawmakers to consider the negative side effects that legislation produces, which have been discussed in Chapter 7.

Unavailability of Less Restrictive Alternatives. Simpler and less restrictive methods that would accomplish the same purposes must be unavailable. Where fraud and deceit are the inherent dangers, the enforcement of existing statutory law is probably a better course of action than licensing. Even when some form of licensing appears warranted, it may be that registration or restrictions against title usage will provide the requisite protection, without the necessity of also restricting practice. A number of others have suggested this as an alternative (see, e.g., Shimberg, Esser, and Kruger, 1972: 222; New Jersey Bateman Commission, 1971: 6; Council of State Governments, 1952: 47).

Significant and Documented Potential for Harm. The potential for significant harm from incompetent or unethical practitioners must exist and must be extremely well documented. Until recently, legislatures have been more than willing to pass licensing laws, as long as some possibility of harm could be demonstrated. Since virtually all occupations involve some danger, this does not provide a very good guideline.

Since it is generally the profession itself that is seeking licensure, and since there is good reason to believe that economic self-interest may be involved, it should be incumbent upon the profession to demonstrate that licensure is actually necessary. This means that the dangers involved without licensure should be easily recognizable and not based on tenuous or remote argument. It means that both the magnitude and the probability of harm should be reasonably large. Isolated instances of severe harm should not constitute sufficient grounds for licensure. A criterion similar to this has been advocated by the Council of State Governments (1952: 57); the New Jersey Bateman Commission (1971: 6); Shimberg, Esser, and Kruger (1972: 222); Gellhorn (1956: 146); and others.

Practitioner Incompetence as Source of Harm. A reasonable consensus must exist as to what causes harm, the causes of harm must be related to professional functioning, and adequate mechanisms

for identifying those who are causing harm must exist. If no consensus exists as to what causes harm, then it is unlikely that licensure laws will mitigate the dangers involved. If the causes of harm are related to environmental or client factors, then professional regulation will likewise have little impact. Even if the cause of harm is related to professional practice, a means of identifying those who are dangerous must exist if regulation is to accomplish its purpose.

Purpose as Prevention of Harm. Where licensing laws require certain standards to be met, these standards must be related to the prevention of harm, not the insurance of high-quality practice. The police power of the state is designed to protect the public from harm. It is not meant to ensure high-quality professional practice. The efforts by various professional associations to require high standards of practice should be restricted because of the negative side effects inevitably engendered.

Adequate Enforcement Mechanisms. Adequate mechanisms for disciplining those who violate the law must exist. Licensing laws must possess comprehensive grounds for discipline that include the right to revoke licenses for incompetent, unethical, or repeatedly negligent practice. Licensing boards should have the necessary powers to take action against practitioners who are practicing illegally. The current tendency, however, of licensing boards to take action to protect the economic interests of the profession, rather than to protect the public from dangerous practitioners (as when lawyers attack real estate brokers for practicing law), needs to be minimized.

Adequate Financial Resources. Adequate financial resources must be committed to ensure proper administration and enforcement of the licensing laws. In the past, licensing laws have often been pushed through legislatures simply because it was guaranteed that administration of the laws would not involve extra state funds. Thus, most licensing boards function almost solely on the basis of licensing fees. It is clear that this policy inevitably results in relative nonenforcement of the laws and places an unnecessary financial burden on those taking the licensing examination. If a legislature truly believes that licensing is necessary to protect the public, then it should budget an adequate amount of funds to do the job properly.

Psychotherapy and Laws Prohibiting Unlicensed Practice. Psychotherapy does not meet the criteria for licensing through laws that restrict a person's right to practice.

Psycho-analysis is something so new in the world, the mass of mankind is so little instructed about it, the attitude of official science to it is still so vacilating, that it seems to me over-hasty to intervene in its development with legislative regulations. Let us allow patients themselves to discover that it is damaging to them to look for mental assistance to people who have not learnt how to give it. If we explain this to them and warn them against it, we shall have spared ourselves the need to forbid it.—Sigmund Freud (1950: 80), in *The Question of Lay Analysis.*

Unlike medicine and the law, psychotherapy is clearly a young and developing profession for which licensing would be premature. Sound and integrated training programs have not yet been developed, an adequate supply of practitioners does not exist, and the profession is already fragmented by existing licensing laws that carve up the practice of psychotherapy among psychology, medicine, social work, and a variety of other professions. Commenting on the inadvisability of licensing legislation for psychologists, Rollo May (1954: 586) states that "in general, legislation is a by-product of the development of a profession rather than a 'cause.' The public is to be protected from quack-

ery, first by our training enough competent helpers with high standards, secondly by public education, and only thirdly by legislation" (see also Kubie, 1955: 160-61).

It is also evident that the profession of psychotherapy cannot yet be adequately defined and has not yet differentiated itself sufficiently from other professions. Whether defined by goals, methods, structure, or theoretical base, psychotherapy is impossible to clearly delimit, except through arbitrary determinations. A committee of the American Medical Association (Gerty, Holloway, and MacKay, 1952: 272), for instance, concluded that "after a great deal of discussion . . . psychotherapy could not be defined satisfactorily, at least for legal purposes, though persons and groups, both medical and nonmedical, often put forward definitions which suit their own purposes." And Arthur Combs (1953: 562), discussing the attempts to enact a psychology law in New York State, has declared:

No problem in licensing has proven to be a greater bone of contention than the matter of psychotherapy. Although everyone has his [or her] own private opinion of what psychotherapy is, no one has yet come forward with a definition of psychotherapy sufficiently precise to stand in a court of law.[3]

Chief Justice Burger, while a judge on the U.S. Court of Appeals for the District of Columbia, concluded that, given the state of psychiatric and psychological knowledge, even the most commonly used terms such as "mental illness" lacked adequate legal meaning:

No rule of law can possibly be sound or workable which is dependent upon the terms of another discipline whose members are in profound disagreement about what those terms mean. . . . This is not simply a matter of experts disagreeing on opinions or on diagnosis, which often occurs, but disagreement at the threshold on what their own critical terms mean. [*Blocker v. United States*, 288 F.2d 853 860 (1961).]

Other statements commenting on the impossibility of defining the term psychotherapy, especially for legal purposes, abound.[4]

The problems involved in defining psychotherapy and their implications for regulation were recognized by organizations such as the American Psychological Association[5] when it originally began to seek legislation. The passage of time, however, has seen the APA and others ignore these implications.[6] It has become apparent that political considerations of power and control have outstripped concerns about the value and quality of regulation. The result has been a thirty-year conflict between major professions over who has the right to practice psychotherapy.

In the fifties the battle was fought between the American Psychological Association and medicine. Eventually the APA and its component state associations were successful in their efforts at licensing, despite the resistance of the American Psychiatric Association and American Medical Association. In the sixties and seventies the battle has been fought among psychologists, social workers, and marriage and family counselors.[7]

Recently the medical profession and psychiatry have reentered the battle—this time in an attempt to prevent other professionals from being considered as independent health care providers under various programs of private and public health insurance. The net result has been a proliferation of licensing laws, as the many professional groups with even a tangential claim to psychotherapy race to protect their legal right to practice.

These events parallel the history of medical licensing. The American Medical Association's attempts to exclude other professional groups through strict licensing laws only led to further laws, as chiropractors, osteopaths, optometrists, and others battled for their existence through fighting for their own licensing laws.

On the other hand, attempts to write narrow and precise definitions of practice present equally serious problems. Shakow (1969: 191) points out that:

There is great danger . . . in an era of great expansion and growth such as the present, of defining a field too narrowly and too rigidly. It is difficult to predict just what clinical psychology will be like ten years from now, and it would be regrettable to let our present ignorance or prejudice or compulsive need burden the natural development of the field.

Despite the advances made in therapeutic practice since 1950, definitional problems have not been alleviated and are likely to persist.[8] The New Jersey Bateman Commission (N.J., 1971: 30), in fact, recommended the delicensing of marriage counselors precisely for this reason:[9]

A chief problem in this area is that so many people practice marriage counseling—friends, relatives, social workers, clergymen, bartenders, attorneys, health and medical care personnel. It is likely that far more marriage counseling is done by others than by marriage counselors. And to license everyone who practices marriage counseling would be patently unrealistic. An argument can be made that protecting the health and welfare of the public is an issue. By the same reasoning, however, it would then be necessary to regulate employment and career-guidance counselors, newspaper columnists who give family advice, case workers who advise welfare recipients, and police officers who deal with family quarrels. The Commission recommends that marriage counselors not be regulated. The many kinds of counseling in our society present too broad and ill-defined a field to be subject to state regulation.

Apart from the definitional quagmire, psychotherapy does not meet many of the other criteria to warrant restrictive licensing. Although the degree of public impact of psychotherapy is sufficient for licensure to be warranted, the evidence from Chapter 7 indicates that the negative impact of licensing is more likely to outweigh the positive benefits that are likely to flow therefrom. In addition, as will be suggested below, other methods of regulation are available that promise adequate protection, but with less adverse impact.

One of the basic reasons that licensing laws restricting practice to the credentialed few have little to recommend them is that sufficient information is not available about the extent and type of danger involved in the therapeutic process, whether the dangers are attributable to actions on the part of the therapist, and what specific activities lead to dangerous results.[10] Since so much disagreement exists on these fundamental issues, the value of licensing is seriously jeopardized. Until a consensus exists on how to identify those therapists who are not dangerous, licensing standards will continue to be arbitrary and capricious. Their actual effect will be to mislead the public into thinking it has protection from the incompetent practitioner.

If one looks at the available empirical evidence, current licensing laws, which rely on possession of academic credentials from accredited institutions, are difficult to defend. First of all, psychotherapy, whether traditionally defined or including the newer encounter groups and humanistic therapies, does not appear to be gravely dangerous. This is not to deny the existence of isolated instances of serious harm, but to suggest that overall the dangers may be overstated.

The percent of people who deteriorate as a result of psychotherapy is somewhere around 5 percent, while the research on encounter groups generally reports figures of 1 percent or less. These dangers are not of such epidemic proportions that the arm of the law should intervene to curb the problem. In agreement with this point of view is a committee of distinguished psychologists and physicians of the American Orthopsychiatric Association (Harrison et al., 1970: 558):

The extent to which the public is hurt by

quackery advertised under the rubric of psychotherapy appeared to be minimal. Although the shortage of data about who helps people and who hurts people presents difficulties, we nevertheless concluded that there was scant evidence of the title "Psychotherapist" being abused.

Assuming, however, that psychotherapy represents a significant public danger, the lack of consensus as to what causes danger and how to measure it should prevent the enactment of laws restricting a person's right to practice.[11] The existing empirical evidence suggests that licensing efforts to date have focused on the wrong variables. No evidence exists that possession of academic credentials protects the public. Surprisingly, little if any evidence exists that the particular school of the therapist, the techniques used, the amount of knowledge, diagnostic ability, or extent of training makes any difference in achieving minimal therapeutic results. Instead, the findings indicate that personality factors may be the most influential in determining whether a therapist is competent to practice.

Specifically, in the encounter group field, empirical research suggests that highly aggressive, intrusive, judgmental, and rejecting group leaders will often precipitate harm, while loving and accepting leaders do not. In more traditional individual therapy, lack of empathy appears to be a good sign that a therapist will bring about untoward results. Yet licensing laws do little to measure these qualities in license applicants. More damaging still is the evidence that factors quite apart from the practitioner, such as the initial level of a patient's mental health, may account for a large share of the harm that occurs in therapy.

Psychotherapy and Title-Protection Acts. Psychotherapy should not be regulated through licensing laws, even if it is only the use of certain titles and representations that is restricted. Even where licensing laws do not restrict a person's right to practice, requiring certain standards to be met before a person has the right to use specific titles is not advisable. Although title-protection acts have fewer disadvantages than laws restricting practice, their positive utility probably does not outweigh their negative potential.

It is true that title-protection acts do not present problems in defining what constitutes psychotherapy, since it is only the use of certain titles that is in question. It is also true that their impact in terms of raising the cost of services and restricting the supply of practitioners is less, since nonlicensed persons are not prohibited from practicing.[12] On the other hand, if no impact occurs, the value of the law disappears.

The critical question is whether states are performing a valuable service by identifying practitioners possessing certain credentials as being competent. The problem is that little consensus exists as to what credentials are a sound measure of therapeutic competence, and the skills that seem important, such as empathic ability, are difficult to operationalize. Thus, it is premature and misleading for the state to give approval to any one set of standards at this time. Instead, its policy should be to recognize this state of affairs and to teach the public that not enough is yet known about the ingredients of therapeutic success to warrant the use of restrictive licensing.

There is another political reason against title-protection laws. Professional associations are generally the sponsors of licensing. When initially seeking licensure it is common to recommend title-protection acts, since they generate less political opposition. Once these laws have been enacted, however, these same associations frequently seek amendments to transform the law into one that prohibits unlicensed practice as well. These amendments often only involve minor word changes, and it is difficult to organize opposition to such changes. If for no other reason, this danger warrants extreme circumspection in advocating the adoption of any title-protection acts.

Psychotherapy and Registration Laws. Registration is the third major alternative in the licensure field. Under a system of registration a person who desires to practice as a therapist must register with the state. Registration generally entails the payment of a small fee. However, it should also require practitioners to provide the state with information relevant to a therapist's competence to practice. This information should include a person's name, address, training, relevant experience, customary methods, and other pertinent data, such as membership in or certification by professional associations. Coupled with this should be a requirement to disclose specific information to all clients and in all advertising (see below). To be registered with the state one should not have to possess any academic credentials or experience, nor should one have to pass an examination. As part of the registration system, an active disciplinary board should possess the power to punish unethical or incompetent practitioners, including the power to revoke a person's right to practice (see below).

As a method of regulation, registration has much to recommend it. Entry into the field is not restricted, utilization of paraprofessionals is not inhibited, and the cost of services is not artificially increased. In fact, a system of registration produces few of the negative side effects created by traditional licensure. Registration recognizes that a consensus does not exist as to what standards and criteria are appropriate for measuring therapist effectiveness. Perhaps most important, rather than having the state make decisions for the consumer, registration laws allow the state to provide clients with relevant information and encourage the potential consumer of services to use careful judgment in selecting a professional.

Although registration does not initially prevent unqualified people from practicing, it does make provision for preventing those who have a record of harming clients from continuing to practice. Thus, some people will be injured by the quack and the charlatan. The thesis of this book, however, is that this danger is less than the risks entailed in more restrictive forms of licensing, where substantial harm results because persons in need of services are unable to afford or find help. As the problems of restrictive licensing become more apparent, political scientists and sociologists are increasingly supporting some form of registration (see Clark, 1974; Friedman, 1962: 144-46; Gellhorn, 1956: 105-51; Lieberman, 1970: 247; Massarik, 1974; Phelan, 1974: 48-50).

Improvements in Traditional Licensing Laws. Although restrictive licensing is not to be recommended, political realities suggest that it will be prevalent for some time. For this reason it is essential to develop a model law that minimizes the negative impact of licensure, while retaining its positive value. The following guidelines should help in framing such a law.

Laws Restricting Practice and/or Title Usage. Where licensing laws require certain standards to be met, laws prohibiting only the unlicensed use of certain titles are preferable to those prohibiting unlicensed practice. Such laws allow nontraditionally trained professionals to continue this work.

Definitions of Practice. Where a determination has been made to prohibit the unlicensed practice of psychotherapy, definitions of psychotherapy should be narrowly drawn. Specific mention should be made as to what activities are included and excluded. Broad phrases restricting general activities to licensed professionals (such as the right to diagnose or treat an emotional problem) should be avoided.[13] Definitions of practice should not restrict

the ability to make independent judgments to professionals only. This restriction has seriously undermined the effectiveness of paraprofessionals, and does not recognize the fact that paraprofessionals are fully capable of making competent independent judgments. Especially where statutory definitions are general and imprecise, licensing agencies should be required to promulgate rules containing more exact definitions.

Delegation of Functions to Paraprofessionals.[14] Laws prohibiting unlicensed practice should allow licensed persons to delegate any and all functions to paraprofessionals or appropriate others. Delegation provisions should only require direct, over-the-shoulder supervision where absolutely necessary. Otherwise, periodic supervision with regular monitoring and review of services should be sufficient. The type of supervision should depend on the function being delegated.

In other countries various methods of resolving the issues involving delegation have been attempted. Ruth Roemer's (1968) comparative study of the laws of seven countries found that all defined with varying detail the general functions that allied and auxiliary personnel could perform. France uses a professional committee to develop a list of those tasks that qualified paraprofessionals may perform on prescription of a physician or under a physician's direct surveillance. This list is revised periodically. In the United Kingdom, on the other hand, the functions of the auxiliary are defined by the practicing physician in accordance with the relevant statute. The Russians and Chinese, with their systems of socialized medicine, have given paraprofessionals enormous responsibility and the capacity to perform virtually any activity of which they are capable. This has proved especially fruitful in rural areas where a lack of highly trained personnel exists.

Since methods of controlling the quality of paraprofessional practice have not yet been adequately investigated, various alternatives should be explored, including: (1) allowing licensed practitioners to delegate functions at their discretion; (2) requiring licensed persons to submit job descriptions of the functions their assistants are to perform and to receive approval of the board that their assistants are qualified to perform those functions; and (3) allowing licensed practitioners to delegate functions to persons who have been certified by organizations approved by licensing boards. The important matter is to experiment with a variety of methods of delegation to determine which has maximum value with minimum risk.[15]

Requirements for Licensure. The requirements for entrance into the profession of psychotherapy should, in so far as possible, be related to the competencies needed to perform effectively.

Level of Competence. Licensure laws should only require minimal competence, which should be defined as the ability not to do harm. Licensing laws should not attempt to ensure that all practitioners are functioning at a high level of competence. Requirements for licensure should be related to the skills needed to perform at a minimum level of effectiveness.

Proficiency Testing. The use of proficiency examinations should be encouraged.[16] Such examinations are designed to determine whether someone has the necessary skills to perform effectively. Methods of proficiency testing are varied. Some rely on analyses of role-playing. Others depend on the evaluations of peers. Still others are based on an analysis of a person's written response to how she or he would handle critical incidents.

Each of these methods, and others, deserve consideration, since proficiency testing is only in its infant stages. Because the state of the art is still rudimentary, care needs to be taken before adopting any one measure as the most preferred. Licensing boards across the country should experiment with different measures and careful research should document the impact of each test.

Attempts at developing competency-based measures have been proceeding slowly, and their quality varies widely. Among professional groups, physical therapy, practical nursing, medical laboratory technicians, and psychiatric technicians have developed some form of competency-based examination processes (U.S. DHEW, 1973: 35). Unfortunately, many of these examinations are still limited to tests of knowledge through multiple choice examinations. Government agencies have also begun to require such exams. The Social Security Amendments of 1972, for instance, contain provisions for proficiency examinations for various categories of health personnel to satisfy Title 18 regulations, and Florida provides for such tests in its laws regulating emergency medical technicians (U.S. DHEW, 1973: 36).

Academic Credentials and Educational Equivalency Measures. Since little evidence exists that academic credentials are a valid measure of therapeutic ability, their use should be supplemented. At the very least, educational equivalency measures should be allowed to substitute for these credentials.[17] This means that credit should be given for knowledge and skills learned outside of academia. In particular, credit should be given for training acquired in some nonaccredited programs, through military service, or in on-the-job training provided in government and nongovernment programs. The determination of whether to give credit should be based on the results of an educational equivalency examination.

Accreditation. In the field of psychiatry, accreditation of programs rests with the American Medical Association, the American Association of Medical Schools, and the Residency Review Committee of the American Board of Psychiatry and Neurology. In psychology the American Psychological Association accredits programs in clinical and counseling psychology. In social work a similar function is performed by the Council on Social Work Education. Licensing boards frequently rely on the determination of these organizations. Otherwise they make their own determination or frequently rely on whether a program or school is accredited by a regional accreditation agency, the state department of education, or the U.S. Office of Education.

There is little evidence that the accreditation procedures of these organizations constitute a valid or useful measure of the quality of professional training. For this reason they should be supplemented.[18] Licensing should depend on the quality of the individual's practice, irrespective of where that person obtained training. At the very least, provision should be made to allow accreditation by organizations that are attempting to evaluate professional training on the basis of whether graduates are actually competent to practice. In addition, licensing boards should not be given the power to conduct the actual evaluation of what schools or programs are accredited. Instead, "schools offering training in licensed occupations and teachers in such schools should be regulated by the state department of education rather than by the board which licenses practitioners in each occupation" (Shimberg, Esser, and Kruger, 1972: 235).

Standardized National Examinations. In recent years an effort has been made to standardize licensing examinations among states.[19] In the medical field, for instance, almost all states allow doctors to substitute the examination of the National Board of Medical Examiners for the local state examination. Both psychology and social work have taken steps to create national examinations that would be administered by each state licensing board. Such examinations have been recommended because they encourage geographic mobility, they are liable to be more reliable, they help ensure uniformity in skill levels, and they result in substantial economic saving for most licensing boards. The U.S. Department of Health, Educa-

tion, and Welfare (1971: 73) claims that a broad consensus exists that such standards would be useful.

In the field of psychotherapy and those related professions that claim psychotherapy as part of their practice, national standards are premature. The wide disagreement as to what makes a therapist competent means that a variety of tests should be developed to determine whether a therapist is qualified to practice. Only in this way can it ultimately be determined whether one test is to be preferred over all others.

Because therapeutic competence may not be reducible to a single common denominator, it may turn out that no one test is capable of measuring even minimal therapeutic skill. Current tests, such as those administered by the Educational Testing Service, Professional Examination Service, Psychological Corporation, National Board of Medical Examiners, and American College Testing, have serious drawbacks since no evidence exists that they bear any relationship to professional competence, despite the fact they exhibit high content validity.

Elimination of Irrelevant Requirements. Requirements that license applicants be state residents, U.S. citizens, twenty-one years of age, and other irrelevant or arbitrary prerequisites should be eliminated.[20]

Selection Methods. Since little agreement exists about what methods of selection are best for determining therapeutic competence, licensing boards should experiment with a variety of procedures. Methods worthy of exploration include supervisor evaluation, recommendations from therapists acknowledged as expert, evaluations of role-playing, and evaluations of taped samples of recorded therapy interviews. The reinstituting of apprenticeships as a vehicle for licensing is especially worthy of exploration.

Endorsement Policies. All state licensing laws should allow endorsement of another state's license. In other words, an applicant licensed in one state should not have to take an examination to be licensed in a second state, so long as the standards of the first state are comparable to the second's. This policy promotes geographic mobility and minimizes the cost of licensing. It is preferable to the requirement of reciprocity, in which one state will only endorse another state's license if the latter state also endorses the former's.

Relicensure and Continuing Competence. A growing consensus exists that professionals should be required to demonstrate periodically that they are still competent to practice (see, for instance, American Hospital Association, 1971; American Medical Association, 1970: 7; Goldberg, 1975; Lurie, 1970; Sanford, 1951: 670; Shimberg, Esser, and Kruger, 1972: 224-25; U.S. DHEW, 1973: 53; U.S. DHEW, 1971: 76-77; U.S. National Advisory Commission on Health Manpower, II, 1967: 331). The reason for such a requirement is fairly obvious and compelling: the fact that a person was licensed forty years ago is no guarantee that she or he is still qualified to practice. The rapid expansion of knowledge and the technological innovations in methods and techniques means that previous training is often quickly outmoded. Speaking about the profession of medicine, Carmichael (1970: 1656) has written: "So challenging is the information explosion in medicine and the advent of the newest technologies that it is said, with some justice, that the 'half-life' of a physician's knowledge and skills is now about ten years."

The most frequently mentioned method of demonstrating this competence is through successful completion of a continuing education requirement.[21] A legitimate argument can be made that courses in continuing education are not a useful means of pursuing this goal, however. The most basic criticism is that evidence does not exist that the typical continuing education course makes any difference. Allowing credit for attending a symposium or half-day seminar at a professional associa-tion's annual meeting, which licensing boards frequently agree to, is especially questionable. In fact, perhaps the only benefit of continuing education requirements accrues to professional associations and continuing educators, who have been provided with a highly profitable and persuasive method of increasing attendance at annual meetings and professional symposiums.

In theoretical terms, the problem with continuing education requirements is that they constitute an input measure, and research has not been conducted to determine whether that input is related to the relevant output—professional functioning. Ideally, relicensure would simply be based on whether a practitioner was able to pass a competency-based examination that was known to be related to minimally competent performance. In fact, no logical reason exists why this examination should be any different from the initial licensure examination. Professional associations, nonetheless, have strongly resisted proposals for relicensing examinations, arguing that it is impossible for such exams to adequately assess a professional's competence.[22]

The only proper concern involved in relicensure is whether the professional is still at least minimally competent to practice. How persons have maintained their competence should be of no concern to licensing boards, as long as practitioners can pass an examination demonstrating minimal mastery of their craft. If licensing boards choose to rely on continuing education requirements, they should also make provision for alternative routes to demonstrating continued competence. The New Jersey Professional and Occupational Licensing Study Commission (1971: 62) recommends credit for publication of professional and scholarly papers, engaging in research; teaching; and successful completion of oral examinations to ascertain growth and understanding of new developments as useful means of demonstrating competence.

"Grandparent" Clauses. When a new licensing law is enacted or when a title-protection act is amended to prohibit unlicensed practice as well, all those practicing psychotherapy at the time the law was passed should be licensed without being required to pass an examination or meet any other requirements. This is in line with the basic policy position against restrictive licensing, since such licensing seriously curtails the supply of practitioners, and does so on the basis of irrelevant standards.

Licensing Fees. If the state believes that licensing is important to protect the public, then it should be willing to underwrite the costs of that protection. For this reason and because high licensing fees operate in discriminatory fashion, licensing fees should be minimal. Funding for the administration of the licensing process should be derived from general state funds.

General and Specialty Licenses. Where licensing boards have the power to grant general licenses to practice psychotherapy or a more broadly defined field of professional practice, they should also have the power to grant specialty licenses for specific areas of practice.[23] This protects the right to practice of those who are demonstrably competent in a narrow field of practice, but who may not have the broad knowledge or wide-ranging skills necessary for general practice. Boards should establish different requirements for these narrow areas of practice.

Alternate Paths to Licensure. Especially where academic credentials are the main prerequisite for licensure, alternate paths should be open for nontraditionally trained persons. In particular, boards should be required to accept satisfactory training and experience in lieu of any degree requirements. All licensing boards should have discretionary power to issue a license without examination to any person who adequately demonstrates competence to practice.

Exemptions. Ample exemptions are required to protect the many people who have a legitimate interest and skill in practicing psychotherapy. This means that all professional groups should be exempt when practicing within the standards and ethics of their profession. What constitutes a profession should not be limited to "recognized" or "licensed" professions, but should include less well-defined professions. Perhaps the criteria for inclusion should be whether a group has some form of regional or national association with written standards and criteria for admission, along with a method for disciplining wayward or unethical members. The recently formed National Commission for Health Certifying Agencies has been created to address, in part, this very problem. Licensing boards should publish rules and regulations that elaborate on these criteria for recognition and that list professional associations that qualify.

In addition, broad exemptions should be granted to the employees of various organizations, including government agencies, educational institutions, research laboratories, business corporations, and nonprofit organizations. Within a profession itself, exemptions should be made for students, interns, nonresidents temporarily practicing in a state, lecturers, and recent residents who have applied for licensure, pending disposition of their applications.

Disciplinary Enforcement. To date, licensing agencies have done a poor job of discipline, seriously undermining whatever small value such agencies have had.[24] Drastic changes are needed if this situation is to improve.

Education of the Public and Profession as a Central Function. One reason why licensing boards have failed at their task is that little effort has been made to educate properly the profession and the public. The profession needs to be informed and educated as to its legal duties, what activities are unethical, and what constitutes sound practice. The public needs education as to what constitutes a disciplinary violation and how to obtain redress. In addition, it should be a matter of public record who is disciplined and for what reasons.

These recommendations imply the need for simply designed pamphlets summarizing the salient features of licensing laws and their grounds for discipline. In addition, the existence, addresses, and easiest means of access to licensing boards should be widely advertised. An excellent means of doing this would be to require all practitioners to distribute to all clients information about the licensing board and how to obtain legal redress when dissatisfied with services received.

Licensing boards should also be required to publish an annual report containing complete data on all disciplinary actions taken, including the filing of any complaints. When disciplinary action is taken, the relevant information should be provided to local newspapers in the town in which the disciplined practitioner works. It should also be sent to the proper mental health agencies across the state, to the federal government, to appropriate journals, and to other state licensing agencies. Some of these practices have already been instituted in California, where licensing boards forward press releases to local newspapers about any major disciplinary action taken and send evidence of potential criminal violations to local district attorneys (Phelan, 1974: 11-12).

Although most professions have been loath to publicize unethical or incompetent activity upon a member's part, lack of publication has frequently allowed professionals to obtain licenses in one state when their license has been revoked in a second (see American Bar Association, Special Committee on Evaluation of Disciplinary Enforcement, 1970: 157-60). It has also resulted in public agencies hiring professionals not worthy of the public's trust.

Grounds for Discipline. Licensing statutes should contain complete grounds for discipline. Important grounds that are frequently missing include violation of a professional code of ethics, incompetent practice, practicing outside one's area of competence, and repeated negligence. As well as being more complete, the grounds for discipline should be more precise and more fully detailed. Terms such as "unprofessional conduct" deserve careful definition, which is most appropriately done through board rule or regulation. On the other hand, all restrictions preventing advertising and other restrictions based on economic self-protection of the professions should be repealed.[25]

Adequate Funding. A major reason why disciplinary boards have not been effective is lack of funds. Without reasonable financial resources it is impossible to hire investigative officers, train staff, or prosecute important cases. Even the matter of record-keeping is seriously hampered.

Proactive Stance toward Discipline. Licensing boards should play a highly active role in determining whether disciplinary violations are occurring. Among other things, licensing boards should subscribe to newspaper and magazine clipping services that would provide information on potential disciplinary violations by practitioners. The legislature should require all state courts to report any criminal convictions or civil actions, such as malpractice suits against licensed practitioners, to the appropriate licensing board. In addition, all law enforcement agencies should report instances of unethical or otherwise illegal conduct, and insurance companies should report the filing of any malpractice claims (see American Bar Association, Special Committee on Evaluation of Disciplinary Enforcement, 1970).

A central data bank should exist so that actions taken and information obtained by a state licensing agency are available to similar licensing agencies in other states. California has implemented a number of these suggestions, subscribing to a news clipping agency and making extensive use of the state justice department's criminal identification and investigation division (Marsh, 1972: 125).

Adequate Legal Powers and Staff. Current licensing boards, which are dominated by professionals from the field being regulated, do not have the training or expertise necessary to adequately carry out the disciplinary function. This should be remedied through access to specially trained staff in each state's attorney general's office. In addition, licensing boards should be given adequate legal powers to carry out their mandate. Specifically, licensing boards must have the power to issue subpoenas, and when action is taken against a licentiate, such action should not be stayed pending appeal. A number of states already have such powers. In addition to the board's power to revoke or suspend licenses or to censure a practitioner, it should have the power to formally admonish practitioners for minor offenses. This latter power is especially important, since current legal regulations result in most licensing boards taking action only in cases of gross abuses.

Centralization of Disciplinary Function. The New Jersey Professional and Occupational Licensing Study Commission (1971: 69) points out that the opportunity for licensing boards to abuse their powers is great under the current system, in which a board functions as investigator, prosecutor, judge, and jury. In addition, they do not have many of the skills necessary to carry out any of these functions very effectively. For these reasons efforts have been made to centralize many of the disciplinary functions within a larger branch of the government, such as a department of licensing. Another alternative is to transfer these functions to the office of the attorney general.

Right of Complainant to Standing. Under current law persons who file complaints with licensing boards generally have no right to standing. That is, they have no right to bring witnesses in support of their complaint, they have no legal recourse should a licensing board refuse to act on a complaint, they have no right to see the record, and they do not even have the right to know what action the disciplinary board took, if any. This situation must be rectified, and all complainants should be granted the same standing afforded other legal parties to administrative or judicial actions.

Structure and Functioning of the Licensing Board. Licensing agencies should not be created unless state legislatures have a strong commitment to them and are willing to provide adequate financial resources.[26] Similarly, licensing boards should have clearly outlined plans to ensure their effective functioning. Shimberg, Esser, and Kruger's (1972: 230) recommendation in this regard is excellent:

> Every licensing agency should be required to submit a program budget and clearly indicate its objectives and its plan for achieving these objectives. The budget should be subject to review, approval, and post-audit in exactly the same way as that applied to any state-supported activity. All income from the program should go into a general fund. In this way all licensing agencies would be assured of the support they need.

All licensing boards should have office space in government buildings, instead of the frequent practice today of boards operating out of the home of the chairperson or secretary of the board.

Licensing boards should not only see their purpose as licensing and discipline, but should also have as a central function the education of the public and the profession. In addition to education around the issue of discipline, previously discussed above, informational brochures should be published to inform the public about what possession of a license means.

From a structural standpoint it may be wise to separate out the various functions that a licensing board performs. Specifically, the administration of licensing examinations and the determination of whether applicants have met all the requirements for licensure should be separate from the disciplinary function. Both should be administered by persons skilled in their respective areas, not by professionals in their field. This centralization of functions might apply across all licensing boards within a state, which would generate considerable economic savings and allow the use of highly skilled experts.[27]

Also from a structural standpoint, it may be wise to merge the various professions regulating psychotherapy within a larger licensing board responsible for the mental health field. This has already happened in Virginia where H.B. 378 (1976) has created a behavioral science board to regulate psychology, social work, professional counselors, and other professions in the therapy field. Such a board, if given adequate powers, might begin to bring some unification into the structure of psychotherapy field, while preserving a diversity of standards of practice.

Perhaps the most important recommendation regarding the structure of licensing boards has to do with their composition. Since special technical staff will carry out the day-to-day functions of the board, the board or agency responsible for overseeing the licensing process should concern itself with policy-making and ensuring that its directives are properly executed. A pluralistic agency composed of the appropriate constituencies is likely to be most effective. This means that the administrative agency, whether constituted as a licensing board or administrative department, should have professionals, public members, government officials, testers, administrators, and clients on its staff. In addition, policies should make it mandatory that women, minorities, the aged, and the poor are adequately represented.

Among professional members, it may be wise to seek representatives from the different areas of professional practice, including private practice, teaching, and research. The actual selection of licensing boards should be done by state governors, who should have complete freedom in their selection, and should not be bound by lists submitted by professional associations.

No one group, unless it is the public members, should be in a position to dominate any board. This point deserves special emphasis. Today, licensing boards are dominated by members of the regulated profession. The recent move to include public members has generally resulted in one or two nonprofessionals being placed on the board. It is questionable whether this has any significant impact. Not only are such members in the minority, but they often lack the necessary background to function effectively (Thomson, 1973). Also, without an effectively organized constituency, a public representative has little political leverage to exert (Shimberg, Esser, and Kruger, 1972: 231).[28]

The argument that licensing boards should be dominated by professionals because only professionals are capable of evaluating themselves is not true. First of all, the matter of evaluation is best performed by skilled evaluators and testers. Only in the field of psychology is it likely to be true that the professional is an expert in the area of evaluation. Second, public members may not be able to directly evaluate the competence of a licensed applicant, but they can surely use sound judgment in relying on professionals who serve them in an advisory capacity. Third, as previously mentioned, the board's function should not be to construct the actual tests or to conduct the actual evaluation, but to oversee that process, which would be effected by skilled technical personnel.

More to the point, however, is the convincing evidence that licensing laws will probably never be effective as long as they are profession-dominated. Pfeffer (1974) presents three factors to support this contention. First, whether administrative regulation of any sort ever works is a function of the relative powers of the groups involved. Professional associations have far more power than the consuming public, leading to biased regulation. Second, as public interest in the operation of an agency wanes, which occurs with considerable regularity, the agency must seek support from the organizations it is regulating. To do otherwise risks a considerably reduced budget and the threat of internment. The result is predictable, according to Pfeffer (1974: 476): "Acquiescence to the interests of the regulated is almost an inevitable outcome." Finally, because state governments rarely support state agencies with adequate funds and staff, these agencies must rely on the regulated organizations to obtain the data needed for their functioning, which means that damaging data is likely to be concealed.

Judicial Regulation

Judicial regulation through professional liability suits has limited value. Except for cases of gross abuse, such as sexual or physical attacks, or cases only tangentially involving professional practice, such as inadequate supervision, the malpractice of psychotherapists is unlikely to be affected by judicial regulation. The undisputed fact is that most of what transpires in therapy does not provide a good basis for suit. As long as therapists simply talk to their patients, which is what most of them do, they do not have to worry about being sued, no matter how badly they perform.

Granted the fact that malpractice suits are not a useful means of regulating therapeutic behavior, and given the evidence that the current rash of malpractice suits is probably producing as many harmful results as positive (see Chapter 8), the value of judicial regulation should be seriously questioned. Instead, alternative methods of accomplishing some of its other purposes should be sought. For instance, the value of screening panels to evaluate the merits of individual suits before they reach the court system should be explored. Likewise, the potential or arbitration panels to decide many of the smaller malpractice suits deserves consideration because of their potential for

decreasing the amount of time necessary to decide individual cases.

Since malpractice suits will continue to be brought, however, the findings on what makes therapists harmful contains implications for the standard of care to be applied in such suits. Perhaps most important is the fact that no consensus exists as to what constitutes acceptable practice. The number of legitimate schools of thought existing in the psychotherapy field make it quite impossible to establish a single standard of care. The courts, therefore, should adopt a broad policy of protecting a therapist's right to experiment with new techniques, so long as proper safeguards are employed. Because a technique is new should not be enough in itself to render an adverse judgment. The courts should also broaden their doctrine of what constitutes an acceptable professional school. Only in those instances where a practitioner claims to be one of an extremely few adherents to a school, or where there are no published or established standards of practice, should the courts apply standards drawn from another school.

Related to the above, the courts should allow a practitioner to justify the use of questionable techniques and methods, not only on the basis of what is acceptable practice, but on the basis of empirical evidence documenting the effectiveness of the particular methods employed. Similarly, aggrieved patients should be allowed to present empirical evidence that certain practices are likely to be harmful, even if they represent the standard practice in a particular community.

On this basis, the courts should be careful in the development and application of various legal doctrines related to professional liability suits. The concepts of negligence per se, and *res ipsa loquitur*, should be used sparingly and only in unusual and compelling circumstances. Thus, even physical attacks on a patient should not necessarily be viewed as overwhelming evidence of negligence. Rather, this determination should be based on the soundness of the theory and evidence in support of the use of such methods.

Professional Associations

Left to themselves, professional associations are unlikely to achieve a high level of self-regulation. The historical tendency for such organizations has been to act in their own self-interest at the expense of the public interest, when the two conflict. No reason exists for this to change without outside intervention. In the field of psychotherapy the current course of events indicates that professional associations will continue to raise their standards for admission, that these standards will continue to bear little relationship to the skills required for competent practice, and that the basic goal of associations will be to achieve as much power as possible and to dominate the field as completely as possible.

These directions are precisely the opposite of what is desirable. Instead, professional associations should experiment with a variety of standards and criteria and methods of measuring therapeutic competence. Ideally, the field would be filled with a number of organizations, all with different methods of assessing competence. Some associations would ask of their members that they possess certain knowledge, others would require expertise in the utilization of techniques, and still others would want their members only to possess certain personal qualities such as warmth and empathy.

At the same time, these organizations should experiment with a variety of methods of assessing competence. Some should rely on written examinations, others oral interviews, others role-playing, and still others should utilize peer review of academic credentials.

In addition, these associations should experiment with a variety of methods of ensuring that unethical or incompetent practice did not occur after a person was certified. Moreover, professional associations should make a concerted effort to educate the public on the issues confronting the psychotherapy field. The newly formed National Commission for Health Certifying Agencies has an excellent opportunity to see that these recommendations are implemented.

The ideal picture painted above exists only in dim outline in actuality. While over the short term more organizations may appear, if the history of psychotherapy follows the history of medicine in the United States, one association is likely to predominate. The only effective way of ensuring that this does not happen is for government intervention. Such intervention should not be through prohibition, but through financial encouragement to assist in the growth of numerous professional associations. One criterion for federal or state support should be that an organization is not and will not become so powerful that further support would help it monopolize the field. Over a period of time, based on consumer feedback and empirical research, those associations whose members were functioning most effectively would continue to receive support, while the remainder would cease to exist.

Laws Requiring Full Disclosure

A major problem besetting the field of psychotherapy has been the lack of information available to the public. People enter psychotherapy without a clear picture of the process they are about to undergo. They have little idea of the degree to which therapy is effective, what changes it brings about, and in what situations harm is likely to occur. Potential patients do not even know what questions to ask. They tend to assume that academic degrees and state licensing are clear indications of competence, when no evidence exists that this is so.

A partial remedy to this problem is to

require all therapists to disclose relevant information about their background, skills, and methods. This should include an explicit statement about education, training, experience, and professional credentials. Techniques, the length and cost of treatment, whether physical or sexual contact is likely to be a part of treatment, what results may be expected, and the nature of the changes that the therapist sees as important should also be disclosed. In addition, the therapist should be required to provide all clients with a background statement issued by the state describing what is known about the therapeutic process and what clients may do if dissatisfied or harmed by the services they have received.

Support for such a law has been increasing (see Carlson, 1975: 233). Such a law could be instituted at the state or federal level. Recently a petition was presented to the Federal Trade Commission (FTC) to promulgate a Trade Rule Regulation that would have done precisely this (Georgiades, 1976), but the FTC refused to adopt such a rule, claiming that the "available information concerning the existence and prevalence of deceptive or unfair practices industry-wide is insufficient to warrant institution of rulemaking proceedings" (U.S. FTC, 1977).

Client Evaluation/Enforcement of Existing Laws; and Special Laws for Specific Problems

See the recommendations as they are outlined in the relevant sections of "A Proposed Model for Professional Regulation," above.

Education of the Public

Perhaps the most effective method of regulating psychotherapists and protecting the public is through education. This is especially true of any profession that is young and undeveloped, and where standards of practice are still quite diverse. What is important is to provide potential consumers with an understanding of what

they are buying, what their options are, what they may reasonably expect, and what they may do if dissatisfied with their services. This means disseminating information as to the current state of the psychotherapeutic art, including what little is known about therapist effectiveness.[29]

The public should have ready access to the results of empirical research, as well as expert opinion. The public needs information on available mental health resources, and the differential effectiveness of psychotherapy versus treatment through drugs, electro-convulsive therapy, and other physical techniques. Education is also important concerning the situations in which a therapist is likely to behave unprofessionally, and what behaviors are considered unprofessional. On a broader scale, the public should become more informed about the professions, their importance to society, their power, and the ways in which that power may be abused (Lieberman, 1970: 260–64).

The task of educating the public is not an easy one. Some believe that the task is hopeless, especially if the media is relied upon.[30] Many public education programs have been misdirected, and a general belief has developed that such education is unlikely to achieve anything. The problems are especially severe in the mental health field, since the public has a long-standing distrust of the mentally ill, past programs to educate the public have been small in scale,[31] and the public seems to have many distorted views about the therapeutic process.[32]

Part of the answer to these problems, in the words of one of the best-known antiquackery crusaders, James Harvey Young (1967: 433), is "education more appropriately aimed than in the past." The details of such a program require careful working out and professional expertise. Laws requiring full disclosure should obviously play a role. Lately, a number of guides have appeared that attempt to provide potential consumers with pertinent information on psychotherapists in a specific geographic area (see, for instance, Adams and Orger, 1975; Wallis, 1976), despite receiving considerable resistance from the major professions. An increasing number of books is also appearing that attempt to explain the process of psychotherapy and differentiate the various therapeutic techniques in simple terms (see, for instance, Heck et al., 1973; Howard, 1970; Park and Shapiro, 1976). Lieberman (1970: 257–67) has suggested the introduction of courses in high school on consumer issues and the nature and problems of the professions.

Research and Knowledge Development

> Research in psychotherapy bears a painfully close resemblance to the nightmarish game of croquet in *Alice in Wonderland*, in which the mallets were flamingos, the balls hedgehogs, and the wickets soldiers. Since the flamingo would not keep its head down, the hedghogs kept unrolling themselves, and the soldiers were always wandering to other parts of the field, "Alice soon came to the conclusion that it was a very difficult game indeed." [Frank, 1973: 332.]

In a profession where little concensus exists about critical issues a most important task is to gather new information, conduct further research, and disseminate the results of that research.[33] Studies are needed on what makes therapists effective or ineffective, what methods of selection are most valid and reliable, and what methods of selection are most valid and reliable, and what methods of training are most efficient. Research needs to determine the role of techniques, personal qualities, diagnostic ability, and knowledge in creating competent therapists. The effectiveness of paraprofessionals is especially important to document. Comparisons of academic training, on-the-job training, and various mixes of experiential and didactic teaching need to be made. In addition, research on the regulatory process itself is important. Studies should be conducted to determine the effectiveness of various forms of regulation, including licensure and malpractice suits. Further, research should examine why people go to quacks, how bad practices arise, and ways of preventing professional abuses.

In order to improve the quality and generalizability of this research, better informational and data-gathering systems need to be developed. This is probably best done through agencies such as the National Center for Health Statistics. Once information is gathered and analyzed, the final step will be to improve the communication of that research to the public and professional, so that its results can have maximum impact.

IMPLICATIONS FOR OTHER MEANS OF REGULATION

The means of influencing standards of therapeutic practice are manifold. In addition to direct means such as licensing, there are other methods whose express purpose is to control the quality of services delivered. The most clear-cut example is the use of federally mandated Professional Standards Review Organizations (PSROs) that monitor the cost and appropriateness of medical services. In addition to indirect means, such as education of the public, are other activities that indirectly, but powerfully, influence standards of professional practice. The implications of the findings, conclusions, and recommendations contained in this book are spelled out for the more important of these other means of regulation.

Insurance Coverage

Under current programs of private health insurance, various professional groups are included as primary health care providers. These providers are directly reimbursed for services they perform, and they do not require supervision by other professionals. Psychiatrists and other physicians are generally reimbursable for rendering mental health services where such services are covered by insurance. Psychologists have fought a reasonably successful battle to obtain parity with psychiatrists in this regard, and the enactment of freedom-of-choice legislation in many states has legislatively mandated equality. Social workers are fighting for similar legislation, but most often have to work under the supervision of a psychiatrist for their services to qualify for coverage.

The findings of this book suggest that insurance coverage should not be based on the academic credentials of the person delivering services, nor should it be based on whether that person is licensed. Instead, insurance companies should attempt to use competency-based measures that empirical research demonstrates are connected with effective performance. For instance, an insurance company might choose to require service providers to achieve some minimal score on Truax's (1972) accurate empathy scale, or it might require certification by a professional association that had competency-based membership requirements. Insurance companies might also refuse to reimburse professional services on the basis of degrees or licensing, forcing professional associations to develop competency-based systems of certification.

Insurance companies might also examine the possibility of allowing reimbursement for services performed by paraprofessionals who are graduates of sound training programs or who are working in agencies known for the quality services they provide. At the very least, insurance companies should experiment with lowering their current requirements, allowing master's degree psychologists and social workers to perform as primary health care providers. Such a move could lead to a significant decrease in the cost of services, at least partially—if not wholly—offsetting the increase in overall cost resulting from the greater number of providers.

Professional Standards Review Organizations (PSROs)

PSROs were established by federal mandate in 1972 as part of Public Law 92–603.[34] The purpose of PSROs is to monitor the institutional care provided for Medicare, Medicaid, and Maternal and Child Health patients. The monitoring is carried out by organized groups of physicians, who determine whether the services were performed at a reasonable cost and whether the quality of services met professional standards in the geographic area of the PSRO.

For the most part PSROs have focused on controlling costs, and little has been done to enforce standards of competent practice (Anderson, 1976). Since the process is controlled by physicians, and since the public and other constituencies serve only in an advisory capacity, the likelihood that peer review through PSROs will actually ensure quality is unlikely. The same problems may be expected that have occurred in the licensing process. To prevent this, consumers and other appropriate constituencies must be given adequate representation and power.

The Accreditation Process

Federal, regional, state, and private accreditation agencies have substantial power to affect standards and criteria of professional practice. Unfortunately, neither the accreditation of educational institutions and training programs nor the accreditation of health care facilities, such as hospitals, has utilized criteria based on the quality of the service ultimately delivered. Changes should be instituted to rectify this situation.

Accreditation agencies must attempt to establish methods of evaluating educational programs and service facilities that will show whether they result in quality practice. For academic training programs this means decreased reliance on how much knowledge a program imparts, and increased reliance on what skills it teaches.

For health care facilities it means decreased emphasis on whether staff possess the requisite academic credentials and specialty certification, and increased emphasis on whether they are capable of performing their services effectively, as documented by competency-based measures of performance. Control of the accreditation process should not be placed in the hands of professionals alone, but should be shared by educators, professionals, the public, and government.

Education and Training

The training of psychotherapists, which is currently fragmented among many professions, should be unified and integrated within the mental health field. A diversity of methods should be encouraged, since not enough is known about effective training. Education should be organized around a core curriculum to facilitate vertical and lateral movement of paraprofessionals. Intellectual training should only be emphasized to the extent that it is relevant to the skills needed to perform effectively. A strong emphasis should be placed on clinical work and quality supervision. Personal therapy, which should not be mandatory, should be available as an option. A significant part of the curricula should be devoted to problems in the organization and delivery of mental health services to provide therapists with a clear picture of the overall framework within which they are working. Programs should not be geared to full-time students, but should provide continuing-education services so that working professionals can obtain advance degrees without significant economic hardship or job dislocation.

Other Methods

Other methods of regulation and influencing standards of practice should conform to the guidelines laid down earlier in this chapter. This includes direct means of regulation through professional codes of ethics, peer review in group practice, utili-

zation review committees in hospitals, audits, and institutional licensure. It also includes other indirect means of regulation, such as requirements for professional services to qualify as income tax deductions for recipients, the criteria for determining use of government funds for new health-care facility construction, the determination of who has the right to testify in court on mental health issues, and the criteria government agencies and nongovernment organizations use in determining employment opportunities.

STRATEGIES AND TACTICS

The implementation of the above recommendations will require concerted action on a number of fronts. Government and the private sector must both be involved. Since the critical factor in professional regulation is the licensure process, special emphasis should be given to strategies and tactics designed to bring about constructive changes in this area.

Legislative and Judicial Action Regarding Licensure.

Since licensing laws prohibiting unlicensed practice or title usage are inadvisable, strategies need to be developed to overturn them or at least eliminate some of their negative aspects. Five possibilities exist: (1) direct repeal or amendment; (2) judicial action based on the proposition that licensing laws are unconstitutional; (3) judicial action based on the theory that licensing laws are in violation of federal and state statutory law; (4) the enactment and enforcement of "sunset" laws to lead to an eventual determination by the legislature that licensing laws are not operating in the public interest; and (5) where traditional licensing remains, the enactment of model psychotherapy laws to protect the rights of nontraditionally trained practitioners and otherwise eliminate many of the less desirable aspects of traditional licensing.

Direct Repeal or Amendment. The most direct method of eliminating the negative effects of licensing laws is for state legislatures to vote their repeal, or to radically amend current laws to mitigate some of their negative side effects. Such a move is becoming increasingly likely as the destructive and inhibitory effects of professional licensing become more apparent. The New Jersey Professional and Occupational Licensing Study Commission (1971: 6–7, 29–30) recommended the delicensure of nine professions, including marriage and family counseling. Although the major professions will undoubtedly be against repeal, many of the smaller associations—especially those professional groups now excluded from licensure—may find reason to lobby for repeal. Federal and state agencies involved in consumer affairs or trade regulation should also exert pressure on legislatures for the elimination of licensing. Where repeal is not politically feasible, laws should be amended so that only the use of certain titles is prohibited without a license, and practice is allowed to anyone.

One serious danger needs to be watched. In a given state, repeal of one set of licensing laws affecting psychotherapy may not be advisable unless all relevant laws are repealed. The likelihood of successfully repealing a law is probably inversely proportional to the power of the profession involved. In the mental health field this means that the first laws to be eliminated will be those regulating marriage and family counseling, followed by social work, psychology, and medicine. If all laws except those regulating medicine were repealed, the net effect would be to increase significantly the power of the medical profession—a result opposite of what is desirable. Similarly, if social work and marriage and family counseling laws were repealed, the psychology and medical professions would have a more effective

monopoly. Thus, repeal of one set of laws should only be considered in conjunction with the repeal of all laws, or amendments that would make these other laws inapplicable to the practice of psychotherapy.

Judicial Action Based on Constitutional Law. Where repeal or amendment of laws regulating psychotherapy is not feasible, it may be possible to have such laws overturned because they are in violation of the U.S. Constitution or state constitutions. Several bases exist for this line of attack.

Void for Vagueness. Laws prohibiting the unlicensed practice of a profession depend upon an aedquate definition of the limits of that practice. An argument can be made that current definitions of the practice of medicine, psychology, social work, and other related professions are so vague as to be unconstitutional.[35]

The U.S. Supreme Court has long held that criminal statutes must be drawn with reasonable clarity: "A criminal statute which either forbids or requires the doing of an act in terms so vague that men of common intelligence must necessarily guess at its meaning and differ as to its application, lacks the first essential of due process of law" (*Connally v. General Construction Co.* [1926]). Without such clarity it becomes impossible for persons to determine whether they are committing a crime (*United States v. Cardiff* [1952]; *United States v. L. Cohen Grocery Co.* [1921]). Even where no criminal sanctions exist, reasonable clarity is necessary where vagueness may result in the destruction of the value of an existing investment of time or money (cf. *A.B. Small Co. v. American Sugar Refining Co.* [1925]). Statutes are also meant as guides to adjudication; judges and juries must have objective guidelines that are clear enough to yield uniform results, not ad hoc arguments based on subjective interpretation of vague language (*Harvard Law Review*, 1948: 77).

Several legal foundations exist for this doctrine. In the main, courts have relied upon the due process clauses of state constitutions and the due process clauses contained in the fifth and fourteenth amendments to the U.S. Constitution.[36] Occasionally the courts have based unconstitutionality on the doctrine of nondelegation of legislative power to courts or enforcement agencies,[37] or on the sixth amendment requirement that adequate standards must be provided to test the legality of an indictment (*United States v. L. Cohen Grocery Co.* [1921]).

The criteria that courts have used to determine whether particular statutes are too vague are not readily apparent.[38] Although definitions of practice in health licensing laws have generally been upheld,[39] licensing laws affecting psychotherapists could be ruled unconstitutionally vague on the following grounds: (1) such definitions of practice are unnecessarily broad and should be more narrowly drawn; (2) unlike many other terms upheld in courts of law, no settled meanings exist, either at common law or within the professions themselves, for the terms involved; (3) statutes with language far more definite in meaning have been struck down; (4) such statutes are inimical to national policy and the public interest because of their negative side effects; and (5) the vagueness of language prevents many practitioners from knowing or being able to determine whether specific practices are in violation of the statute.[40]

Economic Due Process. Under the doctrine of economic due process the state may not curtail a person's right to work or earn a living, except where legislation is designed to protect the public health, safety, and welfare (Hetherington, 1958: 13). This means that occupations, such as watch-making, if they do not constitute a danger to the public, may not be legally regulated. If they are found to constitute a public menace, then the restrictions enacted must be reasonably designed to protect the public from the harm involved.[44]

This doctrine originated at the end of the nineteenth century when the United States was concerned with breaking apart monopolies and protecting the laissez-faire philosophy that had dominated during a large part of the eighteenth century. The courts, although never acting consistently, frequently overturned licensing laws in a variety of fields, including horseshoeing (*Bessette v. People* [1901]), land surveying (*Doe v. Jones* [1927]), paperhanging (*Dasch v. Jackson* [1936]), bricklaying (*Wilson v. District of Columbia* [1905]), and heating contracting (*Harrigan & Reid Co. v. Burton* [1923]). The gradual demise of the individualistic, laissez-faire conception of society and the efforts of President Roosevelt to prevent the Supreme Court from striking down New Deal legislation, however, led to the almost total extinction of this doctrine (Lieberman, 1970: 190). The courts became very hesitant about involving themselves in overturning legislative decisions: "Our recent decisions make plain that we do not sit as a superlegislature to weigh the wisdom of legislation nor to decide whether the policy which it expresses offends the public welfare" (*Day-Brite Lighting, Inc. v. Missouri* [1952]).

Although some have argued that this doctrine should not be exhumed (see, for instance, McCloskey, 1962), others believe that "economic due process was abandoned just at the time a refined version was growing necessary" (Lieberman, 1970: 191). Especially in the field of licensing, it can be argued that many professions are not sufficiently or so inherently dangerous as to warrant legislative intervention through restrictive licensing. In particular, it can be argued that those who believe licensing is necessary for psychotherapists have not demonstrated that a sufficiently high level of danger exists. Only through establishing a court-enforceable presumption against licensing will it be possible to protect the public from the professions' abuses of the legislative process.[42]

Procedural Due Process. Although somewhat narrower, the doctrine of procedural due process is closely intertwined with economic due process. In simple terms, this doctrine makes it unconstitutional for a state legislature to enact regulations that do not bear a rational relationship to the dangers being protected against.[43]

In the early part of this century the courts did not hesitate to employ notions of procedural due process to strike down a variety of statutes. In *Smith v. Texas* (1914), for instance, the Supreme Court struck down a statute containing stricter-than-necessary prerequisites for railroad employees:

A statute which permits the brakeman to act—because he is presumptively competent—and prohibits the employment of engineers and all others who can affirmatively prove that they are likewise competent, is not confined to securing the public safety but denies to many the liberty of contract granted to brakemen and operates to establish rules of promotion in a private employment. [*Smith v. Texas*, 233 U.S. 630–641 (1914).]

On this basis courts have struck down questions on examinations for barbers that went into such details as the proper way to cut hair or give a shave, since such questions have nothing to do with the public health (*Timmons v. Morris* [1921]). Similarly, statutes have been struck down requiring hairdressers to possess at least a tenth-grade education (*Beauty Hall v. State Board of Cosmetology* [1964]), or apprentices to serve extremely long periods before being fully licensed (*People v. Brown* [1951]; *People v. Ringe* [1910], or special schooling in one field that is not necessary to the actual work a person does in another field (*Cleere v. Bullock* [1961]).[44]

Although the courts have backed away from using this doctrine, strong recommendations have been made to apply it in the licensing field to counteract the tendency of professional associations to seek the enactment of laws with higher-than-necessary or irrelevant entrance requirements (Friedman, 1962: 144; Lieberman, 1970: 243–44). Even a cursory perusal of the empirical literature on the effectiveness of psychotherapists should provide sufficient evidence that current licensing standards are largely arbitrary, occasionally capricious, and certainly higher than necessary. In particular, the concept of procedural due process should be used to strike down requirements that practitioners possess advanced degrees.

To date, a number of court decisions have used this theory to render various portions of psychology licensing requirements inoperative. For instance, in *Berger v. Board of Psychologist Examiners* (1975), the court held that it was unconstitutional to require an applicant for licensure under the "grandparent" clause to have a doctoral degree and a certain amount of experience. The court said that the applicant must be given a fair opportunity to demonstrate professional skills according to reasonable standards. And in *Cox v. Mississippi Board of Psychological Examiners* (1976), the court directed the board to issue a license to the plaintiff, despite the board's contention that plaintiff's graduate degree was not in psychology, as required by law (cf. *Whittle v. State Board of Examiners of Psychologists* [1971]).

Nondelegation of Power and Separation of Power. The basic tenet of the nondelegation-of-power doctrine is that the legislative branch of government cannot delegate its power to another body (*United States v. Shreveport Grain and Elevator Co.* [1932]).[45] This has been interpreted as meaning that Congress cannot delegate its rule-making and standard-setting functions (*Yick Wo v. Hopkins* [1886]). The idea that such delegation is unconstitutional is said to stem from Article I of the U.S. Constitution and from similar clauses in state constitutions (see, e.g., *Fink v. Cole* [1951]).

Under the separation-of-power doctrine it is argued that the judicial, executive, and legislative branches of government must remain distinct, and that no branch shall exercise the powers of another branch. Lack of such separation has been thought to lead to tyranny and an authoritarian state. Blackstone (1941: 79), for instance, has said: "In all tyrannical governments, the supreme magistracy, or the right of both making and enforcing the laws, is vested in one and the same man, or one and the same body of men, and wherever these two powers are united, there can be no public liberty." Although no explicit requirement of separation exists in the U.S. Constitution, the doctrine has developed from the constitutional provisions for three branches of government, which vest those branches with specific powers (see *Kilbourn v. Thompson* [1881]). Most state constitutions expressly prohibit such lack of separation.

Under these doctrines state courts have held that it is unconstitutional to give licensing boards unrestricted power to make rules and regulations (see, for instance, *State v. Morrow* [1956]; *Harmon v. State* [1902]; *State v. van Keegan* [1945]). General vagueness of statutory language, especially with regard to licensure requirements, will often be looked at as an unconstitutional delegation of power. In *Hoff v. State* (1938), for instance, the Delaware Supreme Court struck down a statute regulating beauticians because this profession was not adequately defined, the nature and scope of the licensing examination was too vague, and rules were lacking with respect to the registration of beauty schools (see also *Banjavich v. Louisiana Board for Marine Divers* [1959]).

Similarly, where a licensing law states that all applicants for licensure must be graduates of a school approved by a particular professional body or association, these provisions may be attacked as an improper delegation of public authority. A quite recent case involving the American Dental Association (ADA) is directly in point. In *Garces v. Department of Registration and Education* (1969), an Illinois Appellate Court overturned a rule requiring all applicants for dental licensure to be graduates of a school approved by the Council of Dental Education of the ADA or a school with rules and curriculum equivalent to those of the University of Illinois College of Dentistry.

Licensing requirements involving supervised experience may also be struck down.[46] In *People v. Brown* (1951), for example, the Court declared unconstitutional a requirement that apprenticeships be served under licensed master plumbers. The law was ruled defective because master plumbers had unrestricted power to dismiss apprentices or simply not accept them in the first place. Where provisions for alternative paths to licensure were not open, the Court said that this amounted to an unconstitutional delegation of power to a private citizen.

These doctrines may also be employed against legal provisions giving professionals control of licensing boards (see *Lasher v. People* [1899]). The *Harvard Law Review* (1963: 1064), noting the example of a medical association being empowered to appoint members of the state board of examiners, argues that constitutional objections based on arbitrary exclusion might be raised where other private associations have a government-delegated power or function which may be exercised discriminatorily to injure a member of the excluded class."

The nondelegation doctrine is in relative disuse today.[47] The demise of this doctrine, and that of separation-of-powers, is largely attributable to the rise of administrative agencies, which would not be able to function effectively if either doctrine was strictly enforced (Davis, 1972: 6). Davis (1972: 43) makes a persuasive argument that the nondelegation doctrine should be revitalized, however, and makes several recommendations so that its primary and necessary function of preventing abuses of discretionary power can be returned. In simplest terms, Davis (1972: 52) argues: "As far as practicable administrators must structure their discretionary power through appropriate safeguards and must confine and guide their discretionary power through standards, principles, and rules." This standard should be applied even more strictly to state agencies than federal, because state legislatures are often less responsible than Congress, less skillful, and more easily swayed by special-interest groups (Davis, 1972: 36-37).[48] On this basis courts might declare licensing boards remiss if they failed to further define what constituted professional practice.

Several nondelegation cases have directly involved laws regulating psychotherapists. In *Bloom v. Texas State Board of Examiners of Psychologists* (1973), the psychology licensing board denied Bloom a license because he lacked the necessary ethical and other professional qualities essential to professional practice. The Texas Supreme Court ruled that the licensing board had abused its discretionary authority through establishing additional requirements for licensure that were not expressly contained in the law itself. In a similar case, the Florida Supreme Court declared the psychology law unconstitutional because the only standard provided for the board in designing the entrance examination was that it be in the field of psychology, the legislature failed to provide standards to guide the board in its accreditation of university programs, and the board had unlimited power to determine what constituted an equivalent degree in the field of psychology (*Husband v. Cassel* [1961]).[49]

Judicial Action Based on Statutory Law. Licensure laws and the standards and criteria they establish for practice may be subject to various state and federal statutes. In particular, antidiscrimination and antitrust law may be especially effective means of eliminating some of the more harmful aspects of current licensing policies.

Antidiscrimination Laws. At both the state and federal levels, statutes exist that make it a crime for, or allow civil suits against, persons, organizations, or government agencies that discriminate against individuals on the basis of race, sex, color, religion, age, or national origin. The various civil rights laws[50] and fair employment practice statutes[51] are probably the best known of these. Three difficult questions must be answered, however, before such laws will be considered applicable to the activities of state licensing boards.[52]

In the first place, the question arises whether licensing boards may be sued. Under Title VII of the Civil Rights Act of 1964 (42 U.S.C. § 2000e et seq., 1970, as amended), for instance, this determination turns on whether licensing boards are considered "employers." Guidelines on employee selection procedures proposed by a staff committee to the U.S. Equal Employment Opportunity Coordinating Council (1975) would definitely bring licensing boards within the scope of the law, and a number of other commentators believe that these laws should or will apply (see Rebell, undated, 1974; and Maslow, 1971a). The most recent guidelines adopted by the Equal Employment Opportunity Commission, Civil Service Commission, Department of Labor, and Department of Justice state that licensing boards are included "to the extent that licensing and certification may be covered by federal equal employment opportunity law" (Federal Register, August 25, 1978: 38296).

Even if they do apply, two other problems must be dealt with. The activities of licensing boards must be shown to result in discrimination, and the standards and criteria that bring about that discrimination must be shown to bear no rational relationship to the intended purposes of the law. If it were not necessary to demonstrate the intention to discriminate, proof of discrimination would be easy to demonstrate, since little doubt exists that minorities, women, the aged, and the poor are disproportionately affected by current laws. Whether licensing requirements are considered to bear a rational relationship with the ultimate purpose of the law will depend on whether courts require content or predictive validity. If predictive validity is required, then the requirements of licensing laws will have a difficult time withstanding scrutiny. Marshall Brown (in Asher, 1974: 4), chairperson of the Pennsylvania psychology boards, for instance, "suspects that the requirement for a doctorate for licensure . . . 'won't stand up in court,' if its validity is challenged."

Antitrust Laws.

The professions have been involved in various activities that appear fraught with antitrust violations. The bar association price schedules utilized by attorneys, *the imposition by both legal and medical associations of unreasonable licensing requirements*, the pharmaceutical associations' restraints on advertising, and the prohibitions of competitive bidding by architecture, accountant, and engineering associations are all possible antitrust violations. [Ellis, 1973: 743–44 (emphasis added).]

At the present time federal law[53] and most state laws[54] prohibit the existence of unjustified or unnecessary monopolies. In addition, the Federal Trade Commission has authority to act on antitrust violations and has its own set of laws regarding unfair trade practices (15 U.S.C. §§ 41-77 [1970], *as amended* [Cum. Supp. 1976]; see also, U.S. FTC, 1975). An argument can be made that these laws should be applied to professional associations for their monopolistic influence over the licensing process, and that they should be applied directly to licensing boards to

overturn various provisions regulating entrance into the profession and regulating the composition and control of the board itself.[55]

Several potential problems must be resolved before antitrust laws are likely to be applied against the professions or licensing boards. First, the general presumption that the professions are specially exempted from the operation of antitrust laws needs to be removed.[56] Second, the assumption that professional services are not "trade or commerce" within the meaning of antitrust law must be overturned.[57] Third, the theory that the activity of professional associations, at least when it is related to the carrying out of government directives, constitutes "valid state action" and hence is exempt, must be altered.[58] And finally, the historical exemption of federal and state governments, and their agencies, departments, and officials, must be eliminated.[59]

In each of these areas current legal decisions are moving toward a theory that may eventually allow full-scale attacks against licensing boards. The recent antitrust suit against the legal profession for minimum-fee schedules (*Goldfarb v. Virginia State Bar* [1975]), for instance, and suits brought against the medical profession and other health professions for restricting a professional's right to advertise,[60] are indicative of this.

Not only has the public become increasingly dissatisfied with the professions and their alleged monopolistic tendencies, but the FTC and Justice Department are also taking action to curb many professional activities that they consider in restraint of trade. Kenneth Ellis (1973: 762) has concluded:

In view of the suppression of competition through controlled admission requirements and the price fixing activities in which the professions are now engaged, per se immunity from the antitrust laws is clearly undesirable. . . . [U]nreasonable restraints upon economic activity, whether by commercial enterprise or professional organization, are patently inconsistent with our economic system. Absent an express contrary congressional intent, any contract, combination, or conspiracy restraining any economic activity should be subjected to the strictures of the Sherman Act.

Sunset Laws. A recent nationwide effort by Common Cause has led to the adoption of so-called sunset laws in many states.[61] These laws provide for the termination of certain state agencies unless they can actively demonstrate the need for their continued existence. Various states have adopted different criteria for determining this need. In many cases licensing boards in the field of psychotherapy, including psychology, social work, and marriage and family counseling, would have a difficult time in justifying the need for their existence.

Model Laws. Where repeal or amendment of existing laws proves impossible or politically unfeasible, the wisest course of action may be to seek the enactment of an additional licensing law specifically designed to regulate psychotherapists. This law should contain provisions incorporating many of the licensing recommendations made above, including no restrictions against unlicensed practice, alternative paths to licensure, and a licensing board consisting of members of the profession, the public, and other involved constituencies. The enactment of a model law may be the only way to protect the rights of groups not traditionally trained to practice, and it may create a positive force for change in existing laws.

Government Action

Federal and state policies must begin to reflect a greater balance between physical and mental health. Data collection needs drastic improvement. Research on therapist effectiveness, the causes of mental illness, methods of cure, and the effectiveness of various means of regulation should be expanded. Instead of establishing uniformity in therapist standards, federal and state agencies should experiment with a diversity of standards in the

hiring of therapists. The use of academic credentials should be deemphasized, and the potential of paraprofessionals should be exploited.

The development of regulatory proposals and their implementation should be carried out by representatives from all appropriate groups, including the public, clients, government officials, and the professions. In no instance should the professions have a dominant position. This implies a significant restructuring of Professional Standards Review Organizations.

Government agencies should also: (1) fund innovative training programs for mental health practitioners; (2) institute long-range planning for the development of a unified mental health profession; (3) fund research to develop competency-based measures for evaluating therapeutic effectiveness; (4) provide special grants to improve the functioning and quality of licensing boards; and (5) fund a variety of professional associations to experiment with different standards and criteria for certifying therapists and accrediting training programs.

A most important recommendation is for the Federal Trade Commission (FTC) to promulgate a trade rule regulation to require all psychotherapists to disclose certain information to their clients. This requirement should apply to all practitioners, including psychiatrists, clinical psychologists, and psychiatric social workers, whether licensed or not. In addition, the FTC should examine the possibility of suits against therapists who employ dubious advertising techniques; and it should explore the possibility of antitrust suits against the mental health professions for any unnecessarily restrictive practices.

National Conferences

National conferences are necessary to bring attention to the many issues that exist in professional regulation and to develop specific proposals for change. In particular there should be conferences on how to unify the mental health professions, how to integrate the mental health field into general medicine, how to improve disciplinary enforcement, and what vehicles are likely to be the most effective in regulating psychotherapists.

National Institute to Study the Professions

To coordinate research efforts, to educate the public, and to bring about the changes recommended in this book, a national institute to study the professions should be created. More than one such institute may be advisable. The National Center for Study of the Professions in Washington, D.C. is an excellent example of such an institute. It is currently the only organization active in this area, and is focusing on research and the dissemination of information.[62] Because of its nonprofit and tax-exempt status, however, it is unable to take direct political action to effect change, so that a companion institute should probably be established to fulfill this need. These institutes deserve long-term and extensive funding support.

Political Lobby by Counseling Groups

The many professional groups involved in counseling and psychotherapy—especially those that are discriminated against by current licensing laws—should form an umbrella organization to lobby for the types of changes recommended in this book. The American Orthopsychiatric Association represents a possible umbrella, but it may be too dominated by the major associations. Some efforts to form such an umbrella group are already underway through the efforts of the International Association of Applied Social Scientists, the Association for Creative Change, the International Transactional Analysis Association, and the American Personnel and Guidance Association.[63]

Model Professional Association

Many of the ideas discussed in this book could be implemented by private associations without waiting for the government to modify restrictive licensing laws or to enact registration laws. An organization could use competency-based criteria to select people for membership; it could require all members to make certain disclosures to clients; it could establish client-feedback mechanisms to provide evaluations of the professional's performance; it could make such evaluations available to the public; and it could provide mechanisms for enforcing discipline. Presently constituted associations could modify their by-laws and organizational structure to adopt one or more of the recommendations made in this chapter. This might represent an excellent avenue to test some of the ideas suggested in this book.

Professional Associations in General

Professional associations need to move to competency-based criteria for membership, instead of academic credentials. Applicants for membership should be able to demonstrate competency through more than one path. No professional association should attempt to dominate the psychotherapeutic field, either through restrictive licensing laws or through convincing employers to hire only their members.

Educational Institutions

Educational institutions must develop a commitment to engage in the political process. When licensing laws are proposed, faculty should testify at hearings and propose positive recommendations. For instance, universities should forcefully challenge the validity of using academic credentials as a measure of professional competence, and should carefully explain precisely what possession of a doctorate does indicate. If academic degrees are used, educational institutions should seek representation on licensing boards to better enable them to influence the administrative process.

Internally, academia should develop a commitment to use the tools of social science research to investigate the effects of licensure and the use of academic credentials in the labor market. If academic institutions decide not to seek changes in the licensing field, then it becomes incumbent upon them to ensure that possession of their degrees is a true mark of competence as a practitioner.

Insurance Companies

Instead of their current reliance on academic credentials and licensing, insurance companies should experiment with a variety of methods for determining whether a practitioner's services are reimbursable under health insurance policies. Specifically, they should move toward competency-based measurements, and they should also reimburse services performed by paraprofessionals when performed in suitable settings. To encourage client responsibility and allow greater client choice, insurance companies should allow policyholders to visit a number of therapists before making a final decision on with whom they will continue.

The Public and Consumer

Both the public and the consumer must assume responsibility for developments in the mental health field. In addition, they must begin to recognize the limits that exist in the field, what is known and not known, and what can be done when dissatisfied or harmed in the therapeutic process. This means the formation of organized groups to take political action. It means that the individual patients must take responsibility to make detailed inquiries into the pertinent background of their therapists.

The Practitioner

One of the purposes of regulation is to minimize potential harm to the public. Individual practitioners can do much on their own to forestall this possibility. Oden (1974: 6) recommends, first of all, that practitioners have "less *hubris*, [and] more self-critical awareness of their own

limitations." Second, practitioners must be aware that whatever success they have may not be due to the skills and knowledge they believe are the causative agents.[64] Rather than assuming their license or academic degree constitutes sufficient proof of competence, practitioners must establish their own feedback mechanisms and methods of evaluating their work. An essential vehicle is client evaluation, as well as the judgment of one's peers. An excellent method of obtaining an outside perspective of one's work is through group practice, periodic supervision, and case discussions. To assist clients in their choice of therapists, practitioners should develop their own disclosure forms. Many other recommendations made in this chapter are quite capable of being implemented by practitioners on their own. Where possible, this should be done.

CONCLUSION

This study of professional regulation has drawn upon social science research to evaluate the impact and effectiveness of traditional means of regulation, such as licensing. Especially in the field of psychotherapy, it does not appear that traditional methods are likely to be effective. Current licensing laws do not appear to have entrance requirements related to competent practice and do little to discipline unethical or incompetent practitioners. In addition, evidence is mounting that they produce unwanted side effects, including a substantial increase in the cost of services. When a profession is in its early stages of development, as is the case with psychotherapy, the problems created by traditional methods become even more severe. Only when a profession is clearly defined in its field of practice and has standards of practice that are both consensually agreed upon and empirically verified is it likely that restrictive licensing laws will prove constructive.

The recommendations presented in this chapter are intended to suggest improvements and to offer an alternative to existing laws. They emphasize the importance of regulating output, not input. They focus on education of the public and the importance of developing consumer skills in evaluating professional services. In addition to the critical task of protecting the public through effective disciplinary methcnisms, these proposals attempt to protect and encourage diversity in the types of therapeutic services available. Although aimed specifically at the mental health field, these ideas will hopefully find applicability in other professions as well.

NOTES

1. Tancredi and Woods (1972) term this type of regulation "output monitoring." They believe that the advent of the computer makes it possible to determine the output of professional care with reasonable accuracy. What needs to occur is an operational definition of health and then accurate measurement of which professional practices lead to improved health. Tancredi and Woods believe that such a system is conceivable for the entire health care field and that it will make licensure obsolete. They also believe that such a system will have a dramatic effect on consumer protection, will lead to a breakdown of the artificial separation of nurses, physicians, and allied health personnel, and will lead to dramatic changes in medical education.

2. The following individuals, organizations, and agencies have also developed guidelines for the licensing of professions and occupations: Council of State Governments (1952: 57-63); Gellhorn (1956: 144-51); Minnesota Department of Health (1976); Monaghan (1961); New Jersey Professional and Occupational Licensing Study Commission (1971).

3. Combs (1953: 562) goes on to argue that "attempts to define psychotherapy on the basis of what is done to the client universally fail," and that psychotherapy, although thought of as a medical specialty, is more akin to the educational process:

> The purpose of this "therapeutic relationship" is to assist the client to a more effective and satisfying way of life for himself and those about him. This means that psychotherapy is essentially a teaching relationship or, if one prefers it so, a situation designed to help a client learn. Psychotherapy is, then, a learning situation in which a therapist seeks to help his client to explore and discover a better way of life. Interestingly enough, this is exactly what education attempts to do, too. Education also seeks through a relationship between teacher and student to assist the pupil to find a better way of life. It is extremely difficult to effectively separate individual therapy from group therapy or group therapy from education. To do this with the degree of exactitude required for inclusion in a licensing law seems clearly impossible.

4. See, for instance, Woltmann (1949: 32) ("It is impossible to give a comprehensive definition of what constitutes psychotherapy. Any definition will depend upon the aims and purposes which various schools of psychology have considered as their theoretical and practical tools"); Welsch (in Welsch et al., 1956: 39) ("I suspect that in our present stage of development no simple declarative sentence can encompass the sum total of goal-directed interacting processes between patient and therapist that we include within the meaning of psychotherapy"); Parloff (1970: 295) ("Psychotherapy cannot be defined either by evidence of its unique effects or by its professionally specialized and restricted techniques"); Oden (1975: 76) ("How can you train someone rigorously in something that cannot be defined?"); Leifer (1969): 155 ("How can a professional group regulate an activity it is unable to define . . . ? The answer, obviously, is that it cannot").

For the problems involved in defining psychology, see Goode (1960); New York State Department of Mental Hygiene (1956: 1928); Saffir (1950); Shakow (1969: 191).

Leifer (1969: 155) notes that "Psychiatrists . . . are unable to agree on a definition of psychotherapy." And he comments further that "after four years of deliberation, a committee of the American Psychoanalytic Association found it impossible to find a definition of psychoanalysis that would be acceptable to a sufficiently large group of Association members (Leifer, 1969: 155)".

The problem is even more severe for encounter groups. Massarik (1972: 68) states flatly that "nobody knows what *the* encounter group really is. At least the lack of agreement on definition is very evident as the human potential movement in its multiplex manifestations, the National Training Laboratories, and its offspring, variously committed humanistic psychologists, and a wide range of psychotherapists converge from all directions on a suddenly ubiquitous encounter group concept."

5. In 1955 the Joint Committees on Legislation of the American Psychological Association (APA and COSL, 1955: 738 and 754) and all state psychological associations had this to say about licensure:

In effect, it would say "anyone doing these things is, *ipso-facto*, practicing psychology no matter what he calls himself and comes under the purview of the law." Such a law requires a comprehensive and precise definition of the practice of the profession and prohibits such activities by anyone but persons granted the license or certificate under the law. This is the pattern of most medical practice acts which begin with a definition of practice and restrict to licensed physicians the exclusive right to engage in such practices. Many psychological practices are engaged in by large numbers of people outside the profession. The Council of Representatives of the American Psychological Association adopted a policy against restrictive legislation for psychology on the grounds that psychology must not interfere with the legitimate use of psychological methods and techniques by other professions.

FOR THE TIME BEING, STATES SEEKING LEGISLATION REGULATING THE PRACTICE OF PSYCHOLOGY SHOULD ATTEMPT TO DEVELOP LAWS FALLING IN THE CATEGORY OF NONRESTRICTIVE LEGISLATION BY TITLE ONLY, OR BY TITLE AND FUNCTION (WITH A GENERAL RATHER THAN A SPECIFIC DEFINITION).

6. Twelve years after coming out against licensing laws restricting practice, the APA (1967: 1097) reaffirmed that such legislation was unwise: "We are opposed to such restrictions on the grounds that many psychological methods, practices and activities are engaged in by large numbers of individuals and groups who are not psychologists." Nonetheless, the APA (1967: 1098) went on to recommend that "states seeking legislation regulating the practice of psychology should attempt to develop laws falling in the category of licensing legislation," and such legislation would have a definition of psychology that was "as broad as possible, in order to cover all activities of psychology as psychologists."

7. See the history of licensing laws contained in Volume II of this series.

8. Strupp (in Bergin and Strupp, 1972: 434–35) provides an historical viewpoint on the change in meaning that the term "psychotherapy" has undergone:

Originally conceptualized as a form of medical treatment, the meaning of the term psychotherapy has become increasingly fuzzy and more than ever defies precise definition. Diverse human interactions, from individual psychotherapy to encounter groups, from aversive conditioning in the laboratory to token economies in mental hospitals are subsumed under the heading of psychotherapy or under the new rubric, behavior modification. To characterize the field as chaotic is hardly an exaggeration.

9. Unfortunately the commission felt that the services of psychologists were of an order different from marriage counselors and did not recommend delicensing, despite the fact that the definitional problem is exactly the same.

10. In a recent report to the California legislature, the Assembly Subcommittee on Health Personnel (Cal. Assembly Comm. on Health and Welfare, 1976: 4-7) came to virtually these same conclusions about the licensing of sex therapists and counselors.

11. Here is what Combs (1953: 558) has to say about the matter:

In a human relationship, just when is a person harmed? How can you prove it? These are difficult questions to answer for the plain fact of the matter is that people are helped by the damndest things. Almost anything may help people to behave more effectively or to feel happier given the right circumstances. Who is to say that a particular idea taught to a client was an act of quackery, especially if the clients swears it was helpful? Much of the business of human relations is carried on through no more than what one person says to another. It is doubtful if we shall ever seriously want to control such intercourse in a free, democratic society. The cure could well prove more fatal than the disease.

12. To the extent that the public is convinced of the special value of using licensed practitioners, and to the extent that government and institutional jobs are dependent upon state certification, restricting only the use of certain titles may well have the same degree of negative impact as licensing laws that restrict practice to those who possess certain credentials.

13. Although the use of broad phrases was originally thought to "facilitate the necessary expansion and accretion of functions over time" (Duke University, 1970: 10), it has created problems in the use of paraprofessionals and has infringed on the rights of related professions.

14. The issues and problems involved in delegating professional functions, along with recommendations, are discussed in the following: Carlson (1970); Cohen and Dean (1974); Duke University (1970); Roemer (1970); Sadler (1974); Tancredi and Woods (1972); U.S. National Advisory Commission on Health Manpower (1967: II, Appendix VII); *Yale Law Journal* (1974a). See also American Hospital Association (1971); American Medical Association, Nat'l Cong. on Health Manpower (1970); U.S. DHEW (1971).

15. Indications exist that the recent attempts by the medical profession to amend the medical practices acts to allow for delegation of functions to assistants have not led to significant improvements:

During the past six years many states have abandoned the "explicit definition" form of statute in favor of more flexible statutory schemes. . . . Despite their broad rulemaking authority, however, the majority of . . . boards have not permitted substantially more responsibility to auxiliaries than was allowed under the older, "special-listing" statutes. As a result, a wide range of expanded functions, which can be safely and efficiently performed by properly-trained auxiliaries, remains legally off-limits to these paraprofessionals. [*Yale Law Journal*, 1974a: 813-14 footnotes omitted.]

16. The advantages and disadvantages of proficiency testing and educational equivalency measures are discussed in AMA, CHMP (1970); Coleman (1970); Egelston (1970); Shimberg et al. (1972); U.S. DHEW (1975; 1973: 33-37, 1971: 53-56, 75). Most of these recommend the use of proficiency testing or educational equivalency measures.

17. Educational equivalency measures provide an excellent method for licensing boards to get around the problem of academic degrees that must be obtained from accredited programs.

18. For discussions of the lack of usefulness of accreditation and the negative effects it can engender, see Bergstrom and Olson (1975); Dickey and Miller (1972); Kaplin and Hunter (1966); Levitov (1976); Moskowitz (1977); National Commission on Accrediting (1972, 1971); Olson (1977); Study Commission on Undergraduate Education and the Education of Teachers (1976).

19. For discussions of the advantages and disadvantages of such standards, see AMA, CHP (1970); Maslow (1971); New Jersey (1971: 42); Rayack (1975: 158); Roemer (1970; 1970: 56); Tancredi and Woods (1972: 104); U.S. DHEW (1971: 73).

20. As mentioned earlier, one of the more interesting, if somewhat questionable, requirements is the necessity of commercial photographers in Georgia submitting to a Wasserman test (Gellhorn, 1956: 125).

21. For continuing education requirements in those professions involving psychotherapy, see the relevant sections of Volume II. For the most current data on the medical profession, see recent issues of the *State Health Legislation Report* published by the American Medical Association. For information on other professions, see Watkins (1977).

22. This is somewhat ironic, since this argument calls into question the entire licensure system itself although professional associations do not seem to recognize this fact.

23. In the medical field, specialty licensing has been traditional in most countries (Roemer, 1968). It is only the United Kingdom and the United States that allow physicians to practice any branch of medicine. In both England and the United States specialty certification is a function of nongovernment organizations.

24. The following articles and books provide representative analyses of the problems involved in disciplinary enforcement: ABA Spec. Comm. on Eval. of Disc. Enforcement (1970); Carlin (1966); Curran (1966); Derbyshire (1965); Gifford (1971); Jervey (1961); Lieberman (1978, 1977, 1970); Marsh (1972); Rayack (1975).

25. Lieberman (1978) presents a strong case suggesting that most disciplinary provisions in the licensing field are designed to protect the profession more than the public. Carlin (1966) provides empirical support for this proposition in the legal field.

26. Shimberg, Esser, and Kruger, (1972: 230) comment:

> The concept that income derived from licensing fees should pay for the operation of the licensing program is objectionable. If licensing is supposed to protect the public, then the public should pay for the cost of implementing a sound licensing program. Licensing fees should not be thought of as a special tax to be levied on practitioners of an occupation. Moreover, if a legislature has decreed that it is in the public interest that practitioners be licensed, how can it then declare that licensing shall be carried out only if there is a sufficient number of candidates to support the cost of testing and other program operations? The folly of this rationale is exemplified by the decision of one board to stop giving examinations to a particular group because there had not been a sufficient number of applicants during the previous year to cover the cost of preparing and administering the test.

27. This recommendation may not work unless properly funded. In Rhode Island, for instance, centralization has not increased the efficiency of the Division of Professional Regulation because adequate investigative staff were not hired (Rayack, 1975: 132).

28. Because past history has demonstrated that licensing boards dominated by professionals from the field licensed operate in a fashion inimical to the public interest, a number of persons believe that public members should control the board, with practitioners serving only in an advisory capacity. See, for instance, Lieberman (1970: 251-54); Phelan (1974: 48-50); Rayack (1975: 158). Others have recommended that there should be more lay representatives, although not recommending domination. See, for instance, American Hospital Association (1971: 11-12); American Medical Association Council on Health Manpower (1970: 5); Gellhorn (1956: 140-44); New Jersey (1971: 7); Shimberg, Esser, and Kruger, (1972: 230-31); U.S. DHEW (1973: 55).

29. A similar recommendation was made concerning the medical profession in the well-known Truman Report, developed by the American Medical Association's Committee on Medical Practices (1955: 854).

30. Through press releases and newspaper articles Morton Schillinger (1974), executive director of the New York State Psychological Association, attempted to educate the residents of New York state on the dangers of encounter groups and nonlicensed psychotherapists, as well as to inform the public of the existence of growth centers using practitioners with bogus doctoral degrees from diploma mills. He did not feel that anything significant was accomplished. Curran (1974) believes that the media is not a good vehicle

for educating the public, since newspapers and television are overly concerned with exposés and exciting stories.

31. The Joint Commission on Mental Illness and Health (1961: 16) cites studies indicating that the number of articles on mental illness, psychiatry, and psychology has not increased in relation to articles on other subjects, and that people have a very difficult time in recalling medical news related to mental illness or other psychological items in the media.

32. The Joint Commission on Mental Illness and Health (1961: 74) found that "the general public regards the mentally ill with fear, distruct, and dislike." Psychologists, psychiatrists, and psychoanalysts were regarded with moderately favorable attitudes, but those health professionals who treated physical problems were held in much higher esteem. Apparently any word containing "psych" to some extent stigmatizes the practitioner as well as the patient.

As long ago as 1946, in a survey of various areas of Illinois, New Jersey, New York, and Pennsylvania, more than half of those questioned believed that psychologists were licensed in their state (Guest, 1948: 138), although only Connecticut had passed such legislation at the time.

33. An examination of the uses involved in conducting research and excellent proposals as to what research ought to be conducted on the effectiveness of psychotherapy can be found in the following sources: Bergin (1971: 256–63); Bergin and Strupp (1972); Joint Commission on Mental Illness and Health (1961: 193–244); Kiesler (1966); Malan (1975); Meehl (1955); Paul (1967); Rickard (1962); Strupp and Bergin (1969); Truax and Mitchell (1971); U.S. National Institute of Mental Health (1975).

34. For descriptions and analyses of the potential problems and value of PSROs, see Anderson (1976); Ball (1976); Etzioni (1974); Gosfield (1975); Havighurst and Blumstein (1975); Segal (1974); Simmons and Ball (1975); Sullivan (1976).

35. For representative law review articles discussing the void-for-vagueness doctrine, see Aigler (1923); Collings (1955); *Harvard Law Review* (1948); *Indiana Law Journal* (1948); *University of Pennsylvania Law Review* (1960).

36. The fifth amendment reads in part, "no person shall be . . . deprived of life, liberty, or property, without due process of law." § 1, V, U.S. Const. The relevant section of the fourteenth amendment reads, "nor shall any State deprive any person of life, liberty, or property, without due process of law. . . ." § 1, XIV, U.S. Const.

37. The basis for invalidation has been said to be that:

The courts [must also] have standards set forth for them in the statute sufficiently definite to enable them to administer justice in accordance with the intent of the legislature. Otherwise the courts would be left in a definitional quandary, the solution of which the principal of the separation of powers denies to the judiciary since it would entail legislating, [Kayton, 1959: 256 (footnotes omitted).]

38. A *University of Pennsylvania Law Review* (1960: 67, 70–71, footnotes omitted) Note has portrayed the problem graphically:

There are places in the law through which a pair of mutually oblivious doctrines run in infinitely parallel contrariety, like a pair of poolhall scoring racks one or the other of which, seemingly at random, cases get hung up. Such is the area of those Supreme Court decisions which purport to turn on the issue of "unconstitutional uncertainty." . . . .

Line-drawing is the nature of the judicial process, constrained as it is to reach some categorical result in each of a series of cases along a continuum. But while the propriety of placing the line at a particular point may not be rationally demonstrable, in the usual line-drawing area judicial opinions do articulate the countervailing pressures which require that a line be drawn somewhere, do explore the considerations which delimit, on either side, at least the broad range within which it must be drawn, and do relate these considerations to the facts of the individual case. Such is not the situation, however, with regard to the void-for-vagueness decisions. What gives these decisions their pool-rack-hung-up appearance is their almost habitual lack of informing reasoning.

39. In *State ex rel. Beck v. Gleason* (1938), for instance, the court upheld a statute licensing osteopathic physicians, although the statute only defined osteopathy as that which is taught in "recognized" osteopathy schools. It stated that the law was not void for uncertainty.

40. Irving Kayton (1959: 261-62, footnotes omitted), writing in the *St. John's Law Review*, has concluded:

This is a constitutional no-man's land; there is no satisfactory general rule. . . . If, as in New York, the members of the organized psychiatric, psychoanalytic, psychological, and related disciplines cannot agree on the definition of the practice of psychology or psychological services, then we are led reasonably to deduce that at least at this time in that particular jurisdiction a definition cannot be formulated which is constitutionally sound. Under such conditions, at least, the dictates of common sense require that the legislature abstain from any attempt to regulate the practice of psychology either by licensing. . . . The legislature may not and cannot exclude individuals from an area of activity when the legislature itself cannot ascertain the nature or bounds of the area.

On the other hand, an early Note on the regulation of psychological counseling and psychotherapy in the *Columbia Law Review* (1951: 486-87, footnotes omitted) argued:

It might be contended that the phrase "recognized principles, methods, and procedures of the science and profession of psychology" is unconstitutionally vague. Although professional disagreement exists as to correct psychological theory, however, it seems possible to determine the various methods commonly employed by competent psychologists. The statute forbids non-licensed persons to engage in professional counseling, interviewing, and administering of tests, and would therefore appear to offer adequate guidance to professionals and nonprofessionals alike. Thus, the two purposes for which due process requires clarity in the definition of criminally proscribed activities are satisfied: adequate warning to those who may be affected is afforded, and the courts are enable to adjudicate the rights and duties created by the statute.

41. The concept of economic due process is discussed in the following: Albertsworth (1926); Fellman (1941); Friedman (1965); Fulda (1973); Gellhorn (1956); Grant (1942); Gunther (1972); Hanft and Hamrick (1938); Hetherington (1958, 1958a); Kikel (1946); Knudsen (1949); McCloskey (1962); Mitchell (1957); Pound (1909); *Yale Law Journal* (1974a).

42. Milton Friedman (1962: 144) writes that:

The only way that I can see to offset special producer groups is to establish a general presumption against the state undertaking certain kinds of activities. Only if there is a general recognition that governmental activities should be severely limited with respect to a class of cases, can the burden of proof be put strongly enough on those who would depart from this general presumption to give a reasonable hope of limiting the spread of special measures to further special interests. This point is one we have adverted to time and again. It is of a piece with the argument for the Bill of Rights and for a rule to govern monetary policy and fiscal policy.

Lieberman (1970: 243-44) reinforces this point:

When the injunction of *Munn v. Illinois* becomes unworkable—when, that is, the people cannot find a remedy at the polls for abuse of legislative power because the legislation complained of itself hinders the development of countervailing political power—the Court must act to repair the balance of power between important competing interests. So with occupational licensing and professional power over fellow practitioners: Legislatures are politically unable to withstand the producer onslaught. In order to redress the balance between expert and layman, it is necessary for the Supreme Court to embark on at least a limited judicial revolution in yet another area: The power of producers must be balanced by setting limits on its exercise. The Court cannot order consumer groups into being, or demand their representation in the legislature, but it can bring consumer power onto the same field as producer power by restricting the scope of the latter.

43. The concept that statutory rules must bear some rational relation with the purposes for which the statute was designed has received considerable discussion. For a sample of analyses involving professional and occupational licensing, see AMA Law Department (1967); Fulda (1973); Grant (1942, 1942a); Hanft and Hamrick (1938); Hetherington (1958); Knudsen (1949); Rebell (undated); *Virginia Law Review* (1973); *Wake Forest Law Review* (1973); White (undated).

44. On the other hand, the courts have upheld statutes, even though they went beyond what was necessary or did not bring about the result that was intended (e.g., *Roschen v. Ward* [1929]).

45. For a further elaboration of the nondelegation doctrine, see Davis (1972: 1-52); Friendly (1962); Gellhorn and Byse (1974: 58-108).

46. Kayton (1959: 257) argues that such statutes should be struck down as "prima facie . . . an unconstitutional delegation of legislative power to an administrative agency." The basis for his argument is that no satisfactory legal definition of psychological services is possible, and hence board-definitions of what constitutes proper experience amount to a usurping of the law-making function of the legislature.

47. Judge J. Skelly Wright (1972: 582) has commented:

Today, most scholars rank the nondelegation doctrine together with substantive due process, nullification, and common law forms of action as arcane notions which inexplicably fascinated an earlier generation but which were given the decent burials they deserved long ago.

48. The doctrine, in so far as it would apply to professional licensing boards, has been succinctly stated in a *Virginia Law Review* (1973: 1111) article:

Given the reduced role of the delegation doctrine's emphasis on statutory standards, courts should feel more compelled than in the past to require greater specificity in the regulations of licensing boards. The expert composition of the board, justifying as it does the demise of the delegation doctrine, also makes it eminently reasonable to demand a higher degree of specificity in the rules promulgated. If boards desire to punish certain marginal activities as unprofessional, courts should require that specific rules be promulgated. Only when a licensee has by his actions shown himself to be a severe threat to the public should a board be permitted to assert its authority through vaguely defined regulations.

49. On the other hand, in *National Psychological Association v. University of New York* (1960), New York's highest court ruled that these types of delegatory provisions were not unconstitutional (see also *Packer v. Board of Behavioral Science* Examiners [1975]).

50. For representative articles discussing the applicability of civil rights laws to employment testing, see Anderson and Rogers (1970); Bartnoff (1973); *Columbia Law Review* (1972); Drexler (1972); *Harvard Law Review* (1975a); Huff (1974); Johnson (1976); Wilson (1972); *Yale Law Journal* (1974).

51. See Hill (1964), Cooper et al. (1975), and Cooper and Sobel (1969) for discussions of these laws.

52. The following articles discuss the potential applicability of antidiscrimination laws to state licensing boards: Bartnoff (1973); Huff (1974); Rankin (1976); U.S. DOJ, DOL,

and Civil Service Commission (1977); U.S. EEOCC (1975); White (undated); White and Francis (1976).

53. The relevant federal statutes are the Sherman Act (26 Stat. 209 [1890]) and the Clayton Antitrust Act (38 Stat. 731 [1914]), which are part of the general law against monopolies and combinations in restraint of trade (15 U.S.C. § § 1-31 [1970]).

54. At the state level antitrust laws appear in some state constitutions (see, for example, Art. 41 of the Md. Decl. of Rts.), while others have been enacted as statutory law (see, for example, Cal. Bus. and Prof. Code § 16720 [West, 1964], or Wis. Stat. Ann. § 133.01 [Supp. 1973]).

55. Several law review articles deal directly with the possibility of applying antitrust laws to professional licensing agencies, including Donnem (1970); Ellis (1973); Freedenberg (1975); Jones (1975); and Stolar (1976).

56. For discussions of this exemption, how it arose, and its advisability, see Adam (1975); Bauer (1975); Coleman (1967); *Texas Tech Law Review* (1974); *University of Florida Law Review* (1974).

57. Whether professional activities are "trade or commerce" within the antitrust laws is considered in Adam (1975); Gaither (1973); *New York University Law Review* (1974); Sennett (1976); *Texas Law Review* (1975); *Yale Law Journal* (1972).

58. The concept of certain professional activities as constituting "valid state action" is discussed in Delahunty (1974); Dusenberg (1970); Etheridge (1975); Handler (1976); *Harvard Law Review* (1976); Simmons and Forniciari (1974); Slater (1974); *University of Pennsylvania Law Review* (1971); *Utah Law Review* (1975).

59. See *Boston University Law Review* (1963); Donnem (1970); *Harvard Law Review* (1975); Holzer (1975); Jacobs (1975); Saveri (1970); Teply (1974); *Texas Law Review* (1975); Tustin (1967).

60. For information on, and discussions of, these suits, see Engman (1974); Mathews (1976); Randal (1975); U.S. FTC (1975); *U.S. News and World Report* (1976).

61. Colorado and Florida were two of the first states in the nation to adopt these laws. For the particular provisions of the Colorado law, see Act of April 22, 1976, Ch. 115, Colo. Sess. Laws (1976). For Florida, see Fla. Stat. Ann. § 11.61 (West Cum. Supp. 1977). For a sample of other laws, see Hawaii Senate Bill 460, Ninth Legislature, 1977; and 1977 Oreg. Laws, Ch. 842 (Enrolled H.B. 2511).

62. The center's executive director, Paul Pottinger, is focusing on licensing in the professions and occupations, with a strong emphasis on the negative impact created by current testing procedures. The center's goal is to increase access to and mobility within professions. Established with an enabling grant from the M.A. Rooney Foundation, it is a nonprofit research and information center. Its monthly newsletter, *Pro Forum*, is a valuable and up-to-date source of information related to professional regulation.

63. Members of the legislative committees of these groups, along with the executive director of the National Center for Study of the Professions, met at the annual meeting of the Association for Creative Change to plan strategies for collective action to improve current licensing laws and to enact a model psychotherapy bill.

64. In their study of encounter group leaders, Lieberman, Yalom, and Miles (1973: 428) found that group leaders had very little idea of why they were successful:

> The implication in our view is that our research demonstrates that there are factors influencing change which occur in the substratum of the group outside of the leader's level of awareness. Given their invisibility, it is not surprising that these factors have not been appreciated in most leadership approaches. Indeed most leaders have fashioned their style and their theory of change from their personal observations of their groups; clinical style has rarely been influenced by research findings. Exceedingly competent leaders may be unaware of significant factors responsible for their success. And the process does not end there. Many highly successful leaders assume a responsibility to transmit their techniques to others. The result is that they establish training institutes in which they teach their techniques as they conceptualize them, and fail to

pass on their intuitive, unconscious utilization of the psychosocial factors which bear on their success. Too often these teachers transmit only epiphenomenal behavioral characteristics which are idiosyncratic and irrelevant or insufficient to explain that leader's effective outcome.

REFERENCES

Books and Articles

Adam, K. "Trade Regulation: The Legal Profession and the Antitrust Laws—Sherman Act Application to Minimum Fee Schedules." *Washburn Law Journal*, 1975, v. 14, pp. 420–28.

Adams, S., and Orger, M. *Through the Mental Health Maze: A Consumer's Guide To Finding a Psychotherapist, Including a Sample Consumer/Therapist Contract.* Washington, D.C.: Health Research Group, 1975.

Aigler, R.W. "Legislation in Vague or General Terms." *Michigan Law Review*, 1923, v. 21, pp. 831–51.

Albertsworth, E.F. "Constitutional Law—Validity of Act Requiring License of Public Accountants—Limitations on the Police Power." *Illinois Law Review*, 1926, v. 21, pp. 269–73.

American Bar Association, Special Committee on Evaluation of Disciplinary Enforcement. *Problems and Recommendations in Disciplinary Enforcement.* Chicago: American Bar Association, 1970.

American Hospital Association, Special Committee on Licensure of Health Personnel. *Statement on Licensure of Health Care Personnel.* (Approved by AHA, November 18, 1970.) Chicago: American Hospital Association, 1971.

American Medical Association, Committee on Medical Practices. "Report to the Board of Trustees of the American Medical Association of the Committee on Medical Practices, November 1954." *Northwest Medicine*, 1955, v. 54, pp. 844–59.

American Medical Association, Council on Health Manpower. *Licensure of Health Occupations.* (Adopted by AMA House of Delegates.) Chicago: American Medical Association, 1970.

American Medical Association, Law Department. *Disciplinary Digest: Court Decisions in Regard to Disciplinary Actions by State Boards of Medical Examiners.* Chicago: American Medical Association, 1967.

American Medical Association, National Congress on Health Manpower. *Expanding the Supply of Health Services in the 1970's.* (Sponsored by The Council on Health Manpower.) Chicago: American Medical Association, 1970.

American Psychological Association, Committee on Legislation. "A Model for State Legislation Affecting the Practice of Psychology, 1967: Report of APA Committee on Legislation." *American Psychologist*, 1967, v. 22, pp. 1095–103.

American Psychological Association and Conference of State Psychological Associations, Committees on Legislation. "Joint Report of the APA and CSPA Committees on Legislation." *American Psychologist*, 1955, v. 10, pp. 727–56.

Anderson, B.R., and Rogers, M.P. (Eds.) *Personnel Testing and Equal Employment Opportunity.* Washington, D.C.: U.S. Government Printing Office, 1970.

Anderson, O.W. "PSROs, the Medical Profession, and the Public Interest." *Milbank Memorial Fund Quarterly*, 1976, v. 54, pp. 379–88.

Asher, J. "Are MA's Undermining Professional Psychology?" *APA Monitor*, March 1974, pp. 4–5.

Ball, J.R. "Quality of Care Through PSRO." *Journal of Legal Medicine*, 1976, v. 4(8), pp. 17–21.

Bartnoff, J. "Title VII and Employment Discrimination in 'Upper Level' Jobs." *Columbia Law Review*, 1973, v. 73, pp. 1614–40.

Bauer, J.P. "Professional Activities and the Antitrust Laws." *Notre Dame Lawyer*, 1975, v. 50, pp. 570-602.

Bergin, A.E. "The Evaluation of Therapeutic Outcomes." In A.E. Bergin and S.L. Garfield (Eds.), *Handbook of Psychotherapy and Behavior Change: An Empirical Analysis*. New York: John Wiley, 1971, pp. 217-70.

Bergin, A.E., and Strupp, H.H. *Changing Frontiers in the Science of Psychotherapy*. Chicago: Aldine-Atherton, 1972.

Bergstrom, R., and Olson, P.A. *A Time Half Dead at the Top: The Professional Societies and the Reform of Schooling in America—1955-75*. Lincoln, Nebr.: Study Commission on Undergraduate Education and the Education of Teachers, 1975.

Blackstone, Sir W. *Commentaries on the Laws of England*. (Edited by B.C. Gavit; from the Abridged Edition of William Hardcastle Browne.) Washington, D.C.: Washington Law Book, 1941.

Blanck, G.S. "The Development of Psychotherapy as a Profession: A Study of the Process of Professionalization." Ph.D. dissertation, New York University, 1963. Abstracted in *Dissertation Abstracts*, 1963, v. 24(07), p. 2974.

Boston University Law Review. "An Application of the Federal Anit-Trust Laws to a State Authority." *Boston University Law Review*, 1963, v. 43, pp. 541-555.

California, Assembly Committee on Health and Welfare. "Final Report on Sex Therapy and Counseling Licensure in California." Mimeographed. Sacramento, Calif., July 1976.

Carlin, J.E. *Lawyers' Ethics: A Survey of the New York City Bar*. New York: Russell Sage Foundation, 1966.

Carlson, R.J. *The End of Medicine*. New York: John Wiley, 1975.

Carlson, R.J. "Health Manpower Licensing and the Emerging Institutional Responsibility for the Quality of Care." *Law and Contemporary Problems*, 1970, v. 35, pp. 849-78.

Carmichael, H.T. "Self-Assessment Tests: The Psychiatric Knowledge and Skills Self-Assessment Program." *Journal of the American Medical Association*, 1970, v. 213, pp. 1656-57.

Clark, D. Personal communication, May 20, 1974.

Cohen, H.S., and Dean, W.J. "To Practice or Not to Practice: Developing State Law and Policy of Physician's Assistants." *Milbank Memorial Fund Quarterly*, 1974, v. 52, pp. 349-76.

Coleman, F.C. "Licensure Problems of Allied Health Personnel." *Federation Bulletin*, 1970, v. 57, pp. 204-13.

Coleman, J.E., Jr. "Antitrust Exemptions: Learned Professions." *American Bar Association Antitrust Law Journal*, 1967, v. 33, pp. 48-55.

Collings, R.A., Jr. "Unconstitutional Uncertainty—An Appraisal." *Cornell Law Quarterly*, 1955, v. 40, pp. 195-237.

Columbia Law Review. "Employment Testing: The Aftermath of *Griggs vs. Duke Power Co.*" *Columbia Law Review*, 1972, v. 72, pp. 900-25.

Columbia Law Review. "Regulation of Psychological Counseling and Psychotherapy." *Columbia Law Review*, 1951, v. 51, pp. 474-95.

Combs, A.W. "Problems and Definitions in Legislation." *American Psychologist*, 1953, v. 8, pp. 554-63.

Council of State Governments. *Occupational Licensing Legislation in the States: A Study of State Legislation Licensing the Practice of Professions and Other Occupations*. Chicago: Council of State Governments, 1952.

Curran, W.J. Personal communication, July 8, 1974.

Curran, W.J. "New Paramedical Personnel—To License or Not To License." *New England Journal of Medicine*, 1970, v. 282, pp. 1085-86.

Curran, W.J. "Legal Regulation and Quality Control of Medical Practice under the British Health Service." *New England Journal of Medicine*, 1966, v. 274, pp. 547-57.

Davis, K.C. *Administrative Law Text.* (3rd ed.) St. Paul, Minn.: West Publishing Co., 1972.

Delahunty, R.C. *"New Mexico v. American Petrofina*—State Immunity from Sherman Act Liability—More Confusion of *Parker." Utah Law Review,* 1974, v. 1974, pp. 592-602.

Derbyshire, R.C. "What Should the Profession Do About the Incompetent Physician?" *Journal of the American Medical Association,* 1965, v. 194, pp. 1287-90.

Dickey, F.G., and Miller, J.W. *A Current Perspective on Accreditation.* Washington, D.C.: American Association for Higher Education, 1972.

Donnem, R.W. "Federal Anti-trust Laws Versus Anticompetitive State Regulation." *Antitrust Law Journal,* 1970, v. 39, pp. 950-67.

Drexler, J.A. "Fair Employment Practices: The Concept of Business Necessity." *Memphis State Law Review,* 1972, v. 3, pp. 76-91.

Duesenberg, R.H. "The Antitrust State Approved Transaction Exemption." *Valparaiso University Law Review,* 1970, v. 4, pp. 239-60.

Duke University, Department of Community Health Services. "Model Legislation Project for Physician's Assistants." Mimeographed. Durham, N.C., 1970.

Egelston, E.M. "Licensure and Career Mobility." *Hospitals,* December 1, 1970, pp. 42-46.

Ellis, K.C. "Antitrust Law: An Application of the Sherman Act to the Professions." *University of Florida Law Review,* 1973, v. 25, pp. 740-62.

Engman, L.A. "A Critical Report on Government Regulation." *U.S. News and World Report,* November 4, 1974, pp. 81-82.

Etheridge, K.C. "Antitrust Law—Governmental Action Immunity—Should State Presence Alone Be Sufficient to Justify the Exemption?" *Mercer Law Review,* 1975, v. 26, pp. 995-1001.

Etzioni, A. "PSRO: A Poor Mechanism and a Possible Alternative." *American Journal of Public Health,* 1974, v. 64, pp. 415 and 507-8.

Federal Register,/vol. 43 (166), pp. 38290-315 August 25, 1978.

Fellman, D. "A Case Study in Administrative Law—The Regulation of Barbers." *Washington University Law Quarterly,* 1941, v. 26, pp. 213-42.

Forgotson, E.H., and Cook, J.L. "Innovations and Experiments in the Uses of Health Manpower—the Effect of Licensure Laws." *Law and Contemporary Problems,* 1967, v. 32, pp. 731-50.

Frank, J.D. *Persuasion and Healing: A Comparative Study of Psychotherapy.* (Rev. ed.) Baltimore, Md.: Johns Hopkins Press, 1973.

Freedenberg, H. "The Sherman Act and Bar Admission Residence Requirements." *University of Michigan Journal of Law Reform,* 1975, v. 8, pp. 615-45.

Freud, S. *The Question of Lay Analysis: Conversations with an Impartial Person.* (Translated and edited by J. Strachey.) New York: W.W. Norton, 1950.

Friedman, L.M. "Freedom of Contract and Occupational Licensing 1890-1910: A Legal and Social Study." *California Law Review,* 1965, v. 53, pp. 487-534.

Friedman, M. *Capitalism and Freedom.* Chicago: University of Chicago Press, 1962.

Friendly, H.J. "The Federal Administrative Agencies: The Need for Better Definition of Standards." *Harvard Law Review,* 1962, v. 75, pp. 863-903.

Fulda, C.H. "Controls of Entry into Business and Professions: A Comparative Analysis." *Texas International Law Journal,* 1973, v. 8, pp. 109-36.

Gaither, J.F., Jr. "The Antitrust Division v. The Professions—'No Bidding' Clauses and Fee Schedules." *Notre Dame Lawyer,* 1973, v. 48, pp. 966-77.

Gellhorn, W. *Individual Freedom and Governmental Restraints.* Baton Rouge, La.: Louisiana State University Press, 1956.

Gellhorn, W., and Byse, C. *Administrative Law: Cases and Comments.* (6th ed.) Mineola, N.Y.: Foundation Press, 1974.

Georgiades, P.N. *Petition to the Federal Trade Commission to Promulgate a Trade Regulation Rule to Regulate the Business Practices of the "Psychological Services Industry."* Washington, D.C.: George Washington University Law School, 1976.

Gerty, F.J.; Holloway, J.W.; and MacKay, R.P. "Licensure or Certification of Clinical Psychologists." *Journal of the American Medical Association,* 1952, v. 148, pp. 271-73.

Gifford, D.J. "Communication of Legal Standards, Policy Development, and Effective Conduct Regulation." *Cornell Law Review,* 1971, v. 56, pp. 409-68.

Goldberg, M. "How Good Is Your Doctor?" *Parade Magazine,* March 23, 1975, p. 14.

Goode, W.J. "Encroachment, Charlatanism, and the Emerging Profession: Psychology, Sociology, and Medicine." *American Sociological Review,* 1960, v. 25, pp. 902-14.

Gosfield, A. *PSROs: The Law and the Health Consumer.* Cambridge, Mass.: Ballinger Publishing Co., 1975.

Grant, J.A.C. "The Gild Returns to America: Part I." *Journal of Politics,* 1942, v. 4, pp. 303-36.

Grant, J.A.C. "The Gild Returns to America: Part II." *Journal of Politics,* 1942, v. 4, pp. 458-77.

Guest, L. "The Public's Attitudes Toward Psychologists." *American Psychologist,* 1948, v. 3, pp. 135-39.

Gunther, G. "The Supreme Court 1971 Term—Foreword: In Search of Evolving Doctrine on a Changing Court: A Model for a Newer Equal Protection." *Harvard Law Review,* 1972, v. 86, pp. 1-48.

Handler, M. "The Current Attack on the *Parker v. Brown* State Action Doctrine." *Columbia Law Review,* 1976, v. 76, pp. 1-20.

Hanft, F., and Hamrick, J.N. "Haphazard Regimentation under Licensing Statutes." *North Carolina Law Review,* 1938, v. 12, pp. 1-18.

Harrison, S.I.; Bordin, E.S.; Holt, R.R.; Linford, A.A.; Mudd, E.H.; Slovenko, R.; and Visotsky, H. "The Feasibility of a Model Statute Licensing the Practice of Psychotherapy." *American Journal of Orthopsychiatry,* 1970, v. 40, pp. 558.

Harvard Law Review. "The State Action Exemption and Antitrust Enforcement under the Federal Trade Commission Act." *Harvard Law Review,* 1976, v. 89, pp. 715-51.

Harvard Law Review. "Antitrust Laws—Sherman Act—Sherman Act Is Inapplicable to Acts of State Government." *Harvard Law Review,* 1975, v. 88, pp. 1021-28.

Harvard Law Review. "Beyond the Prima Facie Case in Employment Discrimination Law: Statistical Proof and Rebuttal." *Harvard Law Review,* 1975a, v. 89, pp. 387-422.

Harvard Law Review. "Judicial Control of Actions of Private Associations." *Harvard Law Review,* 1963, v. 76, pp. 983-1100.

Harvard Law Review. "Due Process Requirements of Definiteness in Statutes." *Harvard Law Review,* 1948, v. 62, pp. 77-87.

Havighurst, C.C., and Blumstein, J.F. "Coping with Quality/Cost Trade-offs in Medical Care: The Role of PSROs." *Northwestern University Law Review,* 1975, v. 70, pp. 6-67.

Heck, E.T.; Gomez, A.G.; and Adams, G.L. *A Guide to Mental Health Services.* Pittsburgh, Pa.: University of Pittsburgh Press, 1973.

Hetherington, J.A.C. "State Economic Regulation and Substantive Due Process of Law, Part 1." *Northwestern University Law Review,* 1958, v. 53, pp. 13-32.

Hetherington, J.A.C. "State Economic Regulation and Substantive Due Process of Law, Part 2." *Northwestern University Law Review,* 1958, v. 53, pp. 226-51.

Hodgson, E.L. "Restrictions on Unorthodox Health Treatment in California: A Legal and Economic Analysis." *UCLA Law Review,* 1977, v. 24, pp. 647-96.

Holzer, J.C. "State Immunity from the Antitrust Laws." *Houston Law Review,* 1975, v. 12, pp. 742-50.

Howard J. *Please Touch: A Guided Tour of the Human Potential Movement.* New York: Dell, 1970.

Huff, S. "Credentialing by Tests or by Degrees: Title VII of the Civil Rights Act and *Griggs v. Duke Power Company.*" *Harvard Educational Review,* 1974, v. 44, pp. 246-69.

Indiana Law Journal. "Constitutional Law—Void for Vagueness: An Escape from Statutory Interpretation." *Indiana Law Journal*, 1948, v. 23, pp. 272-85.

Jacobs, L.W. "State Regulation and the Federal Antitrust Laws." *Case Western Reserve Law Review*, 1975, v. 25, pp. 221-57.

Jervey, H.E., Jr. "A Survey of Medical Discipline." *Federation Bulletin*, 1961, v. 48, pp. 83-95.

Johnson, J.G. "Albermarle Paper Company v. Moody: The Aftermath of Griggs and the Death of Employee Testing." *Hastings Law Journal*, 1976, v. 27(6), pp. 1239-62.

Joint Commission on Mental Illness and Health. *Action for Mental Health*. (Final report.) New York: Basic Books, 1961.

Jones, R.T. "Licensing in the USA: Anti-trust Aspects." *New Law Journal*, 1975, v. 125, pp. 625-28.

Kaplin, W.A., and Hunter, J.P. "The Legal Status of the Educational Accrediting Agency: Problems in Judicial Supervision and Governmental Regulation." *Cornell Law Quarterly*, 1966, v. 52, pp. 104-31.

Kayton, I. "Statutory Regulation of Psychologists: Its Scope and Constitutionality." *St. John's Law Review*, 1959, v. 33, pp. 249-63.

Kiesler, D.J. "Some Myths of Psychotherapy Research and the Search for a Paradigm." *Psychological Bulletin*, 1966, v. 65, pp. 110-36.

Kikel, M.J. "Statutory Regulation of Photography." *Rocky Mountain Law Review*, 1946, v. 18, pp. 421-26.

Knudsen, R.A. "Licensing of Professions and Occupations in Nebraska." *Nebraska Law Review*, 1949, v. 29, pp. 146-52.

Kubie, L.S. "The Pros and Cons of a New Profession: A Doctorate in Medical Psychology." *Texas Report on Biology and Medicine*, 1954, v. 12, pp. 692-737. Reprinted in M. Harrower (Ed.), *Medical and Psychological Teamwork in the Care of the Chronically Ill*. Springfield, Ill.: Charles C. Thomas, 1955, pp. 125-70.

Leifer, R. *In the Name of Mental Health: Social Functions of Psychiatry*. New York: Science House, 1969.

Levitov, B. (Ed.), *Licensing and Accreditation in Education: The Law and the State Interest*. Lincoln, Nebr.: Study Commission on Undergraduate Education and the Education of Teachers, 1976.

Lieberman, J.K. *Crisis at the Bar: Lawyers' Unethical Ethics and What To Do About It*. New York: W.W. Norton, 1978.

Lieberman, J.K. "How to Avoid Lawyers." In R. Nader and M. Green (Eds.), *Verdicts on Lawyers*. New York: Thomas Y. Crowell, 1976, pp. 105-17.

Lieberman, J.K. *The Tyranny of the Experts: How Professionals Are Closing the Open Society*. New York: Walker, 1970.

Lieberman, M.A.; Yalom, I.D.; and Miles, M.B. *Encounter Groups: First Facts*. New York: Basic Books, 1973.

Lurie, M. "Physician Licensing Policy." In American Medical Association, National Congress on Health Manpower, *Expanding the Supply of Health Services in the 1970's*. (Sponsored by The Council on Health Manpower.) Chicago: American Medical Association, 1970.

McCloskey, R.G. "Economic Due Process and the Supreme Court: An Exhumation and Reburial." In P.B. Kurland (Ed.), *The Supreme Court Review*. Chicago: University of Chicago Press, 1962, pp. 34-62.

Malan, D.H. "The Outcome Problem in Psychotherapy Research: A Historical Review." *Archives of General Psychiatry*, 1973, v. 29, pp. 719-29.

Marsh, H.M. "California Board of Medical Examiners." *University of California, Davis Law Review*, 1972, v. 5, pp. 114-29.

Maslow, A.H. *The Farther Reaches of Human Nature*. New York: Viking Press, 1971.

Maslow, A.P. *Licensing Tests—Occupational Bridge or Barrier?* Proceedings, Third Annual Conference, National Council on Occupational Licensing, Lansing, Mich., 1971a.

Massarik. F. Personal communication, May 18, 1974.

Massarik, F. "Standards for Group Leadership." In L.N. Solomon and B. Berzon (Eds.), *New Perspectives on Encounter Groups.* San Francisco: Jossey-Bass, 1972, pp. 68-82.

Mathews, L. "Supreme Court Ends Ban on Prescription Price Ads." *Boston Globe,* May 25, 1976.

May, R. "Psychology and Legislation." *American Psychologist,* 1954, v. 9, pp. 585-86.

Meehl, P.E. "Psychotherapy." *Annual Review of Psychology,* 1955, v. 6, pp. 357-78.

Minnesota, Department of Health, Health Manpower Program. *Credentialing Document.* St. Paul, Minn.: Department of Health, 1976.

Mitchell, H.T., Jr. "Administrative Law: Constitutionality of Statutes Licensing Occupations." *North Carolina Law Review,* 1957, v. 35, pp. 473-76.

Monaghan, H.P. "The Constitution and Occupational Licensing in Massachusetts." *Boston University Law Review,* 1961, v. 41, pp. 157-82.

Moskowitz, D.B. "Will the ABA Lose Its Accreditation Power?" *Juris Doctor,* November 1977, pp. 27-35.

National Commission on Accrediting, Study of Accreditation of Selected Health Educational Programs (SASHEP). *Accreditation of Health Educational Programs: Part I: Staff Working Papers.* Washington, D.C.: SASHEP, 1971.

National Commission on Accrediting, Study of Accreditation of Selected Health Educational Programs (SASHEP). *Accreditation of Health Educational Programs: Part II: Staff Working Papers.* Washington, D.C.: SASHEP, 1972.

New Jersey, Professional and Occupational Licensing Study Commission. *Regulating Professions and Occupations.* (Reported submitted to the governor and Legislature, State of New Jersey.) Trenton, N.J., 1971.

New York University Law Review. "Portrait of the Sherman Act as a Commerce Clause Statute." *New York University Law Review,* 1974, v. 49, pp. 323-42.

Oden, T.C. "Consumer Interests in Therapeutic Outcome Studies: A Reply to Herron." *Journal of Humanistic Psychology,* 1975, v. 15(3), pp. 75-84.

Oden, T.C. "A Populists's View of Psychotherapeutic Deprofessionalization." *Journal of Humanistic Psychology,* 1974, v. 14(2), pp. 3-18.

Olson, P.A. "Credentialism as Monopoly, Class War, and Socialization Scheme: Some Historical Reflections on Modern Ways of Determining Who Can Do a Job." Paper presented at the Conference on Credentialism, University of California, Berkeley, April 28-30, 1977.

Park, C.C., and Shapiro. L.N. *Your Are Not Alone.* Waltham, Mass.: Little, Brown, Atlantic Monthly Press, 1976.

Parloff, M.B. "Group Therapy and the Small-Group Field—An Encounter." *International Journal of Group Psychotherapy,* 1970, v. 20, pp. 267-304.

Paul, G.L. "Strategy of Outcome Research in Psychotherapy." *Journal of Consulting Psychology,* 1967, v. 31, pp. 109-18.

Pfeffer, J. "Administrative Regulation and Licensing: Social Problem or Solution?" *Social Problems,* 1974, v. 21, pp. 468-79.

Phelan, J.J. *Regulation of the Television Repair Industry in Louisiana and California: A Case Study.* (Staff Report to the Federal Trade Commission.) Washington, D.C.: U.S. Government Printing Office, 1974.

Pound, R. "Liberty of Contract." *Yale Law Journal,* 1909, v. 18, pp. 454-87.

Randal, J. "FTC Says AMA Ban on Ads Restrictive." *Boston Globe,* December 23, 1975.

Rankin, J.W. "Proposed EEOC Guidelines." *Federation Bulletin,* 1976, v. 63, pp. 268-76.

Rayack, E. "An Economic Analysis of Occupational Licensure." Unpublished manuscript, U.S. Department of Labor, Manpower Administration (Grant No. 98-02-6851), 1975.

Rebell, M. *Teacher Credentialling Reform in New York State: A Critique and a Suggestion for New Directions.* Lincoln, Nebr.: Study Commission on Undergraduate Education and the Education of Teachers, 1974.

Rebell, M.A. "The Law, the Courts, and Teacher Credentialling Reform." Mimeographed. New York, undated.

Rickard, H.C. "Selected Group Psychotherapy Evaluation Studies." *Journal of General Psychology*, 1962, v. 67, pp. 35-50.

Roemer, M.I. "Controlling and Promoting Quality in Medical Care." In C.C. Havighurst, "Health Care: Part I." (Special issue.) *Law and Contemporary Problems*, 1970, v. 35, pp. 284-304.

Roemer, R. "Legal Systems Regulating Health Personnel—A Comparative Analysis." *Milbank Memorial Fund Quarterly*, 1968, v. 46, pp. 431-71. Reprinted in J.B. McKinlay (Ed.), *Politics and Law in Health Care Policy.* New York: Prodist, 1973, pp. 233-74.

Roemer, R. "Legal Regulation of Health Manpower in the 1970's." *HSMHA Health Reports*, 1971, v. 86, pp. 1053-63.

Roemer, R. "Legal and Other Institutional Impediments to Realignment of Health Service Functions." In American Medical Association, National Congress on Health Manpower, *Expanding the Supply of Health Services in the 1970's.* (Sponsored by The Council on Health Manpower.) Chicago: American Medical Association, 1970, pp. 43-64.

Sadler, B. "Recent Legal Developments Relative to Physician's Assistants and Nurse Practitioners." *Physician's Assistant Journal*, Winter-Spring 1974, pp. 35-44.

Saffir, M.A. "Certification versus Licensing Legislation." *American Psychologist*, 1950, v. 5, pp. 105-6.

Sanford, F.H. "The Criteria of a Good Profession." *American Psychologist*, 1951, v. 6, pp. 668-70.

Saveri, G. "The Applicability of the Antitrust Laws to Public Bodies." *University of San Francisco Law Review*, 1970, v. 4, pp. 217-28.

Schillinger, M. Executive Director, New York State Psychological Association. Personal communication, September 5, 1974.

Segal, M.B. "A Hard Look at the PSRO Law." *Journal of Legal Medicine*, 1974, v. 2(5), pp. 16-22.

Sennett, M. "Antitrust—*Goldfarb v. Virginia State Bar*—Professional Legal Services Are Held to be Within the Ambit of Federal Antitrust Laws." *Loyola University Law Journal*, 1976, v. 7, pp. 254-76.

Shakow, D. *Clinical Psychology as Science and Profession: A 40-Year Odyssey.* Chicago: Aldine, 1969.

Shimberg, B.; Esser, B.F.; and Kruger, D.H. *Occupational Licensing: Practices and Policies.* (A Report of the Educational Testing Service.) Washington, D.C.: Public Affairs Press, 1972.

Simmons, H.E., and Ball, J.R. "PSRO and the Dissolution of the Malpractice Suit." *University of Toledo Law Review*, 1975, v. 6, pp. 739-63.

Simmons, R.C., and Fornaciari, J.R. "State Regulation as an Antitrust Defense: An Analysis of the *Parker v. Brown* Doctrine." *University of Cincinnati Law Review*, 1974, v. 43, pp. 61-99.

Slater, P.E. "Antitrust and Government Action: A Formula for Narrowing *Parker v. Brown.*" *Northwestern University Law Review*, 1974, v. 69, pp. 71-109.

Stolar, K.S. "Occupational Licensing: An Antitrust Analysis." *Missouri Law Review*, 1976, v. 41, pp. 66-79.

Strupp, H.H., and Bergin, A.E. "Some Empirical and Conceptual Bases for Coordinated Research in Psychotherapy: A Critical Review of Issues, Trends, and Evidence." *International Journal of Psychiatry*, 1969, v. 7, pp. 18-90.

Study Commission on Undergraduate Education and the Education of Teachers. *Teacher Education in the United States: The Responsibility Gap.* Lincoln, Nebr.: University of Nebraska Press, 1976.

Sullivan, F.W. "Peer Review and PSRO: An Update." *American Journal of Psychiatry*, 1976, v. 133, pp. 51-55.

Tancredi, L.R., and Woods, J. "The Social Control of Medical Practice: Licensure Versus Output Monitoring." *Milbank Memorial Fund Quarterly*, 1972, v. 50, pp. 99-125.

Teply, L.L. "Antitrust Immunity of State and Local Governmental Action." *Tulane Law Review*, 1974, v. 48, pp. 272-98.

Texas Law Review. "Antitrust—State Exemption—the Sherman Act Does Not Apply to State Activity Regardless of Its Commercial Nature: *New Mexico v. American Petrofina, Inc.*, 501 F.2d 363 (9th Cir. 1974)." *Texas Law Review*, 1975, v. 53, pp. 566-77.

Texas Tech Law Review. "Antitrust—Minimum Fee Schedules—the 'Learned Profession,' Recognized as an Exemption to Section 1 of the Sherman Act." *Texas Tech Law Review*, 1974, v. 6, pp. 189-200.

Thomas, R. "The Whys and Why Nots of Consumer Participation." *Community Mental Health Journal*, 1973, v. 9, pp. 143-50.

Truax, C.B. "The Meaning and Reliability of Accurate Empathy Ratings: A Rejoinder." *Psychological Bulletin*, 1972, v. 77, pp. 397-99.

Truax, C.B., and Mitchell, K.M. "Research on Certain Therapist Interpersonal Skills in Relation to Process and Outcome." In A.E. Bergin and S.L. Garfield (Eds.), *Handbook of Psychotherapy and Behavior Change: An Empirical Analysis*. New York: John Wiley, 1971, pp. 299-344.

Tustini, K.A. "Immunity of Federal Officials from Civil Liability in Antitrust Suits." *Stanford Law Review*, 1967, v. 19, pp. 1101-9.

U.S. Deparment of Health, Education and Welfare. "Credentialing of Drug Abuse Treatment and Rehabilitation Workers." (Discussion draft, prepared by S.S. Steinberg, A.L. Batista, A.S. Bisconti, and I.L. Gomberg.) Mimeographed. University Research Corp., Washington, D.C., February 1975.

U.S. Deparment of Health, Education, and Welfare. *Developments in Health Manpower Licensure: A Follow-up to the 1971 Report on Licensure and Related Health Personnel Credentialing, June 1973*. (Prepared by H.S. Cohen and L.H. Miike.) Washington, D.C.: U.S. Government Printing Office, 1973.

U.S. Department of Health, Education, and Welfare. *Medical Malpractice: Report of the Secretary's Commission on Medical Malpractice*. (DHEW Publication No. OS 73-88.) Washington, D.C.: U.S. Government Printing Office, 1973a.

U.S. Department of Health, Education, and Welfare. *Report on Licensure and Related Health Personnel Credentialing* (to the Congress of the United States.) Washington, D.C.: U.S. Government Printing Office, 1971.

U.S. Department of Justice, Department of Labor, and Civil Service Commission. "Questions and Answers on the Federal Executive Agency Guidelines on Employee Selection Procedures." *Federal Register*, 1977, v. 42, pp. 4052-58.

U.S. Equal Employment Opportunity Coordinating Council. "Uniform Guidelines on Employee Selection Procedures: Staff Committee Proposal." Mimeographed. Washington, D.C., September 24, 1975.

U.S. Federal Trade Commission. Personal Communication to P.N. Georgiades, September 8, 1977.

U.S. Federal Trade Commission. *Prescription Drug Price Disclosures*. (Staff Report to the Federal Trade Commission.) Washington, D.C.: Federal Trade Commission, 1975.

U.S. National Advisory Commission on Health Manpower. *Report of the National Advisory Commission on Health Manpower*. (Vol. 1.) Washington, D.C.: U.S. Government Printing Office, 1967.

U.S. National Advisory Commission on Health Manpower. *Report of the National Advisory Commission on Health Manpower*. (Vol. 2.) Washington, D.C.: U.S. Government Printing Office, 1967.

U.S. National Institute of Mental Health. *Research in the Service of Mental Health: Report of the Research Task Force of the National Institute of Mental Health*. (DHEW

Publication No. ADM 75-236.) Rockville, Md.: National Institute of Mental Health, 1975.

U.S. News and World Report. "Clamor Grows Across U.S. to Let Professionals Advertise." *U.S. News and World Reports*, January 26, 1976, pp. 60-61.

University of Pennsylvania Law Review. "Governmental Action and Anti-trust Immunity." *University of Pennsylvania Law Review*, 1971, v. 119, pp. 521-26.

University of Pennsylvania Law Review. "The Void-for-Vagueness Doctrine in the Supreme Court: A Means to an End." *University of Pennsylvania Law Review*, 1960, v. 109, pp. 67-116.

Utah Law Review. "Federal Antitrust Policy v. State Anticompetitive Regulation: A Means Scrutiny Limit for *Parker v. Brown.*" *Utah Law Review*, 1975, v. Spring 1975, pp. 179-98.

Virginia Law Review. "Due Process Limitations on Occupational Licensing." *Virginia Law Review*, 1973, v. 59, pp. 1097-129.

Wallis, C. (Ed.) *Directory of Humanistic Psychotherapists: Greater Boston Area.* Boston: Constance Publishing Co., 1975.

Wake Forest Law Review. "Constitutional Law—The Validity of Restrictions on Aliens Entering the Professions." *Wake Forest Law Review*, 1973, v. 9, pp. 589-97.

Watkins, B.T. "States Sending Professionals Back to the Classroom." *New York Times*, September 11, 1977.

Welsch, E.E.; Bernard, V.W.; Austin, L.N.; and Schlesinger, H.J. "Qualifications for Psychotherapists: Symposium, 1954." *American Journal of Orthopsychiatry*, 1956, v. 26. pp. 35-65.

White, D.M. "Legal Approaches to Credentialing." (Appendix F in Refunding Proposal Submitted to the Carnegie Corporation.) Mimeographed. Berkeley, Calif., undated.

White, D.M., and Francis, R.L. "Title VII And the Masters of Reality: Eliminating Credentialism in the American Labor Market." *Georgetown Law Journal*, 1976, v. 64, pp. 1213-44.

White, W.D. *Public Health and Private Gain: The Economics of Licensing Medical Laboratory Personnel.* Chicago: Maaroufa Press, forthcoming.

Wilson, H.S. "A Second Look at *Griggs v. Duke Power Company:* Ruminations on Job Testing, Discrimination, and the Role of the Federal Courts." *Virginia Law Review*, 1972, v. 58, pp. 844-74.

Wisconsin, State of. *Licensing by the State of Wisconsin.* (Research Bulletin No. 108.) Madison, Wis.: Wisconsin Legislative Reference Library, 1952.

Woltmann, A.G. "Problems Involved in the Training of Psychologists as Nonmedical Psychotherapists." *American Journal of Orthopsychiatry*, 1949, v. 19, pp. 32-35.

Wright, J.S. Review of K.C. Davis, *Beyond Discretionary Justice: A Preliminary Inquiry. Yale Law Journal*, 1972, v. 81, pp. 575-97.

Yale Law Journal. "Business Necessity under Title VII of the Civil Rights Act of 1964: A No-Alternative Approach." *Yale Law Journal*, 1974, v. 84, pp. 98-119.

Yale Law Journal. "Restrictive Licensing of Dental Paraprofessionals." *Yale Law Journal*, 1974a, v. 83, pp. 806-26.

Yale Law Journal. "The Applicability of the Sherman Act to Legal Practice and Other 'Non-commercial' Activities." *Yale Law Journal*, 1972, v. 82, pp. 313-37.

Young, J.H. *The Medical Messiahs: A Social History of Health Quackery in Twentieth-Century America.* Princeton, N.J.: Princeton University Press, 1967.

Cases

A.B. Small Co. v. American Sugar Refining Co., 267 U.S. 233 (1925).

Banjavich v. Louisiana Board for Marine Divers, 237 La. 467, 111 So.2d 505 (1959).

Beauty Hall, Inc. v. State Board of Cosmetology, 82 Dauph. 294 (Pa. Dauph. Cty. Ct. 1964).

Berger v. Board of Psychologist Examiners, 521 F.2d 1056 (D.C. Cir. 1975).

Bessette v. People, 193 Ill. 334, 62 N.E. 215 (1901).

Blocker v. United States, 288 F.2d 853 (D.C. Cir. 1961).

Bloom v. Texas State Board of Examiners of Psychologists, 475 S.W.2d 374 (Tex. Civ. App. 1972), reversed, 492 S.W.2d 460 (1973).

Cleere v. Bullock, 146 Colo. 284, 361 P.2d 616 (1961).

Connally v. General Construction Co., 269 U.S. 385 (1926).

Cox v. Mississippi Board of Psychological Examiners, No. 4013 (Chanc. Ct., Harrison Cty., 2d Jud. Dist., Miss., May 6, 1976).

Dasch v. Jackson, 170 Md. 251, 183 A. 534 (1936).

Day-Brite Lighting, Inc. v. Missouri, 342 U.S. 421 (1952).

Doe v. Jones, 327 Ill. 387, 158 N.E. 703 (1927).

Fink v. Cole, 302 N.Y. 216, 97 N.E.2d 873 (1951).

Garces v. Department of Registration and Education, 118 Ill. App. 2d 206, 254 N.E. 2d 622 (1969).

Goldfarb v. Virginia State Bar, 421 U.S. 773 (1975), rehearing denied, 423 U.S. 886 (1975).

Harmon v. State, 66 Ohio St. 249, 64 N.E. 117 (1902).

Harrigan & Reid Co. v. Burton, 224 Mich. 564, 195 N.W. 60 (1923).

Hoff v. State, 39 Del. 134, 197 A. 75 (1938).

Husband v. Cassel, 130 So.2d 69 (Fla. 1961).

Kilbourn v. Thompson, 103 U.S. 168 (1881).

Packer v. Board of Behavioral Science Examiners, 52 Cal. App. 3d 190, 125 Cal. Rptr. 96 (1975).

Parker v. Brown, 317 U.S. 341 (1943).

People v. Brown, 407 Ill. 565, 95 N.E.2d 888 (1951).

People v. Ringe, 197 N.Y. 143, 90 N.E. 451 (1910).

Lasher v. People, 183 Ill. 226, 55 N.E. 663 (1899).

Roschen v. Ward, 279 U.S. 337 (1929).

Smith v. Texas, 233 U.S. 630 (1914).

State ex rel. Beck v. Gleason, 148.Kan. 1, 79 P.2d 911 (1938).

State v. Morrow, 231 La. 532, 92 So. 2d 70 (1956).

State v. Van Keegan, 132 Conn. 33, 42 A.2d 352 (1945).

Timmons v. Morris, 271 F. 721 (W.D. Wash. 1921).

United States v. Cardiff, 344 U.S. 174 (1952).

United States v. L. Cohen Grocery Co., 255 U.S. 81 (1921).

United States v. Shreveport Grain and Elevator Co., 287 U.S. 77 (1932).

Whittle v. State Board of Examiners of Psychologists, 483 P.2d 328 (Okla. 1971).

Wilson v. District of Columbia, 26 App. D.C. 110 (1905).

Yick Wo v. Hopkins, 118 U.S. 356 (1886).

Subject Index

Academic credentials
and competence, 112, 159-60, 255, 268, 345-46, 357, 364-65, 370-71
and discrimination, 280-82, 348
and guidelines for regulatory proposals, 364-65
and licensing laws, 141-42, 249-51, 268, 370
and policy recommendations, 357
and recommendations for licensing laws, 373
as selection criteria, 157-58, 170
Accreditation process, 238, 249, 268-71, 373-74
and professional associations, 330
recommendations for, 384-85
Acting out, 47
Administrative regulation, 237, 270, 379
Advertisements, for therapy, 71 n.8, 348
Affect, 3
Affective Sensitivity Scale, 167
Age, as selection criteria, 157
Aged, and licensing laws, 239, 265, 280-82, 348
Agencies, administrative, 218, 237, 379
Aggressive-stimulators, 106, 133, 179 n.61
Alienation, 53, 62, 64
American Academy of Psychotherapists, 333
American Association of Marriage and Family Counselors (AAMFC), 244, 333
American Association of Medical Schools, 373
American Association of Pastoral Counselors, 333
American Association of Psychotherapists, 333
American Association of Sex Educators, 333
American Bar Association, 257, 261, 269
American Board of Psychiatry and Neurology, 158, 162-63, 334, 373
American Group Psychotherapy Association, 158, 333
American Medical Association (AMA), 1, 3, 253, 265, 337, 368-69
and accreditation, 268-69, 334, 373
Committee on Medical Practice, 261
on cost, and licensure, 275
Department of Medical Ethics, 259
formation of, 227
on illegal practice, 263
innovations and licensing, 280

Medical Disciplinary Committee, 257
power of, 229 n.5, 330-32
American Orthopsychiatric Association, 26, 29 n.1, 333, 370
American Psychiatric Association, 67-70, 112-16, 125, 143, 222, 266, 332-35
Professional Liability Program, 315
on practice of psychotherapy, 369
American Psychoanalytic Association, 162, 332-33
American Psychological Association, 29 n.1, 66-67, 113, 128, 145-47, 222, 334-35
and accreditation, 373
CSPEC, 334
on practice of psychotherapy, 369
Annual Review of Psychology, 23-24
Antidiscrimination laws, 390-91
Anti-intellectual attitude, group as, 64, 131
Antitrust laws, 391
Anxiety, 25
Apprenticeships, 365
Archives of General Psychiatry, 21
Association of American Medical Colleges, 143, 269
Association of Applied Social Scientists, 222
Association for Creative Change, 222, 335-36
Attack, by group leader, 132, 134, 137-38
Attitude
anti-intellectual, of encounter groups, 64, 131
and mental health, 207 n.3
Attitude changes
and encounter groups, 55-59, 62, 72 n.25-n.26, 344
and role of therapist, 90, 106, 204, 345
Australian Institute of Human Relations, 335
Authenticity groups, 40, 43
Autonomy, and mental health, 207 n.3
Aversive therapy, 127

Balanced representation, 4, 356, 365, 379
Bateman Commission, 263, 290 n.33, 367, 369
Behavior changes
and encounter groups, 55-63, 72 n.25-n.26, 344

Author Index

Case Index

About the Author

After graduating from Yale University in 1965, Dan Hogan was a Peace Corps volunteer in rural community development in Lesotho, Africa. He subsequently obtained a master's degree in education from Boston University and in 1972 received his law degree from Harvard Law School. Since then he has been a consultant in the small-group field, with the main focus of his work on T-groups and the training of small-group leaders. In this capacity he has been an Associate of McBer and Company in Boston and has been a consultant to various government and nongovernment agencies, including the Department of Health, Education, and Welfare and the Office of Minority Business Enterprise.

Hogan's major current interest is the development and regulation of the mental health profession. He is also extremely interested in the role of the professions in society and in establishing sound mechanisms for determining professional competence. Hogan serves on the Board of Directors of the National Center for the Study of Professions, the International Association of Applied Social Scientists, and the New England Training Institute. For the past three years he has been a Research Fellow in the Department of Psychology and Social Relations at Harvard University, where he is currently completing his Ph.D. in Social Psychology.